Cognitive
Anthropology

Cognitive Anthropology

Readings edited by

STEPHEN A. TYLER

Tulane University

Holt, Rinehart and Winston, Inc.

New York   Chicago   San Francisco   Atlanta   Dallas
Montreal   Toronto   London   Sydney

Foreword

The last decade has been a most seminal period in anthropology. Among the developments with greatest potential for changing the future shape of cultural anthropology is the one subsumed in this volume under the heading, Cognitive Anthropology. Like most significant movements in letters and sciences, it is led by a handful of scholars. Those of their writings that fall under this heading often use terminology and concepts that are unfamiliar to many of us. These terminologies and concepts derive in part from the language of other sciences, from formal logical analysis, and from mathematics. From within anthropology structural linguistics and studies of kinship terminology have contributed models, methods, and data. And although anthropologists are presumably familiar with these sectors of their discipline, neither of the above is noted for its nontechnical nature.

For these reasons the potential impact of cognitive anthropology (including formal ethnography, semantic analysis, ethnoscience, and componential analysis) upon the study of culture and the building of cultural theory is not widely understood. One suspects, also, that as with most innovative movements in science, prejudices have formed unhampered by careful analysis. When we read the papers in this volume and the Introduction by the editor, we are led to the conclusion that cultural anthropology may undergo indeed, as he states, a drastic reorganization of its methods, theories, and even its facts.

Consider, for example, the proposition that cultural anthropology should not be considered a natural science but a formal science and that its data can be analyzed by formal methods. As perceived by some of our colleagues, these methods if applied widely would destroy cultural anthropology. The more moderate among us at least protest that humanistic values tend to be lost in a formal analysis of cultural data, and that these values are basic to the character structure of anthropology and its contribution to the understanding of man. Opinions about why formal methods are effective and desirable or ineffective and undesirable are plentiful. This volume provides a documentation of what such methods can do at this point in the development of the field. It is biased positively towards the utility of these methods but it makes this bias available for scrutiny.

Or consider another proposition: An approach based upon comparison of substantive variables (household composition, corporate lineages, aggression training), or indices of such variables from various tribes or communities must be abandoned, because these variables have been described in the categories provided by the anthropologist's language, and not those provided by the language of the culture. This assertion makes sense if we grant that the principles used by the native to order phenomena and not the "material phenomena" themselves are the critical variables, and the proper object of study by the cultural anthropologist. Although this postulate has its roots in ideational definitions of culture that have been influential in American anthropology for some time, its full implications were only realized when controlled methods of eliciting relevant data and formal methods for analyzing it were developed. Surely these propositions will be contested and the validity of the methods will be examined. The purpose of this volume is to make it possible for more people to argue their cases better.

It is perhaps unfair to cast, by implication, the authors of the separate papers in this volume in a revolutionary role. All of them are modest about the significance of their work and its possible influence upon the future shape of anthropology. Most of them do more than one kind of anthropology. Nor are all of the authors whose work is represented in this volume of one mind. Papers reflecting varying points of view are included. It is also true that cognitive anthropology is still characterized more by way of programatic statements than by substantive analyses and that no one can yet judge the ultimate significance of the developments brought together under this title.

This volume makes it possible for anyone who will do serious reading to become acquainted with cognitive anthropology and judge for himself its potential significance. The papers are drawn from nine different publications, and four of them have not been published before. The recency of the field is obvious: Although the earliest publication represented is 1956, the majority of the papers were published for the first time during 1964 or later. Of the twenty-nine articles in the volume fifteen have been published in the *American Anthropologist* suggesting that this movement is not on the periphery of our discipline.

The volume is one that anthropologists, graduate students, and undergraduate majors in anthropology should read. It is also one that should be of interest to our colleagues in other disciplines. There is an explicit collaboration with cognitive psychology invited by this collection of papers, and psycholinguistics and sociolinguistics are already siblings to cognitive anthropology. Communications research may profitably employ some of its formulations. Many other sectors of the behavioral sciences will find this conception of the study of man's culture and mind relevant.

The editor, Dr. Stephen Tyler, is to be applauded for selecting, grouping, and commenting on the papers in this volume and for so forthrightly stating what he believes to be their significance. He was trained in cognitive anthropology and his field experience among the Koya of India has resulted in some exceptional papers that fall within this framework, one of which is represented in this volume. He received his graduate training at Syracuse University and at Stanford University where he acquired his Ph.D. in 1964. He has been an assistant professor at the University of California at Davis and is now an associate professor at Tulane University.

George D. Spindler

Stanford, California
February 1969

Preface

In compiling this anthology I have had two related goals in mind. First, I have attempted to provide a basic text in cognitive anthropology for undergraduate and graduate students. The materials have been arranged so that information contained in earlier papers provides a framework for problems and procedures in later papers. Each section is preceded by an editor's introduction which outlines the major topic discussed in each section. Since the papers included cover topics discussed in a number of anthropology courses this volume could also serve as a supplementary text for a wide variety of courses. I have also attempted to make readily available to anthropologists and scientists in related disciplines contributions which are representative of assumptions, methods, problems, and results in cognitive anthropology. Hopefully, the easy accessibility of these papers will facilitate further research and encourage interdisciplinary cooperation. These goals reflect my conviction that the aims and procedures of cognitive anthropology have profound implications not only for anthropology, but for many allied disciplines as well.

As I see it, cognitive anthropology entails four related operations: (1) *acquisition* of data; (2) *discovery* of semantic features; (3) *arrangement* of features; (4) a statement of *relevance*. This does not imply that these are rigid, airtight compartments, for the process of fieldwork entails constant checking back and forth among these operations. This in itself provides a useful method for evaluating data. Discovery of a semantic feature may, for example, lead to a search for new data or a rechecking of the original data. In fact, procedures for acquiring data are also procedures for discovering semantic features and for data evaluation. Fieldwork and analysis should be carried out simultaneously. Yet, for purposes of exposition, it is convenient to look at semantic analysis as if its operations are isolable. Although most of the papers in this book deal to some extent with problems related to all of these topics, they have been selected and arranged to illustrate only a single problem or operation. Each chapter is designed to present a discussion of one of these operations. Since an intuitive grasp of these procedures is most easily acquired through a discussion of problems of arrangement, the organization of the book departs from the sequence given above.

Chapter 1, instead of acquisition, deals with the problems of feature arrangement. The papers focus on the way individual semantic features and lexemes combine to produce various types of semantic arrangements. Chapter 2 is concerned with techniques designed for the acquisition of data. The papers in this section demonstrate methods used by cognitive anthropologists in developing replicable and culturally sensitive eliciting and field procedures. Chapter 3 treats discovery procedures with major emphasis on isolating semantic features by formal methods. The remaining chapters are devoted to the problem of relevance. Relevance is considered in two aspects: psychological reality and contextual sensitivity. Chapter 4 examines relevance from the standpoint of psychological reality, and Chapter 5 examines relevance in terms of context.

I wish to acknowledge with gratitude the advice and counsel of George and Louise Spindler and the editorial and secretarial assistance of my wife Martha. Without their assistance this book would not have been completed. All errors, however, are my responsibility and cannot be attributed to them.

Stephen A. Tyler

New Orleans, Louisiana
February 1969

Contents

Cognitive
Anthropology

Introduction

The history of all scientific disciplines is marked by periods of intense theoretical innovation followed by relatively quiescent periods of consolidation and refinement. When the descriptive facts of science no longer fit the older explanatory models, it becomes necessary to discover new theories which will more adequately explain the accumulated data. Anthropology is currently in one of these periods of innovation. On every hand, the various subdisciplines of anthropology are astir with new formulations challenging and supplementing established concepts and methods. The very lexicon of anthropology reflects this ferment. The journals are full of articles on *formal analysis, componential analysis, folk taxonomy, ethnoscience, ethnosemantics,* and *sociolinguistics,* to list but a few. Nearly all of these topics have appeared in the brief span of approximately ten years, with increasing frequency in the last three or four years.

Assessment of such new departures is always difficult. What are their historical antecedents and what do they augur for the future of anthropology? Are these genuinely viable reformulations or are they simply short-lived fads and blind alleys, detrimental in the long run to significant research?

Enough has been presented in symposia and journals for us to feel that we are witnessing a quiet revolution in anthropology—

1

quiet because the new departures are firmly rooted in the past. Formal analysis derives in part from the work of such anthropological titans as Radcliffe-Brown, Lévi-Strauss, and Nadel. Folk taxonomies are foreshadowed in the writings of Mauss, Boas, and Evans-Pritchard. That great ethnographer Malinowski would have been no stranger to recent developments in sociolinguistics. The concern for psychological validity is congruent with much of Sapir's work and, to a lesser extent, with some of Kroeber's. And, perhaps, most relevant of all is the work of Bateson.

Yet, these developments constitute more than a disconnected reworking of disparate themes from out of the past. These new formulations contrast sharply with many of the aims, assumptions, goals, and methods of an earlier anthropology. Previous theoretical orientations in anthropology can in a very general way be classed into two types—those concerned primarily with change and development and those concerned with static descriptions. Thus, the evolutionists and the diffusionists concentrated on patterns of change, while the functionalists eschewed this work as mere "speculative history," and focused on the internal organization and comparison of systems, hoping thereby to discover general laws of society. Some culture and personality studies attempted to characterize whole cultures with such concepts as "national character" and "modal personality type," while other culture and personality studies utilized a comparative approach in an attempt to correlate psychological and cultural features.

These formulations were attempts to construct universal organizational types which were linked either by similar processes of change or by similarities of internal structure. In order to achieve this goal, only certain kinds of information were accepted as relevant, and concrete ethnographic data had to be elevated to more abstract forms such as index variables and typological constructs. Consequently, abstract definitions of these features were necessary, and much of the discussion in books and journals concerned the adequacy of these definitions. Once a corporate lineage, for example, had been defined in a particular way, it was only a matter of time before some fieldworker returned to his desk and elatedly reported that his tribe did not conform to the received definition. One way around this problem was to construct more types and subtypes, and broader, more abstract definitions. It was generally accepted that neither the types nor the definitions actually corresponded to anything in the "real world." They were merely convenient methods of ordering the data at hand. Proliferation of types, however, was dangerous, for as the types proliferated, so did the processes linking the types and their constituents. Contrary to expectations, anthropology became more and more particularistic rather than more general and universal.

This concern with typology and definition is an index to another feature characteristic of this period in anthropology. Anthropologists were really much more concerned with discovering what anthropology was than, for example, what an Eskimo was. In a sense anthropologists were studying only one small culture—the culture of anthropology.

Aside from the diffusionists, these earlier theories can be characterized as attempts to construct monolithic, unitary systems which purported to either explain cultures or their development. Such concepts as cultural core, cultural norm, structure, modal structure, pattern, and others were used to describe these systems. These ideas are symptomatic of a quest for the typical, the normal, the usual, for those definitely bounded phenomena which would systematically differentiate one culture from another. In fact, the very concept of culture is but another of these labels for some arbitrarily bounded unit within which certain types of behavior, norms, artifacts, and emotions are typical (cf. Sapir 1932:515; 1934:593–595). The atypical, especially as expressed in patterns of variation, were either simply dismissed or artifically worked into the scheme as indices of change, diffusion, survival, innovation, dysfunction, abnormality, cultural disintegration, opportunities for the exercise of social control and the like. The only important variations were variations between cultures.

In contrast to these approaches, cognitive anthropology constitutes a new theoretical orientation. It focuses on *discovering* how different peoples organize and use their cultures. This is not so much a search for some generalized unit of behavioral analysis as it is an attempt to understand the *organizing principles underlying* behavior. It is assumed that each people has a unique system for perceiving and organizing material phenomena— things, events, behavior, and emotions (Goodenough 1957). The object of study is not these material phenomena themselves, but the way they are organized in the minds of men. Cultures then are not material phenomena; they are cognitive organizations of material phenomena.[2] Consequently, cultures are neither described by mere arbitrary lists of anatomical traits and institutions such as house type, family type, kinship type, economic type, and personality type, nor are they necessarily equated with some over-all integrative pattern of these phenomena. Such descriptions may tell us something about the way an anthropologist thinks about a culture, but there is little, if any, reason to believe that they tell us anything of how the people of some culture think about their culture.

In essence, cognitive anthropology seeks to answer two questions: What material phenomena are significant for the people of some culture; and, how do they organize these phenomena? Not only do cultures differ among one another in their organization of material phenomena, they differ as well in the kinds of material phenomena they organize. The people of different cultures may not recognize the same kinds of material phenomena as relevant, even though from an outsider's point of view the same material phenomena may be present in every case. For example, we distinguish between dew, fog, ice, and snow, but the Koyas of South India do not. They call all of these *mancu*. Even though they can perceive the differences among these if asked to do so, these differences are not significant to them. On the other hand, they recognize and name at least seven different kinds of bamboo, six more than I am accustomed to distinguish. Similarly, even though I know that my cousin George is the son of my mother's sister, while my cousin Paul is the son of my mother's brother, this objective difference is irrelevant to my system of classification. They are both "cousins." If I were a Koya, however, this difference would be highly important. I would call my mother's brother's son *baaTo* and my mother's sister's son *annaal*. Even though the same material phenomena are objectively present, they are subjectively perceived and organized differently by Koyas than they are by Americans.[3] Furthermore, there is no apparent over-all integrative pattern which relates the classification of bamboo to the classification of relatives. These are separate classes of phenomena with distinctive and unrelated principles of organization.

Not only may the same phenomena be organized differently from culture to culture, they may also be organized in more than one way in the same culture. There is, then, *intracultural* variation as well as *intercultural* variation. Some intracultural variations may be idiosyncratic, but more important from the anthropologist's point of view are those variations which are used by different classes of people and/or occur in different situations and contexts (cf. Goodenough 1963:257–264). For example, if we are interested in describing the way people classify colors we may discover that there are variant patterns dependent upon the sex or age of our informant as well as his general experience with colors. Thus, females in our culture can generally discriminate and name more colors than males. Or, to take another example, the classification of relatives may be partially dependent on the social statuses of the people talking about relatives, the relationship between them, and the social context in which they are conversing. A Telugu refers to his younger sister as *celli* when talking to another member of his family, but when speaking to a person outside his family group, he uses the term *cellelu*, which may mean younger sister, or mother's sister's daughter, or father's brother's daughter.

A consequence of this interest in variation is the idea that cultures are not unitary phenomena, that is, they cannot be described by only one set of organizing principles. For each class of relevant phenomena there may be several alternative organizations. The realization or choice of one alternative to the exclusion of some other is dependent upon a variety of factors. For example, some people have more or less knowledge of some phenomena, or certain alternatives may be acceptable only in particular contexts (cf. Hymes 1964b:41). If these variants are used only in certain identified situations, or if there is a hierarchy of choice so that variants are ordered on the basis of their relative desirability, we can say that they are in complementary distribution and do not conflict with one another. In such a situation it is possible for a large number of variants to coexist. But, if these variants conflict in their organization and the situations in which they occur, there must be some means of harmonizing the contrast. This can be achieved by some change in the principles of organization or in the situations in which they occur. For example, among the Koyas, the pig is classed as an edible animal, but among neighboring Muslims the pig is classed as inedible and defiling. Suppose a Koya woman were married to a Muslim man. While in her husband's home she could not act on her classification of the pig as an edible by eating pork; while visiting her parents in the absence of her husband she could. So long as the two systems of classification can be realized in these isolated contexts there is no necessary conflict between them, and both may persist. If these contexts were not in complementary distribution, some rearrangement of the two contrasting systems of classification would have to take place if the marriage were to persist.[4]

In fact, this is an argument for a different kind of unitary description which sees unity as emerging from the ordered relations between variants and contexts. Variants are not mere deviations from some assumed basic organization; with their rules of occurrence *they are the organization*. (Wallace 1961:29–41; Hymes 1964a:386–387). It must be emphasized, however, that such a unitary description can be achieved only by the anthropologist. It is highly unlikely that the members of a culture ever see their culture as *this kind of* unitary phenomenon. Each individual member may have a unique, unitary model of his culture, but is not necessarily cognizant of all the unique, unitary models held by other members of his culture. He will be aware of and use some, but it is only the anthropologist who completely transcends these particular models and constructs a single, unitary model. This cognitive organization exists solely in the mind of the anthropologist (cf. Bateson 1958:294). Yet, to the extent that it will generate conceptual models used by the people of a particular culture, it is a model of their cognitive systems.[5]

The "theory" here is not so much a THEORY OF CULTURE as it is *theories of cultures*, or a theory of descriptions. The aim of such a theory is to provide answers to the questions: How would the people of some other culture expect me to behave if I were a member of their culture; and what are the rules of appropriate behavior in their culture? Answers to these questions are provided by an adequate description of the rules used by the people in that culture. Consequently, this description itself constitutes the "theory" for that culture, for it represents the conceptual model of organization used by its members. Such a theory is validated by our ability to predict how these people would expect us to behave if we were members of their culture.

ORDER OUT OF CHAOS

In a sense, cognitive anthropology is not a new departure. Many anthropologists have expressed an interest in how the natives see their world. Yet, there is a difference of focus between the old and the new. Where earlier anthropologists sought categories of description in their native language, cognitive anthropologists seek categories of description in the language of their natives.[6] Ultimately, this is the old problem of what do we describe and how do we describe it? Obviously, we are interested in the mental codes of other peoples, but how do we infer these mental processes? Thus far, it has been assumed that the easiest entry to such processes is through language, and most of the recent studies have sought to discover codes that are mapped in language. Nearly all of this work has been concerned with how other peoples "name" the "things" in their environment and how these names are organized into larger groupings. These names are thus both an index to what is significant in the environment of some other people, and a means of discovering how these people organize their perceptions of the environment. Naming is seen as one of the chief methods for imposing order on perception.[7]

In a very real sense, the anthropologist's problem is to discover how other people create order out of what appears to him to be utter chaos. Imagine, for a moment, a being from another planet equipped with all our sensory apparatus who perceives for the first time the infinite variety of sight and sound in which we live. Suppose further that he is attempting to describe this world in a scientific report for his colleagues at home. At first, everything would be chaotic. Each sound and object would seem to be unlike any other. His experience would be similar to what we feel the first time we hear a language we have never heard before. But, with infinite time and patience, let us assume that he is able to describe everything he perceives—that is, the total environment of earth. Probably he would eventually be able to organize his report around concepts acceptable to his world or devise new ones as he saw fit. Yet, would anyone of us accept his report as an accurate account of the world as we see and live in it? If he in fact describes everything, we would not. Nor would we accept his organization of the things he perceived, for they would almost certainly not fit our own system of organization. Unlike this mythical creature, we do not live in a world in which we discriminate among all the possible sensory stimuli in our environment, nor do we react to each stimulus as if it were totally new and foreign. In effect, we choose to ignore many of those perceptual differences which make each object unique. In large part, we do this by naming. By naming we classify and put objects which to us are similar into the same category, even though we can perceive differences among them (cf. Boas 1938:208–214). For example, the chair in which I sit has a nick in the left leg, yet I class it as a "straight chair" no different from others like it in the room.

We classify because life in a world where nothing was the same would be intolerable. It is through naming and classification that the whole rich world of infinite variability shrinks to manipulable size and becomes bearable. Our methods of classification are entirely arbitrary and subjective. There is nothing in the external world which demands that certain things go together and others do not. It is our perception of similarities and differences together with a set of hierarchical cues that determine which things go together. We not only react to certain discriminable stimuli as if they were the same, we name them and organize them into groupings. Thus, for example, there are objects with a seat, a back and four legs which we label *chairs*, even though no two of these objects are exactly alike. The word *chair* then stands as a sign for a whole class of objects with a seat, a back, and four legs. This sign, too, is arbitrary—we might as well call these objects *argoboos*. Just as there is no inherent quality in an object that forces us to perceive it in exactly one way, neither is there an intrinsic characteristic associating an object with its name. Consequently, with the passage of time, a class of objects may be renamed, but the class of objects denoted by this name does not change, or, conversely, the class of objects denoted by a name may change, but the name does not.

Thus, we subjectively group the phenomena of our perceptual world into named classes. These classes are not disparate and singular. They are organized into larger groupings. To the extent that these groupings are hierarchically arranged by a process of inclusion, they form a *taxonomy*. To continue the example of chairs, there are other objects in our homes which are not chairs. There are sofas, tables, desks, cabinets, and the like. Each of these constitutes a separate class, some with many subclasses. For example there are end tables, dining tables, and coffee tables, but each of these is also a member of some more inclusive class—the class of things called "furniture." A portion of this taxonomy is shown in Fig. 1.

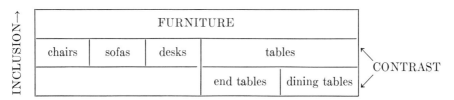

Figure 1.   Taxonomy of furniture.

Figure 1 illustrates two processes characteristic of taxonomies: (1) items at the same level contrast with one another; (2) items at different levels are related by inclusion. At the bottom level are the more highly discriminated classes, at the top is the most inclusive class. Thus, end tables are kinds of tables as tables are kinds of furniture; end tables are not the same as dining tables just as tables are not the same as chairs. These relationships could also be represented in a branching diagram as in Fig. 2.

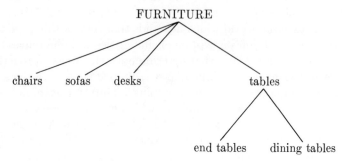

Figure 2.   Branching diagram.

This particular taxonomy constitutes one *semantic domain* in our culture. A sematic domain consists of a class of objects all of which share at least one feature in common which differentiates them from other semantic domains. Chairs, sofas, desks, end tables, and dining tables have in common the designation *furniture*.

Note that Fig. 2 tells us nothing of the things which distinguish a chair from a table. It tells us only that they are different. Suppose you had to tell someone how you know that one object is a chair and the other is a table. In the process of doing this, you might describe certain underlying features, some of which both chairs and tables share and some of which they do not. For example, you might say a chair has four legs, a seat, and a back, but a table has four legs and a top. Chairs would thus differ from tables by the presence of two features—a seat and a back, and the absence of one feature— a top. These underlying features are *components* or *features* of meaning. They are some of the dimensions of meaning underlying the general domain of *furniture*. That these are not the only dimensions is apparent in the contrasts between desk and table. Both pieces of furniture have four legs and a top. Using only the two features you have isolated, it is not possible to say how a table differs from a desk. Should you wish to show how each of these items differs from the other you would have to discover other features of meaning.

Semantic features, like labels, are also organized. A part of the taxonomy of "animals" in American English consists of the following lexemes: cow, bull, heifer, calf, steer, mare, stallion, filly, foal, colt, gelding, sow, boar, gilt, barrow, shoat, piglet, ewe, ram, wether, lamb, livestock, cattle, swine, horse, sheep. This taxonomy is arranged in Table 1.

On even casual examination the items occurring in the lowest level of Table 1 seem to be related in some way. Closer inspection reveals that

Table 1.   Taxonomy of "Livestock"*

	ANIMAL		
	Livestock		
cattle	horse	sheep	swine
cow	mare	ewe	sow
bull	stallion	ram	boar
steer	gelding	wether	barrow
heifer	filly	lamb	gilt
calf	colt		shoat
	foal		piglet

* CF. Lamb 1964:68.

similar distinctions are made under each major category of livestock. The contrast between cow and bull, for example, is the same as the contrast between boar and sow; ram and ewe; stallion and mare. We can readily identify this contrast as one of sex or gender, male versus female. Similarly, there is an identical contrast between bull and steer; ram and wether; stallion and gelding; boar and barrow. Again, we would identify this as a contrast between male animals versus neutered animals. In addition to this sex contrast there is a further contrast between mature and immature animals. A calf is an immature cow or bull and a heifer is an "adolescent" cow. All the lexemes in the lowest level of Table 1 reflect the two semantic features of sex and maturity. Each of these has three values: sex (male, female, neuter); maturity (adult, adolescent, child). Note, however, that horse and pig have an additional feature of maturity denoting "newborn" or "baby" (piglet and foal).

Using symbols: $\male$—male; $\female$—female; $\emptyset$—neuter; M^{-1}—adult; M^{-2}—adolescent; M^{-3}—child; M^{-4}—baby; H—horse; P—swine; C—cattle; S—sheep; the distribution of features for each label can be stated in formulae as follows:

stallion	H $\male$ M^{-1}	boar	P $\male$ M^{-1}
mare	H $\female$ M^{-1}	sow	P $\female$ M^{-1}
gelding	H $\emptyset$ $M^{-1}M^{-2}$	barrow	P $\emptyset$ $M^{-1}M^{-2}$
filly	H $\female$ M^{-2}	gilt	P $\female$ M^{-2}
colt	H $\male$ $\female$ M^{-3}	shoat	P $\male$ $\female$ M^{-3}
foal	H $\male$ $\female$ M^{-4}	piglet	P $\male$ $\female$ M^{-4}

The first formula reads: a stallion is a horse, male, adult, or more appropriately, a stallion is an adult male horse. Such formulae are simply expressions of the distribution of features for each separate label. A box figure shows how these features distribute across the whole set of labels.

Reading from the diagram, a stallion is an adult male horse and a mare is an adult female horse. The features "adult" and "male" *intersect* at the space containing the label "stallion," while the features "adult" and "female" intersect at the space containing the label "mare." Since this diagram has two major features (maturity and sex) which cut across (intersect) one another, it is a *paradigm*. Features are paradigmatically arranged when they are: (1) multiple; (2) intersect.[8]

Paradigms and taxonomies are different kinds of semantic arrangements. In contrast to a paradigm, a taxonomy orders its labels by contrast and inclusion. A taxonomy typically asserts that items in lower levels are *kinds of* items in higher levels. A horse, for example, is a *kind of* livestock. A paradigm makes no such assertion. In Fig. 3 for example, a shoat is not necessarily a kind of boar.

		SEX		
		male ♂	female ♀	neuter ∅
MATURITY	adult M-1	stallion boar	mare sow	gelding barrow
	adolescent M-2		filly gilt	
	child M-3	colt shoat		
	baby M-4	foal piglet		

Figure 3.   Paradigm of features for "horse" and "swine."

For cattle and sheep the contrast between baby and child would be omitted. Sheep also omits the adolescent distinction. There is however an archaic form for newborn sheep *viz.* "Yeanling."

In addition to taxonomies and paradigms semantic features may be arranged on a branching diagram called a *tree*. Features in a tree are ordered by sequential contrast of only one feature at a time. Trees are thus based on successive choices between only two alternatives. Such a semantic arrangement is most frequently encountered in zoological or botanical texts. Figure 4 is a simplified example of a tree.

A reading of Fig. 4 would be: Are the flowers spurred? If yes, are the flowers regular? If they are regular, then this is a delphinium. Unlike a paradigm, the features of a tree do not intersect, and unlike a taxonomy items at lower levels are not included in higher levels. Consequently, paradigms, taxonomies and trees are fundamentally different kinds of semantic arrange-

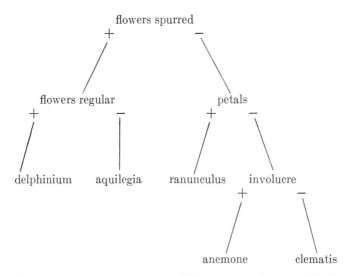

Figure 4.   A tree arrangement. (Adapted from Porter 1967:83)

Plus (+) indicates presence of the feature, minus (−) its absence. Thus, if a flower is not spurred, has no petals, and no involucre, it is a clematis.

ments. Each semantic domain of a culture may be ordered by one or more of these arrangements.

A culture consists of many semantic domains organized around numerous features of meaning, and no two cultures share the same set of semantic domains or features of meaning, nor do they share the same methods of organizing these features. The problem for the anthropologist is to discover these semantic domains and their features, for an anthropologist in the field is much like our interplanetary visitor. There is no familiar order to the way these strange people organize their world. But, unlike our visitor, the anthropologist must avoid imposing his own semantic categories on what he perceives. He must attempt to discover the semantic world in which these people live. There are, then, two ways of bringing order out of apparent chaos—*impose* a preexisting order on it, or *discover* the order underlying it.[9] Nearly all of earlier anthropology was characterized by the first method. By contrast, cognitive anthropology seeks to develop methods which can be used for discovering and describing these principles of organization.

Since such semantic systems are implicit in our use of language, they constitute one of the most significant features of human communication. Yet, what can be communicated and how it is communicated is not solely determined by this kind of semantic feature. Other semantic features deriving from the context of communication are equally important. Context includes the manner of communication (for example, verbal and written), the social setting, and the linguistic repertories of speaker and hearer.

Contextual semantic features and their mutual interdependence are as much a part of the cognitive system as taxonomies and semantic domains.

There still remains the question of how we discover features in cultures other than our own. If you will attempt to complete the statement of semantic features for the taxonomy of furniture, you will see that the discovery of these features is difficult enough in your native language. It is even more difficult in a strange language. As a consequence, new fieldwork techniques and methods have had to be devised. Most important among these are techniques of *controlled eliciting* and methods of *formal analysis*.

Controlled eliciting utilizes sentence frames derived from the language of the people being studied. The aim of such eliciting is to enable the ethnographer to behave linguistically in ways appropriate to the culture he is studying. This involves the use of linguistically correct questions which relate concepts meaningful in that culture. Suppose you are a foreigner attempting to learn something about American culture. On seeing an object for which you do not know an English term, one possible sequence of related questions and responses might be:

Q. What is this?
A. This is a sow.
Q. Is that a sow, too?
A. No, that's a boar.
Q. Is a boar a kind of sow?
A. No, a boar is a kind of livestock.
Q. Is a sow a kind of livestock?
A. Yes.
Q. How many kinds of livestock are there?
A. There are pigs, horses, mules, sheep, goats, and others.

This sequence indicates that sows and boars are conceptually linked and that there are numerous other things grouped with them in the taxonomy of livestock. Note that decisions concerning the inclusion of items within this taxonomy are made by the informant, not by the investigator. Contrast this procedure with a familiar questionnaire technique derived from handbooks on social science methodology. Is the cow __very like; __somewhat like; __only a little like; __not at all like a god (check one). Aside from the spurious scaling, this question would be meaningful only in societies of English speakers in which there were: (a) cows, (b) gods, (c) some evidence that gods and cows were conceptually linked, or (d) sociologists. In this technique, the investigator has already made all the decisions about conceptual relevance. The informant's responses can only be replications in one way or another of the investigator's judgments about conceptual relevance. In a sense, such a method merely tells you what you already know. Controlled eliciting, on the other hand, is designed to provide the ethnographer with not only the answers, but also to assist him in discovering the

relevant questions. It clearly derives from the fact that the questioning process is itself the dominant factor in scientific investigation (Collingwood 1929:29–43). Where the procedures and results of controlled eliciting are contained in the report, two things are achieved: (1) there is an explicit record of how the data were gathered; (2) a public record of the results is available.

Formal analysis is simply one method of stating the results of such controlled eliciting. It differs from other methods in its emphasis on internal consistency, completeness, and form. A particular set of data relating to some semantic domain must be explained by the relationship between units comprising that domain—not by determinants outside it. The problem of external determinants is delayed until internal determinants are analyzed. For example, the question of whether I call my mother's sister's son "cousin" because he is outside my nuclear family cannot be determined until I know the system of relations between cousin, brother, and all the other kin terms in the English system. A formal analysis is complete when the relations among all the units comprising a semantic domain are described.

THE NEW ORDER

The aims and methods of cognitive anthropology have important implications for cultural anthropology. They entail a rethinking of the culture concept, the comparative method, and of ethnography.

In this discussion culture has been identified with cognition. This must strike some cultural anthropologists as a truncated version of the culture concept, for it neglects many of their traditional interests. They might well ask, What about process? What about behavior? What about motivation? Implicit in these questions is an assumption that in addition to cognitive systems a theory of culture must explain cultures as systems emerging from patterned frequencies of observed behavior and processes of development and change (cf. Goodenough 1964). *As a general statement of anthropological goals, these are relevant considerations, but they are not relevant to a theory of culture.* There is no necessity to assume that the cognitive order is either systematically a derivative of or a predictor of substantive actions. Just as the grammar of a language provides no information on what an individual speaker will say on any given occasion, so too a cognitive description of a culture does not pretend to predict the actual behavior of any individual. The formal analysis of culture, like a grammar, is concerned only with what is expected and appropriate. And just as an adequate grammar is neither contingent upon prior assumptions concerning developmental processes nor necessarily explains them, a grammar of culture need make no assumptions about nor attempt to explain these processes. So construed, neither prediction of actual events nor specification of developmental process is a necessary component of a theory of culture.[10] To paraphrase Collingwood (1956:217), cultural anthropology is not a description of events or an account of change. The cultural anthropologist is only concerned with those events which are expressions of underlying thoughts. His aim is to penetrate beyond mere material representation to the logical nexus of underlying concepts.

Culture, conceived as the totality of human behavior, ideas, history, institutions and artifacts has never been particularly useful as a meaningful method of explaining ethnographic facts. Such a conception merely asserts that culture is equivalent to the whole of human knowledge. As a device which purports to explain all of man's learned behavior, motivations, prehistoric record, ecological adaptations, biological limitations, and evolution it attempts too much. What we need is a more limited notion of culture which stresses *theories of culture*. Rather than attempt to develop a general THEORY OF CULTURE, the best we can hope for at present is particular theories of cultures. These theories will constitute complete, accurate descriptions of particular cognitive systems. Only when such particular descriptions are expressed in a single metalanguage with known logical properties will we have arrived at a general theory of culture. Such a general theory will be equivalent to the language in which we describe cultures (Kay 1965:112). In effect we already have a pseudometalanguage. It is for this reason that nearly all ethnographies have similar chapter headings. The problem with this metalanguage is that it assumes universality without prior demonstration. Its universality inheres in the language of description and not necessarily in the object being described.[11]

At issue here are two contrasting views of cultural anthropology. The central issue is, Is cultural anthropology a *natural* or a *formal* science? Traditional cultural anthropology is based on the assumption that its data are discrete material phenomena which can be analyzed like the material phenomena of any other natural science. Cognitive anthropology is based on the assumption that its data are mental phenomena which can be analyzed by formal methods similar to those of mathematics and logic.[12] Each particular culture consists of a set of logical principles which order relevant material phenomena. To the cognitive anthropologist these logical principles rather than the material phenomena are the object of investigation. For the cognitive anthropologist cultural anthropology is a formal science. It seems likely that the logical operations underlying principles of ordering are finite and universal, but capable of generating an infinite number of possible specific orderings (cf. Lévi–Strauss 1966:268). In this limited sense, cognitive anthropology constitutes a return to Bastian's search for the "psychic unity of mankind."

The implications for the comparative method follow directly from the above. The central issue in comparative analysis is, What is the unit of comparison? There have been many attempts to specifically delimit the

unit of comparison. Yet most so-called cross-cultural comparisons have really been nothing more than cross-tribal or cross-community comparisons. Obviously, if a culture is the unit of comparison, then we must compare whole systems which are bounded in space and time or demonstrate that the parts of systems we are comparing are justifiably isolable (cf. Boas 1940:275). Since most ethnographies are not sufficiently complete for either of these possibilities, the whole comparative approach based on substantive variables must be abandoned if our aim is indeed cultural comparison. Those who insist that no fact has meaning except by comparison are right, but the implication that comparison can occur only between similar facts from different systems does not follow. It is much more pertinent to compare similar, but not identical facts within the same system. This is not so much a total abandonment of the comparative method; it is a matter of priorities. Comparisons between systems can only be useful if the facts compared are truly comparable, and we cannot know what facts are comparable until the facts themselves are adequately described. When this is achieved, the units of comparison will be formal features rather than substantive variables.

PROBLEMS AND PROSPECTS

A major indication of vitality in any new orientation is its capacity to generate new problems, and new ways of looking at old problems. Although cognitive anthropologists have made great strides in the study of semantic organization and formal analysis there still remains a vast and only partially explored territory. How current procedures and assumptions will be modified in the attempt to explore these areas is an open question. Clearly, methods and procedures are not adequate for all of the problems that will be encountered. A few of these problems and some of the potential means of looking at them are outlined in the following section.

Arrangements

Taxonomies, paradigms, and trees do not exhaust the domain of semantically significant cognitive orderings. In fact, they represent only a small portion of cognitive processes, and probably occur only when the number of properties or the relations among properties are few. In more complex domains properties are only partially ordered. The structure of such domains is characterized by discontinuous and partial combinations of a large number of features. These are probably best represented as discontinuous arrays of features in a matrix, each row uniquely defining a single lexeme. Although some of the features of such a domain may be dichotomously opposed, intersect paradigmatically, or be related by inclusion, it is not possible to order the entire domain by any one of these principles of ordering. It seems likely that most semantic domains will display this kind of partial ordering and will not strictly conform to any one of the three preceding kinds of arrangement. If this is true, such domains should probably not be analyzed in terms of features and feature organization. The multiplicity of relations and properties probably signifies some other type of ordering unrelated to the isolation and organization of features.

Perception and Conception

The problem of partially ordered domains discussed above is partially a reflex of a related problem—the problem of the relation between perception of attributes or features ("identification") and conceptual knowledge. So far anthropologists seem to have assumed a direct connection between attribute perception and conceptual ordering. In many semantic domains this assumption is probably unjustified. Some semantic domains (for example, the classification of deities) may lack obvious perceptual attributes. Other semantic domains may be conceptually ordered without reference to perceptual attributes. Even though it may be possible to isolate perceptual attributes in such cases they are not semantically relevant. It is also possible that the organization of attributes and the organization of concepts ultimately refer to different semantic domains. Where this is the case both conceptual and perceptual orderings may merely be surface structures deriving from even more complex underlying forms.

Discourse Analysis

In part the difficulties inherent in the perception-conception problem arise from the cognitive anthropologist's enthrallment with the lexeme as a basic unit of analysis. As yet, few anthropologists have attempted to investigate either larger linguistic units or nonlinguistic units. What semantic information, for example, is transmitted by the occurrence of a lexeme in sequences of discourse larger than a sentence (cf. Harris 1952)? In connected discourse speakers and authors deliberately manipulate semantic features in order to convey nuances of meaning often quite opposed to the overt content of individual lexemes. Essentially, discourse analysis is one more aspect of the problem of context.

Propositional Analysis

When lexemes occur in a sentence, it is obvious that some aspect of meaning is conveyed by the sentence as a whole. The meaning of the sentence is not simply the sum of the meanings of its constituent lexemes. One convenient approach, which has a long-standing usage, is to assume that the sentence is an assertion about the relationship among the semantic components of its constituent lexemes. The sentence "germs cause colds" asserts a relation between germs and colds—in this case a causal relation. It can also be seen as a statement about disease *beliefs*. Underlying this sentence is the prior semantic information to the effect that there are things called colds and there are things called germs. Such sentences can be succinctly stated in logical form.

(1) $(\exists x)(\exists y)(xCy)$

Where x stands for germs, y for colds and C for the relation of causality, this formula reads, There is an x (germs) and there is a y (colds) such that x causes y. In this same domain of analysis, the sentence "germs cause disease" also occurs, symbolized as follows (z stands for disease):

(2) $(\exists x)(\exists z)(xCz)$

Except for the substitution of z this formula is identical with (1). Note however that there is a special relation between z and y. A cold is a kind of disease. Using the notation for set inclusion $(\in)$ this taxonomic relation can be symbolized as:

(3) $(\exists y)(\exists z)(y \in z)$

This formula asserts that there are colds (y) and there are diseases (z) and that colds are a kind of (are included in the set of) disease. Since (3) is equivalent to a statement of taxonomic categorization it is apparent that all taxonomies are derived from propositions of this type.[13] A more interesting feature is that because y is included in z we might infer without prior knowledge:

(4) $(\exists x)(\exists y)(\exists z)(xCz)$ & $(y \in z) \rightarrow (xCy)$

That is, if there are germs, diseases and colds, and germs cause diseases, and colds are a kind of disease, then germs also cause colds. If we did not already know that germs cause colds, on the basis of this inference we would be prompted to ask our informant if this were the case. As a matter for further investigation we would want to discover whether or not the relation of germ causation holds for all lexemes included in the category of diseases. In other words, we are interested in the domain of the relation C. It would also be interesting to know if C holds for all lexemes included in the category of "illness." Since mental illness is a kind of illness (is included in the set of illnesses) and we would not normally assert that germs cause mental illness, one of the chief semantic contrasts between illness and disease is the belief that germs cause disease but not all illnesses. Put another way, the domain of C does not include cases in which the ordered couples are germs and illness.[14]

An important point is implicit in the preceeding illustration. Since germs are not an attribute of disease we would probably not have arrived at this statement of contrast between illness and disease if we had remained at the level of identifying those perceptual attributes which differentiate diseases from illnesses or one kind of disease from another. Perceptual attributes are irrelevant to beliefs (conceptual knowledge) about diseases— at least in this example (cf. D'Andrade and others 1966). Recognition of propositional analysis and its importance for understanding cognitive orderings is recent, but it seems certain that it will play an important role in the development of cognitive anthropology (cf. Kay 1965).

Metamessages

A much more difficult area of research is the analysis of what I shall here refer to as "metamessages." In a common sense way, metamessages are what we are talking about when someone says, How are you? and we say to ourselves, Now I wonder what he *really* meant by that? Metamessages communicate semantic information which does not seem to be at all related to the overt content of an utterance. Under these circumstances an apparently simple sentence like "it's cold in here" could mean "bring me my coat," "turn up the heat," or "you've had enough to drink and its time to go home." The pioneering work of Bateson (1956) remains the most important contribution to this kind of analysis.[15] As a speculative aside (deriving from Bateson's work) it is possible that all such metamessages ultimately derive from a restricted set of propositions in the imperative mood expressing dominance, dependency, aggression, and submission (Love me! Hate me! Don't hurt me! Be nice!). If this is true, then it is in this area that studies of animal communication can make a significant contribution to cognitive anthropology.

Historical Linguistics

Application of formal semantic analysis to problems of linguistic reconstruction should yield significant results. Historical linguistics has made great progress in the reconstruction of phonology and grammar, but its attempts to reconstruct meanings are generally unimpressive. Too often semantic reconstructions are either based on the notion that the most frequently occurring glosses represent basic meaning or that certain glosses are derivative extensions of other glosses. The fallacy in much of this stems from a failure to recognize the arbitrary nature of the relation between linguistic signs and their denotata. Attempts to reconstruct the meanings of words are symptomatic of a preoccupation with the lexeme rather than the organization of semantic domains. Recent work in the semantic reconstruction of kinship terminologies indicates that semantic domains can be reconstructed without reference to their constituent lexemes (cf. Voorhees 1960; Tyler 1965). The basic procedure consists of a comparison and reconstruction of semantic categories. The structure of the rules which transform one genetically related system into another constitutes a description of historical process. An interesting feature emerging from these studies is that the semantic structure of such systems display a remarkably conservative nature. The parameters of the system are relatively impervious to change despite the fact that individual lexemes denoting semantic categories frequently undergo rapid and dramatic change. Changes occur in the variables of the system, not in its parameters (cf. Bateson 1958:292). Preliminary reconstructions of Dravidian, Athapascan, Yuman, and Indo-European kinship systems all agree in manifesting this trait. Such evidence, preliminary as it may be, is certainly sufficient to challenge many of our assumptions about change in kinship as a result of changes in other features of social organization. Whether such persistence is characteristic of other semantic domains remains to be seen, but it seems apparent that structural semantics can make an important contribution to linguistic reconstruction. And, if the structure of transform rules linking the semantic domains of separate languages are in fact a description of historical process, this should be of enormous significance to lexicostatistics and glottochronology.

Semantic Ontogenesis

Finally, we need research on the development of cognitive categories. How does the child acquire semantic features? What is the significance of rote versus rule learning in semantic analysis? What is the relation between the derivation of semantic features and their order of acquisition in the learning process? A common assumption in philosophy (cf. Quine 1960:80–124) and psychology (cf. Church 1963:68–78) is that the child first acquires concepts for concrete objects and gradually expands its semantic domain by extension and generalization to include more abstract conceptions. There is little real evidence to support this developmental sequence and despite its obvious appeal to intuitive notions, it seems suspect. Given the primacy of spatiotemporal orientation over language acquisition, an equally good a priori argument could be made for the prior learning of relational concepts. It is quite likely that the ontogenesis of semantic categories will bear little significance in the analysis of semantic domains among adult speakers. Since different individuals probably arrive at similar semantic structures by widely variant ontogenetic pathways the relation between ontogenesis and semantic structure will probably remain indeterminant. Disparity of ontogenetic sequences may, however, be related to the occurrence of multiple formal solutions in some indirect fashion.

These comments are intended as speculations on the possible areas of future development in cognitive anthropology. They do not pretend to be exhaustive nor even representative. Nonetheless, they do indicate that cognitive anthropology has moved into a secondary stage of development. We have a few tentative answers, some new questions, and a host of old questions still unanswered. Fresh ground has been broken and new areas occupied, but still more remote territories have opened up for further research.

Explicit here is a view of culture derived from a kind of ethnography in which the methods of description are public and replicable, and the results predictive of expectations of appropriate behavior. Implicit is the cognitive reorganization of our categories of description and analysis. Cognitive anthropology entails an ethnographic technique which describes cultures from the inside out rather than from the outside in. Categories of description are initially derived from relevant features in a culture rather than from the lexicon of anthropology.

Cognitive reorganization is a familiar process in the history of anthropology—in fact of any scientific discipline. The history of science is but the record of constant reexamination of assumptions, methods, and data. Such new developments in science do not take place in a vacuum. Innovations in one branch of science are complemented by convergent developments in other branches.

The psychologist's renewed interest in cognition, the linguist's rediscovery of semantics, the biologist's recent emphasis on taxonomy and species specific behavior, and the sociologist's concern with the presentation of the self all reflect a set of recent developments complementary to one another and to those in anthropology. To be sure, among these disciplines there are differences in emphasis and method, yet each shares with the other a common orientation—the discovery of the organizing principles used by individuals, cultures, and species in manipulating and adapting to their particular life-space.

NOTES

[1] I wish to thank the following people who commented on previous versions of this paper: Brent Berlin, Mary Black, Charles Frake, John Gumperz, Dell Hymes, Paul Kay, Floyd Lounsbury, Ronald Rohner, George and Louise Spindler. I hope it is evident that the views in this chapter are those of the editor and do not necessarily represent a consensus of opinion among the above nor among those whose papers comprise subsequent chapters.

[2] In this, and in much of what follows, there is a pronounced neo-Kantian flavor.

[3] For an instance of a similar distinction between "objective environment" and "perceived life-space," see von Uexküll (1957).

[4] The processes involved in this example are related to theories of cognitive dissonance (cf. Festinger 1957).

[5] The line of argument here derives mainly from Russell (1929:92–98), but see also Bateson (1958:294) and Sapir (1932:515–519).

[6] The most notable exception to this statement is Boas.

[7] It is probably not true that all named things are significant, just as it is not the case that all significant things are named. Yet, as a point of departure, named categories are of primary importance.

[8] Note the two empty spaces in Fig. 3. These indicate that this is not a perfect paradigm. The empty spaces are the result of incomplete combination of semantic components. The combinations $\male$ M^{-2}; $\varnothing$ M^{-3}; $\varnothing$ M^{-4} do not occur. In a perfect paradigm all possible combinations would be realized. Perfect paradigms occur less frequently than imperfect paradigms. It should also be noted that in some contexts the lexemes "boar" and "stallion" denote not only $\male$ M^{-1} but $\male$ $M^{-1}M^{-2}$. For "horse" the lexeme "yearling" may sometimes denote $\male$ M^{-2}; $\female$ M^{-2}; $\varnothing$ M^{-2}. Historically it is interesting to note that all the lexemes denoting "newborn" ($\male$ $\female$ M^{-4}) except piglet are derived from verbs denoting "to give birth to." A cow "calves," a mare "foals," a ewe "lambs," or "yeans," but a sow "farrows." As might be expected the archaic term for a newborn pig is "farrow." The lexeme piglet is recent. Also relevant is the fact that the "wild animal" category denoted by the lexeme "deer" has, except for the neuter category, the same semantic features as the category denoted by cattle. Formerly deer denoted "animal." Finally, the features male, female, neuter correspond to the generalized Indo-European classification of nouns as masculine, feminine, neuter.

[9] This distinction between a priori and a posteriori models is difficult to maintain, for it impinges directly on the philosophical problem of "other minds." If the mind imposes its own order on the disorderly happenings of the universe, then the investigator of necessity imposes his own logical constructs on the world he believes he is exploring. From this point of view there is no evidence for a belief in the existence of other minds except by analogy. Yet, granted the existence of other minds it is possible to assume that since the logical constructs of an informant and of an investigator are both products of a mind, these constructs are knowable insofar as they are communicable. Hence, the cognitive anthropologist's emphasis on language as both a method of discovery and an object of investigation (cf. Russell 1929:99–103).

[10] This is not to imply that such a theory is incompatible with the study of change and development. The point is that a theory of description constitutes a different order of theory than that required for processes of change (for a discussion of this point, see Bateson 1958:296–300). A theory of change emphasizing cognitive organization would probably demonstrate that most anthropological data on change relate not to cultural change, but merely to epiphenomenal fluctuations.

[11] This is misleading. Scientific laws are of necessity statements of universals in the language of description. All talk of "objects" and an hypothesized relation between "objects" and the language of description is symptomatic of a pernicious kind of dualism. The point is that our current language of description is inadequate either for the description of particular cultures or the development of universals simply because its assumptions are implicit and its operations (when specified) are contradictory. The continuing argument in descent "theory" is a classic example of the inadequacy of our current "metalanguage." The misleading statement reflects my own vaccilation between an "intuitionist" (conceptualist) and "logicist" (realist) point of view (cf. Quine 1952). In general, this chapter is intuitionist with occasional logicist lapses. The lapses create problems like the one referred to above.

My assertion that the description of a culture is really a description of the an-thropologist's cognitive ordering is pure intuitionism which does not square directly with the Lévi-Straussian quest for a universal pan-human logic expressed in other sections. In a sense, the psychological reality problem is a confrontation between intuitionism and realism or perhaps formalism (nominalism). My belief in the relevance of relevance as an aspect of cognitive anthropology is probably creeping realism.

[12] Leach (1961:6–21) makes a similar point, but with different emphasis. For two discussions of the distinction between formal and factual or natural sciences, see Carnap (1953) and Quine (1960:270–276). The distinction may be somewhat overdrawn, but this should not obscure the fact that cultural anthropology has traditionally emulated a model of scientific method derived from a rather naive nineteenth century scientific materialism. Harris's (1962) quest for elementary units of cultural "matter" is a recent example of this attitude.

[13] For more complete formalization of taxonomies, see Gregg (1954), and Woodger (1952).

[14] These assertions are illustrative. Whether they hold true for disease and illness is a matter for research. The main point is that the domain of a relation may be of greater importance in establishing semantic contrast than the distribution of features.

[15] For additional research of this kind, see the bibliography under "expressive language" in Hymes (1964a).

REFERENCES CITED

Bateson, Gregory, 1958, Naven, 2d ed. Stanford, Stanford University Press.

———, D. D. Jackson, J. Haley, and J. H. Weakland, 1956, Toward a theory of schizophrenia. Behavioral Science 1:250–264.

Boas, Franz, 1938, The mind of primitive man. London, Macmillan.

———, 1940, Race, language and culture. New York, Macmillan.

Carnap, Rudolf, 1953, Formal and factual science. In H. Feigl and M. Brodbeck, eds., Readings in the philosophy of science. New York, Appleton.

Church, Joseph, 1961, Language and the discovery of reality. New York, Random House.

Collingwood, R. G., 1939, An autobiography. New York, Oxford University Press.

———, 1956, The idea of history. New York, Oxford University Press.

D'Andrade, Roy G., N. Quinn, S. B. Nerlove, and A. K. Romney, 1966, Categories of disease in American-English and Mexican-Spanish. Unpublished manuscript.

Festinger, Leon, 1957, A theory of cognitive dissonance. New York, Harper & Row.

Goodenough, Ward H., 1957, Cultural anthropology and linguistics. In Paul Garvin, ed., Report of the seventh annual round table meeting on linguistics and language study. Georgetown University Monograph Series on Language and Linguistics No. 9.

———, 1963, Cooperation in change. New York, Russell Sage.

———, 1964, Introduction. In W. H. Goodenough, ed., Explorations in cultural anthropology. New York, McGraw-Hill.

Gregg, John R., 1954, The language of taxonomy: an application of symbolic logic to the study of classificatory systems. New York, Columbia University Press.

Harris, Marvin, 1964, The nature of cultural things. New York, Random House.

Harris, Zellig, 1952, Discourse analysis. Language 28:1–30.

Hymes, Dell, ed., 1964a, Language in culture and society. New York, Harper & Row.

———, 1964b, Directions in (ethno-) linguistic theory. American Anthropologist 66 Pt. 2 No. 3:6–56.

Kay, Paul, 1965, Does anthropology need a metalanguage? Paper presented at the Southwestern Anthropological Association Annual Meeting, 1965.

———, 1966, Ethnography and theory of culture. Bucknell Review 14:106–113.

Lamb, Sydney, 1964, The sememic approach to structural semantics. American Anthropologist 66 Pt. 2 No. 3:57–78.

Leach, E. R., 1961, Rethinking anthropology. London School of Economics Monographs on Social Anthropology No. 22. London, University of London Press.

Lévi-Strauss, Claude, 1966, The savage mind. Chicago, University of Chicago Press.

Porter, C. L., 1967, Taxonomy of flowering plants. San Francisco, Freeman.

Quine, Willard Van Orman, 1960, Word and object. New York, Wiley.

———, 1952, On what there is. In L. Linsky, ed., Semantics and the philosophy of language. Urbana, University of Illinois Press.

Russeil, Bertrand, 1929, Our knowledge of the external world. New York, Norton.

Sapir, Edward, 1932, Cultural anthropology and psychiatry. In D. G. Mandelbaum, ed., Selected writings of Edward Sapir. Berkeley, University of California Press.

———, 1934, The emergence of the concept of personality in a study of cultures. In D. G. Mandelbaum, ed., Selected writings of Edward Sapir. Berkeley, University of California Press.

Tyler, Stephen A., 1965, Proto-central Dravidian kinship terminology. Paper presented at a symposium on kinship in India at the American Association for the Advancement of Science Annual Meeting, 1965.

Uexküll, Jakob Von, 1957, A stroll through the world of animals and men: a picture book of invisible worlds. In C. H. Schiller and K. S. Lashley, eds., Instinctive behavior: the development of a modern concept. New York, International Universities.

Voorhees, Thomas, 1959, The formal analysis and comparison of Yuman kinship systems. Unpublished MA Thesis, Stanford University.

Wallace, A. F. C., 1961, Culture and personality. New York, Random House.

Woodger, J. H., 1952, Biology and language: an introduction to the methodology of the biological sciences including medicine. Cambridge, the University Press.

1 Arrangements

Even the most rigorous method of data acquisition will not necessarily reveal relationships among facts. Consequently, we must discover that method of arrangement which provides the best statement of relationships. Since our concern is only with relationships among facts which can be demonstrated to comprise a single domain, the problem of functional or other relations with facts external to this domain is irrelevant—at this stage of analysis. We are interested then only in the question of internal orderings. Since it is evident that there is a great number of possible semantic features, which may enter into a variety of relations with one another it might be supposed that orderings too are exceedingly diverse. This statement is true insofar as it pertains to the over-all organization of a semantic domain. Yet, it is paradoxical that these diverse organizations appear to result from relatively few principles of ordering. The principles of ordering which cognitive anthropologists have so far dealt with most frequently are: (1) taxonomies; (2) paradigms; (3) trees. No one denies the existence of other principles of ordering, but they have not yet been widely used in the analysis of ethnographic data (cf. Conklin, this volume, Chapter 1). The important point is that the principles of ordering, though derived from a set of finite logical operations are capable of producing an infinite variety of specific organizations. In this respect Boole's quest for the universal laws of human thought cannot be said to have been in vain.

TAXONOMIES

A folk taxonomy constitutes a description of relevant conceptual categories. It tells us what the categories are and how they are related to one another. In a taxonomy, categories are hierarchically ordered by relations of contrast and inclusion. Categories at the same level contrast with one another while categories at lower levels are included in categories at higher levels. Categories at the same level differ from one another, but when included in the same higher level category are somehow like one another. It is for this reason that a folk taxonomy is but the first step in a semantic analysis, for there must be some reason behind this arbitrary neutralization of difference at higher levels. In general, this corresponds to our intuition that certain things go together because they share some underlying element. The next step in semantic analysis then is to discover these elements. By discovering the underlying features shared by things which are alike, but not shared by things which are not alike, we complete the second stage of semantic analysis. This process is discussed in detail in chapter three.

PARADIGMS AND TREES

Just as the relationship between categories is ordered, relations between features too are ordered. Thus far, only two types of feature arrangement have been systematically investigated. These are paradigms and trees. Like a taxonomy, a paradigm arranges its components on the basis of their sameness and difference. But, unlike a taxonomy, the multiple components of a paradigm cannot be arranged hierarchically, for they are not ordered by *inclusion*. Instead, they are ordered by simultaneous *intersection*. By contrast, the features in a tree do not intersect one another simultaneously and they contrast on only one dimension at a time. Relationships in a tree are expressed as dichotomous oppositions of components selected one at a time (cf. Kay, this volume, Chapter 1, Conklin, this volume, Chapter 1; Wallace, this volume, Chapter 4).

Taxonomies, paradigms and trees, though different, are all semantic structures derived from the continuous combination of relations among properties. Properties may be lexemes or semantic features.

Problems of domain overlap between lexemes, isolation of lexical items, unlabeled categories, and multiple levels of contrast are difficult to resolve. The papers by Frake and Conklin delineate the basic features of taxonomic ordering and discuss some approaches to the solution of these problems. Bright's paper provides a detailed example of nonhierarchic ordering derived from domain overlap and multiple levels of contrast. Kay presents a most useful formalization of types of arrangement and should be read in conjunction with Conklin (this volume, Chapter 2) and Wallace (this volume, Chapter 4). Other useful discussions not included in this volume are: Conklin (1962), Durbin (1966). Berlin and colleagues show how proliferation of taxonomic categories reflects areas of high cultural interest. The problem of unlabeled categories is discussed in Black (this volume, Chapter 2; see also Berlin 1966).

REFERENCES CITED

Berlin, Brent, 1966, Unlabelled taxons in folk taxonomies. In manuscript.
Conklin, H. C., 1962, Comment on the "Ethnographic study of cognitive systems" by C. O. Frake. *In* Thomas Gladwin and William C. Sturtevant, eds. Anthropology and human behavior. Washington, D.C., Anthropological Society of Washington.
Durbin, Marshall, 1966, The goals of ethnoscience. Anthropological Linguistics 8:22–41.

The Ethnographic Study of Cognitive Systems[1]

Charles O. Frake

WORDS FOR THINGS

A relatively simple task commonly performed by ethnographers is that of getting names for things. The ethnographer typically performs this task by pointing to or holding up the apparent constituent objects of an event he is describing, eliciting the native names for the objects, and then matching each native name with the investigator's own word for the object. The logic of the operation is: if the informant calls object X a *mbubu* and I call object X a *rock*, then *mbubu* means *rock*. In this way are compiled the ordinary ethnobotanical monographs with their lists of matched native and scientific names for plant specimens. This operation probably also accounts for a good share of the native names parenthetically inserted in so many monograph texts: "Among the grasses (*sigbet*) whose grains (*bunga nen*) are used for beads (*bitekel*) none is more highly prized than Job's tears (*glias*)." Unless the reader is a comparative linguist of the languages concerned, he may well ask what interest these parenthetical insertions contain other than demonstrating that the ethnographer has discharged a minimal obligation toward collecting linguistic data. This procedure for obtaining words for things, as well as the "so-what" response it so often evokes, assumes the objective identifiability of discrete "things" apart from a particular culture. It construes the name-getting task as one of simply matching verbal labels for "things" in two languages. Accordingly, the "problem-oriented" anthropologist, with a broad, cross-cultural perspective, may disclaim any interest in these labels; all that concerns him is the presence or absence of a particular "thing" in a given culture.

If, however, instead of "getting words for things," we redefine the task as one of finding the "things" that go with the words, the eliciting of terminologies acquires a more general interest. In actuality not even the most concrete, objectively apparent physical object can be identified apart from some culturally defined system of concepts (Boas 1911:24–25; Bruner *et al.*, 1956; Goodenough 1957). An ethnographer should strive to define objects[2] according to the conceptual system of the people he is studying. Let me suggest, then, that one look upon the task of getting names for things not as an exercise in linguistic recording, but as a way of finding out what are in fact the "things" in the environment of the people being studied. This paper consists of some suggestions toward the formulation of an opera-

From *Anthropology and Human Behavior*. Washington, D.C., Anthropological Society of Washington, 1962. Used by permission of the author and the Anthropological Society of Washington.

tionally-explicit methodology for discerning how people construe their world of experience from the way they talk about it. Specifically these suggestions concern the analysis of terminological systems in a way which reveals the conceptual principles that generate them.

In a few fields, notably in kinship studies, anthropologists have already successfully pushed an interest in terminological systems beyond a matching of translation labels. Since Morgan's day no competent student of kinship has looked upon his task as one of simply finding a tribe's words for "uncle," "nephew," or "cousin." The recognition that the denotative range of kinship categories must be determined empirically in each case, that the categories form a system, and that the semantic contrasts underlying the system are amenable to formal analysis, has imparted to kinship studies a methodological rigor and theoretical productivity rare among ethnographic endeavors. Yet all peoples are vitally concerned with kinds of phenomena other than genealogical relations; consequently there is no reason why the study of a people's concepts of these other phenomena should not offer a theoretical interest comparable to that of kinship studies.

Even with reference to quite obvious kinds of material objects, it has long been noted that many people do not see "things" quite the way we do. However, anthropologists in spite of their now well-established psychological interests have notably ignored the cognition of their subjects. Consequently other investigators still rely on stock anecdotes of "primitive thinking" handed down by explorers, philologists, and psychologists since the nineteenth century (Brown 1958:256; Hill 1952; Jespersen 1934:429; Ullman 1957:95, 308). Commonly these anecdotes have been cited as examples of early stages in the evolution of human thought—which, depending on the anecdote selected, may be either from blindly concrete to profoundly abstract or from hopelessly vague to scientifically precise. A typical citation, purporting to illustrate the primitive's deficient abstractive ability, concerns a Brazilian Indian tribe which allegedly has no word for "parrot" but only words for "kinds of parrots" (Jespersen 1934:429ff.). The people of such a tribe undoubtedly classify the birds of their environment in some fashion; certainly they do not bestow a unique personal name on each individual bird specimen they encounter. Classification means that individual bird specimens must be matched against the defining attributes of conceptual categories and thereby judged to be equivalent for certain purposes to some other specimens but different from still others. Since no two birds are alike in every discernable feature, any grouping into sets implies a selection of only a limited number of features as significant for contrasting kinds of birds. A person learns which features are significant from his fellows as part of his cultural equipment. He does not receive this information from the birds. Consequently there is no necessary reason that a Brazilian Indian should heed those particular attributes which, for the English-speaker, make equivalent all the diverse individual organisms he labels "parrots." Some of this Indian's categories may seem quite specific, and others quite general, when compared to our grouping of the same specimens. But learning that it takes the Indian many words to name the objects we happen to group together in one set is trivial information compared to knowing how the Indian himself groups these objects and which attributes he selects as dimensions to generate a taxonomy of avifauna. With the latter knowledge we learn what these people regard as significant about birds. If we can arrive at comparable knowledge about their concepts of land animals, plants, soils, weather, social relations, personalities, and supernaturals, we have at least a sketch map of the world in the image of the tribe.

The analysis of a culture's terminological systems will not, of course, exhaustively reveal the cognitive world of its members, but it will certainly tap a central portion of it. Culturally significant cognitive features must be communicable between persons in one of the standard symbolic systems of the culture. A major share of these features will undoubtedly be codable in a society's most flexible and productive communication device, its language. Evidence also seems to indicate that those cognitive features requiring most frequent communication will tend to have standard and relatively short linguistic labels (Brown 1958:235–241; Brown and Lenneberg 1954). Accordingly, a commonly distinguished category of trees is more likely to be called something like "elm" by almost all speakers rather than labelled with an ad hoc, non-standardized construction like, "You know, those tall trees with asymmetrical, serrated-edged leaves." To the extent that cognitive coding tends to be linguistic and tends to be efficient, the study of the referential use of standard, readily elicitable linguistic responses—or *terms*— should provide a fruitful beginning point for mapping a cognitive system. And with verbal behavior we know how to begin.

The beginning of an ethnographic task is the recording of what is seen and heard, the segmenting of the behavior stream in such a way that culturally significant noises and movements are coded while the irrelevant is discarded. Descriptive linguistics provides a methodology for segmenting the stream of speech into units relevant to the structure of the speaker's language. I assume that any verbal response which conforms to the phonology and grammar of a language is necessarily a culturally significant unit of behavior. Methodologies for the structural description of non-verbal behavior are not correspondingly adequate in spite of important contributions in this direction by such persons as Pike and Barker and Wright (Barker and Wright 1955; Pike 1954; cf. Miller *et al.* 1960:14–15). By pushing forward the analysis of units we know to be culturally relevant, we can, I think, more satisfactorily arrive at procedures for isolating the significant constituents of analogous and interrelated structures. The basic methodological concept advocated here—the determination of the set of contrasting responses appropriate to a given, culturally valid, eliciting context—should ultimately be applicable to the "semantic" analysis of any culturally meaningful behavior.

SEGREGATES

A terminologically distinguished array of objects is a *segregate* (Conklin 1954, 1962; cf. Lounsbury 1956). Segregates are categories, but not all categories known or knowable to an individual are segregates by this definition. Operationally, this definition of a segregate leaves a problem: how do we recognize a "term" when we hear one? How do we segment the stream of speech into category-designating units?

The segmentation of speech into the grammatically functioning units revealed by linguistic analysis is a necessary, but not sufficient, condition for terminological analysis. Clearly no speech segment smaller than the minimal grammatical unit, the morpheme, need be considered. However, the task requires more than simply a search for the meanings of morphemes or other grammatical units. The items and arrangements of a structural description of the language code need not be isomorphic with the categories and propositions of the message. Linguistic forms, whether morphemes or larger constructions, are not each tied to unique chunks of semantic reference like baggage tags; rather it is the use of speech, the selection of one statement over another in a particular socio-linguistic context, that points to the category boundaries on a culture's cognitive map (Chomsky 1955; Haugen 1957; Hymes 1961; Joos 1958; Lounsbury 1956; Nida 1951).

Suppose we have been studying the verbal behavior accompanying the selection and ordering of items at an American lunch counter.[3] The following text might be typical of those overheard and recorded:

"What ya going to have, Mac? Something to eat?"

"Yeah. What kind of sandwiches ya got besides hamburgers and hot dogs?"

"How about a ham 'n cheese sandwich?"

"Nah . . . I guess I'll take a hamburger again."

"Hey, that's no hamburger; that's a cheeseburger!"

The problem is to isolate and relate these speech forms according to their use in naming objects. Some, but apparently not all, orderable items at a lunch counter are distinguished by the term *something to eat*. A possibility within the range of 'something to eat' seems to be a set of objects labelled *sandwiches*. The forms *hamburger, hot dog, ham 'n cheese sandwich,* and *cheeseburger* clearly designate alternative choices in lunch-counter contexts. A customer determined to have a 'sandwich' must select one of these alternatives when he orders, and upon receipt of the order, he must satisfy himself that the object thrust before him—which he has never seen before—meets the criteria for membership in the segregate he designated. The counterman must decide on actions that will produce an object acceptable to the customer as a member of the designated segregate. The terminological status of these forms can be confirmed by analysis of further speech situations, by eliciting utterances with question frames suggested to the investigator by the data, and by observing non-verbal features of the situation, especially correlations between terms used in ordering and objects received.

In isolating these terms no appeal has been made to analysis of their linguistic structure or their signification. *Sandwich* is a single morpheme. Some linguists, at any rate, would analyze *hot dog* and even *hamburger* as each containing two morphemes, but, since the meaning of the constructions cannot be predicted from a knowledge of the meaning of their morphological constituents, they are single "lexemes" (Goodenough 1956) or "idioms" (Hockett 1958:303–318). *Ham 'n cheese sandwich* would not, I think, qualify as a single lexeme; nevertheless it is a standard segregate label whose function in naming objects cannot be distinguished from that of forms like *hot dog*. Suppose further utterances from lunch-counter speech show that the lexically complex term *something to eat* distinguishes the same array of objects as do the single morphemes *food* and *chow*. In such a case, a choice among these three terms would perhaps say something about the social status of the lunch counter and its patrons, but it says nothing distinctive about the objects designated. As segregate labels, these three frequently-heard terms would be equivalent.

Although not operationally relevant at this point, the lexemic status of terms bears on later analysis of the productivity of a terminological system. In contrast, say, to our kinship terminology, American lunch-counter terminology is highly productive. The existence of productive, polylexemic models such as *ham 'n cheese sandwich* permits the generation and labelling of new segregates to accommodate the latest lunch-counter creations. However, the non-intuitive determination of the lexemic status of a term requires a thorough analysis of the distinctive features of meaning of the term and its constituents (Goodenough 1956; Lounsbury 1956). Such an analysis of the criteria for placing objects into categories can come only after the term, together with those contrasting terms relevant to its use, has been isolated as a segregate label.

CONTRAST SETS

In a situation in which a person is making a public decision about the category membership of an object by giving the object a verbal label, he is selecting a term out of a set of alternatives, each with classificatory import. When he asserts "This is an *X*," he is also stating that it is *not* specific other things, these other things being not everything else conceivable, but only the alternatives among which a decision was made (Kelly 1955). In lunch-counter ordering, 'hamburger,' 'hot dog,' 'cheeseburger,' and 'ham and cheese sandwich' are such alternatives. Any object placed in one of these segregates cannot at the same time belong to another. Those culturally appropriate responses which are distinctive alternatives in the same kinds of situations—or, in linguistic parlance, which occur in the same "environment"—can be said to *contrast*. A series of terminologically contrasted segregates forms a *contrast set*.

Note that the cognitive relation of contrast is not equivalent to the relation of class exclusion in formal logic and set theory. The three categories 'hamburger,' 'hot dog,' and 'rainbow' are mutually exclusive in membership. But in writing rules for classifying hamburgers I must say something about hot dogs, whereas I can ignore rainbows. Two categories contrast only when the difference between them is significant for defining their use. The segregates 'hamburger' and 'rainbow,' even though they have no members in common, do not function as distinctive alternatives in any uncontrived classifying context familiar to me.

TAXONOMIES

The notion of contrast cannot account for all the significant relations among these lunch-counter segregates. Although no object can be both a hamburger and a hot dog, an object can very well be both a hot dog and a sandwich or a hamburger and a sandwich. By recording complementary names applied to the same objects (and eliminating referential synonyms such as *something to eat* and *food*), the following series might result:

>Object A is named: *something to eat, sandwich, hamburger*
>Object B is named: *something to eat, sandwich, ham sandwich*
>Object C is named: *something to eat, pie, apple pie*
>Object D is named: *something to eat, pie, cherry pie*
>Object E is named: *something to eat, ice-cream bar, Eskimo pie.*

Some segregates include a wider range of objects than others and are sub-partitioned by a contrast set. The segregate 'pie' *includes* the contrast set 'apple pie,' 'cherry pie,' etc. For me, the segregate 'apple pie' is, in turn, sub-partitioned by 'French apple pie' and 'plain (or 'ordinary') apple pie' Figure 1 diagrams the sub-partitioning of the segregate 'something to eat' as revealed by naming responses to objects A—E.[4]

Again it is the use of terms, not their linguistic structure, that provides evidence of inclusion. We cannot consider 'Eskimo pie' to be included in the category 'pie,' for we cannot discover a natural situation in which an object labelled *Eskimo pie* can be labelled simply *pie*. Thus the utterance,

something to eat				
sandwich		pie		ice-cream bar
hamburger	ham sandwich	apple pie	cherry pie	Eskimo pie
A	B	C	D	E

OBJECTS:

Figure 1.   Sub-partitioning of the segregate 'something to eat' as revealed by naming responses to objects A—E.

"That's not a sandwich; that's a pie," cannot refer to an Eskimo pie. Similar examples are common in English. The utterance, "Look at that oak," may refer to a 'white oak' but never to a 'poison oak.' A 'blackbird' is a kind of 'bird,' but a 'redcap' is not a kind of 'cap.' For many English speakers, the unqualified use of *American* invariably designates a resident or citizen of the United States; consequently, for such speakers, an 'American' is a kind of 'North American' rather than the converse. One cannot depend on a particular grammatical construction, such as one of the English phrasal compounds, to differentiate consistently a single cognitive relation, such as that of inclusion (cf. Hockett 1958:316–317). Because English is not unique in this respect (Frake 1961), the practice of arguing from morphological and syntactic analysis directly to cognitive relations must be considered methodologically unsound.

Segregates in different contrast sets, then, may be related by inclusion. A system of contrast sets so related is a *taxonomy* (Conklin 1962; Gregg 1954; Woodger 1952). This definition does not require a taxonomy to have a unique beginner, i.e., a segregate which includes all other segregates in the system. It requires only that the segregates at the most inclusive level form a demonstrable contrast set.

Taxonomies make possible a regulation of the amount of information communicated about an object in a given situation (compare: "Give me something to eat" with "Give me a French apple pie a la mode"), and they provide a hierarchal ordering of categories, allowing an efficient program for the identification, filing, and retrieving of significant information (Herdan 1960:210–211). The use of taxonomic systems is not confined to librarians and biologists; it is a fundamental principle of human thinking. The elaboration of taxonomies along vertical dimensions of generalization and horizontal dimensions of discrimination probably depends on factors such as the variety of cultural settings within which one talks about the objects being classified (Frake 1961:121–122), the importance of the objects to the way of life of the classifiers (Brown 1958; Nida 1958), and general properties of human thinking with regard to the number of items that the mind can cope with at a given time (Miller 1956; Yngve 1960).[5] Determining the precise correlates of variations in taxonomic structure, both intra-culturally and cross-culturally, is, of course, one of the objectives of this methodology.

In order to describe the use of taxonomic systems and to work out their behavioral correlates, evidence of complementary naming must be supplemented by observations on the socio-linguistic contexts that call for contrasts at particular levels. One could, for example, present a choice between objects whose segregates appear to contrast at different levels and ask an informant to complete the frame: "Pick up that ____." Suppose we have an apple pie on the counter next to a ham sandwich. The frame would probably be completed as "Pick up that pie." If, however, we substitute a cherry pie for the ham sandwich, we would expect to hear "Pick up that apple pie." Variations on this device of having informants contrast particular objects can be worked out depending on the kind of phenomena being classified. Some objects, such as pies and plants, are easier to bring together for visual comparison than others, such as diseases and deities.

Another device for eliciting taxonomic structures is simply to ask directly about relations of inclusion: "Is X a kind of Y?" Since in many speech situations even a native fails to elicit a term at the level of specification he requires, most, if not all, languages probably provide explicit methods for moving up and down a taxonomic hierarchy:

"Give me some of that pie." "What kind of pie d'ya want, Mac?"

"What's this 'submarine' thing on the menu?" "That's a kind of sandwich."

Once a taxonomic partitioning has been worked out it can be tested systematically for terminological contrast with frames such as "Is that an X?" with an expectation of a negative reply. For example, we could point to an apple pie and ask a counterman:

1. "Is that something to drink?"
2. "Is that a sandwich?"
3. "Is that a cherry pie?"

We would expect the respective replies to reflect the taxonomy of lunch-counter foods:

1. "No, it's something to eat."
2. "No, it's a pie."
3. "No, it's an apple pie."

(Admittedly it is easier to do this kind of questioning in a culture where one can assume the role of a naive learner.)

In employing these various operations for exploring taxonomic structures, the investigator must be prepared for cases when the same linguistic form designates segregates at different levels of contrast within the same system ('man' vs. 'animal,' 'man' vs. 'woman,' 'man' vs. 'boy') (Frake 1961:119); when a single unpartitioned segregate contrasts with two or more other segregates which are themselves at different levels of contrast ("That's not a coin; it's a token." "That's not a dime; it's a token."); and when incongruities occur in the results of the several operations (terminological contrasts may cut across sub-hierarchies revealed by complementary naming; explicit statements of inclusion may be less consistent than complementary naming).

ATTRIBUTES

Our task up to this point has been to reveal the structure of the system from which a selection is made when categorizing an object. When you hand a Navajo a plant specimen, or an American a sandwich, what is the available range of culturally defined arrays into which this object can be categorized? Methodological notions of contrast and inclusion have enabled us to discern some structure in this domain of cognitive choices, but we still have not faced the problem of how a person decides which out of a set of alternative categorizations is the correct one in a given instance. How does one in fact distinguish a hamburger from a cheeseburger, a chair from a stool, a tree from a shrub, an uncle from a cousin, a jerk from a slob?

A mere list of known members of a category—however an investigator identifies these objects cross-culturally—does not answer this question. Categorization, in essence, is a device for treating new experience as though it were equivalent to something already familiar (Brown 1958; Bruner 1957; Bruner et al. 1956; Sapir 1949). The hamburger I get tomorrow may be a quite different object in terms of size, kind of bun, and lack of tomatoes from the hamburger I had today. But it will still be a hamburger—unless it has a slice of cheese in it! To define 'hamburger' one must know, not just what objects it includes, but with what it contrasts. In this way we learn that a slice of cheese makes a difference, whereas a slice of tomato does not. In the context of different cultures the task is to state what one must know in order to categorize objects correctly. A definition of a Navajo plant category is not given by a list of botanical species it contains but by a rule for distinguishing newly encountered specimens of that category from contrasting alternatives.

Ideally the criterial attributes which generate a contrast set fall along a limited number of dimensions of contrast, each with two or more contrasting values or "components." Each segregate can be defined as a distinctive bundle of components. For example, the plant taxonomy of the Eastern Subanun, a Philippine people, has as its beginner a contrast set of three segregates which together include almost all of the more than 1,400 segregates at the most specific level of contrast within the taxonomy. This three

Table 1.   Defining Attributes of the Contrast Set of Stem
Habit in the Subanun Plant Taxonomy

CONTRAST SET	DIMENSIONS OF CONTRAST	
	Woodiness	Rigidity
gayu 'woody plants'	W	R
sigbet 'herbaceous plants'	W̄	R
belagen 'vines'		R̄

member contrast set can be generated by binary contrasts along two dimensions pertaining to habit of stem growth (see Table 1). Applications of componential analysis to pronominal systems and kinship terminologies have made this method of definition familiar (Austerlitz 1959; Conklin 1962; Goodenough 1956; Lounsbury 1956; McKaughan 1959; Thomas 1955; Wallace and Atkins 1960). The problem remains of demonstrating the cognitive saliency of componential solutions—to what extent are they models of how a person decides which term to use?—and of relating terminological attributes to actual perceptual discriminations (Frake 1961; Wallace and Atkins 1960). As a case of the latter problem, suppose we learn that informants distinguish two contrasting plant segregates by calling the fruit of one 'red' and that of the other 'green.' We set up 'color' as a dimension of contrast with values of 'red' and 'green.' But the terminology of 'color' is itself a system of segregates whose contrastive structure must be analysed before color terms can serve as useful defining attributes of other segregates. Ultimately one is faced with defining color categories by referring to the actual perceptual dimensions along which informants make differential categorizations. These dimensions must be determined empirically and not prescribed by the investigator using stimulus materials from his own culture. By careful observation one might discover that visual evaluation of an object's succulence, or other unexpected dimensions, as well as the traditional dimensions of hue, brightness, and saturation, are criterial to the use of "color" terms in a particular culture (Conklin 1955).

Whether aimed directly at perceptual qualities of phenomena or at informants' descriptions of pertinent attributes (Frake 1961:122–125), any method for determining the distinctive and probabilistic attributes of a segregate must depend, first, on knowing the contrast set within which the segregate is participating, and, second, on careful observations of verbal and non-verbal features of the cultural situations to which this contrast set provides an appropriate response.

This formulation has important implications for the role of eliciting in ethnography. The distinctive "situations," or "eliciting frames," or "stimuli," which evoke and define a set of contrasting responses are cultural data to be discovered, not prescribed, by the ethnographer. This stricture does not limit the use of preconceived eliciting devices to prod an informant into action or speech without any intent of defining the response by what evoked it in this instance. But the formulation—prior to observation—of response-defining eliciting devices is ruled out by the logic of this methodology which insists that any eliciting conditions not themselves part of the cultural-ecological system being investigated cannot be used to define categories purporting to be those of the people under study. It is those elements of *our informants'* experience, which *they* heed in selecting appropriate actions and utterances, that this methodology seeks to discover.

OBJECTIVES

The methodological suggestions proposed in this paper, as they stand, are clearly awkward and incomplete. They must be made more rigorous and expanded to include analyses of longer utterance sequences, to consider non-verbal behavior systematically, and to explore the other types of cognitive relations, such as sequential stage relations (Frake 1961) and part-whole relations, that may pertain between contrast sets. Focussing on the linguistic code, clearer operational procedures are needed for delimiting semantically exocentric units ("lexemes" or "idioms") (Goodenough 1956; Nida 1951), for discerning synonomy, homonymy, and polysemy (Ullman 1957:63), and for distinguishing between utterance grammaticalness (correctly constructed code) and utterance congruence (meaningfully constructed message) (Chomsky 1957; Joos 1958). In their present form, however, these suggestions have come out of efforts to describe behavior in the field, and their further development can come only from continuing efforts to apply and test them in ethnographic field situations.

The intended objective of these efforts is eventually to provide the ethnographer with public, non-intuitive procedures for ordering his presentation of observed and elicited events according to the principles of classification of the people he is studying. To order ethnographic observations solely according to an investigator's preconceived categories obscures the real content of culture: how people organize their experience conceptually so that it can be transmitted as knowledge from person to person and from generation to generation. As Goodenough advocates in a classic paper, culture "does not consist of things, people, behavior, or emotions," but the forms or organization of these things in the minds of people (Goodenough 1957). The principles by which people in a culture construe their world reveal how they segregate the pertinent from the insignificant, how they code and retrieve information, how they anticipate events (Kelly 1955), how they define alternative courses of action and make decisions among them. Consequently a strategy of ethnographic description that gives a central place to the cognitive processes of the actors involved will contribute reliable cultural data to problems of the relations between language, cognition, and behavior; it will point up critical dimensions for meaningful cross-cultural comparison; and, finally, it will give us productive descriptions of cultural behavior, descriptions which, like the linguists' grammar, succinctly state what one must know in order to generate culturally acceptable acts and utterances appropriate to a given socio-ecological context (Goodenough 1957).

NOTES

[1] In preparing this paper I have especially benefited from suggestions by Harold C. Conklin, Thomas Gladwin, Volney Stefflre, and William C. Sturtevant.

[2] In this paper the term *object* designates anything construed as a member of a category (Bruner *et al.* 1956:231), whether perceptible or not.

[3] Because this is a short, orally presented paper, suggested procedures are illustrated with rather simple examples from a familiar language and culture. A serious analysis would require much larger quantities of speech data presented in phonemic transcription. For a more complex example, intended as an ethnographic statement, see Frake 1961.

[4] This example is, of course, considerably over-simplified. If the reader does not relate these segregates in the same way as our hypothetical lunch-counter speakers, he is not alone. Shortly after I completed the manuscript of this paper, a small boy approached me in a park and, without any eliciting remark whatsoever on my part, announced: "Hamburgers are more gooder than sandwiches." One could not ask for better evidence of contrast.

[5] At least in formal, highly partitioned taxonomic systems an ordering of superordinates according to the number of their subordinates appears to yield a stable statistical distribution (the Willis distribution) regardless of what is being classified or who is doing the classifying (Herdan 1960:211–225; Mandelbrot 1956).

REFERENCES CITED

Austerlitz, Robert, 1959, Semantic components of pronoun systems: Gilyak. Word 15(1):102–109.

Barker, Roger G. and Herbert F. Wright, 1955, Midwest and its children, the psychological ecology of an American town. New York, Harper & Row.

Boas, Franz, 1911, Introduction. *In* Handbook of American Indian languages, Bureau of American Ethnology Bulletin 40, Pt. 1, 1–83.

Brown, Roger, 1958, Words and things. New York, Free Press.

Brown, Roger and Eric H. Lenneberg, 1954, A study in language and cognition. Journal of Abnormal and Social Psychology 49(3):454–462.

Bruner, Jerome S., 1957, Going beyond the information given. *In* Contemporary approaches to cognition; a symposium held at the University of Colorado. Cambridge, Harvard University Press, 41–70.

Bruner, Jerome S., J. J. Goodnow, and G. A. Austin, 1956, A study of thinking. With an appendix on language by Roger W. Brown. New York, Wiley.

Chomsky, Noam, 1955, Semantic considerations in grammar. Georgetown University Monograph Series on Language and Linguistics, No. 8, 141–150.

————, 1957, Syntactic structures. The Hague, Mouton.

Conklin, Harold C., 1954, The relation of Hanunóo culture to the plant world. Unpublished Ph.D. dissertation. New Haven, Yale University.

————, 1955, Hanunóo color categories. Southwestern Journal of Anthropology 11(4):339–344.

————, 1962, Lexicographical treatment of folk taxonomies. Work paper for Conference on Lexicography, Indiana University, Nov. 11–12, 1960. *In* Fred W. Householder and Sol Saporta, eds., Problems in lexicography. Supplement to International Journal of American Linguistics, Vol. 28, No. 2—Indiana University Research Center in Anthropology, Folklore and Linguistics, Publication 21. Bloomington.

Frake, Charles O., 1961, The diagnosis of disease among the Subanun of Mindanao. American Anthropologist 63(1):113-132.

Goodenough, Ward H., 1956, Componential analysis and the study of meaning. Language 32(1):195–216.

————, 1957, Cultural anthropology and linguistics. Georgetown University Monograph Series on Language and Linguistics, No. 9, 167–173.

Gregg, John R., 1954, The language of taxonomy, an application of symbolic logic to the study of classificatory systems. New York, Columbia University Press.

Haugen, Einar, 1957, The semantics of Icelandic orientation. Word 13(3):447–459.

Herdan, Gustav, 1960, Type-token mathematics, a textbook of mathematical linguistics. The Hague, Mouton.

Hill, A. A., 1952, A note on primitive languages. International Journal of American Linguistics 18(3):172–177.

Hockett, Charles F., 1958, A course in modern linguistics. New York, Macmillan.

Hymes, Dell H., 1961, On typology of cognitive styles in language (with examples from Chinookan). Anthropological Linguistics 3(1):22-54.

Jesperson, Otto, 1934, Language: its nature, development, and origin. London, Allen & Unwin.

Joos, Martin, 1958, Semology: a linguistic theory of meaning. Studies in Linguistics 13(3):53–70.

Kelly, George, 1955, The psychology of personal constructs. New York, Norton.

Lounsbury, Floyd G., 1956, A semantic analysis of the Pawnee kinship usage. Language 32(1):158–194.

Mandelbrot, Benoit, 1956, On the language of taxonomy. *In* Colin Cherry, ed., Information theory. New York, Academic Press 135–145.

McKaughan, Howard, 1959, Semantic components of pronoun systems: Maranao. Word 15(1):101–102.

Miller, George, 1956, Human memory and the storage of information. IRE transactions on information theory IT, 2:129–137. New York, Institute of Radio Engineers.

Miller, George, Eugene Galanter and Karl Pribram, 1960, Plans and the structure of behavior. New York, Holt, Rinehart and Winston.

Nida, Eugene, 1951, A system for the description of semantic elements. Word 7(1):1–14.

————, 1958, Analysis of meaning and dictionary making. International Journal of American Linguistics 24(4):279–292.

Pike, Kenneth, 1954, Language in relation to a unified theory of the structure of human behavior. Part 1. Glendale, Summer Institute of Linguistics.

Sapir, Edward, 1949, The psychological reality of phonemes. In David G. Mandelbaum, ed., Selected writings of Edward Sapir in Language, culture, and personality. Berkeley, University of California Press, 46–60.

Thomas, David, 1955, Three analyses of the Ilocano pronoun system. Word 11(2): 204–208.

Ullman, Stephen, 1957, The principles of semantics, New York, Philosophical Library.

Wallace, Anthony and J. Atkins, 1960, The meaning of kinship terms. American Anthropologist 62(1):58–80.

Woodger, J. H., 1952, Biology and language, an introduction to the methodology of the biological sciences including medicine. Cambridge, The University Press.

Yngve, Victor H., 1960, A model and an hypothesis for language structure. Proceedings of the American Philosophical Society 104(5):444–466.

Lexicographical Treatment of Folk Taxonomies[1]

Harold C. Conklin

INTRODUCTION

Many lexical problems are of considerable importance to linguists and ethnographers. With the interests of both groups in mind, I would like to discuss certain aspects of folk classification which I feel deserve more rigorous lexicographic attention than they have typically received.

An adequate ethnographic description of the culture (Goodenough 1957) of a particular society presupposes a detailed analysis of the communications system and of the culturally defined situations in which all relevant distinctions in that system occur. In this regard, accurate knowledge of both the grammar and lexicon of the local spoken language constitutes a minimum requirement. When the ethnographer works in an area for which adequate

From F. W. Householder and S. Saporta, eds., Problems in Lexicography. Bloomington, Indiana University Research Center in Anthropology, Folklore, and Linguistics, 1962. Used by permission of the author and Indiana University Research Center in Anthropology, Folklore, and Linguistics.

statements about the local language are unavailable in published sources, his first and often continuing task is the construction of a set of valid rules for the interpretation of the local language. In his phonological and grammatical analysis of new speech forms, he may find many helpful models in the descriptive linguistic literature. In attempting, however, to account for the obligatory semantic relations inherent in his lexical corpus, he may not be so fortunate. While extant dictionaries and vocabularies do provide glosses and definitional information, many of the nontrivial, and often essential, semantic and contextual relationships obtaining among lexical items are often either neglected or handled in an imprecise and unsystematic manner (cf. Newman 1954:86).

For formal linguistic analysis it is necessary that utterances be acceptable and interpretable grammatically. For ethnographic (including lexicographic) analysis utterances must also be acceptable and interpretable semantically. While an "appeal" to meaning does not improve grammatical analysis, neither does an intuitive appeal to morphosyntactic form yield the most appropriate analysis of meaning and reference (see 1.5. below). In fact, an adequate grammar may generate semantically unacceptable propositions (Chomsky 1955:149, 1957:103–104; cf. Landar 1960:352; Frake 1961:113). Results of some recent attempts to develop nonintuitive procedures for the evaluation of the grammaticalness and meaningfulness of sentences (e.g., Maclay and Sleator 1960; cf. Joos 1958) indicate that this difference is of considerable importance. The distinction between these two aspects of the analysis of speech is apparent even in the treatment of isolated forms.

In the course of several years of linguistic and ethnographic field work among the Hanunóo in the Philippines, it became abundantly evident that providing such segments as *sah, tabākuq, samparansisku-qalistun*, and *lāda. balaynun. tagnānam. qiruŋ-pādiq* each with the same gloss '(distinct) kind of plant' was—while adequate for certain syntactic purposes—most unsatisfactory for the task of semantic analysis. Had I not modified this procedure, I would have ended up with more than 2000 lexical items (including several hundred referential synonyms) each labeled identically. While employing glosses like 'tea' and 'tobacco' (in the first two cases above) proved useful in labeling familiar objects, the majority of these culturally significant Hanunóo designations referred to entities which to me were quite unfamiliar. In this type of ethnographic context one finds many instances where the problems faced traditionally by the compilers of bilingual dictionaries are considerably magnified (Nida 1958). For the ethnographer, the semantic structure of such folk classification is of paramount significance. Upon his analysis of it depends the accuracy of many crucial statements about the culture being described. Problems of analyzing and presenting such structures in a succinct fashion may be of interest even to lexicographers who work only in relatively familiar cultural surroundings.

1. FOLK CLASSIFICATION

In the lexicographic treatment of folk classification, we are concerned primarily with (1) the identification of relevant syntactic segments, (2) the identification of fundamental semantic units in specific contexts, (3) the delineation of significant sets of semantic units in particular domains, and (4) the translation (and marking) of these units so that important semantic relationships will not be obscured. In discussing different systems of classifying segments of the natural and social environment, the neutral term *segregate* (Conklin 1954) serves as a label for any terminologically-distinguished (i.e., conventionally-named) grouping of objects.

1.1. LINGUISTIC STRUCTURE   The shape and combinatorial structure of the linguistic forms which designate folk segregates are irrelevant, in a strict sense, to the analysis of the system of classification itself; i.e., to the semantic structure (Conklin 1957). Labels and categories can change independently and therefore must be analyzed separately. On the other hand, a knowledge of the linguistic structure involved is essential for understanding the principles of folk *nomenclature;* and in working out this structure, clues for isolating folk segregate labels and for eliciting information about such segregates may be found.

1.2. LEXICAL UNITS AND CONTEXTS   A full lexical statement (i.e., an adequate dictionary) should provide semantic explanation, as well as phonological and grammatical identification, for every meaningful form whose signification cannot be inferred from a knowledge of anything else in the language. It is convenient to refer to these elementary lexical units as *lexemes* (cf. Swadesh 1946; Newman 1954; Jorden 1955; Goodenough 1956), although other terms have been suggested (e.g., *idiom* [Hockett 1956; cf. Householder 1959:508–524; Weinreich 1960:337]). So far as lexemic status is concerned, the morphosyntactic or assumed etymological relations of a particular linguistic form are incidental; what is essential is that its meaning cannot be deduced from its grammatical structure. Single morphemes are necessarily lexemes, but for polymorphemic constructions the decision depends on meaning and use (implying an analysis of the constraints imposed by the semantic structure, and the specification of relevant immediate contexts).

Formal segments such as *black bird* (vs. *blackbird*) or *in the old house* (vs. *in the doghouse*) can be excluded from the lexical statement because they are predictable, meaningfully, in that they can be considered *semantically endocentric* (Nida 1951:12–13, 1958:286; cf. Chao 1953:385). Put another way, those constructions which are never *semantically exocentric* may be classed as *nonlexemic* forms (e.g., *sunburned face, long pink strand*). Problems do arise, however, in degrees of lexemic *exocentricity* (Nida 1958:286) and, again, if caution is not exercised in distinguishing clearly between grammatical and semantic criteria. The compounds *firewater* and *silverfish*, for example, are endocentric morphosyntactically (either on an attribute-plus-head basis or on the perhaps stronger grounds of formal selection rules [Lees 1960:128, 158]), but semantically they are as exocentric as *vodka* and *moth*.

In the study of segregate labels in folk classification, and despite some of the difficulties of technical definition noted, I find it useful to distinguish by explicit semantic criteria two kinds of lexemic units: *unitary lexemes* (no segments of which may designate categories which are identical with, or superordinate to, those designated by the forms in question) and *composite lexemes* (one or more segments of which, under specified conditions, may (a) designate the same categories as those designated by the forms in question (abbreviation), or (b) designate categories superordinate to those designated by the forms in question (generalization), see 2.-2.2.) Unitary lexemes may be either *simple* (unsegmentable) or *complex* (segmentable). These distinctions are exemplified below:

LEXEMES

Unitary Simple	Unitary Complex	Composite
oak	poison oak	white oak
pine	pineapple	pitch pine
son	grandson	son-in-law
dart (an artifact)	darts (a game)	Baldwin apple
Jack	jack-in-the-pulpit	Port-orford cedar
dandelion	black-eyed Susan	black-crowned night heron
caterpillar (larva)	cat's-eye	caterpillar tractor

For contrast, consider a few similar but *nonlexemic* forms: *cheap pine, pine and oak, black-eyed Joe, darts* (plural of *dart* [Hockett 1956:229]). For a native speaker, such distinctions cause little concern, but in new linguistic and cultural environs difficulties may arise.

For example, on first inspection, the following partially-identical Hanunóo forms (Conklin 1954) might appear to belong to a simple paradigm (they could all be recorded during a conversation about rice cultivation and weeding problems):

1	paray:paray	'cattail'
2	pāray˙māyah	'immature wild pādaŋ (plant)'
3	pāray˙qiŋkantuh	'kind of wild sedge'
4	pāray˙bīhud	'kind of rice'
5	pāray˙tāwuh	'some one (else)'s rice'
6	pāray˙tīdah	'that rice'

The glosses, however, indicate that several types of lexical units may be involved. Are there any formal linguistic clues?

Each of the six forms is easily segmented into two morphs, as I have indicated by the use of dots. Loose-joining, phonemically, is represented by a single raised period. Except for the closely-joined doubling in item number *1*, the forms in this set provide no obligatory intonational or junctural contrasts. Furthermore, each form occurs in many identical frames such as *tūhay ŋāni ti* _____. '_____ is (are) certainly different.' Thus, for most of the semantically distinct types of joining suggested by the glosses, there are no phonological clues and few, if any, immediate, formal indications. (A full syntactic statement covering the structure of compounds would separate out some of these forms on grammatical grounds [cf. Lees 1960].) Given the necessary semantic information, however, these distinctions can be noted easily for lexicographical purposes by rewriting the forms as follows:

1 *parayparay*
2 *pāray-māyah*
3 *pāray-qiŋkantuh*
4 *pāray.bīhud*
5 *pāray tāwuh*
    (5a) *(5b)*
6 *pāray tīdah*
    (6a) *(6b)*

This procedure clearly marks *1*, *2*, and *3* semantically exocentric, unitary lexemes; *4* as a composite lexeme; and *5* and *6* as nonlexemic, semantically endocentric constructions the initial lexeme of which is superordinately related to *4*. Minimally, forms *1*, *2*, *3*, *4*, *5a*, and *6a* could be labeled 'kind of plant,' but by not attending to essential semantic distinctions this type of short cut would obscure such important contrastive relations as the mutual exclusion of coordinate categories (*1*:[*pādaŋ*, implied—but not covered—by the specific growth stage term number *2*]:*3*:*5a* or *6a*), and the possible total inclusion of subordinate categories (*4* by *5a/6a*; but *not 1*, *2*, or *3* by *5a/6a*). Statements about such relations, hinted at in some glosses and definitions, may be demonstrated only by systematic pairing in minimal, and relatively controlled, linguistic and semantic contexts.

1.3. LEXICAL SETS AND DOMAINS.   In many ways it can be said that the more discrete the phenomena referred to, the simpler the task of treating the associated terminology in a lexicographically adequate manner (cf. Wallace and Atkins 1960). If this is true for particular lexical items it is equally true for the semantically structured sets which such items may comprise (Frake 1961). Minimally, a *lexical set* consists of all semantically contrastive lexemes which in a given, culturally relevant context share exclusively at least one defining feature (Lounsbury 1956:61–62). The semantic range of all such lexemes defines the *domain* of the lexical set. The initial establishment of domain boundaries, while widely recognized as an ideal goal; is often a very difficult task (cf. Voegelin and Voegelin 1957). Effective eliciting frames and procedural tests used to determine such boundaries, and convincing demonstrations of their intracultural reality, are subjects not often discussed in the linguistic or ethnological literature. Some of the essential factors involved in this type of analysis are treated briefly below under "levels" (2.) and "dimensions" (3.) of contrast. In general, the number and complexity of boundary problems increases as one moves from the investigation of lexical domains within a particular language to an attempt to "match" the domains of different languages (Öhman 1953; cf. Quine 1960:26–79). This does not, however, preclude rigorous contrastive analysis.

1.4. TRANSLATION AND SEMANTIC STRUCTURE. With few exceptions, the lexical items employed in systems of folk classification always comprise a segment of the everyday vocabulary of the particular language (Conklin 1957). The rules governing the obligatory semantic relations among the categories in such lexical sets are thus to be determined, evaluated, and described for each language. Such rules cannot be prescribed merely on the basis of familiarity *in another system* with the "concrete" denotata of the sets involved. In the case of folk botany, for example, this means that a local system of plant classification cannot be described accurately by attempting to obtain only vernacular "equivalents" for botanically recognized species. Translation labels (glosses) are frequently necessary, but they should be considered neither as definitions nor as exact equivalents (Lounsbury 1956: 163; for an attempt to use acronyms as a partial mnemonic solution to such translation problems, see Landar *et al.* 1960:371). This well-established and perhaps obvious semantic principle is sometimes forgotten where the assumed absolute nature (in a cross-linguistic sense) of "scientific" names or of other long-established traditional distinctions in certain Western languages is involved (Öhman 1953; cf. Simpson 1961:11).

1.5. SYNTACTIC VS. SEMANTIC STRUCTURE. Implicit in the preceding remarks is the assumption that the relation between formal linguistic (syntactic, in the general, semiotic sense [Morris 1946]) structure and semantic structure need not be isomorphic (Lounsbury 1956:189). If this assumption is taken seriously, a full dictionary should state explicitly the necessary and sufficient conditions for the unambiguous structural interpretation of each included lexeme in the context of the total lexicon as well as in that of the grammar. While such coverage has rarely been achieved, even for relatively small lexical domains, I feel that recognition of this goal has considerable relevance for this discussion. A brief illustration may help to indicate the kind of crucial lexical data that are often ignored, especially where meanings are either assumed on the basis of semantic patterning in a more familiar language, or where they are treated only partially (as in the derivation of definitional statements from translational labels).

Consider the following situation (which, with minor differences, I have encountered on a number of occasions): a woman, whose brother (x) and husband (y) are both named Juan, has a son, also named Juan (z) and a daughter who in turn has a son named Pedro (P). The genealogical situation is diagrammed in Fig. 1 (we can ignore the broken lines for a moment). Two fluent speakers of English, F, a Filipino whose first language was Tagalog, and A, a native speaker of a dialect of American English, both know Pedro and the specified members of his family. The fact that one of the Juans (x, y, or z) has died is known only to A (or F) who in turn wishes to relate this circumstance to his friend F (or A). A straightforward statement completing the sentence *P's _____ Juan died* would seem to do the trick; and, depending on the circumstances, one of two unitary lexemes (*grandfather, uncle*) might be used to fill the blank:

1   *Pedro's Grandfather Juan died.*
2   *Pedro's Uncle Juan died.*

However, if A uses *Grandfather*, F may ask *Which grandfather?*; if F uses *Uncle*, A may ask *Which uncle?* indicating a kind of two-way ambiguity which can only be resolved by recognizing that despite their unquestionable grammaticality and morphosyntactic identity, A's sentences 1 and 2 and F's sentences 1 and 2 differ semantically:

SENTENCE	KIN TERM USED	KIN TYPE(S) INCLUDED (PR = PARENT'S)	
A1	*Grandfather*	y	(PrFa)
F1	"	x and y	(PrFa, PrPrBr)
A2	*Uncle*	x and z	(PrBr, PrPrBr)
F2	"	z	(PrBr)

This, of course, reflects only a small part of a very fundamental structural difference in Central Philippine and North American systems of kinship classification: universal terminological recognition of generation in the former vs. universal terminological recognition of degree of collaterality in the latter (these two "limits" to the lexical extension of kin class membership are indicated on the kinship diagram in Fig. 1 by the horizontal and diagonal broken lines, respectively). Although any careful investigator might learn this systematic distinction after a few days of field work, the principle goes unaccounted for in the relevant and extant bilingual dictionaries. The restrictions involved in this illustration are just as obligatory and inescapable within the respective semantic systems represented as is the distinction of singular vs. plural in English grammar.

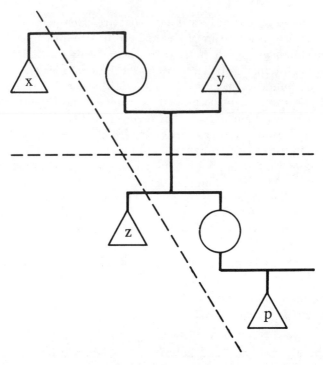

Figure 1.   A genealogical illustration of contrasting systems of kinship classification.

2. LEVELS OF CONTRAST

Folk categories within the same domain may be related in two fundamentally different ways: by *inclusion*, which implies separate levels of
contrast, and by *exclusion*, which here applies only within single-level contrast sets. There may also be subcategoric, or componential, *intersection* (see
3. below). In studying semantic relationships, as among folk categories, it
has often been demonstrated that likeness logically and significantly implies
difference (Kelly 1955:303–305). It is also pertinent, however, to note that
total contrast (complete complementary exclusion)—which logically relates
such segregates as *ant* and *ship* or *cough* and *pebble*—is less important than
restricted contrast within the range of a particular semantic subset (compare
the relations within and between the partial sets *robin - wren - sparrow;
spaniel - terrier - poodle;* and *bird - dog*). When we speak of the category
dime being included in the category *coin* we imply that every dime is also a
(kind of) coin—but not necessarily the reverse. Furthermore, when we state
(a) that the category *dime* contrasts with that of *quarter* and (b) that the
category *coin* contrasts with that of *bill* we are speaking of two instances of
relevant mutual exclusion at two different levels of contrast (Conklin 1955,

1957; Frake 1961). Such alignments of folk categories are common to all languages, though systematic indications of these relationships are rare even in the more detailed monolingual dictionaries.

2.1. HIERARCHIC STRUCTURE   Where the articulation between successive levels, each consisting of a set of contrastive lexical units, is ordered vertically by inclusion such that each monolexemic category at one level is totally included in only one category at the next higher level, we can speak of a lexical hierarchy. The two axes of such a structure involve the horizontal *differentiation* of contrastive but coordinate categories and the vertical increase of *generalization* or *specification* resulting from ascent to superordinate (including) or descent to subordinate (included) levels, respectively (Gregg 1954; Conklin 1957; Beckner 1959; 55–80; Frake 1961:117). These axes are fixed and cannot be merged or interchanged, nor can the succession of levels be modified. *Dime* is not contrasted with *coin*, but at the same level with *nickel*, *quarter*, *penny*, etc. Subhierarchies of varying "depths" are often discernible within larger hierarchic structures. The depth (in levels) of the subhierarchy including the categories *hawk*, *pigeon*, and *starling* is less than that of the subhierarchy including *hawk*, *horse*, and *crocodile*; i.e., the first three segregates are included in a superordinate category at a lower level than that of the segregate ultimately including *hawk*, *horse*, and *crocodile*. The embedding of subhierarchies within increasingly deeper ones is characteristic of many systems of folk classification.

2.2. FOLK TAXONOMY   A system of monolexemically-labeled folk segregates related by hierarchic inclusion is a *folk taxonomy;* segregates included in such a classification are known as *folk taxa* (Conklin 1957; cf. Lawrence 1951:53; Simpson 1961:19). Some of the additional requirements of "model" or "regular" taxonomic systems (Woodger 1952:201ff.; Gregg 1954; Beckner 1959:55–58; Simpson 1961) are: (1) at the highest level, there is only one maximal (largest, unique) taxon which includes all other taxa in the system; (2) the number of levels is finite and uniform throughout the system; (3) each taxon belongs to only one level; (4) there is no overlap (i.e., taxa at the same level are always mutually exclusive). Folk systems vary widely with respect to these more specific "requirements," but the presence of hierarchically arranged though less "regular" folk taxonomies is probably universal. Most of the examples given here are taken from folk botany, but similar illustrations could be taken from other domains (Thomas 1957; Frake 1961).

Several important differences distinguish folk taxa from the taxonomic groups of biological systematics (Conklin 1957; Simpson 1961). The former usually relate only to locally relevant or directly observable phonomena. They are defined by criteria which may differ greatly from culture to culture. The number and position of levels of contrast may change from one sector of a folk system to another. There are no formal rules for the nomenclatural recognition or rejection of taxa (cf. Lawrence 1951:213–215), though new groupings may be added productively with considerable ease. In respect to any particular local biota, there is no reason to expect the folk taxa to match those of systematic biology—either in number or in range. The Hanunóo classify their local plant world, at the lowest (terminal) level of contrast, into more than 1800 mutually exclusive folk taxa, while botanists divide the same flora—in terms of species—into less than 1300 scientific taxa.

2.3. SPECIAL PROBLEMS   Although they cannot be discussed here at length, a number of lexicographically important problems encountered in the analysis of folk taxonomies include:

(1) Multiple and interlocking hierarchies. Unlike scientific taxa, folk segregates may belong simultaneously to several distinct hierarchic structures. The same segregates may be classed as terminal categories in a taxonomy based on form and appearance and also as terminal or nonterminal categories in another taxonomy based on cultural treatment (e.g., morphologically distinguished kinds of floral segregates vs. functional categories of plants as food cultigens, medicines, ornamentals, etc.) (Conklin 1954). Subhierarchies may be interarticulated in numerous ways (e.g., Joos 1956:296–297) and there is always the potentiality of partial inclusion or domain overlap.

(2) Extrahierarchic relations. Not all folk categories are directly related by class inclusion or contrast within the range of a particular superordinate category. For example, numerous difficulties may arise if lexemes designating separate ontogenetic stages or parts of members of particular segregates (see 1.2. above) are not distinguished from hierarchically arranged folk taxa (Chao 1953:387–389; Conklin 1954, 1957; Frake 1961). *Part-of* (part-whole) relations are often complicated by ambiguities (Nagel 1961:381–383) not encountered in the analysis of *kind-of* (class inclusion) relations (e.g., the segregates *plant, stem, sap* are not related taxonomically like *plant, tree, elm*).

(3) Synonymy and homonymy. When, within the context of a particular folk taxonomy, a single taxon may be labeled by phonemically distinct forms, as in the case of minor dialect variants or abbreviated terms (see 1.2.), we may speak of referential synonyms (or synonymous lexemes); e.g., *fin, finnif, five, fiver, five-spot, five-dollar bill*. In many such cases, it may be difficult to demonstrate taxonomic identity and the absence of categoric overlap. Alternative substructuring of the subhierarchy may be involved. Phonemically identical (homonymous) lexemes may designate separate taxa of different ranges of generalization at successive levels. Such situations (e.g., *animal* and *man* in the following partial contrastive sets: *animal*[1] vs. *plant*, *animal*[2] vs. *man*[1], *man*[2] vs. *woman* [cf. Frake 1961:117–119]) are not uncommon but they require careful contrastive pairing and testing for inclusion at

each level involved. Similar steps must also be taken in working out problems concerned with distinguishing polysemy from homonymy (Wells 1958:662–663; cf. Chomsky 1957:95; Garvin 1960:147).

(4) Types of contrast. Paired folk taxa of some lexical subsets are related by simple, binary, segregate opposition. Many larger sets and some dyadic ones involve important types of semantic contrast other than antonymy (cf. Lyons 1960:622). Structurally, for example, taxa may be contrasted in serial, complementary, or discontinuous arrays. (For subcategoric attribute relations, see 3. below.)

2.4. FOLK VS. BOTANICAL TAXONOMY   Ideally, in the study of interrelated lexical sets in folk taxonomies, priority and preference should be given to unanimously-agreed-upon, obligatory distinctions in specified contexts. When tested by means of what are essentially crucial experiments—by pairing and contrasting negatively and positively—one should be able to construct a model (i.e., a theoretical statement) of the hierarchic structure such that assertions of membership and inclusion in any of the implied taxa are unanimously and unambiguously denied whenever such assertions are incongruent (i.e., meaningless within the system) (cf. Joos 1958:65). The assertion 'Poodles, dogs, and animals are kinds of snails' would thus be rejected by speakers of my dialect of English—and on very easily specified semantic grounds. Within a particular universe of discourse (a taxonomic domain) how can one construct a nontrivial model by means of which only semantically acceptable, congruent propositions may be generated? An example from Hanunóo folk botany may serve as a partial answer.

In a situation where one Hanunóo farmer wishes to draw another's attention to a particular individual pepper bush Q, he may, of course, attempt to describe some of Q's unique attributes without naming the plant. Much more often, however, even in the course of a "unique" description, he will resort to the use of one or more of at least eight lexical units each of which might complete the frame *māluq, qinda pag* _____, 'Hey, take a look at this _____,' but at different levels of contrast (allowing for different degrees of desired or required specificity):

I	*kuwaq*	'entity' (i.e., something that can be named)
II	*bāgay*	'thing' (not a person, animal, etc.)
III	*kāyuh*	'plant' (not a rock, etc.)
IV	*qilamnun*	'herbaceous plant' (not a woody plant, etc.)
V	*lādaq*	'pepper (plant)' (not a rice plant, etc.)
VI	*lāda. balaynun*	'houseyard pepper (plant)' (not a wild pepper plant)
VII	*lāda. balaynun. mahārat*	'houseyard chili pepper (plant)' (not a houseyard green pepper plant)

VIII   *lāda. balaynun.*   ' "cat-penis" houseyard chili pepper (plant)'
      mahārat.   (not a member of any of five other ter-
      qūtin-kutiq   minal houseyard chili pepper taxa such
                      as *lāda. balaynun. mahārat. tāhud-manuk,*
                      the "cock's-spur" variety).

Within the domain of Hanunóo plant taxonomy, from level III down, and specifically within the range of *lādaq*, from level V down, conversations recorded during many similar situations would ultimately provide the lexicographer with fifteen unitary and composite lexemes (including a terminal set of eleven 'pepper plant' names) arranged at four levels in the form of a discrete subhierarchy (Fig. 2). Specification below the level of the terminal taxa noted in the diagram (Fig. 2:1–11), and hence outside this system of classification, may be provided only by semantically endocentric constructions describing individual plant variations, on which unanimous accord is rare and unpredictable. In this particular case, folk taxa 15, 14, and 11 happen to correspond rather closely with the scientific taxa *Capsicum*, *C. annuum* L., and *C. frutescens* L., respectively; but the twelve remaining folk taxa involve distinctions not recognized as significant botanical subspecies by taxonomic botanists who have classified the same flora. Structurally speaking, however, some of the most important patterns of semantic contrast involve not only the hierarchic separation of these varied, lower-level, folk taxa (i.e., 1–10, 12–13), but also a large number of nonhierarchic relations governed by sublexemic class intersection (see 3.2). Although such relations cannot be diagrammed with the taxonomic implications of Fig. 2, nor can they be treated effectively at all in terms of our hierarchic model, they should nevertheless be of considerable interest to linguists and others concerned with systems of folk classification.

3. DIMENSIONS OF CONTRAST

At any given level within a well-defined folk-taxonomic subhierarchy, the relations obtaining among three or more coordinate taxa may involve varying dimensions, or kinds of subcategory contrast. The conjunction of these dimensions, or more precisely, of the values (or specific attributes [cf. Bruner *et al.* 1956:26–30]) along the several dimensions, define the categories involved within an essentially paradigmatic (i.e., nonhierarchic) subsystem (Lounsbury 1956, 1960:27–28; for a discussion of the structurally similar though more typologically-oriented procedures of attribute space substruction and reduction see Greenberg 1957 and Lazarsfeld 1961).

3.1. NONHIERARCHIC STRUCTURE   Such multidimensional contrasts do not imply, and indeed do not allow, the ordering of the resultant categories by hierarchic inclusion. These features of nonhierarchic semantic structures,

Figure 2. A segment of Hanunóo plant taxonomy. All folk taxa included in the taxon *lādaq*, are indicated.

kuwaq

bāgay

kāyuh

qilamnun

lādaq

lāda. balaynun

lāda. balaynun. mahārat						*lāda. balaynun. tagnānam* 13				
l.b.m. batūnis	*l.b.m. hapun*	*l.b.m. pasītih*	*l.b.m. pinasyak*	*l.b.m. gūtin-kutiq*	*l.b.m. tāhud-manik*	*l.b.t. mali-puŋkuk*	*l.b.t. pasītih*	*l.b.t. patuktuk*	*l.b.t. qarābaq*	
1	2	3	4	5	6	7	8	9	10	

lāda. tirindukun-tigbayaq   11

15

14

12

53

while not always sharply distinguished from the principles inherent in
hierarchic systems, have been recognized and carefully analyzed in a number
of domains, notably in kinship (Goodenough 1951:92–110, 1956; Lounsbury
1956; Frake 1960; Wallace and Atkins 1960), color (Conklin 1955; cf.
Lenneberg and Roberts 1956; Landar *et al.* 1960), orientation (Haugen 1957),
disease (Frake 1961), and, beginning with Jakobson's pioneering efforts, in
such partly modulational (Joos 1958:70) paradigms as case and pronoun
systems (Jakobson 1936; Sebeok 1946; Harris 1948; Lotz 1949; Wonderly
1952; Austerlitz 1959). The following example of multidimensional contrast
in a regular paradigmatic structure will illustrate some of these points.

3.2. SIGNIFICANT CLASSIFICATION VS. CATALOGUING   If, omitting the
high-level, wide-ranging *kuwaq* (see 2.4), we list all the Hanunóo personal
name substitutes occurring in various frames such as *māluq, qinda pag
binwat ni* _____, 'Hey, take a look at what _____ did (here),' we will
invariably end up with an exhaustive and mutually exclusive lexical set
consisting of just eight units (in each case representing a single morpheme).
Arranged in the least meaningful type of catalogue, an alphabetical *index*
(as in a dictionary), these lexical units are:

dah	'they'
kuh	'I'
mih	'we'
muh	'you'
tah	'we two'
tam	'we all'
yah	'he, she'
yuh	'you all'

The shapes provide little that is structurally suggestive, but the glosses
do indicate that an ordering in terms of eight "traditional" distinctions
along three quasi-semantic dimensions

(1) first person : second person : third person
(2) singular   : dual ·   : plural
(3) exclusive   : inclusive

might be attempted. But the resulting applied structure is hardly elegant,
economical, or convincing:

kuh	1s	*tah*	1d	*mih*	1pe
- - -		- - -		*tam*	1pi
muh	2s	- - -		*yuh*	2p
yah	3s	- - -		*dah*	3p

If a close examination is made of the distinctive contrasts involved, not in terms of labels but in terms of actual, minimal, obligatory differences, a more satisfactory, economical, and semantically verifiable solution is reached. The necessary and sufficient conditions for defining each of the eight categories depend on the regular intersection of six components which comprise three simple oppositions:

minimal membership : nonminimal membership $(M:\bar{M})$

inclusion of speaker   : exclusion of speaker $(S:\bar{S})$

inclusion of hearer   : exclusion of hearer $(H:\bar{H})$

These relations can be represented in list or diagrammatic form (Fig. 3). Even without further elaboration, the basic semantic structure of this

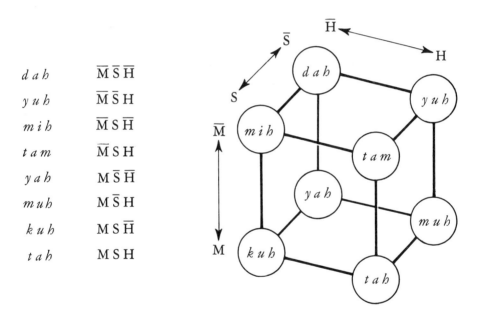

$d\,a\,b$	$\bar{M}\,\bar{S}\,\bar{H}$
$y\,u\,b$	$\bar{M}\,\bar{S}\,H$
$m\,i\,b$	$\bar{M}\,S\,\bar{H}$
$t\,a\,m$	$\bar{M}\,S\,H$
$y\,a\,b$	$M\,\bar{S}\,\bar{H}$
$m\,u\,b$	$M\,\bar{S}\,H$
$k\,u\,b$	$M\,S\,\bar{H}$
$t\,a\,b$	$M\,S\,H$

Figure 3.   Paradigmatic structure of a Hanunóo pronominal set.

lexical set should now be clear. (In passing, it may be noted that pronoun systems in Tagalog, Ilocano (Thomas 1955), Maranao (McKaughan 1959), and some other Philippine languages exhibit very similar, if not identical, obligatory semantic relationships.)

This example also illustrates a very important, though perhaps less obvious, characteristic of paradigmatic relations at one level in a taxonomic subhierarchy in contrast to the noncommutative relations of class inclusion governing the larger taxonomic system. Within such a contrastive lexical set (as in Fig. 3), ordered by class intersection, the constituent categories cannot be arranged in a taxonomic hierarchy. Any arrangement (e.g., a circular, block, or branching diagram) superficially appearing to contradict this statement will prove on closer inspection either (a) to constitute what the biologists call a *key* (Mayr *et al.* 1953:162–8; Simpson 1961:13–6), essentially another kind of catalogue or finding list ordered by successive— but not necessarily taxonomically significant—dichotomous exclusion, or (b) to be based on some other artificially imposed, and hence semantically nonsignificant, classification.

4. LEXICOGRAPHIC TREATMENT

The ways in which the problems mentioned in this paper may be treated in bilingual dictionaries, especially ethnographic dictionaries, are practically unlimited. That very few of the possibilities have been explored to date is disappointing, but not discouraging. There have been a number of new attempts at expanding the analytic procedures of descriptive linguistics to include a more rigorous, thorough, and theoretically rewarding analysis of semantic structure (e.g., Goodenough 1956; Lounsbury 1956; Nida 1958; Frake 1961). Despite these more encouraging signs, I realize that most dictionaries will continue to be organized primarily as alphabetical indices. Suggestions regarding the ways in which structural semantic information (especially with reference to folk taxonomies) might be more adequately covered in such dictionaries would include, wherever possible: (1) consistent marking of each entry as to its status as a lexical unit and taxon, its immediately subordinate taxa and superordinate taxon, and all coordinate taxa included with it in this next higher taxon (simple diacritics and abbreviations can be devised for systematic use in compilation and checking); (2) differential marking of translation labels and of definitions; (3) concise indication of distinctive attributes which define categories belonging to analyzed lexical sets; (4) systematic cross-referencing to maximal taxa in all major subhierarchies, to referential synonyms, and to all units involved in categoric overlap; and (5) frequent use of structural charts and diagrams. Where only limited opportunities are available for accomplishing such tasks, priority might be given to those parts of the lexicon which, on the basis of nonintuitive and intracultural criteria, appear to involve semantic relations of an everyday, obligatory nature. In number of segregates, paradigmatic complexity, and hierarchic depth, certain lexical domains are likely to be more highly structured than others (Brown 1956:307; Nida 1958:283–284; Worth

1960:277; Frake 1961:121–122). For the student of folk taxonomy, focusing attention on these domains should lead not only to more interesting analytic problems but also to results of greater lexicographical and general cultural relevance.

NOTES

[1] The work on which most of this paper is based has been supported by the National Science Foundation. A number of students and other friends have offered constructive criticism of an earlier draft of this statement. For especially helpful and more detailed comments I am particularly indebted to Y. R. Chao, David Crabb, Arthur Danto, C. O. Frake, Paul Friedrich, W. H. Goodenough, J. H. Greenberg, Einar Haugen, P. F. Lazarsfeld, F. G. Lounsbury, and Volney Stefflre.

REFERENCES CITED

Austerlitz, Robert, 1959, Semantic components of pronoun systems: Gilyak. Word 15:102–109.
Beckner, Morton, 1959, The biological way of thought. New York, Columbia University Press.
Brown, Roger W., 1956, Language and categories. *In* Jerome S. Bruner and others, A study of thinking. New York, John Wiley.
Bruner, Jerome S., Jacqueline J. Goodnow, and George A. Austin, 1956, A study of thinking. New York, Wiley.
Chao, Yuen Ren, 1953, Popular Chinese plant words, a descriptive lexicogrammatical study. Language 29:379–414.
Chomsky, A. Noam, 1955, Semantic considerations in grammar. Washington, Georgetown University Monograph Series on Languages and Linguistics No. 8:141–150.
———, 1957, Syntactic structures. 's Gravenhage, Mouton.
Conklin, Harold C., 1954, The relation of Hanunóo culture to the plant world. Unpublished Ph.D. dissertation in anthropology, Yale University.
———, 1955, Hanunóo color categories. Southwestern Journal of Anthropology 11:339–344.
———, 1957, Ethnobotanical problems in the comparative study of folk taxonomy. Paper read at the Ninth Pacific Science Congress.
Frake, Charles O., 1960, The Eastern Subanun of Mindanao. *In* G. P. Murdock, ed., Social structure in Southeast Asia. Chicago, Quadrangle Books.
———, 1961, The diagnosis of disease among the Subanun of Mindanao. American Anthropologist 63:113–132.
Garvin, Paul L., 1960, On structuralist method. Washington, Georgetown University Monograph Series on Languages and Linguistics No. 11:145–148.

Goodenough, Ward H., 1951, Property, kin, and community on Truk. Yale University Publications in Anthropology, No. 46.

———, 1956, Componential analysis and the study of meaning. Language 32: 195–216.

———, 1957, Cultural anthropology and linguistics. Washington, Georgetown University Monograph Series on Languages and Linguistics No. 9:167–173.

Greenberg, Joseph H., 1957, The nature and uses of linguistic typologies. International Journal of American Linguistics 23:68–77.

Gregg, John R., 1954, The language of taxonomy: an application of symbolic logic to the study of classificatory systems. New York, Columbia University Press.

Harris, Zellig, 1948, Componential analysis of a Hebrew paradigm. Language 24:87–91.

Haugen, Einar, 1957, The semantics of Icelandic orientation. Word 13:447–459.

Hockett, Charles F., 1956, Idiom formation. In For Roman Jakobson. The Hague, Mouton.

Householder, Fred W., Jr., 1959, Review of Charles F. Hockett, A course in modern linguistics. Language 35:503–527.

Jakobson, Roman, 1936, Beitrag zur allgemeinen Kasuslehre. Travaux du Cercle Linguistique de Prague 6:240–288.

Joos, Martin, 1956, Review of William N. Locke and A. Donald Booth, eds., Machine translation of languages: fourteen essays. Language 32:293–298.

———, 1958, Semology: a linguistic theory of meaning. Studies in Linguistics 13:53–70.

Jorden, Eleanor Harz, 1955, The syntax of modern colloquial Japanese. Language 31, No. 1, Pt. 3:1–135.

Kelly, George A., 1955, The psychology of personal constructs. Vol. 1., A theory of personality. New York, W. W. Norton.

Landar, Herbert J., 1960, A note on accepted and rejected arrangements of Navaho words. International Journal of American Linguistics 26:351–354.

Landar, Herbert J., Susan M. Ervin, and Arnold E. Horowitz, 1960, Navaho color categories. Language 36:368–382.

Lawrence, George H. M., 1951, Taxonomy of vascular plants. New York, Macmillan.

Lazarsfeld, Paul F., 1961, The algebra of dichotomous systems. In Herbert Solomon, ed., Studies in item analysis and prediction. Stanford, Stanford University Press.

Lees, Robert B., 1960, The grammar of English nominalizations. International Journal of American Linguistics 26, No. 3, Pt. 2:1–205.

Lenneberg, Eric H., and John M. Roberts, 1956, The language of experience, a study in methodology. International Journal of American Linguistics Memoir No. 13.

Lotz, John, 1949, The semantic analysis of the nominal bases in Hungarian. Travaux du Cercle Linguistique de Copenhague 5:185–197.

Lounsbury, Floyd G., 1956, A semantic analysis of the Pawnee kinship usage. Language 32: 158–194.

———, 1960, Similarity and contiguity relations in language and culture. Washington, Georgetown University Monograph Series on Languages and Linguistics No. 12:123–128.

Lyons, J., 1960, Review of Henry M. Hoenigswald, Language change and linguistic reconstruction. Bulletin of the School of Oriental and African Studies 27: 621–622.

Maclay, Howard, and Mary D. Sleator, 1960, Responses to language: judgments of grammaticalness. International Journal of American Linguistics 26:275–282.

Mayr, Ernst, E. Gorton Linsley, and Robert L. Usinger, 1953, Methods and principles of systematic zoology. New York, McGraw-Hill.

McKaughan, Howard, 1959, Semantic components of pronoun systems: Maranao. Word 15:101–102.

Morris, Charles W., 1946, Signs, language, and behavior. New York, Prentice-Hall.

Nagel, Ernest, 1961, The structure of science: problems in the logic of scientific explanation. New York, Harcourt.

Newman, Stanley, 1954, Semantic problems in grammatical systems and lexemes: a search for method. In Harry Hoijer, ed., Language in culture. Chicago, University of Chicago Press.

Nida, Eugene A., 1951, A system for the description of semantic elements. Word 7:1–14.

――――, 1958, Analysis of meaning and dictionary making. International Journal of American Linguistics 24:279–292.

Öhman, Suzanne, 1953, Theories of the 'linguistic field.' Word 9:123–134.

Quine, Willard Van Orman, 1960, Word and object. Cambridge, The Technology Press of M.I.T.

Sebeok, Thomas A., 1946, Finnish and Hungarian case systems: their form and function. Acta Instituti Hungarici Universitatis Holmiensis, Series B, Linguistica 3.

Simpson, George Gaylord, 1961, Principles of animal taxonomy. New York, Columbia University Press.

Swadesh, Morris, 1946, Chitimacha. In Harry Hoijer and others, Linguistic structures of native North America. New York, Viking Fund.

Thomas, David, 1955, Three analyses of the Ilocano pronoun system. Word 11: 204–208.

――――, 1957, An introduction to Mansaka lexicography. Nasuli, Philippines, Summer Institute in Linguistics.

Voegelin, Charles F. and Florence M., 1957, Hopi domains, a lexical approach to the problem of selection. International Journal of American Linguistics Memoir No. 14.

Wallace, Anthony F. C., and John Atkins, 1960, The meaning of kinship terms. American Anthropologist 62:58–80.

Weinreich, Uriel, 1960, Mid-century linguistics: attainments and frustrations. Romance Philology 8:320–341.

Wells, Rulon, 1958, Is a structural treatment of meaning possible? Proceedings of the Eighth International Congress of Linguists, Oslo, 1957.

Wonderly, William L., 1952, Semantic components in Kechua person morphemes. Language 28:366–376.

Woodger, J. H., 1952, Biology and language: an introduction to the methodology of the biological sciences including medicine. Cambridge, The University Press.

Worth, D. S., 1960, Review of A. I. Smirnickij, Lekiskologija anglijskogo jazyka. Word 16:277–284.

Folk Taxonomies and Biological Classification[1]

Brent Berlin,
Dennis E. Breedlove,
Peter H. Raven

The finding that lower-level categories of native folk taxonomic systems sometimes correspond with biological species in a one-to-one relation has often been used as evidence that biological species reflect objective natural groupings of organisms (Diamond 1966). Unfortunately, most of the data contributing to our understanding of the structure of folk taxonomies are casually collected, nonsystematic, incomplete, and anecdotal (for an exception, see Conklin 1954). These deficiencies tend to obscure the relation between folk and biological classification. They also make the solution of many questions of great interest difficult, such as the correspondence between lexical differentiation and cultural significance in a well-defined semantic domain.

Our data have been drawn from nearly 10,000 botanical collections made with one to several native informants. The research was done over an 18-month period in and near the Tzeltal-speaking municipio of Tenejapa, Chiapas, Mexico. This region, approximately 160 km² in area, ranges from 900 to 3000 m in elevation; it lies on a sloping plane of north-south orientation. Speaking generally, vegetation of the municipio includes cloud forest at the highest elevations; mixed pine-oak-liquidambar forest at the more temperate middle regions; legume-deciduous forest on drier slopes of the lower elevations; and tropical evergreen forest in more moist areas, such as along rivers, at the lowest elevations. More than 1500 species of vascular plants probably occur in the municipio of Tenejapa.

Repeated interviews with native informants suggest that our sample of more than 1100 Tzeltal plant names, at least 1000 of which are Tzeltal specifics, is nearing completion. We have defined a Tzeltal specific as any taxon which includes no other taxa. For the purposes of this report we have taken a sample of about 20 percent of our data by including the first 200 Tzeltal specific names in our alphabetical files. We have no reason to believe that such a procedure biases the results in any significant manner.

In examining the extent to which the Tzeltal taxonomy of plants corresponds with standard botanical classification, we first divided Tzeltal specifics into three categories. The first category, which we refer to as underdifferentiated, is composed of Tzeltal specifics which include two or more botanical species. Category 2 includes those Tzeltal specifics which correspond in a one-to-one fashion with botanical species. Category 3, which we refer to as overdifferentiated, includes those Tzeltal specifics which exhibit a many-to-one relation with botanical categories—that is, when more than one Tzeltal specific maps to one botanical species. These three categories are illustrated in Table 1. Using these standards of classification for our sample of 200 names, we find that 82 are underdifferentiated, 68 map in a one-to-one fashion, and 50 are overdifferentiated. Tzeltal specifics clearly do not correspond in a predictable way with botanical species.

In an effort to identify the reasons for the different lexical treatment accorded various plant species, we scored the 200 Tzeltal specifics in terms

Table 1. Examples of the Three Categories of Tzeltal Specific Plant Names

TZELTAL SPECIFIC NAME	BOTANICAL CLASSIFICATION
	Underdifferentiation
ʔahateʔes	$\left\{\begin{array}{l}\textit{Archibaccharis flexilis} \text{ Blake (Compositae)} \\ \textit{Gaultheria odorata} \text{ Willd. (Ericaceae)} \\ \textit{Ugni montana} \text{ (Benth.) Berg (Myrtaceae)} \\ \textit{Vaccinium leucanthum} \text{ C. \& S.ʹ (Ericaceae)}\end{array}\right.$
ʔičil ʔak'	$\left\{\begin{array}{l}\textit{Clematis dioica} \text{ L. (Ranunculaceae)} \\ \textit{Clematis grossa} \text{ Benth. (Ranunculaceae)} \\ \textit{Serjania} \text{ spp. (Sapindaceae)}\end{array}\right.$
	One-to-one correspondence
balamk'in	*Polymnia maculata* Cav. (Compositae)
kašlan bok	*Brassica oleracea* L. (Cruciferae)
çaʔteʔ	*Ateleia pterocarpa* Sessé & Moc. (Leguminosae)
weʔbalil çib	*Marattia weinmaniifolia* Liebm. (Marattiaceae)
	Overdifferentiation
çahal šču ʔil čenek' k'anal šču ʔil čenek' ʔihk'al šlumil čenek' çahal šlumil čenek' sakil šlumil čenek'	*Phaseolus vulgaris* L. (Leguminosae)
k'atk'at bohč sepsep bohč çu čahk'oʔ	*Lagenaria siceraria* (Mol.) Standl. (Cucurbitaceae)

of high, moderate, and low cultural significance. Assignment was made as follows: category 1, plants of low cultural significance, includes plants of little or no utility for the Tzeltal; category 2, plants of moderate cultural significance, includes species used for food, firewood, or other purposes but not cultivated; and category 3, plants of high cultural significance, encompasses all plants intensively cultivated by the Tzeltal—such as corn, beans, chilis, and squashes. These plants are primarily food or cash crops and clearly are of great importance.

The relation between lexical diversity and plant utilization is shown in Table 2; about a third of the Tzeltal specifics in our sample fall in each of

Table 2. Relation of cultural significance to differentiation (in terms of botanical categories) of Tzeltal specific plant names

UNDERDIFFER-ENTIATION	ONE-TO-ONE CORRESPONDENCE	OVERDIFFER-ENTIATION
	Low cultural significance	
49	10 (2)	5
	Moderate cultural significance	
31 (1)	31 (14)	5
	High cultural significance	
2	27 (24)	40

Numbers in parentheses indicate number of plants which were presumably introduced into Tenejapa after the Spanish conquest.

the three groups of cultural significance. There is a strong positive correlation between cultural significance and degree of lexical differentiation; for example, 40 of the 50 species which were overdifferentiated were judged to be of high cultural significance.

In analyzing the degree of correspondence between Tzeltal specific names and botanical species, it is useful to consider the examples of overdifferentiation in greater detail. The simplest case is exemplified by "white zapote," *Casimiroa edulis:*

$$
\left.
\begin{array}{l}
ba\mathcal{c}'il \; {}^{\textit{?}}ahate{}^{\textit{?}} \\
\mathcal{c}ahal \; {}^{\textit{?}}ahate{}^{\textit{?}} \\
k'anal \; {}^{\textit{?}}ahate{}^{\textit{?}} \\
\mathcal{c}elum \; {}^{\textit{?}}ahate{}^{\textit{?}}
\end{array}
\right\}
\;
\begin{array}{l}
Casimiroa \; edulis \\
\text{Llave \& Lex.}
\end{array}
$$

Linguistically, the Tzeltal specific lexemes comprise an attributive plus a head, the attributive referring to frequency of occurrence or dominance (*baȼ'il* "true"), color (*ȼahal* "red," *k'anal* "yellow"), or shape (*ȼelum* "elongated"). The head, *ʔahateʔ*, is also a free form which acts as the including taxon at the next taxonomic level. The four Tzeltal specifics are, therefore, "kinds" of *ʔahateʔ*, and in this case, the higher level taxon, *ʔahateʔ*, would stand in a one-to-one relation to *Casimiroa edulis*.

Although the example of *Casimiroa* represents a common case of over-differentiation, it must be noted that more complicated situations are often encountered. For example, the Tzeltal plant name *čenekʼ* (see Table 1) includes all varieties of *Phaseolus vulgaris*. In addition, however, it includes some (but not all) other species of *Phaseolus* as well as *Vigna sinensis* (L.) Savi ex Hassk., *Vicia faba* L., *Pisum sativum* L., *Arachis hypogaea* L., and *Lupinus* sp. Thus there is no complete correspondence between *čenekʼ* and any recognized botanical category.

The Tzeltal classification of the common bottle gourd, *Lagenaria siceraria*, presents a less common situation. We note the following Tzeltal specifics.

$$\left. \begin{array}{l} k'atk'at\ bohč \\ sepsep\ bohč \\ \not{c}u \\ č'ahk'oʔ \end{array} \right\} \begin{array}{l} Lagenaria\ siceraria \\ (\text{Mol.})\ Standl. \end{array}$$

Although the first two forms, *k'atk'at bohč* and *sepsep bohč* are "binomials," each being a "kind-of" *bohč*, there remain the specifics *ɗu* and *č'ahk'oʔ*. These forms are clearly, from the Tzeltal point of view, not "kinds-of" *bohč*. They are likewise distinct from one another. There is, then, no named Tzeltal higher level taxon which corresponds in a one-to-one fashion with *Lagenaria siceraria* and which includes as well all Tzeltal specifics which are identified as *Lagenaria siceraria*.

There are good morphological grounds to justify each group of the above Tzeltal categories, given the specialized attributes which characterize the Tzeltal system of classification. Thus the fruits of *bohč* are large and round and are used, for example, as containers for tortillas and drinking water; those of *ɗu* are long-necked gourds used mainly as carrying vessels for liquids; the small oval fruits of *č'ahk'oʔ* have no known utility. Nonetheless, these groupings do not correspond to botanical categories in any meaningful fashion.

An unexpected result of our investigations was the realization that a high proportion—40 out of 68—of the plants for which there was a one-to-one correspondence were introduced to Tenejapa after the Spanish conquest. Twenty-four of the 27 species of high cultural significance for which there is a one-to-one correspondence belong to this group. All 40 species came as a part of Hispanic culture and the majority of their Tzeltal names are derived from Spanish (see Table 3). Presumably the one-to-one relation in the names of these plants exists because they were introduced as named

Table 3.   Examples of Tzeltal specific plant names which are of high cultural significance, show one-to-one correspondence, and are introduced flora

TZELTAL SPECIFIC NAME	DERIVATION AND BOTANICAL NAME
waneš	<OSp./rábano̱s/rabanos "raddishes" *Raphanus sativus* L.
wéna	<Sp./yérba buéna/yerba buena "mint" *Mentha* sp.
ʔašuš	OSp./ášo̱s/ajos "garlics" *Allium sativum* L.
kašlan bok	(Lit. "Castillian vegetable") <OSp./kaštilyáno/*castillano* "Castillian" + *bok* "vegetable" *Brassica oleracea* L.
šʔawaš čenek'	(Lit. "broad-bean bean") <OSp./ábas̱/abas ("broad-bean" + *čenek'* ("bean") *Vicia faba* L.
kašlan č'opak'	(Lit. "Castillian soaproot") <OSp./kaštilyáno/*castillano* "Castillian" + *č'opak'* "soaproot" *Ricinus communis* L.
ʔiko	Sp./ígo/*higo* "fig" *Ficus carica* L.

entities. They are invariably used today for the same purposes for which they were originally introduced and in many instances retain the same names.

The data presented in this report show that although botanical species may be recognized in folk systems of classification, this is not necessarily reflected linguistically in a one-to-one fashion. One native category may correspond to several species, genera, or families, or portions of these taxa, or one species may correspond to several native categories. Even though about a third of the species in the total inventory of Tzeltal specifics map in a one-to-one fashion onto botanical species, some 59 percent of these correspondences are best thought of as artifacts of Hispanic culture. Only 14 percent of the Tzeltal specifics in our sample refer to native plants and exhibit a one-to-one correspondence with botanical species.

What is the basis for the correspondence, or lack of correspondence, between the lower levels of native folk taxonomic systems and biological species? Many groups of organisms do occur in nature in well-defined clusters, often separated by clearly recognizable discontinuities in the pattern of variation. When species of plants occur in the same place, they are usually easily separated; when they do not, the assignment of populations to the category "species" often becomes more arbitrary.

Taking these facts into consideration, there are still several possible sorts of classificatory systems for organisms. Among these, most biologists would understand a *natural* taxonomic grouping to be one which reflects the phylogenetic and genetic relations of the organisms being classified. This is quite apart from the use of the term "natural" in logic. On the other hand, a system of classification is said to be *general* ("natural" in a logical sense) insofar as its members possess many attributes in common, and *special* ("artificial" in a biological sense) when it is based on a few attributes that are of special interest for a particular purpose.

In a general or, as it is sometimes called, a "general-purpose" classification, the members of a group share many correlated attributes; the information content of the group and, by implication, the classificatory scheme which gave rise to it, is high (Sneath 1957). On the other hand, a general classification can never be perfect for all purposes. As emphasized by Sokal and Sneath (1963), when we put together entities with the highest proportion of shared attributes, we debar ourselves from insisting that these entities share any one particular attribute. Thus a special classification is demonstrably the best one for the limited purpose for which it was constructed, a general one the best for a wide range of potential purposes.

Viewing the problem in this light, we can readily comprehend the distinction between our usual Linnaean system of classification and any particular folk system of classification. The former, by continual review, is consciously made more and more general (Sokal and Sneath 1964; Davis and Heywood 1963); the latter, perhaps unconsciously, is made more and more special—hence specific—and with the highest possible predictive value with respect to the operations for which it is employed. It is hardly surprising that the special classification will often be concerned with characteristics that are also reflected in the general one and, insofar as this is true, mirror it. This clearly tells us nothing about the structure of nature itself, but a great deal about our own view of this structure.

NOTES

[1] Supported by NSF grant GS-383 (A. K. Romney and P. H. Raven, principal investigators). We are grateful to many botanists, but especially to L. O. Williams of the Field Museum of Natural History, Chicago, and to R. McVaugh of the University of Michigan for assisting with identification of plant materials, and to R. W. Holm of Stanford University for his critical review of the manuscript. We also thank J. Brukman and R. Ornduff of the University of California, Berkeley, and P. Kay, Center for the Advanced Study of Behavioral Sciences, who have read an earlier version of the paper. The work reported here is being continued and supported under the following National Science Foundation grants: GS-1183 and GS-2280. Additional support is provided by The Center for Advanced Study in the Behavioral Sciences where one of the authors is currently a Fellow. This support is gratefully acknowledged. Further materials bearing directly on the point at issue in this paper may be found in Brent Berlin, Dennis Breedlove, and Peter H. Raven, "Covert categories and folk taxonomies," American Anthropologist 70:290–299 (1968). Relevant bibliographic material on the ethnobotanical work now in progress may be obtained by writing to the authors at The Center for Advanced Study in the Behavioral Sciences, Stanford, California.

REFERENCES CITED

Conklin, Harold C., 1954, The relation of Hanunóo culture to the plant world. Unpublished Ph.D. Dissertation, Yale University.
Davis, P. H., V. H. Heywood, 1963, Principles of angiosperm taxonomy. Edinburgh, Oliver and Boyd.
Diamond, J., 1966, Zoological classification system of a primitive people. Science 151:1102.
Sneath, P. H. A., 1957, Some thoughts on bacterial classification. Journal of General Microbiology 17:184.
Sokal, R. R., P. H. A. Sneath, 1963, Principles of numerical taxonomy. San Francisco, Freeman.

Semantic Structures in Northwestern California and the Sapir-Whorf Hypothesis[1]

Jane O. Bright
William Bright

The Indian tribes of northwestern California constitute a well recognized culture area, first defined by A. L. Kroeber. The groups which best typify the northwestern California culture are the Yurok, the Karok, and the Hupa; slightly peripheral are the Smith River Indians (Tolowa), the Wiyot, and the Chilula. The nonlinguistic culture of the area is quite homogeneous, so that Kroeber felt justified in stating (1925:5) that "The Yurok shared this civilization in identical form with their neighbors, the Hupa and Karok. The adjacent Tolowa, Wiyot and Chilula adhere to the same culture in every essential trait." Linguistically, however, the area is probably as heterogeneous as any of comparable size in the world. Yurok and Wiyot are related to the Algonkian languages of eastern and central North America; but despite their geographical proximity, it is far from clear that they are more closely related to each other than either is to Algonkian (Teeter 1964:189). Karok is Hokan, but only remotely related to its nearest Hokan neighbors, Shasta and Chimariko. Hupa and Smith River are both Athabascan, but the division of Pacific Coast Athabascan languages into two groups falls between them, so that the closest relatives of Hupa extend southward into Central California, while Smith River has its closest kin in southwestern Oregon.

Reproduced by permission of the authors and the American Anthropological Association from the *American Anthropologist*, Vol. 67, no. 5, part 2 (Special Publication), pp. 249–258 (October 1965).

The paradoxical combination of cultural unity with linguistic diversity in other areas has been commented on by anthropologists—notably in the Southwestern United States where Pueblo groups with similar cultures speak diverse languages. The northwestern California case was cited by Sapir (1921:214) as illustrating his point that "language and culture are not intrinsically related." He noted that speakers of the clearly unified Athabascan language family adapted themselves, evidently with considerable speed, to four very different culture areas of North America. "The Hupa Indians," he wrote, "are very typical of the culture area to which they belong. Culturally identical with them are the neighboring Yurok and Karok. There is the liveliest tribal intercourse between the Hupa, Yurok, and Karok, so much so that all three generally attend an important religious ceremony given by any one of them. It is difficult to say what elements in their combined culture belong in origin to this tribe or that, so much at one are they in communal action, feeling and thought. But their languages are not merely alien to each other; they belong to three of the major American linguistic groups . . . "[2]

Compare this with Sapir's more famous statement, the basis of the Sapir-Whorf (or Whorfian) hypothesis (1929:209):

> Human beings do not live in the objective world alone, nor alone in the world of social activity as ordinarily understood, but are very much at the mercy of the particular language which has become the medium of expression for their society. . . . The fact of the matter is that the "real world" is to a large extent unconsciously built up on the language habits of the group. No two languages are ever sufficiently similar to be considered as representing the same social reality. The worlds in which different societies live are distinct worlds, not merely the same world with different labels attached.

When this statement, the basis of the Sapir-Whorf or Whorfian hypothesis, is compared to the previous quotation, a certain discrepancy is apparent. If the Sapir-Whorf hypothesis is maintained, then the Yurok, for example, are seen as being "at the mercy of" their Algonkian-like linguistic heritage; the Smith River and Karok are similarly dominated by Athabascan and Hokan structures, respectively. Given this linguistic diversity, how can these tribes be "culturally identical"? Or is it possible that they do after all share "the same world with different labels attached," contrary to our expectations derived from Sapir and Whorf?

Perhaps we can answer part of this question by suggesting that the languages are more similar than their diverse genetic backgrounds indicate. This is reasonable in terms of Whorf's specific recognition (1941:91) that linguistic structures and other cultural patterns "have grown up together, constantly influencing each other." The mutual assimilation of languages under the influence of a broader cultural unity is, of course, observable in many parts of the world, and we can expect to find the same phenomenon in northwestern California. Loan words between languages in the area are few: we know of only ten between Yurok and Karok, and fewer between Yurok and Smith River. But there are a number of grammatical similarities between Yurok and Karok (cf. W. Bright 1959:103): possessive and locative inflection of nouns, but plurality only for a limited group of them; inflection of verb forms for pronominal object as well as subject; the use of nominalized verb forms as heads of equational sentences; the redundant marking of plurality in verbs by an extended stem; and the use of preverbal particles to mark tense and aspect. Smith River shares a number of these features: nouns are sometimes inflected for possession and location, but never for plurality; verbs are inflected for pronominal object as well as subject; and verbal prefixes are used to mark tense and aspect. Impressionistically, we may say that Yurok shows more structural similarities with Karok than with Smith River, although the three languages still show many more differences than similarities. The similarities may be accidental; this could be proved only if they were reconstructable in the grammatical systems of Proto-Algonkian, Proto-Hokan, and Proto-Athabascan. Some of the similarities appear to be due to diffusion. If this is true, we may reason that the uniformity of culture has tempered language diversity in the area to the point where the reverse effect—the diversification of culture patterns under the influence of linguistic differences—is partly inhibited.

The apparent incompatibility of cultural identity and linguistic diversity is also mitigated by the possibility that the linguistic diversity of the area may have conditioned certain nonlinguistic differences between the Yurok and their neighbors—differences in cognitive habits, perhaps, which have not received adequate attention from ethnographers. This amounts to testing the Sapir-Whorf hypothesis itself; if full data on the northwestern California tribes revealed no cultural differences correlative with linguistic differences, then we would be strongly influenced to abandon the view of Sapir and Whorf. The difficulty in making the test, however, is that available ethnographic data emphasize only the uniformity of the area. After some brief remarks on the Karok, Kroeber states (1925:108): "Data are scarcely available for a fuller sketch of Karok culture. Nor is such an account necessary in the present connection. In at least ninety-five institutions out of every hundred, all that has been said of the Yurok or is on record concerning the Hupa applies identically to the Karok." Cultural diversity in the area was described mostly in terms of unsystematized data: "Hupa alone has a first-fruits feast for the acorn crop" (Kroeber and Gifford 1949:4). The few general statements available about differences between tribes are vague and hard to apply—for example, the comment of a Karok informant that the Hupa are lazier than the other tribes in the area. Furthermore, aboriginal cultures are now nearly extinct, making it difficult to gather new data on intertribal differences.

A topic on which some data are still collectable, however, is the taxonomy applied by the Indians to the physical world around them. This taxonomic system survives precisely because of its close correspondence to the vocabulary of the aboriginal languages, which have lasted longer than other aspects of native life.[3] Such folk taxonomies should be examined in the light of Sapir's statement that "the worlds in which different societies live are distinct worlds, not merely the same world with different labels attached."

An example of such a taxonomy is spatial orientation: the inland Yurok and the Karok, living on either side of the Klamath River, oriented themselves not to the apparent motion of the sun, which Europeans use to define the terms "north, south, east, west," but to the direction of river flow. This is reflected in the Yurok and Karok terms for cardinal directions, words translatable as "upriver, downriver, towards the river, away from the river." The morphemes used by these languages for a given meaning have no similarity in their phonemic shape (cf. Yurok *wonew*, Karok *maruk* "away from the river"): it is rather that both languages reflect the same conceptual structure.

More complex systems are to be found in what we may call the ethnobiotaxonomy of these northwestern California tribes—the folk classification of their plant and animal world. Stimulated by the recent work by Conklin (1962a) and Frake (1962) in this area of "ethnoscience," we tried to discover the principles underlying the coastal Yurok and Smith River classifications of their biosphere.[4] Following suggestions made by Metzger (1963), questioning was conducted as much as possible in the Indian language, and features of taxonomic structure were approached repeatedly from a number of different angles. A typical series might be: (a) a wild strawberry is shown to an informant, with the question (in the Indian language), "What's this?" (b) Several kinds of berries are shown, with the question, "What are these?" (c) The questioner asks, "Is a strawberry a berry?" (d) A deliberately foolish question is asked, such as, "Is a strawberry a tree?" (e) Receiving a negative answer to the previous question, the investigator asks, "What *is* a strawberry then?" The informants preferred were those who knew least English, to keep the Indian view as pure as possible. Informants were encouraged to comment as they went along; tape-recorded interviews were later transcribed and translated with the help of informants who spoke good English.

Various difficulties were encountered: informants displayed, at one time or another, lapse of memory, contamination by white man's categories, and lack of attention. The most knowledgeable informant was a Yurok, Mrs. Alice Spott Taylor, aged 95 years. She was the sister of Robert Spott,

Kroeber's informant for many years. Mrs. Taylor was the most "Indian" informant who could be found, but her very "Indianness" was sometimes troublesome, as when her answers refer less to taxonomy than to mythology. Witness the following exchange:

Q. nunepuy hes wiʔ kʼi loʔcoʔm "Is a toad a fish?"[5]
A. paaʔ, nimiʔ nunepuy kʼi loʔcoʔm "No, a toad isn't a fish."
Q. tiʔ ni šoˑ wiʔ kʼi loʔcoʔm "What *is* a toad?"
A. loʔcoʔm kʷel wencoks wiʔ "A toad is a woman."

This is, of course, a myth reference, and is reminiscent of Kroeber's statement: "In trying to obtain ordinary ethnographic data on Yurok, I have had to listen time and again to myths which I had already heard, before I could come to the contemporary facts; and sometimes these had to be elicited by prodding" (Spott and Kroeber 1942:214). Many misleading answers were clarified by the cross-checking built into the routine of questioning, and by consulting several informants. To be sure, there are discrepancies between informants, but these are probably inherent in any taxonomy. English speakers do not agree, for instance, on whether avocados and tomatoes are fruits or vegetables; California Indians may surely be allowed a similar lack of unanimity.[6]

One fact emergent from a study of the Yurok and Smith River taxonomic systems is that they are less hierarchically organized than our own. We nearly exhaust the universe of living things with multileveled hierarchical classifications such as "plant, bush, berry bush, gooseberry bush" or "animal, insect, louse, body louse." The Indians, by contrast, have relatively few generic terms, and many terms which do not fall into any hierarchy. The generic terms noted, with rough English equivalents, are as follows: Yurok has *hoˑreʔmos* "quadruped mammal," *nunepuy* "fish," *leyes* "snake," *cʼucʼiš* "bird, especially small bird," *tepoˑ* "fir tree, tree," *kaˑpʼeɬ* "bush," *ʔɹˑwɹh* "grass," *ciˑšep* "flower," and *nɹhpɹy* "berry." Smith River has fewer terms: *tʼaaɣəš* "snake," *tšʼeeyáš* "duck, bird," *tšʼaamé* "fir tree, conifer," *tšéeneh* "bush, nonconiferous tree," *xəmšən* "grass," *tšʼabáayuh* "flower," and *deetšíh* "berry." The terms available from Karok (although they were not collected with taxonomic structures in mind) are comparable in number to those of Smith River: *ʔápsuˑn* "snake," *ʔačiˑʋ* "bird," *ʔíppaha* "tree," *píriš* "bush, grass," *ʔiθríha* "flower," and *ʔuxraˑh* "berry." We note a considerable core of agreement in these three systems.

In this framework, a term like Yurok *wɹˑgɹ* "body louse" cannot be subsumed in larger classes "louse" or "insect," since none exist; nor is the classification *hoˑreʔmos*, sometimes translated "animal," conceded to apply to it. The answer to the question *tiʔ ni šoˑ wiʔ kʼi wɹˑgɹ* "What *is* a body louse?" is simply *wɹˑgɹ wiʔ* "It's body louse." Furthermore, Yurok informants, asked to identify a plant or animal for which they know no name, often say that it is "like such-and-such," rather than assigning it to a class: thus several flowering bushes were described as *sahsip segon* "like wild lilac," although they bore little resemblance to the wild lilac, from a white man's point of view. (A similar response was reported by David French [1960] for the Sahaptin Indians in Oregon.) Where generic terms exist, they may also refer to a specific member of the class. This parallels the use of English "man" to refer both to human beings as a class and to adult males as a subdivision of that class; but the phenomenon is commoner in the Indian languages. Thus Yurok *tepo·* refers to "fir tree" or "tree" in general; Smith River *tš'eeyáš* is "duck" in particular or "bird" in general.

We see, then, that a hierarchical model, which shows only the relationship of *domination* ("A dominates B" = "B is an A"), cannot account adequately for the Indian taxonomies. In a hierarchy, an item either is or is not a member of the class named by the next higher node. But there is no way of indicating, in a hierarchical tree, the situation where a specific term like Yurok *tepo·* "fir, tree" or Smith River *tš'aamé?* "fir, conifer" can also be used as a generic term, thus including other trees which resemble the fir by being coniferous. In addition, there is no way of indicating when an item is classified in a certain way because it is "like" another item which is more central to the focus of the domain in question. Therefore, although our European hierarchic taxonomies can be represented for the most part by a branching tree (see the English chart in Fig. 1), the aboriginal taxonomies of northwestern California can be represented more faithfully by a kind of "sphere of influence" model. Figure 1 compares a section of the taxonomies for "(woody) plants," first giving the English hierarchical taxonomy for the items in question, and then sphere of influence diagrams for parts of the Yurok and the Smith River systems. These charts are designed to point out the few differences between the two Indian systems as contrasted to the English. An example of a term also standing for the generic label of its class is found in Y1 where *tepo·* is the tree par excellence, namely the fir tree; and also in SR1 and SR2, where woody plants are *tš'aamé?* if they are conifers like the fir, or *tšéeneh* if they are bushy and nonconiferous like the oak—the focus of its domain. Y2 illustrates the classification of numerous bushes which are *ka·pet* because they are like *sahsip*, the lilac, although there is no morpheme for them in the language. Our sphere of influence model, a type not referred to by Conklin or Frake, is then only partly hierarchical.[7]

At this point we may raise the question: do semantic structures, such as these biotaxonomies, belong to language or do they belong to nonlinguistic culture? (The term "culture" alone is used hereafter in the sense of "everything in culture except language.") Both points of view have been held widely. On the one hand, many linguists have applied the term "lexical structure" to taxonomies such as these, and have included this structure, along with phonology and grammar, as the three main parts of descriptive

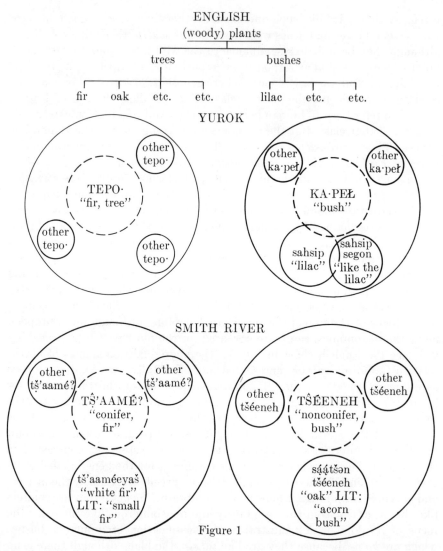

ENGLISH
(woody) plants

trees   bushes

fir   oak   etc.   etc.   lilac   etc.   etc.

YUROK

other tepo·

TEPO·
"fir, tree"

other tepo·

other tepo·

other ka·peł

other ka·peł

KA·PEŁ
"bush"

sahsip
"lilac"

sahsip segon
"like the lilac"

SMITH RIVER

other tṣ̌'aamé?

other tṣ̌'aamé?

TṢ̂'AAMÉ?
"conifer, fir"

tṣ̌'aaméeyaš
"white fir"
LIT: "small fir"

other tšéeneh

other tšéeneh

TŠ́EENEH
"nonconifer, bush"

sáátšən tšéeneh
"oak" LIT:
"acorn bush"

Figure 1

linguistics. On the other hand, structural semanticists such as Frake have proposed their techniques as specifically ethnographic. We would like to consider semantic structure as a part of culture; the model we have in mind is shown in Fig. 2. There is here a very close correspondence between certain linguistic items—those morphemes and constructions of morphemes which we call lexemes—on the one side, and certain units of nonlinguistic behavior on the other side. Following Goodenough (1956:208), the latter can be called sememes. Thus the English morpheme and lexeme "uncle" corresponds to a particular point in nonlinguistic behavior patterns, namely the

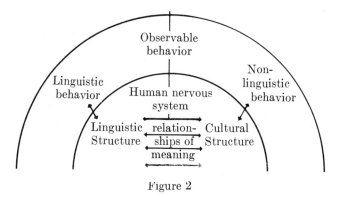

Figure 2

sememe which we may define as the role of an "uncle" in our culture. Although normally these correspondences are one-to-one, there are exceptions: thus Goodenough's analysis of Trukese kinship has to recognize several "zero lexemes"—points in the semantic pattern with no corresponding morphemic material. The general regularity of these relations, however, leads to differences of opinion as to whether semantic structure is part of language or part of culture.[8]

If we accept the view that semantic structure is part of nonlinguistic culture, we may attempt to confirm this from the particular case of northwestern California taxonomy. Specifically: Do the biotaxonomies of the Yurok, the Smith River, and the Karok reflect the diversity of their languages, or the relative uniformity of their culture? As we have seen, Yurok has nine taxonomic terms, Smith River seven, and Karok six, but most of these correspond to specific Yurok terms. All three tribes are alike in their lack of classifications corresponding to English terms such as "insect, worm, shellfish, lizard, plant, fern, weed." It appears that the biotaxonomies of these tribes are much more similar than are their languages. They show, in fact, the kind of near-uniformity which characterizes the nonlinguistic culture of the area. We may take this as support for our choice of assigning semantic structure to culture rather than to language. In addition, we may say that the Sapir-Whorf hypothesis is not strongly applicable to our data; Yurok, Smith River, and Karok speakers do not appear to live in such "distinct worlds" after all, at least as far as their views of the northwestern California biosphere are concerned.

Since we are looking for subtle differences in the cultures of these tribes, we cannot neglect the fact that the Yurok stand out from the others by having a somewhat more complex biotaxonomy, containing more generic terms, as well as some classifications based on the "is like a" relationship. Perhaps this is not surprising, since the Yurok are generally conceded to represent the climax or culmination of the northwestern California culture area. We are now, however, sharpening our focus, replacing the broad notion of "cultural climax" by the specific one of "greater elaboration of generic terms in biotaxonomy." Pursuing our interest in the Sapir-Whorf hypothesis, we may ask if there is anything in the Yurok, as opposed to the Smith River, language, which corresponds to this greater taxonomic complexity. No correspondences with specific grammatical features have suggested themselves, but certain broad traits of Yurok and Smith River grammar may be contrasted usefully. (Our approach is comparable to the overview of Chinook grammar made by Hymes [1961].) Yurok syntax is characterized by loose order, creating many ambiguities to be resolved by context, and has little cross-referencing through the morphology. Smith River, on the other hand, has rigid syntactic ordering, with extensive morphological cross-referencing. In morphology, Yurok has few obligatory categories: verbs have suffixes for person and number, but tense and aspect are indicated by particles; nouns have possessive prefixes indicating person but not number. Smith River morphology, by contrast, shows many obligatory categories: verb forms have up to 11 prefix positions, marking person, number, tense, and aspect; nouns have possessive prefixes which indicate both person and number.

At first glance, there seems to be a paradoxical inverse relation between the two cultures. In Yurok, a relatively complex taxonomy is associated with a loose grammatical structure, whereas in Smith River a less complex taxonomy goes with a very rigid grammar. But it is possible to resolve the paradox: the Yurok have more generic classifications, which means that they have more *choice* when they refer to plants and animals. Thus the Yurok fisherman can refer to his catch either as *ckʷoʈ* "steelhead" or, generically, as *nunepuy* "fish." This is consistent with the high degree of choice afforded in Yurok grammar, with its nearly-free word order and its optional morphological categories. The Smith River taxonomic system offers less choice: a steelhead is called *ṭislih* and nothing else—just as in Smith River grammar the basic sentence order is Indirect Object, Direct Object, Subject, Verb, and none other. Here the lack of choice in the linguistic structure corresponds to the constraint imposed by the taxonomic structure. (As for Karok, the grammar is intermediate in rigidity between Yurok and Smith River, but both taxonomy and grammar seem to approximate the Smith River more than the Yurok situation.) The Yurok "is like a" relationship also may be correlated with the greater freedom already noted in Yurok grammar. For Smith River, woody plants are either *tš'aamé?* or *tšéeneh;* there is a choice only of these two generic terms or of specific lexemes. In Yurok, classification does not fall into such strict lines: an item may be included in the *ka·p'eʈ* "bush" domain if it is merely *like* another member of that class. This is an example of a sememe with no lexemic correspondent—Goodenough's "zero lexeme" (1956:203).

We may now make a specific hypothesis about language-and-culture relationships in northwestern California: namely, a principle of choice inherent in Yurok linguistic structure has conditioned a similar degree of choice in biotaxonomy, manifested by a greater richness of generic terms; whereas the relative absence of choice in Smith River and Karok grammar has conditioned a corresponding poverty in taxonomy. This statement, like most of the applications of the Whorfian point of view, is probably not provable in itself. It may have a value, however, if taken together with other hypotheses pointing in the same direction, providing that each is based on solid data. The very effort to develop such hypotheses will stimulate the collection of valuable information which otherwise could be overlooked.[9]

SUMMARY

Northwestern California offers a case of aboriginal groups living in nearly identical cultures but speaking languages which differ considerably in structure. This situation can be used as a sort of test of the Sapir-Whorf hypothesis, especially of Sapir's claim that groups speaking diverse languages necessarily classify phenomena into "distinct worlds." The extreme genetic differences between the northwestern California languages are tempered somewhat by a few rather striking linguistic similarities—perhaps an indication of mutual linguistic influence. On the other hand, the cultures may not be as identical as has been thought. This possibility can be investigated more thoroughly by study of the semantic structures of the tribes concerned, in particular of their folk classifications of the biosphere. Study of three tribes shows that folk taxonomies are not necessarily hierarchical; they are better represented by a "spheres of influence" model than by a "family tree" model. The final question posed is: Are these taxonomies relatively similar to each other, like the cultures of the area; or are they diverse, like the linguistic structures? We find them quite similar, contrary to prediction from the Sapir-Whorf hypothesis. However, the greater choice in the Yurok taxonomic system can be correlated with the relatively greater choice allowed within Yurok grammar—a conclusion which supports Sapir and Whorf.

NOTES

[1] This paper is based on field work with the Smith River and Yurok conducted in the summer of 1963 under a grant from the Penrose Fund of the American Philosophical Society. We express our gratitude in particular for the cooperation of Amelia Brown and Alice Spott Taylor, highly knowledgeable representatives of the Smith River and Yurok cultures respectively; for the assistance of Minnie Macomber and Florence Shaughnessy in interpreting Yurok data; for the initial inspiration for this paper, provided by Philip L. Newman; and for the valuable suggestions of Dell H.

Hymes and Albert Anderson. Additional thanks are due Hymes for presenting this paper at the Stanford Conference, which we were not able to attend, and to the other members of the Conference for their constructive criticism.

[2] The Smith River Indians also were close to the focal point of northwestern California culture: they intermarried with the Yurok, joined with them in warfare, and enjoyed the prestige of being regarded by the Yurok as rich.

[3] We here assume that taxonomic systems are best regarded not as part of language itself, but as part of nonlinguistic culture, albeit a part having especially close relations with language. This view is developed more fully below.

[4] The coastal Yurok and Smith River peoples lived in almost identical natural environments. The Smith River villages were located primarily upcoast and downcoast from the mouth of the Smith River itself. Farther south, the Yurok clustered around the mouth of the Klamath River. Both groups had settlements some miles up their respective rivers—one of the largest Yurok villages was far inland, adjacent to Karok territory.

[5] Yurok forms are cited in the phonemic system of Robins (1958); Karok forms are as in W. Bright (1957); Smith River forms are as in J. Bright (1964).

[6] In discussing this paper, Floyd Lounsbury made the point that disagreements among English speakers as to avocados and tomatoes may be due not to any inherent loose ends in our taxonomy, but rather to a cross-cutting of two taxonomic systems, one concerned with plant products, the other with prepared foods. In any case, we agree with other participants in the discussion at Stanford who suggested (1) that we cannot exclude the possibility that probabilistic considerations are involved in some folk-taxonomic systems, and (2) that some cultures recognize some classes defined not by their boundaries, but by their centers. Such center-oriented classes are well-known in folk-taxonomies of color, and we believe they are also relevant to the northwest California classification of plants and animals.

[7] A center-oriented classification, such as proposed here, can be converted into a hierarchical classification by putting a single term on several hierarchical levels, as Frake (1961:119) has done: English "man" (vs. "animal") dominates "man" (vs. "woman"), which dominates "man" (vs. "boy"), which dominates "man" (vs. "unmanly male"). We feel, however, that the investigator who follows this procedure runs the risk of imposing a scientific taxonomy, or some other system which he knows, upon the folk-taxonomic data that he is studying. Where members of a culture use a single term to classify objects at different levels of generalization, it may be that the very concept of levels and of hierarchy is irrelevant to their semantic structure.

[8] We here regard linguistic structure as comprising those patterns which account for verbal behavior and certain types of response to verbal behavior. We regard semantic structure as nonlinguistic insofar as it may operate independently: thus one may sort out the produce of a garden plot in terms of culturally-defined categories such as "fruit" and "vegetables," without any verbal behavior being involved.

[9] We feel that the recent statement by Robbins Burling (1964:26) that "Whorf's ideas have fallen into disrepute" is exaggerated. As evidence we may cite recent publications, all sympathetic to the Whorfian hypothesis, by Hymes (1961), Fishman (1960), Kluckhohn (1961), and Mathiot (1962). Carroll (1964:12) offers a statement of what we may call the neo-Whorfian position: "Insofar as languages differ in the

ways they encode objective experience, language users tend to sort out and distinguish experiences differently according to the categories provided by their respective languages. These cognitions will tend to have certain effects on behavior."

REFERENCES CITED

Bright, Jane O., 1964, The phonology of Smith River Athabascan (Tolowa). International Journal of American Linguistics 30:101–107.

Bright, William, 1957, The Karok language. University of California Publications in Linguistics 13.

———, 1959, Review of R. N. Robins, The Yurok language. Language 35:100–104.

Burling, Robbins, 1964, Cognition and componential analysis: God's truth or hocuspocus? American Anthropologist 66:20–28.

Carroll, John B., 1964, Linguistic relativity, contrastive linguistics, and language learning. International Review of Applied Linguistics in Language Teaching 1:1–20.

Conklin, Harold C., 1962, Comment (on the ethnographic study of cognitive systems, by C. O. Frake). In T. Gladwin and W. C. Sturtevant, eds., Anthropology and human behavior. Washington, Anthropological Society of Washington.

Fishman, Joshua, 1960, A systematization of the Whorfian hypothesis. Behavioral Science 5:323–339.

Frake, Charles O., 1961, The diagnosis of disease among the Subanun of Mindanao. American Anthropologist 63:113–132.

———, 1962, The ethnographic study of cognitive systems. In T. Gladwin and W. C. Sturtevant, eds., Anthropology and human behavior. Washington, Anthropological Society of Washington.

Goodenough, Ward H., 1956, Componential analysis and the study of meaning. Language 32:195–216.

Hymes, Dell H., 1961, On typology of cognitive styles in language. Anthropological Linguistics 3:1. 22–54.

Kluckhohn, Clyde, 1961, Notes on some anthropological aspects of communication. American Anthropologist 63:895–910.

Kroeber, A. L., 1925, Handbook of the Indians of California. Bureau of American Ethnology Bulletin 78. Washington, The Smithsonian Institution.

Kroeber, A. L., and E. W. Gifford, 1949, World renewal, a cult system of native northwest California. University of California Anthropological Records 13:1–156.

Mathiot, Madeleine, 1962, Noun classes and folk taxonomy in Papago. American Anthropologist 64:340–350.

Metzger, Duane, 1963, Asking questions and questioning answers in ethnography. Paper presented at the Spring Meeting of the Southwestern Anthropological Association, Riverside, California.

Robins, R. H., 1958, The Yurok language. University of California Publications in Linguistics 15.

Sapir, Edward, 1921, Language: an introduction to the study of speech. New York, Harcourt, Brace.

Teeter, Karl, 1964, Wiyot and Yurok. *In* W. Bright, ed., studies in Californian Linguistics. University of California Publications in Linguistics 34.

Whorf, Benjamin L., 1941, The relation of habitual thought and behavior to language. *In* L. Spier and others, Language, culture and personality. Menasha, Wisconsin, Banta.

Comments on Colby

Paul Kay

The following comments are intended not as criticism of Colby's paper but as supplement. As Colby is aware, there have been significant advances in the field of ethnographic semantics since his paper was drafted (see his addendum). It is appropriate to review some of the results of this work here, however briefly, because they lead to certain reinterpretations and clarifications of the literature covered in Colby's excellent review.

On the theory side, the field of ethnographic semantics now contains a relatively small number of clearly understood, related notions. The first and most important two, *domain* and *lexeme*, will not be discussed in detail in these comments. Problems remain both with the theoretical definition and operational isolation of these units. Nevertheless, we assume for present purposes that a basic problem of ethnographic semantics is the following: given a finite set of lexical units (*lexemes*) (Conklin 1962) that share some feature of meaning, we say (a) that the set of lexemes form a *domain* (Lounsbury 1964b) and (b) that our task is to discover something about the formal pattern of meanings underlying the domain (Colby, 1966:6–7).

The remaining basic notions of ethnographic semantics are *componential analysis, paradigm, taxonomy, key, tree, dimension* of meaning, *feature* of meaning, *inclusion of reference, level of contrast, etic grid*, and *contrast set*.

The first useful distinction is between (1) *componential analysis* and (2) the formal structure of the domain under analysis. Componential analysis is best conceived as an analytic *process* in which the investigator searches for (a) the *dimensions* of meaning underlying the domain and (b) the mapping of the values on these dimensions (the *features of meaning*) onto *the set of lexemes*. The process of looking for these mappings is not to be confused with particular types of such mappings such as paradigm and tree.

Componential analysis may be, and has been, performed with or without the aid of an a priori *etic grid*. All of the well-known kinship componential

From Comment on "Ethnographic Semantics: A Preliminary Survey," by B. N. Colby. *Current Anthropology*, Vol. 7, No. 1, pp. 20–23, 1966. Used by permission of the author and *Current Anthropology*.

analyses use the kin-type etic grid. Examples of ethnosemantic componential analyses not employing a priori etic grids include Hanunóo and Tzeltal pronominals (Conklin 1962; Berlin 1963, respectively). Frake's (1961) analysis of Subanum disease terms is in part a componential analysis (without etic grid) in that he includes a partial discussion of the features of meaning on which the disease names contrast.

A lexical domain may be analyzed with or without reference to the dimensions of meaning (and their component features) that underlie it. When an attempt to discover the underlying dimensions either is not made or is not successful, the semantic analysis is not, properly speaking, componential. In this case, the major concept ordinarily used to represent "something about the formal pattern of meanings underlying the domain" is the notion *inclusion of reference*. When a lexical domain is organized according to inclusion of reference, the resulting structure is a *taxonomy*. When there are many levels of inclusion, as in the case of Hanunóo plants or Subanun diseases, we may say there is a deep taxonomy. Deep taxonomies are probably empirically rare but are nevertheless interesting. Inclusion of reference, *not* absence of componential definitions, is the distinguishing feature of taxonomy; whether or not the feature definitions of the lexemes are known is logically irrelevant to the question of whether a taxonomy exists. An example of a taxonomy in which the feature definitions are known is the complete domain of American kin-terms including such subsets as {relative, blood relative, ancestor, grandparent, grandfather}, in which each lexeme in the sequence properly includes the designatum of the following lexeme. The basic point was made by Conklin (1962:135) but for one reason another seems frequently to have been ignored (cf. Colby 1966:7–8).

A characteristic of all taxonomies is that they contain *levels of contrast*. The notion is familiar to workers in the field of ethnographic semantics (see, for example, the expositions in Frake 1961, 1962; Conklin 1962). However, a problem connected with this notion that does not seem to be generally appreciated is the following: in taxonomies where the feature definitions of the lexemes are not known, there is no established procedure for assigning levels of contrast to all the lexemes on the basis of the inclusion-of-reference relations alone. (This problem is treated in the additional note at the end of the reading.)

In some, but not all, ethnosemantic studies of lexical domains, the signification of each lexeme can ultimately be referred to a finite set of semantic dimensions each containing a finite number of values (features, components). The dimensions may be obvious functions of an etic grid (e.g., generation, sex of referent) or functions of an etic grid which are not obvious (e.g., *agnatic rank*, Lounsbury 1956; *generalized cross-parallel*, Kay 1965), or they may involve no a priori etic grid (e.g., *minimalness of membership*, Conklin 1962, *inclusion of speaker*, Berlin 1963). The following comments apply regardless of whether an etic grid is in any way involved in the setting up of the semantic dimensions. (Isolation and justification of semantic dimensions in the case where there is no readily available etic grid is an extremely important methodological problem. Major contributions in this area have been made by Metzger and Williams (1962; 1963a,b,c).

However, the discussion here is limited to the formal relations of the lexemes to the dimensions and does not cover the very important problem of the ethnographic operations for obtaining these relationships.

When the feature definitions of all the lexemes are known, the basic problem for representing the cognitive structure of the domain is to decide whether, or to what extent, informants apply the semantic dimensions *simultaneously* as against *sequentially*. Formal relationships among the componential definitions can provide suggestive, *but not conclusive*, evidence on this point.

The simplest and most elegant formal structure consonant with a psychological theory of simultaneous application of dimensions is the paradigm. In order to define the notion of paradigm, we first consider a set of things we may call "minimal classification events." If we select any one feature from each of the semantic dimensions and take the intersection (conjunction) of all the features we have selected, the result is a minimal classification event. For example, with two binary dimensions A and B, the set of minimal classification events is $\{a_1b_1, a_1b_2, a_2b_1, a_2b_2\}$ (where concatenation symbolizes intersection).

The semantic structure of a domain is characterized by a perfect paradigm if and only if each componential definition corresponds to a unique minimal classification event, and conversely. An interesting result of this definition is that in a perfect paradigm, for any pair of features (a_1, a_2) on a given dimension A, there exists a pair of lexemes in the domain whose componential definitions are identical except for differing on that pair of features (a_1, a_2).[1] (See Fig. 1.)

Perfect paradigms have zero redundancy in the sense that a change in a single feature of a componential definition changes it into the componential definition of another lexeme in the domain. It is probably for this reason that perfect paradigms are empirically rare. Naturally evolved symbol systems—as opposed to self-consciously invented ones—seem usually to contain a fair amount of redundancy (see, for example, Shannon 1948; Greenberg, Osgood, and Saporta 1945, Colby 1958).

In polar opposition to the minimally redundant (paradigmatic) system of feature definitions, there is a maximally redundant system in which no two componential definitions contrast on more than one dimension. Such a system may be called a *tree* (Fig. 2b). A tree requires representation by a *key*. A semantic key is a branching structure (similar to the "tree diagrams" of stochastic processes) where the first node indicates the "root" or domain

Domain: $\{L_1, L_2, \ldots, L_8\}$ (i.e. the domain contains 8 lexemes)

Dimensions: $\{D, A, B, C\}$, where the features are given by

$D = \{d\}$
$A = \{a_1, a_2\}$
$B = \{b_1, b_2\}$
$C = \{c_1, c_2\}$

Componential definitions

$$L_1 > d \ a_1 \ b_1 \ c_1$$
$$L_2 > d \ a_1 \ b_1 \ c_2$$
$$L_3 > d \ a_1 \ b_2 \ c_1$$
$$L_4 > d \ a_1 \ b_2 \ c_2$$
$$L_5 > d \ a_2 \ b_1 \ c_1$$
$$L_6 > d \ a_2 \ b_1 \ c_2$$
$$L_7 > d \ a_2 \ b_2 \ c_1$$
$$L_8 > d \ a_2 \ b_2 \ c_2$$

Box Diagram:

	a_1	a_2	
c_1	L_1	L_5	b_1
c_2	L_2	L_6	
c_1	L_3	L_7	b_2
c_2	L_4	L_8	

Figure 1.   A perfect paradigm.

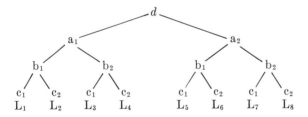

Note:
1. In each row of the tree, only one dimension occurs, and that dimension occurs only in that particular row.
2. There is no reason to diagram this structure by this particular key in preference to any of the other five keys that could be constructed by interchanging rows. This feature is characteristic of paradigms and makes the representation of any empirical paradigm by a key quite misleading (unless there is some kind of evidence for a relative primacy of dimensions).
3. Only the bottom row of nodes is labeled; hence no taxonomy.

Figure 2a.   Key diagram of a perfect paradigm (without taxonomy). The structure diagrammed is exactly the same as the one diagrammed in Figure 1.

Domain: $\{L_1, L_2 \ldots, L_8\}$

Dimensions: $\{D, A, B, C, D, E, F\}$ where features are given by

$D = \{D\}$

$A = \{a_1, a_2\}$

.

.

.

$F = \{f_1, f_2\}$

Componential definitions:

$$L_1 > d\ a_1\ b_1\ d_1$$
$$L_2 > d\ a_1\ b_1\ d_2$$
$$L_3 > d\ a_1\ b_2\ e_1$$
$$L_4 > d\ a_1\ b_2\ e_2$$
$$L_5 > d\ a_2\ c_1\ f_1$$
$$L_6 > d\ a_2\ c_1\ f_2$$
$$L_7 > d\ a_2\ c_2\ g_1$$
$$L_8 > d\ a_2\ c_2\ g_2$$

Key:

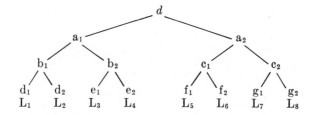

Note:

1. Each dimension occurs at one and only one node; e.g., dimension B occurs at (descends from) the unique node labeled a_1.
2. Except for the trivial alteration of interchanging features on the same dimensions, this is the only possible key for this structure.
3. A box diagram is impossible for this structure.
4. Only the bottom row of nodes is labeled; hence no taxonomy.

Figure 2b.   Key diagram of a perfect tree (without taxonomy).

feature (Lounsbury 1964b) and each succeeding node represents a selection of a single feature from some particular dimension. (Paradigms can also be represented by keys, but there is no reason to so represent them unless there is behavioral—as contrasted to linguistic-cultural—evidence that the dimensions are in fact applied sequentially [see Fig. 2a, especially Note 2].)

It should be clear that taxonomies, paradigms, and trees are kinds of semantic structures whereas a key is a kind of representation of a semantic structure. It is a particularly interesting kind of representation because, by representing the three major kinds of semantic structure on a key, it is easy to display their differences. In brief, a perfect *paradigm* is represented by a key in which a given dimension occurs in only one row (horizontal slice) of the diagram and a given row contains only one dimension (Figs. 2a and 2c). A perfect *tree* is represented by a key in which, for any dimension, there is a unique node at which it is applied (Figs. 2b and 2d). A perfect taxonomy is represented by a key in which each node corresponds to a lexeme (Figs. 2c and 2d). In summary, paradigms and trees are logically incompatible, but either may occur in a taxonomy (Figs. 2c and 2d respectively).[2] The structures discussed here and pictured in Figure 3 are, of course, ideal types. All sorts of intermediate types occur empirically.

These brief comments in no way exhaust either the known problems or the known solutions in the field of formal theory in ethnosemantics. In particular, limitation of space here has precluded any systematic attempt to relate this discussion to previous discussions of the same topics (especially Wallace and Atkins 1960; Conklin 1962, 1964; Lounsbury 1964b). Some of the topics covered in those papers are covered in this comment and some are not. I have only tried briefly to sketch the outlines of the most important kinds of structural differences among discrete semantic domains. The problem of continuous models of semantic structure has not even been considered (Kay 1963b).

Domain: $\{L_1, L_2, \ldots, L_{15}\}$

Dimensions: as in Figures 1 and 2a

Componential definitions:

(1) $L_1, L_2, \ldots, L_8$ as in Figures 2 and 3a

(2) $L_9 > d$ a   b   c*
$L_{10} > d$ a_1 b   c
$L_{11} > d$ a_2 b   c
$L_{12} > d$ a_1 b_1 c
$L_{13} > d$ a_1 b_2 c
$L_{14} > d$ a_2 b_1 c
$L_{15} > d$ a_2 b_2 c

Key:

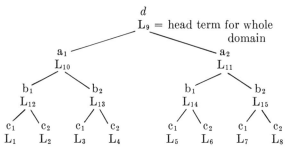

Note: All nodes are labeled; hence perfect taxonomy.

Figure 2c.   Key diagram of a perfect paradigm (with perfect taxonomy).

* Absence of subscript on a letter indicates the union of all features on the dimension indicated.

Domain: $\{L_1, L_2, \ldots, L_{15}\}$

Dimensions: as in Figure 2b

Componential definitions:

(1) $L_1, L_2, \ldots, L_8$ as in Figure 2b
$L_9 > d$ a_1 b_1 d or d a_1 b_2 e or d a_2 c_1 f or d a_2 c_2 g^*
$L_{10} > d$ a_1 b_1 d or d a_1 b_2 e
$L_{11} > d$ a_2 c_1 f or d a_2 c_2 g
$L_{12} > d$ a_1 b_1 d
$L_{13} > d$ a_1 b_2 e
$L_{14} > d$ a_2 c_1 f
$L_{15} > d$ a_2 c_2 g

Key:

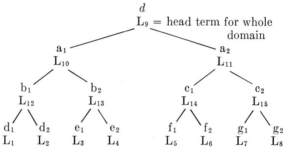

d
L_9 = head term for whole domain

Note: All nodes are labeled; hence perfect taxonomy.

Figure 2d.   Key diagram of a perfect tree (with perfect taxonomy).

* "or" means logical union, that is "and/or."

Another important recent development in the field of ethnographic semantics requires mention. Following the pioneer work of psychologists Roger Brown and Eric Lenneberg and the anthropologist John M. Roberts (Brown and Lenneberg 1964, Lenneberg and Roberts 1956), anthropologists are beginning to investigate the psychological implications of various semantic structures by accompanying their structural semantic analysis with parallel studies correlating speech and nonspeech behavior with the results of the formal analysis (Romney and D'Andrade 1964b). The work in this area of which I am aware is currently being performed by B. Berlin, C. Frake, W. Geoghegan, June Nash, A. K. Romney, and V. Stefflre. There is doubtless other research of this type going on of which I am not aware.

ADDENDUM

Since the original publication of this paper several advances have occurred in the formal theory of the structure of lexical domains. Space prevents even a summary mention of all such work in this brief note. Moreover, the results mentioned below are treated only superficially and the reader is urged to consult the source documents if he wishes to apply them to his own data.

The most important advance in this area is represented by the work of W. H. Geoghegan (1968). Geoghegan presents an axiomatic theory of semantic domains by treating them as coding rules, that is, sequenced decisions about the applicability of semantic features in the cognitive process of categorization. Geoghegan shows that the set-theoretic structure he postulates for such rule-processes is based on thoroughly plausible empirical assumptions. In addition to its explicit, mathematical character, this approach presents several advantages over the "classical" taxonomic, paradigmatic, and tree models: (i) the provision of a formal mechanism for expressing the interlocking character of semantic domains through explicit incorporation of G. A. Miller's intuitive notion of recoding; (ii) a straightforward theoretical, rather than programmatic, treatment of the "psychological reality" problem by incorporation in the semantic model of a sequence of real time cognitive decision procedures; (iii) a demonstration of the empirical power of the formulation to handle situations of greater formal complexity than can be treated by the standard componential and inclusion-hierarchy analyses; and (iv) a proof that the rather abstract set-theoretical character of the model can be represented by a certain sub-class of flow diagrams with explicitly designated properties. The last advantage is of practical interest because it makes Geoghegan's mathematical approach available to students of ethnographic semantics who lack mathematical background. However, some applications by other scholars which have already been made suggest two caveats: (i) careful attention should be paid to the *allowable* subclass of flow-diagrams if the empirical presentation is to be given meaning within Geoghegan's framework; (ii) the empirical entities formalized in the boxes of the flow charts must all be entities of the same sort—sets of mutually exclusive semantic components—if the diagrams are to have meaning as semantic-cognitive analyses. (Cf. Ervin-Tripp 1968, Keesing in Press).

Berlin, Breedlove, and Kay (1968) attack certain problems of ambiguity in the literature on folk taxonomies and suggest remedies which include definitions of several special types of semantic contrast relations within the general framework of taxonomy. Most of the problems treated involve ambiguities in the term "level of contract." There are five major points:

(1) Despite Conklin's (1962) warning to the contrary, taxonomic structure and nomenclature are not always strictly separated. That is, cognitive categories, (*taxa*), must always be kept distinct from their labels, (*lexemes*). (For empirical motivation of this theoretical point see most recently Berlin, Breedlove, and Raven 1968). In particular the frequently heard expressions of the form, "X contrasts with Y at one level and with Z at another level," embody such a confusion. Consider Figures 3 and 4.

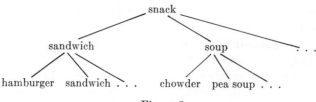

Figure 3

In Figure 3, two distinct taxa are labeled by the lexeme *sandwich*, one of which includes hamburgers and one of which excludes hamburgers. It is sometimes said in such situations that, *"Sandwich* contrasts at one level with *hamburger* and at another level with *soup."* The quoted expression has reference to the fact that a single lexeme is the overt marker for two distinct taxa (covert categories).

However, the same expression is also frequently employed to refer to the fact that not all terminal taxa in a given taxonomy are at the same level (counting down from the unique beginner).

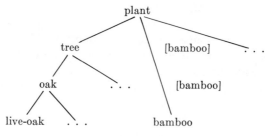

Figure 4

It is also said, with reference to situations such as that shown in Figure 2 that, *"Bamboo* contrasts with *tree* at one level, with *oak* at another, and with *live-oak* at a third."* However, in this case what is being referred to is *not,* as in the previous case, a mapping of one lexeme onto two or more distinct taxa. Rather we have here a one-one mapping of lexemes onto taxa. The circumstance to which attention is being called is simply that two terminal taxa, *bamboo* and *live-oak,* are at different levels, two and four respectively. (*Level* is counted down from the unique beginner.)

The proposal here is to restrict use of the term level to taxa, and not apply it to lexemes. Thus, the lexeme *sandwich* applies to two (distinct) taxa, one of which includes the other; the unique taxon labeled *bamboo* is terminal and is one of the few taxa occurring at level two in American folk-botanical taxonomy which is also terminal. (A *terminal* taxon is one which includes no other taxon.)

(2) It is misleading to say that the labels of two segregates, one of which includes the other, "do not contrast." This is sometimes done nevertheless.

Consider the following two assertions:

(2.1) All *live-oaks* bear acorns.

(2.2) All *trees* bear acorns.

Since the first is true and the second false, *tree* and *live-oak* contrast semantically.

(3) Problems such as those described above led Berlin, Breedlove, and Kay to define formally several different types of contrast relations among taxa. They consider these formal definitions to be empirically motivated.

(3.1) *Direct Contrast:* Two taxa are in the same *contrast set* if and only if they are immediately dominated by the same taxon. For example, in Figure 5, the pairs of taxa (X, Y), (P, Q), and (R, S) constitute all the contrast sets. In particular the set of taxa {P, Q, R, S} is *not* a contrast set. Two distinct taxa are said to be in *direct contrast* just if they are in the same contrast set.

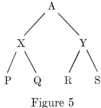

Figure 5

(3.2) *Inclusion Contrast:* e.g. tree and live-oak (cf. (2) above).

(3.3) *Indirect Contrast:* This is essentially a quaternary (rather than binary relation) which involves (a) two taxa which are not in the same contrast set and (b) two taxa which dominate the aforementioned two taxa and which *are* in direct contrast (i.e., in the same contrast set). In Figure 6, taxa X and Y are said to be in indirect contrast via taxa P and Q.

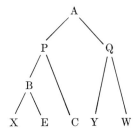

Figure 6

If we metaphorically equate a taxonomic hierarchy with a genealogy on which only, say, males are shown, the relation of indirect contrast can be phrased as that obtaining between two collaterally related individuals via the pair of brothers one of whom is ancestral to each. In Figure 6, the brothers P and Q would be respectively grandfather and father to individuals X and Y. (Actually this is a bit of an oversimplification in that one, *but not both*, of the "related individuals" may be identical to his "ancestral brother"; for example X and Q are in indirect contrast via P and Q.)

(3.4) *Terminal Contrast*: Any two terminal taxa are defined to be in *terminal contrast*. In Figure 2 the taxon labeled *bamboo* is in direct contrast with the one labeled *tree* and in *terminal contrast* with the taxon labeled *live-oak*. Taxa in terminal contrast may or may not be in direct-contrast, and conversely. Terminal taxa are *not*, in general, all at the same level.

(4) One of the several consequences of these definitions is the following: If two taxa are in the same contrast set (that is, are in direct contrast), then they are at the same level. But the converse is *not* true in general. That is, it is not the case that any two taxa at the same level are in direct contrast. One of the many usages to which the phrase "contrast at the same level" has been put treats that phrase as synonymous with "are in the same contrast set" (hence are in direct contrast). It should be clear from the above that this usage is misleading and should be abandoned since it suggests that direct contrast is a matter of level, which it is not. For example, empirical investigation might reveal that the taxa labeled *oak* and *wisteria* are at the same level in an American folk-botanical taxonomic structure, but these are not in any particular relation of contrast other than indirect contrast via *tree* and *vine*. More precisely they are not in direct, inclusion, or terminal contrast. The general recommendations may be summarized as follows:

(a) It is necessary to maintain a strict separation of classificational hierarchy and the associated nomenclature. A hierarchy of classes conforming to certain axioms and having a certain empirically determined cognitive status is called a *taxonomic structure*. The term *taxonomy* is reserved for a mapping of a finite set of lexemes onto the elements (taxa) of a taxonomic structure.

(b) The technical term "level of contrast" should be dispensed with because of its ambiguity. The levels at which two taxa occur give little information concerning the particular relations of contrast which may obtain between them.

(c) The following terms, whose definitions are suggested above, but not made fully explicit, are recommended:

   (i) direct contrast;

   (ii) indirect contrast via . . . and . . .;

   (iii) inclusion contrast; and

   (iv) terminal contrast.

NOTES

[1] e.g., pair of features (σ, φ):

Componential definitions   *Lexemes*
(kinsman, G^{+1}, lineal, σ) < "father"
(kinsman, G^{+1}, lineal, φ) < "mother"

[2] It is sometimes said of the kind of structure shown in Figure 2b that it is a "taxonomy in which the lexemes at the lowest level of contrast form a paradigm."

REFERENCES CITED

Berlin, B., 1963, A possible paradigmatic structure for Tzeltal pronominals. Anthropological Linguistics 5:1–5.

———, D. E. Breedlove, and Paul Kay, ms., n.d. Folk taxonomy and semantic contrast.

———, D. E. Breedlove, and P. H. Raven, 1968, Covert categories and folk taxonomies. *In* American Anthropologist 70, 2:290–299.

Brown, R. W., E. H. Lenneberg, 1954, A study in language and cognition. Journal of Abnormal and Social Psychology 49:454–462.

Colby, B. N., 1958, Behavioral redundancy. Behavioral Science 3:317–322.

———, 1966, Ethnographic semantics: a preliminary survey. Current Anthropology 7:3–17.

Conklin, H. C., 1962, Lexicographical treatment of folk taxonomies. *In* F. W. Householder and S. Saporta, eds., Problems of lexicography. Indiana University Research Center in Anthropology, Folklore and Linguistics, Publication No. 21.

———, 1964, Ethnogenealogical method. *In* W. H. Goodenough ed., Explorations in cultural anthropology. New York, McGraw-Hill.

Ervin-Tripp, Susan, 1968, Sociolinguistics. Language-Behavior Research Laboratory, University of California, Berkeley, Working Paper No. 3. *In* L. Berkowitz, Advances in Experimental Social Psychology, Vol. 4, Academic Press, (in press).

Frake, Charles O., 1961, The diagnosis of disease among the Subanun of Mindanao. American Anthropologist 63:11–32.

———, 1962, The ethnographic study of cognitive systems. *In* Anthropology and human behavior. Washington D.C., The Anthropological Society of Washington.

Geoghegan, W. H., 1968, Information processing systems in culture. Language-Behavior Research Laboratory, University of California, Berkeley, Working Paper No. 6. *In* P. Kay, ed., Explorations in Mathematical Anthropology, MIT Press (in press).

Greenberg, J. H., C. E. Osgood, and S. Saporta, 1954, Language change. *In* C. E. Osgood ed., Psycholinguistics. International Journal of American Linguistics Memoir 10.

Kay, Paul, 1963, Race and class in Papeete. Appendix 1 of Some aspects of social structure in Manuhoe. Unpublished Ph.D. Dissertation, Harvard University, Cambridge, Mass.

Kay, Paul, 1965, A generalization of the cross/parallel distinction. American Anthropologist 67:30–43.

Keesing, Roger M., Formalization and the construction of ethnographies. *In* P. Kay, ed., Explorations in Mathematical Anthropology, MIT Press, in press.

Lenneberg, E. H., J. M. Roberts, 1956, The language of experience: a study in methodology. International Journal of American Linguistics Memoir No. 13.

Lounsbury, Floyd, 1956, A semantic analysis of the Pawnee kinship usage. Language 32:158–194.

————, 1964, The structural analysis of kinship semantics. *In* Horace G. Lunt, ed., Proceedings of the ninth international congress of linguists. The Hague, Mouton.

Metzger, Duane, Gerald E. Williams, 1962, Patterns of primary personal reference in a Tzeltal community. Anthropological Research Projects, Stanford University.

————, 1963a, Tenejapa medicine: the curer. Southwestern Journal of Anthropology 19:216–234.

————, 1963b, A formal ethnographic analysis of Tenejapa Ladino weddings. American Anthropologist 65:1076–1101.

————, 1963c, Procedures and results in the study of native categories: Tzeltal firewood. Anthropological Research Projects, Stanford University.

Romney, A. K., R. G. D'Andrade, 1964, Cognitive aspects of English kin terms. American Anthropologist 63 No. 3, Pt. 2:146–170.

Shannon, Claude, Warren Weaver, 1948, The mathematical theory of communication. Urbana, University of Illinois Press.

Wallace, A. F. C., J. Atkins, 1960, The meaning of kinship terms. American Anthropologist 62:57–80.

2 Data Acquisition

It is axiomatic in all scientific investigation that the kind of question asked determines the response. This is an infinitely more crucial factor in anthropology, for responses in anthropology are determined not only by the kind of question, they are even more powerfully determined by the linguistic and extralinguistic context in which questions are asked.

Since an adequate semantic analysis presupposes the existence of adequate data there is now a renewed interested in the process of data collection. How does the anthropologist get his data? What techniques will ensure that the kinds of questions anthropologists ask discover concepts that are cognitively related in the culture being studied? Can the results be replicated? In an effort to resolve these problems cognitive anthropologists have developed procedures which focus on specifying the linguistic context in which data are gathered. The basic tool is a set of linguistic frames derived from the language of the people being studied. This procedure aims at: (1) specification of linguistic context in terms of grammatical features; (2) specification of cognitive context in terms of concepts; (3) specification of response in terms of questioning procedures. Some authors include an additional dimension of extralinguistic context which takes into account such features as the social identities and social settings involved in a linguistic exchange. This aspect of context is taken up in more detail in the final chapter.

Among cognitive anthropologists there are differences of opinion about the extent to which eliciting procedures can be formalized. Both Frake and Conklin rely upon less formal procedures, taking their eliciting cues directly from patterns of question and response in natural settings whereas Black and Metzger utilize a more formal procedure which is still response sensitive but discounts the natural setting. The method of Frake and Conklin is more naturalistic and sensitive to cultural nuances, but what it gains in this category is lost by being less capable of replication. The Black-Metzger method is just the reverse. It is highly replicable but less responsive to cultural nuances. Cognitive anthropologists are not forced to choose between these methods, for my own field experience indicates that it is possible to use both methods in conjunction with one another. In fact, this procedure provides a useful internal method of quality control.

Ethnogenealogical Method[1]

Harold C. Conklin

INTRODUCTION

In one way or another, all societies recognize assumed birth and mating relations. And virtually every modern ethnographer investigates "the kinship system" during the course of his fieldwork. It would seem appropriate here, therefore, to reconsider critically some of the more salient attributes of anthropological research on kinship, with particular focus on those procedures employed in the collection, description, and interpretation of genealogical information. The principal aims of this paper are to provide such a review of the genealogical approach to kinship, and to consider certain ways in which this approach may be improved. In reexamining various notions commonly used in this type of research and in discussing specific procedural details, I shall refer with some regularity to a sample set of kinship data taken from my recent field work among the Hanunóo. This material may also help to demonstrate, as well as to illustrate, the more general suggestions I should like to make for achieving greater analytic depth and precision in ethnography.

At this point, I feel I should be explicit about my assumptions regarding the nature and purpose of ethnography (Goodenough 1956a; cf. Conklin 1962a; Frake 1962a, 1964). This seems especially important when one considers that ultimately all kinship data derive from ethnographic contexts.

An adequate ethnography is here considered to include the culturally significant arrangement of productive statements about the relevant relationships obtaining among locally defined categories and contexts (of objects and events) within a given social matrix. These nonarbitrarily ordered statements should comprise, essentially, a cultural grammar (Goodenough 1957; Frake 1962a). In such an ethnography, the emphasis is placed on the interpretation, evaluation, and selection of alternative statements about a particular set of cultural activities within a given range of social contexts. This in turn leads to the critical examination of intracultural relations and ethnotheoretical models (Conklin 1955; Goodenough 1961c). Demonstrable intracultural validity for statements of covert and abstracted relationships is a primary goal. The structural description of such relationships should be based on prior analysis of particular and generalized occurrences in the ethnographic record (Lounsbury 1955:163–164, 1956; cf. Morris 1946). Criteria for evaluating the adequacy of ethnographic statements, with reference to the cultural phenomena described, include: (1) productivity (in terms of appropriate anticipation if not actual prediction), (2) replicability or testability, and (3) economy. In actual field situations, recording activities, analytic operations, and evaluative procedures (in short, the application of ethnographic technique, method, and theory) can, and I think should, be combined. The improvement and constant adjustment of field recording is, in fact, dependent upon simultaneous analysis and evaluation.

GENEALOGICAL METHOD

One approach to certain problems in ethnographic description is known widely as the "genealogical method." This usually refers to techniques for recording and summarizing field notes on the kinship relations of some particular social unit. Despite the label, however, actual methodological (or theoretical) considerations are not always implied.

There is, of course, nothing intrinsically sacrosanct about genealogies, kinship, or any other traditional anthropological rubric. In ethnography, significant categories and relations are derived from intracultural analysis; they are not determined by the application of a previously designed typological grid. Prior category assumption is ruled out, and, instead, we try to base our work on such concrete realities as a local group of people and the kinds of objects and events the members of this group treat as culturally significant (Goodenough 1956a; Leach 1961c:4–5, 26–27, 104). After beginning a field investigation with kinship analysis, one may find that political alignment, economic activities, or religious demands are determinant of rights and duties among members of the society far more often than are kin ties. Nevertheless, there are three things which do make the study of genealogical relations important for the anthropologist:

1. Kinship connections are universally recognized, although the cultural significance associated with such recognition is not universally similar.

2. Kinship relations are almost universally discussed in contemporary ethnographic literature.

3. Attention to genealogical connections is a long-standing disciplinary tradition dating well back into the last century.

The "genealogical method" is often taken for granted, but this should not be considered as evidence for general agreement among anthropologists as to what this "method" actually includes. In a recent seminar on ethnographic theory, methods, and techniques, I found that among the advanced graduate student participants, the genealogical method was one of the least well agreed upon anthropological approaches we discussed. In part, this may be due to a time lag in that some of the questions now being asked had not been formulated in Morgan's time, or when Rivers was at work among the Toda.

Based on explicit statements by Rivers (1900, 1906, 1910, 1912), Radcliffe-Brown (1941), and others (e.g., Royal Anthropological Institute, 1951:42, 50–55, 79–82), one learns that the "classical" genealogical method included the following:

1. The study of social correlates of genealogical linkage within the system by the plotting of individuals and their respective social identities in time and space. (This sometimes included the study of associated rights, duties, and privileges with special regard for associated economic and political powers and liabilities.)

2. The taking of a sociological census in which a careful check is made of adoptions, local groups (households, residential units, etc.), deaths, marriages, births, multiple kin ties between relatives, and social group affiliations (including totems, etc.).

3. The analysis of various systems of folk taxonomy used in classifying individuals and in categorizing groups of individuals by noting the use of personal names, name taboos, name changing, different modes of specification (of relatives) and last, but by no means least, the terms of relationship themselves.

4. The perhaps accidental, but unfortunate, unilineal and historical bias of many investigators who had not worked ethnographically on the analysis of cognatic systems. [This has led some to consider "our" cognatic system as aberrant (Fortes 1959, cf. Arensberg 1961).]

5. Much concern with recording, but little attention paid to evaluations, testing, rethinking, and reworking of the analysis.

6. The use of dyadic and prearranged questionnaires, grids, and charts [which rarely allow the productive analysis of levels of contrast or hierarchic relations (Frake 1962b), though they may provide some useful hints].

How does this approach stand up against our requirements for an adequate ethnography? As was already implied, some (namely, the first three of the characterizations just listed) stand up fairly well, but the last three obviously leave much to be desired. And, in practice, an "ethnogenealogical" component is noticeably lacking despite Rivers' early statements:

> In acquiring a knowledge of the pedigrees, the inquirer learns to use the concrete method of dealing with social matters which is used by the natives themselves and is able to study the formation and nature of their social classification and to exclude entirely influence in civilized categories [Rivers 1912:119];

and

> While actually working it would be fatal to attempt to use any other than the native name for any social group [Rivers 1912:144; cf. Radcliffe-Brown 1941; Leach 1961c:29].

In discussing and rethinking ways in which genealogical recording and analysis can be made more effective ethnographically I should like to draw attention to four problems (none of which, of course, is limited to kinship):

1. CRITERIA OF RELEVANCE How do we know the labeled categories or relations we speak about are culturally significant? Are the descriptive rubrics we employ derived only from a priori notions of expected occurrences on a prearranged grid? Ideally, we hope to describe "what the significant social categories are; not . . . what they ought to be" (Leach 1961c:27). Commitment to received definitions, past or present, cannot serve as tests of relevance in ethnography. While useful for certain kinds of subsequent comparative research, cross-cultural ethnological categorization and sociological typologizing—or substructuring—of various pertinent attribute spaces (Lazarsfeld 1937) are of little direct assistance in increasing the analytic power or productivity of ethnographic methods (Conklin 1955, 1961; Goodenough 1956a:37; Frake 1961, 1962a:54; Needham 1962:4).

2. DOMAIN DEMARCATION How do we recognize culturally significant boundaries? How are they established, checked, modified? Are there different types of delimitation, under varying circumstances? The mapping of domains is greatly facilitated by discovering locally important frames of reference and by testing for lexically contrasted categories within such frames (Conklin 1960, 1962b; Conant 1961; Frake 1962b).

3. ANALYTIC CATEGORIZATION How can we achieve total accountability and maximum resolution of ambiguities, and still adhere to reasonable canons of clarity and parsimony? Effective recording of particular events and of recurrences of culturally important classes of events depends partly on the precision and economy of the analytic operations employed (Lounsbury 1956:158–168; cf. Lazarsfeld 1961:142–157).

4. TRANSLATION LABELING How can we translate category labels without distorting distinctive semantic relations? Abstract symbols may be helpful, and when translation labels must be used, they should be clearly distinguished from valid definitions (Lounsbury 1956:163; Conklin 1962a:124).

We should like especially to avoid the pitfalls of (1) *translation-labeling analysis* wherein the *units* are provided not by the culture studied but by the metalanguage given before the investigation begins; (2) *translation-domain analysis,* wherein the boundaries and establishment of larger contexts are similarly provided by prior agreement instead of by ethnographic investigation; and (3) *etymological involvement,* wherein valuable space and time are wasted tracing down the putative and often highly incomplete and speculative history of particular technical terms instead of focusing on the data at hand and the socially and culturally relevant interrelations they reflect. Our task is not so much the prescription of accepted versus unaccepted meanings in the metalanguage (cf. Freeman 1961:192–202), as it is the establishment of demonstrated versus undemonstrated social relationships (Frake 1960; Leach 1961c; Conklin 1962a).

"ETHNOGENEALOGICAL METHOD"

While the most efficient model for any particular cultural subsystem may be characterized as that which accounts for all and only those instances within that subsystem, the delineation and testing of such a model is rarely a simple task.

It is frequently highly instructive to examine the explicit models constructed by one's informants—especially when such abstractions are used by the informants themselves and in natural settings. Dimensions of contrast unfamiliar to the ethnographer and important cultural "distortions" of measurable or "etically"[2] discriminable contextual features may thus be revealed. As Lévi-Strauss has noted:

> Even if these models are biased or erroneous, the very bias and the kind of errors which they contain are an integral of the facts to be studied; they may even perhaps be counted among the most significant models.
> [*Même si les modèles sont tendancieux ou inexacts, la tendance et la genre d'erreurs qu'ils recèlent font partie intégrante des faits à étudier; et peut-être comptent-ils parmi les plus significatifs* (Lévi-Strauss 1958:309).]

Ethnographically, the "inexactness" referred to here is often due to imprecise translation; but whatever the facts may be, one cannot afford to neglect such information. Both the explicit ethnomodels and the implicit principles on which they are based are well worth investigating. Where this is done systematically in the study of kinship linkages, and where intracultural validity is a goal in ethnographic inquiry, I consider the approach to be "ethnogenealogical." If the recording procedures employed in the field have built-in restrictions on the interpretation of responses, as would be the case in the exclusive use of a questionnaire for eliciting kinship terminology, one may never succeed in adequately describing the intracultural relationships of such a system. By reviewing various steps in my own work on Hanunóo social structure I shall try to demonstrate a few procedural devices which, I think, may help to avoid some of these pitfalls and which will permit more rigorous ethnographic analysis. Though not previously published, most of this analysis was worked out in its present form while I was still in the field (1957–1958; see Conklin 1959).

Before turning to the genealogical corpus, we should first note for the Hanunóo that (1) everyday, obligatory social relations require an exact knowledge of kinship; (2) the most complete role network, affecting all segments of the society, is based on kin ties; and (3) the reckoning of precise degrees of relationship is of crucial importance in regulating marriage (as is well indicated below where I consider the apparent paradox in which an individual always marries a kinsman, though ideally he never should). Verbal recognition of kinship statuses is often obligatory, and there is almost unanimous agreement on the internal and external boundaries of the kinship system from one region to another within the Hanunóo area. Thus, on the basis of frequency, universality, and social significance, we may continue this discussion with the knowledge that kinship is a wide-ranging and important domain in Hanunóo culture (Conklin 1954:45–47, 78–80; 1957:12–19, 1959).

It must be emphasized that in the following paragraphs many details have necessarily been left out. The analysis, however, is based on my attempts to account systematically for all available and pertinent information. To facilitate diagrammatic expression and evaluative criticism of the procedures used, I shall discuss four main stages or aspects of this analysis, in terms of:

1. Genealogical positions
2. Kin categories
3. Abstract principles
4. Correlates

At each of these stages, I have arranged in chart or list form at least a sample of the results of my analysis up to that particular point (Figs. 1 to 4). The sector marked B in each of these figures illustrates the use of different types of ethnogenealogical information derived largely from unsolicited Hanunóo statements (including overhead conversations) about kinship.

1. Genealogical Positions

Conventional charting devices including numbers and other symbols for proper names are widely used to map the interrelationship of the particular denotata in a kin network. An example of this first step of kinship investigation is shown in Fig. 1A, which consists of a partial segment of an actual Hanunóo genealogy. As even casual inspection would suggest, this segment has been very much simplified.

Enclosures (△ = male, ○ = female) represent specific genealogical positions occupied by particular individuals (numbers corresponding to personal names). They stand for concrete entities in a known social context. Single lines indicate cognatic linkage; double lines stand for links between spouses. The vertical grid on the left indicates generation in relation to that of ego (number 38). The original genealogy from which these 63 related positions were taken included 443 positions. Some notion of its general form may be gained from the observation that it resembles an expanded and cross-referenced version of the 200-odd-position Sinhalese genealogy recently published by Leach (1961a: chart *i*). All positions are or were occupied by identifiable individual kinsmen, of which only 39 were not known to ego by a specific personal name. [Included in this latter category are positions in the two most senior and the two most junior generations in Fig. 1*A*; positions in generations 7 and 6 were identified by one of ego's elder kinsmen, those in generations —3 and —4 were added by ego as hypothetical (i.e., future) kinsmen.]

By generation, the actual distribution of kinsmen in this personal genealogy is as follows:

Generation	:	Number of kinsmen
7	:	1
6	:	2
5	:	4
4	:	9
3	:	16
2	:	60
1	:	118
0	:	141
−1	:	71
−2	:	18
−3	:	2
−4	:	1

Thus, the main simplification was to leave out 85 per cent of the individual positions which were on the original chart. Secondly, almost all multiple and sequential linkages were dropped. Thirdly, such additional information as the indication of death, residence, and inheritance was excluded. Nevertheless, enough relational data remain so that every basic Hanunóo kin class is exemplified from one to several times. And though it is partial, this section of a personal genealogy does illustrate the difficulties encountered when one focuses on elements instead of on relations within a system. Reading "raw" data from such charts is much like reading certain portions

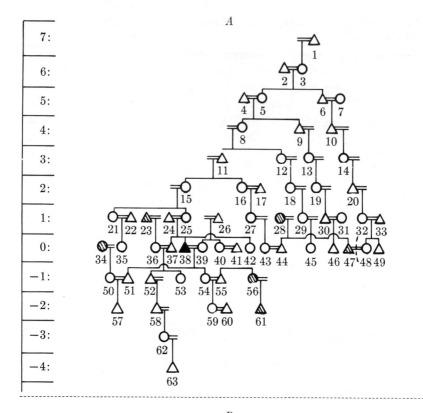

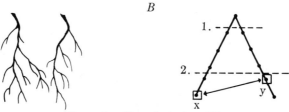

Figure 1.   Genealogical positions.

of Biblical narrative; by itself, such activity does not lead to ethnographic statements of general interest. Only particular details within ambiguous or boundless categories can be provided in this manner. Fortunately, this kind of necessary, empirical ground plan is only the beginning.[3]

The kind of evidence provided in Fig. 1A does indicate that the Hanunóo probably have a personal- or ego-based kinship category system (Davenport 1959; Murdock 1960; Goodenough 1961b), in which the criteria for membership in socially important kin classes do not depend on fixed lineage or lineage-like affiliation. Most importantly, it provides a map of the actual network within which there are as many potential ego-referents as one would need for testing structurally oriented hypotheses regarding kin categorization.

Before going further, we should note that in Fig. 1B we have two indications of how the Hanunóo themselves handle genealogical problems of interconnection. On the left is a rough sketch of two *kāway* which may be glossed roughly as 'flowering branchlets (of certain plants).'[4] The Hanunóo refer to relations between such adjacent plant structures when discussing the boundaries of their maximal kinship groupings; in fact, the term *kāway* is used at at least two levels of contrast to designate such ego-defined social categories (Conklin 1954). Marriages between a member of one's own *kāway* (in the less general sense) and a nonmember extend kinship ties into, but not beyond, the in-law's 'branchlet.' Thus, for example, if ego (38) were not related to 48 and 49 as a fifth cousin, but only by 48's marriage to 47, 48, and 49 would be *nonkinsmen* with respect to ego. Then, from the standpoint of ego, the dotted line in 1A would be universally recognized as a finite boundary, beyond which individuals are excluded from the general category, *kinsman*. In this system a cousin's cousins are kinsmen, but a cousin's cousin's cousins (if not more directly related) are not. Theoretically, or ethnotheoretically at least, this is an open system (cf. Romney and Epling 1958).

On the right is my diagram of a frequently observed practice of "tracing back" genealogical relations. When x and y meet but do not know what to call each other, they work "backwards" in their own *kāway* until siblinghood or a same-generation, finite degree of cousinship is established for specific ascendants of both parties. If a parent of x is known to y as a third cousin, at the level below broken line 2, the x-y relationship is determined (see d or e, Fig. 2), and no further inquiry is necessary. They may have to push back to the original or "truncal" sibling pair (cf. Freeman 1961:204) at the level just below line 1. Whatever the situation, specification of the links separating the determinant set is not required. This sketch reflects common knowledge and frequently observed practice among the Hanunóo. Of comparative interest is a remarkably similar diagram published together with an explanatory note on "The Mathematics of American Cousinship" in a recent issue of the *Kroeber Anthropological Society Papers* (Roark 1961). There, the purpose in providing such a device is explicitly the resolution of a frequently met ambiguity and lack of common knowledge among American anthropologists as to the steps required in reckoning degrees of cousinship in English!

However illustrative it may be, the display of genealogical details in Fig. 1A—essentially a case history (Leach 1961a:11–12; cf. Gluckman 1961)—does not in itself constitute a description or demonstration of structurally important kinship relations. The marked positions represent individual variants within a set of as yet unanalyzed but significantly more invariant categories (cf. Nadel 1957:8). Nevertheless, this type of over-differentiated mapping of objectively determined denotata does permit at least a partial solution to the many problems of indeterminacy in translation envisioned by such writers as Quine (1960:26–79; cf. Naess 1953). In fact, it provides the kind of information needed for a nonintuitive investigation of the proposition, which I accept, that all lexical domains are not equally indeterminate (cf. Quine 1960:78). This consideration leads us directly to stage two.

2. Kin Categories

In Fig. 2 we move from the positions occupied by identified individuals, from the denotata of the system, to their folk categorization into contrastive kin classes; from individual exemplars to categories. Although we must skip many operations, failures, and retestings, several points should be emphasized. Depending largely on recorded conversations in local settings and on unintentional as well as intentional "mistakes," I tallied and checked the use of kin terms, personal names, nicknames, etc. with known genealogical positions. Nominal usage (specifying individuals) was distinguished from designative (class, category) reference; only the latter will be treated here in detail. Suffice it to say that, in Hanunóo, recurrent exchanges such as the example below yield a set $[z]$ of maximally distinctive monolexemic responses which designate a finite number of mutually exclusive kin classes at one level of contrast (Conklin 1955, 1962a; Frake 1961, 1962a):

A. *May kalabutan qaw si x sa kan y?*	Is x related to y?
A. *Huq.*	Yes.
A. *Kabitay?*	How?
B. *Kan y [z] si x.*	x is y's $[z]$.

At this most frequently used, basic level of contrast, **23** categories are distinguished under two general sets of circumstances: to classify individuals in relation to a given referent (as in the frame above), and to describe step-by-step genealogical connections between individuals and categories of individuals. In other words, from the information included in—or added to—Fig. 1, we derive the core of what is represented in Fig. 2, a set of designata consisting of **23** kin classes. In passing from column 1 to column 5—and on to column 6—the intended progression is toward greater analytic rigor and ethnographic precision.

1. The numbers in column 1 correspond to those in Fig. 1*A*. All positional numbers in Fig. 1*A* are included.

2. In column 2 I list 23 Hanunóo kin terms (monolexemic designations for each of the contrastive categories in this set). In each case, the form given is the designative term most frequently recorded in the field; many referential synonyms were recorded but are not indicated here (cf. Schneider and Homans 1955; Frake 1960). That there is no one-to-one relation between morpheme and lexeme is well illustrated by the forms in this lexical set (one term is a compound, and seven others are morphologically—or at least etymologically—complex).

3. In column 3, to facilitate further and more formal analysis, each of the kin classes listed in column 2 is symbolized by an italicized lowercase letter.

4. In column 4 each of the 23 categories is given an English designative gloss or "translation label."

   a. Abbreviations should be self-explanatory. A slash (/) may be read "and/or."

   b. A useful cover term for nephew and niece, "nibling," was first suggested by Samuel E. Martin in 1951. It has since gained some acceptance by anthropologists, e.g., Frake (1954:324).

   c. The term "sibling" refers here only to brother or sister, not to cousins.

   d. The precise meaning of "consanguineal" with respect to this system is discussed below (page 111).

5. The formulas in column 5 are written in one of the commonly used notational systems for kin-type analysis (e.g., Murdock 1949:100): Fa, Mo, Br, Si, So, Da, Hu, and Wi for father('s), mother('s), brother('s), sister('s), son('s), daughter('s), husband('s), and wife('s), respectively. Single-letter designators are employed similarly by some writers (e.g., Lounsbury 1956:163; Needham 1962:32–33).

   a. Mn and Wm stand for man's and woman's.

   b. A terminal period indicates that for this particular kin class there is a finite number of possible kin types. No further marking is provided where all possible kin types are listed (6 categories). The terminal period is preceded by a parenthesized figure where I give only a partial listing of the total but finite numbers of possible kin types (4 categories). In such cases, the figure indicates the missing number of kin types (676 in all).

   c. A terminal sequence of three periods indicates that for this par-

Figure 2.   Kin Categories.

			A		B
(1)	(2)	(3)	(4)	(5)	(6)*
51, 54	*qanak*	*a*	child	So, Da.	C
24	*qamaq*	*b*	father	Fa.	f
25	*qīnaq*	*c*	mother	Mo.	m
22, 30, 33, 52, 53	*bāpaq*	*d*	uncle/nibling	MoSiHu, MnBrDa, MoMoFaMoMo-BrSoDaSoDaHu; FaBr, ...	**Pb**/m(w)**SC**
21, 27, 29, 31, 32	*bāŋih*	*e*	aunt/nibling	MoSi, MoMoFaMoBrDaDaSoWi; MoBrWi, WmSiSo, ...	**Ps**/w(h)**SC**
17, 20, 57, 58, 59	*lakih*	*f*	grandfather/grandchild	MoMoSiHu, MnDaDa, MnBrSoSo; MoFa, ...	**Pf**/m**CC**
15, 16, 18, 19	*qiduh*	*g*	grandmother/grandchild	MoMo, MoMoSi; WmDaDa, WmBrSoSo, ...	**Pm**/w**CC**
11, 12, 13, 14, 62	*qumput*	*h*	gr.gr.parent/gr.gr.child	MoFa, MoMoFaMoMoBrSoDa; SoDaSo, ...	**PPP**/**CCC**
8, 9, 10, 63	*pūpuh*	*i*	gr.gr.gr.parent/gr.gr.gr.child	MoMoFaMo, BrSoSoDaSo; ...	**PPPP**/**CCCC**
1, 2, 3, 4, 5, 6, 7	*qapuh*	*j*	remote ancestor/remote descendant	MoMoFaMoMoMoFa; ...	**PPPPP**$_n$/**CCCCC**$_n$
42	*qāriq*	*k*	younger sibling	YoSi; YoBr.	y-S
37	*qākaq*	*l*	elder sibling	ElBr; ElSi.	e-S
35	*qinsan*	*m*	first cousin	MoSiDa; (7).	PSC
43	*qarvah*	*n*	second cousin	MoMoSiDaDa; (31).	PPSCC
45	*qatluh*	*o*	third cousin	MoFaSiDaDaDa; (127).	PPPSCCC
46	*bāliv-sayah*	*p*	fourth cousin	MoMoFaMoBrDaDaSoSo; (511).	PPPPSCCCC
48, 49	*tarqāriq*	*q*	distant cousin	MoMoFaMoMoBrSoDaSoDaSoDa; ...	PPPP$_n$SCCCCC$_n$
39	*qasāvah*	*r*	spouse	Wi; Hu.	M
50, 55, 60	*qumāgad*	*s*	child-in-law	SoWi, DaDaHu; ...	**C**$_n$**M**
26	*manūgaŋ*	*t*	parent-in-law	WiFa, HuFaMoSi; ...	**MP**$_n$
36, 40, 44	*bayaw*	*u*	sibling-in-law	BrWi, WiSi, MoMoSiDaDaHu; ...	**MS**/**SM**
41	*bilas*	*v*	spouse's sibling's spouse	WiSiHu; WiFaMoBrSoSoWi, ...	MSM
23, 28, 34, 47, 56, 61	*balāyih*	*w*	consanguineal's spouse's consanguineal	BrWiFa, MoMoSiDaDaHuMo, SoWi-Mo, MoMoSiDaDaHuBr, DaHuSi, DaHuSiSo; ...	BMB

* C, child; P, parent; S, Sibling; M, spouse; B, consanguineal; f, father; m, mother; b, brother; s, sister; h, husband; w, wife; m, man's; w, woman's; y-, younger; e-, elder; /, and, or; $_n$, unbounded vertical extension, for n (may = O) generations, in the same direction indicated; **boldface**, unbounded horizontal extension to all of ego's collateral consanguineals of the same generation (and sex) indicated.

NOTE: Nonfinal, nonhyphenated letter symbols read: ———'s. And letter symbols in parentheses read facultatively; i.e., the formulas apply both with and without these symbols.

ticular kin class, there is theoretically an infinite number of proper kin types (13 categories).

d. A semicolon separates kin types exemplified in Fig. 1A, and hence also in column 1 in Fig. 2A, from kin type not previously illustrated.

e. Note that it is impossible to give either a complete or economical listing of this kind. However, column 5 does provide a good example of what often exasperates the structurally oriented anthropologist who consults lexical sources which depend heavily on this device in "defining" kin terms (e.g., Leach 1961c:42).

f. More specifically, note the positions listed in column 1 for category w, and then check their positional plotting in Fig. 1A. To help visualize the difficulty in attempting to define this kin class by means of kin types such as are listed at the lower end of column 5, I have—on Fig. 1A—crosshatched the individual enclosures to which this category label applies.

By employing kin categories already noted in this basic contrast set together with other terms used by the Hanunóo in discussing kinship relations (including some superordinate kin terms like *guraŋ* 'parent') it is relatively easy to revise and improve our kin-type definitions. By combining certain of these Hanunóo relationship categories, selected partly on the basis of the results of detailed genealogical checking, one may derive the succinct and more powerful ethno-kin-type and ethno-kin-class formulas listed in Fig. 2B. This reformulation reduces significantly the complexity and inefficiency of the kin typing exemplified in column 5, and allows us to go beyond the limitations of expanded but nondefining translation labeling. The result is a precise and verifiable set of "statements," symbolically noted in column 6. The notation is explained at the bottom.

One example may help to show the utility of this kind of relisting. The terminological categorization of all parent's brothers/parent's male same-generation cousins/parent's sister's husbands/parent's female same-generation cousin's husbands, a well as of all wife's sibling's children/wife's same-generation cousin's children, and, for a man, all sibling's children/same-generation cousin's children, as members of kin class d (*bāpaq*), is covered adequately and exclusively by the formula: Pb/m(w)SC. [This reads: 'parent's brother (or male cousin) *or* parent's sister's (or female cousin's) husband, *or* man's or man's wife's) sibling's (or cousin's) child.']

Although we have not yet indicated the elementary abstract principles underlying this system, we have reduced the endlessness of traditional kin-type listing. The categoric distinctions employed in Fig. 2B are restricted to those whose explicit or implicit importance in Hanunóo usage has been

repeatedly tested. [In fact, one of these distinctions—even at this stage—
requires special comment. Consanguineals in the Hanunóo system, as in
our own, must be defined so that spouses of all ascendant cognates, and
all descendant cognates of one's spouse, are included (see category w
in column 6 and the explanation of **boldface**).]

Before we move on to stage three, several points should be understood:

1. The 23 basic categories in column 2 comprise a single contrast set,
one "rank" within one subhierarchy of a particular folk taxonomy (that
which the Hanunóo employ for making decisions in the realm of kinship
classification).

2. For any subhierarchy in a folk taxonomy (of artifacts, statuses,
kin classes, plant segregates, etc.), the *basic level* of contrast is probably
best defined as the lowest level at which all folk taxa are labeled by unitary
lexemes (Conklin 1962a:122). In English, for example, the more specific
term *first cousin* is a composite lexeme for which the basic-level unitary
term *cousin* may be substituted; i.e., if x is a first cousin of y, he is also
necessarily a cousin of y. Furthermore, even though there may be a superficial similarity between the paired terms, *grandfather:father* and *grand-
uncle:uncle,* only the latter two kin classes are semantically related in
the same manner as first cousin and cousin. Neither first cousin nor granduncle is a basic-level category, whereas grandfather is; i.e., we cannot
substitute father for grandfather because it is never the case that if x
is a grandfather of y, he is also necessarily a father of y. Testing to establish basic-level contrast sets, then, does not depend upon the morphological
construction of linguistic forms, but upon the demonstrable semantic relations of generalization (or specification) and differentiation (Conklin
1962:128).

3. To be useful, the distinctions referred to above (and elsewhere in
this paper) must be clearly understood with respect to various alternative
methods of classification (Kluckhohn 1960). In very general terms, five
kinds of arrangement (index, key, paradigm, taxonomy, and typology)
may be distinguished by such criteria as inclusion, dimensionality, binary
opposition, and arbitrariness.

    i. A *taxonomy,* or taxonomic hierarchy, differs from the other four
    in that its constituent entities, or taxa, are arranged vertically
    by nondimensional class inclusion (Gregg 1954; Conklin 1954,
    1961, 1962a; Frake 1961; Simpson 1961). Hierarchic positions
    in a taxonomy—biological or otherwise—are not permutable,
    and so far as folk taxonomies are concerned, the definition and
    arrangement of included taxa are nonarbitrary. The Hanunóo
    kin classes discussed in this paper are coordinate folk taxa,

categories which are unambiguously and nonarbitrarily determined by Hanunóo usage. Such cultural entities are necessarily "given," not "imposed." In one sense they can be considered "natural."

ii. Of the dimensional forms of arrangement, only an *index* can be considered unidimensional. This simplest form of catalogue (Conklin 1962a), or finding list, usually appears as a sequence of entities arranged in accordance with one arbitrary dimension such as alphabetic order (e.g., the arrangement of names in a telephone directory, or of words in a dictionary).

iii. A *key* is a multidimensional, and hence often permutable, arrangement of attribute oppositions (couplets), which, by their hierarchic application, help to locate (key out) the entities being identified (Mayr and others 1953; Conklin 1962b; Schwartz 1962). The selection and arrangement of dichotomous exclusions may result in a branching structure resembling a taxonomy, but the geometrical similarity is illusory. In the construction or "repartment" (Gilmour 1961) of a key, the selection of the attributes and of a particular sequence of oppositions may be arbitrary.

iv. Both *paradigms* and *typologies* are multidimensional forms of arrangement organized by class intersection. Paradigmatic classification arranges entities which are known (1) to share a certain common feature (Lounsbury 1956), and (2) to constitute a contrast set (Conklin 1962a). Typological classification, on the other hand, is based primarily on extrinsically defined attribute dimensions. In a typology, the cells represent "attribute combinations" (Spaulding 1960), subpartitions of an "attribute space" (Greenberg 1957; Lazarfeld 1937, 1961). In a paradigm, the entities to be classified (e.g., folk taxa) provide the necessary contrasts from which relevant and defining attributes are derived; in a typology this process is usually reversed.

These distinctions can be illustrated quite easily if we let i to iv represent the major contrasts just outlined, and use capital and lowercase letters to indicate entites classified and attributes, respectively, with *italics* marking "given" or "natural" elements (as distinct from "imposed" ones) in the otherwise identical graphs under iv.

There is an obvious formal similarity between a paradigm and a typology, but not between either of these and a taxonomy. A coordinate set of entities such as A–B–C–D in a taxonomy may be internally arranged

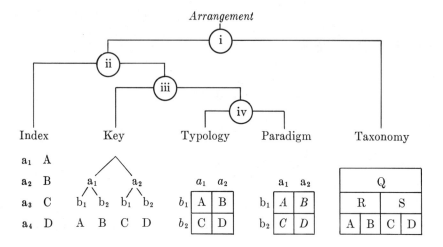

as in a paradigm. It may also be efficiently subdivided and differentiated with the aid of an arbitrarily constructed key, but a paradigm by itself cannot be transformed into a taxonomy (Conklin 1962a, 1962b; cf. Leach 1961c:2–3, 5; Wallace 1961a, 1962). In other words, any taxonomy may contain one or more paradigmatic structures, but no paradigm can include or be equivalent to a taxonomy. If these distinctions are recognized, a three-way ambiguity in the anthropological use of "type" can be discerned: (1) type as *paragon* ("type specimen," achetype, etc.; not included above); (2) type as *attribute combination* (or bundle of attributes, as in a typology); and (3) type as *taxon* or kind (illustrated by kin categories, or by the entities in any taxonomy or paradigm).

3. Abstract Principles

At this third stage in our analysis (Fig. 3), I attempt to reduce to a minimum the remaining complexities in our data, to move from extensional to intensional definitions by identifying the necessary and sufficient conditions for membership in each of the contrastive kin classes, and to represent parsimoniously and productively the abstract principles on which the terminological system is based.

I have tried to indicate in an effective and economical way the paradigmatic relations which obtain between and among these categories, as this set of categories appears to be generated by the intersection of certain dominant and nondominant dimensions. Note that the kinship space division is neither an arbitrary reduction of such a domain nor a direct replica of a Hanunóo model; but it is an analytic model (Leach 1961c; Goodenough 1957, 1961a; cf. Nadel 1957) which has been tested and proved adequate to meet our criteria of economy, productivity, and accuracy (i.e., replicabil-

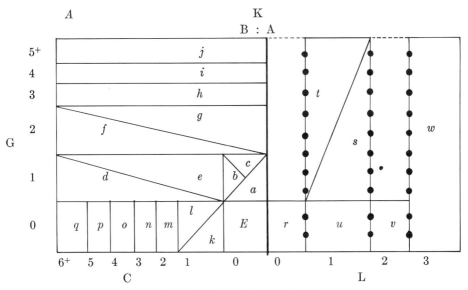

Dimensions of Hanunóo Kinship (K):

1. Affinity (B, consanguineal: A, affinal)   4. Linkage (L: degree)
2. Generation (G: degree)   5. Age $(+/-)$
3. Collaterality (C: degree)   6. Sex (m\f)

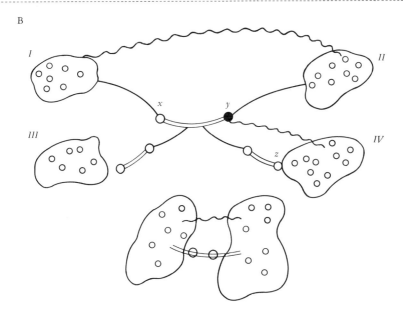

Figure 3.   Abstract principles.

ity, making it possible to drive verifiable deductions from it semantically). In particular, note the following:

1. Each enclosure other than that marked E (for a given point of reference, or ego) defines one of the 23 categories derived from steps one and two (Figs. 1 and 2). No category is represented more than once, and all 23 categories are indicated.

2. Unbroken horizontal- and vertical-line boundaries of these enclosures indicate, in addition to the B:A (consanguineal-affinal) opposition discussed below, three major contrastive dimensions:

    a. G: *Generation,* i.e., degree of generational removal from ego's own (or zero generation, indicated by positions bounded by horizontal lines $[0, 1, 1^+, 2, 3, 4, 5^+$ (where $n^+ = \geq n)]$);

    b. C: *Collaterality,* i.e., degree of collaterally including lineality or zero-degree collaterality (Lounsbury, 1956:168), indicated by positions bounded by plain vertical lines $[0, 1, 1^+, 2, 3, 4, 5, 6^+,$ (where $n^+ = \geq n)]$; and

    c. L: *Linkage* or *consanguineal linkage,* i.e., the status of plural-member consanguineal sets through which an affinal is related to ego, indicated by enclosed positions bounded on at least one side by "knotted" vertical lines (0 zero, 1 terminal, 2 medial, 3 double).

3. Slanting lines indicate minor contrasts by *age* and *sex* within four of the rectangular subspaces produced by the intersections of values of B, G, and C or L:

    a. A Z-slant line ($/$) indicates the elder/younger age distinction based on the relative structural seniority of the elder member of the ego-alter pair.

    b. An S-slant line ($\backslash$) indicates a male/female sex distinction always based on the sex of the higher generation member of the ego-alter pair (or dyad).

Note that because the Z-slant distinction implies polarity, the kin classes within rectangular attribute spaces so divided are nonreciprocal categories:

    bc/a (parents/children)

    l/k (elder siblings/younger siblings)

    t/s (parents-in-law/children-in-law)

The S-slant distinction does not imply polarity. Therefore, all kin classes within rectangular attribute spaces which remain undivided, or are divided only by S-slant (or sex) diagonals, are characterized implicationally by the merging of polar types, or reciprocity.

4. Thus, six dimensions suffice to chart adequately the relevant kinship space. For accurate interpretation, however, the specific intracultural defini-

tions of consanguinity and affinity must be made explicit. In this analysis, the following distinctions must be recognized:

a. *Cognate,* a kinsman by assumed birth linkage only

b. *Affine,* a kinsman by marriage

c. *Consanguineal,* a cognate or an ascendant cognate's spouse (or reciprocal, i.e.; a spouse's descendant cognate)

d. *Affinal,* an affine who is not a consanguineal

Although it appears that *a* and *b* contrast with *c* and *d* in more or less etic-emic terms, the distinctions involved in defining the latter pair of concepts are also of some comparative interest.

With supporting data derived largely from unilineal category systems, Radcliffe-Brown (1941, 1950; cf. Dumont 1953:39) and others have long stressed the unity, identity, equivalence, or solidarity of siblings. With reference to cognatic systems such as those reported from various parts of Malaysia, a working definition of consanguinity often appears to require recognition of the structural equivalence of spouses, or more specifically, of the structural equivalence of ascendant, collateral spouses. This certainly holds for the Hanunóo and it seems to do likewise for the Iban (Freeman 1960:81, 83, 87), the Sagada Igorot (Eggan 1960:32–34), the Eastern Subanun (Frake 1960:60, 64), the Tagalog, and other similar kinship systems, including that shared by many native speakers of English. Essentially, this recurrent categorization seems to illustrate what might be called the "principle of senior spouse-set unity." (Note that where such conditions obtain there is no structural equivalence of spouses in ego's, or in a descending, generation.) This principle may be restated in several ways. Formally, the terminological situation may be accounted for by means of a single reduction or substitution rule (cf. Lounsbury 1964; Keesing, n.d.): Let any ascendant collateral cognate's spouse be rewritten as that ascendant collateral cognate of the opposite sex; e.g., MoFaBrWi → MoFaSi. In a more generalized notation, this rule may be symbolized very simply (though with far-reaching consequences)

$$-C_x S_y. \rightarrow -C_y.$$

where C = child, S = spouse, subscripts x and y indicate sex opposition but not specification, a hyphen stands for cognatic linkage, and a period indicates termination of the kin type in an ascending generation. Thus $PPPC_x S_y \rightarrow PPPC_y$ (in which P = parent) would be covered by the rule cited above.

5. Within any paradigm or paradigm-like structure (Lounsbury 1956: 162, 192), contrasting units can be described componentially. Thus, from the information provided in Fig. 3*A* one could easily derive a list

of componential definitions (in one of several possible notations) for this set of kin categories (cf. Goodenough 1951, 1956b; Lounsbury 1956; Wallace and Atkins 1960; Wallace 1961b, 1962).[5] Mere transcription, however, may not add significantly—or at all—to our analysis. For purposes of deriving valid ethnographic statements about the Hanunóo kinship system, our Fig. 3A diagram actually provides more readily visualized information regarding such matters as total accountability, boundary phenomena, and articulation of categories, than can be displayed by lists of conjunctive formulas (cf. Frake 1960:60, 1961). And just as it is possible to construct a number of alternative keys (see above), none of which may show a very close fit with the natural taxonomic units it "arranges," so also is it possible to use a number of componential dimensions, not all of which may be ethnogenealogically valid, in writing formulaic definitions of kin classes. In view of the increasing number of published "componential analyses" based on quite disparate criteria of relevance (cf. Conant 1961; Epling 1961; Grimes and Grimes 1962; Pospisil 1960; and Wallace 1961a, 1961b, 1962), it is useful to refer back to the essentials of submorphemic, distinctive-feature analysis as first applied by linguists to relatively simple but complete contrast sets in the form of grammatical paradigms (e.g., Jakobson 1936; Harris 1948:87). As similar efforts have been extended to more complex lexical structures (especially in kinship studies), there has been a tendency to analyze arbitrarily delimited segments rather than complete sets. While such a restriction may simplify componential treatment, its arbitrary quality may also lead to the distortion of significant ethnographic relations. In analyzing actual kinship category systems, the determination of relevant dimensions is achieved neither by the simple mastery of a notational device, nor by the multiplication of possible componential distinctions (cf. Atkins 1959). Solution of such problems depends, instead, on the discovery of locally recognized contrasts, within recurrent ethnogenealogical settings.

6. From additional ethnographic information not provided in the paradigmatic structure outlined in Fig. 3A, one could also place this set of kin categories within the larger framework of the overall Hanunóo folk taxonomy of kinship. In fact, several interlocking hierarchies would have to be described. In other words, for a complete ethnographic statement of Hanunóo kinship categorization, hierarchic (i.e., nonparadigmatic) folk-taxonomic definitions (Conklin, 1962a) would have to be provided for many terms not included in this discussion. It would be noted, for example, that some of the minor contrasts in Fig 3A are ignored at higher levels, while additional distinctions are obligatory under specified circumstances. Categorization of multiple but simultaneous genealogical relations (qúnuŋ, if determined by ego's marriage; dagqup, if not so determined; etc.) and the

initially confusing coexistence of fictive kinship designations (though restricted to relations between Hanunóo and members of other ethnolinguistic groups) could also be explored profitably. The important point to note here is that the basic set of kin categories we have selected to discuss in some detail does have a folk taxonomic position with respect to other levels in the same subhierarchy as well as in relation to other kinds of social-identity networks.

7. Finally, it should be noted that the paradigmatic arrangement in Fig. 3*A* allows a more precise and simplified investigation of social activities wherein kin categorization is essential. By holding certain dimensional contrasts constant while removing others, and by noting various types of articulation of clustered categories, this kind of arrangement provides many suggestions for further intracultural and comparative research (cf. Conklin 1953, 1954:80; Frake 1960:62).

The potato-like sketches in Fig 3*B* exemplify certain explicit Hanunóo principles in reckoning kinship. They were made by informants to illustrate the nature of membership in the *w*, or *baláyih*, kin class. In the field, and as I have indicated indirectly above, I had difficulty defining this category by kin-typing and traditional ego-alter-questioning procedures. In fact, partly because the semantic range of *baláyih* totally includes that of linguistically cognate terms such as *balae*, Tagalog for 'co-parent-in-law,' or more precisely, 'child's spouse's parent' (cf. Eggan 1960:36; Frake 1960:298; Freeman 1960:83–84; and Suttles 1960:298), I failed initially to note that the Hanunóo category was not restricted to ego's generation (Conklin 1953:67; cf. Conklin 1954:79). Nor did I realize at first how important it might be to test kinship assumptions for various ego-referents and to phrase questions polyadically as well as within the traditional dyadic frame (cf. Leach 1961b:12). The drawings represented here did much to clarify my own thinking on these matters in the field and to increase my respect for the study of ethnomodels. In these drawings, large enclosures were sketched to indicate *káway*, or maximal consanguineal categories. Small circles stand for individual kinsmen. As indicated by the informant's use of a wavy line, any member of *I* (*x's káway*; I have added only the letter and number symbols) is a *baláyih* of any member of *II* (*y's káway*), and vice versa. This relationship exists because *I* and *II* were linked by the marriage of *x* and *y*. Similarly, *y* and *x*, together with the combined membership of *I* and *II*, are reciprocally *baláyih* of all members of *IV* (*z's káway*), because of *z's* marriage to a child of *x* and *y*. The lower sketch illustrates the same essential features of linkage (page 111) and of the *w*-category relationship. (These drawings were made by men[6] who had previously observed my diagrammatic efforts in recording genealogies. I had not, however, instructed or trained them in such details. The sketches

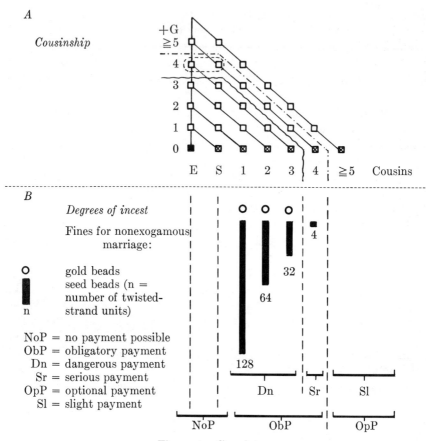

Figure 4. Correlates.

reproduced in Fig. 3B were proffered by them, not at my request, but at their suggestion, after my extensive but narrow type of questioning seemed to be leading nowhere.)

4. Correlates

Now that we have defined the basic kin categories in the Hanunóo system, we may examine briefly some of the nonlinguistic correlates of this particular set of distinctions. While complete isomorphism between semantic and pragmatic structural relations cannot be anticipated, and we do not expect to discover mechanical laws of causality in comparing such structures, we may hope to achieve a productive correlational analysis such that we will first be able to isolate major discontinuities (Kluckhohn

1960) and then be in a position to demonstrate effectively *how* they are interrelated (Lounsbury 1956:189; Mayr 1961:1502–1505).

By looking back for a moment at Fig. 3, we note a very unexpected degree of vertical and horizontal differentiation. Why should this be? In part the answer is pragmatic or behavioral and thus a nonlinguistic and nonsemantic one.

This can be seen, partially, in Fig. 4. Here we have abstracted the essential cousin-differentiating feature of Fig. 3*A*, in a way which displays a very interesting horizontal reflection of the vertical distinctions. Hanunóo "cousins," as in many cognatic systems, are restricted to ego's generation—indicated here by the horizontal row of boxes marked with X's (S, 1, 2, etc. standing for sibling, first cousin, second cousin, etc.). With reference to lineal ascendant- and zero-generation-collateral positions, note that:

1. The heavy broken line indicates the inner boundary in both directions (generationally and collaterally) of *unlimited* categories (*j* and *q* in Fig. 3*A*).

2. The categories represented between the wavy line and the heavy broken line are the most "extended," or distant (in both directions), of the *finite,* consanguineal kin classes in the Hanunóo system (*i* and *p* in Fig. 3*A*).

3. The two fourth-ascending generation kin positions encircled by a dotted line stand for the truncal sibling sets from which all members of any ego's determinable and finite cognatic stock (cf. Freeman 1961) are descended. In ego's generation, this would include all fourth cousins and closer cognates and would exclude all fifth cousins and more distant cognates. For the Hanunóo, however, this unnamed grouping remains essentially an etic potentiality rather than a culturally relevant and pragmatically real social entity. As we have noted above, ascending collaterals are not set off from their spouses in terms of this possible cognatic grouping, and, in fact, the high degree of collateral differentiation indicated in Fig. 4*A* does not extend obligatorily to kinsmen in other than ego's generation. Nevertheless, genealogical distance between same-generation cognates is apparently of considerable significance. Why?

One hint comes from a set of culturally explicit activities in an area where economic transactions, marriage regulations, and kin categorization are involved. This is illustrated in Fig. 4*B*.

Here I have indicated the differential ritual (but real) payments in glass seed-beads and gold beads which are made by newlyweds in return for ceremonial services and feast food. These highly valued goods, the ideal quantities of which do not fluctuate, are paid as "fines" for nonexogamous marriage. It is clear that the precise amounts paid on such occasions are closely correlated with the degree of the particular incest infraction, which, in turn, is determined by the degree of cousinship. (English designations for the various types of payment noted in Fig. 4*B* are glosses for single-term category labels in Hanunóo.) Careful reckoning of such relationships is far from being an esoteric matter for the Hanunóo. This can be more readily appreciated when it is remembered that the local rule of exogamy states that one should never marry a kinsman (cf. Freeman 1961:208–209). As I have stated elsewhere:

> Marriage is traditionally proscribed within the bounds of personally-focused, bilateral, kindredlike categories, which are maximally extended to include all of Ego's consanguineals, their spouses, and the consanguineals of the latter (if not previously [i.e., prior to the connecting marriage] more closely related). Because the members of Hanunóo settlements are usually linked by close bonds of cognatic kinship and the population of Hanunóo hamlets is small (usually less than 50), this prohibition results in strict local exogamy at the hamlet level. However, a marked tendency toward regional endogamy at higher levels leads to frequent [marriages between known kinsmen], requiring ritual cleansing, for which the payment is commensurate with the closeness of the kin tie. There is no formal wedding rite or bride price, though marriage is usually preceded by a long period of courting and bride service, and followed by at least initial uxorilocality [Conklin 1959:634].

This maximal kin category, *katawūhan*, is well defined for any given ego in Hanunóo society. The membership of all 23 basic kin categories is included. It is interesting, but not surprising, to note that this highest-level kin category is never partitioned by the Hanunóo in a manner that would allow it—in part or in whole—to be equated with the restricted "kindred" as currently used by some anthropologists (e.g., Freeman 1961; cf. Mitchell 1959). Although degrees of incest within this maximal category are first calculated on the basis of cousinship in one's own generation, cross-generational marriages do occur, and appropriate extensions of "graded" incest ranges are well established. On a chart similar to but larger than Fig. 4, it would be possible to indicate the explicit means of descriptively designating those kinsmen in adjacent generations who are structurally the incest equivalents of each cousinship degree noted. But even without further discussion of such correlates, the utility of the procedures followed above should now be apparent. It would seem reasonable to hypothesize that wherever the paradigmatic structure of a lexical set shows a high degree of obligatory subdivision we may expect to find external correlations of relatively greater cultural importance than for less divided portions of the same paradigm. Where the contrast set is part of a kinship system, one may anticipate correlations of general social significance.

CONCLUSION

In this paper, I have reviewed some of the steps that may be profitably taken in an ethnographic analysis of one segment of social behavior. I have tried to emphasize that it is possible to put to some useful effect a number of the early aims of the so-called genealogical method. However, I have also tried to demonstrate that it is often necessary to go somewhat beyond meeting those minimum requirements.

The sequence I have followed has led us from specific-to-general-to-abstract-to-correlational substatements of Hanunóo ethnography. We have moved from individuals occupying established genealogical positions in a well-recognized kin net, to the examination of types of kin classes, to the analysis and articulation of the defining features, or significata, which underlie the whole category system; and finally to a brief consideration of one set of significant nonterminological correlates of the more highly structured parts of this system. In each case, I have tried to draw attention to ethnographically effective ways of combining (or using in a complementary fashion) analytic and folk classificatory models. The more strictly ethnogenealogical information I have indicated diagrammatically in the B section of each figure.

In cultural contexts where genealogical connections are of demonstrable social significance, I think that a somewhat broadened and more critical use of the criteria of relevance that I have specified should become an important and continuing ethnographic responsibility. Procedures similar, or analogous, to those suggested here may also be helpful in the study of role networks (e.g., Goodenough 1961c) and other culturally significant relationship patterns aside from those whose major structural features appear to lie within the realm of kinship.

NOTES

[1] Most of the research on which this paper is based has been supported by grants from the National Science Foundation and the Columbia University Council for Research in the Social Sciences. I am also indebted to many students and other friends for their critical comments on various portions of this article, a brief version of which was first read at the Tenth Pacific Science Congress in Honolulu in August, 1961. For especially helpful suggestions in revising earlier drafts of this paper I should like to thank D. Crabb, R. M. Keesing, F. G. Lounsbury, and W. C. Sturtevant.

[2] *Etic* discriminations are presumably culture-free, in contrast to *emic* ones, which are structurally significant within a particular cultural system. This usage, derived and generalized from the phonetic-phonemic contrast in phonology, was first suggested by a linguist (Pike, 1954, pp. 8–28).

[3] Less fortunately, some of the nonproductive, nonessential, and redundant features just noted are occasionally carried over to the analysis of kinship categories. This is usually done in the form of symmetrically arranged kin-element maps

otherwise very much like Figure IA. Two readily available kinship charts (Eggan, 1960, p. 33; Freeman, 1960, p. 78) may serve as illustrations of this tendency in the current literature. Without indications of category boundaries or defining principles, these charts show (*a*) a certain number of terminologically distinct kin classes, (*b*) a total number of kin-term occurrences, and (*c*) a total number of specified genealogical positions, in the following ratios, respectively:

a		*b*		*c*
8	:	93	:	128
12	:	44	:	44

Repetitive and uneconomical charting, even with structural intent, can also lead to apparent error, as in an often-cited diagram of types and "structural groupings" of American families (Parsons 1943:23) where grandnieces and/or grandnephews are listed as *cousins* in one instance and as *cousins "once removed"* in three others. (For a diagram where this error does not occur, see Wallace and Atkins 1960:62.)

[4] Single quotation marks are used to set off translations or glosses of Hanunóo expressions.

[5] If, for example, we use the following notation:

A	:	$a_1 a_2$	(consanguineal, affinal)
B	:	$b_1 b_2 b_3 b_4 b_5 b_6$	(zero to five generations removed from ego's)
C	:	$c_1 c_2 c_3 c_4 c_5 c_6 c_7$	(zero to six degrees of collaterality)
D	:	$d_1 d_2 d_3 d_4$	(zero, terminal, medial, and double degrees of linkage)
E	:	$e_1 e_2$	(senior in structural age, junior in structural age)
F	:	$f_1 f_2$	(male, female)

then we may define componentially the kin-category spaces a to w in Figure 3A as follows (boldface = n^{th} or higher degree):

a	$a_1 b_2 c_1 e_2$	g	$a_1 b_3 f_2$	m	$a_1 b_1 c_3$	s	$a_2 b_2 d_2 e_2$
b	$a_1 b_2 c_1 e_1 f_1$	h	$a_1 b_4$	n	$a_1 b_1 c_4$	t	$a_2 b_2 d_2 e_1$
c	$a_1 b_2 c_1 e_1 f_2$	i	$a_1 b_5$	o	$a_1 b_1 c_5$	u	$a_2 b_1 d_2$
d	$a_1 b_2 c_2 f_1$	j	$a_1 b_6$	p	$a_1 b_1 c_6$	v	$a_2 b_1 d_3$
e	$a_1 b_2 c_2 f_2$	k	$a_1 b_1 c_2 e_2$	q	$a_1 b_1 c_7$	w	$a_2 d_4$
f	$a_1 b_3 f_1$	l	$a_1 b_1 c_2 e_1$	r	$a_2 b_1 d_1$		

[6] At the time of the Eighth Pacific Science Congress (November, 1953), I took Badu', who made the top sketch in Figure 3B, to Manila for a minor medical operation. He recovered rapidly, and between stints as a model for one of the art courses on the university campus, he attended various Congress functions. At one cocktail party held in the home of a Manila newspaperman, Badu' quietly made a floor plan of the apartment, and proceeded, via conversations with Tagalog guests, to record the functional differences associated with each room. Having completed that project to his satisfaction, he settled down with one congenial foreign delegate and through an interpreter began to work out some details of the American kinship system. A lasting friendship was established. Badu' still frequently inquiries, *"Kabitay si murdak?"* (How is Murdock?)

REFERENCES

Arensberg, Conrad, 1961, Structural models of kinship: the algebra of formal systems of interaction. Paper read at the New York Academy of Sciences.

Atkins, John, 1959, The cardinality of a kin relationship, Philadelphia Anthropological Society Bulletin, 13.1:7–10.

Conant, Francis P., 1961, Jarawa kin systems of reference and address: a componential comparison, Anthropological Linguistics, 3.2:19–33.

Conklin, Harold C., 1953, Hanunóo-English vocabulary. University of California Publication in Linguistics, 9:1–290.

———, 1954, The relation of Hanunóo culture to the plant world. Doctoral dissertation, Yale University, New Haven.

———, 1955, Hanunóo color categories, Southwestern Journal of Anthropology, 11:339–344.

———, 1957, Hanunóo agriculture: a report on an integral system of shifting cultivation in the Philippines. United Nations, FAO Forestry Development Paper No. 12.

———, 1959, Linguistic play in its cultural context, Language, 35.4:631–636.

———, 1960, The cultural significance of land resources among the Hanunóo, Bulletin of the Philadelphia Anthropological Society, 13.2:38–42.

———, 1961, The cultural relevance of cognitive contrast. Paper read at Harvard Center for Cognitive Studies Colloquium, April, 1961.

———, 1962a, Lexicographical treatment of folk taxonomies, International Journal of American Linguistics, 28.2:119–141. Part II, supplement, Problems of lexicography, Fred W. Householder and Sol Saporta, eds., Publication 21 of the Indiana University Research Center in Anthropology, Folklore and Linguistics, Bloomington, Ind.

———, 1962b, Comment (on the ethnographic study of cognitive systems, by C. O. Frake). In Thomas Gladwin and William C. Sturtevant, eds., Anthropology and human behavior:86–91. Washington: The Anthropological Society of Washington.

Davenport, William, 1959, Nonunilinear descent and descent groups, American Anthropologist, 61.4:557–572.

Dumont, L., 1953, The Dravidian kinship terminology as an expression of marriage, Man, Vol. 53, article 54:34–39.

Eggan, Fred, 1960, The Sagada Igorots of Northern Luzon. In George Peter Murdock, ed., Social structure in Southeast Asia. Viking Fund Publications in Anthropology, No. 29:24–50, Wenner-Gren Foundation for Anthropological Research, Inc.

Epling, P. J., 1961, A note on Njamal kin-term usage, Man, Vol. 61, article 184:152–159.

Fortes, Meyer, 1959, Primitive kinship, Scientific American, 200.6:146–158.

Frake, Charles O., 1954, Sindangan Subanun word list, The University of Manila Journal of East Asiatic Studies, 3.3:321–324.

———, 1960, The Eastern Subanun of Mindanao. In George Peter Murdock ed., Social structure in Southeast Asia. Viking Fund Publications in Anthropology, No. 29:51–64, Wenner-Gren Foundation for Anthropological Research, Inc.

——, 1961, The diagnosis of disease among the Subanun of Mindanao, American Anthropologist, 63.1:113–132.

——, 1962a, Cultural ecology and ethnography, American Anthropologist, 64.1:53–59.

——, 1962b, The ethnographic study of cognitive systems. *In* T. Gladwin and W. C. Sturtevant, eds., Anthropology and Human Behavior:72–85. Washington Anthropological Society of Washington.

——, 1964, A structural description of Subanun religious behavior. *In* Ward H. Goodenough, ed., Explorations in cultural anthropology: essays in honor of George Peter Murdock, pp. 111–129. New York, McGraw-Hill.

Freeman, J. D., 1960, The Iban of Western Borneo. *In* George Peter Murdock, ed., Social structure in Southeast Asia. Viking Fund Publications in Anthropology, No. 29:65–87, Wenner-Gren Foundation for Anthropological Research, Inc.

——, 1961, On the concept of the kindred, Journal of the Royal Anthropological Institute, 91(part 2):192–220.

Gilmour, J. S. L. (compiler), 1961, The mathematical assessment of taxonomic similarity, including the use of computers, Taxon, 10.4:97–101.

Gluckman, Max, 1961, Ethnographic data in British social anthropology, The Sociological Review, 9.1:5–17.

Goodenough, Ward H., 1951, Property, kin, and community on Truk. Yale University Publications in Anthropology, No. 46.

——, 1956a, Residence rules, Southwestern Journal of Anthropology, 12.1:22–37.

——, 1956b, Componential analysis and the study of meaning, Language, 32.2:195–216.

——, 1957, Sultural anthropology and linguistics. *In* Paul L. Garvin, ed., Report of the seventh annual round table meeting on linguistics and language study. Georgetown University, Monograph Series on Languages and Linguistics, No. 9:167–173.

——, 1961a, Review of Pul Eliya, a village in Ceylon, a study of land tenure and kinship, by E. R. Leach, Science, 133:1816.

——, 1961b, Review of social structure in Southeast Asia, George Peter Murdock, ed., American Anthropologist, 63.6:1341–1347.

——, 1961c, Formal properties of status relationships. Paper read to the annual meeting of the American Anthropological Association, November 16, 1961, Philadelphia.

Greenberg, Joseph H., 1957, The nature and uses of linguistic typologies, International Journal of American Linguistics, 23.2:68–77.

Gregg, John R., 1954, The language of taxonomy: an application of symbolic logic to the study of classificatory systems. New York: Columbia.

Grimes, Joseph E., and Barbara F. Grimes, 1962, Semantic distinctions in Huichol (Uto-Aztecan) kinship, American Anthropologist, 64.1:104–114.

Harris, Zellig, 1948, Componential analysis of a Hebrew paradigm, Language, 24.1:87–91.

Jakobson, Roman, 1936, Beitrag zur allgemeinen Kasuslehre, Travaux du Cercle linguistique de Prague, 6:240–288.

Keesing, Roger M., n.d., Formal and sociological analysis of Ramkokamekra kinship. Unpublished manuscript.

Kluckhohn, Clyde, 1960, The use of typology in anthropological theory. *In* Anthony F. C. Wallace, ed., Selected papers of the Fifth International Congress of anthropological and ethnological sciences, Philadelphia, September 1–9, 1956, 134–140. Philadelphia, University of Pennsylvania Press.

Lazarsfeld, Paul F., 1937, Some remarks on the typological procedure in social research, Zeitschrift für Sozialforschung, 6:119–139.

———, 1961, The algebra of dichotomous systems. *In* Herbert Solomon, ed., Studies in item analysis and prediction, pp. 111–157. Stanford, Stanford University Press.

Leach, E. R., 1961a, Pul Eliya, a village in Ceylon: a study of land tenure and kinship. New York, Cambridge.

———, 1961b. On certain unconsidered aspects of double descent systems. Paper read at the Tenth Pacific Science Congress, August 1961, Honolulu.

———, 1961c. Rethinking anthropology. London School of Economics Monograph on Social Anthropolgy, No. 22.

Lévi-Strauss, Claude, 1958, Anthropologie structurale. Paris, Librairie Plon.

Lounsbury, Floyd G., 1955, The varieties of meaning. Georgetown University, Monograph Series on Languages and Linguistics, No. 8:158–164.

———, 1956, A semantic analysis of the Pawnee kinship usage, Language, 32.1:158–194.

———, 1964, A formal analysis of the Crow and Omaha-type kinship terminologies. *In* Ward H. Goodenough, ed., Explorations in cultural anthropology: essays in honor of George Peter Murdock, pp. 351–393. New York, McGraw-Hill.

Mayr, Ernst, 1961, Cause and effect in biology, Science, 134:1501–1506.

Mayr, Ernst, E. Gordon Linsley, and Robert L. Usinger, 1953, Methods and principles of systematic zoology. New York, McGraw-Hill.

Mitchell, William E., 1959, Theoretical problems in the concept of "kindred." Paper read at the 58th Annual Meeting of the American Anthropological Association, Mexico City.

Morris, Charles W., 1946, Signs, language, and behavior. Englewood Cliffs, Prentice-Hall.

Murdock, George Peter, 1949, Social structure. New York, Macmillan.

———, 1960, Cognatic forms of social organization. *In* George Peter Murdock, ed., Social structure in Southeast Asia. Viking Fund Publications in Anthropology, No. 29:1–14, Wenner-Gren Foundation for Anthropological Research, Inc.

Nadel, S. F., 1957, The theory of social structure. New York, Free Press.

Naess, Arne, 1953, Interpretation and preciseness: a contribution to the theory of communication. Oslo, Jacob Dybwad.

Needham, Rodney, 1962, Structure and sentiment: a test case in social anthropology. Chicago, The University of Chicago Press.

Parsons, Talcott, 1943, The kinship system of the contemporary United States, American Anthropologist, 45.1:22–38.

Pike, Kenneth L., 1954, Language in relation to a unified theory of the structure of human behavior, Part I. Preliminary ed. Glendale, Summer Institute of Linguistics.

Pospisil, Leopold, 1960, The Kapauku Papuans and their kinship organization, Oceania, 30.3:188–205.

Quine, Willard Van Orman, 1960, Word and object. New York, Wiley.

Radcliffe-Brown, A. R., 1941, The study of kinship systems, Journal of the Royal Anthropological Institute, 71:1–18. Reprinted in Structure and function in primitive society, 1952:48–89. New York, Free Press.

———, 1950. Introduction. In A. R. Radcliffe-Brown and Daryll Forde, eds., African systems of kinship and marriage, pp. 1–85. New York, Oxford.

Rivers, W. H. R., 1900, A genealogical method of collecting social and vital statistics, Journal of the Royal Anthropological Institute, 30:74–82.

———, 1906, The Todas. New York, Macmillan.

———, 1910, The genealogical method of anthropological inquiry, Sociological Review, 3.1:1–12.

———, 1912, The genealogical method. In B. Freire-Marreco and J. L. Myres, eds., Notes and queries on anthropology, 4th ed. London: The Royal Anthropological Institute, pp. 119–122, and other sections of Part III, Sociology, pp. 108–180.

Roark, Richard, 1961, The mathematics of American cousinship. The Kroeber Anthropological Society Papers, No. 24:17–18.

Romney, A. Kimball, and Philip J. Epling, 1958, A simplified model of Kariera kinship, American Anthropologist, 60.1:59–74.

Royal Anthropological Institute of Great Britain and Ireland, 1951, Notes and queries on anthropology, 6th ed. London, Routledge.

Schneider, David M., and George C. Homans, 1955, Kinship terminology and the American kinship system, American Anthropologist, 57:1194–1208.

Schwartz, Douglas W., 1962, A key to prehistoric Kentucky pottery, Transactions of the Kentucky Academy of Science, 22.3–4:82–85.

Simpson, George Gaylord, 1961, Principles of animal taxonomy. New York, Columbia.

Spaulding, Albert C., 1960, The dimensions of archaeology. In G. E. Dole and R. C. Carneiro, eds., Essays in the science of culture, in honor of Leslie A. White, pp. 437–456. New York, Crowell.

Suttles, Wayne, 1960, Affinal ties, subsistence, and prestige among the Coast Salish, American Anthropologist, 62.2:296–305.

Wallace, Anthony F. C., 1961a, On being just complicated enough, Proceedings of the National Academy of Sciences, 47.4:458–464.

———, 1961b. The psychic unity of human groups. In Bert Kaplan, ed., Studying personality cross-culturally. New York, Harper & Row.

———, 1962. Culture and cognition, Science, 135:351–357.

Wallace, Anthony F. C., and John Atkins, 1960, The meaning of kinship terms, American Anthropologist, 62.1:58–80.

Notes on Queries in Ethnography[1]

Charles O. Frake

The only existing field manual for ethnographers, *Notes and Queries on Anthropology* (Royal Anthropological Institute 1951), presents a list of queries that an investigator can take to the field, present to his informants, and thereby produce a set of responses.[2] His ethnographic record, then, is a list of questions and answers. (The tradition in modern anthropology, however, is not to make such a record public but to publish an essay about it.) The image of an ethnography we have in mind also includes lists of queries and responses, but with this difference: both the queries and their responses are to be discovered in the culture of the people being studied. The problem is not simply to find answers to questions the ethnographer brings into the field, but also to find the questions that go with the responses he observes after his arrival.

Ethnography, according to this image, is a discipline which seeks to account for the behavior of a people by describing the socially acquired and shared knowledge, or culture, that enables members of the society to behave in ways deemed appropriate by their fellows. The discipline is akin to linguistics; indeed, descriptive linguistics is but a special case of ethnography since its domain of study, speech messages, is an integral part of a larger domain of socially interpretable acts and artifacts. It is this total domain of "messages" (including speech) that is the concern of the ethnographer. The ethnographer, like the linguist, seeks to describe an infinite set of variable messages as manifestations of a finite shared code, the code being a set of rules for the socially appropriate construction and interpretation of messages.

Accounting for socially meaningful behavior within a given society is not the sole aim of ethnography. By developing methods for the demonstrably successful description of messages as manifestations of a code, one is furthermore seeking to build a theory of codes—a theory of culture. Since the code is construed as knowledge in people's heads, such a theory should say something of general relevance about cognition and behavior.

A familiar model for behavior is the stimulus-response frame: if a person encounters stimulus X, he will do Y. To account for behavior we need only observe the input and the output. We can ignore whatever might be going on inside the actor's head. This model has had some success under conditions in which the investigator defines the stimulus beforehand and strives to

Reproduced by permission of the author and the American Anthropological Association from the *American Anthropologist*, Vol. 66, no. 3, part 2 (Special Publication), pp. 132–145 (June 1964).

eliminate from the situation anything else that might impinge on the subject as a stimulus. The model is somewhat less successful in accounting for what people do during those intervals of life spent outside the psychologist's laboratory. In the natural settings of behavior, it is difficult to determine which of a multitude of potential stimuli confronting a subject evoke a particular response and which portion of the subject's behavior is a response to some stimulus (Chomsky 1959). If we want to account for behavior by relating it to the conditions under which it normally occurs, we require procedures for discovering what people are attending to, what information they are processing, when they reach decisions which lead to culturally appropriate behavior. We must get inside our subjects' heads. This should not be an impossible feat: our subjects themselves accomplished it when they learned their culture and became "native actors." They had no mysterious avenues of perception not available to us as invesigators.

The aims of ethnography, then, differ from those of stimulus-response psychology in at least two respects. First, it is not, I think, the ethnographer's task to predict behavior per se, but rather to state rules of culturally appropriate behavior (Frake 1964). In this respect the ethnographer is again akin to the linguist who does not attempt to predict what people will say but to state rules for constructing utterances which native speakers will judge as grammatically appropriate. The model of an ethnographic statement is not: "if a person is confronted with stimulus X, he will do Y," but: "if a person is in situation X, performance Y will be judged appropriate by native actors." The second difference is that the ethnographer seeks to discover, not prescribe, the significant stimuli in the subject's world. He attempts to describe each act in terms of the cultural situations which appropriately evoke it and each situation in terms of the acts it appropriately evokes.

There are a variety of methods one might use to discover those aspects of cultural situations relevant to rendering appropriate performances—many more, I am sure, than I am concerned with here.[3] The method considered here attends to the way people talk about what they do. Since the knowledge that enables one to behave appropriately is acquired from other people, it must be communicable in some symbolic system which can travel between one mind and another as code signals in a physical channel. The procedures of this paper seek to reveal the knowledge that is communicated by talking. This may not include everything a person knows which is relevant to his cultural performances, but it will certainly include a sizable chunk of it. Actually, I find it difficult to conceive of any act, object, or event which can be described as a *cultural* artifact, a manifestation of a code, without some reference to the way people talk about it. This is the case because the informants' interpretation of a socially meaningful act (a message) is the key to the discovery of code rules. An informant makes an interpretation by applying code rules to the observable message. Therefore, if one knows the message and the interpretation, one can infer the relevant code rules (Ebeling 1962:13). (Let me emphasize, however, that I do not believe an adequate ethnography can be produced from a record only of what people say, most especially it cannot be produced from a record only of what people say in artificial interviewing contexts removed from the scene of their ordinary cultural performances.)

What we want to do, then, is to discover how a person in a given society finds out from one of his fellows what he knows. In general, if you want to find out what someone knows, you ask him. This suggests that the informative utterances produced by native actors be matched with the inquiries which elicit them. For every response, discover the set of inquiries which appropriately evokes it; and for every inquiry, discover a set of responses it appropriately evokes.

By presenting an inquiry (e.g., "What kind of tree is that?"), a native inquirer seeks to restrict the appropriate responses to a given set of responses (e.g., tree names), so that the selection of a particular response (e.g., "elm tree") by alter from the set conveys information significant to the inquirer. A description organized by linked queries and responses is simultaneously a program for finding out information, a program which can be replicated and tested by the reader of the description. An inquiry about a given topic also instructs alter to attend to certain features of the topic and to ignore others. Consequently, knowing the queries that can be appropriately posed about a given topic reveals the features of that topic that are relevant to the inquirer. Furthermore, the topic of a given query will be a response to some other query, making it possible to produce lists of utterances *interlinked* as topics and responses of specified queries. A pair of queries which interlink utterances as mutual topics and responses constitutes the basic unit of these procedures, a unit which we will call an *interlinkage*.

If "meaning" has to do with (extra-grammatical) rules of use, then to the extent to which the conditions for the use of an utterance are verbally constrained or verbally specifiable, the interlinking of queries and responses says something about the meaning of utterances even if we cannot as yet identify the nonverbal objects and events (if any) to which these utterances apply. For example, even if we cannot identify an instance of a "tree," if we learn the verbal response *tree* is interlinked with *plant* by one pair of queries, to *elm, oak, pine,* etc. by another, to *leaf, stem, branch, trunk, root,* etc. by another, to *lumber, firewood,* etc. by another, then we have discovered some of the kinds of relationships that can exist among categories of things in a culture.

As an attempt to apply these notions to the analysis and display of ethnographic data, let me refer to a small segment of a descriptive statement I have been trying to formulate off and on for several years. What we seek to describe here is one phase of the selection of ingredients for the manufacture of *gasi*, a fermented beverage which is the major lubricant of inter-family social relations among the Eastern Subanun of the Philippines (Frake 1960, 1964). Wishing to reserve the term 'wine' for another drink, I gloss[4] *gasi* as 'beer,' a somewhat inappropriate label since the starchy mash is not reduced to sugar by malting as in the West, nor by saliva as in parts of the New World, but by certain fungi grown with yeast in cakes of rice flour. These fungi reduce the starch to sugars upon which the yeast can then act. This method of fermenting starchy mashes occurs widely in the Orient (Burkill 1935:1604–1607). Subanun 'beer,' drunk with bamboo straws from Chinese jars, is prepared for consumption by adding water to a wort which has fermented aerobically for several hours and anaerobically in the sealed jar for at least several weeks, generally much longer. The wort is prepared by adding rice chaff and powder from pulverized 'yeast cakes' to a mash of cooked rice, manioc, maize, and/or Job's tears. The 'yeast cakes,' prepared

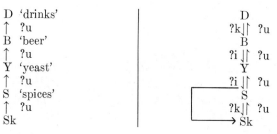

D 'drinks'	D
↑ ?u	?k↓↑ ?u
B 'beer'	B
↑ ?u	?i ↓↑ ?u
Y 'yeast'	Y
↑ ?u	?i ↓↑ ?u
S 'spices'	S
↑ ?u	?k↓↑ ?u
Sk	→ Sk

   a. *Discovering linking queries*   b. *Discovering reciprocal queries*

D ginumen 'drinks'

?k↓↑ ?u

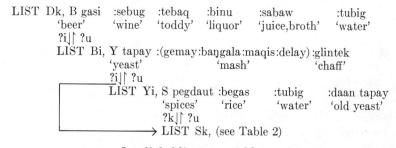

       LIST Dk, B gasi   :sebug   :tebaq   :binu   :sabaw   :tubig
                'beer'   'wine'   'toddy' 'liquor' 'juice,broth' 'water'
                ?i↓↑ ?u
            LIST Bi, Y tapay :(gemay:baŋgala:maqis:delay) :glintek
                   'yeast'   'mash'   'chaff'
                   ?i↓↑ ?u
                LIST Yi, S pegdaut :begas   :tubig   :daan tapay
                    'spices' 'rice'   'water'   'old yeast'
                    ?k↓↑ ?u
                    → LIST Sk, (see Table 2)

         c. *Interlinked lists generated by queries*

Figure 1.   Discovery and display of lists and queries (for queries see Table 1)

in advance and stored for use as necessary, are made by mixing an assortment of 'spices' with a dough of uncooked rice flour and an infection of old yeast. We will focus the present description on these yeast cakes, ignoring the complex routines of processing the ingredients and attending only to a relatively simple and, at first sight, trivial little problem: the selection of 'spices' to add to the other yeast ingredients.

One task is to specify operationally the relations among 'spices,' 'yeast,' and 'beer.' That there is some relation seems apparent from observation. Fig. 1a shows that beginning with a term for some item (Sk) used for 'spice,' the successive application of query ?u 'what is X used for' will link any Sk with 'yeast,' 'yeast' with 'beer,' and 'beer' with 'drinks.' (The arrow travels from topic to response.) Next we seek to discover the reciprocals of ?u in each case, e.g., if 'yeast' is the response to 'what are spices used for,' then what can be asked about 'yeast' to elicit 'spices' as a response? Interlinking queries, displayed in Fig. 1b, enable one to proceed by queries from any item in the chain to any other item. In traveling down the chain, three noteworthy things happen. First, the reciprocals of ?u are not all the same. Thus 'beer' will be included in the response to query ?kD 'what kinds of drinks are there,' but 'yeast' will not occur as a response when the same question is asked of 'beer' (?kB); instead there will occur the names of the plants that provide starch for the mash. A different query, ?i 'what are the ingredients of X,' is required to get from 'beer' to 'yeast.' Our operations demonstrate that each of the pairs in the chain are not linked by equivalent relations as appeared at first sight. A second event in downward querying in this chain is that ?i asked of 'yeast' (?iY) may yield List Sk instead of 'spices' as a response. The reasons for this will be apparent shortly, but had we proceeded in one direction only, we might have missed one link in the chain (especially if we were interviewing an informant outside the context of using the referents of these terms). Third, downward queries in this chain produce responses other than those shown in Figs. 1a and 1b; they produce *lists*. (The list may be elicited by a single query such as 'what kinds of X are there' or by successive applications of a query such as 'what kind of X is that' (Table 1). (The notation of Fig. 1 does not distinguish list-eliciting from item-eliciting queries.) Fig. 1c displays the lists and the queries that interlink an item in a given list with the list below it. Colons separate *contrasting* items in a list (Frake 1961, 1962; Conklin 1962). The parsing of lists into contrast sets (see 'mash' in Fig. 1c) must be performed by further inquiries; it cannot be assumed that all responses elicited by a given inquiry contrast at the same level (Frake 1961).

The list (Sk) of items used for 'spices' presented in Table 2 is a composite list produced by asking ?iY and ?kS of all available yeast makers (a subset of women) and by recording actual recipes of items used as spices on given occasions. The complete list was then cross-checked with informants to determine which items, if any, were consistently judged as unfamiliar, idiosyncratic, or inappropriate by informants other than the original respondee. Idiosyncratic items are enclosed by parentheses in Table 3. Certain

Table 1.   Queries and Interlinkages

QUERIES

?u: ditaq ig baalan dun X?	'What is X used for?'
?k: ditaq X ai run ma iin?	'What kind of X is it?'
ditaq dega X ai run?	'What all kinds of X are there?'
?i: ditaq ma kig baalan X-en kin?	'What is that ingredient of X?'
ditaq dega ig baalan X-en?	'What all are the ingredients of X?'
ditaq ig baalan mu rin X-en?	'What are you using there for making X?'
?w: ditaq alandun ma X?	'What is X (a kind of)?'
?p: ditaq ginalapan dun X ma iin?	'What (separated) part of X is it?'
ditaq kaqalapan dun X ma iin?	'What (separable) part of X is it?'
ditaq dega i kaqalapan dun X?	'What are the (potentially separable) parts of X?'
?s: ditaq ma bwat kini?	'What does this come from?'

INTERLINKAGES

?k/?w	species—genus
?k/?u	species—use
?i/?u	ingredient—use
?p/?s	part—source
?u/?s	use—source

---

items occur in every recipe, and some of these are consistently regarded as necessary (starred items in Table 3). One item, *palay* 'rice,' is always used if the appropriate parts ('roots') are available (they are available in the post-harvest season, the usual time for yeast making). Note that, for a Subanun, the identification of an item in List Sk is, because of the length of the list and the unpredictability of the constituents of a given recipe, generally much more informative than the identification of an item in List Yi. It is apparently for this reason that in many contexts ?iY elicits an item in Sk, skipping List Yi (see Fig. 1).

Since a particular recipe contains only about half the number of items included in the composite List Sk, the next task of description is to specify how, and from what set of objects, a particular selection of 'spices' is made. What information about the items in List Sk is relevant to this decision? Of the many information-probing questions entertainable about an item in List Sk, we will describe the results of applying a few general queries: ?w, ?k, ?p, and ?s (Table 1).

The query ?w, 'what is X (a kind of),' will yield for any Sk(x): *gayu* 'tree' (rigid-stemmed woody plant); *sigbet* 'herb' (rigid-stemmed nonwoody plant); or *belagen* 'vine' (nonrigid-stemmed plant). The reciprocal link is

?k, 'what kind of X is it (are there)':

List Sk   ?w/?k   List Pt, gayu:sigbet:belagen

(In this representation of an interlinkage, the query symbol (e.g., ?w) appears on the same side of the slash as its topic and on the opposite side from its response.)

Table 2. Yeast Spice Ingredients

LIST SK:	BOTANICAL IDENTIFICATION OF AT LEAST THREE SPECIMENS OF THE EQUIVALENTLY-NAMED PLANT CATEGORY (LIST PK):[5]
1. belili	*Eleusine indica*, (L.) Gaertn. (Gram.)
2. belurus	*Ficus saherthwaitei*, Elm. (Mor.)
3. bilaw	? (Zingiber.)
4. busyuŋ	*Ficus botryocarpa*, Miq. (Mor.)
5. deluyut	*Saurania glabrifolia*, Merr. (Dillen.)
6. gebul	*Solanum ferox*, L. (Solan.)
7. geleŋug	*Champereia manillana*, (Blm.) Merr. (Opil.)
8. gimit	*Ficus minahassae*, (Teysm. and De Vr.) Miq. (Mor.)
9. glabana	*Anona muricata*, L. (Apon.)
10. gleknu	*Cyclosorus unitus*, Ching. (Aspid.)
11. glempiq	*Vernonia cinerea*, (L.) Less. (Composit.)
12. glimbuŋa	*Macaranga tanarius*, (L.) Muell.-Arg. (Euphor.)
13. glinda	*Macaranga hispida*, (Blume) Muell.-Arg. (Euphor.)
14. glumbilan	*Leucosyke capitellata*, (Poir.) Wedd. (Urt.)
15. gluntud-ulaŋan	*Buddleia asiatica*, Lour. (Logan.)
16. gluya	*Zingiber officinale*, Roscoe (Zingiber.)
17. guburubud	*Oreocnide rubescens*, (Blume) Miq. (Urt.)
18. guleŋkem	*Mismosa pudica*, L. (Legum.)
19. gupa	*Litsea garciae*, Vidal. (Laur.)
20. mendyabaw	*Wendlandia luzoniensis*, DC. (Rub.)
21. naŋka	*Artocarpus heterophyllus*, Lam. (Mor.)
22. niup	*Callicarpa* sp. (Verben.)
23. palay	*Oryza sativa*, L. (Gram.)
24. payaw	*Homalomena philippinensis*, Engl. (Ar.)
25. peŋgya	*Ananas comosus*, (L.) Merr. (Bromel.)
26. sagiŋ tubali	*Musa* sp. (Musac.)
27. sili	*Capsicum* sp. (Solan.)
28. tebu belekbut	*Saccharum officinarum*, L. (Gram.)
29. tetibeg	*Ficus carpentariana*, Elm. (Mor.)
30. tuba	*Derris elliptica*, (Roxb.) Benth. (Legum.)
31. tubayag	*Piper umbellatum*, L. (Piper.)
32. tuyabaŋ	*Spathoglottis plicata*, Blume. (Orchid.)

Table 3.   Intersection of List Sk (Kinds of Yeast Spices) with List Pt
(Plant Types), List Pp (Plant Parts), and Category C 'cultigens'

	'YOUNG LEAVES'	'UNDERGROUND PARTS'	OTHER
'TREES'	belurus busyuŋ deluyut gimit glimbuŋa glindaŋ glumbilan guburubud gupa mendyabaw tetibeg tubayag	gluntud-ulaŋan (geleŋug) (glabana) C (naŋka) C	*sili C (niup)
'HERBS'	(gebul) (guleŋkem) gleknu	(guleŋkem) belili bilaw glempiq *gluya C palay C payaw peŋgya C sagiŋ tubali C tuyabaŋ	*tebu belekbut C
'VINES'		(tuba)	

Query ?k, asked about items in List Pt, yields (eventually) a 1,500+
member list, Pk. List Sk is a subset of List Pk. One can infer, then, that List
Pk represents the universe of objects from which a particular spice recipe
is selected.

One thing apparent from observation, however, is that objects represented by forms in List Sk differ radically in appearance from other things
called by the same terms, objects pointed out as examples of Pk. Forms in
List Sk denote bits and pieces of things that can be picked up by the hand-
fuls; forms in List Pk denote entire plants, including large trees. This
observation suggests a 'part of' question. The appropriate Subanun question
in this case is ?p which inquires about the 'separable' or 'separated' constituents of an object:

List Pk   ?p/?s   List Pp (a long list of plant parts)

If we restrict ourselves to those Pk occurring also in List Sk, then we elicit a much reduced subset of Pp: *gekbus* 'young leaves'; *gaŋet* 'root'; *gabi* 'corm'; *guned* 'tuber'; *buŋa* 'fruit'; *gayu* 'stem.' Further querying, which we will not display here, will reveal that not all of these terms for plant parts contrast as different parts of a single plant. Thus a given plant may have both 'fruit' and 'stem,' but it has either a 'root' or a 'tuber' or a 'corm.' In contexts involving the selection of a part from a given plant, there can be no choice among the last three items. Consequently, we can rewrite the portion of List Pp that concerns this description (List Pp(Sk)) as follows:

List Pp(Sk), *gekbus* 'young leaves' :(*gaŋet:guned:gabi*)
'underground parts':*buŋa* 'fruit':*gayu* 'stem.'

Table 3 displays the intersection of List Sk with Lists Pp and Pt, showing what parts of what type of plants are selected as yeast spices. It reveals sufficient patterning to suggest some preliminary rules of selection:

To construct a 'yeast spice' recipe, select a subset of plant parts which include

1) the 'fruits' of *sili* 'chili,'
2) 'stem' pieces of *tebu* 'sugar cane,'
3) 'young leaves' of selected 'trees,'
4) 'underground parts' of selected 'herbs' (including *gluya* 'ginger' and, if available, *palay* 'rice').

If these rules do not perfectly determine a recipe selection, they at least predict idiosyncratic responses with considerable accuracy, e.g., *tuba* 'Derris,' a 'vine'; *naŋka* 'jackfruit,' a 'tree' whose roots are used.

To improve these rules many further questions could be asked, questions of treatment, habitat, properties, etc. For example, items marked *C* in Table 3 are those that receive the response *pemulanan* 'cultigen' in answer to a query about treatment. All items considered necessary (starred in Table 3) are 'cultigens.' If List Sk is divided into three groups, 'cultigens,' 'wild trees,' and 'wild herbs,' then it is the case that any given recipe will contain at least three but not more than nine items from each group. The following diagram displays the appropriate combinations, for all but a few items, of plant type (T 'tree,' H 'herb'), treatment (C 'cultigen,' W 'wild'), and part used (L 'young leaves,' R 'underground parts'): (Read across.)

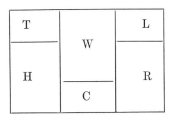

A habitat query reveals that all source plants grow in secondary forest, fallow fields, or cultivated fields; none are primary forest plants. Consequently an appropriate selection of ingredients (always picked fresh before use) can be made within close range of a household. In contrast to the case of 'medicines,' for example, no value is placed on rare, unusual, or difficult-to-obtain items in the selection of yeast ingredients. Questions about the desirable properties of yeast spices would point up attributes such as 'sweetness,' 'piquancy,' 'flossiness,' 'milky sap,' and, for one idiosyncratic maker, 'toxicity' (*tuba* and *niup* are fish poisons). Continued questioning would reveal that yeast making is considered to be the critical stage of brewing and that the selection of ingredients properly combined under a set of compulsively observed routines and taboos is essential to the desired strength and flavor of the final product. Still other questions would lead into social structure (e.g., the social relations among yeast makers and users), religion (gods as well as men are inveterate drinkers), and magic (yeast is a ritual object of considerable potency; its improper handling can cause grave misfortune).

One does not have to attempt very many descriptive statements of this type to realize that any concept is interlinked by a variety of relationships to a large number of other concepts, which, in turn, are interlinked with still other concepts. If a semantic domain is a set of related concepts, then it is clear that there is no one way to separate the conceptual structure of a people into a finite number of discrete, clearly delimited, domains. Rather, we have a network of relations whose links enable us to travel along a variety of paths from one concept to another.

The utility of the exercise in description, however, goes beyond explicating the ramifications of Subanun yeast making. We have succeeded in isolating some of the basic types of relationships linking concepts among the Subanun. Each pair of interlinking queries defines such a relationship. These relationships are of interest because of their applicability throughout many domains of the culture and because of the implications they have for the ways people talk about the things so interlinked. The interlinkages isolated thus far and some of their implications are:

1. X ?k/?w Z 'X is a kind of Z.' Implication: Any object, a, called X can also be called Z, and there is some object, b, which can be called Z but which cannot be called X. Z is the *head term* for List Zk (produced by ?kZ), that is, the items of List Zk, considered collectively as well as individually, can be called Z.

2. X ?i./?u Z 'X is an ingredient of Z.' Implication: An object called X cannot be called Z, nor can List Zi taken as a collectivity be called Z. Thus List Bi (Figure 1) is not equivalent to 'beer,' for 'beer' results only after the items named in List Bi have been subjected to processing whereby they lose their identity. In the case of Bi, Yi, and most ingredient lists, the head term

for the list depends on the *stage* of processing, revealing another type of relationship, 'X is a stage of Z' (cf. Frake 1961).

  3. X ?k/?u Z 'X is something used for Z.' Implication: Similar to that of ?k/?w rather than of ?i/?u. (?k/?w appears generally, perhaps always, substitutable for ?k/?u, but the converse is not true.)

  4. X ?p/?s Z 'X is a part of Z.' Implication: X is 'separable' or 'separated' from Z at some conventional point. List Zp, if separated parts, cannot collectively be called Z and there is no processing by which they can become Z. An object named X cannot be called Z.

  One of the practical problems to which this approach can contribute is that of sorting out the different but related concepts which a single linguistic form can represent without relying on the number of equivalents required to translate the form into some other language. In a previous paper (Frake 1961:120–121), I discussed a case in which a single Subanun disease term, *nuka*, labels three concepts, X, Y, Z, where Y is a *kind* of X, and Z is an initial *stage of* some but not all X. The following is a somewhat more complex example involving the use of the Subanun form *buŋa* to mean:

  B1. A kind of 'tree,' the 'areca palm.'
  B2. A plant part, 'fruit.'
  B3. A category of betel quid constituents.
  B4. A kind of 'fruit,' the 'areca nut.'
  B5. One member of category B3, the 'areca nut.'

Figure 2 displays the queries that interlink these concepts. (Note a new interlinkage of familiar queries, ?u/?s.) If the full lists, rather than single responses, generated by these queries were displayed, then each occurrence of *buŋa* would be as a member of a different list. Thus although B4 and B5 denote the same objects, 'areca nuts,' they have different meanings in that the contrasting categories are different: other 'fruits' in one case and other substances used for constituent category B3 in the other.

  Figure 2 also suggests the possibility of formulating logical rules of interlinkage general for the culture. It appears to be the case, for example, that

  if A is interlinked with B by some query pair ?x/?y
  and A is interlinked with C by ?k/?w,
  and B is interlinked with D by ?k/?w,
  then C is interlinked with D by ?x/?y.

(Compare 'tree,' B2, B1, and B4 in Fig. 2.) This example is a demonstration of one of the semantic properties of a 'kind of' (?k/?w) relation, namely any property of a superordinate will also be held by its subordinates (but not the converse).

  Because of inadequacies in the ethnographic record (obtained before these analyses were attempted), both the descriptive examples in this paper may contain errors. However, the errors could be easily discovered and corrected by testing the description with informants. To produce ethnographic statements that can be demonstrated to be *wrong*, and not simply judged to

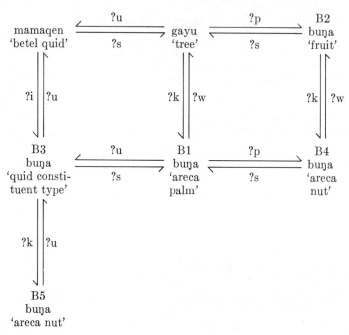

Figure 2.   Interlinkages of categories labeled *buŋa* (for queries see Table 1).

be unpersuasively written, is, I think, some advance over the production of most current statements. Also, the probable deficiencies in the present examples demonstrate the need to carry out and test analyses as part of data collecting procedures. Only in this way can errors be detected, gaps filled, and, through successively better approximations, an adequate descriptive statement be produced.

These procedures are intended not only to be replicable and testable, but also perfectly general. They are procedures for describing anything people talk about, be it plants, kinsmen, or gods. There is no argument that any one aspect of culture should be selected as the focus of a description. Indeed, short of a "complete" description of a culture, the preferable strategy is probably to focus in depth on a variety of domains in order to reveal the kinds and range of patterns in the culture for construing the world. No one working with procedures similar in intent to these has yet described a complete culture, but some have succeeded in producing descriptions of a remarkable variety of cultural manifestations. Metzger and Williams, for example, emerged from one field session with descriptions of firewood (1963b), terms of personal reference (1962), curers (1963c), and weddings (1963a). Conklin has described ethnobotanical systems, agriculture, betel chewing, pottery, verbal play, color, kinship, and water (see Conklin 1962 for methodological statement). None of these descriptions, whatever its faults, can be called superficial, and each says a great deal not only about the topics at hand but also about the cultures being investigated and about culture in general.

At this point the reader himself may have a query: "All this is fine, but how do I go about finding appropriate queries?" Even though it is somewhat fashionable these days to dismiss "discovery procedures" as something not amenable to statement, we consider such a query appropriate and will attempt a response.

Two tasks are assumed to be completed or at least well under way: an analysis of the phonology and grammar of the language being investigated, and an ability of the ethnographer to produce utterances that are phonologically and grammatically acceptable. In the course of language learning and analysis, the ethnographer will learn some basic query frames which can be checked for appropriateness with specific topics. The ethnographer can listen for queries in use in the cultural scenes he observes, giving special attention to query-rich settings, e.g., children querying parents, medical specialists querying patients, legal authorities querying witnesses, priests querying the gods. He can take advantage of the power of language to construc settings: hypothetical information-eliciting situations can be described or even staged with native actors, a technique especially useful when working with informants removed from their society. When using interpreters, instead of relying on contact-language questions to elicit native equivalents, one can describe situations in the contact language and inquire how one would ask questions about features of the situation. Once a few general queries such as "What is it called?" or "What kind of X is it?" are discovered, these can be used to elicit lists which in turn can be used in the search for other queries to which items in the list are topics and responses.

Discovered queries must be tested for appropriateness with respect to particular topics. To learn to distinguish appropriate from inappropriate queries, the ethnographer can try apparently inappropriate questions on informants to determine the pattern of their response. Typical cues of appropriateness are length of response (in number of forms and/or elapsed time), consistency of response across informants or across time, and nonverbal aspects of the response such as laughter, frowning, or raised eyebrows. As a test, the reader with a chair and an English speaking informant handy might try to detect which of the following queries are inappropriate:

What kind of chair is it?
What does a chair taste like?

What is a chair used for?
What sex is that chair?
What part of a chair is this?
How fast is this chair?
Is that a couch?

One can, of course, contrive to evoke concise responses to inappropriate questions: "This is a psychological test; answer 'yes' or 'no': Is a chair sexy?" A response to such a query may be revealing to some investigations (any selection of alternative responses is presumably informative of something), but not to what the ethnographer seeks to describe: the relations between appropriate behavior and the cultural settings for such behavior.

NOTES

[1] These procedures are an outgrowth of those employed in Frake 1961. The present formulation owes a great deal to discussions with Duane Metzger and Gerald Williams, whose writings exemplify intensive application of similar methodological notions (Metzger and Williams). I am also indebted to the editor of this volume, Roy D'Andrade. This paper was written with the support of USPHS Grant M-6187, under the direction of the National Institute of Mental Health.

[2] This characterization of *Notes and Queries* is more apropos of earlier editions (1874, 1892, 1899, 1912, 1929) than of the sixth edition (1951).

[3] Any representation of an object or an event by an informant, for example, can be useful (for use of native drawings and models by Harold Conklin, see Rockefeller Institute 1961). In this paper we are concerned with verbal descriptions as representations of objects and events.

[4] English forms enclosed by single quotation marks are *glosses*, devices to enable talking about Subanun concepts without using the Subanun forms that represent them. They are selected for their mnemonic, not their defining, value. Thus 'beer' represents the Subanun concept labeled *gasi*, not the English concept labeled *beer*.

[5] Identifications by the Philippine National Museum from specimens collected by the writer. Listing partially matching botanical identifications is the only way the referents of plant categories can be identified with any accuracy. Although there are many reasons why botanical identifications are necessary in ethnobotanical descriptions, it should be emphasized that they do not provide *definitions* of Subanun categories, nor can defining features of Subanun categories be extracted from matched botanical identifications with procedures analogous to those used in performing componential analyses of kinship categories from matched lists and kin terms and kin types (Frake 1961).

REFERENCES CITED

Burkhill, I. H., 1935, A dictionary of the economic products of the Malay Peninsula. London Crown Agents for the Colonies. 2 vols.

Chomsky, Noam, 1959, *In* B. F. Skinner, ed., Review of verbal behavior. Language 35.1:26–58.

Conklin, H. C., 1962, Lexicographical treatment of folk taxonomies. *In* F. W. Householder and Sol Saporta, eds., Problems in lexicography. International Journal of American Linguistics 28.2 Part IV.

Ebeling, C. L., 1962, Linguistic units. Janua Linguarum 12, 's-Gravenhage, Mouton & Co.

Frake, C. O., 1960, The Eastern Subanun of Mindanao. *In* G. P. Murdock, ed., Social structure in Southeast Asia, pp. 51–64. Chicago, Quadrangle Books.

———, 1961, The diagnosis of disease among the Subanun of Mindanao. American Anthropologist 63.1:113–132.

———, 1962, The ethnographic study of cognitive systems. *In* Thomas Gladwin and William C. Sturtevant, eds., Anthropology and human behavior. Washington, Anthropological Society of Washington.

———, 1964, A structural description of Subanun "religious behavior." *In* Ward Goodenough, ed., Explorations in cultural anthropology. New York, McGraw-Hill.

Metzger, Duane, Gerald E. Williams, 1962, Patterns of primary personal reference in a Tzeltal community. Anthropology Research Projects: Preliminary Report No. 10. Stanford.

———, 1963a, A formal ethnographic analysis of Tenejapa Ladino weddings. American Anthropologist 65.4.

———, 1963b, Procedures and results in the study of native categories: Tzeltal firewood. Anthropology Research Projects: Preliminary Report No. 12. Stanford.

———, 1963c, Tenejapa medicine I: the curer. Southwestern Journal of Anthropology 19:216–234.

Rockefeller Institute, 1961, Visiting anthropologist shows drawings clue to form of culture. The Rockefeller Institute Quarterly 5.4.

Royal Anthropological Institute, 1951, Notes and queries on anthropology. Sixth edition. London, Routledge and Kegan Paul Ltd.

Ethnographic Description and the Study of Law

Mary Black
Duane Metzger

For all their lack of "shared meanings," vagueness of definitions, and multiplicity of structural solutions, participants in the world's cultures do in fact draw inferences, promulgate plans, and act with a considerable degree of consistency. Complex, habitual patterns of inference and action survive

Reproduced by permission of the authors and the American Anthropological Association from the *American Anthropologist*, Vol. 6, part 2 (Special Publication), pp. 141–165 (December 1965).

through many generations. Pattern analysis has become a well developed science in recent years, and ethnographic pattern-finding procedures are being reformulated in order to utilize available approaches and technology.

This paper will describe two occasions when a recently developed eliciting procedure was used to gather information related to the ethnography of law. The resulting ethnographic descriptions will then be discussed in terms of the kind of eliciting, the kind of information, and the kinds of "law" involved. The format of the descriptions is also of interest.

Ethnography has traditionally meant the study of individual cultures. An ethnographic description of law, then, is an ethnographer's attempt to learn about and describe whatever behavior, if any, is found to fall within what people conceive "law" to be in the culture he is studying. This implies (1) that these people conceive of a domain that is "law"; (2) that an anthropologist can tap, or inventory, their relevant conceptions; and (3) that he can report this ideology to his fellow anthropologists in a way that is both understandable and subject to precise verification or disproof by colleagues who do not wish to take his word for it. These requirements are formidable. An attempt to meet them includes the following considerations:

1) DOMAIN   Our approach is not designed to contribute very much to the definition of universally applicable boundaries of any domain of culture, so the much-disputed boundary of the "legal" as a cross-cultural category is not an a priori concern. The approach is designed to discover boundaries of particular conceptual subsystems within particular cultures. It is a search for sets of questions that the people of a society are responding to when they behave in systematic ways, and for the relations existing among these questions and responses. To determine the relevant stimuli in the scenes that he observes—the things that make a difference—is the job of the ethnographer as interpreted here. To the extent that he predetermines his descriptive units (including the domain itself) on the basis of things that make a difference in some other system, he defeats his objective. The eliciting heuristic starts of necessity with Western categories, but the ethnographer can discard this position once he has an initial set of responses, and from then on everything he does depends on the last thing he did. The boundaries of the system he explores are revealed as he proceeds. (See Metzger 1960, Frake 1963, and Nader and Metzger 1963 for some explorations of "legal" boundaries.)

2) ELICITING OF NATIVE CONCEPTS OR IDEOLOGY   The ethnographer takes as the basic unit of an ideology (or set of expectations for behaviors) a stable question-and-response pair produced spontaneously by native informants. A native concept is thus operationally defined as a Q-R unit in the native language that remains stable with several informants and with repeated elicitations from the same informant. The procedures for actual eliciting of such verbal material, and plans for putting it into correspondence

with observations of nonverbal behavior, will be discussed and illustrated in this paper.

3) DESCRIPTIVE FORMAT   The present development of systematic ethnographic procedures aims to provide simultaneously for formalizing eliciting technique and for reporting data in a public scientific language. The point in "formal descriptions" where description ends and analysis begins has been difficult to determine. In the approach described in this paper, the procedures both for gathering ethnographic data and for their storage and retrieval as well have been explicitly formalized, with a strict cost-accounting of the empirical bases for investigators' inferences and conclusions. Attention to descriptive format is being pushed back to the first stages of data-collecting, for we believe that a formal description of part of a culture is a public scientific document only to the extent that the data on which it is based and the procedures followed in gathering and analyzing them are made public along with the results of the analysis. This notion has been expressed in the past, but the unwieldiness of its execution has usually been discouraging. It now appears that computers can help reduce such an approach to manageable proportions—if the data have been systematically gathered and recorded. The clerical function of the machine is undisputed, its contribution being proportionate to the orders of magnitude of data to be stored and processed. Computational routines can also perform complicated sorting tasks, reassembling the data for analysis in ways that would be prohibitive manually; for example they can produce concordances of all the significant units in an analysis (see section on the analysis of Tenejapa law materials).

For an initial contribution toward an ethnography of law, the ideas and methods presented above have been turned on two problems: (1) mapping the variable codification of concepts regarding remedial measures for settlement of disputes and trouble-making within one cultural group (Čahpanel in Tenejapa), and (2) discovering within another cultural group the structure of a segment of the categorization of legal role types (American law terms). Each of these two applications has produced a body of verbal data. Both might be termed monolingual eliciting, though in one case the native language was the ethnographer's own and in the other it was the informants' only. The goal in both studies was to develop techniques for eliciting and describing the more or less well codified inference structures that order people's expectations of their own and others' cultural roles and behavior. (This is, in general, what is meant here by "ideology." It is similar to Goodenough's "ideational order" [1964:11–12].) One powerful instrument for symbolic expression of such structures is language, and work on the ethnography of law to date has been directed to the indexing of verbal material. Setting this material into correspondence with observation of other expressions of cultural patterns is foreseen as a desirable further step.[1]

BACKGROUND

Some recent work in ethnography has been directed toward devising better systematic ways of finding out how people in alien cultures arrange their knowledge of the world. It is of primary importance to have reliable methods of learning how they sort out the raw data of experience, and especially of determining which features have significance for them and which go unnoticed. Hymes (1964a) has described the acquiring of such a methodology as "the devising of improved techniques for tapping, through linguistically expressed categories, the cognitive worlds of participants in the culture," and has called it an "ethnographic semantics." Sturtevant (1964) has published a survey of this and related work entitled "Studies in Ethnoscience," which title refers to descriptions of "the system of knowledge and cognition typical of a given culture." The goal is an ethnographic description that parallels the classifications, or the system of concepts, of the people described.

Investigators in this field generally agree that it is the ethnographer's duty to report the significant dimensions as perceived and reacted to by participants in the culture, and that discovery of people's cognitive arrangements has relevance not for psychology alone but for ethnography as well (cf. D'Andrade and Romney 1964). Members of a subject culture base their inferences, their plans, and their actions and reactions on observable cues in their environment, which the ethnographer can perceive as well as they, once trained by them to do so. His resulting analysis then is expressed in *their* meaningful units, derived not from their awareness of these as units, nor from their explicit knowledge of the system as finally described but from informants' reactions to situations of controlled variation when they are presented with the potentially significant stimuli of the environment.

Environments employed in this work have been largely linguistic: native terminological systems, or "folk taxonomies," have been elicited and analyzed by Conklin and by Frake, while pioneering studies by Lounsbury and by Goodenough were focused on kinship terms. (For methodological statements and bibliographies, see Conklin 1962, 1964; Frake 1962, 1964; Sturtevant 1964; Goodenough 1964.) More general ethnographic domains, such as weddings, firewood, and curers, have been described by Metzger and Williams (1962a,b, and 1963a,b) using distributional analyses of linguistic contexts. (For discussion of procedures, see Metzger 1963.)

Intensive work is being continued by these and other investigators in the development of field procedures for simultaneous data eliciting, data analysis, and validation or testing of interpretations. These procedures are designed to be self-corrective in the field, and the resulting statements to be replicable and precise rather than persuasive and plausible—statements with implications for behavior that are so explicit as to allow correction or addition at any future time by the same or other investigators.

THEORETICAL BASIS FOR QUESTION-RESPONSE PROCEDURE

As has been stated, the basic investigative unit of the procedure is Question-and-Response. The ethnographer's questions as well as the informants' answers are reported, in compliance with the notion that a scientifically useful report carries an account of the activities of the observer, or measuring instrument, in interaction with the subject matter. But there are more notions than that one involved. There is, for example, the notion of the primacy of the questioning activity. It is basic to communications theory that you don't start getting any information from an utterance or event until you know what it is in response to—you must know what question is being answered. It could be said of ethnography that until you know the question that someone in the culture is responding to you can't know many things about the response. Yet the ethnographer is greeted, in the field, with an array of *responses*. He needs to know what question people are *answering* in their every act. He needs to know which questions are being taken for granted because they are what "everybody knows" without thinking. To find out these implicit questions is not easy. When anthropologists say they are describing a people's "world view" they are saying in essence: "These are the big questions asked of the world by this people, and these are this people's answers." But when for comparative purposes the ethnographer proposes one set of so-called universal questions that are relevant in all cultures, including concepts such as "man's relation to the supernatural," he may be obscuring rather than illuminating the world view. For example, some people appear not to make our distinction between the natural and the supernatural (cf. Hallowell on the Ojibwa, 1960), and so a question meant to relate these two European concepts will not produce any sort of stable and reliable response from these people. Thus the task of the ethnographer is to discover questions that seek the relationships among entities that are conceptually meaningful to the people under investigation.

It is noteworthy that as early as World War I, the British philosopher R. G. Collingwood (1939) was formulating a new "logic of question and answer," insisting that the basic unit of thought was not the proposition (as was then held), but "propositions . . . together with the questions they were meant to answer." Collingwood wrote, "A logic in which the answers are attended to and the questions neglected is a false logic." Note that he was referring to the question, usually unstated, that the proposition is *intended* to answer. The question is implicit, as far as the speaker is concerned:

he assumes it is known to the hearer. It was Collingwood's thesis that the question may actually be unknown or mistaken by the hearer and, if so, he is incapable of understanding and responding appropriately. It was not until World War II that social scientists fully grasped this as a basic principle of codification of information (Reusch and Bateson 1951). For ethnography this principle has a special relevance. Whereas the ordinary speaker normally assumes knowledge of his implicit question on the part of his hearer, the ethnographic approach used here assumes lack of knowledge of the questions on the part of the anthropologist, who must proceed systematically to learn them from informants.

THE ELICITING PROCESS

The discovery of ways of formulating questions in the informant's language is critical to the eliciting process described here. The basic formula might be stated as follows: The ethnographer is being trained by the informant to behave linguistically or verbally in ways which the informant considers appropriate. An early search for question words and the syntax of interrogative sentences is indicated—without, however, making a complete grammatical analysis of the language. When the language is unknown to the investigator, the use of bilingual informants speeds up the gathering of data in early stages, but it is in no way a necessary condition, as will be shown in the Tzeltal study to be described. The American law study was conducted in a language native to both the investigators and the informants, yet presented similar problems in the learning and testing of appropriate verbal behavior.

In any case, the early stages of eliciting the forms are the most difficult, for the ethnographer begins his pattern searching knowing neither the forms nor the functions of the events he observes. Like a child of the culture, he starts to look for units that remain stable across a variety of contexts and to determine which forms have similar value. His problem is to avoid two types of error: forms which have similar value must not be identified as different; forms which have different values must not be identified as similar. The ethnographer, in dealing with both linguistic and nonlinguistic events, knows that what appear to him to be meaningful and well-defined examples of similarity may from the native's point of view be different. His task is to be alert to the distributional patterns of signs and to the native's responses to these signs. He can start, like the child, searching out modes of inquiry that bring stable responses.[2]

A primary reason for working with native-language questions from the very beginning is that they constitute reliable, reconstructible, congruent patterns of stimulation for the native speaker.

At first, the investigator directs the informant's attention to some question he (the investigator) has formulated in the native language. The ethnographer needs to test the question in two ways: Is it grammatically correct? Is it semantically construable, and, if so, ambiguously or unambiguously? He can test its grammaticality by asking the informant to repeat the question or to paraphrase it. He can test its semantic status by (1) observing the ease with which the informant responds, (2) direct questioning of the informant, (3) examining the linguistic form of the response, and (4) examining the semantic content of the responses. These tests are, of course, only heuristic. The final test of the appropriateness of the question is the stability with which it elicits the same responses across eliciting sessions with the same informant, and across informants.

Informants rapidly become trained in the method, distinguishing when they are being asked to improve on the phrasing of a question from when a response is desired. Soon they can produce their own questions with only slight and indirect prompting from the ethnographer. A few of the ways this can be done are (1) to ask the informant "what is an interesting question about _____?", (2) to ask the informant "what is a question to which the answer is _____?", and (3) to ask the informant to write a text in question-and-answer form on some topic of interest to the investigator. Informants who know or can be taught to write their language can be put to work producing texts that provide new source material for eliciting.

Questions consist of two parts. The first and more general part of the question is called the frame (F). The frame may be considered as the interrogative skeleton of the question. An example of a frame used in the American law study was:

(F) Does X take cases to court?

The second and more specific part of the question is called the term (T). The term directs the informant's attention to some specific area of content. An example of one of the terms used with the frame above was:

(T) Attorney General.

Hence the entire question presented to the informant was:

(Q) Does the Attorney General take cases to court?

The actual responses elicited by this question illustrate an important aspect of the procedure. On one occasion the informant answered "Yes" and on another "No." This pattern of responses immediately indicates that there is something wrong with the question as a whole. It might be that the frame, or the term, or some part of either was an ungrammatical or anomalous whole (that is, that the term was inappropriate for the frame). In the above case, part of the frame needed revision. The informant subsequently produced the following two frames to replace the defective one:

(F) Does X press litigation?

(F) Does X try cases?

Both new frames then produced consistent responses with respect to the term Attorney General and to other terms as well.

The example above illustrates one kind of continuity in the eliciting process. The ethnographer simultaneously corrects his earlier work and moves closer to the precise concepts being employed by his informant.

Another kind of continuity in the eliciting process is provided by constructing new questions out of the material obtained as responses to earlier questions. As responses are obtained, they are entered as terms in previously existing frames to form new questions. An example of this frame-term-response productivity can be provided by the following excerpt from an elicitation session in Tenejapa Tzeltal:

> (Q) /bi ya yak' ta čahpanel te kunerol e/
> 'When does the Mayor give justice?'
> (R) /ha? te me ?ay mač'a ya sle mulil e/
> 'If there is someone who commits a crime.'

This response permitted the reuse of a previously formulated frame to elicit the informant's concept of categories of crimes:

> (Q) /binti sbil huhuten te mulil e/
> 'What are the names of each kind of crime?'
> (R) /?ay č'in mulil/
> 'There are small (minor) crimes.'
> /?ay muk'ul mulil/
> 'There are large (major) crimes.'

An extended illustration of this productivity of the frame-term distinction is given in the Tzeltal study, where nearly the entire corpus of material gathered to date was constructed from a few sets of responses to initial questions, including those just given. This was possible even though one ethnographer began with no knowledge of the language and at the end of two months of eliciting could employ it to only a limited extent. This illustration will show that by carefully controlling the eliciting process, it is possible to link together frames, terms, and responses in ways that show both the relations of independence and those of dependence that exist between them. Kinds of distributional analysis possible with data elicited in this way will be discussed with regard to the Tzeltal study.

ČAHPANEL IN TENEJAPA

ELICITING   A study was recently initiated which undertakes to use these procedures to learn something of the ideology of "conflict-resolution" in the municipio of Tenejapa in highland Chiapas, Mexico. The Mayan language spoken by the Tenejapanecans is Tzeltal. Although the informants were bilingual, one of the ethnographers whose work is presented here knew neither Tzeltal nor the contact language (Spanish), and was therefore left with the most radical form of the eliciting procedure: monolingual eliciting in the unknown language. That prior linguistic work on this language was available (Berlin 1962a, b; 1963a, b; Berlin and Romney 1964) and that some informants had learned to write it alleviated the situation somewhat, for the immediate problem with monolingual eliciting is to develop a beginning description of the informant's grammar as well as a beginning description of some aspect of his culture. It has been demonstrated that ethnographic description of semantic or cognitive systems can be productively carried out as part of the language-description process at whatever stage is necessary.

The initial problem in eliciting involves discovering the modes of stimulation which will produce responses of a certain type on the part of the informant. As has been noted, the investigator can observe proper kinds of responses before he can observe (and hence record) proper patterns of stimulation. In fact, in monolingual eliciting, the first stimuli may have to be either actions (pointing) or visual materials, and the interrogative material can only follow upon some analysis of responses. That is what was referred to earlier as the eliciting heuristic: any device to aid the informant in producing an initial set of responses. The ethnographer can then record the shape of the responses by some systematic notation, and move toward determining and constructing appropriate stimulus units. Use of bilingual informants (and in this case a Spanish-English dictionary) allows an early search for possible question words, such as the who, what, when, where, why, etc., series in English (or the /mač'a/, /bi-binti/, /bi?ora/, /banti/, /bi yu?un/, etc., series in Tzeltal). After constructing tentative questions, and testing their appropriateness (both grammatical and semantic) with the informant, the ethnographer can begin addressing such questions to informants and recording both questions and responses formally. The subsequent construction of second-order questions, and analysis of distributions, can proceed, already focusing on semantic patterns in the relevant domain, though knowledge of the language is yet minimal. Thus the ethnographer can concentrate almost from the beginning on the potentially available set of questions in the unknown language that is in fact used to direct inquiry in some particular domain of content.

THE CORPUS   The difficulty—as well as the possibility—of learning systematically, in an unknown language, something so complex as the concepts held by Tenejapanecans regarding proper and expected manners of disposing of trouble-making in their community, is shown by examining the results of the first two months of this field study. Coverage of content is wide and thin, reflecting the investigator's concentration on running several "contrast sets" of terms, originally obtained as series of responses, through as many different frames as possible with each of three informants in the time allowed.

A Tzeltal term, /čahpanel/, obtained from informants, appeared to be in some correspondence with the English domain of 'law, justice.' Investigation of the range and structure of this Tzeltal domain in Tenejapa began with eliciting the classes of /čahpanel/ using the frame:

(Q) /binti sbil huhuten te čahpanel e/
'What is the name of each kind of law?'
(R) /ʔay čahpanel yuʔun kirsanuetik/
'There is law of the Tenejapa people.'
(R) /ʔay čahpanel yuʔun kašlanetik/
'There is law of the ladinos.'
(R) /ʔay čahpanel ta č'ulna/
'There is church law.'
(R) /ʔay čahpanel ta husgaro/
'There is civil law.'

Focusing for the moment on the last response of this list, /čahpanel ta husgaro/, a list of the administrators of this type of law was produced in responses to the frame:

(Q) /mač'a ya yak' čahpanel ta husgaro/
'Who administers the civil law?'
(R) /te tatik kunerol e/
'Mr. Mayor.'
(R) /te sekretaryo e/
'The municipal secretary.'
(R) /te bankilal rehrol e/
'The senior regidor.'
(R) /te sintiko e/
"The sindico.'
(R) /te hwes e/
'The judge.'

Rank ordering within the group of administrators was determined by means of the frame:

(Q) /mač'a sbabi ya yak' čahpanel ta husgaro/
'Who is the first administrator of the law?'

in which the underlined slot is filled successively by the ordinal numbers "first" through "fifth," /sbabi, ščebal, ʔošebal, ščanebal, hoʔebal/. The rank order is the same as the order in which the responses were given to the question, "Who administers the civil law?"

Investigating the functions of the administrators of justice with the frame:

(Q) /bi ya yak' ta čahpanel te kunerol e/
'When does the Mayor give justice?'

produced the following response.

(R) /haʔ te me ʔay mač'a ya sle mulil e/
'If there is someone who commits a crime.'

Classes of crimes were established as follows:

    (Q) /binti sbil huhuten te <u>mulil</u> e/
        'What is the name of each kind of crime?'
    (R) /ʔay č'in <u>mulil</u>/
        'There are minor crimes.'
    (R) /ʔay <u>muk'ul mulil</u>/
        'There are major crimes.'

Classes within these types of crimes were elicited with further questions constructed in combination with these responses:

    (Q) /binti sbil huhuten te <u>muk'ul mulil</u> e/
        'What is the name of each kind of major crime?'
    (R) /ʔay <u>miltomba</u>/
        'There is killing.'
    (R) /ʔay <u>ʔelek'il</u>/
        'There is stealing.'
    (R) /ʔay <u>¢ak'an¢</u>/
        'There is rape.'
    (R) /ʔay <u>poh k'inal</u>/
        'There is land robbery.'
    (R) /ʔay <u>mahtomba</u>/
        'There is fighting.'
    (Q) /binti sbil huhuten te <u>č'in mulil</u> e/
        'What is the name of each kind of minor crime?'
    (R) /ʔay <u>ʔaʔynomil</u>/
        'There is gossip.'
    (R) /ʔay <u>net'tomba ta tiʔ ¢'akan</u>/
        'There is moving of land markers.'
    (R) /ʔay <u>ʔutomba</u>/
        'There is quarreling (scolding).'
    (R) /ʔay <u>laʔbanwaneh</u>/
        'There is criticism (mockery).'
    (R) /ʔay <u>tok'tawaneh</u>/
        'There is verbal insult (cursing).'
    (R) /ʔay <u>paslot</u>/
        'There is lying.'

and again, using the new responses as terms in the same frame:

    (Q) /binti sbil huhuten te <u>miltomba</u> e/
        'What is the name of each kind of killing?'
    (R) /ʔay <u>tuhk'ael</u>/
        'There is shooting.'
    (R) /ʔay <u>bohel</u>/
        'There is machete-ing.'
    (R) /ʔay <u>lowel</u>/
        'There is knifing.'

(R) /ˀay pič'el ta nuk'il/
'There is strangling.'
(R) /ˀay hohk'anel ta teˀ/
'There is hanging.'
(Q) /binti sbil huhuten te ˀelek'il e/
'What is the name of each kind of stealing?'
(R) /ˀay ˀelek' tak'in/
'There is stealing money.'
(R) /ˀay ˀelek' čambalam/
'There is stealing animals.'
(R) /ˀay ˀelek' k'uˀil pak'al/
'There is stealing clothing.'
(R) /ˀay ˀelek' ˀišim čenek'/
'There is stealing corn and beans.'
(R) /ˀay ˀelek' čiˀpah/
'There is stealing fruit.'
(Q) /binti sbil huhuten te ¢akˀan¢ e/
'What is the name of each kind of rape?'
(R) /ˀay hun naš/
'There is only one kind.'

The productivity of this particular frame is obvious, in its establishing contrast sets and hierarchical (taxonomic) relations. Before English glosses had been worked out for most of the Tzeltal responses, they were being used as terms in further questions, and their distributional meanings were becoming clearer. Also, certain regularities and partial similarities in the forms of the language could be examined.

Eventually, each of the "kinds of crimes" was inserted as a term in a variety of other frames. For example, the frame:

(Q) ·/bi ya spas te kunerol te me ˀay mačˀa ya sle mulil e/
'What does the Mayor do when someone commits a crime?'

produced the following responses:

(R) /ya ščuhkotik/
'He puts us in jail.'
(R) /ya yičˀ sk'anel smulta/
'He levies a fine.'

From these responses, new frames were constructed in which the kinds of crime were substituted as follows:

(Q) /hayeb stohol multa ta me ya smah sbaik/
'What is the fine if they fight with each other?'
(R) /čaˀwinik pešu/
'40 pesos.'

(R) /ʔošwinik pešu/
'60 pesos.'
(R) /hoʔwinik pešu/
'100 pesos.'
(Q) /hayeb stohol multa ta me ya smil sbaik/
'What is the fine if they kill each other?'
(R) /čeʔsiento pešu/
'200 pesos.'
(R) /mil pešu/
'1,000 pesos.'
(Q) /hayeb stohol multa ta me ya yelek'anik/
'What is the fine if they steal?'
(R) /lahuniš čaʔwinik pešu/
'30 pesos.'
(Q) /hayeb stohol multa ta me ya yak' čamel/
'What is the fine if they commit witchcraft?'
(R) /maʔyuk multa/
'There is no fine.'

Another set of frames elicited the sequence of events following a crime, as follows:

(Q) /mač'a ya sba yal parte te k'alal lah htul winik/
'Who notifies the authority when a man dies?'
(R) /te stat e/
'His father.'
(R) /te šnič'an e/
'His son.'
(R) /te yinam e/
'His wife.'
(R) /mač'auk smolol sȼakil/
"Some members of his family.'
(Q) /mač'a yik' ya šbahtik yilel ʔanima te k'alal lah htul winik/
'Who goes to investigate a death when a man dies?'
(R) /te hwes e/
'The judge.'
(R) /te bankilal rehrol e/
'The senior regidor.'
(R) /te sintiko e/
'The sindico.'
(R) /te ʔalkal kašlan e/
'The ladino alcalde.'
(R) /te bankilal ʔalkal e/
'The senior alcalde.'
(R) /te čantul ʔihȼ'inal rehroletik e/
'Four junior regidores.'

(Q) /bi ya spasik te čukawaletik e te k'alal ya štal ta sna ʔanima/
'What does the investigating commission do when it arrives at the house of the dead person?'

(R) /ya stiʔik mut/
'They eat chicken.'

(R) /ya yuč'ik maȼ'
'They drink pozol.'

(Q) /bi ya spasik te čukawaletik e ta patil ya stiʔik mut sok ya yuč'ik maȼ'/
'What does the investigating commission do after they eat chicken and drink pozol?'

(R) /ya šhilik ta ʔanima te hwes sok te sintiko e/
'The judge and the sindico go to where the body is.'

(R) /ya šbahtik ta sleel ta hmilawal te šan yan rehroletik e/
'The rest of the regidores go to look for the killer.'

(Q) /bi ya spasik te hwes sok te sintiko e ta patil ya šhilik ta ʔanima/
'What do the judge and the sindico do after they go to the body?'

(R) /ya yiltikla batik ʔehčinahem/
'They look for the wounds (the cause of death).'

(Q) /bi ya spasik te šan yan rehroletik e ta patil ya šbahtik ta sleel ta hmilawal/
'What do the rest of the regidores do after they go to look for the killer?'

(R) /ta me ya sleik ta hmilawal ya suhtik tal ta sna ʔanima sole hmilawal/
'If they find the killer they return with him to the dead person's house.'

(R) /ta me ma sleik ta hmilawal ya suhtik tal ta sna ʔanima/
'If they don't find the killer they return to the house of the dead person.''

(Q) /bi ya spasik te hwes sok te sintiko e ta patil ya yiltik la batik ʔehčinahem/
'What do the judge and the sindico do after they inspect the body for the cause of death?'

(R) /ya snakan ta hun/
'They write a report.'

(Q) /bi ya spasik te hwes sok te sintiko e ta patil ya snakan ta hun/
'What do the judge and the sindico do after they write a report?'

(R) /ya šlihk yalik sok smolol ʔakil te me yakbel ta lum/
'They begin to discuss with the relatives whether or not they will take the body back to the town center.''

(Q) /bi ya spasik te hwes sok te sintiko e ta patil ya šlihk yalik sok smolol ʔakil te me yakbel ta lum/
'What do the judge and sindico do after they begin to discuss with the relatives whether or not they will take the body back to the town?'

(R) /ya šlihk yal tal hayeb multa/
'They begin to talk of the payment (for not taking the body to the town center to be buried there).'

(Q) /hayeb stohol multa ta smukenal/
'How much is the payment (which the family makes to the investigating commission) for the privilege of burying the body (in the paraje)?'

(R) /ho?winik pešu/
'100 pesos.'

(R) /čanwinik pešu/
'80 pesos.'

(Q) /bi ya spasik te čukawaletik e te me ma yak'be smulta ta smukenal/
'What does the investigating commission do if the family does not make the burial payment?'

(R) /ya šbahtik ta lum sok ?anima/
'They take the body back to the town center.'

(Q) /bi ya spasik te čukawaletik e te me yak'be smulta ta smukenal/
'What does the investigating commission do if they (the family) make the burial payment?'

(R) /ya šlihk shok'obe te me ?ay stohol shatobil/
'They begin to discuss the amount of the autopsy (payment).'

(Q) /hayeb stohol multa ta shatobil/
'How much is the autopsy payment (a payment which prevents the commission from doing an autopsy)?'

(R) /lahuneb yoš winik tak'in/
'50 pesos.'

(Q) /bi ya spasik te čukawaletik e te me yak'be smulta/
'What does the investigating commission do if they (the family) make the autopsy payment?'

(R) /tey ya smuhk te sna e/
'He is buried in his house.'

(Q) /bi ya spasik te čukawaletik e te me ma yak'be smulta ta shatobil/
'What does the commission do if the autopsy payment is not made?'

(R) /ya shat ta pwérsa/
'The autopsy is required.'

(Q) /banti ya smuk te ?anima e/
'Where do they bury the dead person?'

(R) /ya smuk ta yutna/
'He is buried inside the house.'

(R) /ya smuk ta kapasánto/
'He is buried in the cemetery.'

(Q) /mas lek bal ya smuk ta yutna mak ya smuk ta kapasánto/
'Is it better to bury a person in the house or in the cemetery?'

(R) /mas lek ta yutna/
'It is better in the house.'

(Q) /bi yu?un mas lek ta yutna/
'Why is it better in the house?'

(R) /melel k'ušobel sba yu?un ha?al/
'Because otherwise he will feel the rain.'

(Q) /bi ya spas te hmilawal e te me lom p'ih/
'What does the killer do if he is smart?'

(R) /ya š?an/
'He flees.'

(R) /ya spakan hilel te ?anima e/
'He turns the dead man face down.'

(Q) /te me ya š?an hmilawal banti ?an/
'If the killer flees, where does he go?'

(R) /ya šbaht ta pinka/
'He goes to work on a ranch.'

(R) /ya šbaht ta sk'inal ?oščuhk/
'He goes to Oxchuc.'

(R) /ya šbaht ta sk'inal k'ankuhk/
'He goes to Cancuc.'

(Q) /bi yu?un ya spakan hilil te ?anima e/
'Why does he turn the dead man face-down?'

(R) /ma sk'an ta ščuhk/
'He does not wish to be captured.'

(R) /ma ba ya stak yil šč'ulel ?anima/
'The soul of the dead person will not be able to see him (and help in his capture).'

(Q) /bi ya spas te hmilawal e te me lom bol/
'What does the killer do if he is stupid?'

(R) /biluk naš ta šhil ta ?anima/
'He does not turn the dead man face-down.'

(Q) /bi ya spasik te čukawaletik e ta patil ya sta hmilawal/
'What does the commission do after they find the killer (if they do)?'

(R) /ya ščukik ta ?ora/
'They tie him up.'

(Q) /bi ya spasik te čukawaletik e ta patil ya ščukik ta ?ora/
'What does the commission do after they tie him up?'

(R) /ya snitik bel ta lum/
'They lead him to the town center.'

(Q) /bi ya spasik te čukawaletik e ta patil ya snitik bel ta lum/
'What does the commission do after they lead him to the town center?'

(R) /ya sk'ot ta čukel/
'They put him in jail.'

This sample of the type of corpus obtained from eliciting is sufficient to indicate that it will be possible to infer certain structural relations (see next section on analysis), and also that a wealth of questions is waiting to be constructed from the material now at hand.

Many of the responses raise further questions. For example, why is there no fine for cases of witchcraft? Why is there such considerable variation in the size of fines for killing? A systematic substitution of question words in all the frames used has not yet been attempted. Also, distinctions in criteria between different sets and between members of one set were sought in some cases in a systematic manner, but others are yet to be completed. For example, some time was spent trying to elicit the features by which informants distinguish /ʔaʔynomil/'gossip' from /paslot/'lying' as these glosses were suspected of being inadequate, but the distinctive features by which 'crimes' are assigned to the 'major' or the 'minor' categories were only just begun. Analysis will indicate precisely what further eliciting will be needed in order to get or test informants' critical discrimination among all such items of the present corpus. Furthermore, it is clear that the sets themselves are not exhaustive; though informants indicated they had finished giving 'kinds of killing,' and the ethnographer let the list be closed in order to get on with the next level of questioning, additional 'kinds' actually were mentioned later (but were arbitrarily excluded); more could surely be elicited.

Moreover, the corpus is enriched by a number of texts written by the informants telling of actual cases of crimes and how they were settled. These will provide new forms, potential structural slots, and other source material for further eliciting. A rough English glossing of one of these texts can be given here:

> It happened that a man from the paraje Tzahalchen was scolded by another man, and they quarreled. The man from Tzahalchen accused the second man's bull of eating his corn. The second man denied his bull was loose. They both grew angry and they decided to come to Tenejapa to talk to the Mayor.
>
> So the owner of the cornfield said, "Mr. Mayor, I've come to speak to you concerning this man's bull who ate the corn in my cornfield." The Mayor answered, "And why didn't you ask the man to repay you for your loss, right then and there?" The man said, "He didn't want to pay me right then and there, because he's got a very bad character."
>
> And then the Mayor said to the owner of the bull: "Why didn't you take care of your bull?" "Well, Mr. Mayor, it's because his lasso tore, and he went loose. Shall I repay the loss of corn?" "If it's the truth, you must repay the loss of corn," the Mayor said. "All right, then, Mr. Mayor," the man said. Thus it was settled, and the man wasn't fined.
>
> All of this is the work of the Mayor, to settle the cases that need to be settled, under his authority. Because he is like our father, the Mayor, for all the people of Tenejapa. If there were not a person who is there to think about all the people, no one would know where to go to settle a matter. But instead, he is the great father of the people, no matter from what parajes they come to ask his aid.

ANALYSIS   Although it is probably spurious to separate "analysis" from "corpus" we intend now to describe some of the analytic aids provided by machine processing. (The corpus of all eliciting and texts is stored on IBM cards, in Tzeltal and in English, coded for a number of different sortings including identification of frames, terms, and responses. After approximately one month, the ethnographer was able to elicit directly onto layout sheets for card-punching.)

At the simplest level, the computer produces printouts which tell the ethnographer what questions he has asked what informant, and in what order. Ideally, machine processing is begun at once, on the records of the first formal eliciting sessions, so that while still in the field the ethnographer can receive information about the state of his corpus which will allow him to cover gaps and also to make inferences which can then be tested with informants. It is true that this is what ethnographers and linguists always have done in the field, on paper or in their heads. However, (1) machines can do it faster and more accurately; (2) the corpus is at once in a form ready for more sophisticated analysis, by the same or by other investigators; (3) the record is public and available, from raw data through each operation and inference of the investigator, and (4) the amounts and detailed nature of data required for good pattern analysis, which were prohibitive manually, can now be handled by computers. For example, the present corpus is about as large as can be kept track of manually; the ethnographer kept charts on questions asked and on informants, but systematic inspection of responses became unwieldy. Yet this corpus is now only a springboard for finding out about Tenejapa law.

At another level, the problem mentioned above of isolating some distinctive features by which people of Tenejapa recognize and assign great crimes and small, or differentiate acts called /ʔaʔynomil/ from those called /paslot/, can be greatly facilitated by computer routines. All instances of the occurrence of one of these forms in the question-response units can be printed out for examination. Concordances can also be assembled of each type of descriptive unit: frames, terms, responses, or sets consisting of a frame and all of the terms inserted in it, or a single question and all of its responses (sorted as to informant, if desired). Hence the relations of co-occurrence in a question-response unit may be examined for a large number of frame-term, term-response, and frame-response pairs.

Other kinds of formal distributional relationships are also subject to analysis. E.g., frame-sets, term-sets, and response-sets may be defined as the set of units of the named type such that each member co-occurs in the same environment (defined in terms of the two other types of units). These sets form distributionally defined domains whose internal structure may be further analyzed. Since lexical material which occurred first in a response was often inserted later as a term, and forms which had served in the status of term could be added to existing frames, it can be seen that complex distributional patterns may be found. The kind of "meaning" discovered in such distributional relationship contributes to a structural analysis (and of course to a linguistic analysis) independently of knowledge of the content, or translated, meaning. The latter, in fact, may never be precisely ascertainable, from one language to another. We feel that the monolingual eliciter, working without a contact language, has the advantage of avoiding translation misinterpretations of what his informants tell him, and in fact learns his "meanings" contextually—in much the same manner that his subjects learned them.

It may also be of interest to the investigator to distinguish two types of questions: those responded to with substantive information, and those that receive a "yes" or "no" response.[3] The latter type can be constructed out of information received from the former, and used as validation questions at a later date. However, they are also useful in gaining specific information not already known. In Tzeltal this latter type of question can be easily sorted out on the basis of question-word, which is coded for all data: only "yes-no" questions utilize the question-word /bal/. A sorting of the corpus on the basis of all question-words could be interesting as well.

AMERICAN LAW TERMS[4]

Table 1 below is a chart on which an ethnographer has displayed all the information formally elicited on the subject of one informant's terminological categorization of "lawyers." The chart represents a stage in the eliciting-analysis-validation process. It is neither the complete corpus of frames, terms, and responses by which the information was obtained, nor a final elegant analysis of minimal differences in criteria governing selection of lawyer reference terms. It is simply a working device constructed by the ethnographer in the field at a point in the eliciting where a systematic validation of data was desired. A summary statement of the information was accomplished by hazarding the beginning of an analysis that named dimensions of difference, or components. The nature of the corpus and analysis will be discussed after some consideration of eliciting, though in practice these three are not separated.

ELICITING   The informant was an American law student in California. His native language was English, as was the ethnographer's. The subculture under investigation was one known already in some degree to the ethnographer, though not as a specialist. This presents important differences from the Tzeltal study just described, namely, eliciting in the ethnographer's own language, and sharing with the informant a large number of over-all cultural patterns or codings, though not those restricted to the subculture under investigation.

It was not "monolingual eliciting" in the sense employed earlier. The problem of learning to use the language, in the grammatical sense, was eliminated. This offers an advantage for proceeding to less trivial types of infor-

Table 1.   Reference Terms for Lawyers

TERMS	Kind of Term 1.1	Settings 2.1	2.2	Kinds of Practice 3.1	3.2	3.3	3.4	3.5
*Lawyer	C	BC	AB	X	X	X	X	X
Attorney-at-law	C	C	C	X	X	X	X	X
*Lawyer	B	C	AB	0	C	0	BaBb	0
*Corporation lawyer	B	C	AB	Aa	C	A	Ba	C
Personal injury lawyer	B	C	AB	Ab	Aa	A	Aa	C
Insurance lawyer	B	C	AB	Ac	C	A	Ba	C
Insurance Co. lawyer	B	C	AB	Ac	Ab	A	Aa	C
*Tax lawyer	B	C	AB	Ad	C	A	Ba	C
Contract lawyer	B	C	AB	Af	C	?	B?	?
Property lawyer	B	C	AB	Ag	C	?	B?	?
*Divorce lawyer	B	C	AB	Ah	C	A	Ac	C
Gas & oil lawyer	B	C	AB	Aj	C	A	B?	C
*Trial lawyer	B	C	AB	AbBAc	AbAa	A	Aa	C
Criminal lawyer	B	C	AB	B	Ab	A	Aa	C
*Appellate lawyer	B	C	AB	C	B	A	Ad	C
*Defense lawyer	B	BC	AB	AcB	Ab	A	Aa	C
Prosecuting attorney	Aa	ABC	ABCD	B	Aa	Bb(2)	Aa	Ba
Prosecutor	Aa	ABC	ABCD	B	Aa	Bb(2)	Aa	Ba
District attorney	Aa	ABC	ABCD	C	Aa	Bb(3)	Aa	Ba
D.A.	Aa	BC	AB	C	Aa	Bb(3)	Aa	Ba
State's attorney	Aa	ABC	ABCD	B	Aa	Bb(2)	Aa	Ba
U.S. attorney	Aa	ABC	ABCD	C	Aa	Bb(3)	Aa	Ba
Asst. district attorney	Aa	ABC	ABCD	C	Aa	Bb(3)	Aa	Bb
Deputy prosec. attorney	Aa	ABC	ABCD	B	Aa	Bb(2)	Aa	Bb
U.S. attorney general	Aa	ABC	ABCD	C	C	Bb(3)	Bb	A
State attorney general	Aa	ABC	ABCD	C	C	Bb(2)	Bb	A
Solicitor general	Aa	ABC	ABCD	C	?	Bb(3)	Bb	Ba
U.S. commissioner	Aa	ABC	ABC?	?	?	Bb(3)	Bb	B?
Corporation counsel	Aa	ABC	ABCD	C	C	Bb(1)	Bb	A
General counsel	Ab	C	AB	Aa	C	Ba	Bb	A
Trial counsel	Ac	ABC	?	D	Ab	C	Ae	?
Counsel for the state	C	Ab	D	B	Aa	Bb(2)	Aa	BaBb
*Counsel for plaintiff	D	Ab	D	0	0	0	0	0
Plaintiff's counsel	D	Ab	D	0	0	0	0	0
*Counsel for defendant	D	Aa	D	0	0	0	0	0
Defense counsel	D	Aa	D	0	0	0	0	0

LEGEND: *—"Attorney" may be substituted for "Lawyer" or "Counsel." (Possibly "Attorney" more likely when talking to profession, "Lawyer" to laymen. Needs testing.)

AB—A and/or B
0—not relevant
X—any or all
?—information lacking

Table 1A.   Code for Reference Terms for Lawyers

Ego: Lawyers or law students
Informant: Second-Year Law Student, Stanford University

1.1 If you or any other lawyer referred to a person as a _____, you would be
calling him by a term that is:
  A: a title of a job
      a: given by the courts of some sovereignty.
      b: given by a private company or corporation.
      c: given by the military.
  B: descriptive of his kind of practice.
  C: a general term descriptive of all persons who have passed their bar exams
      and are members of the bar.
  D: restricted to a particular setting or situation.

2.1 A lawyer would be referred to as a _____ when:
  A: he is named in the formal process of courtroom proceedings on a case.
      a: representing defense.
      b: representing plaintiff.
  B: the speaker is referring to his work on a particular case.
  C: no reference to a particular case is involved.

2.2   A: the speaker is talking to other lawyers.
      B: the speaker is talking to non-lawyers.
      C: the term is written in a letter or printed in a letterhead.
      D: the term is written in official court records about a case.

3.1 If you or other lawyers referred to a lawyer as a _____, this would indicate
that he:
  A: has a civil practice and specializes in the area of civil law called

a: corporation law	f: contract law
b: personal injury law	g: property law
c: insurance law	h: domestic relations law
d: tax law	i: water law
e: admiralty law	j: gas and oil law

  B: specializes in the criminal field.
  C: is unspecialized, as to civil work or criminal work.
  D: is working under the Uniform Code of Military Justice.

3.2   A: does a lot of trial work
      a: for plaintiffs
      b: for defendants
      B: does a lot of appellate work.
      C: does neither trial nor appellate work to any great extent.

3.3   A: has clients who retain his services individually.
      B: is employed
      a: by a company or private corporation.
      b: by a sovereignty, namely (1) the city.
                                  (2) the state.
                                  (3) the Federal Government.
      C: is a member of the Armed Forces.

Table 1A.   Code for Reference Terms for Lawyers (*Continued*)

3.4   A: appears in
        a: trial court   c: divorce court
        b: probate court   d: appellate court
               e: military court
   B: does his legal work in his
        a: own office
        b: employer's office
3.5   A: is the head, or overlord, of the legal office of a corporation or sovereignty.
   B: works on the staff of the head of the legal office of a corporation or sovereignty,
        a: and also has lawyers working under him.
        b: and does not have any other lawyers working under him.
   C: has an independent practice or is a member of a private law firm.

---

mation than are initially possible in an exotic language, but it also holds pitfalls for trying to detect and avoid a priori assumptions as to what are the relevant questions, or stimuli. A false sense of communication and of familiarity with structure (both linguistic and cultural) has to be countered with the constant self-reminder: to the extent that the ethnographer knows precisely the question that the behavior was trying to answer, he understands—and no more. The self-corrective function of the formal eliciting procedure is here more indispensable than ever, and, in a sense, smaller knowledge of American law made for easier application.

The ethnographer first learned that "What kinds of lawyers are there?" is not a native-language question that the informant considered appropriate. The informant would instead ask, "What kinds of practice" lawyers had. He was asked that question. The first hour of eliciting provided such an array of relevant responses that all subsequent time was spent going narrower and deeper: that is, learning the proper questions to appropriately discriminate the phenomena already encountered. Five more hours sufficed to bring the corpus to the stage of refinement shown on the chart. (For comparison, as many as 100 hours of eliciting went into the present state of the Tzeltal corpus, comparable in many respects to the lawyer data at the end of one hour. Use of the same questions with several Tzeltal informants accounted for a part of the time difference; in Tzeltal, however, nearly as much eliciting time was spent in constructing questions as in responding to them, especially at the beginning. The Tzeltal material is only now approaching the scope necessary for going narrower and deeper.)

Starting with the second eliciting session, what has been termed 'validation' actually began. This means constructing a question-and-response unit that can be accepted or rejected by the informant—in other words, predicting the informant's response to either the same or reformulated questions. The self-corrective nature of the procedure involved the recognition, when the informant diverged from a predicted response, that it is the *question* that needs improving—that the question, as stated, was ambiguous. This is not to deny that people in everyday life often ask ambiguous questions; it is only that the responses to such questions are governed by something outside the content-value of the question, by some context in which the question or the questioning is embedded. The operation needed here was one that would eliminate such lack of control, either by constructing context-free questions or by identifying the controlling context.

An example where a "no" response was received when "yes" had been predicted was given earlier in this paper. The question was whether the Attorney General "takes cases to court." At stake was whether the Attorney General is referred to as a "trial lawyer." The discrepancy showed that "takes cases to court," when applied to the Attorney General, was considered by the informant to control either of the alternative responses, "yes" and "no," the determining factor having been included in some larger context of the questioning which the investigator had no way to detect until faced with the second response. A comparison of the two questionings revealed that this phrase could be construed to refer both to the actual trial work (which is what the investigator supposed she was asking about), and the official responsibility for bringing the action. The ethnographer learned from this not only that the Attorney General does one of these things and not the other, but more about what constitutes an appropriate question to ask this informant. "Tries cases" replaced "takes cases to court" as a criterion for "trial lawyer." A later rewriting of "takes cases to court" as "presses litigation" on the one hand, and "tries cases" on the other, accounted for the alternation and made future responses more predictable. (For the fate of the original utterance, "Takes cases to court," see next section.)

This simple rewriting exercise reduced the ambiguity with regard to three operational problems of persons learning to use these terms: (1) criteria for use of or reaction to the term "trial lawyer"; (2) criteria for identification of and reference to "Attorney General"; (3) decoding of the much-used but context-dependent phrase "takes cases to court." For the last phrase, the ethnography will show that the hearer of this utterance must look to its larger context—linguistic or nonlinguistic—for the factors that condition its criterial significance in the situations in which it is encountered.

The chart in Table I is composed of such "validating" questions. It is at the points where the next informant disagrees with the responses that new information will be added. In this type of controlled eliciting, *validation as part of the eliciting process*[5] is made explicit, and a basic principle of learning is specified as part of the operation of the ethnographer.

THE CORPUS   The corpus has been contrasted to that of the Tzeltal study in terms of time spent eliciting. Type of content also probably contributed to the difference found. The narrower content focus, "reference terms for lawyers," means the ethnographer was seeking the internal structure of a subset of terms bounded by the cover term "lawyer," and thus that the system had already been specified and a rule stated for determining its boundary. Formal descriptions of terminological systems have probably enjoyed the greatest success precisely because they can be arbitrarily delimited in this manner without too much offending our sense of reporting phenomenological reality; at the least, the arbitrariness can be made explicit in the report. Though choice of this domain accelerated the appearance of systematization, the use of systematic eliciting procedures is applied equally with both types of content.

If the chart in Table 1 were taken as the total corpus, it could be argued that information about decoding such phrases as "takes cases to court" had been lost—unless rewrite rules were included to show it as an empirically occurring reduction of "presses litigation" and "tries cases." The provisions for machine retention and retrieval of each step of eliciting, as described in the preceding section, act as the rewrite rules for the material that has subsequently been analyzed into finer information-giving units; the rules and the latest material *together* comprise the description. The points to be made here are: (1) statements that purport to be ethnographic descriptions, but lack the rules or other means for translating back into empirically obtained data, are not in any sense scientific reports; (2) formal analytic descriptions carry this requirement, but usually do not carry it far enough; their rewrite rules translate into the original corpus, but to the question of how the corpus related to empirical situations they are often indifferent. We argue that until the discovery procedures also are formalized, the data on which such analyses rest have no guarantee of validity.

ANALYSIS   It is clear from the chart that "analysis" has begun. First, as just pointed out, the procedures have led *away* from what the informant "would say in natural situations" in order to record the canonical form of his knowledge of discriminations, and these latest make up the chart's code. In addition, some dimensions of difference have been isolated and are being tried out. The dimensions used are those that have occurred in the data, and it is hoped that further eliciting will introduce terms and refinements that will lead to correcting the dimensions rather than to distorting new forms in a rigid analytic grid. Though this description may eventually provide a "corpus of lawyer terms" to be analyzed, "corpus" in the present writing refers to the questions and responses through which the information was received.

A sample reading of the chart might indicate some of the kinds of inferences made possible by displaying the material in this way. Take, for example, the term *defense lawyer* on the left-hand axis of the chart and the code which defines the symbols that have been inserted in the cells; the chart tells the following information about *defense lawyer:*

When a lawyer (law student) calls a person a "defense lawyer," he is is using a term

—that is descriptive of the man's practice (B on 1.1);

—that is not used in court proceedings, but may be said about a lawyer on a case, and also where no particular case is involved (B and C, on 2.1);

—that is used when the speaker is talking to other lawyers; also when he is talking to nonlawyers (A and B, on 2.2);

The referent of the term:

—(3.1) may be specializing in criminal work (B), or else in the area of civil practice called "insurance law" (Ac);

—(3.2) does a lot of trial work, representing defendants (Ab);

—(3.3) has clients who retain his services individually (A);

—(3.4) appears in trial court to do his work (Aa);

—(3.5) has an independent practice (C)

A comparison of the whole pattern across the board with that of some other terms, will show, for example, that anyone who is called a "defense attorney" may also be called "trial lawyer" or "criminal lawyer," though the reverse is not true. (Relations of inclusion and hierarchy could be shown on taxonomic charts for most of the terms.)

The code for the chart takes the form of a minimal set of frames and responses that generates all the data from this informant relevant to a classification of this corpus of lawyer reference terms. It will generate some frames that have never been asked him but have been inferred from the structure.

The organization of the informant's knowledge that these frames have elicited is shown in the *contrast sets*, which result from selecting all terms substitutable in a single frame of the code (on the chart, the terms showing the same symbol down one dimension, or vertical column). Overlapping of membership in contrast sets shows relations of terms with one another. Any two terms that share all memberships appear to be in free variation of usage—at least under the dimensions of contrast so far used. An example of such randomly selected usage is "defense counsel" and "attorney for defendant" as used in courtroom formalities.

The "0" symbol reflects something about dimensions: there proved to be three different types of dimensions (which might be classed as three types of semantic categories) and they are not cross-comparable. Thus, the pattern of nonrelevant 0 shows that terms used for roles in court do not indicate anything about the regular practice of the lawyer filling the role. The first category is different again: it sorts "kinds of terms," and also takes care of the special rule that "job title" terms are used invariantly, so that a "prosecuting attorney," though he meets all the other criteria for "trial lawyer" and for "criminal lawyer," is not called by those terms. It can also be seen that category 2, "settings," differs from the others in having choices of frame that are not mutually exclusive. (Thus, three "systems" were isolated from the data, each of which can be analyzed internally.)

The symbol "?" indicates lack of information, and its pattern shows readily where more work is needed. It is clear, from the "?" pattern that "kinds of practice" dimensions have been more fully covered than "settings," and that certain of the terms have not had much attention.

The symbol "X" was required because of the multilevel terms "lawyer" and "attorney," which are sometimes used in a general sense for the entire domain, so that all other terms are "included" in them, and sometimes in contrast with other terms along some of the dimensions. (E.g., the referents of any of the terms of the corpus may also be referred to as 'lawyer'; but the informant also contrasted 'trial lawyer'/'appellate attorney'/'lawyer' on dimension 3.2.)

RELEVANCE AND USEFULNESS TO SOCIAL SCIENCE

Thus the formally correct native language questions, along with the stable set of responses that they call up, are the basic building blocks of this type of ethnography. Such ethnography has the essential advantage of being replicable and containing within it all the information necessary for its testing. The gain in reliability, plus the opportunities presented by present-day high-speed recording and computational devices for processing the orders of magnitude of detailed data required for good pattern analysis, are features that will have to be taken into account by some ethnographers in the future.

Further, there is available from this type of ethnographic data the information necessary for the estimation of the generality of sets across informants, and the distinction thereby of significant subcultural and individual differences. From such an analysis can come "common-core" and "over-all pattern" descriptions, reflecting the real subcultural diversity and the differential accessibility of knowledge that mark even the simplest of societies.

Finally, this type of material and methodology should be of interest to other anthropologists and to other social scientists for two reasons: (1) It can examine in great detail some dimensions of the phenomenological world (or any specified subportion) of any speaker of any language, and it can do so by means of specifiable operations under a relatively severe cost-accounting regime; and (2) it provides the phenomenological content in a format well suited for mastery of the relevant patterns by nonnative speakers, by other ethnographers and behavioral scientists whose special interest may not be in the revelation of the patterns themselves. Such a scientist need not engage in performances such as those described here. He would, instead, under the guidance of linguist and ethnographer, be treated with the necessary introductory language contexts to master the basic relevant grammatical patterns as well as the structuring of the domain of content that happens to concern him (as informants structure this content in speech). With properly programmed teaching materials, this learning period need not take more than a month or six weeks, and the gain in power to elicit valid and relevant information, once he begins his work in the field settings, should more than repay the initial investment.

NOTES

[1] This task is being carried out under a Ford Foundation Grant by Charles Gibson, Duane Metzger, and Fred Strodtbeck. The completed study will be prepared for publication.

[2] This is not to say that the ethnographer can or should learn his subject culture in the same way as a child of the culture does, nor that he is freed entirely of the enduring problem and paradox of ethnography: translating his understandings in the field into terms understandable to his colleagues. But of the devices anthropologists have employed to circumvent this paradox, the present one tries harder to avoid obstructing the vision with preset categories or analytic models—perhaps in the only way possible, by reporting all of the observations, instruments, and operations, and identifying the stimulus for each response. This is a large task, even when formally limiting the observations to linguistic units, and the need for that limitation becomes apparent in this context. (See Black 1963b.)

[3] These two types of question function differently in different stages of the eliciting. In order to ask a question which has a 'yes-no' response, one must already have gained control over the information that makes up the entire content of the question. It is precisely the previous substantive responses which provide this information. One way of viewing the process of eliciting is that the first type of question and its response can be used to construct propositions whose truth value is tested in the 'yes-no' questions. This is one manner of validating the ideology (see note 5). Another, of course, is testing the stability of response to the same question across informants and over time. The latter operation can reveal subcultural variation in access to knowledge or in emphasis or interest, and could be pursued for the purpose of securing "common core" or "over-all pattern" delineations.

[4] Material from this study was presented at Spring Meetings, Southwestern Anthropological Association, April 1963, in Symposium on Ethnographic Procedures and Descriptive Format, "Establishing Units in the Ethnography of American Law" (Black 1963a).

[5] The test of an adequate ethnography, according to Goodenough (1957) and others, is whether it enables one to anticipate and interpret what goes on in a society as appropriately as one of its members. It has been stated above that without rewrite rules translating the canonical forms back into something that is likely to happen,

the description, as ethnography, is inadequate. It should also be emphasized here that the statement that "validation" begins with the ethnographer's first prediction of responses, *as part of the interview eliciting process*, need not imply that validation also ends there. It is agreed that final validation would involve trying out the knowledge—or observing its truth value—in "real," noninterview situations. Then, when some responses (events) do not occur as predicted from elicited information, the ethnographer can discover the additional determinants of response-variation which had not been encountered in interview, to complete his description of ideology. The authors of the present procedures are attempting to develop an observation format for accomplishing this important kind of validation.

REFERENCES CITED

Berlin, B., 1962a, An outline of Tenejapa Tzeltal morphology. Ms. Anthropology Research Projects. Stanford University.

———, 1962b, Esbozo de la fonologia del Tzeltal de Tenejapa, Chiapas. Estudios de Cultura Maya, Vol. II. México.

———, 1963a, A possible paradigmatic structure for Tzeltal pronominals. Anthropological Linguistics 5(2):1–5.

———, 1963b, Some semantic features of reduplication in a dialect of Tzeltal. International Journal of American Linguistics 29:211–218.

Berlin, B., A. K. Romney, 1964, Descriptive semantics of Tzeltal numeral classifiers. American Anthropologist 66(3) Part 2:79–98.

Black, M., 1963a, Establishing units in the ethnography of American law. Ms. read at annual meeting of Southwestern Anthropological Association, Riverside, California, April 11–13.

———, 1963b. On formal ethnographic procedures. American Anthropologist 65(6):1347–1351.

Collingwood, R. G., 1939, An autobiography (Ch. V). London, New York, Oxford University Press.

Conklin, H., 1962, Lexicographical treatment of folk taxonomies. *In* International Journal of American Linguistics 28(2) Part II supplement, Problems in lexicography, F. W. Householder and S. Saporta, eds, Publication 21. Bloomington, Indiana University Research Center in Anthropology, Folklore and Linguistics, pp. 119–141.

———, 1964, Ethnogenealogical method. *In* Explorations in cultural anthropology, W. H. Goodenough, ed. New York, McGraw-Hill, pp. 25–55.

D'Andrade, R. G., A. K. Romney, 1964, Summary of participants' discussion. American Anthropologist 66(3) Part 2:230–242.

Frake, C. O., 1962, The ethnographic study of cognitive systems. *In* Anthropology and human behavior. T. Gladwin and W. C. Sturtevant, eds. Washington, Anthropological Society of Washington, pp. 72–85.

———, 1963, Litigation in Lipay: a study in Subanun law. *In* Proceedings of the Ninth Pacific Science Congress of the Pacific Science Association, Bangkok, 1957, Vol. 3:217–222.

————, 1964, Notes on queries in ethnography. American Anthropologist 66(3) Part 2:132–145.

Goodenough, W. H., 1957, Cultural anthropology and linguistics. *In* Report of the 7th Annual Round Table Meeting on Linguistics and Language Study, Paul L. Garvin, ed. Monograph Series on Languages and Linguistics No. 9. Washington, Institute of Languages and Linguistics, Georgetown University, pp. 167–173.

————, 1964, Introduction. *In* Explorations in cultural anthropology, W. H. Goodenough, ed. New York, McGraw-Hill.

Hallowell, A. I., 1960, Ojibwa ontology, behavior, and world view. *In* Culture in history, S. Diamond, ed. New York, Columbia University Press.

Hymes, D., 1964a, A perspective for linguistic anthropology. *In* Horizons of anthropology, S. Tax, ed. Chicago, Aldine Publishing Company.

————, 1964b, Directions in (ethno)-linguistic theory. American Anthropologist 66(3) Part 2:6–56.

Metzger, D., 1960, Conflict in Chulsanto. Alpha Kappa Deltan, Wtr., pp. 35–48.

————, 1963, Some ethnographic procedures. Ms. read at annual meeting of Southwestern Anthropological Association, Riverside, California, April 11–13.

Metzger, D., G. E. Williams, 1962a, Patterns of primary personal reference in a Tzeltal community. Ms. Anthropology Research Projects No. 10, Stanford.

————, 1962b, Procedures and results in the study of native categories: Tzeltal firewood. Ms. Anthropology Research Projects No. 12, Stanford.

————, 1963a, A formal ethnographic analysis of Tenejapa ladino weddings. American Anthropologist 65(5):1076–1101.

————, 1963b, Tenejapa medicine I: the curer. Southwestern Journal of Anthropology 19(2):216–234.

Nader, L., D. Metzger, 1963, Conflict resolution in two Mexican communities. American Anthropologist 65(3):584–592.

Ruesch, J., G. Bateson, 1951. Communication, the social matrix of psychiatry. New York, Norton.

Sturtevant, W. C., 1964, Studies in ethnoscience. American Anthropologist 66(3) Part 2:99–131.

Eliciting Folk Taxonomy in Ojibwa

Mary B. Black

I. INTRODUCTION: SEMANTIC ETHNOGRAPHY

Ethnography has traditionally referred to the description of individual cultures. Such descriptions lie at the base of all anthropological work. One approach to ethnography is called ethnoscience, or ethnographic semantics. It deals with describing a culture as a system of meanings which the people of one group "know" and use in their interactions with each other. This knowledge represents their basic view of what the world is like, and it facilitates their "understanding" each other in a way an outsider does not.

Like the forms of their language, they use it as a code for communicating, although they may not be aware of its structure.

How does the ethnographer, an outsider, learn the semantic systems used by the people of a particular cultural group? More likely than not, he doesn't even know their language, at first. Since ethnoscience is a study of a society's "particular ways of classifying its material and social universe" (Sturtevant 1964:100), the ethnographer may be interested in learning what things in the world are grouped together, in a taxonomic sense, by a certain society on the explicit, talked-about level: what classes or concepts their words refer to. A folk taxonomy has been described as "the grouping of entities according to the category labels given to them by the culture" (Mathiot 1962:343). The labels will be words in the native language. Thus the language itself may be one avenue of access to a semantic system.

Some ethnographic field procedures will be described in the next section, which were designed specifically to exploit the native language as a means of getting at some part of the cultural system of its speakers. Then a segment of an Ojibwa folk taxonomy of "living things" will be given, which was elicited in 1965 from Ojibwa Indians living in northern Minnesota, using these procedures.

II. FIELD PROCEDURES: ELICITING

The eliciting process described here serves to formalize somewhat an activity that is a part of nearly all ethnographic field research, talking with informants. Unless we choose to eliminate the questioning of people as a source of information, this activity takes place, and it always causes a certain amount of disturbance or distortion of the "natural history" we are trying to record. That is, the presence of the ethnographer introduces an "artificial" effect on the normal everyday situation of the culture, and the informant is asked to engage in behavior that is novel, not contained in any of his usual cultural scenes. To treat this behavior as part of the natural history, included in the events of the culture which make up the ethnographic record, is somewhat different from treating it as a secondhand report of typical (or particular) events of the culture. Yet if one is looking for knowledge of the semantic structure as carried in the cognitive content of speech, an informant's talk can be firsthand data as such.

To formalize this part of the fieldworker's activity means, for one thing, to keep track and to specify what manner and degree of artificiality is being introduced. It makes explicit what things the observer has selected to observe. It aims to control the effect of the observer, and to identify the stimulus to which the observed behavior is a response. These are ethnographic goals in all types of observational setting. Talking with informants is considered here as one type of observational situation. When controlled for the eliciting of purely semantic distinctions, it yields data that may be considered firsthand natural history.

Formalization further means "making explicit the logical structure of a set of assertions" (Berger and others, 1962). One aspect of such structure can be described as the *sets of questions* which correspond to the assertions (beliefs and actions) of a cultural group. With these eliciting procedures we try to learn the questions that go with native assertions,[1] *in the logic of the culture under study*, and to report these explicitly. That is, we assume that whatever we see happening when visiting an alien culture consists of *responses*, TO WHICH WE DO NOT YET KNOW THE QUESTIONS. We need to discover the significant stimuli in the scene, from the point of view of the actors. This statement employs a metaphorical extension of "question" to include all kinds of stimulus or triggering conditions, and is one way of talking about the ethnographer's expectation that he is going to find his data and his ultimate descriptive units arranged, in this alien culture, in patterns and categories and relations that he could not have predicted in advance. However, when seeking cognitive categories and semantic distinctions, the method of securing data can literally concentrate on formulation of verbal questions. It would seem that cognitive distinctions are largely "questionable," whether that is the usual form of their occurrence or not. Formal field procedures can therefore force them into the semantic expression of language, and then, once learned, they can be recognized in their other expressions and contexts.

The procedures described here were developed by D. Metzger and G. E. Williams and are described in several of their joint publications (1963a, 1963b; 1966a, 1966b) as well as in Black and Metzger (1965), Williams (1966), and Black (1963, 1967). The brief exposition in the following pages will serve to introduce the data-gathering situation of the Ojibwa study.

As stated above, the ethnographer aims to discover those things that culture-participants already "know" in order to communicate with each other, in order to anticipate adequately each other's actions and reactions. How does one go about doing this, using the procedures mentioned above? Having informants teach you how to ask reasonable questions in their language is one first step. Learning from them what constitutes a "correct" response is another, and this involves training them and yourself to work simultaneously on several levels of pattern-finding. This is discussed further under *Training of Informants*, below, but the importance of the native actor-speaker cannot be too much stressed. It is his reactions to the phenomena of his experience that will tell you what you want to know. For this, you must be a sensitive, as well as a systematic observer, and you must be able to count on the intelligence and the integrity and good will of your informants.

I spent one year on an Ojibwa Indian reservation[2] doing field research that was limited to questioning informants. I wanted to find out how much I could learn, through formal eliciting alone, about Ojibwa categorization of all 'living things.' Since it turned out that the classification, when elicited in Ojibwa from older residents, still conformed to a considerable extent to the "Indian" rather than the "white" view of the world, it is concluded that in this case other observational settings might have supplemented the eliciting, but only minimally. They could not have substituted for it. That is, the Indian view of the world is not current among the younger members of the community and informants' responses were largely based upon the daily life of "their own childhood." (In cases of ongoing semantic systems, it should be noted that observation of naturally occurring events may provide an essential corrective step in eliciting semantic structures. See Note 3.)

Finding and Keeping Informants

In a community that is largely bilingual, I looked for people who could teach me something about the Indian language, who had "talked Indian" before they learned English. I professed to be interested only in the language, and asked for persons who would be good at teaching me. Three men and two women, between the ages of 62 and 85, were my "teachers" throughout the study. All had been born in this reservation community; none of their parents had ever learned English. I saw them on a schedule of about four hours a week each, paid them a dollar an hour, and made a great effort to be reliable about our appointments. After four to five months, I could be certain I had five dependable co-workers and loyal friends, whose interest was engaged both in the regular small income and in the work itself, and who were proof against certain animosities, jealousies and fears of others in the Indian community. None were people who had retired from active life, in spite of their years; all but one were the chief supporters of their housholds, held other better-paying jobs, and worked long exhausting hours at the commercial fishing which is one of the industries of the reservation. During the first half of my stay, perhaps a third of my time was spent in keeping the channels open and holding onto my informants. It was time well spent, if not well afforded. Keeping the same informants, once trained, is rather basic to this kind of fieldwork. "Rapport" is not to be underrated; having respect for informants and earning theirs won't ever be old-fashioned. And in some kinds of communities this could take several months to establish.

Location of Eliciting Sessions

Eliciting can take place nearly anyplace there is a table to write on and relative freedom from interruption. I would argue for the "unnatural" setting of a private room or office, a desk and two chairs, one informant, and one ethnographer with notebook. (A tape recorder is desirable, *if* it does not inhibit responses. It cannot, however, replace the notebook.) This may be what is sometimes called "white room" or "hotel room" fieldwork, in contrast to the "grass hut" variety. (Any derogatory intent in this contrast, directed toward the white room, is in my opinion misplaced and uninformed, as will become apparent.)

The scene of most of the Ojibwa sessions was literally a white room, a small windowless office in the basement of the Public Health Service clinic, a modern building used by the medical people only one day a week. The privacy and reduced distraction which this setting afforded were valuable assets. This fact was established by its contrast with some of the other settings where eliciting took place: in informants' homes, in my car parked in their yard or by their fishing dock, or partaking of nature's blessings to these northern interior peoples—relaxing on the shore of the lake (in summer).

It was in the white room that I feel I "got inside" the Indian belief system. The argument in favor of this setting, however, is based on the aim of these eliciting procedures to control the governing conditions of the responses. In order to assume that responses are varying with the change in semantic content of the questions, and not with something else, one must control the effect of other variables. (This is, of course, an ideal not ever totally achieved.) Linguistic context is held constant by the frame (see below), and by relative isolation or independence of each question. Situational context of speech events also is known to have systematic effects over and above the content meaning of what is said. This context is held constant in the eliciting by unchanging personnel, relationship, and locale, as much as possible.

The other work settings were illuminating, of course. They contributed an order of knowledge about informants' lives and community dynamics which supplemented and sometimes corrected the information received in the white room. However, their effect on the formal eliciting was marked. The stimuli in the scene became so varied, as to possible effects on responses, that there was a feeling of everything going out of control. Since the events which were the subject of our dialogue seldom took place while so eliciting, these sessions did not supply to any large extent the corrective by "participant-observation" which might be systematically employed for semantic descriptions.[3]

On the other hand, within the formal eliciting itself there occurred some direct behavioral validation of the semantic information. This was due in part to the character of the subject matter. When asked, "Is it dangerous to talk about X?" one informant first tried responding "No," or "I don't know" (regarding a number of especially sensitive X's). She then broke down and asked in English that we stop talking about this, since it made her too "scared." (This was in part a means of informing me that her responses had been inaccurate, I believe, as other informants had selected out these entities as the most dangerous to talk about.) When the subject matter was "talking," we were of course directly engaging in the activity while we worked. Our talk about the 'spirits' was itself considered dangerous. Additional events corroborated this. Two other informants each let me know one stormy cloudy day that they considered it an inappropriate time to elicit material regarding the powers of 'Thunderbirds,' because there were Indians fishing out on the lake who might suffer retaliation if the 'spirits' considered our talk to be offensive. ('Thunderbirds,' especially, cause storms, as the name implies.) Thereafter, the weather became a factor in my choice of subject. I was learning to apply the rules of Ojibwa talking behavior.

Also, the increasing ability of the ethnographer to use Ojibwa terms in a semantically correct or meaningful way is itself behavioral participation in the subject culture. I think, therefore, that in a somewhat wider sense also, "participation" takes place in the white room. The process of understanding, of communication, of sharing meanings, was being enlarged at every session. Informants were beginning to speak to me as they would to one of their group. It has sometimes been charged that formalization dehumanizes the ethnographic report, and the ethnographer's relations in the field, and that it is employed by those who don't care to learn about people and the way people relate to one another, about "their values, emotions, attitudes, and self-conceptions; their hopes and fears." (Berreman 1966:349) This is a strange notion, indeed, and hardly deserves an answer. But the opposing of "scientistic" and "humanistic" anthropologists is false as well as foolish, in my opinion. Berreman hopes we can combine the virtues of both, yet he makes this supposed polarity the basis for his critique. I agree with him that those who do not wish to take the "formal" methodological road should, instead of being "dazzled" or behaving defensively, proclaim loudly what methods they do intend to use and defend them passionately. But unless or until they have tried the field procedures which they think have nothing to do with "people," their authority on *this* subject is less than established.

My own feeling is that belief systems (communication) are so much at the center of the most intimate knowledge of and interactions with people, that other more peripheral cultural levels seem pallid and sterile by comparison. It would take a great amount of participant-living in this reservation community, I believe, to bring me closer to the essence of what it is (or was) to be an Ojibwa Indian than did ten intensive months of learning to communicate with a handful of its citizens in a white room, across a metal desk. But then, ethnographers may differ in what they find exciting. I find people exciting, and I find structure exciting, mainly because communicating with people is the point, and communication is structure. (And culture is communication; that is why being an anthropologist is exciting.)

Training Informants and Self: Multiple Levels

LANGUAGE   Although your learning takes place on several levels at once, even from the beginning—levels of linguistic structure, question-response pattern, content-focus, semantic categories—a first requirement is to become able to hear and write down the language of the informants well enough to say it back, and eventually to write it phonemically and construct new utterances. Any degree of prior knowledge of the language is helpful, particularly the phonology. A linguist working on the scene is someone to cultivate. Being a linguist yourself is probably best, but this is not an all-or-nothing requirement.

The question of the linguistic capability and preparation of the fieldworker for this native-language ethnographic procedure has received little explicit attention to date. There are two considerations:

1) how much knowledge of the subject language you should have before starting the study

2) your level of linguistic sophistication, both in ability to interpret a linguist's description of the language and in ability to perform linguistic eliciting and analysis in the field.

There arises a practical third question: how much time should be allocated during the field operation for strictly linguistic investigation? This last will depend on both (1) and (2), and (2) depends somewhat on (1).

Initial language-learning can take place while already collecting data on the subject-focus, and without a contact language if necessary. It has been stated in a previous publication that the eliciting procedures are designed to be productive of semantic ethnography "as part of the language-description process at whatever stage is necessary." (Black and Metzger 1965:147.) However, the radical stage of being confronted with a completely unknown informant language and having no contact language in which to start work is fairly slow and painful. Good bilingual informants hasten the initial progress considerably.

The first answer to both (1) and (2) above is "the more the better." For minimal requirements, it seems clear that a *lack of both* could not be considered. Assuming a lack of prior acquaintance with the native language the fieldworker should have had at least one or two courses in descriptive linguistics, including field methods, working with informants. A complete description of the phonology and grammar, however desirable, may not be necessary, but the operational principles involved in the structural description of languages are basic, to both linguistic and semantic eliciting. This is requisite for either of the tasks of interpreting a linguist's work, or producing some description yourself by working with informants. Thus the minimum condition, for an ethnographer working alone, is the capability either to do some field linguistics or to apply the work of others, but it should be added that a certain amount of the former will be required anyway, for example in the matter of question-construction which is seldom covered in linguists' reports to the extent needed for developing the frames used here. In addition, if we go back and assume some degree of a prior acquaintance with the language, either this has been acquired through the abilities mentioned, or you have a "native speaker" grasp of it, in which case the principles of phonemic orthography and of eliciting for contrastive analysis will still have to be learned.

The ethnographer, then, must have the capability either to learn a certain amount of the structure of the language by informant work, or to understand and utilize a linguist's report at this level. If the former is necessary, the time allocated to it will vary with your degree of competence, and while it can be done concurrently with ethnosemantic data-gathering, some special sessions will probably have to be devoted to purely linguistic work. (Another suggestion is an ethnographer-linguist team, in the field; however, both should be considerably aware of each other's tasks in this case.) These requirements should not be interpreted as formidable by the novice who finds the semantic approach to ethnography agreeable but who has no linguistic training as yet. The principles of structural description are not that "complex"—indeed their very difficulty for some students seems to lie in grasping the *simplicity* of the basic notions. The very best way to incorporate these notions into your working and thinking toolbox is the experience of performing the operations. That is probably why most classes in descriptive linguistics confront you with a native-speaker informant before you think you know what it's all about. This is often frightening, as is the first ethnographic field experience, but both have that gratifying consequence, that "rite of passage" function, of initiating you into the direct knowledge that the world is there,[4] amenable to your queries and probes, ready to teach you what it is all about. Linguistics, for the anthropologist especially, is not some esoteric, ivory tower intellectual discipline, but rather a systematic way of finding out, *in situ*, how people code their experience. As such, it has everything to do with ethnography.

"CORRECT" RESPONSES TO REASONABLE QUESTIONS   The informant (or any spontaneous source from the culture) provides at first some askable and correctly constructed questions, and will later judge your construction of additional ones on levels of grammaticality and semantic sensibleness. He also provides responses to each, assumed to be "correct" in one or more of the following ways:

1) correct grammatically, and forming a proper unit with the question form;

2) correct in that it can count as one of the possible answers to that question, from the point of view of the questioner; thus that it is sensible

and semantically appropriate, and is evidence that the question was not meaningless but was answerable or reasonable.[5]

3) correct in the sense of its truth value: some responses might be correct in the above senses (grammatical, sensible) but be false statements. When an informant rejects an utterance as incorrect, it may be because it is untrue, according to his beliefs or knowledge. This type of response is that usually requested of ethnographic informants. Their responses are their report of how things truly happen in their culture.

There is an additional sociolinguistic or pragmatic level for correctness of questions and responses, about which my informants felt obliged to instruct me. It turns out that asking direct or unambiguous questions is bad form in Ojibwa etiquette, and not the most successful gambit for acquiring reliable information. This was revealed when my query, Is this a good question? or Could I ask this question? or, What would someone answer to this question? stimulated responses of the following type:

"No, that wouldn't be polite."
"Oh, he'd probably answer 'I don't know' or 'It's none of
your business.' "

Here the informant has taken the task at the pragmatic level, and is responding in terms of situational context and appropriateness of the questioning. Although this was both interesting and pertinent,[6] informants had to be trained to ignore any possible scene of the questioning, for the moment, in order to provide the other levels of instruction for their "pupil."

It is seen from the above that there are actually four levels or kinds of correctness possible.[7] Informants need to know which kind of correctness you are expecting, and you need to know which kind they are providing, in any given instance. It is clear that training of informants for multi-level eliciting involves a more intricate communication situation than is normally the case when talking with a native about his culture. It is more complex, also, than purely linguistic eliciting. Linguists have explicitly warned against the danger of misinterpreting the level of informants' judgments, wishing to abstract out only judgments of grammaticality. (Gleason 1961:198–200.) The present type of eliciting, however, may be concerned with all four kinds, as has been seen. The problem amounts to a self-training of the ethnographer to carry out both linguistic and ethnographic eliciting more or less simultaneously and to be able to detect at which of the four levels the informant is responding. It is necessary to keep them separate, or communication breaks down.

Informants for the Ojibwa study, in addition to providing judgments of acceptability on linguistic, semantic, and pragmatic levels, also acted as ethnographic informants and provided "true" responses to the questions they had aided in constructing. While they were very much aware of this last distinction, and made sure which responses were being entered in the "true" record, they varied in becoming trained to discriminate the first three tasks.[8] Of course, you as ethnographer must first of all be clear in your own mind what you are asking for, but also you will have to find ways to make certain which kind of acceptability is being judged at any given time. Mistaking the level can result in wrong analysis and unreliable ethnography.

At each level, what you need finally is some idea of the set of all possible correct responses (or correct questions). This provides some of the kinds of classes which will comprise your data.

Distributional Data: Frames, Terms, Responses

As described on pages 145–147 of Black and Metzger (1965), the eliciting format I used consists of asking questions which are composed of a *frame* and a *term*, the latter filling any one substitution slot of the former. Thus a number of terms judged by the informant to be suitable in the X slot of the frame

/a.ndi endažiwi.siniwa.d X/   'Where do X's eat?'

form a set or class, at some level (depending on kind of suitability or correctness, again), and can then be used to make up a set of minimally varying questions, the *responses* to which will be assumed to covary with the terms. The above-referenced paper gives some of the distributional analyses possible with the manipulation of these three units, and also gives examples of the *productivity* of the process (how new frames can be constructed from data received in responses). Black (1967) gives in detail the steps for generating frames, including a typology of kinds of frames and their functions in eliciting.

Classes are also obtained by examining the sets of responses to a "list" question such as,

/awenenag dinowag X eya.wa.d/   'What kinds of X are there?'

Responses to this frame may be inserted by pairs into the additional frame,

/mi.na bežig dinowa Y aʔa Z/   'Is Z one kind of Y?'

These two frames can elicit, sort, and check inclusion-classes for a taxonomic hierarchy.[9]

In the Ojibwa study, taxonomic relations were first elicited regarding 84 Ojibwa lexical terms which were each a *kind of* "living thing." Only the taxonomy proper will be under discussion here. (Some other ways that the Ojibwa classify these terms were explored, after the taxonomy had been elicited.)[10] A portion of the elicited taxonomy is given in III below, where a special problem of labelling is described.

It is now clear that data-collecting and data-analysis are not separated in this kind of eliciting. Analysis depends upon how informants perform specified tasks, which build each on the last so that they cannot be decided in advance.

III.   OJIBWA TAXONOMY OF 'LIVING THINGS': PROBLEMS OF AN "UNLABELED TAXON"

In the course of learning from informants how to construct proper questions and recognize "correct" responses in the Minnesota dialect of Ojibwa, I was introduced to some of their phonology, grammar, and lexicon, and to some of the semantic contrasts which they use. In this study, I applied the eliciting procedures just described in a search for some locally relevant semantic structures (or native classifications) of an Ojibwa lexical domain bounded by a term which can be glossed in English as 'living things' ('those who are living'). The Ojibwa word is /bema.diziwa.d/.[11] It stands as the head-term of the taxonomic universe under discussion, and is shown at the top of both charts, in Tables 1 and 2.

(Please note the use of single quotation marks, in the charts and in the text, for English glosses of material which occurred in Ojibwa. See note in Table 1. Ojibwa forms omitted from this paper are available from the author. Also the Minnesota-Chippewa phoneme inventory, for which the help of C. E. Fiero, field linguist with the Christian and Missionary Alliance, is acknowledged and appreciated.)

The present paper deals with a segment of the Ojibwa taxonomy, and with a particular problem about an unlabeled category, which arose in eliciting. I want to describe both the empirical and the formal aspects of this problem, that is, the solutions available both in eliciting (or speaking) and in analysis.

The problem centers on the semantic condition which ethnographers have sometimes reported as They have no word for 'people,' or, Their word for themselves is the same as their word for 'human beings.' This condition appears true for the Ojibwa term /anišina.beg/, which functions semantically as 'Indians' when contrasted with 'white people,' 'Negroes,' 'Asiatics'; but which also can function as 'people' or 'human beings' when contrasted with 'large animals,' 'small animals,' 'insects,' 'birds,' etc.[12] To put this in a way less dependent on English glosses, one could say that /anišina.beg/ in some contexts specifically *excludes* the terms glossed as 'white people,' 'Negroes,' 'Asiatics,' but in other contexts it can generalize so that it excludes specifically 'large animals,' 'small animals,' 'insects,' etc., and in the latter case it stands for the entire class of which it is a member. The same *cannot* be said for the words glossed as 'white people,' 'Negroes,' 'Asiatics,' which in all of *their* contexts are limited to excluding only each other and 'Indians.'

Table 1. Section of Ojibwa Taxonomy Showing Only Unambiguously Labeled Categories

	t.1 /bema.diziwa.d/ 'living things'							
t.2 /anišina.beg/	t.3 /gičimoko-ma.nig/	t.4 /makade-wiya.sag/	t.5 /ani.bi.ške-wininiwag/	t.6 /awesi.yag/	t.7 /manido.-weyišag/	t.8 /manido.-šag/	t.9 other
'Indians'	'white people'	'Negroes'	'Asiatics'	'large animals'	'small animals'	'insects'	

NOTE: "t" numbers are *category* or *taxa* identification.
Ojibwa *labels* are in phonemic orthography, between diagonals.
English *glosses* do not represent exact translations or semantic equivalents, that is, they do not necessarily designate, in their English usage, the same range of referents. They are printed in single quotation marks, as is all English substituted for utterances which occurred in Ojibwa.

176

Table 2. Section of Ojibwa Taxonomy Showing Category 'Human Beings' Inferred from Semantic Contrasts of Two Double-Level Labels

t.1 /bema.diziwa.d/ 'living things'

t.2 /bema.diziwa.d/ /aniŝina.beg/ 'human beings'	t.3 /awesi.yag/ 'large animals'	t.4 /manido.weyiŝag/ 'small animals'	t.5 /manido.ŝag/ 'insects'	t.6 /bineŝi.yag/ 'birds'	t.7 /gi.go.yag/ 'fish'	t.8 /adiso.ka.nag/ 'spirits'
t.9 /aniŝina.beg/ 'Indians'	t.13 /makwa/ 'bear'	t.17 /žiga.g/ 'skunk'	t.21 /ğinebi.g/ 'snake'	t.25 /migizi/ 'bald eagle'	t.29 /na.me/ 'sturgeon'	t.33 /nenaboŝo/ (culture hero)
t.10 /ği.čimo.koma.nig/ 'white people'	t.14 /mo.ns/ 'moose'	t.18 /agakoji.ŝi./ 'woodchuck'	t.22 /obegomagaki/ 'toad'	t.26 /go.ko.ko?o/ 'owl'	t.30 /oga/ 'pike'	t.34 /mikinak/ (great turtle)
t.11 /maka.dewiya.sag/ 'Negroes'	t.15 /atik/ 'caribou'	t.19 /ža.ngweŝi/ 'mink'	t.23 /o.ji.ns/ 'fly'	t.27 /wi.na.nge/ 'buzzard'	t.31 /asa.wens/ 'perch'	t.35 /binesiwag/ 'thunderbirds'
t.12 /ani.bi.ŝkewininiwag/ 'Asiatics'	t.16 other	t.20 other	t.24 other	t.28 other	t.32 other	t.36 /memegwesiwag/ 'paddlers'
						t.37 /gi.zis/ 'sun'
						t.38 /no.dino.g/ 'winds'
						t.39 /ba.na.be/ 'mermaid'
						t.40 other

This double meaning does not normally cause confusion or misunderstanding, since the context in which the speaker uses the word (linguistic, semantic, or situational context) generally indicates which meaning is intended. Unfortunately, the contexts of my usage did not provide resolution of this ambiguity, so operationally, in the subsequent questioning regarding each of the terms of the domain, it worked something like this: each time I wanted to ask about 'human beings' I asked instead about 'Indians,' 'white people,' 'Negroes,' 'Asiatics'—and then 'large animals,' 'small animals,' 'birds,' 'insects,' 'fish,' and so forth. This was my operational solution to the problem, but Ojibwa speakers may choose one of several other possible solutions, as will be shown. (Thus, Table 1 was the model for questioning informants about attributes of the taxonomic classes, rather than Table 2 which, I hope to show, better represents their conceptual categories and folk taxa, and their use of labels.)

The problem, however, turned out to be more complex than the common label for 'Indians' and 'human beings.' It appears one can also report that the Ojibwa have the same word for 'human beings' as they do for all living creatures. Their term /bema.diziwa.d/ also is taxonomically homonymous; sometimes it is taken to refer to just people, other times it includes all living things. Addition of category t.2 in Table 2 is based on the inference that Ojibwa speakers recognize a subclass of living things that includes all the named classes of people (that is, t.2 through t.5 of Table 1) and excludes all other classes at this level, but for which their language does not provide a unique label; and that they deal with the empirical situation in at least two ways:[13] by borrowing a label from among the members of the subclass, namely the word for 'Indians,' *or* by using the label of the next superclass, the word for 'living things.' That is, the label for either t.9 or t.1 is used. There are then really two labels in use for this category, each of which is taxonomically ambiguous by virtue of its serving to label two separate categories at different levels, and each of which is apparently the only label in use in its other position. This compounds the ambiguities to be resolved (or perpetuated) by the speaker's choice of how to refer to 'human beings' in any given context.

There is both a formal and an empirical problem here, although to separate them may be somewhat spurious. What I mean by the formal taxonomic problem is whether such a category can be justified in the analysis—whether these Ojibwa speakers do in fact hold a concept of *people* distinct from that of 'Indians' and from that of 'living things.' In other words, is the taxonomic chart of Table 1, or the one in Table 2, the better analysis? And if there is such a semantic category, how to talk about it: unlabeled, double-labeled, or nonuniquely labeled? By "empirical problem" I mean, what do Ojibwa speakers do about it, when referring to this concept which lacks a proper or unique label?

It has already been stated what the ethnographer did about it; the chart of Table 1 contains all the categories used. No other labels were available for insertion in the eliciting frames. To ask about 'human beings' was not possible, as the eliciting context was precisely the type that did *not* provide resolution of the taxonomic ambiguity represented by either label. Informants were thus trained to expect that in the formal questioning /aniŝina.beg/ *always* referred to 'Indians' and /bema.diziwa.d/ *always* meant 'living things,' although their own usage in responses and elsewhere was not so strict.

An examination of what Ojibwa speakers normally do about it, when referring to this category (if indeed they do so refer) will provide the evidence needed to resolve the formal problem. That is, instances of their usage of these terms must show either *inclusion relations*, involving two taxonomic levels, or *exclusion relations* (contrast) vis-à-vis the other categories on the level of t.2 'human beings' in Table 2. These kinds of evidence will be given shortly.

Two points first about analytic procedures:

1) *Labels* and *categories* are not the same thing. "Taxon" refers to a category or class concept in the semantic system. These are numbered with *t*'s in Tables 1 and 2. When you see the Ojibwa word or lexeme designating a category, that is a *label*. These are given in Ojibwa on the charts of the figure with English glosses in single quotes. Citing Conklin on this: "The shape . . . of the linguistic forms which designate segregates is irrelevant . . . to . . . the semantic structure (or) system of classification . . . labels and categories can change independently and therefore must be analyzed separately." (1962:121) Thus there is the possibility of an "unlabeled taxon," as well as referential synonyms (more than one label for the same taxon), and homonymous lexemes (which label two or more taxa). It appears that /aniŝina.beg/ and /bema.diziwa.d/ qualify as candidates for both of the latter, and that the concept corresponding to English "people" or "human beings" cannot be called "unlabeled," since there are actually two labels in use for it.

2) The other point is that translation labels (or English glosses—see note on Table 1 about glosses) do not play the decisive role in determining the folk classification. A contact language may be useful in communicating with informants and getting initial clues, but when a bilingual Ojibwa-English speaker is asked to construct an Ojibwa question regarding "kinds of people," and he uses the word /bema.diziwa.d/, this is not evidence for an Ojibwa category equivalent to "people" in English. However, the Ojibwa responses to the Ojibwa question 'Can you name me all the kinds of *bema.diziwa.d* that exist?' did tell something about semantic structure and labels, for together the question and responses provided information regarding an inclusion relation among a number of Ojibwa lexemes. Ojibwa ques-

tions and responses designed to elicit this relation, and also that of direct contrast or exclusion (*if it's an X, it isn't a Y* information), can be used to sort taxonomic classes and may indicate possible unlabeled categories (for example when circumlocutions are used to respond to a question such as 'what kind of thing is an X?').

Here are some of the things that initially happened which pointed to the ambiguities under discussion:

When asked to help construct an Ojibwa question which might request information as to "all the kinds of people," one informant produced a construction using animate gender but no referent noun at all that could be glossed 'what kinds are there?' His example of a good response: 'there is one kind of man, Indian; there is another kind of man, white; there is another kind of man, Negro; there is another kind of man, Asiatic.' Then he explained that the word he had used, /inini/, means just 'man' and doesn't really cover it. (So far he avoided the "people" slot, except to fill it ineffectually with 'man.') At a later date, in another construction, this same informant changed the word for 'man' /inini/, to the word /bema.dizid/ and glossed it 'person,' explaining that this was a better word since it did not specify man, woman, or child, but covered them all. (/bema.dizid/ is the singular of /bema.diziwa.d/.)

Another informant produced the question about "kinds of people," using much the same construction but inserting /bema.diziwa.d/ for 'people,' so that it came out 'what are all the kinds of people that exist in the world?', Her response simply listed: /anišina.beg/ 'Indians'; /mi.nawa. gičimokoma.-nig/ 'also white people'; /mi.nawa. makadewiya.sag/ 'also Negroes'; /mi.nawa. ani.biškewininiwag/ 'also Asiatics.'

Now these, so far, are instances of a weak sort of evidence (listed below as number 2), since the category was introduced in English. However, four months later this query was put to all informants cold, in Ojibwa, first in the form 'what kinds are there?' They said this could not be answered until it specified "kinds of what." Next, /bema.diziwa.d/ was inserted, so that the question asked 'what are all the kinds of *bema.diziwa.d?*'

The first informant responded with Ojibwa terms for 'white people,' 'Indians,' 'men,' 'women,' 'children,' 'teenagers.' After a pause, he added 'large animals,' 'small animals,' 'those things that fly,' 'fish,' 'those things that crawl.'

The second informant gave just 'white people,' 'Indians,' and stopped.

Another went right through these:

'all the tribes of Indians'	Thunderbirds'
"including Orientals" (in English)	'fish'
'all the kinds of white people'	'the Mink' (mythological)
'Negroes'	/Nenabošo/ (mythological)

'Canadian Indians'	'trees'
'Eskimos'	'stones'
'Philippinos'	'leaves'
'Germans'	'flowers'
'small animals'	'grass'
'large animals'	'berries'
'birds'	'vegetables'

The last agreed to all of the above, and added:

'spirits'	'frogs'
'thunder gods'	'toads'
'forest dwarves'	'snakes'
'canoe-paddling spirits'	'ants'
'dogs'	'grasshoppers'
'cats'	'butterflies'
'boys'	'owls'
'girls'	'eagles'
'babies'	'golden eagles'
'cows'	'swans'
'horses'	'sun'
'rabbits'	'moon'
'porcupines'	'winds'
'skunks'	'shells'
	'ocean'

Inclusion-levels within this set obviously needed to be sorted. But this kind of eliciting provided the broad membership data on /bem.diziwa.d/ for its more inclusive class, t.1, and also it gave an indication that the term was sometimes reacted to in a more restricted way. Direct inclusion-testing was done on all 84 terms of the inventory with the Ojibwa question 'Is X a kind of *bema.diziwa.d?*' (as well as application to each pair of the frame 'Is X a kind of Y?')

/anišina.beg/ was in the same way established as the label for the class t.9 'Indians,' both by inclusion and contrast evidence.

Thus these two terms as labels for t.1 and t.9, while not unique to the categories, appear to be unique for the categories, since each stands alone as a speaker's only choice when wishing to refer to these classes.

It is their use as alternative labels for category t.2 'human beings' which requires evidence now to support my thesis that there exists a category in the Ojibwa semantic system that subsumes the four named classes of people and contrasts as a unit with other classes, and that speakers deal with its labeling in the above-described manner. As has been stated, evidence for *contrast* horizontally, and for *inclusion* vertically, is required, showing the use of each of these words as a label for the inferred category. The types of evidence found for documenting the existence and labeling of t.2 could be graded for strength as follows:

(1) THE FIRST AND WEAKEST   When the ethnographer introduced either term, the logic of the response cannot count as evidence. This is because my usage was reserved for the unique labelings; to reduce ambiguity I treated the system as if there were no such category as t.2, and informants soon expected this.

(2) THE SECOND TYPE   English-Ojibwa translation by informants, as when telling how to say "what are the kinds of people," is hardly good evidence but may provide clues. The category in this kind of case in introduced in English. (For example, when queried how to express in Ojibwa, Are X's birds or people? all informants used /aniši̱na.beg/ for 'people.')

(3) THE THIRD TYPE   Ojibwa-English translation by informants, as when providing an English gloss after having given an Ojibwa response to an Ojibwa question. This might be considered evidence, for here the category was introduced by them in Ojibwa. One informant made the following response to an Ojibwa question: /dibiško anišinabe/ and then said it meant 'like a human being' or 'the same as a human being.' (—/dibiško/ generally refers to a state of equality or near-equality between two different things.) Another informant responded /dibiško bema.dizid/ and said it meant 'the same as a human being.' Thus, 'human being' was given as the gloss for two different Ojibwa words, the singular of /anišina.beg/ and the singular of /bem.diziwa.d/.

(4) THE FOURTH TYPE   The evidence is stronger when only one of the categories of the label is logically possible. In the last example, there occurred both type 3 and type 4 evidence. First, /dibiško anišinabe/, though interpreted by the speaker as 'like a human being,' *might* make as much sense if glossed 'like an Indian,' for the question had been, 'In what way does Mikinak change his form?' Mikinak is a turtle, who has special powers in certain situations including transforming himself to become like an Indian in the sense of taking on human form and powers. So /anišinabe/ here could logically stand for either category, and it is only the gloss which is cited as evidence of the type 3 variety in favor of the existence of t.2. However, in the other instance, /dibiško bema.dizid/ was a response to the question 'What does Nenabošo eat?' Now, Nenabošo, the culture hero, has already been established as one of the /bema.diziwa.d/—at some level. Also it is known he is *not* in the class of /anišina.beg/. (Nor, incidentally, in those of 'white,' 'Negro,' or 'Asiatic.') Thus he is not in t.2. In fact, as can be seen on the chart, he is an /adiso.ka.n/ or 'spirit,' and *as such* in the

superclass /bema.diziwa.d/ 'living things,' t.1. The response then that
Nenabošo eats 'the same as /bema.dizid/' can reasonably refer only to the
subclass 'human beings,' and the informant's gloss supports this. Added
support comes from the knowledge that there is no standard gustatory fare
for all members of t.1 'living things,' so that 'eating the same as living things'
would make little sense. This appears to be fairly strong evidence for an
occurrence of /bema.diziwa.d/ as a label for category t.2.

(5) THE FIFTH TYPE   The strongest type of evidence would come from
situations where direct contrast or inclusion relations are tested in Ojibwa
with no English gloss. This was illustrated in the eliciting for inclusion and
contrast for t.1 and t.9. It was not followed through for t.2 systematically,
since this category was dropped from explicit questioning. The present data
are culled mainly from other contexts. /bema.diziwa.d/ appeared to be
taken as 'human beings' and to include /anišina.beg/ as 'Indians' in the
response which listed only the four "races" as kinds of /bema.diziwa.d/.
/anišina.beg/, however, cannot be tested for its inclusion of 'white people,
Negroes, Asiatics,' since its direct contrast with them seems to be dominant
over its inclusion relation to them. It is its contrast with 'large animals,'
'small animals,' etc. that serves as evidence. This is analogous to our men
versus animals, men versus women. "Men" can substitute for other subset
members (for example, "women") by covering them too in this higher-
level contrast, but it would be no more sensible in ordinary conversation
to say that a 'white person' is a kind of /anišina.beg/ than it is to say that
a "woman" is a kind of "man." (It follows that speakers will choose
/bema.diziwa.d/ for indicating the class of which 'white people' is a member,
since they have this option. However, in most contexts it would not then be
clear which level of /bema.diziwa.d/ had been intended. (See IV 7/5 data
on Table 3 for structural pressure toward t.2, in placing 'Germans.') As
for /bema.diziwa.d/ including /anišina.beg/ where the latter is a label for
t.2, no cases were found.[14]

(6) THERE MIGHT BE ADDED A SIXTH TYPE OF EVIDENCE   Type 5 carried
out with monolingual informants. But for two reasons that is omitted.
First, to avoid the question of whether bilingual Ojibwa-English speakers
have acquired a new category by diffusion or interference from their English.
For present purposes the category is viewed as part of the present dialect
of these Minnesota Chippewa Indians, however they got it. The problem of
historical change is of interest, of course; and choosing to call the t.2 category "unlabeled" rather than the t.9 (thus assuming generalization upward
of /anišina.beg/)could be quite wrong, viewed historically. I have tried
to deal with the present choices of present speakers, rather than to trace
independent changes in labels and categories. The second reason is that
my one monolingual informant seems never to have felt the need to use

Table 3.   Contrast and Inclusion Data for Category t.2 'human beings'

/aniŝina.beg/ as t.2 'human beings'	/bema.diziwa.d/ as t.2 'human beings'
Contrast Relation	
II 10/12: Q 'In what way does *mikinak* change his form?' R /dibiŝko aniŝinabe/ 'like a human being' (3)	VII 9/22: Q 'What does Nenaboŝo eat?' R /dibiŝko bema.dizid/ 'The same as a human being.' (3, 4-see page 35)
IV, II 6/3: English: "How would you ask in Ojibwa, 'Is it a bird or a person?'" Ojibwa: Both IV and II used /aniŝina.be/ for 'person.' (2)	II 7/27: Regarding 'sparrows,' already a member of t.1: /ga.wi.n igo awe ogosagiwawan ono bema.dizinid../ 'They are not afraid of people . . .' (3)
V 8/16: /giba.gin a?aniŝina.be/ 'Lightning struck that person.' (3)	IV 9/21: "They don't give offerings to human beings." Q "How would you say that in Ojibwa?" R /ga.wi.n win obagijidawasiwawan ini bema.dizinid/
II 8/3: English, discussing /andomakomeŝi.yag/ 'monkeys' vs. /memegwesiwag/ (hairy man-like beings seen on the lake in canoes) Q "Are *memegwesiwag* monkeys?" R "No. That's a different class. Like people." Ojibwa, immediately following: Q 'Are *memegwesiwag aniŝna.beg?*' R 'yes.' (2, 3)	(NOTE: They do give offerings to other 'living things' (2, 4-see footnote 13)
	IV 9/23: "How do you say in Ojibwa 'Where do people eat?'" R /a.ndi endaẑiwi.siniwa.d bema.diziwa.d/ (2)
	II 9/28: "How do people get around?" /a.ni.n nagakeya eẑičigewa.d ba.ba.ma.diziwa.d bema.diziwa.d/ (2)
	IV 2/16: /mewi.ẑa gabima.diziwa.d/ 'People who lived a long time ago' (3)
	IV 2/11: "What are the kinds of people here on earth?" /awenenag dinowag bema.diziwa.d eya.wa.d oma?aking/ (2)

(NOTE: /memegwesiwag/ are not 'Indians.' Neither are they generally said to be 'people.' Here he was contrasting them with 'monkeys,' indicating "like people." /aniŝina.beg/ is ambiguous here, without the gloss. Category introduced in English, by informant.)

Inclusion Relation

Inclusion relation not directly testable. However, II 8/3 above is a possible exception.

In the following, it appears that both /aniśina.beg/ (because of contrast) and /bema.diziwa.d/ (because it occurs in the Q) are being avoided:

IV 6/3: Q 'What kind of *bema.diziwa.d* is a pike?'
R 'A fish.'
Q 'What kind of *bema.diziwa.d* is an Englishman?'
R 'A white person.'

Whereas, the same kind of structural pressure, but without /bema.diziwa.d/ in the Q, received the R: /bema.diziwa.d/ from IV on 7/15 (see opposite column).

II 6/1: 'What are the kinds of *bema.diziwa.d?*'
R /giĉimokoma.nig/ 'white people'
/aniśina.beg/ 'Indians'
/abino.ji.yag/ 'children'
/ikwewag/ 'women'
/ininiwag/ 'men' (5)

II 2/4: "What are some kinds of people?" (English)
R /bema.dizid/ 'living person'
/gibana.dizid/ 'dead person' (2)

V 6/4: 'What are the kinds of *bema.diziwa.d?*'
R /giĉimokoma.nig/ 'white people'
/aniśina.beg/ 'Indians' (5)

II 4/20: /odaśwagiman gego idodawa.d ono bema.dizinid/
'He threatens to do something to a person.' (3)

(NOTE: /bema.dizinid/ was substituted for the word for 'man,' as it "does not specify 'man' 'woman' or 'child' but covers them all.")

IV 7/15: Q 'What kind of thing is a sheephead?'
R /gi.go/ 'fish'
Q 'What kind of thing is *Nenaboǒo?*'
R /adiso.ka.n/ 'spirit'
Q 'What kind of thing are Germans?'
R /bema.diziwa.d/ 'human beings' (??) *
Q 'What kind of thing are woodchucks?'
R /manido.weyiśag/ 'small animals'

LEGEND
Roman numerals: Informant number, plus date
Kinds of evidence:
(1) investigator's use, ignoring category t.2
(2) category introduced in English
(3) category introduced in Ojibwa, glossed in English
(4) t.2 the only logical choice of category
(5) inclusion relation, no English used

* (Structural pressure would indicate t.2; no glosses were given.) (Absence of /bema.diziwa.d/ in Q allowed this R; see IV 6/3 in opposite column.)

either of these labels for the 'people' category during his relatively brief work with me, and in fact on the one occasion where it is reasonable to think he wished to refer to the category, he replied with /inini ikwe gaye/ which says 'man, woman also.' This is interesting, but hardly sufficient data even for speculation. Monolingual speakers of today may or may not have a different way of dealing with category t.2 and its subclasses from that of bilinguals, and this would be something to investigate.

The remaining evidence which occurred in my data is shown in Table 3, according to label and taxonomic relation, and with the type of evidence as just described coded 1 through 5. The Roman numerals I–VIII are informant numbers.

These are relatively fragmentary occurrences of evidence,[15] but I hope the evidence and the general argument are in a form to be tested more thoroughly and systematically by any interested ethnographer or linguist. There are additional possibilities for structural description here; for example, the pragmatic rules regarding choice of label. It is apparent that the choice for the speaker of which label to use when wishing to refer to the category 'human beings' is dictated by context and type of contrast or relation demanded by the communication, as well as by the possibility of some logically unlikely combinations. For example, a speaker contrasts 'human beings' with 'fish' and 'birds' by using /aniši̇na.beg/ usually, for these other classes are also kinds of /bema.diziwa.d/. Also, one avoids saying /aniši̇na.beg/ is a kind of /aniši̇na.beg/ and so forth. Some examples of these choices have been given here, but no attempt at formal description has been made at this level.

NOTES

[1] According to my usage of "assertions" as "beliefs and actions," this statement refers to *all possible native assertions*, whether verbally asserted or not.

[2] In the community of Ponemah, Red Lake Chippewa Reservation, in northern Minnesota. "Chippewa" is the term for the Minnesota and Wisconsin tribes of Ojibwa Indians. Their language is a dialect of Ojibwa, a Central Algonkian language, and is referred to here as the Minnesota-Chippewa dialect.

[3] From Goodenough 1951:9:

"Our attempts at participation also revealed unsuspected aspects of the internal organization of the extended family. Rules of conduct which informants had given frequently turned out to be inaccurate generalizations or approximate rules of thumb when the responses which the writer's behavior evoked proved quite different from those he had been told it would evoke. While in this way the writer unquestionably made a fool of himself in native eyes on more than one occasion, his *faux pas* provided a basis for straightening out many misconceptions which no amount of straight interviewing would have clarified. They revealed that many of his questions of informants had been beside the point, had failed to allow for necessary distinctions, or had left a confused impression as to what he was driving at."

This is a concrete description of the way in which information given in eliciting sessions can be corrected by participation. A systematic use of such procedures, including assessment by native observers of natural scenes and occurring "errors," is being developed currently for descriptions of semantic structuring.

[4] I would like to leave the arguments as to whether "the world" exists in the data, in the ethnographer's descriptive analysis, or in the language used by one or the other, to the philosophers' offices and behavioral science graduate seminars, where such matters are of consequence. While these decisions may be basic to what an ethnographer does, the experience of confronting the "raw" material and learning from it something you had not known before need not wait upon their resolution.

[5] That the question asked for some definable type of information, and was not ambiguous, can be tested by repetition with the same or different informants; when responses are stable in type of information, the frame construction is unambiguous; when responses are stable in content, (give the same answer), the question is unambiguous semantically. The matter of clarifying the question-frames used in the present ethnographic procedures is illustrated in Black and Metzger 1965:146, and in Black 1967.

[6] Informants' own responses on the "truth" level had later to be examined for adherence to the Ojibwa rules of questioning-and-responding etiquette; their "tip-off" as to how Ojibwa responders manage to give informationless answers to questions considered to be out-of-line was of some aid in dealing with informants during eliciting about "sensitive" issues, but for the most part it seemed reasonably certain they were going along with the "white man's" etiquette, and providing reliable information.

[7] Three of these kinds of correctness correspond to the three-fold division of semiotics (sign theory) first advanced by Morris (1938) and now widely employed: *syntactics*, or the formal relations between signs; *semantics*, or the relations of signs to the things they refer to; and *pragmatics*, or the relations of users of signs to the signs they use. This division does not take account specifically of the "truth" level, which might be a subdivision of pragmatics, in that an utterance can be chosen as appropriate in a given situation and yet be judged untrue by the speaker (for example, proclaiming "such a beautiful baby" to proud new parents).

[8] The training proceeded in somewhat the same order as given here. Informants first learned the task of linguistic or grammatical judgment, abstracting from sense, truth, and use; they secondly added the abstracting of sense from truth. But then, under the impression they were training me to go out in the community and ask questions of people, they took pains to warn of pragmatic consequences. Only last did they learn that the questions would be asked of *them*, and then "true" responses became of importance. (It was less easy to reverse this order, once the ethnographer's interest in their belief system was unveiled.)

[9] Definitions here follow Conklin (1962): "taxonomic relations" means, first inclusion of reference, or *class-inclusion*, implying separate hierarchical levels; and second, exclusion, or *direct contrast* among members of a subset at a particular level.

Contrast refers to two items which are mutually exclusive in some context, e.g. X contrasts with Y if "X" implies "not Y."

The above two frames are sufficient to obtain a folk taxonomy; that is, to elicit sets of terms and to determine inclusion and contrast relations among all terms elicited.

Semantic analysis of the *features* of contrast which differentiate co-members of a taxonomic subset (paradigmatic, or componential) is not being considered here as part of the taxonomy proper nor as indicative of taxonomic relations. Such analyses give further information *about* a taxonomy, in other words, the rules for assigning members to classes, but they are performed on sets of terms whose inclusion and contrast status has already been determined (cf. Conklin 1962:132).

[10] An attempt was made in the Ojibwa study not to prejudge semantic structures by the ethnographer's procedures, but to remain in opportunistic readiness for clues from informants as to alternative means of classifying which they might employ in other contexts. Grounds for starting with taxonomic questions rested on the fact that it has been taken as a semantic universal of languages that there will be generic terms and hierarchic class-inclusion relations (Conklin 1962:128; Weinreich 1963).

[11] The fact that the word /bema.diziwa.d/ is not a single lexeme (its meaning can be deduced from its grammatical structure), and therefore is not properly a category label (cf. Conklin 1962:128), is discussed in Black 1967 and will not be dealt with here. It did function semantically as described, in the usage of Minnesota Ojibwa speakers.

[12] Hallowell (1955), in reporting on the Canadian Ojibwa of the Berens River dialect of the 1930's, gives this same word as "human beings," then adds in parentheses "that is, Ojibwa Indians." Minnesota speakers of 1965 included all varieties of Indians under this label.

[13] Other ways included switching to English. At one point, an informant was apparently impatient with my four-fold repetition through 'Indians,' 'white people,' 'Negroes,' 'Asiatics,' and being asked in Ojibwa 'Do they make offerings to *aniŝina. beg?*' (aniŝina.beg filling the X slot in this frame), she broke into English with "They don't make offerings to any human beings." When asked how that would be said in Ojibwa, she used /bema.diziwa.d/.

[14] Semantic usage of /bema.diziwa.d/ is more complex than has been indicated in this paper. A description of its derivation, inflections, contrasts and usages, as far as the writer has analyzed these, is found in Black 1967, Appendix A.23. Its most *salient* reference, when it stands unqualified by another noun, seems to be to the category 'human beings,' in the Minnesota usage. That it properly extends to all 'living things' is immediately acknowledged, however, by informants.

[15] The inference of t.2 was based also on evidence of intersecting categories such as the set 'men, women, children, teenagers, babies,' which set off the four classes of 'people' from other classes in the taxonomy.

REFERENCES CITED

Berger, J., B. P. Cohen, J. L. Snell and M. Zelditch, Jr., 1962, Types of formalization in small-group research. Boston, Houghton Mifflin.

Berreman, Gerald D., 1966, Anemic and emetic analyses in social anthropology. American Anthropologist 68:346–354.

Black, Mary B., 1963, On formal ethnographic procedures. American Anthropologist 65:1347–1351.

——, 1967, An ethnoscience investigation of Ojibwa ontology and world view. Unpub. Ph.D. Dissertation, Stanford University.

Black, Mary B., Duane Metzger, 1965, Ethnographic description and the study of law. *In* Nader, L., ed., The ethnography of law, American Anthropologist 67, No. 6, Pt. 2.

Conklin, Harold C., 1962, Lexicographical treatment of folk taxonomies. *In* Householder, Fred W. and Sol Saporta, eds., Problems in lexicography. Bloomington, Indiana, Research Center in Anthropology, Folklore and Linguistics, Pub. 21.

Gleason, H. A., 1961, An introduction to descriptive linguistics. New York, Holt, Rinehart and Winston.

Goodenough, Ward H., 1951, Property, kin, and community on Truk. Yale Univ. Pubs. in Anthropology, No. 46.

Hallowell, A. I., 1955, Culture and experience. Philadelphia, Univ. of Pa.

Mathiot, Madeleine, 1962, Noun classes and folk taxonomy in Papago, American Anthropologist 64:340–350. (Also in Hymes, D., ed., Language in culture and society, 1964:161.)

Metzger, D., G. E. Williams, 1963a, A formal ethnographic analysis of Tenejapa ladino weddings. American Anthropologist 65:1072–1101.

——, 1963b, Tenejapa medicine I: the curer. Southwestern Journal of Anthropology 19:216–234.

——, 1966a, Procedures and results in the study of native catagories: Tzeltal firewood. American Anthropologist 68:389–407.

——, 1966b, Patterns of primary personal reference in a Tzeltal community. Estudios de la cultura Maya, Vol. VI.

Morris, Charles W., 1938, Foundations of a theory of signs. Chicago, Univ. of Chicago Press.

Sturtevant, W. C., 1964, Studies in ethnoscience. *In* Romney, A. K. and R. G. D'Andrade, eds., Transcultural studies in cognition. American Anthropologist 66, No. 3, Pt. 2.

Weinreich, U., 1963, On the semantic structure of language. *In* J. H. Greenberg, ed., Universals of language. Cambridge, M.I.T. Press.

Williams, G. E., 1966, Linguistic reflections of cultural systems. Anthropological Linguistics 8:13–21.

3 Discovery

of Semantic Features:

Formal Analysis

A formal analysis presumes that the items to be analyzed are part of some legitimate semantic domain, and that the data are adequately described. Formal analysis is basically a translation procedure. It seeks to explain the semantic features of one language (the target language) by reference to features whose values are known in some other language (the reference language). The aim of formal analysis is to discover and state the relation of features in the reference language as parsimoniously as possible. Since the features available in the reference language are always more numerous than those in the target language, this is a two-step procedure which entails: (1) listing the features of the reference language relevant to each semantic category of the language to be translated: (2) elimination of redundant features in the reference language (cf. Hammel 1965:4–5). A third step— the arrangement of features—has already been discussed in chapter one.

Procedures for eliminating redundant features are based on one or more kinds of formal rules. One kind of formal rule consists of a set of operations derived from algebraic factoring and substitution. Basically this is the technique employed intuitively in componential analysis (cf. Lounsbury this volume, chapter 3; Goodenough this volume, chapter 3). A different type of rule consists of an instruction to rearrange features of the reference language in set patterns and usually in a given order. Since they may be repeatedly applied over the appropriate sequence of features, rules of the latter type are similar to recursive functions. Lounsbury's Crow-Omaha paper utilizes rules of this type (see also Hammel 1965; Kay 1965, 1967; Lamb 1965; Romney 1965; Tyler 1966). Both kinds of rules achieve similar results, but differ in their implications. Algebraic rules tend to be finite. Unless modified by additional rules they will only generate back the original data. Without restrictions recursive rules will go beyond the original data to generate new expressions. The significance of these differences is not yet fully understood.

Since a formal analysis emphasizes internal consistency, completeness, and form, it must first be evaluated in these terms. Is the analysis consistent? Is it complete? Is it parsimonious? In other words, the analysis is first evaluated in terms of criteria relevant to its internal elements and operations. The question of external relevance is no more significant at this stage than is the question: "Does the 'real world' correspond to the operations of algebra?" The question of external relationships constitutes a further step in the analysis and is discussed in chapters 4 and 5.

REFERENCES CITED

Hammel, E. A., 1965, A transformational analysis of Comanche kinship terminology. American Anthropologist 67 No. 5, Pt. 2, 65–105.
——, 1965, Introduction. *In* E. A. Hammel ed., Formal semantic analysis. American Anthropologist Special Publication. 67; Pt. 2, No. 5:1–8.
Kay, Paul, 1965, A generalization of the cross-parallel distinction. American Anthropologist 67:30–43.
——, 1967, On the multiplicity of cross-parallel distinctions. American Anthropologist 69:83–85.
Lamb, Sydney M., 1965, Kinship terminology and linguistic structure. American Anthropologist Special Publication. 67; Pt. 2, No. 5:29–64.
Romney, A. K., 1965, Kalmuk mongol and the classification of lineal kinship terminologies. American Anthropologist 67 No. 5, Pt. 2, 127–141.
Tyler, Stephen A. 1966, Parallel/cross: an evaluation of definitions. Southwestern Journal of Anthropology 22:416–32.

The Structural Analysis of Kinship Semantics[1]

Floyd G. Lounsbury

The set of KIN-TYPE designations—such as *father, father's brother, mother's brother, father's sister's son,* etc.—specifying the genealogical positions of one's known kin in relation to himself, can be regarded as constituting a semantic field. Linguistic usage, in any given community, groups these kin types into a smaller number of labeled KIN CLASSES, such as "father," "uncle," "cousin," etc. The set of linguistic forms employed to designate such kin classes in a speech community constitutes its KINSHIP VOCABULARY. Any one of the forms is a KIN TERM. The classificatory structure imposed on this semantic field by conventional usage of kinship vocabulary varies greatly from society to society. We shall consider one single instance of such usage—that of the Seneca Indians, an Iroquois tribe of western New York State, as documented by Lewis Henry Morgan in the middle of the nineteenth century.

A kinship vocabulary can be regarded as constituting a paradigm. It can be subjected to a kind of analysis similar to that given other paradigmatic sets in a language. The Seneca data will be analysed in this manner. The application of the method yields results which are not common knowledge and which run counter to a classic but erroneous anthropological view concerning the nature of the "Iroquois type" of kinship system. Our interest in this paper, however, is not in correcting an anthropological error, but in illustrating a method of semantic analysis.

PRELIMINARY NOTIONS

PARADIGM   We shall regard as a paradigm any set of linguistic forms wherein: (a) the meaning of every form has a feature in common with the meanings of all other forms of the set, and (b) the meaning of every form differs from that of every other form of the set by one or more additional features. The common feature will be said to be the ROOT MEANING of the paradigm. It defines the semantic field which the forms of the paradigm partition. The variable features define the SEMANTIC DIMENSIONS of the paradigm.

DIMENSION; FEATURE   A dimension of a paradigm is a set of mutually exclusive (i.e., non-cooccurent) features which share some or all of the same privileges of combination ("bundling") with features not of this dimension. A feature is an ultimate term of characterization in a set of descriptive

From *Proceedings of the Ninth International Congress of Linguists,* 1964. The Hague, Mouton and Co. Used by permission of the author and Mouton and Co.

terms appropriate for the analysis of a particular given paradigm. A dimension is thus an "opposition," and the features of a dimension are the terms of the opposition. Reduction to dichotomous oppositions is always possible, but is normally carried out only when a resulting increase in clarity and simplicity warrants it.

MEANING   In paragraph 1 above, where we have written "meaning," one may read "meaning and/or distribution" without departing from the sense intended. The term is meant to be interpreted broadly, covering both (a) objects and conditions of reference, and (b) restrictions and special privileges of context. In the instance of the kinship paradigm given below, however, we have only to deal with reference.

COMPONENTIAL DEFINITIONS   A term belonging to a paradigm can be defined componentially in terms of its coordinates in the paradigm. The definition represents a bundle of features: one from each of several, or of all, of the dimensions of the paradigm. This bundle of features states the necessary and sufficient conditions which an object must satisfy if it is to be a DENOTATUM of the term so defined. Terms having single denotata are the exception; multiple denotation is more generally the case. The class of all possible denotata of a term constitutes its DESIGNATUM. The defining features of this class—i.e. the necessary and sufficient conditions for membership in it—are its SIGNIFICATUM (Morris 1938, 1946). The componential definition of a term is the expression of its significatum.

CONJUNCTIVE DEFINITIONS   A componential definition represents a Boolean class product, and is thus a "unitary" or "conjunctive" definition. It is assumed that the meaning of any term belonging to a properly defined paradigm—one whose semantic field is itself unitary—will be susceptible to such a definition. This is perhaps a stronger item of faith than we have a right to hold at this moment: but it furnishes the motivation for the analysis of kinship systems at least. We proceed from extensional definitions (definitions by listing of denotata) to intensional definitions (definitions by specification of distinctive features). We feel that we have failed if we cannot achieve conjunctive definitions for every terminological class in the system. Were we to compromise on this point and admit disjunctive definitions (class sums, alternative criteria for membership) as on a par with conjunctive definitions (class products, uniform criteria for membership), there would be no motivation for analysis in the first place, for definitions of kin classes by the summing of discrete members—as in the table of Seneca data given below—are disjunctive definitions par excellence.

SENECA KINSHIP DATA

Following is a list of the Iroquois kinship terms, given in the language of the Seneca. Each term designates a class of one's kinsmen. The reference of each term is defined by naming all of the more closely related types of kinsmen, as well as a small sample of the more distant ones, to which the term is applied. We restrict our discussion here to consanguineal types.

ABBREVIATIONS   Primary kin types are abbreviated as follows: F = *father;* M = *mother;* B = *brother;* S = *sister;* s = *son;* d = *daughter.*[2] Higher-order kin types are abbreviated with compound symbols, e.g.: Bd = *brother's daughter;* FSs = *father's sister's son;* MMBsd = *mother's mother's brother's son's daughter;* etc. Since we shall deal here only with the consanguineal system, we shall not need to employ the additional symbols H (= *husband*) and W (= *wife*) which are necessary in the writing of affinal and step types.

SEX OF PROPOSITUS   All kin types listed after any given kinship term are assumed to be possible referents of that term in relation to a propositus *of either sex,* except when otherwise indicated. Such indication is either written out (unabbreviated), as in the list of data at the close of this section, or is indicated by the prefixed signs ♂ and ♀, as in some of the later discussion. Thus; ♂s = *a man's son;* ♀s = *a woman's son;* ♂Ss = *a man's sister's son;* etc.

TRANSLATION LABELS   English labels are also given for the Seneca terms. In each case the label is the word which we would use in English, in our kinship usage, to refer to the pivotal member or members of the class—that one which is (or those which are) the most closely related to the propositus. It should be borne in mind that these English labels are *not* proper English translations, for they do not cover the same areas of denotation. English translations can be achieved only by descriptive circumlocution after the classificatory features defining the Iroquois kin classes have been discovered. The purpose of the English labels is merely to save the reader the task of learning an Iroquois vocabulary, and also to identify the pivotal member or members, i.e., the focus or foci, of each class. Translation labels will always appear in double quotation marks (e.g., "my father") to mark them as Iroquois concepts and to distinguish them from the normal English meanings of the same words.

hakso:t "my grandfather"	FF, MF; FFB, FMB, MFB, MMB, FFFBs, etc.; *also* FFF, MMF, etc.
akso:t, "my grandmother"	FM, MM; FFS, FMS, MFS, MMS; FFFBd, etc.; *also* FFM, MMM, etc.
ha²nih, "my father"	F; FB; FMSs, FFBs, FMBs, FFSs, FFFBss, etc.
no²yēh, "my mother"	M; MS; MMSd, MFBd, MMBd, MFSd, MMMSdd, etc.
hakhno²sēh, "my uncle"	MB; MMSs, MFBs, MMBs, MFSs; MMMSds, etc.

ake:hak, "my aunt"	FS; FMSd, FFBd, FMBd, FFSd; FFFBsd, etc.
hahtsi², "my elder brother"	B; MSs, FBs; MMSds, FFBss, MFBds, FMSss, MMBds, FFSss, MFSds, FMBss; MMMSdds, etc., *when older than Ego.*
he²kē:², "my younger brother"	Same, *when younger than Ego.*
ahtsi², "my elder sister"	S; MSd, FBd; MMSdd, FFBsd, MFBdd, FMSsd, MMBdd, FFSsd, MFSdd, FMBsd; MMMSddd, etc., *when older than Ego.*
khe²kē:², "my younger sister"	Same, *when younger than Ego.*
akyä:²se:², "my cousin"	MBs, FSs; MMSss, FFBds, MFBss, FMSds, MMBss, FFSds, MFSss, FMBds; MMMSdss, etc.; *and* MBd, FSd; MMSsd, FFBdd, MFBsd, FMSdd, MMBsd, FFSdd, MFSsd, FMBdd; MMMSdsd, etc.
he:awak, "my son"	s; Bs; MSss, FBss, MBss, FSss; MMSdss, etc., *of a man; but:* s; Ss; MSds, FBds, MBds, FSds; MMSdds, etc., *of a woman.*
khe:awak, "my daughter"	d; Bd; MSsd, FBsd, MBsd, FSsd; MMSdsd, etc., *of a man; but:* d; Sd; MSdd, FBdd, MBdd, FSdd; MMSddd, etc., *of a woman.*
heyē:wõtē², "my nephew"	Ss; MSds, FBds, MBds, FSds; MMSdds, etc., *of a man.*
hehsõ²neh, "my nephew"	Bs; MSss, FBss, MBss, FSss; MMSdss, etc., *of a woman.*
kheyē:wõ:tē², "my niece"	Sd; MSdd, FBdd, MBdd, FSdd; MMSddd, etc., *of a man.*
khehsõ²neh, "my niece"	Bd; MSsd, FBsd, MBsd, FSsd; MMSdsd, etc., *of a woman.*
heya:te², "my grandson"	ss, ds; Bss, Bds, Sss, Sds; FBsss, etc.; *also* sss, dds, etc.
kheya:te², "my granddaughter"	sd, dd; Bsd, Bdd, Ssd, Sdd; FBssd, etc.; *also* ssd, ddd, etc.[3]

ANALYSIS

THE ROOT OF THE PARADIGM   An individual related to a propositus in any of the ways specified by the various kin-type designations given under the kin terms of the above list is also *akyatēnõhk*, "my kinsman," and can be referred to as such. This general term subsumes all of the special terms of the kinship vocabulary, each of which in turn subsumes all of the kin types listed after it. It thus defines the common feature of meaning required of a set of forms if they are to be regarded as constituting a paradigm. It represents, therefore, the root of the paradigm. This feature will be written as K (for *kinsman*) in the kin-class definitions below.

THE DIMENSION OF GENERATION   Inspection of the data shows that one of the dimensions of the system is obviously GENERATION. This presents a set of five features, which represent obligatory categories in the system. These are: *second-or-higher ascending generation; first ascending generation; the generation of the propositus; first descending generation;* and *second-or-lower descending generation*. In the kin-class definitions below, these will be written as G^2, G^1, G^0, G^{-1}, G^{-2}, respectively.

The categories of generation in Seneca, unlike those in our own system of kinship terminology, are overriding categories. Seneca kin-classes do not cross generation lines, whereas some of ours do (e.g., our classes cousin, uncle, aunt, etc.). Seneca kin classes, on the other hand, cross degrees of collaterality, whereas none of our English classes transgress the boundaries of the three DEGREES OF COLLATERALITY obligatorily distinguished in our system, viz.: the *zero degree* (i.e., lineal kin); *first degree* (brother, sister, uncle, aunt, nephew, niece); and *second-or-higher degree* (cousin).

THE DIMENSION OF SEX   Another obvious dimension of the system is that of SEX. Its features are *male* and *female*. In the kin-class definitions below, these will be written as ♂ and ♀ respectively.

The features from the dimensions of generation and sex are sufficient to distinguish and define four of the kin classes of the list:

hakso:t, grandfather"	♂·G^2·K.
akso:t, `grandmother"	♀·G^2·K.
heya:te², 'grandson"	♂·G^{-2}·K.
kheya:te², "granddaughter"	♀·G^{-2}·K.

Note that, unlike the analogous terms in English, these four Seneca terms include known collateral kin of all degrees, as well as lineal kin. The componential definitions given here recognize this fact, inasmuch as they do not incorporate any features drawn from a dimension of collaterality distinctions, as definitions for our English terms must.

THE CLASSIFICATION IN THE FIRST ASCENDING GENERATION   Four kin classes are distinguished in the first ascending generation: *ha²nih* ("father"), *no²yēh* ("mother"), *hakhno²sēh* ("uncle"), and *ake:hak* ("aunt"). Assuming that we may be dealing with two dimensions of dichotomizing features, we may try pairing the terms.

Given any four terms, there are three possible ways of pairing them. In the present case, we might first pair "father" with "uncle" and oppose these to the remaining pair consisting of "mother" and "aunt." Inspection of the data will show that, if we do this, the oppostion is in the dimension of sex. (It should be noted that we *must* inspect the data to determine this; we cannot simply assume it as natural, or infer it from the translation labels. Anthropological literature furnishes many examples of systems that have both females and males in the "mother" class, and both males and females in the "father" class.)

Inspection of the data also suggests another plausible pairing: that of "father" with "aunt," as opposed to "mother" and "uncle." In this case the dimension can be characterized as SIDE, and the opposed features which constitute it as *patrilateral* and *matrilateral*. These we may write as π and μ. As can be seen from the table, the types of kinsmen who are called by the "father" term, *ha?nih*, in Seneca are male first-ascending-generation kinsmen related to the propositus on his father's side (patrilateral), while those called "uncle," *hakhno?sēh*, are all on his mother's side (matrilateral). Similarly, all of those who are "aunt," *ake:hak*, are female kin of that generation on the father's side, while those that are "mother," *no?yēh*, are on the mother's side. These features from the dimension of side, together with those from the dimension of sex, suffice to differentiate the kin classes of the first ascending generation. The definitions are as follows:

ha?nih, "father"	$\male \cdot \pi \cdot G^1 \cdot K.$
ake:hak, "aunt"	$\female \cdot \pi \cdot G^1 \cdot K.$
hakhno?sēh, "uncle"	$\male \cdot \mu \cdot G^1 \cdot K.$
no?yēh, "mother"	$\female \cdot \mu \cdot G^1 \cdot K.$

There is however a third possible way of pairing these terms, which, because it may appeal to us as a more or less reasonable and natural kind of pairing, at least should not be overlooked. This is to pair "father" with "mother," and to oppose them to the pair consisting of "uncle" and "aunt." Study of the data, with the aim of discovering a feature shared by all of the members of both the "father" and the "mother" classes, and some other opposed feature common to the members of the "uncle" and "aunt" classes, shows that, from the standpoint of the data, this is a less obvious manner of pairing and will require a more contrived set of features. It is possible, nonetheless, to define such features. And this fact suffices to show that this is indeed a natural pairing; for arbitrary and unnatural pairings never allow the discovery of common features.

Accordingly we may define a feature, $L^=$, which will be said to inhere in any kin type in which *the sex of the designated kin is the* SAME *as that of the first link;* and an opposed feature, $L^{\neq}$, which will be said to inhere in any kin type in which *the sex of the designated kin is* OPPOSITE *to that of the first link.* Now, the second of these features is common to all of the members of both the "uncle" and the "aunt" classes, while the first is common to all of the members of both the "father" and "mother" classes. Thus, in the types MB, MMSs, MFBs, MMBs, MFSs, etc. ("uncles"), and in the types FS, FMSd, FFBd, FMBd, FFSd, etc. ("aunts"), it is true that the sex of the designated kinsman or kinswoman (given by the last term in any kin-type abbreviation) is in every case opposite to that of the first link to the propositus (given by the first term in the abbreviation). *The sexes of intervening links, when present, are irrelevant to the reckoning.*[4] Similarly, in the types F, FB, FMSs, FFBs, FMBs, FFSs, etc. ("fathers"), and in the types M, MS, MMSd, MFBd, MMBd, MFSd, etc. ("mothers"), the sex of the designated kinsman or kinswoman is in every case the same as that of the first link. [Note: F and M are the limiting cases, where "designated kin" (last term) and "first link" (first term) coincide. In the case of coincidence, the condition of equality of sex can of course be said to be satisfied.]

With three possible pairings of the four G^1 kinship terms, we are now in possession of one more dimension than is necessary for uniquely characterizing them. The features from any two of these dimensions might be chosen as defining features, and those of the third dimension regarded as "redundant." ("Redundant" in a logical sense, not merely in an empirical sense, since the features of any one of the dimensions can be defined in terms of those of the other two.) It may be objected that in the case of the third pair of features we are attempting to impose on the Seneca system a pairing which is natural and reasonable from our point of view, as members of our society, but which, because of its contrived nature, may be inappropriate to the Seneca system. We can leave the judgment on that point until later. For the time being, we recognize that there are three possible alternative definitions for each of the first-ascending-generation kin classes:

ha²nih, "father"	$\male \cdot L = \cdot G^1 \cdot K,$	*or*	$\male \cdot \pi \cdot G^1 \cdot K,$	*or*	$\pi \cdot L = \cdot G^1 \cdot K.$
no²yêh, "mother"	$\female \cdot L = \cdot G^1 \cdot K,$	*or*	$\female \cdot \mu \cdot G^1 \cdot K,$	*or*	$\mu \cdot L = \cdot G^1 \cdot K.$
hakhno²sêh, "uncle"	$\male \cdot L^{\neq} \cdot G^1 \cdot K,$	*or*	$\male \cdot \mu \cdot G^1 \cdot K,$	*or*	$\mu \cdot L^{\neq} \cdot G^1 \cdot K.$
ake:hak, "aunt"	$\female \cdot L^{\neq} \cdot G^1 \cdot K,$	*or*	$\female \cdot \pi \cdot G^1 \cdot K,$	*or*	$\pi \cdot L^{\neq} \cdot G^1 \cdot K.$

THE CLASSIFICATION IN THE FIRST DESCENDING GENERATION   Six kin terms are given in the list for kin types of the first descending generation, but only four of them are available to any given propositus.

First let us consider the four terms for the kin of a male. As before, we seek all possible ways of pairing the terms. We may begin with the sex pairing, of "son" (*he:awak*) with "nephew" (*heyê:wõ:tê²*), as opposed to "daughter" (*khe:awak*) and "niece" (*kheyê:wõ:tê²*).

A second possible pairing is that of "son" with "daughter," these being opposed to "nephew" and "niece." This pairing, as can be seen from the list, opposes a class consisting of the children of a male propositus and of all of his male generation-mates,[5] to a second class consisting of the children of his female generation-mates.[6] The features of this opposition we may symbolize with the letters ϕ and σ (suggested by the partially—though not completely—descriptive terms "fratrifilial" and "sororifilial").

There should be a third manner of pairing these four kin terms. This can only be to set "son" with "niece," and to oppose these to "daughter" and "nephew." While this might not appeal to us (or to the Iroquois either) as a natural pairing, it is nonetheless possible to define a feature which would unite the "son" and the "niece" classes (viz., sameness of sex of designated kin and last link), and an opposing feature which would unite the "daughter" and "nephew" classes (viz., oppositeness of sex of designated kin and last link). We might symbolize these features as P= and P≠, respectively (suggested by: *kinsman's* PARENT *of* SAME *sex as kinsman*, and *kinsman's* PARENT *of* OPPOSITE *sex to kinsman*).

Thus, one may write three alternative definitions of each of the four G^{-1} kin classes for a *male propositus:*

he:awak, "son"	$\male \cdot \phi \cdot G^{-1} \cdot K,$	*or* $\male \cdot P^= \cdot G^{-1} \cdot K,$	*or* $\phi \cdot P^= \cdot G^{-1} \cdot K.$
khe:awak, "daughter"	$\female \cdot \phi \cdot G^{-1} \cdot K,$	*or* $\female \cdot P^{\neq} \cdot G^{-1} \cdot K,$	*or* $\phi \cdot P^{\neq} \cdot G^{-1} \cdot K.$
heyʔ:wõ:tẽʔ, "nephew"	$\male \cdot \sigma \cdot G^{-1} \cdot K,$	*or* $\male \cdot P^{\neq} \cdot G^{-1} \cdot K,$	*or* $\sigma \cdot P^{\neq} \cdot G^{-1} \cdot K.$
kheyẽ:wõ:tẽʔ, "niece"	$\female \cdot \sigma \cdot G^{-1} \cdot K,$	*or* $\female \cdot P^= \cdot G^{-1} \cdot K,$	*or* $\sigma \cdot P^= \cdot G^{-1} \cdot K.$

If we consider now the classification of kin in relation to a *female propositus*, we find we can write the following definitions:

he:awak, "son"	$\male \cdot \sigma \cdot G^{-1} \cdot K,$	*or* $\male \cdot P^{\neq} \cdot G^{-1} \cdot K,$	*or* $\sigma \cdot P^{\neq} \cdot G^{-1} \cdot K.$
khe:awak, "daughter"	$\female \cdot \sigma \cdot G^{-1} \cdot K,$	*or* $\female \cdot P^= \cdot G^{-1} \cdot K,$	*or* $\sigma \cdot P^= \cdot G^{-1} \cdot K.$
hehsõʔneh, "nephew"	$\male \cdot \phi \cdot G^{-1} \cdot K,$	*or* $\male \cdot P^= \cdot G^{-1} \cdot K,$	*or* $\phi \cdot P^{\neq} \cdot G^{-1} \cdot K.$
khehsõʔneh, "niece"	$\female \cdot \phi \cdot G^{-1} \cdot K,$	*or* $\female \cdot P^{\neq} \cdot G^{-1} \cdot K,$	*or* $\phi \cdot P^= \cdot G^{-1} \cdot K.$

It will be seen that none of these definitions are invariant to the sex of the propositus. In fact, the definitions of "nephew" (*hehsõʔneh*) of a female are identical to those of "son" (*he:awak*) of a male, while those of "son" (*he:awak*) of a female are identical to those of "nephew" (*heyẽ:wõ:tẽʔ*) of a male. Preferable, surely, would be definitions invariant to the sex of the propositus—at least where the same linguistic forms are involved (*he:awak, khe:awak*).

These can be obtained by employing a pair of features which are the reciprocals of those used to obtain the pairing of "mother" with "father," and "uncle" with "aunt" in G^1, as follows. Let us define a feature $\lambda^=$, which will be said to inhere in any kin type in which *the sex of the last link is the* SAME *as that of the propositus;* and an opposed feature, $\lambda^{\neq}$, which will be said to inhere in any kin type in which *the sex of the last link is* OPPOSITE *to that of the propositus.* The first of these features is common to all the members of both the "son" (*he:awak*) and the "daughter" (*khe:awak*) classes, regardless of whether this be in relation to a male or to a female. Inspection of the data will verify that this is so. E.g., σBs, ♀Ss, σMBss, ♀MBds, etc. [Note: s (i.e., σs and ♀s) and d (i.e., σd and ♀d) are the limiting cases, where last link (second-last term) coincides with the propositus. In such a case it can of course be said that their sexes are the same.]

We may redefine the G^{-1} terms as follows:

> *he:awak,* "son" $\sigma \cdot \lambda = \cdot G^{-1} \cdot K.$
> *khe:awak,* "daughter"   ♀$\cdot \lambda = \cdot G^{-1} \cdot K.$
> *heyẽ:wõ:tẽˀ / hehsõˀneh,* "nephew" $\sigma \cdot \lambda \neq \cdot G^{-1} \cdot K.$
> *kheyẽ:wõ:tẽˀ / khehsõˀneh,* "niece" ♀$\cdot \lambda \neq \cdot G^{-1} \cdot K.$

Now, instead of having *he:awak* a being a pair of homonymous words, it is just one word with one signification; and similarly with the *khe:awak.* And we get a bonus out of it besides: the two "nephew" terms end up being synonyms of a sort, differing only by an additional component specifying the sex of the propositus; and similarly the two "niece" terms. [This is a useful bonus, especially in a related language such as Tuscarora, which lacks the extra synonym and has but one term (Tusc. *kheyēhwaˀnẽˀ*) undifferentiated for either sex of propositus or sex of kin, for the meaning $\lambda \neq \cdot G^{-1} \cdot K.$)]

THE CLASSIFICATION IN EGO'S GENERATION   Five kin terms are employed in $G°$. Four of them, the "sibling" terms *hahtsiˀ, heˀkẽ:ˀ, ahtsiˀ, kheˀkẽ:ˀ,* form a readily analysable set based on the differentiations of RELATIVE AGE and SEX. The fifth term, *akyä:ˀse:ˀ,* "cousin," has a range of denotation comparable in magnitude to that of the four "sibling" terms conjointly. Within this range, no distinctions are made either for sex or for relative age.

We wish now to find out the dimension of difference that opposes the combined "sibling" class (the sum of the four special "sibling" classes) to the "cousin" class. Study of the data reveals one, and only one, possibility. Let us accordingly define a feature, $\Lambda =$, which will be said to inhere in any kin type in which *the sex of the last link is the* SAME *as that of the first link;* and an opposed feature, $\Lambda \neq$, which will be said to inhere in any kin type in which *the sex of the last link is* OPPOSITE *to that of the first link.* The second of these features is common to all of the members of the "cousin" class (e.g., MBs, FSs, FFSds, FMSds, etc.), while the first is common to all of the members of the four "sibling" classes (e.g., MSs, FBs, FFSss, FMSss, etc.). [Note: B and S are the limiting cases, where the last link and the first link coincide—a fact that is not obvious simply from the writings B and S but that can be readily seen when it is remembered that B is Fs and/or Ms, and that S is Fd and/or Md. (There are empirical reasons why B and S are admitted as "primary" kin types in kinship reckoning, and why the ambiguity inherent in them can be tolerated.)]

Now we may write the definitions for the $G°$ terms. (A^+ and A^- are for the features of RELATIVE AGE.)

hahtsi?, "elder brother"	$A^+ \cdot \male \cdot \Lambda^= \cdot G° \cdot K.$
he?kē:?, "younger brother"	$A^- \cdot \male \cdot \Lambda^= \cdot G° \cdot K.$
ahtsi?, "elder sister"	$A^+ \cdot \female \cdot \Lambda^= \cdot G° \cdot K.$
khe?kē:?, "younger sister"	$A^- \cdot \female \cdot \Lambda^= \cdot G° \cdot K.$
akyä:?se:?, "cousin"	$\Lambda^{\neq} \cdot G° \cdot K.$

THE DIMENSION OF BIFURCATION   Reviewing the definitions given in preceding paragraphs for kin classes in G^1, G^{-1}, and $G°$, it is seen (a) that the features $L^=$ and $L^{\neq}$ occur only in the context G^1; (b) that the features $\lambda^=$ and $\lambda^{\neq}$ occur only in the context G^{-1}, and (c) that the features $\Lambda^=$ and $\Lambda^{\neq}$ occur only in the context $G°$. They are thus in complementary distribution. This may suggest that they may be but conditioned variants of one basic pair of features; and that they may, if the similarity condition can be met, be grouped into a single pair of units in the metalanguage which we use to spell out the semantic content of the Seneca kin terms. They may thus be reduced to one opposition of wider applicability in the system, instead of three oppositions of more limited applicability.

The condition of similarity can indeed be met (all three contrasts involve comparisons in the generation just above the lowest represented by propositus and/or kin), and we may take $L^=$, $\lambda^=$, and $\Lambda^=$, as defined previously, to be conditioned variants of one basic feature. Similarly, $L^{\neq}$, $\lambda^{\neq}$, and $\Lambda^{\neq}$ can be taken as conditioned variants of the opposed feature. These features we can call by the traditional names of *parallel* and *cross*, respectively, although the real meanings of these terms in their application to Iroquois-type kinship systems have been rather poorly understood in the past. And the dimension which these features constitute can similarly be called by the traditional name of BIFURCATION. The symbols $\parallel$ and $\times$ will be used to represent the features in the writing of definitions.

THE STRUCTURE OF THE FIELD   The definitions of the kin classes in the middle three generations may now be rewritten; and the entire paradigm may be presented, so as to show the structure of its semantic field, in a four-dimensional diagram, a four-column matrix, or a four-margin outline.

The field dealt with up to this point has been that of the consanguineal kin-types. The step-kin and in-law types, and the terms that classify them, can be dealt with in a similar fashion. Step and in-law categories are obligatorily distinguished from the consanguineal ones, as well as from each other, and their classification is peculiar to the Iroquois system.

Also not dealt with yet are the many forms designating the superclasses which are obtained by neutralizing the oppositions of sex, relative age, and generation "direction"—i.e., *ascending* vs. *descending*. These neutralizations are accomplished by grammatical devices provided in the Iroquoian inflectional and derivational systems. The existence of these does not invalidate the claim to "obligatoriness" that was made for the distinctions drawn in the sections above, for the neutralizing forms are cover-terms that are appropriate only to rather particular contexts, having a status in usage (though not in grammar) somewhat comparable to our cover-terms "parent," "child," "parent-and-child," "sibling," and such artificial ones like "grand-kin"—as anthropologists occasionally employ.

These various aspects of the Iroquois kinship system cannot be treated here. To do so would expand this article to a length inappropriate to the present occasion. One matter of some general interest deserves comment however. It will be noted that, of the four dimensions employed in the analysis of the consanguineal system, three of them—sex, bifurcation, and relative age—were dimensions representing a *dichotomous opposition* of just two features; but one of them—generation—was a dimension whose variable could assume five values. Two questions may be raised. One of these is whether the five-valued dimension is reducible in fact to a larger number of dimensions of dichotomous oppositions. The other is whether, in dichotomous oppositions, one member of the opposition can be said to be the marked member (a positive feature), and the other the unmarked member (the absence, or negation, of the positive).

In regard to the first question it may be remarked that, since kinship terms come in reciprocal sets, it is always possible to analyse out the polarity between the reciprocals as a separate dimension of opposition. Thus, in place of the five-valued dimension of GENERATION (G^2, G^1, G^0, G^{-1}, G^{-2}), we may have a three-valued dimension of GENERATION DISTANCE (consisting of the absolute values G^2, G^1, G^0) and a dimension of POLARITY (*senior* vs. *junior*) or GENERATION DIRECTION (*plus* vs. *minus*). This is especially appropriate in Iroquoian where, for example, a set such as that consisting of the two "parent" terms, together with their reciprocal "child" terms, is covered by a single cover-term that neutralizes the generation direction (or polarity), as well as the sex, of the basic terms. Thus:

$$\{[ha^{\textit{?}}nih + no^{\textit{?}}y\tilde{e}h] + [he\text{:}awak + khe\text{:}awak]\} = \{akyatathawak\},$$

i.e., $\{[(\male \cdot \| \cdot G^1 \cdot K) + (\female \cdot \| \cdot G^1 \cdot K)] + [(\male \cdot \| \cdot G^{-1} \cdot K) + (\female \cdot \| \cdot G^{-1} \cdot K)]\} = \{\| \cdot G^{\pm 1} \cdot K\}$; and similarly with the other reciprocal sets of the system.

This new dimension can be equated with that already set up for RELATIVE AGE, for the polarity relation between the "parent" and "child" terms is similar to that between the "elder sibling" and "younger sibling" terms. Thus also:

$$\{[hahtsi^{\textit{?}} + ahtsi^{\textit{?}}] + [he^{\textit{?}}k\tilde{e}\text{:}^{\textit{?}} + khe^{\textit{?}}k\tilde{e}\text{:}^{\textit{?}}]\} = \{akyatate^{\textit{?}}k\tilde{e}\text{:}^{\textit{?}}\},$$

i.e., $\{[(\male \cdot \| \cdot A^+ \cdot G^0 \cdot K) + (\female \cdot \| \cdot A^+ \cdot G^0 \cdot K)] + [(\male \cdot \| \cdot A \cdot G^0 \cdot K) + (\female \cdot \| \cdot A^- \cdot G^0 \cdot K)]\}$
$= \{\| \cdot G^0 \cdot K\}$.

Thus the analytic simplification of the dimension of generation can be accomplished at no cost to economy in the total number of dimensions.

As for the possibility of reducing the remaining three-valued dimension of GENERATION DISTANCE still further, I know of no *good* natural basis for doing this; though it can, of course, always be done by fiat. One might cut it in either of two places: between G^2 and all else, or between G^0 and all else. More-or-less plausible arguments might be adduced for either of these, but it can be done only at the expense of adding a dimension to the system. This *is* an 'expense,' for it would take two dimensions of dichotomous opposition to account for only three values.

As for the second of the questions posed above, viz. whether a distinction can be made between a 'marked' and an 'unmarked' member of every opposition, it may be stated that there are good reasons—primarily semantic-structural, but with strong linguistic as well as social correlates—for regarding the *first* term of each of the following oppositions as the *marked* member:

> POLARITY: *senior*, vs. *junior*
> SEX: *male*, vs. *female*
> BIFURCATION: *cross*, vs. *parallel*.

The fourth dimension of the system, GENERATION DISTANCE, remains a three-valued one unless reduced by fiat. Just as I have not yet found any good basis, linguistic or social, for dividing this into two taxonomic dichotomies, so I am also without any basis for determining which features might best be regarded as marked and which as unmarked if this were done.

To justify the above choices of "marked" members (*senior, male, cross*) would require an extended treatment of the transitive pronominal prefix system, the gender system, and the stem-derivational system of Iroquois grammar, together with a "Whorfian" exegesis of the same, and an additional discussion of the typology of so-called Iroquois-type' kinship systems. It must suffice here to say that in each case the marked member is a "special" one in some sense, that is opposed to a "general" or "common" one. In positions or contexts of contrast, the unmarked member is specific. In positions or contexts of no contrast, it is general.[7] Thus, the "common gender" of Iroquois is the feminine (not the masculine as in English); the general root for the parent-child relation is -*hawak;* and the extension of bifurcation into G^0 (making the system "Iroquois type" as opposed to "Cheyenne type") in fact rests rather lightly on the Iroquois.

CONCLUDING REMARKS

This paper is presented as an example of the structural analysis of a lexical set which covers and partitions a semantic field. It was noted that this particular kind of lexical set can be regarded as constituting a paradigm, and that it can be subjected to a kind of analysis similar to that given other paradigmatic sets in a language. Certain common linguistic notions basic to this treatment were also defined, or briefly discussed, with special reference to their use in semantic analysis. These included the notions of semantic field, paradigm, root, dimension, feature, componential definition, the route from extensional to intensional definitions, the possibility of dichotomous dimensions of contrast, and the identification of the marked feature of an opposition. Also, something of the reason for the desideratum of conjunctive definitions was indicated.

A rather frequent response of linguists to such kinship exercises, I have found, is that they are of limited interest so far as the general problems of semantic analysis are concerned because, it is said, kinship vocabularies and their meanings are something special in lexicology, permitting as they do, the specification and analysis of reference with a satisfactory degree of rigor; but it is felt that they are, for this very reason, unrepresentative of linguistic-semantic, or lexicological, problems in general. I would not care to make any exaggerated claims for the particular methods that are of utility in the analysis of systems of kinship terminology, though I do think that their potentialities are rather generally underestimated. In any case, I would like to comment on a few further points of general relevance that arise out of the exercise presented in the preprint paper.

The first of these is the question of whether there are other content fields represented in language that are susceptible to this kind of analysis. On this point I will only say that anthropologists have applied this or similar sorts of analysis to the vocabularies representing a number of lexical and cultural domains of special interest to them. Among them are color vocabularies, native ethnobotanical terminologies, vocabularies of disease taxonomy in primitive societies, those of primitive cosmologies, systems of religious concepts, etc. The work is still new, and much needs to be done yet in the development of the method. A review of this work and a bibliography of some relevant items are contained in a recent paper by Harold Conklin (1962).

The second point has to do with the formal characteristics of the structure of semantic fields. There *is* something a bit special about the structure of kinship systems, viz., that their structure is in large part that of the "paradigm." While there are numerous sets of this sort in lexicon, this is by no means the general case. More typical, perhaps, is the "taxonomy." In the perfect paradigm, the features of any dimension combine with *all* of those of any other dimension. In the perfect taxonomy on the other hand, they never do; they combine with *only one* feature from any other dimension. In the perfect paradigm there is no hierarchical ordering of dimensions that is not arbitrary; all orders are possible. In the perfect taxonomy there is but one possible hierarchy. To illustrate the difference we may consider a set of eight elements constituting a field F. If these represent a paradigm, it takes but three dimensions of dichotomous opposition to fully characterize them (Fig. 1). If they represent a taxonomy, it takes seven (Fig. 2). Kinship terminologies usually represent something intermediate between these, the imperfect or asymmetrical paradigm, which combines principles of both kinds. In the analysis of content fields other than kinship, one must be prepared to find both kinds of structures. Anthropological work on folk taxonomies reckons with both.

F							
a_1				a_2			
b_1		b_2		b_1		b_2	
c_1	c_2	c_1	c_2	c_1	c_2	c_1	c_2

Figure 1

F							
a_1				a_2			
b_1		b_2		c_1		c_2	
d_1	d_2	e_1	e_2	f_1	f_2	g_1	g_2

Figure 2

A third point has to do with the question of metaphor, the delimitation of a semantic field, and the possibility of conjunctive definitions. I should confess at once that I have not included *all* of the meanings of the Iroquois kinship terms in the tabulation of data given in the paper. Not included, for example, are *the moon* in the list of denotata of the "grandmother" term, or *the thunderers* amongst the "grandfathers," or *the earth* as our "mother," or *the sun* as our "elder brother." Nor have I included the metaphoric uses of the "brother" and "cousin," "father" and "son," "elder brother" and "younger brother" terms, in ceremonial discourse, for divisions of the Longhouse and of the political confederacy of the Six Nations; or that of the "uncle" term for the Bigheads (certain masked dancers at Midwinter ceremonies) or, formerly, for prisoners at the stake. There is no difficulty here in identifying these as marginal" or "transferred" meanings, to use Bloomfield's terms. Metaphoric extensions can be expected for any lexical item. In the structural analysis of a semantic field, however, they are excluded. We have not intended to deal with all of the meanings of the Iroquois kinship terms here, but only with those that fall within the field defined as *genealogical kin*. All of these have one common feature of meaning which is lacking from the metaphoric extensions. Determining the criteria for the delimitation of fields is the first important step in semantic analysis. Determining the bases for metaphoric extensions beyond the field is one of the last, and sometimes one of the most interesting. Normally it is not possible to subsume *all* of the meanings of a lexical item under one *conjunctive* definition. We expect that it should be possible to do this, however, for all of those meanings of an item *that lie within a properly defined field.*

A fourth point has to do with the way of entry into a problem of meaning. Bloomfield was of the opinion that "signals can be analyzed, but not the things signalled about," and that "this reinforces the principle that linguistic study must always start from the phonetic form and not from meaning" (1933:162). The entry into phonology for Bloomfield was the same-or-different test applied to the meanings (1933: Chapter 5, esp. pp. 74–78). I have suggested elsewhere that the entry into *semantics* could be a same-or-different test *applied to forms,* and that this also offered a possible starting place (1956:158–194, esp. pp. 190–192). C. M. Ebeling has an important and interesting discussion of this possibility, and of the symmetry, or parallelism, between the analytic constructs of semantics and those of phonology (1960, Chapter III). And a comment by Jakobson, that "meaning can and must be stated in terms of linguistic discriminations and identifications, just as, on the other hand, linguistic discriminations are always made with regard to their semantic value," is fundamental to this view (1959:139–145; quote from p. 143). For purposes of the analysis of the Iroquois kinship semantics that has been made in this paper, it was not really necessary for us to know anything about the Seneca forms other than whether any two responses of Morgan's informants were *the same* or *different.*

A fifth and final point has to do with the analysis of multiple denotation *within a field.* It should be noted that dimensional analysis of a field, and componential definitions of the elements that constitute it, are as applicable to sets of forms having only single denotata as to sets of forms having multiple denotata. Only in the latter case—of which the Seneca kinship vocabulary has furnished an example—does one face the typical *"allo-*unit" problem. I want to point out that there are two ways of handling this, at least in kinship analysis. One is by the method of *total class definitions;* the other is by a method of *basic member definitions* and supplementary *rules of extension.* Much of linguistic method as we have known it in the recent past is based on the former method. The first attempts at componential analysis of kinship terminologies (Goodenough 1951; 1956: Lounsbury 1956), as well as the present paper, take an analogous approach in the handling of multiple denotata. Differences of degree within the class of denotata of a term are of course recognized, but these are treated as "nondistinctive."

There is, as was mentioned, another way of handling this. It is to regard one, or sometimes two, members of a terminological kinclass as the basic members and to fit the definition of the kinship term to these. The other members of the class are then treated as extensions ("metaphoric" in relation to the narrow field covered by the basic types and their definitions, but yet not "metaphoric" when considered in relation to the wide field which is the subject of analysis). These extensions are then accounted for by rules.

The rules may be written either as expansion rules or as reduction rules. In the former case they derive distant members of the class from the basic member or members; in the latter they reduce the distant ones to the basic ones.

To illustrate this method let us take an example of a type of system somewhat more complicated than that of the Iroquois, for it will allow perhaps a more convincing demonstration of the potentialities of the method. There are kinship systems called "Crow" type (after the Crow Indians, whose system was one of the first of these to receive notice) which are found in many parts of the world. Actually, the Crow type is not one, but many. Let us consider one particular subvariety, which we might as well call the Choctaw subtype. It will suffice here to mention only the classification of two particular kin-types (cousins to us), viz., *father's sister's son* [FSs] which goes by the "father" term in these systems, and *father's sister's daughter* [FSd] which goes by the "grandmother" term. These two can usually be taken as quick diagnostics of this particular variety of kinship system.

This system can be generated by a set of three rules, which I shall write here as reduction rules. These account not only for FSs and FSd, but for the whole system. They are:

(1) Skewing Rule: *Let any woman's brother, as linking relative, be regarded as equivalent to that woman's son, as linking relative.*

$$♀B \ . \ . \ . \ → \ ♀s \ . \ . \ .$$

From this follows a corollary stating the consequent relationship of the reciprocals: *Any male linking relative's sister will then be equivalent to that male linking relative's mother.*

$$. \ . \ . \ ♂S → \ . \ . \ . \ ♂M$$

(2) Merging Rule: *Let any person's sibling of same sex, as linking relative, be equivalent to that person himself directly linked.*

$$♂B \ . \ . \ . \ → \ ♂ \ . \ . \ . \ ; \ ♀S \ . \ . \ . \ → \ ♀ \ . \ . \ .$$

From this follows the corollary pertaining to the reciprocals: *Any linking relative's sibling of same sex as himself (or herself) will then be equivalent to that relative himself (or herself) as an object of reference.*

$$. \ . \ . \ ♂B → \ . \ . \ . \ ♂; \ . \ . \ . \ ♀S → \ . \ . \ . \ ♀$$

(3) Half-sibling Rule: *Let any child of one of one's parents be regarded as one's sibling.*

$$Fs → B; Fd → S; Ms → B; Md → S$$

This rule contains its own reciprocal corollary.

Of these three rules, the third one is almost universal in kinship systems; the second is widespread, applying to many systems besides the one now under consideration, but is by no means universal; while the first of these is the one of most restricted occurrence, being peculiar to this particular subvariety of so-called "Crow" systems, but being found in quite a number of unrelated systems in many parts of the world nonetheless.

The rules constitute an unordered set. When we scan the rules for applicability in reducing a kin-type, if any is applicable, there is never more than one that is applicable at any particular step in the reduction. And if we write them as expansion rules rather than as reduction rules (which can be done by merely reversing the arrows), all possible orders of application of the rules must be exploited in generating a system. Since the rules cannot come into conflict, there is no basis for ordering.

We may apply them now to the kin-types *father's sister's son* [FSs] and *father's sister's daughter* [FSd]:

FSs → FMs	(by skewing rule corollary),
→ FB	(by half-sibling rule),
→ F	(by merging rule),
→ "father"	(by definition).
FSd → FMd	(by skewing rule corollary),
→ FS	(by half-sibling rule)
→ FM	(by skewing rule corollary),
→ "grandmother"	(by definition).

Thus there is a logic by which one's father's sister's son may be classified as "father" and one's father's sister's daughter as a "grandmother."[8]

I have mentioned this alternative method not just to exhibit a bit of the variety in systems of kinship semantics, or the methodological resources of their devotees, but to raise also a more general point concerning the possible nature of relationships *between* the various denotata of a form. I am not prepared at this point to show that there are other semantic fields where a few generative rules may account for all instances of multiple denotation for all of the forms of an entire lexical set; but I think it might be suggested that the derivation of denotatum from denotatum, and the formulation of the principles involved, is a rather general problem in structural semantics.

NOTES

[1] Earlier versions of this paper, or of parts of it, were presented at the Fifth International Congress of Anthropological and Ethnological Sciences in Philadelphia, September 5, 1956 (under the title, "The Componential Structure of the Iroquois-

type Kinship System"); at the Tenth Conference on Iroquois Research, Redhouse, N.Y., October 13, 1956; and at the Yale Linguistic Club, November 11, 1957.

[2] As a mnemonic device one can remember that lower case means lower generation.

[3] The data are from Lewis Henry Morgan's *Systems of Consanguinity and Affinity of the Human Family*. The items listed here are attested there either directly or by reciprocal, or both. The spelling of the kinship terms is after Wallace Chafe, *Handbook of the Seneca Language*, 1963, with but minor modifications.

[4] The italicization, for emphasis, is to call this point to the attention of anthropologists. The "classic but erroneous anthropological view concerning the nature of the 'Iroquois type' of kinship systems," to which reference was made at the beginning of this paper, is that this kind of system classifies kin by membership in unilineal descent groups. Thus, given exogamous matrilineal moieties (as the Seneca are said to have had), all of one's "fathers" should be found in one's father's moiety, and all of one's "maternal uncles" should be found in one's own moiety. A glance at the data shows that this theory of the Iroquois system gives about fifty percent right predictions and nearly fifty percent wrong predictions. Of the "maternal uncles," for example, MB, MMSs, and MFBs would indeed be found in one's own exogamous matrilineal moiety, but MMBs and MFSs would be in the opposite moiety. Similarly one has classificatory "fathers" in *both* moieties, his own as well as his father's. Another version of the theory, thought to be applicable where matrilineal clans (sibs) exist but moieties do not, or where kinship is reckoned to clan limits but not to moiety limits, is that the "father" term refers to men of one's father's clan in his generation or age grade, and that the "maternal uncle" term refers to men of one's own clan in the generation or age grade of one's mother's brother. The facts, however, correspond as little to the predictions of this clan theory of Iroquois kinship as they do to those of the moiety theory; for one may have ' fathers" in any clan, and one may also have "maternal uncles" in any clan. The predictions of these theories are as far off for the other kin-classes of the system as they are for these. These facts are true not only of the Iroquois Indians themselves, but also of every "Iroquois-type" system included in Morgan's tables in *Systems of Consanguinity and Affinity*. While I was becoming acquainted with this for the first time in 1954–55 by reading these tables, my colleague Leopold Pospisil was finding out the same thing for the Kapauku Papuans while engaged in field work in the highlands of the (then) Netherlands New Guinea. (Cf. L. Pospisil, 1960, 188–205.) My astonishment at discovering the real principle operative in the reckoning of bifurcation in an Iroquois-type kinship system was matched by his. It was contrary to all of the expectations to which we had been led by the anthropological theoretical writings on the subject. It is surprising that the essential data pertinent to a subject about which so much has been written should have been in print and available to all for nearly a century without anyone's having taken account of the classification of any but the closest collateral kin-types. The classic theory predicts correctly only to the immediate (closest) uncles and aunts [FB, MB, FS, MS] and first cousins. Beyond this its predictions are half right and half wrong. Morgan himself, already under the influence of a clan theory of kinship (of his own making), is partly responsible for this error. Statements in Chapter IV, Book I, of his *League of the Ho-de-no-sau-nee or Iroquois* (1851) can be derived from a metaphoric use of "sibling" terms and from the ignoring of all

but the closest kin-types included in his own tables of data that he published in *Systems*.

There *do* exist systems which classify kin-types in the way that the Iroquois type was imagined to. These are the "Dravidian" type of systems. Interestingly, they are *not* generally founded on clan or moiety reckoning, but on a mode of reckoning of bifurcation that, unlike the Iroquois, takes account of the sexes of all intervening links. The Dravidian and Iroquois types are rarely distinguished in anthropological literature, all passing under the label "Iroquois type." Actually, they are systems premised on very different principles of reckoning, and deriving from social structures that are fundamentally unlike.

⁵ I.e., the children of his brother and of *all* of his male cousins, regardless of whether the latter be classificatory "brothers" to him (e.g., MSs, FBs) or "cousins" to him (e.g., MBs, FSs).

⁶ I.e., the children of his sister and of *all* of his female cousins, regardless of whether the latter be classificatory "sisters" to him (e.g., MSd, FBd) or "cousins" to him (e.g., MBd, FSd).

⁷ ". . . a marked category states the presence of a certain (whether positive or negative) property A; . . . the corresponding unmarked category states nothing about the presence of A, and is used chiefly, but not exclusively, to indicate the absence of A. On the level of general meaning the opposition . . . may be interpreted as 'statement of A' vs. 'no statement of A', whereas on the level of 'narrowed,' nuclear meanings, we encounter the opposition 'statement of A' vs. 'statement of non-A'." (Roman Jakobson 1957).

⁸ A full presentation of the method of reduction rules is given in my paper "A Formal Account of the Crow and Omaha-type Kinship Terminologies," reprinted here, Chapter 3.

REFERENCES CITED

Bloomfield, Leonard, 1933, Language. New York, Holt, Rinehart and Winston.

Conklin, Harold C., 1962, Lexicographical treatment of folk taxonomies. *In* F. W. Householder and S. Saporta, eds., Problems of lexicography. Indiana University Research Center in Anthropology, Folklore and Linguistics, Publication No. 21.

Chafe, Wallace, 1963, Handbook of the Seneca language. New York State Museum and Science Service, Bull. No. 388.

Ebeling, C. M., 1960, Linguistic units. The Hague, Mouton.

Goodenough, Ward H., 1951, Property, kin, and community on Truk. Yale University Publications in Anthropology No. 46.

———, 1956, Componential analysis and the study of meaning. Language 32: 195–216.

Jakobson, Roman, 1957, Shifters, verbal categories, and the Russian verb. Harvard University, Russian Language Project.

———, 1959, Boas' view of grammatical meaning. Memoir 89, American Anthropological Association.

Lounsbury, Floyd G., 1951, A semantic analysis of the Pawnee kinship usage. Language 32:158–194.

————, 1964, A formal account of the Crow and Omaha-type kinship terminologies. *In* W. H. Goodenough, ed., Explorations in cultural anthropology. New York, McGraw-Hill.

Morgan, Lewis Henry, 1831, League of the Ho-de-no-sau-nee or Iroquois. New York.

————, 1871, Systems of consanguinity and affinity of the human family. Smithsonian contributions to knowledge, No. 218. Washington, D.C., Smithsonian Institution.

Morris, C. W., 1938, Foundations of the theory of signs. International encyclopedia of unified science, vol. 1, No. 2. Chicago, University of Chicago Press.

————, 1946, Signs, language, and behavior. New York, Prentice-Hall.

Pospisil, Leopold, 1960, The Kapauku Papuans and their kinship organization. Oceania 30:188–205.

A Formal Account of the Crow- and Omaha-Type Kinship Terminologies

Floyd G. Lounsbury

I

Let us distinguish at the outset between a "formal account" of a kinship terminological system, and such other kinds of accounts as anthropologists may be interested in—e.g., a functional account, a historical account, or any other kind of causal account.[1]

We may consider that a "formal account" of a collection of empirical data has been given when there have been specified (1) a set of primitive elements, and (2) a set of rules for operating on these, such that by the application of the latter to the former, the elements of a "model" are generated; which model in turn comes satisfactorily close to being a facsimile or exact replica of the empirical data whose interrelatedness and systemic nature we are trying to understand. A formal account is thus an apparatus for predicting back the data at hand, thereby making them "understandable," i.e., showing them to be the lawful and expectable consequences of an underlying principle that may be presumed to be at work at their source.

A formal account should be distinguished both by its sufficiency and by its parsimony. Its "sufficiency" consists in its ability to account *in toto* for what is at hand in the empirical data, with no elements of this collection wrongly predicted or left unpredicted in the model, and with none of the predictions of the model remaining empirically unverifiable (assuming adequate documentation or documentability of the source). That is to say, the model should not underpredict, overpredict, or wrongly predict. To the extent that it achieves this goal, it satisfies the requirement of sufficiency. Theories, formal or otherwise, purporting to account for the application of terms of relationship in Crow- and Omaha-type systems,[2] including the ones proposed in this paper, can and should be judged against this criterion of sufficiency.

The "parsimony" of a formal account consists in its specifying only the absolute minimum of assumptions that are necessary to account for the data of the empirical collection, or to generate an exact replica thereof. The theories just mentioned may be judged against this criterion also. One that purports to be "formal" is expected to be so judged.

Now it is a fact, deriving from this very parsimony, that formal accounts are likely to be peculiarly unsatisfying to many anthropologists. Thus, for example, a simple rule that tells one the exact minimum he needs to know in order to predict what relationships are to be assigned to what categories in such and such a system of kinship terminology, *and nothing else*, is quite likely to be rejected because it fails to tell him other (and doubtless more important) things that he wants to know about the society, its culture, its legal structure, its patterns of social interaction, value orientations, etc. In fact, it may well reinforce in him the common prejudice that kinship terminologies are of no importance to the study of social structure—"so why bother with the kinship algebra?"

This, I hope to convince the reader, would be a premature and unfortunate conclusion. It is the parsimony of formal accounts—the fact that they do not tell one more than the barest necessary minimum—that is precisely the characteristic that can give them their value in terms of cross-culture generality; and it is the habit of overexplanation, so common in attempts at functional description, that robs the latter of their generality. I suggest, then, that it is only the parsimonious "formal" account that can point to the common and essential features of the various causal matrices out of which any given type of kinship terminology crystalizes.

This is not meant to disparage functional accounts. Quite to the contrary, it is a hope and a legitimate expectation that a formal analysis will be of help—as a kind of direction indicator—in getting functional analyses profitably oriented. All of us, surely, formalist and functionalist alike, have this as an objective. It is something of a commonplace in linguistics that the functional account of a system requires, or is at least facilitated by, a prior formal account; and that the functional account is but a part of the formal account of some larger system within which the first is embedded.

II

The classic labels "Crow" and "Omaha" obscure a host of differences between the individual systems covered by these terms. They are differences that are rarely given any attention. A few of them will be singled out in the sections that follow, and will be the basis for a tentative and partial typology of subvarieties. We mention one of these points of variation now, by way of illustration.

There are "Crow-type" systems in which one's father's sister and one's father's sister's daughter, together with their female parallel collaterals, uterine descendants, and certain other kin types, are given a *first*-ascending-generation classification either as part of a separate "paternal aunt" class (in a fully bifurcate system) or as part of an undifferentiated "mother" class (in a semibifurcate or a nonbifurcate system[3]). But there are also "Crow-type" systems in which these same kin types are given a *second*-ascending-generation classification and become one's classificatory "grandmothers"[4]—i.e., fall into the same class and under the same label as one's "real" grandmothers (father's mother and mother's mother).

Reciprocally, a woman's brother's children, her mother's brother's children, etc., are classed as her "nephews and nieces" (fully bifurcate) or her "sons and daughters" (semibifurcate and nonbifurcate) in systems of the first of these varieties, but as her "grandchildren" in systems of the second variety.

There are also mirror images[5] of these subvarieties among "Omaha-type" systems. Thus, in some of these the mother's brother, mother's brother's son, etc., are given a *first*-ascending-generation classification in a separate "maternal uncle" class (fully bifurcate) or as part of an undifferentiated "father" class (nonbifurcate), whereas in others, belonging to the second variety, these same types of kin are accorded a *second*-ascending-generation status in the terminological usage, being called by the "grandfather" term. The reciprocals follow accordingly, so that in the former variety a man's sister's children, his father's sister's children, etc., are his "nephews and nieces" or his "children," whereas in the second variety they appear as his "grandchildren."

Radcliffe-Brown, in discussing this latter variety of "Omaha"—wherein one's mother's brother is a "grandfather" and a man's sister's children are his "grandchildren"—attempts a functional explanation of this apparent generation anomaly in terms of his alternating-generation theory of affect, the "grandfather" classification being a device that, to quote, "removes him [the mother's brother] from that generation-category to which there is a tendency to attach superiority of interpersonal rank and places him, by a fiction, in one towards which the relation is one of easy familiarity, approximate equality, or privilege."[6] Now, this function may indeed be present. But the functional explanation applies only to this particular kin type, the mother's brother, or at most to the class of such persons and their male agnatic descendants (mother's brother's son, etc.), whereas in a formal account this classification of the mother's brother as "grandfather" is merely one among many automatic results of the operation of a rule that generates the entire system. The particular detail is satisfactorily explained when that rule is explained; it does not need a separate explanation.

III

There have been a number of attempts to specify the basis for the classification of kin given by Crow- and Omaha-type systems. The best known, perhaps, is Radcliffe-Brown's unity-of-the-lineage theory, wherein it is held that the members of a corporate unilineal descent group, though differentiated in status when seen from a vantage point within the lineage group, tend to present a unity, undifferentiated, when seen from without. Thus, kinsmen of one sex who belong to one such lineage group which is not ego's should all stand in the same kind of status relation to ego and should be expected to receive a common kin-term designation. For example, all the men of ego's father's matrilineage—to which, of course, ego does not belong—would stand in the same kind of relation to ego and would all be called by the same "father" term by him, and he would accordingly be a "son" to all of them in a Crow-type system.[7]

Although there can hardly be much question that strong corporate unilineal kin groupings may sometimes—and perhaps often—provide conditions favorable to the development of Crow-type or Omaha-type classifications (i.e., Crow with matrilineal and Omaha with patrilineal groupings), the situation is really not that simple. For there are societies without such lineage structure that have Crow- or Omaha-type classifications, and there are those that do indeed have strong corporate unilineal kin groups but employ quite different systems of kin classification.[8] And there are at least five cases on record of societies that have Crow-type systems of terminology in association with patrilineal kin groupings (some of these, at least, being strongly corporate property-holding groups), rather than the Omaha type as would be expected according to the unity-of-the-lineage theory; and there is at least one case of what looks like the opposite arrangement, with matrilineal kin groupings, matrilineal inheritance of property, and matrilineal succession to kingship, but yet with what appears to be a variety of Omaha kinship reckoning instead of the Crow manner that one would expect.[9]

Beside these deviant examples of whole systems, there is a further difficulty with the unity-of-the-lineage theory in that only rarely, i.e., only in a few particular instances, does it correctly account for the application of kin terms to the various types of kinsmen in one's genealogy, even where the right kind of lineages exist. Thus, for example, the proposition that "the meaning of the 'father' term in a Crow-type kinship terminology is *male member of my father's matrilineage*" is false, as can be seen by close examination of *all* of the data from carefully documented systems; for "being a member of the father's matrilineage" is neither a necessary condition nor a sufficient condition for being designated by the "father" term of a Crow-type kinship system. In the first place, one has classificatory "fathers" who are not members of the father's matrilineage. The father's father's sister's son's son is such a type, i.e., one normally falling under the "father" classification (if the system reaches out that far), but yet not normally a member of the father's matrilineage (except in the case of a matrilateral cross-cousin marriage in the preceding generation). Thus, being a member of the father's matrilineage is not a *necessary condition* for falling into the "father" class of a Crow-type kinship terminology. Further, in many Crow-type systems not all members of the father's matrilineage are in fact classificatory "fathers." The father's mother's brother is such a type. In a few systems, one of which is that of the Crow Indians themselves, the father's mother's brother is indeed a classificatory "father." But in most Crow-type systems he is not; he is a classificatory "grandfather" instead. Therefore, "being a member of the father's matrilineage" is not a *sufficient condition*, either, for falling within the terminological "father" class of most of the Crow-type systems (although it is, apparently, for the Crow Indians themselves).[10]

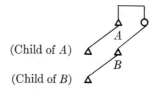

(Child of *A*)

(Child of *B*)

Figure 1.   The offspring of a man and of his sister's son.

Just as it has been classic doctrine about Crow-type systems that all the men of one's father's matrilineage are one's "fathers," so it has been maintained, as a corollary, that the offspring of all the men of a man's own matrilineage are his classificatory "children." But this is not true either. Consider a simple case: that of the offspring of two men who themselves are related to each other as mother's brother and sister's son (Fig. 1). By the classic theory, not only should the child of *A* be a classificatory "child" of *B*, but the child of *B* should also be a classificatory "child" of *A*. Now, while the first of these statements is true (to the best of my knowledge) of all systems which anthropologists are agreed in calling "Crow," the second is not. It is true only of a minority (a minority including that of the Crow Indians, however). In the majority of systems of the Crow type, on the other hand, the child of A (in Fig. 1) is a classificatory "child" of B, but the child of B is a classificatory "grandchild" of A.

There is one main point which the above enumeration of discrepancies between factual data and theory-based expectation is intended to emphasize. It is that a close attention to the details of data available on well-documented Crow-type and Omaha-type systems of kinship terminology shows that the lineage theory of these systems does not of itself account correctly for all of the data. An *adequate* theory, on the other hand, must make no wrong predictions. In the sections that follow, some formal theories that are adequate to certain particular cases will be presented. We keep to the simpler varieties here. Some more complex ones will be dealt with in separate papers which are in preparation and are expected to appear elsewhere.

IV

The reader was warned in advance that he is likely to be disappointed when the formal rules that generate Crow- and Omaha-type systems are finally unveiled; for on the face of it they will appear to tell him very little about the societies that have these systems. One might well regard this "formal rule" business as little more than a trick. But it is not a bad trick, judged in relation to its limited aims; for it works in reducing the seeming complexity and voluminousness of detail of these systems to a few fairly simply stated underlying principles, showing the former to be merely the automatic consequences of the latter.

The simpler forms of Crow- and Omaha-type kinship systems can be accounted for by means of three equivalence rules which are to operate on genealogical types before submitting these to labeling in accordance with kin-term definitions. These equivalence rules may be written either as reduction rules or as expansion rules. Written as reduction rules, they operate always on more remote kin types to "reduce" them to the genealogically closer kin types to which they are terminologically equivalent. For example, repeated applications of the reduction rules to the various denotata of the "father" term of a Crow-type kinship system will "reduce" or "transform" all of these into the primary kin type *father*, to which they are terminologically equivalent. Written as expansion rules, on the other hand, they operate always on genealogically closer kin types to "expand" these,[11] i.e., to derive from them more distant kin types which are their terminological equivalents. Thus, operating on the primary kin type *father*, they generate the specification of all of the other kin types to which the "father" term is extended. A rule can be changed from one of reduction to one of expansion, or vice versa, merely by reversing its arrow. Here they will be written as reduction rules.

The three equivalence rules will be referred to as a "skewing rule," a "merging rule," and a "half-sibling rule," respectively. The skewing rule expresses the formal equivalence, in specified contexts, between two kin types of different generations. Among its effects are the skewing of the relation between terminological generation and natural generation (assuming, perhaps ethnocentrically, that our notion of generation is somehow more "natural" than that expressed in one of the kinship systems we are concerned with here). Hence the name given to this rule.

The merging rule expresses the formal equivalence, in specified contexts, between siblings of the same sex. It is a formalization of Radcliffe-Brown's famous principle of the "equivalence of brothers" and that of sisters. But whereas Radcliffe-Brown apparently saw it as a general tendency of some sort, no such assumption is made here. A merging rule is written for systems that require it, and in the form required, but is not written for systems in which none is operative.

The half-sibling rule expresses the formal equivalence between half siblings and full siblings. In its algebraic form, it says that the expression *father's son* can always be rewritten as *brother*, and *father's daughter* as *sister;* and similarly also *mother's son* and *mother's daughter.*

The half-sibling rule, to the best of my knowledge, is universal in kinship systems. By this I mean that I have not yet come across an account of a system in which an *obligatory* terminological distinction is drawn between half siblings and full siblings. Apparent instances to the contrary turn out, on examination, to be based on some other criterion than that of *half* versus *full.* Usually this is *uterine* versus *nonuterine*, or *agnatic* versus *nonagnatic.*[12] In our own terminology the distinction between half and full siblings is of course optional. Our usage allows us to obscure it in the general terms "brother" and "sister."

The merging rule, while not universal in kinship systems, is nonetheless of very wide generality. It is operative in many systems other than those of the Crow and Omaha types that concern us in this paper. And it may assume more than one form, necessitating its proper specification for any given kinship system under analysis. It is not operative in our own kinship system.

The skewing rule is, of the three kinds under discussion, the one of most limited generality. And it can assume a very large number of different forms, with correspondingly different consequences for the termino-logical classification of kin types. It also, then, must be properly specified for any given skewed stem under analysis. Some of the commoner varieties will be illustrated in this paper.

V

In the remaining sections it will be necessary to employ a number of abbreviating symbols and conventions. Those which apply to kin types, and which will appear in the reduction formulas, are the following:

1. Primary kin types:

F = father
M = mother
B = brother
S = sister
H = husband
W = wife
s = son[13]
d = daughter

2. Secondary and further-degree kin types are written with combinations of these symbols, juxtaposition indicating the relative product, thus:

FS = father's sister
MB = mother's brother
FSs = father's sister's son
MMBdd = mother's mother's brother's daughter's daughter
HS = husband's sister
WBs = wife's brother's son
etc.

3. Sex is implicit in all of the above symbols. In addition to these, the Mars and Venus symbols are used respectively for male and female, designating either ego (the propositus) or a kinsman or a linking kinsman, and in each case specifying the sex of the party designated. Thus:

♂ = male (ego, kinsman, or linking kinsman)
♀ = female (ego, kinswoman, or linking kinswoman)

These symbols are used to designate ego only in cases where it is intended that the sex of ego be restricted. Otherwise ego is unwritten, but is to be understood as preceding any kin-type designation. Thus:

♂ MBs = a man's (or boy's) mother's brother's son
♀ MBs = a woman's (or girl's) mother's brother's son
MBs = one's mother's brother's son (i.e., of either a male or a female)

The Mars and Venus symbols are used to designate a kinsman or linking kinsman only when it is intended to specify the sex but to leave the genealogical position unrestricted. It is used in this way only in the reduction formulas and not in the abbreviations of kin types in other contexts. For examples see below.

4. In the reduction rules it is necessary to distinguish specifically non-terminal positions in the genealogical chain from those that are unrestricted

as to whether they are terminal (i.e., ego, or the designated kinsman) or nonterminal (i.e., a linking kinsman). A sequence of three dots (. . .) is used for this purpose.

When the dots are preposed to a male or a female sign it means that this sign cannot be interpreted as ego, but must be restricted to interpretation at a linking kinsman of the appropriate sex but of unspecified genealogical position. Contrast the following:

> . . . ♂ Ss = male linking relative's sister's son (where the dots imply that the male sign cannot represent ego, i.e., that it cannot be the initial terminus of the genealogical chain)
>
> ♂ Ss = any male person's sister's son (where the male in question may be *either* ego *or* a linking relative standing in the chain between ego and the designated kin type)

When the dots are postposed to a kin-type abbreviation it means that the given abbreviation cannot be interpreted as referring to the designated relative, but must be restricted to interpretation as a linking relative. Contrast the following:

> MB . . . = mother's brother's . . . (i.e., mother's brother as a link in the genealogical chain between ego and a kinsman to be designated, the dots implying that something else *must* follow in the spelling of the kin type)
>
> MB = mother's brother, *or* mother's brother's (i.e., mother's brother *either* as the designated relative *or* as a link to some other designated relative traced through him)

As noted, these conventions are to apply only in the statement of the reduction formulas.

VI

One of the simple varieties of Omaha-type systems is generated by the following rules (*a*, *b*, and *c* below). But for one minor detail (which will be discussed for the light that it throws on the application and the resources of our method) the data generated by this set of rules coincide exactly with the very full schedule of consanguineal data published by Sol Tax (1937b) for the Fox Indians.

(*a*) SKEWING RULE (Omaha Type I): FS . . . → S . . .

This is to be read: *Let the kin type* FATHER'S SISTER, *whenever it occurs as a link between ego and any other relative, be regarded as structurally equivalent to the kin type* SISTER *in that context.*

If this rule be specified as operative, then it follows as a corollary that a similar equivalence must exist between the reciprocals of the types covered by the rule. This may be expressed as follows:

COROLLARY: . . . ♀ Bs → . . . ♀ B; and . . . ♀ Bd → . . . ♀ S

This is to be read: *One's female linking relative's* BROTHER'S CHILD (BROTHER'S SON *or* BROTHER'S DAUGHTER) *is therefore to be regarded as structurally equivalent to that female linking relative's* SIBLING (BROTHER *or* SISTER, *respectively*). Since the original rule was unspecific as to sex of ego, allowing either possibility, so the corollary describing the reciprocals must be unspecific as to the sex of the relative. We find it somewhat more convenient to write the formula twice, once for each sex, rather than to introduce cover symbols for "child" and "sibling."

(*b*) MERGING RULE: ♂ B . . . → ♂ . . . ; and ♀ S . . . → ♀ . . .

This is to be read: *Let any person's sibling of the same sex as himself (or herself), when a link to some other relative, be regarded as equivalent to that person himself (or herself) directly linked to said relative.* Again we find it convenient to write the rule twice, once for each sex, instead of introducing cover symbols for the "person" and the "sibling of same sex."

From this follows a corollary stating the equivalence between the reciprocals.

COROLLARY: . . . ♂ B → . . . ♂ ; and . . . ♀ S → . . . ♀

This is to be read: *Any linking relative's sibling of the same sex as himself (or herself) is to be regarded as equivalent to that linking relative.*

As noted in section V, the merging rule is a formal paraphrase of Radcliffe-Brown's principle of the equivalence of siblings of the same sex. The rule is expressed, and the formula written, in the manner given here only for the sake of removing an absurd logical consequence that would follow if the dots were omitted and the statement taken literally; for among the consequences of the rule written in such a simplified form (e.g., ♂ B → ♂ ; ♀ S → ♀) would be the unwanted ones in the case where ♂ is ego and B is the designated kinsman, and where ♀ is ego and S is designated kin, in which case ego would be applying the first-person pronoun to his sibling.

(*c*) HALF-SIBLING RULE: Fs → B; Ms → B; Fd → S; Md → S

This is to be read: *Let one's parent's child be considered to be one's sibling.* The formula is written four times, once for each of the possibilities obtained by commuting the sexes of both parent and child, since we have chosen not to add cover symbols to our list of kin-type abbreviations.[11]

The reciprocal of "one's *parent's child*" is "one's *parent's child*," and the reciprocal of "one's *sibling*" is "one's *sibling*." Since the types are self-reciprocal, the rule as stated contains its own reciprocal corollary.

As noted previously (section IV), this rule expresses the fact that no obligatory distinction is drawn between half siblings and full siblings. Although possibly universal and not a peculiarity of the type of kinship system under discussion, it still must be written. Otherwise it would be impossible to carry out some of the reductions called for by the data of these systems. Every kind of operation that is to be carried out must be specified.

FURTHER COROLLARIES AND DERIVATIONS FROM RULES *a*, *b*, AND *c*. In the paragraphs above, there have been written only the corollaries that concern the reciprocals of the kin types expressed in the original statements of the rules. Other consequences, concerning hundreds of other kin types, can be written also as corollaries or as derivations from these rules taken singly or as an assemblage constituting an unordered set. These corollaries and derivative statements constitute the set of equivalences in a kinship system of the type under discussion.

For example, consider the "uncle" class (kin types labeled by the "mother's brother" term, *nehcihsähA*) of the Fox Indians. Tax reports the following in his data[15] (which we segregate by "natural" generation in this list):

G^2:	MMFSs
G^1:	MB, MFBs, MMSs
G^0:	MBs, MFBss, MMSss, MMBds
G^{-1}:	MBss
G^{-2}:	MBsss

By repeated applications of the rules, all of these kin types reduce to the one kin type MB (mother's brother), which may be considered as the *focal type* within the class—the 'real' *nehcihsähA* perhaps, or at least the closest one. The reductions are statements of the terminological equivalence of the other more distant genealogical types to this closest "uncle" of all.

We illustrate the reductions by applying the rules to four of the most remote "uncles" in this list.

1. MMFSs	→ MMSs	[by the skewing rule]
	→ MMs	[by the merging rule]
	→ MB	[by the half-sibling rule].
2. MMSss	→ MMss	[by the merging rule]
	→ MBs	[by the half-sibling rule]
	→ MB	[by the skewing rule corollary].
3. MMBds	→ MMSs	[by the skewing rule corollary]
	→ MMs	[by the merging rule]
	→ MB	[by the half-sibling rule].
4. MBsss	→ MBss	[by the skewing rule corollary]
	→ MBs	[by a second application of the same]
	→ MB	[by a third application of the same].

In the same way the remaining "uncle" types of the Fox reduce to MB. They are terminological "uncles," then, by virtue of the operation of the three basic equivalence principles expressed in the skewing rule, the merging rule, and the half-sibling rule. The application of the "uncle" term to these types can be considered as an "extension" of that term from its primary or focal meaning. The various instances in the list can be regarded as one-step, two-step, or three-step extensions, depending on the number of steps in the derivation of the term from MB by means of the expansion rules, which is the same as the number of steps in the reduction of the kin type to MB by means of the reduction rules.

In similar fashion and by use of the same rules, all of the extensions of the other kin terms reduce to the primary meanings, or foci (of appropriate "natural" generation), of their respective terminological classes. Specifically: all "uncles" (*nehcihsähA*) reduce to MB; all "paternal aunts" (*neshegwisA*) to FS; all "fathers" (*no·hsA*) to F; all "mother's sisters" (*negi·HA*) to MS, and then to M (see discussion of this point at the end of this section); all "sons" (*negwihsA*) to ♂ s or ♀ s; all "daughters" (*netanehsA*) to ♂ d or ♀ d; all "nephews" (*nenegwa·HA*) to ♂ Ss or ♀ Bs; all "nieces" (*nehcemi·HA*) to ♂ Sd or ♀ Bd; all "siblings" (*netehgwämA* "man's sister," *netawämA* "woman's brother," *neto·tämA* "man's or woman's sibling of same sex"; or, alternatively, *nesese* "older sibling of same sex," *nemise* "older sibling of opposite sex," *nesime* "younger sibling") to B or S; all "grandfathers" (*nehmehco*) to male kin types of second or higher ascending generation; all "grandmothers" (*no·hgomehsA*) to female kin types of second or higher ascending generation; and all "grandchildren" (*no·hcihsemA*) to kin types of second or lower descending generation.

It has already been noted that the rules stated above are an unordered set. This statement can be made, and no hierarchical order of preference given to the rules, because of the fact that when applied as reduction rules no conflict is ever possible, and when applied as expansion rules all possible orders are permissible and required.

In using them as reduction rules—as we have here—the procedure for reducing any given kin type is to scan the set of rules to see which if any of the rules is applicable to the kin type at hand. If none is applicable, then no reduction can be made and the kin type stands as written. If, on the other hand, one is found to be applicable, then it is applied, and the resulting reduction is written. In this case, the rules are then to be scanned again to see if any of them is applicable to the reduced form now at hand. If not, the reduction has come to an end. If, however, one is, it is to be applied. And so on, until the possibilities for reduction are exhausted. It is an empirical fact that if any rule is found to be applicable at any point in this process, there is never any other rule that is also applicable at that same point. Consequently, as just noted, a conflict among them is not possible.

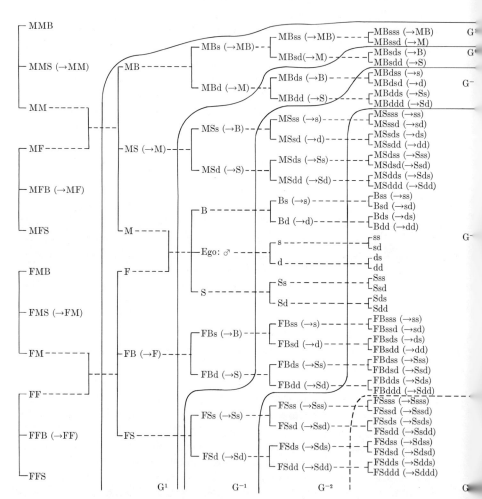

Figure 2.   Omaha reductions, type I, ego being male.

A necessity to choose among them does not arise. Therefore no priorities need be attached to them, and we may regard them as an unordered set.[16]

Figure 2 gives all of the reductions that follow from these rules for the kin types contained in the genealogical diagram used here. (This is a somewhat abridged version of the genealogical diagram. The one published by Tax for the Fox Indians is larger, containing all of the first-cousin types of both parents, and all of the second-cousin types of ego, in addition to the types given here. But our rules account for these additional items of data as well as they do for the ones presented in Fig. 2.) Onto the genealogical diagram there are added other lines that segregate the skewed "terminological generations" (or "social generations," if this is not reading too much content into the formal categories of the system) which result from the consistent application of the reduction rules.

As noted briefly somewhat earlier, there is one minor detail in which the Fox terminological system differs from that determined by our rules. These rules, as written here, generate a "mother" class consisting of M, MS, MFBd, MMSd, MMFSd, MBd, MFBsd, MMSsd, MMBdd, MBsd, MBssd, etc., of which the focal type—that to which all of the others reduce—is M, viz., own mother. But in the Fox terminology published by Tax, M is given a separate designation, *negyA*, while all of the remainder receive the designation *negi·HA* and thus constitute a kin class whose focal member is MS.

This point is illustrative, in a small way, of a quite frequently occurring phenomenon in the structure of kinship terminologies. What the rules generate here is, for the case of the Fox, a superclass: the sum of the "mother" class (here a class of one) and the "mother's sister" class. This generated class must then be subdivided by the introduction of an additional taxonomic diagnostic (here *lineal* versus *collateral*) which yields the two labeled subclasses. In keeping with this structural feature it is perhaps appropriate to gloss these two Fox classes as "lineal mother" and "collateral mother" respectively (rather than "mother" and "maternal aunt"), indicating that we shall regard them as subclasses of a more general and hypothetical superclass "MOTHER" which is determined by the equivalence rules.

The forms of the words thus glossed, *negyA* and *negi·HA* respectively, suggest that this may not be a farfetched interpretation. They appear to contain a common root—perhaps something like -GI- (*ne-* is the first-person prefix)—but this cannot be said with certainty until inquiry is made into the morphology and morphophonemics of Fox, and perhaps also of comparative Algonkian. But the etymological consideration is not crucial in any case. Far more significant is the fact that *negyA* ("lineal mother") and *negi·HA* ("collateral mother") have common reciprocals, *negwihsA* ("son") and *netanehsA* ("daughter"), which are also the reciprocals of *no·hsA* ("father"). Their sharing of common reciprocals suffices to define them as a superclass ("MOTHER"), just as the sharing of the same reciprocals by *no·hsA* ("father") defines a still-higher-order superclass ("PARENT"). Thus we have in Fox the reciprocal set shown in Fig. 3. Thus, the reciprocal

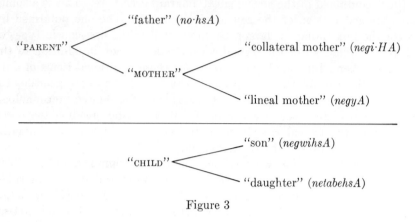

Figure 3

of the superclass "CHILD," which is subject to one subdivision on the basis of sex, is a superclass "PARENT" which is subject to two successive subdivisions, first on the basis of sex, and then—amongst females only—on the basis of collaterality.

This is a common enough state of affairs in kinship structures. Sometimes such a superclass is itself labeled in the native language with a "cover term"; in other instances it is not covered by a free form but is the meaning of a common underlying root, a bound form, common to the specific terms which label the subclasses; in still other instances it is simply an unlabeled superclass in the taxonomic hierarchy, verbalizable (by the native) only with a descriptive circumlocution.

The Fox distinction between "lineal mother" and "collateral mother" might suggest that the merging rule was written above in too strong a form to suit the Fox system and that the female portion of the rule should be in a weaker form (. . . ♀ S . . . → . . . ♀ . . .) instead of in the form given above. While this would yield the desired results for the "lineal mother" and "collateral mother" classes of Fox, preventing reduction of MS to M, while permitting all of the other reductions, and obviating the necessity of a separate taxonomic rule to introduce the consideration of collaterality, it would result also in an unwanted reciprocal distinction between a woman's "lineal children" and her "collateral children." In this case we would need to introduce the merger of these, again by a separate taxonomic rule.

We conclude in this case, as in many others that present analogous kinds of problems, that the set of reduction rules must take priority, and that additional taxonomic rules, expressing the definitions of classes and subclasses, are to be brought in when necessary only after the reduction rules have been applied.

When we speak of "simple" varieties of Crow- or Omaha-type systems, we have in mind those that present no taxonomic differentiation *below* the level attained by the application of reduction rules of one of the ordinary varieties outlined in this paper. Taxonomic merging *above* the level attained by applying these reduction rules will not be considered a mark of complexity, however.

Simple varieties, or relatively simple ones, will be used as examples whenever possible in this paper. The Fox is a relatively simple one. The utility of the method of reduction rules is not limited to these simple cases, however. In fact, the strength and the validity of the approach receive their most convincing demonstration in those very systems that are the most complex. There are some extreme cases of systems in which the classes produced by the reduction rules are in almost all instances superclasses, each of which gets subdivided in its own idiosyncratic way on the basis of its own special criteria for subclassification. The results can appear especially confusing when reciprocal superclasses are subdivided in different manners, making it appear superficially as though the law of the consistency of reciprocals did not hold. Yet at the hierarchical level represented by the superclasses determined by the basic set of reduction rules, this law does hold. The use of the rules brings out this fact better, and enables one to discover the structure more quickly, than any other method known to me.

VII

The mirror image of the "Omaha" variety just illustrated is the "Crow" variety given by the following:

SKEWING RULE (Crow Type I): MB . . . → B . . .

This is to be read: *Let the kin type* MOTHER'S BROTHER, *whenever it occurs as a link between ego and any other relative, be regarded as structurally equivalent to the kin type* BROTHER *in that context.*

COROLLARY: . . . ♂ Ss → . . . ♂ B; and . . . ♂ Sd → . . . ♂ S

One's male linking relative's SISTER'S CHILD (SISTER'S SON *or* SISTER'S DAUGHTER) *is to be regarded as structurally equivalent to that male linking relative's* SIBLING (BROTHER *or* SISTER, *respectively*).

This rule and its corollary are to be taken together with the same merging rule and the same half-sibling rule as given in section VI above.

This Crow skewing rule is the mirror image of the Omaha rule given in section VI, as are its results in the reduction of kin types. The merging rule and the half-sibling rule given in section VI are their own respective mirror

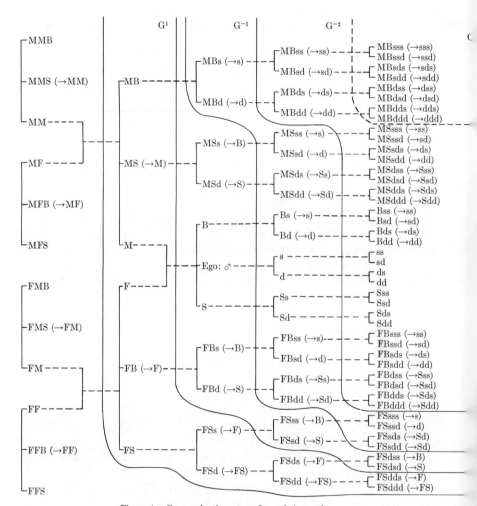

Figure 4.   Crow reductions, type I, ego being male.

images, and consequently apply regardless of whether the skewing be of an Omaha or a Crow variety.

The reductions resulting from these rules are given, for a male ego, in Fig. 4.

The only simple example of this variety of Crow-type system that I have at hand is an unpublished schedule of data obtained by Alexander Alland from the Abron of the Ivory Coast. Published literature, however, furnishes several more complex ones that are based on this particular skewing rule. An unusual and interesting one is in the set of data published by Georges Condominas (1960) for the Mnong Gar of Viet Nam.

For the Mnong Gar, a further restriction must be placed on the skewing rule, as follows: MyB . . . → eB . . . *Let the kin type* MOTHER'S YOUNGER BROTHER, *whenever it occurs as a link between ego and any other relative be regarded as equivalent to the kin type* ELDER BROTHER *in that context.*

Its corollary then takes the form: . . . ♂ eSs → . . . ♂ yB, and . . . ♂ eSd → . . . ♂ yS. *One's male linking relative's* ELDER SISTER'S CHILD (ELDER SISTER'S SON *or* ELDER SISTER'S DAUGHTER) *is to be regarded as equivalent to that male linking relative's* YOUNGER SIBLING (YOUNGER BROTHER *or* YOUNGER SISTER, *respectively*).

The result of this is to produce a system for the Mnong Gar that has both Crow-type and Hawaiian-type classifications. For example, one's father's elder sister's son is a classificatory "father," while one's father's younger sister's son is a classificatory "brother." Similarly, one's (either a man's or a woman's, since it is a semibifurcate system) mother's younger brother's son is one's classificatory "son," while one's mother's elder brother's son is one's "brother."

Other special features of the Mnong Gar system are that: (1) the merging rule must be differently written (in the "Cheyenne" manner[17]) in order to accomplish the appropriate reductions of the residue of cross-collaterals that are unaffected by the more limited skewing rule; (2) subsidiary taxonomic rules must be written to achieve the subclassifications peculiar to the system—as for example those of the "parental," i.e., first ascending, terminological generation shown in Fig. 5; and (3) provision for mirror-image reversal upon decedence of certain links must also be included, thus giving the system an additional "Omaha" character in some of its parts under certain conditions.

Also to be noted in this system is the fact that in the ordinary Crow-type system, by repeated applications of the skewing rule, the "father" status passes from F to FSs, to FSds, etc., down a line of matrilineally related males, and also the kinship status assigned to FS passes on to FSd, to FSdd, etc. (thus doubtless having given rise to the notion that lineage membership was the criterial attribute for these statuses). However, the Mnong Gar skewing rule permits a maximum of only one application and

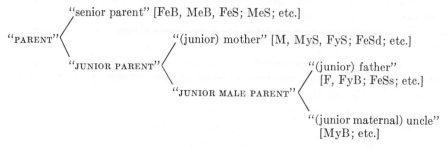

Figure 5

cannot transmit a particular status on down to several successive generations of a matriline. For example, whereas in an ordinary Crow-type system we have the reduction:

FSds → FSs   [by skewing rule corollary]
    → FB   [by a second application]
    → F   [by merging rule]

in the Mnong Gar system two cases of the type FSds must be distinguished, viz., FeSds and FySds, only the former of which is subject to the Mnong Gar skewing rule, which yields

FeSds → FySs

the result of which is not susceptible to a second application of this rule. The next reduction is by a merging rule of wider scope ("Cheyenne" form, as noted above), which yields

FySs → B

VIII

The Omaha and Crow skewing rules presented in sections VI and VII generate four first-ascending-generation kin classes by leaving four G^1 types invariant—F, M, FS, MB—and by reducing numerous other kin types of several "natural" generations to these. Thus, F, M, FS, and MB become the foci of what may quite properly be called the "father," "mother," "(paternal) aunt," and "(maternal) uncle" classes, respectively. These may undergo yet further mergings (e.g., FS with M in semibifurcate or non-bifurcate systems; and MB with F in nonbifurcate systems), or subdivisions (as already noted and illustrated), by virtue of special taxonomic rules that apply to the end products of the reductions.

There are some Omaha-type systems, however, that lack a "paternal aunt" class altogether, not by virtue of any special taxonomic rule, but by virtue of a stronger skewing rule that reduces the whole "paternal aunt" class of our first system, as well as some of the "grandmother" types of that system, to S, making classificatory "sisters" of all of these. This variety of Omaha is generated by the following rule, which is like our first one except that here we remove the restriction implied by the dots in the first rule.

SKEWING RULE (Omaha Type II): FS → S.

The phrasing of the rule reads as before, except that the relevant cases are no longer limited to those in which FS appears as a linking relative. Now it applies to FS in any context, and reads: *Let the kin type* FATHER'S SISTER *be equivalent to the kin type* SISTER.

COROLLARY: ♀ Bs → ♀ B; and ♀ Bd → ♀ S.

Let a woman's BROTHER'S CHILD *be equivalent to that woman's* SIBLING. The female sign may now refer to ego, as well as to linking female relatives. (In the earlier rule this sign was restricted to links.)

The reductions produced by this rule, taken together with the merging and half-sibling rules as previously stated, are illustrated in Fig. 6 for the case where ego is male.

The kinship terminology of the Tzeltal (Chiapas, Mexico) may be cited as an example of a system that is based on this stronger Omaha skewing rule.[18]

IX

The mirror image of this stronger Omaha skewing is given by the following Crow rule:

SKEWING RULE (Crow Type II): MB → B.

COROLLARY: ♂ Ss → ♂ B; and ♂ Sd → ♂ S.

The results, for a male ego, are illustrated in Fig. 7. It will be noted that the terminological-generation lines drawn on Fig. 7 are not an exact mirror reflection of those drawn on Fig. 6. This is because both figures are made out for a male ego. The mirror reflection of the Omaha diagram for male ego (Fig. 6) would be a Crow diagram for female ego. And the mirror reflection of a Crow diagram for male ego (Fig. 7) would be an Omaha diagram for female ego.

The Crow Indians themselves offer an example of a system based on this stronger skewing rule.[19]

Just as the stronger Omaha variety lacks a "paternal aunt" class, so this analogous stronger variety of Crow—its mirror image—lacks a "maternal uncle" class. MB and other types that are "uncles" in the weaker variety of Crow as well as some types that are "grandfathers" in that variety, reduce to B and now become classificatory "(elder) brothers."

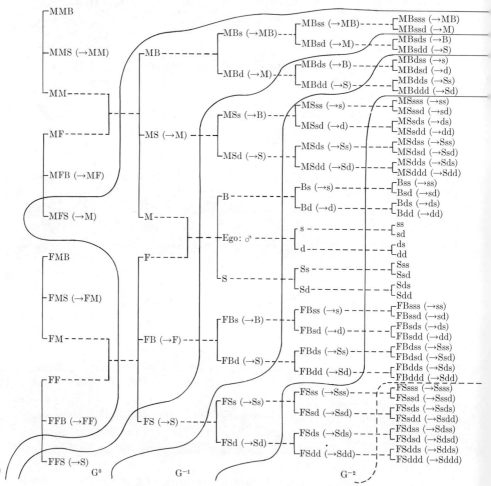

Figure 6. Omaha reductions, type II, ego being male.

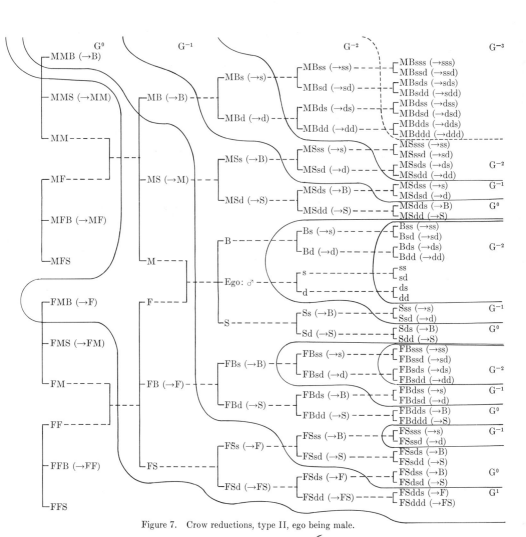

Figure 7.   Crow reductions, type II, ego being male.

X

So far we have seen (1) that there are some Omaha-type systems and some Crow-type systems that have four first-ascending-generation classes, "father," "mother," "paternal aunt," and "maternal uncle" (deriving by extension from F, M, FS, and MB, respectively); and (2) that there are other Omaha-type systems that eliminate the "paternal aunt" category altogether, and other Crow-type systems that similarly eliminate the "maternal uncle" category, by bringing FS in the first instance and MB in the second, together with their derivative types and certain others, down to the level of ego's generation and putting them into "sibling" categories. Now we are to introduce a third variety (3) of these systems, that eliminates the "maternal uncle" category from the Omaha type and the "paternal aunt" category from the Crow type by lifting MB in the first instance, and FS in the second, together with the extensions from these, up to the second ascending terminological generation and putting them into "grandfather" and "grandmother" categories. This third variety of 'Omaha' is given by the following rule:

SKEWING RULE (Omaha Type III): $\male$ S . . . $\rightarrow$ $\male$ d . . .

I.e., *let a man's* SISTER, *as linking relative, be regarded as equivalent to that man's* DAUGHTER *as linking relative.*

COROLLARY: . . . $\female$ B $\rightarrow$ . . . $\female$ F.

I.e., *let any female linking relative's* BROTHER *be regarded as equivalent to that female linking relative's* FATHER.

To illustrate the operation of this rule, taken together with the usual merging and half-sibling rules, let us consider the kin types MBs, MBd, and FSs. They reduce as follows:

MBs	$\rightarrow$ MFs	[by skewing rule corollary]
	$\rightarrow$ MB	[by half-sibling rule]
	$\rightarrow$ MF	[by skewing rule corollary].
MBd	$\rightarrow$ MFd	[by skewing rule corollary]
	$\rightarrow$ MS	[by half-sibling rule]
	$\rightarrow$ M	[by merging rule].
$\male$ FSs	$\rightarrow$ $\male$ Fds	[by skewing rule]
	$\rightarrow$ $\male$ Ss	[by half-sibling rule]
	$\rightarrow$ $\male$ ds	[by skewing rule].
$\female$ FSs	$\rightarrow$ $\female$ Fds	[by skewing rule]
	$\rightarrow$ $\female$ Ss	[by half-sibling rule]
	$\rightarrow$ $\female$ s	[by merging rule].

Thus MBs, like MB, goes into the "grandfather" category by virtue of its equivalence, under this skewing rule, to one of the second-ascending-generation male types; while MBd goes into the "mother" class by virtue of its reduction, under the same rule, to M. And a man's FSs, like a man's Ss, becomes a "grandson"; while a woman's FSs, like her Ss, becomes a classificatory "son."

The reductions obtained under this rule are illustrated in Fig. 8.

It is systems of this variety that Radcliffe-Brown (1950:34) referred to as "a special variety of the Omaha type of terminology found in the Shona, Ndau, and Shangana-Tonga peoples of Southern Rhodesia and Portuguese East Africa" and to which reference was made in section II of this paper. We quote further from Radcliffe-Brown (1950:34–35):

> The other tribes of this cluster [i.e., other than Ronga, the southernmost tribe of the Shangana-Tonga group] have a different system involving an extended use of the term for grandfather. The mother's brother is called 'grandfather'—*sekuru* in Shona, *tetekulu* in Ndau, *kokwana* in Lenge and other tribes of the Shangana-Tonga group; both the Shona and the Ndau terms are derived from a stem meaning 'father' and *kulu* or *kuru* meaning 'great.' The sons and son's sons of the mother's brother are also called 'grandfather.' The reciprocal of 'grandfather' is, of course, 'grandchild'—*muzukuru* in Shona, *muzukulu* in Ndau, *ntukulu* in Shangana-Tonga. This term, which is used by a man for the children of his son or daughter, is thus also applied to his father's sister's child and his sister's child, both of whom call him 'grandfather.' A man thus may have 'grandchildren' who are older than himself and 'grandfathers' who are younger.
>
> In these tribes, as in the Ronga, the daughter and the son's daughter of the mother's brother are called 'mother'—*mayi* or *mayi nini* (little mother) in Shona, *mai* in Ndau, *manana* in Shangana-Tonga. The children of these women are therefore called 'siblings' (*makwabu* or *makweru* in Shangana-Tonga).
>
> This terminology expresses the unity of the mother's lineage. All the female members of a man's mother's lineage in her own and succeeding generations are his 'mothers.' All the men of the lineage through several generations fall into a single category, but instead of being called 'mother's brother' they are called 'grandfather.' The male members of the lineage are placed in a category that refers primarily to the second ascending generation, while the females are placed in one that refers primarily to the first ascending generation. . . .
>
> These systems of terminology are clearly based on the principle of the unity of the lineage. But that does not explain why the mother's brother is called 'grandfather.' To understand that we must refer to certain features of the social relationship between mother's brother and sister's son in these tribes.

It was to answer this question that Radcliffe-Brown adduced the MB/Ss relationship of familiarity (found in certain patrilineal societies[20]) and his alternating-generation theory of affect. As noted in section II, however, we are not in need of a separate explanation for this particular terminological merger. It follows, as do all of the other generation assignments of the entire system, from the skewing rule that has just been written.

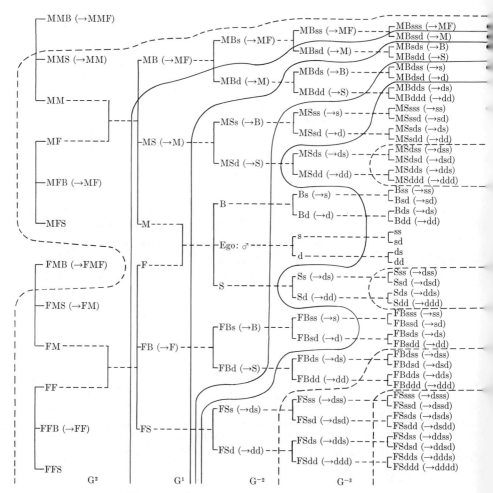

Figure 8. Omaha reductions, type III, ego being male.

Data at hand on the kinship terminology of the Kamba, collected by Robert Dentan (unpublished ms.) in Kenya, present an unusually complex system (complex in the sense defined in section VI) based on this skewing rule. And to move out of Africa, it is abundantly clear that the early Latin and the early Germanic kinship systems were Omaha systems based on this skewing rule. It is no accident that mother's brother was *avunculus* (diminutive of *avus*, "grandfather") in Latin, or that a man's sister's children were, like his daughter's children and his son's children, *nepos* and *neptis* ("grandson" and "granddaughter")—whence, via French, we have our present-day English words *nephew* and *niece*. And like Latin *nepos* and *neptis*, the Old English cognate words *nefa* and *nift* (which antedated our borrowed French words) also referred both to one's grandchildren and to a man's sister's children. Moreover, the reciprocal of *nefa* and *nift*, viz., *eam* (from Proto-Germanic **auhaima-*, with a Pre-Germanic root **au-*, cognate to that of Latin *avus* and *avia*) was used with both the meaning of mother's brother and that of grandfather.

XI

The mirror image of this second stronger variety of Omaha skewing is given by the analogous Crow rule:

SKEWING RULE (Crow Type III): ♀ B . . . → ♀ s . . .

I.e., *let a woman's* BROTHER, *as linking relative, be regarded as equivalent to that woman's* SON *as linking relative.*

COROLLARY: . . . ♂ S → . . . ♂ M.

I.e., *let any male linking relative's* SISTER *be regarded as equivalent to that male linking relative's* MOTHER.

Just as the rule of section X produces an Omaha-type system in which MB and equivalents are classed as "grandfathers" and a man's sister's children as "grandchildren," so this rule produces a Crow-type system in which FS and equivalents are turned into "grandmothers" and a woman's brother's children into "grandchildren." For example:

♀ Bs → ♀ ss   [by this skewing rule].

The reductions given by this rule are illustrated in Fig. 9, for a male ego. The diagram for a female ego is the mirror reflection of Fig. 8. Similarly the female-ego diagram corresponding to the male-ego one of Fig. 8 is the mirror reflection of Fig. 9.

The Oklahoma Seminole system reported by Alexander Spoehr furnishes an excellent and very thoroughly documented example of a system of this variety (Spoehr 1942). It is also a relatively simple instance of it, since the only supplementary taxonomic rules required are to add a diminutive suffix to the "father" and "mother" terms when denoting collateral members of these classes, and also to the "child" term when denoting collateral "children" of a female ego.

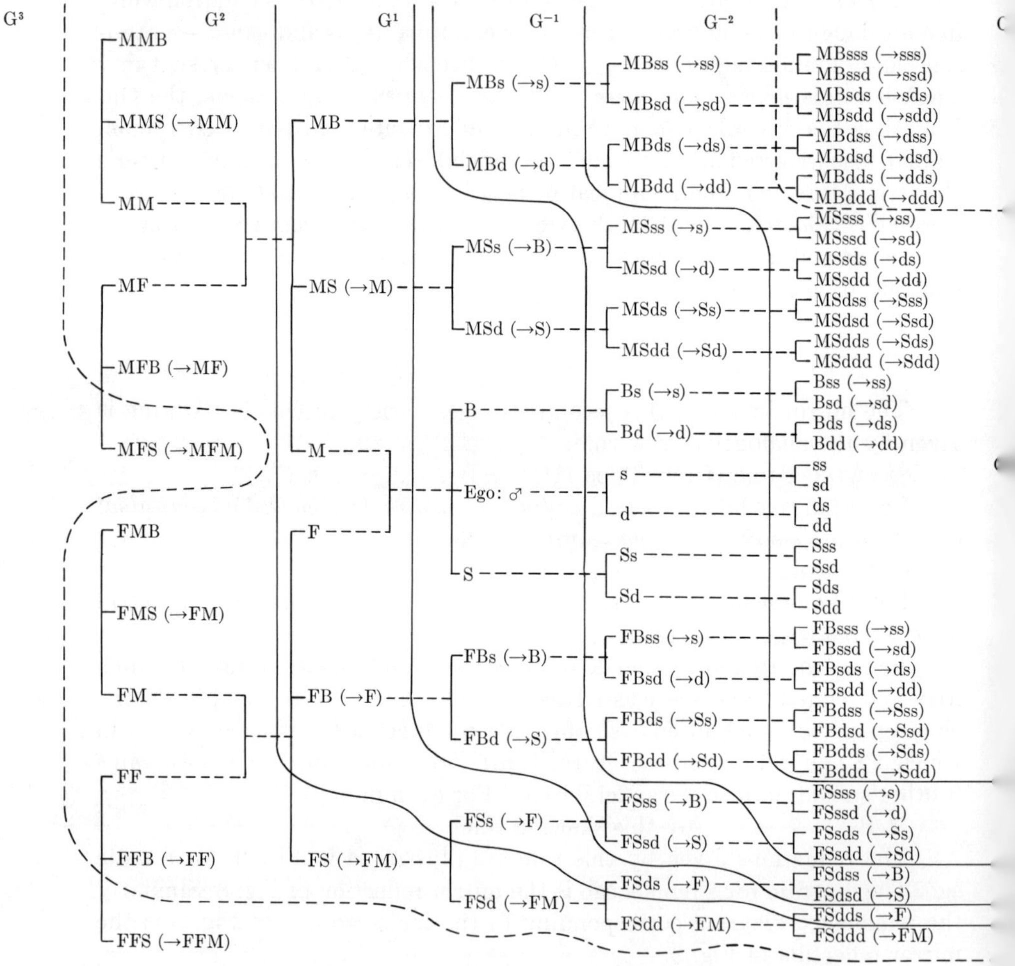

Figure 9. Crow reductions, type III, ego being male.

The Trobriand system is also based on this rule. The now famous category *tabu* of the Trobrianders is nothing more or less than a self-reciprocal "grandkin" term, representing a taxonomic merger of the "grandfather," "grandmother," "grandson," and "granddaughter" classes generated by the skewing rule of this section. Sociological explanations based on lineage theory have either been embarrassed by the inclusion of the mother's mother in the Trobriand category *tabu* (Fathauer 1961) or have expended admirable but unnecessary ingenuity to account for it (Leach 1962). In terms of the theory put forth here, however, the mother's mother is as good a "grandmother" as the father's mother, the father's sister, or the father's sister's daughter. As with the mirror-image situation that Radcliffe-Brown was trying to explain in his way, so also here a separate sociological explanation is not called for. All that needs explaining is the skewing rule itself.

XII

A fourth major subvariety of the Omaha type combines the extreme features of skewing given by both the Type II skewing rule (section VIII) and the Type III skewing rule (section X). Both rules must be written for these systems, even though they overlap in their implications. Both of the stronger forms produce all of the skewings (i.e., generation-altering reductions) of the initial or weak form, but produce others in addition. This fourth and strongest variety (we shall call it Type IV) includes all the additional skewings given by both of the intermediate stronger forms. Thus, both the "paternal aunt" class and the "maternal uncle" class are eliminated, the former by being lowered a generation to "sister," and the latter by being raised a generation to "grandfather." The only first-ascending-generation categories remaining in this type of system are "father" and "mother." All cross-kin categories are evacuated. The cross-cousin category is emptied by all of the forms of Omaha and Crow skewing that have been discussed here, and is of course absent from most Crow-type and Omaha-type systems. In this strongest form of skewing, the evacuation of cross-kin categories is complete: the cross-uncle, cross-aunt, cross-nephew, and cross-niece categories are all empty, and labels for such concepts are missing from systems of this type.

Figure 10 presents some of the results of this strongest Omaha skewing, for a male ego. The Southeastern Wintu of California furnish an example of such a system (cf. Gifford 1922).

XIII

The analogous fourth and strongest form of Crow-type skewing is illustrated in Fig. 11, for male ego. The female-ego diagram is a mirror reflec-

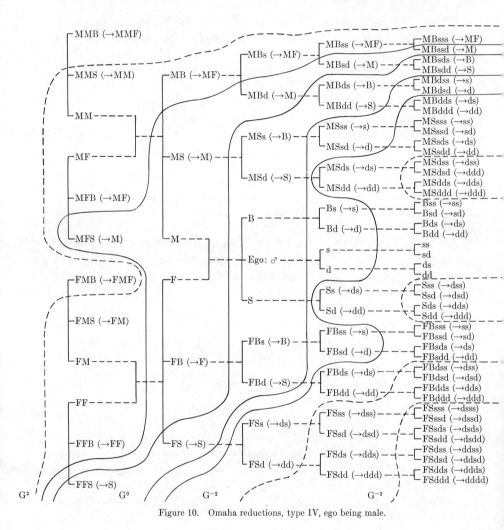

Figure 10.   Omaha reductions, type IV, ego being male.

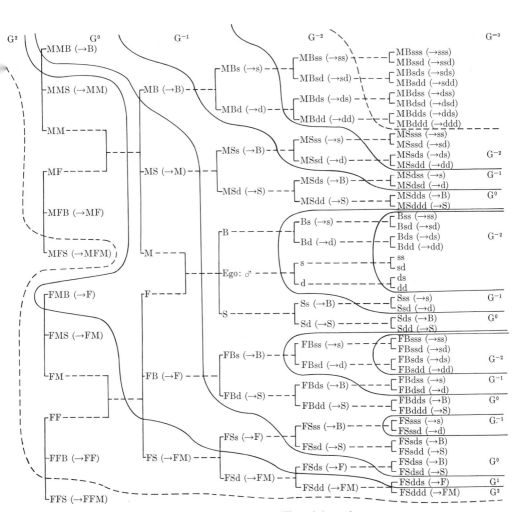

Figure 11.   Crow reductions, type IV, ego being male.

tion of Fig. 10. Similarly, the female-ego diagram corresponding to Fig. 10 (strongest form of Omaha) is a mirror reflection of Fig. 11. A well-known system and another less well known that we might cite as examples of this strongest Crow form would require too much explaining here to substantiate the claim, for they are both complex in the sense defined in section VI. In the absence of the examples, this form can be listed merely as a theoretical possibility.

XIV

The foregoing survey of major varieties of Omaha and Crow skewing is by no means exhaustive of the subject. In the first place, we have dealt so far only with consanguineal kin types. But the assignment of whatever affinal categories (spouse, in-law, and step) as are provided by the vocabulary and taxonomic principles of a given kinship system must also be done in accordance with the same reduction rules as are operative in the consanguineal part of that system. Consequently the rules for any system must be written in such a way that this will result from them. This is a subject which has not been touched on yet, and which, for reasons of space, will not be treated here. It must suffice to say that affinal systems show great variety also, and that if we were to review this, and to write rules to account for it, we should have not four forms each for the Crow- and Omaha-type skewing rules, but eight. For example, there are Crow-type systems in which one's mother's brother's wife (MBW) is given the status of a classificatory "wife" or "sister-in-law," being brought down to ego's own terminological generation; but there are other Crow-type systems in which she is left in the first ascending terminological generation as a "stepmother" or "mother" (the latter depending on whether or not the taxonomic principles of the system maintain or obliterate a distinction between step and consanguineal types[21]). Thus, MBW is "wife" to a man and "sister-in-law" to a woman by Pawnee reckoning, but "mother" (to a man or a woman) by Trobriand reckoning. The skewing rules for these systems must be written in ways that will include these as well as all other assignments (consanguineal, step, and in-law) among their predictions.[22]

Another matter not dealt with here is the generation skewing of certain parallel-collateral kin types which is found in a few systems along with the more usual skewing that affects some or all of the cross-collateral kin types. Both asymmetrical and symmetrical varieties exist. It has been possible to account for a few of these through the discovery of reduction rules that produce the desired results. Some of them, however, are still unsolved.

Another topic that needs fuller treatment than has been given to it here is the subject of taxonomic principles, their variety, their treatment in dimensional analysis of systems and in componential definitions of categories, and the relation of these to reduction rules.

Still another is what happens to Omaha- or Crow-type systems when a consanguineal marriage prescription (or consanguineal-affinal equation) is imposed. In cases such as this another equivalence rule must be added to the set. This must usually take priority over all other rules, so that we deal then with an ordered set. This rule has the effect of transforming certain consanguineal types into affinal types, and other consanguineal types of one sort into closer consanguineal types of a different sort. Among these results is usually the transformation of MBd into another type so that it is not available for reduction to M by the Omaha rule that is most often operative in these systems. Thus one is usually spared the embarrassment of marrying a "mother" under the matrilateral cross-cousin prescription.

Beside all of these, there is a good deal of business that has to do with fundamental postulates, the ultimate primitives, and the logical structure of kinship reckoning as a mathematical system, that has been completely passed over in this paper in order to reach more quickly the kind of data that falls into the hands of the ethnologist.

Finally and most important, one will wish to know something about the relevance, if any, of these formal analyses of kinship terminological systems to the sociology of kinship. Much will have to be done yet—in the structural and comparative analysis of many systems of terminology, in the analysis of the social systems where these are found, and in the testing of hypotheses concerning the relation of sociological factors to the formal principles underlying kinship reckoning—before anything can be said with a comfortable sense of certainty on this subject. However, it may not be amiss to register, although prematurely, a few tentative hypotheses and general ideas concerning this relation. It should be understood that these are little more than guesses at the possible significance of the results obtained by formal analysis of the terminologies. The best that can be said for them is that they appear (at the moment) to be not unreasonable, and that the very little bit of preliminary testing that has been done so far has not yet dealt too badly with them.

XV

First of all it may be remarked that the formal analyses of Crow-type and Omaha-type systems of kinship terminology such as have been illustrated here, as well as similar analyses of a number of other kinds of terminological systems, predispose us rather strongly in favor of an "extensionist" theory of kinship systems.

Secondly, it can be noted that this view is, in certain of its aspects, at once Murdockian and Malinowskian: Murdockian in its accord with the assumption of the importance and near universality of the nuclear family as a social institution,[23] and Malinowskian in its deriving the relations of kinship from the primary relations within the nuclear family.[24] (The *real* "father" is F, the *real* "mother" is M. These are *basic* meanings; others are *extensions*. *Real* "uncles" and "aunts" are [unmerged] siblings of parents, etc.)

Thirdly, in this view, kinship reckoning is based squarely on genealogical reckoning. Extensions are not seen as blanket labelings of "social groups" characterized by lineage, locality, age grade, etc., but rather as resulting from a series of derivations, reckoning genealogically[25] from one individual to another in accordance with the principles that are normal for any given system.

Perhaps no set of views could be more at variance with the received notions in the social-anthropological theory of kinship today or more inviting of a ready-made judgment of "naïve" than these. For the current doctrine is characterized by an antiextensionist and antigenealogical bias and prefers to deal in "social categories" instead.[26] This current theory is supposed to apply to "noncognatic" systems, a category including the "unilineal." The imposition of genealogical reckoning on such systems is viewed as an anthropological error, resulting from the carry-over of a mode of thought peculiar to our own cognatic system, and thus revealing a lack of social-anthropological sophistication. I suspect, however, that the systems described from this point of view may yet profit from being looked at rigorously from the opposed point of view presented here, and I know of two cases where this can be shown to be a fact.[27] In any case, every system ought to be looked at from all available theoretical points of view, if only not to prejudge the situation. I suspect, though, that there are not very many truly "noncognatic" systems, in the sense of their *lacking* a bilateral genealogical reckoning of personal kinship, however skewed their generation reckoning or unilineal their appearance.[28] Rather, the "noncognatic" systems of kinship appear to be a social-structural overlay having to do with kin-based corporations of some sort. This has been repeatedly mistaken for the essence of kinship. And one of the most persistent errors in the study of kinship terminologies has been the assumption—authored perhaps by Morgan in his *League of the Iroquois* but contradicted by his own data in *Systems of Consanguinity and Affinity*—that the function of classificatory kinship terms is to delineate membership in unilineal descent groups.[29] On the basis of all of the analyses of kinship terminological systems that I have carried out so far, however, I incline strongly to the assumption that the *primary* function of kinship terminologies is to delineate the relation of ego to the members of his personal bilateral kindred in such a way as to express some socially and legally important aspect of each of these relationships. From the kindred, these terms can be extended and reextended till they reach the sky (as they often do, literally, to include the sun, moon, thunderers, and other deities and heavenly beings). For example, at least five different varieties of such metaphoric extension, in as many different social contexts, can be distinguished for the secondary uses of the Iroquois kinship terms. One of these gave rise to Morgan's error.

XVI

So much for the generalities concerning a point of view that seems congenial to the results obtained by formal analysis of terminologies. Now a few more specific hypotheses concerning the systems themselves and their differences can be suggested.

As noted above, we see the *basic meanings* of such primary category terms as "father," "mother," etc. (in whatever language) as the primary kin types F, M, etc. Other referents of these terms are *extensions*. Secondary categories—"uncles," "grandparents," and the like—derive from the overlap of the nuclear families of orientation and procreation[30] of linking individuals. The catch comes with the extensions. These result from shunts across the genealogical network that put secondary or more distant kin types into primary categories, etc. To Malinowski this was an "anomaly of the language"—doubtless because it had such bizarre results in Trobriand as applying the "father" term, a term laden with intensive positive affect in its primary application, to a "predestined enemy" (FSs) in a secondary application of the term.[31]

Our problem then is to inquire into the nature and function of these "shunts" across the genealogical net. The shunts are those that are effected by equivalence rules like those described in this paper. A hypothesis that is being considered seriously at the moment is that the transformational rules express laws of succession: lineal succession (uniform for the two sexes) in the skewing rules, and lateral succession (perhaps along with other things) in the merging rules. Extensions of a kinship term, then, would define a class of potential legal successors—and successors to successors—to statuses held by one's nearer kinsman.[32]

If this first hypothesis be entertained as plausible, then it might be supposed also that differences in the skewing rules—from one variety or subvariety of these to another—ought to reflect differences of some sort either in these laws of succession or in the context in which they operate.

The statuses involved might be of various sorts: head of family, other positions in the domestic group, headship of a lineage or kin-based corporation, hereditary political office, religious office, etc. The exact specifications may be different from case to case, and it is well to leave these somewhat flexible. The kinship terminology may follow one of these while ignoring or running counter to another. The "deviant" examples referred to earlier (section III) should warn us not to restrict the interpretation of "status" to "membership in a unilineal descent group." Such groups may provide excellent contexts for statuses important enough to have their succession reflected in kinship terminology, and so we might expect a certain correlation of Crow-type terminology with matrilineal descent groups, and of Omaha-type terminology with patrilineal descent groups (without the necessity, however, of assuming that it is descent-group categories that are being labeled by the kinship terms). But the existence of patrilineal succession to important offices in societies with matrilineal descent groups, and vice versa, and of unilineal successions in societies without any descent groups, would allow for the cases of Crow- and Omaha-type terminologies that run counter to this association.

By way of illustration of how skewing rules might express laws of succession (and the variability in the meaning of these), we may consider a hypothetical case involving a Crow rule together with the usual merging and half-sibling rules. By virtue of the merging rule, I (male ego) am a terminological "father" to my brother's children, and they are in turn my "children." And by virtue of the skewing rule, I am also a terminological "father" to my mother's brother's children, and they are thus also my "children." We ask now what it means to be a terminological "father" to my mother's brother's children. Ethnographies suggest that this can mean many different things in different societies, depending apparently on what the social statuses are whose transmission the skewing rule recognizes. It is fairly clear, for example, that it meant something rather different in Trobriand from what it meant in Pawnee.

On the one hand, it might mean that I am a legal potential "social father" to my mother's brother's children: I may succeed to my mother's brother's position as head of his family upon his death, or perhaps even share with him, as a junior partner of sorts, some of the responsibilities of that position while he is still living. Similarly, in a case like the Pawnee where my mother's brother's wife is my terminological "wife" and I am a terminological "husband" to her, I may legally succeed to the position of husband to her upon her own husband's death, and I might even share with this husband some of the responsibilities, not to mention privileges, of that status while he is living.[33]

On the other hand, it may not mean at all that I ever assume the role of a husband to my mother's brother's wife or of social father in relation to my mother's brother's children, but only that I am the legal heir to their father's rights over certain "home property" and that, while I may respect their widowed mother's dowager rights (until she remarries, if she does) and assume some responsibility for her support, I am uneasy about the continued presence there of her adult children—especially sons—and can, if provoked, throw them off the place and terminate their privileges there.[34]

By either the weak Crow skewing rule (section VII) or the second stronger form (section XI), it is important to note, the children of my brother and of my mother's brother become my "children," but the children of my sister's son do not—even though they, like the others, are the offspring of a man of my own matriline and matrilineage (if lineage structures are present), which, by the lineage theory of these things, should make them equally my "children." Instead, they are my "grandchildren" (see Figs. 1, 4, and 9). By the succession theory, on the other hand, this appears reasonable enough. It may simply mean that although I may succeed to a brother's status or to that of my mother's brother, the latter does not succeed to mine; and although my sister's son may be my successor, I am not his. In systems of the first stronger form, however (section IX, Fig. 7), the lineage theory seems more appropriate. In these, my sister's son's children are in fact my classificatory "children." The research which will be necessary to determine whether or not there is any significance to this difference has not been done. Until it is, one can only wonder.

The above argument has been framed in terms of matrilineal succession to both male and female positions (sister's son follows brother; sister's daughter follows sister) and Crow-type terminologies. Analogous arguments can apply to patrilineal succession (brother's son follows brother; brother's daughter follows sister) and Omaha-type terminologies. It has to be recognized that rules of succession to female statuses can be as important for determining terminological generation skewing as rules of succession to male statuses.

In regard to the possible significance of the difference between the second stronger form (section XI, Fig. 9) and the weak form (section VII, Fig. 4), the following hypothesis is suggested—very tentatively. Professor Murdock (1949, chap. 4) has distinguished between two varieties of unilineal descent groups: the "consanguineal" and the "compromise." We should like to generalize the application of this contrast so that it will apply to unilineally determined kin aggregates of any sort, whether they merit being called "descent groups" (by whatever criteria one may wish to invoke in the definition of that concept), or not. The former variety, so far as the relationship between its adult members of opposite sex is concerned, can be viewed as made up of successive generations of unilineally connected sibling sets, while the latter variety must be seen as made up of successive generations of unilineally connected spouse pairs. In the former, individuals of both sexes—as they become adults—attain to the adult social statuses and positions of authority and responsibility in their own natal group. In the latter variety this is not the case. As a pair of siblings of opposite sex become adults, the one of lineal sex attains to the adult statuses of his sex in his natal group, while the other does not. He has no legal status within that group other than the one of his childhood: he remains, as it were, a "child" in relation to that group, and attains to adult statuses only in the group which he enters upon marriage. (The grammatical "he" of these sentences is of course that of the indefinite gender, and is to be understood as he or she, depending on whether the compromise group is defined matrilineally or patrilineally.) Perhaps it is arrangements such as this that give social meaning to the skewing rule, *let a woman's brother, as linking relative, be equivalent to that woman's son, as linking relative* (Crow, second stronger form; section XI, Fig. 9), and to the rule, *let a man's sister, as linking relative, be equivalent to that man's daughter, as linking relative* (Omaha, second stronger form; section X, Fig. 8).[35] Possibly this is what can be understood if, as is said, the early Romans referred collectively to the women born into a gens as "the daughters of the gens." They did not succeed to adult legal statuses in their natal gens, for these were taken by the women who were married in. A woman lost her membership in her natal gens upon marriage, to become a member of her husband's gens, assuming its name, performing its religious rituals, and filling the important position of a woman in that group. As once before (section X), it may be suggested again that it is perhaps not an accident that in early Latin a man's sister's children were *nepos* and *neptis* ("grandson" and "granddaughter"), for if sister is as daughter (to an adult brother), then sister's child must be as daughter's child, i.e., "grandchild."

XVII

It is by no means certain that the speculations ventured here, concerning possible social bases for the equivalence rules, and also concerning the possible significance of differences between the various forms of skewing rules, are in the right direction. But at least they lead to testable hypotheses. The testing, however, may require more careful observation and documentation than is generally available in ethnographic accounts on such topics as the composition of domestic and any larger kin groups, their charter, spatial distribution, and relations to property, the native legal concepts pertaining to them, the distribution of authority and responsibility within them, the definitions of legal statuses in them and of the expected roles of their occupants, the legal norms and other considerations that enter into the determining of successors, etc. But whatever the merits or shortcomings of this first attempt to read sociological meaning from the formal rules underlying systems of terminology, it must be emphasized that the validity of the rules or of the method does not depend on this. The validity of an analysis of this kind rests only upon its sufficiency and its parsimony in accounting for the application of terms of relationship to one's relatives in whatever society's usage is being described. Similarly, its utility should be judged in relation to its originally stated limited aims (section I), viz., to tell one the exact minimum he will need to know in order to predict accurately what relationships are assigned to what categories in such and such a system of kinship terminology. Anything beyond this that may eventually come from it I shall regard as a bonus.

NOTES

[1] A preliminary version of this paper, entitled Equivalence Principles and Reduction Rules in the Analysis of Kinship Systems, was presented in the symposium on *Methods of Formal Analysis in Anthropology* at the meeting of the American Anthropological Association, Nov. 16, 1961, in Philadelphia. The method of analysis that is presented here grew out of an attempt to find a better kind of solution for Crow- and Omaha-type systems than that exemplified in my Semantic Analysis of the Pawnee Kinship Usage (1956). The first results of this search were presented in a paper prepared for the panel on *Anthropology and Linguistics* at the Ninth Annual Round Table Meeting on Linguistics and Language Studies at Georgetown University, Apr. 11, 1958, in Washington, D.C., but because of difficulties arising from a still inadequate understanding of the rules at work in these systems, the paper could not be brought to a form which I considered suitable for publication at that time, and was not included in the published *Report* of that meeting.

[2] For the historical record, the following attempts to account for Crow- and Omaha-type kinship systems deserve mention: Kohler (1897), Durkheim (1898), Rivers (1914), Gifford (1916), Seligman (1917), Lowie (1930, 1932), Tax (1937a), White (1939), Radcliffe-Brown (1941, 1950), Murdock (1949:166–169), Lane and Lane (1959), Eyde and Postal (1961), and Moore (1963). For brief reviews see Tax (1937a:12–15) and Radcliffe-Brown (1941:56). Most of these attempt causal accounts of one sort or another. Radcliffe-Brown (1941) disavowed a causal account and professed to offer only a structural account; but it amounts to a social-causal account after all. His primary concern was to eschew conjectural history as a causal explanation. Recent descriptions by Goodenough (1951, 1956) and myself (1956), influenced by the linguistic methods of componential analysis, are "structural" in a more formal and literal sense, as well as noncausal. They have attempted to give theories of particular Crow-type systems that satisfy the requirement of sufficiency.

[3] A fully bifurcate system is one that distinguishes between "cross" and "parallel" kin types for both males and females in the first ascending generation, and in relation to both a male ego and a female ego for kin types of the first descending generation. An example of a fully bifurcate Crow-type system is Cherokee (cf. Morgan 1871; and Gilbert 1937, 1943). A semibifurcate system is one that distinguishes between "cross" and "parallel" kin type only among males in the first ascending generation, and only in relation to a male ego for kin types of the first descending generation. An example of a semibifurcate Crow-type system is Pawnee (cf. Lounsbury 1956). A nonbifurcate system is one that makes no distinctions between "cross" and "parallel" kin types. An example of a nonbifurcate Crow-type

system is Trukese (cf. Goodenough 1951, 1956). These characterizations are applicable also to nonskewed systems. E.g., among the Iroquois tribes, the Seneca, Wyandot, and Tuscarora systems are fully bifurcate, while the Mohawk, Oneida, Onandaga, and Cayuga are semibifurcate (cf. Morgan 1871; Lounsbury 1962). The so-called Hawaiian-type systems are the nonbifurcate analog to these.

[4] E.g., Seminole (cf. Spoehr 1942), and Trobriand (Malinowski 1929). Readers will be quick to object to this statement, sensing a translation fallacy in the use of the word "grandmother" here. However, I mean exactly this, and would like to ask them to hold their objections in abeyance until they have read through the arguments of this paper.

[5] The mirror image of a system is another system in which the structural positions of the sexes are reversed throughout, in comparison with the first. The mirror image of a particular kin type is one in which all of the sexes in the genealogical chain are reversed. The mirror image of the Crow treatment of a man's mother's brother's son as *his* classificatory "son" is the Omaha treatment of a woman's father's sister's daughter as *her* classificatory "daughter."

[6] Radcliffe-Brown (1950:34–38; quotation from p. 38).

[7] Although the appeal in these explanations has repeatedly been to clan or lineage membership as the basis for the application of kin terms (e.g., Radcliffe-Brown 1941, 1950; Eggan 1955; Spoehr 1942), exceptions have been acknowledged in these same discussions. Thus, Radcliffe-Brown (1950:33): "By the terminology he treats all the members of that group [his mother's lineage], through *three* (or *more*) *generations, beginning with that of his mother,* as belonging to a single category"; Eggan (1955:504): "The basic Fox kinship structure still corresponds to a lineage pattern, *except for the grandparent-grandchild extensions*"; Spoehr (1942:64): "Within these two groups of kin it is obvious that the basis of classification was sex and that generation was disregarded. *The statement requires some modification,* . . . in Fig. 3 [the genealogical diagram] I have designated the father's mother's brother as 'grandfather.' This is certainly correct, and I suspect there may have been some slight difference in usage for direct blood relations and classificatory kin. In any case the use of the grandfather and grandmother terms in this way *introduces some qualification* to the statement that sex rather than generation formed the basis of terminological classification of the two groups here examined"; and further (Spoehr 1942:68): "As in the case of the father's clan, *the statement needs qualification*. Examination of the genealogical chart (Fig. 3) shows that the children of those 'nephews' belonging to ego's clan were called 'grandchild.' " [Italics ours in these quotations.] Tax (1937b: 277–282) challenged this appeal to clan or lineage membership as a general explanation, pointing out its irrelevance in the case of the Fox (p. 282): "In combination with actual clans or moieties, the Omaha and Crow types assume new and different meanings, and they fit so nicely that one is tempted to explain one in terms of the other. Fox material gives some strong indications, however, that this is an erroneous approach."

[8] Thus Tax (1937b:280) raised the question, "why do not the Ojibwa (with clans very much stronger than those of the Fox) have this type [Omaha type] of kinship system?"

[9] Murdock (1949:168) lists Bachama, Koranko, and Seniang as having "Crow terms with patrilineal descent and patrilocal residence." Some of his double-descent cases (p. 167), e.g., Manus, are also relevant examples. I think Yap might also be

mentioned (cf. Schneider 1953). It appears as though the Kuanyama might be an example of the opposite arrangement. They are matrilineal in the ways mentioned above, but the kinship terminology has certain marks of 'Omaha' classification (e.g., MB MF). There are gaps in the data, however, so one cannot be sure (Loeb 1962).

[10] Lowie (1935:19–20); Morgan (1871).

[11] The terms "expand" and "expansion" are taken from linguistic usage. Cf. Wells (1947).

[12] Thus, for example: *"Para medios-hermanos se emplean los mismos términos que para hermanos, añadiendoles el prefijo čab. Entiendase por medios-hermanos los hijos de la madre de ego y de padre diferente (aquellos hijos del padre con otra mujer son considerados como verdaderos hermanos de ego)."* Guiteras Holmes (1948:157). Similarly, Latin *germanus*, inapplicable to a uterine half sibling, was applicable to a full sibling, an agnatic half sibling, or a patrilateral parallel first cousin. Thus the distinction is agnatic versus nonagnatic; not full versus half. A number of African systems, in societies with polygynous families, furnish examples where the uterine half sibling is classed with the full sibling and opposed to the agnatic half sibling, resulting in the distinction of uterine versus nonuterine, rather than full versus half.

[13] For the values of S and s one may remember, as a mnemonic device, that *lowercase* means *lower generation*.

[14] Cover symbols would make for more compact symbolization of some of the rules. However, collections of raw data are generally given in a notation based on maximum differentiation, and there is a certain practical advantage to having the rules symbolized in the same notation.

[15] All but the first of these is given directly. The first is given by reciprocal only.

[16] This is true for Crow and Omaha rules, which include only a skewing rule, a merging rule, and a half-sibling rule. It is understood, of course, that these equivalence rules take priority over the taxonomic rules, i.e., the kin-term definitions, of the system. (For examples of some of the ways in which these can vary, see the discussion of the Fox parental terms and of the Mnong Gar first-ascending-generation terms above.) There exist systems, however, which require in addition to these a rule of prescriptive affinity, allowing for consanguineal marriages (e.g., MBd → W) and establishing a set of equivalences of various consanguineal kin types with corresponding affinal types, and vice versa. To generate the terminological assignments of such systems, the affinity rule must take precedence over the other rules. In this case we deal with an ordered set in which one rule ranks above the other rules, which latter amongst themselves constitute an unordered subset. A further qualification might also be noted. In this paper I have written the merging rule in "Dravidian" fashion, which eliminates links that are same-sexed siblings. It could also have been written in the "Iroquois" fashion which establishes a wider set of equivalences, eliminating links that are same-sex and same-generation kin of any degree of collaterality, and of any kind ("parallel" or "cross"). In this case, however, the rules would have to be listed as an ordered set, the skewing rule always taking precedence over the merging rule. (For the nature of the Iroquois equivalence, see my paper prepared for the Ninth International Congress of Linguists, 1962.)

[17] The "Cheyenne" reduction rule is a stronger form of the "Iroquois" rule (cf. note 16), and like that one, it must also be ordered to yield precedence to the merging rule. For an account of the Cheyenne kinship system, see Eggan (1937).

[18] For data see Castro (1957:109–123) and Sousberghe and Robles (1962). The latter have also collected variant usages which illustrate the still stronger skewing discussed in section XII.

[19] For data see Lowie (1935) and Morgan (1871).

[20] Cf. Radcliffe-Brown (1924).

[21] "Step" relatives are kinsmen's spouses in the first ascending generation, and spouse's kinsmen in the first descending generation. "In-law" relatives are spouse's kinsmen in the first ascending generation, and kinsmen's spouses in the first descending generation. In ego's generation "in-laws" are both of these categories, while "step kin" are kinsmen's spouse's kinsmen, reckoned up, over, and down. These definitions are quite general in systems where the distinctions are made. Thus, in Iroquois, MH', MSH, and FSH are all "stepfather," while WF, WFB, and WMB are all "father-in-law." Our own system does not normally extend the *step versus consanguineal* distinction or the *in-law versus consanguineal* distinction to collaterals, although occasionally one hears, or sees in print, such expressions as "stepuncle" and "uncle-in-law." Some systems terminologically merge step relatives with consanguineal relatives throughout. Some, with rules of cross-cousin marriage, merge in-laws with cross consanguineals. Anthropologists usually "merge" step types with in-law types in their loose use of the term "affinal." This is appropriate only in systems of prescriptive alliance. Otherwise it is not a merger found in natural systems.

[22] The correct rule for the Trobriand system will be presented in another paper, to appear at a later date in the *American Anthropologist*. If we attend only to consanguineal kin, as in the present paper, it suffices to cite Trobriand as illustrative of the rule of section XI.

[23] Cf. Murdock (1949:2–3): "The nuclear family is a universal human social grouping. Either as the sole prevailing form of the family or as the basic unit from which more complex familial forms are compounded, it exists as a distinct and strongly functional group in every known society. No exception, at least, has come to light in the 250 representative cultures surveyed for the present study. . . . The view of Linton that the nuclear family plays 'an insignificant role in the lives of many societies' receives no support from our data."

[24] Cf. Malinowski (1929:525–526; 1932, 3d ed.:442–443): "I have intentionally and carefully distinguished this from so-called classificatory kinship ties; for the mixing up of the individual and the 'classificatory' relation, kept apart by the natives in law, custom, and idea, has been a most misleading and dangerous cause of error in anthropology, vitiating both observation and theory on social organization and kinship. . . . The child is taught by its elders to extend the term *inagu* to her [mother's sister], and this extension is made natural and plausible to the child by the considerable similarity between its relations to mother and mother's sister. But there can be no doubt that the use of the word remains always what it is, an extension and a metaphor." It is in a way ironic that an exercise in kinship algebra—a thing odious to Malinowski—should be used to support a view of kinship that is fundamentally closer to his than to that which has unseated and replaced it in contemporary social-anthropological thought.

[25] In "genealogical" reckoning, adoptive kin are counted *as if* consanguineal. By this, however, I do not concede the completely nonbiological view of kinship that current social-anthropological doctrine ascribes to its subjects. Rather, I would

view the recognized kinship statuses of any system as deriving from the constituents of the biological family, with adopted relatives being assimilated to these *as substitutes.*

[26] Cf., for example, Leach's introductory note to the reprinting of his paper, Jinghpaw Kinship Terminology (1961:28–29), his interpretation of Trobriand (1962), and Needham's of the Wikmunkan (1962).

[27] These two cases are the subjects of separate papers now in preparation.

[28] For an authentic example, however, see Gough (1952).

[29] Evidence showing that this cannot be the function of the kinship terms is given in my paper, The Structural Analysis of Kinship Semantics (1962).

[30] Cf. Murdock (1949:94).

[31] Cf. Malinowski (1929:16).

[32] This idea is not new. Fortes (1950:270–271) writes of the Ashanti: "The critical element in the relation of mother's brother and sister's son is the latter's status as the former's prospective heir. This comes out in the kinship terms used in addressing or referring to them by their non-lineage kin. Thus a man's children address his sister's son as father (*agya*) if they wish to show respect to him, since he might well step into their father's position some day."

[33] Cf. Lesser (1930).

[34] Cf. Malinowski's account of such an incident (1929:12–16).

[35] The "second stronger form" is Type III, of both the Crow and the Omaha varieties. The "first stronger form" is Type II. The "weak form" is Type I.

REFERENCES CITED

Castro G., Antonio, 1955, Hablemos en Tzeltal. San Cristobal Las Casas, Chiapas, Instituto Nacional Indigenista.

————, 1957, El Tzeltal Hablado (Adapted from Castro, 1955, by members of the Department of Anthropology, University of Chicago). Chicago, University of Chicago, Department of Anthropology.

Condominas, Georges, 1960, Les Mnong Gar du Centre Viêt-Nam. *In* G. P. Murdock, ed., Social structure in Southeast Asia. Viking Fund Publications in Anthropology, Wenner-Gren Foundation for Anthropological Research, Inc., No. 29:15–23.

Durkheim, E., 1898, Review of J. Kohler, Zur Urgeschichte der Ehe, Année Sociologique, 1:306–319.

Eggan, Fred, 1937, The Cheyenne and Arapaho kinship system. *In* Fred Eggan, ed., Social anthropology of North American tribes: 35–98. Chicago, The University of Chicago Press.

————, 1955, Social anthropology: Methods and results. *In* Fred Eggan, ed., Social anthropology of North American tribes, 2d ed.: 485–554. Chicago, The University of Chicago Press.

Eyde, David B., and Paul Postal, 1961, Avunculocality and incest, American Anthropologist, 63:747–771.

Fathauer, George H., 1961, Trobriand. *In* D. M. Schneider and Kathleen Gough, eds., Martilineal kinship: 234–269. Berkeley, University of California Press.

Fortes, Meyer, 1950, Kinship and marriage among the Ashanti. *In* A. R. Radcliffe-Brown, Daryll Forde, eds., African systems of kinship and marriage, 252–284. Fair Lawn, Oxford University Press.

Gifford, E. W., 1916, Miwok moieties. University of California Publications in American Archaeology and Ethnology, Vol. 12, no. 4.

———, 1922, California kinship systems. University of California Publications in American Archaeology and Ethnology, Vol. 18, no. 1.

Gilbert, W. H., 1937, Eastern Cherokee social organization. *In* Fred Eggan, ed., Social anthropology of North American tribes, pp. 285–338. Chicago, The University of Chicago Press.

———, 1943, The Eastern Cherokees. Bureau of American Ethnology Bulletin 133:169–414.

Goodenough, Ward H., 1951, Property, kin, and community on Truk. Yale University Publications in Anthropology, no. 46.

———, 1956, Componential analysis and the study of meaning, Language, 32:195–216.

Gough, E. Kathleen, 1952, Changing kinship usages in the setting of political and economic change among the Nayars of Malabar, Journal of the Royal Anthropological Institute, 82:71–87.

Guiteras Holmes, C., 1948, Sistema de Parentesco Huasteco, Acta Americana, 6:152–172.

Kohler, J., 1897, Zur Urgeschichte der Ehe, Zeitschrift für Vergleichende Rechtswissenschaft, vol. 12:187–353.

Lane, Robert, and Barbara Lane, 1959, On the development of Dakota-Iroquois and Crow-Omaha kinship terminologies, *Southwestern Journal of Anthropology*, 15:254–265.

Leach, E. R., 1961, Rethinking anthropology. London School of Economics Monographs on Social Anthropology, no. 22.

———, 1962, Concerning Trobriand clans and the kinship category Tabu. *In* Jack Goody, ed., Cambridge Papers in Social Anthropology, no. 1, pp. 120–145.

Lesser, Alexander, 1930, Levirate and fraternal polyandry among the Pawnees, Man, 30:98–101.

Loeb, Edwin M., 1962, In feudal Africa. Indiana University Research Center in Anthropology, Folklore, and Linguistics, Publication 23.

Lounsbury, Floyd G., 1956, A semantic analysis of the Pawnee kinship usage, Language 32:158–194.

———, 1962, The structural analysis of kinship semantics. Preprints of Papers for the Ninth International Congress of Linguists, pp. 583–588. Cambridge, Massachusetts Institute of Technology. To appear in Proceedings of the Ninth International Congress of Linguists. The Hague: Mouton & Co. (in press).

Lowie, Robert H., 1930, The Omaha and Crow kinship terminologies. *In* R. Grossmann and G. Antze, eds., Verhandlungen des 24. Internationalen Amerikanistenkongresses. Hamburg: Friederichsen, De Gruyter, pp. 103–107.

———, 1932, Kinship. Encyclopaedia of the Social Sciences, Vol. 8:568–572.

———, 1956, The Crow Indians. 1935, reissued 1956. New York, Holt, Rinehart and Winston.

Malinowski, Bronislaw, 1929, The sexual life of savages. London, Routledge.

Moore, Sally Falk, 1963, Oblique and asymmetrical cross-cousin marriage and Crow-Omaha terminology, American Anthropologist, 65:296–311.

Morgan, Lewis H., 1871, Systems of consanguinity and affinity of the human family. Smithsonian Contributions to Knowledge, no. 17.

Murdock, George Peter, 1949, Social structure. New York, Macmillan.

Needham, Rodney, 1962, Genealogy and category in Wikmunkan society, Ethnology, 1:223–264.

Radcliffe-Brown, A. R., 1924, The mother's brother in South Africa, South African Journal of Science, 21:542–555, 1924. Reprinted in A. R. Radcliffe-Brown, Structure and Function in Primitive Society, New York, pp. 15–31. Free Press.

————, 1941, The study of kinship systems, Journal of the Royal Anthropological Institute. 1941. Reprinted in A. R. Radcliffe-Brown, Structure and Function in Primitive Society. New York: Free Press, pp. 49–89.

————, 1950, Introduction. In A. R. Radcliffe-Brown and Daryll Forde, eds., African systems of kinship and marriage, pp. 1–85. New York, Oxford University Press.

Rivers, W. H. R., 1914, Kinship and social organization. London, London School of Economics.

Schneider, David M., 1953, Yap kinship terminology and kin groups, American Anthropologist, 55:215–236.

Seligman, Brenda Z., 1917, The relationship systems of the Nandi Masai and Thonga, Man, 17, art. 46.

de Sousberghe, L., and C. Robles Uribe, 1962, Nomenclature et structure de parenté des Indiens Tzeltal, L'Homme, 2:102–120.

Spoehr, Alexander, 1942, Kinship system of the Seminole. Field Museum of Natural History Anthropological Series, Vol. 33, no. 2.

Tax, Sol, 1937a, Some problems of social organization. In Fred Eggan, ed., Social anthropology of North American tribes, pp. 3–34. Chicago, The University of Chicago Press.

————, 1937b, The social organization of the Fox Indians. In Fred Eggan, ed., Social anthropology of North American tribes, pp. 243–284. Chicago, The University of Chicago Press.

Wells, Rulon S., 1947, Immediate constituents, Language, 23:81–117.

White, Leslie A., 1939, A problem in kinship terminology, American Anthropologist, 41:566–573.

Yankee Kinship Terminology:
A Problem in Componential Analysis[1]

Ward H. Goodenough

I

The method of descriptive semantics known as "componential analysis" has been described and illustrated only in part (Goodenough 1956, 1957, 1964; Frake 1960, 1962; Wallace and Atkins 1960; Conklin 1962a, 1962b,

Reproduced by permission of the author and the American Anthropological Association from the *American Anthropologist*, Vol. 67, no. 5, part 2 (Special Publication), pp. 259–287 (October 1965).

1964; Burling 1962, 1963, 1964a; Pospisil 1964). The number of reasonably adequate analyses published is very small (Goodenough 1956, 1964; Frake 1960; Conant 1961; Burling 1962, 1963; Conklin 1964; Pospisil 1960, 1964). Even in relation to kinship materials these few analyses hardly begin to illustrate the various operations that may be involved. The structure of componential matrices and the principles governing the manipulation of columns and rows within them have yet to be discussed. Only one such matrix has been published (Goodenough 1964). The use of equivalence rules and transformation rules in conjunction with componential analysis has not been explored.[2] As Wallace and Atkins (1960), Burling (1964a), and I (1956) have all observed, moreover, it is possible to devise at least several different models of the semantic structure of a terminological system, any one of which will predict adequately the permissible denotata[3] of its terms. The criteria by which one chooses one model over another, however, remain to be determined. The very fact that it is possible to construct more than one *valid* model of a semantic system has profound implications for cultural theory, calling into question the anthropological premise that a society's culture is "shared" by its members.[4] Until these matters are more fully explored, debates about the relationship of componential analysis to cognitive processes (Burling 1964a, 1964b; Hymes 1964; Frake 1964) must remain inconclusive.

This account of Yankee kinship settles none of these questions. It is offered as a contribution toward their clarification and ultimate resolution.

II

The kinship terminology analyzed here is the one with which I grew up and with which I continue to operate. It is not shared by all North Americans or by all native speakers of English. I have encountered many fellow Americans who reckon degrees of cousinship differently and others who confine cousins to ego's generation entirely, regarding all collaterals in their parents' generation as their aunts and uncles rather than as their cousins. There are evidently significant subcultural differences not only in the selection of linguistic forms to designate the same relationships—as with the preference in much of the southern United States for *daddy* over *father* as a standard term of reference—but in the classes of kin types[5] that a given term may designate.

III

That I have been my own informant should require no apology. Indeed, it has been exceedingly useful, for it has helped me to discover some of the criteria for rejecting what appear to be minimally adequate componential models.

Considering only the distribution of kin terms with respect to consanguineal kin types, I arrived at a "solution" of Yankee terminology similar to that published by Wallace (1962). It made a basic three-way cut of the universe of kin types in terms of degree of collaterality, with a "lineal" set, a "first-degree collateral" set (including the designata of *aunt, uncle, nephew, niece, brother, sister*), and a "second or further-degree collateral" set (consisting of the designatum of *cousin*). The lineal and first-degree collateral sets were further partitioned by considerations of generation removal, generation seniority, and sex of alter in the relationship. The model perfectly predicted the consanguineal kin types that were permissible denotata of the terms, but it bothered me. It didn't feel right to have the major taxonomic level in the system (as represented by degree of collaterality) separating the terms *brother* and *sister* from *father, mother, son,* and *daughter,* with which I felt they somehow belonged as a distinct subset of terms. Grouping them with *aunt, uncle, nephew* and *niece* just didn't sit right.

An analysis that does violence to the informant's subjective feel for the appropriateness of things is presumably suspect, especially if a satisfactory alternative analysis is available with which the informant is more comfortable. That there was objective structural reason for my discomfort in this case became apparent when I undertook an analysis that included affinal as well as consanguineal kin types. The terms *brother* and *sister* had to be considered as part of a subset with the terms *father, mother, son,* and *daughter* because, like them, they were subject to transforming operations signalled by the affixes *step-* and *-in-law*, and at the same time no other terms were subject to these transforming operations. This observation made it immediately apparent that Yankee terminology consists of a set of basic terms and of another set of expressions that are derivatives of the basic terms. The basic terms fall into distinctive subsets according to the kinds of derivatives that can be built on them. By insisting that analysis preserve the integrity of these subsets, I arrived at the componential models presented here. What preserving the integrity of subsets means operationally can be demonstrated readily in the course of analysis when we consider the structure of componential matrices.

By dealing with my own kinship terminology, then, and serving as my own informant, I was able to objectivize something in my own culture for which I had had only a subjective "feel." I should add that my first rough formulation of componential analysis as a method (Goodenough 1951:103–110) was in response to an effort to make objective something about Trukese kinship for which I had developed a subjective feel also. I knew that some Trukese kinship terms went together to form a system of terminology and that others were what I called "special" terms that did not fit into the system. By what criteria was I deciding that some terms were special and that others belonged together in a system of terms? It presumably involved the way in which the meanings (to me) of the terms were interrelated structurally. My effort to find a way of making these interrelationships explicit opened up for me the possibility of a rigorous descriptive semantics. My own experience leads me to conclude that asking questions of oneself as an informant is not necessarily an unsound procedure. On the contrary, it can be highly productive, especially if it allows us to convert subjective and intuitive processes within us into objectivized analytical operations.

IV

Ordinarily it is my objective as an English-speaking ethnographer to describe in English the culture of a non-English speaking people for the information of fellow speakers of English, who presumably know no more about the culture described than I did before I went out and tried to learn it. Such an account inevitably appears highly informative to those who read it. By contrast, an account of my own culture in my own language must appear highly uninformative to fellow speakers of English with much the same culture. It says what the audience already largely knows. Interest focuses on the variations of detail that reveal subcultural differences between ethnographer and audience. The ethnographer is inclined to omit consideration of the things that would be most informative to someone entirely unfamiliar with the culture he is describing. The language of description in this case, moreover, is at the same time a code for the cultural concepts described. Unless special care is taken, description can lapse into meaningless tautology.

To avoid these pitfalls and to make my account comparable with my accounts of alien cultures, I have taken as my audience a reader for whom English is a second language. Until now he has attributed to English kinship terminology, insofar as he has encountered it at all, significations corresponding to the meanings of kinship terms in his native language and culture. My object is to explain to him the meanings of my kinship terms.

The utility of this approach is obvious. One test of the adequacy of this account, I have said, is that it not do violence to my own feel, as informant, for the structure of what is described. This is the subjective test of adequacy. An equally important test is that it provide an alien with the knowledge he needs to use my kinship terminology in a way I will accept as corresponding with the way I use it. This is the objective test of adequacy. An account is deficient to the extent that it fails the test.

V

The description and analysis presented here are concerned only with kinship expressions used in reference. The data analyzed, furthermore, have only to do with the situation in which someone inquires of another, not in the presence of the person being inquired about, "What kin relationship, if any, is he (she) to you?" This invites the answer, "He (she) is my _____," or "He (she) is not a relative." The importance of controlling the context in which data are elicited is obvious when one considers how personal considerations affect the use of kinship terms in address[6] or in the presence of the person being inquired about, as illustrated by Schneider and Homans (1955). As this controlling question suggests, I am concerned in this paper with the context in which information is asked and truthfully given about the nature of the kin connection between two persons.

The number of possible answers is finite. To establish levels of contrast, we can then ask for any relative, "Is she (he) your _____?" in connection with every expression. The answer can be "Yes" or "No" (with a qualification to be noted below). When the same person can be referred to by more than one kinship expression, the several expressions are synonyms, belong to different terminological systems relating to the same domain (not a problem in the present case), or are at different levels of contrast in the taxonomy of kin relationships (as with *uncle* and *mother's brother*). Otherwise, the informant can trace his relationship to the person in question in different ways; a different kin type is in fact being denoted by each kinship expression (as when one of the informant's kinsmen has married another).

Some of the expressions we obtain are lexemes in that they signify what cannot be predicted from the significata and arrangement of their constituent parts (Goodenough 1956: 199, 206–208). Others are not lexemes, having significata that may be understood as relative products of lexemes. Thus *uncle* and *halfbrother* are lexemes, but *mother's brother* is not. Analysis need be concerned only with the lexemes of a terminological system, since their relative products need no further definition.

VI

A system of kin relationships rests on the established institutions and customs relating to membership in households, sexual rights, the definition of procreation, the legitimization of progeny as members of a jural community, and the like. My own kinship system is no exception. The very definition of kin-types requires that we take account of certain principles of family organization in my particular subculture.

Kinship is regarded as following from biological procreation. Conception is seen as resulting from a single sexual union of a man as genitor and woman as genetrix; and prenatal growth is independent of subsequent sexual unions. My culture allows for an individual to have only one genitor as well as only one genetrix, unlike Lakalai culture in New Britain, which allows for the possibility that several men may be cogenitors of the same individual. My culture also disallows the possibility of conception without a genitor, unlike Trobriand Island culture, which has the dogma that men play no essential part in procreation (Malinowski 1932). Each individual must have a genitor as well as a genetrix.

As genitor and genetrix of joint progeny, a man and woman are supposed to have established a common household independent of the household of any other adults. Following traditional procedures known as *marriage* they are supposed to have entered into lifelong agreement to maintain such a household, to confine their sexual relations to one another, and to be jointly responsible for the care, socialization, education, and sponsorship of their joint progeny. No man may be married to more than one woman, or woman to more than one man, at a time. Remarriage by the survivor following the death of his (her) marriage partner is permitted. Although marriage is ideally for life, there are formal procedures for terminating a marriage, *divorce* and *annulment*, after which a man and woman are free to marry again. The common household established by a marriage is dissolved following a divorce or annulment.

The male partner to a marriage is the female partner's *husband* and the female partner is the male partner's *wife*. A husband and wife refer to their joint male progeny as their *son*, to their female progeny as their *daughter*, and to their collective progeny as their *children*. They are their progeny's *father* (genitor)[7] and *mother* (genetrix) respectively and their progeny's *parents* collectively. The joint progeny refer to one another as their *brother* (if the person referred to is male) and their *sister* (if the person referred to is female).

A married man and woman are a single social unit whose solidarity, joint interests, and responsibilities take precedence over obligations and interests either may have in any other relationship. Their relations to their dependent progeny might appear to be an exception to this principle, but ideally their obligations to their progeny are joint and cannot be in conflict with their mutual interests. The unity of married pairs extends to almost all aspects of kin relationships and to many aspects of social relationships generally. Whatever obligation a person may have to kinsmen, for example, his marriage partner must share that obligation as well. A man should be as prepared to give financial aid to a dependent kinsman of his partner as to one of his own.

The foregoing ideal of what is supposed to be does not always obtain in fact. A man and woman may establish a common household without having gone through a formal marriage. Their marriage may be dissolved, formally or informally. Men and women may have sexual relations and procreate with other than their marriage partners. Responsibility for the care, socialization, education, and sponsorship of progeny may be assumed by other than the genitor and genetrix. The cultural principles for classifying kin relationships necessarily take account of such departures from the ideal.

As it turns out, the biological connections of genitor and progeny and of genetrix and progeny take priority, when publicly acknowledged, except under special and very limited conditions. They provide a principle that no ego may acknowledge a relationship with more than one person at a time as *his father* or *his mother*. Furthermore, no ego may ever establish more than one such relationship, except by legal adoption, in which the previous relationship is in effect formally dissolved. The original relationship thus established need not be with the *genitor* or *genetrix*, but once established so that a person says "She is my mother" in answer to the question "What relationship is she to you?," the same answer cannot ever be given with reference to another person (provided, of course, that the person referred to is not within hearing).[8] Only of the genitor and genetrix, finally, can it be said "He (she) is my true (real) father (mother)."

Beyond the relationships between members of the same immediate family is a wider set in which there are ascribed dependency obligations and rights for as long as either party to the relationship lives. And beyond this is another set of relationships in which there are no such lifetime obligations. These categories of relationship can best be described after we have analyzed the kinship terminology.

VII

The lexemes that can be obtained in answer to the question that provides the context for this analysis are presented herewith. After each are listed the denotata that follow from the assumption that biological procreation, marriage, and social responsibility for progeny all go together according to the ideal pattern and usual expectation. The kin-type notation used for this is:

Hu—ego's male partner in marriage
Wi—ego's female partner in marriage
Sp—either Hu or Wi
Fa—ego's genitor
Mo—ego's genetrix
Pa—either Fa or Mo
So—ego's male progeny
Da—ego's female progeny
Ch—either So or Da
Br—male who has same genitor and same genetrix as ego, as distinct from FaSo or MoSo
Si—female who has same genitor and same genetrix as ego, as distinct from FaDa and MoDa
Sb—either Br or Si

All other denotata are represented as relative products of these, e.g. FaBrSo, SpSbCh. Following the denotata noted in this fashion are descriptions of how the kinship terms are used when usual expectations about biological procreation, marriage, etc., are not met.

1. *My father:* Fa. A male who has succeeded ego's genitor by virtue of legal adoption, or who otherwise has fully assumed the genitor's place, provided ego has not previously established a positive relationship with the genitor as *my father* and provided the genitor has fully abdicated (by death or otherwise) all public responsibility for ego, and provided further that ego has been incorporated into the nuclear family of the genitor's substitute. Thus *my father* may sometimes be used for someone who would otherwise be 7 (*my stepfather*) or 19 (*my foster father*), but only under the conditions just indicated. Only of the genitor may it be said "He is my true (real) father." The term *father* may be applied to God and to priests, but these may never be referred to as *my father* and are therefore excluded as possible denotata of "He is my father" in answer to the control question "What relationship is he to you?"

2. *My mother:* Mo. A female who has succeeded ego's genetrix by virtue of legal adoption, or who otherwise has fully assumed the genetrix' place, provided ego has not already established a positive relationship with the genetrix as *my mother* and the genetrix has fully abdicated all public responsibility for ego, and provided further that ego has been incorporated into the nuclear family of the genetrix' substitute. Thus *my mother* may sometimes be used for someone who would otherwise be 8 (*my stepmother*) or 20 (*my foster mother*). Only of the genetrix may it be said "She is my true (real) mother."

3. *My son:* So. Male adoptee.

4. *My daughter:* Da. Female adoptee. The terms *my son* and *my daughter* are always properly used for the biological male and female progeny respectively. They may also be used for an alter who has been incorporated into the nuclear family of which ego is male or female head and for whom ego has become a parental substitute as indicated in connection with terms 1 and 2.

5. *My brother$_1$*: Br, FaSo, MoSo. A male with the same genitor or same genetrix, or both, as ego. A male who has been incorporated into the same nuclear family of orientation as ego so that he, with ego, refers to the same person as *my father* or *my mother* in answer to the control question. Thus *my brother* may sometimes be used for a *stepbrother* (11) or a *foster brother* (23).

5a. *My brother$_2$*: Br. A male with both the same genitor and the same genetrix as ego. It is synonymous with 5b, and on the same level of contrast with 5c, designating a subclass of the designatum of *my brother$_1$*.

5b. *My full brother* or *my fullbrother:* Br. A synonym of 5a. Stress and juncture patterns indicate that this may be either two words or one word in my dialect.

5c. *My halfbrother:* FaSo, MoSo. A male with either the same genitor or the same genetrix as ego, but not both. This is one word in my dialect. Terms 5a, 5b, and 5c are not at the same level of contrast with 5. In response to the question "Is he your brother?" ego cannot say "No, he is my halfbrother" (i.e. not *my brother₁* but some other kind of relative), but can only say "Yes," or "Yes, he is my halfbrother" (i.e. *my brother₁* and the kind of brother who is *my halfbrother*). By way of contrast, it is possible to answer the question "Is he your brother?" by saying "No, he is my stepbrother." This illustrates what may prove to be a useful device in componential analysis. With kinship terms at the same level of contrast, the only possible answers to the question "Is he your A?" are "Yes, he is my A" or "No, he is my B." In such case either A and B are in direct contrast in the same semantic domain or they belong to contrasting domains altogether ("Is he your brother?" "No, he's a stranger"). But if the answer to the question "Is he your A?" is "Yes, he is my B," then B and A are at different levels of contrast within the same semantic domain, B standing for a taxonomic subdivision of A. Thus, to the question "Is he your child?" one can answer "Yes, he is my son," but not "No, he is my son." For this reason it is evident that the designatum of *my halfbrother* is a subset of the designatum of *my brother₁*. But we must take account of a further complication. In answer to the question "Is he your son?" it is not possible to say "No, he is my child." But in answer to the question "Is he your halfbrother?" it is possible to say "No, he is my brother" interchangeably with "No, he is my full brother." This requires us to recognize that the term *my brother* has two distinct designata, one a subset of the other. Therefore, I have listed *my brother₂* (term 5a) as a homonym of *my brother₁* (term 5).

6. *My sister₁:* Si, FaDa, MoDa. A female with the same genitor or same genetrix, or both, as ego. A female so incorporated into the same nuclear family of orientation as ego that she, with ego, refers to the same person as *my father* or *my mother* in answer to the control question. Thus *my sister₁* may sometimes be used for a *stepsister* (12) or *foster sister* (24).

6a. *My sister₂:* Si. A female with both the same genitor and the same genetrix as ego.

6b. *My full sister* or *fullsister:* Si. This is a synonym of 6a. It may be two words or one word in my dialect.

6c. *My halfsister:* FaDa, MoDa. This is one word in my dialect. The same considerations govern the designata of terms 6, 6a, 6b, and 6c as govern terms 5, 5a, 5b, and 5c.

7. *My stepfather:* MoHu, when MoHu is not also ego's genitor and when ego has already established a relationship with the genitor as *my father*. Terms 7–12 are each one word in my dialect.

8. *My stepmother:* FaWi, when FaWi is not also ego's genetrix and when ego has already established a relationship with the genetrix as *my mother*.

9. *My stepson:* SpSo, when ego is not genitor or genetrix and has not become for alter someone who is *my father* or *my mother*.

10. *My stepdaughter:* SpDa, when ego is not genitor or genetrix and has not become for alter someone who is *my father* or *my mother*.

11. *My stepbrother:* PaSpSo who is not also PaSo, and when both ego and alter would not refer to the same person in answer to the control question as *my father* or *my mother*.

12. *My stepsister:* PaSpDa who is not also PaDa, and when both ego and alter would not refer to the same person in answer to the control question as *my father* or *my mother*.

13. *My father-in-law:* SpFa, SpMoHu (if married to SpMo before the marriage of ego and if SpFa is dead or in no way functioning as SpFa).

14. *My mother-in-law:* SpMo, SpFaWi (if married to SpFa before ego's marriage and if SpMo is dead or in no way functioning as SpMo).

15. *My son-in-law:* DaHu, SpDaHu (if married to SpDa after ego's marriage to Sp, and if Sp's former Sp is dead or in no way functioning as a parent to SpDa).

16. *My daughter-in-law:* SoWi, SpSoWi (if married to SpSo after ego's marriage to Sp, and if Sp's former Sp is dead or in no way functioning as a parent to SpSo).

17. *My brother-in-law:* SpBr, SpPaSo, SpPaSpSo (if SpPaSp is referred to as 13 or 14), SiHu, PaDaHu, PaSpDaHu (if alter refers to ego's Pa as 13 or 14). Anyone whom ego's Sp refers to as *my brother*$_1$ in answer to the control question, or Hu of anyone whom ego refers to as *my sister*$_1$.

18. *My sister-in-law:* SpSi, SpPaDa, SpPaSpDa (if SpPaSp is referred to as 13 or 14), BrWi, PaSoWi, PaSpSoWi (if alter refers to ego's Pa as 13 or 14). Anyone whom ego's Sp refers to as *my sister*$_1$ in answer to the control question, or Wi of anyone whom ego refers to as *my brother*$_1$.

19. *My foster father.* Male head of a household in which ego has been incorporated as a dependent juvenile member, but not legally adopted, and when ego has or has had a relationship to someone else as *my father*.

20. *My foster mother.* Female head of a household in which ego has been incorporated as dependent member, but not legally adopted, and when ego has or has had a relationship to someone else as *my mother*.

21. *My foster son.* Any male juvenile incorporated as a dependent member of the household of which ego is male or female head, and for whom ego is neither 1, 2, 7, or 8.

22. *My foster daughter.* Any female juvenile incorporated as a dependent member of the household of which ego is male or female head, and for whom ego is neither 1, 2, 7, or 8.

23. *My foster brother.* Any male who has been incorporated as a juvenile dependent into the household in which ego is also a juvenile dependent or who is a juvenile dependent in the household into which ego has been incorporated as such.

24. *My foster sister.* Any female who has been incorporated as a juvenile dependent into the household in which ego is also a juvenile dependent or who is a juvenile dependent in the household into which ego has been incorporated as such.

25. *My husband:* Hu. A man with whom a female ego has established a common household and assumed the joint responsibilities associated with the marriage agreement without having actually entered into a formal marriage.

26. *My wife:* Wi. A woman with whom a male ego has established a common household and assumed the joint responsibilities associated with the marriage agreement without having actually entered into a formal marriage.

27. *My uncle:* PaBr, PaPaSo, PaSiHu, PaPaDaHu. Anyone to whom ego's Pa refers as *my brother₁* or *my brother-in-law.* A PaSi's or PaPaDa's second Hu is less assuredly *my uncle* than the first Hu if ego has already established a relationship with the first Hu as *my uncle.* I may not refer to PaPaBr as *my uncle,* but must use the construction *my great uncle* in answer to the control question (contrast with Conklin 1964:39).

28. *My aunt:* PaSi, PaPaDa, PaBrWi, PaPaSoWi. Anyone to whom ego's Pa refers as *my sister₁* or *my sister-in-law.* A PaBr's or PaPaSo's second Wi is less assuredly *my aunt* than the first Wi if ego has already established a relationship with the first Wi as *my aunt.* I may not refer to PaPaSi as *my aunt* in answer to the control question.

29. *My nephew:* SbSo, PaChSo, SpSbSo, SpPaChSo. Anyone who is 3 to anyone who is ego's 5, 6, 17, or 18. I may not refer to my SbChSo as *my nephew.*

30. *My niece:* SbDa, PaChDa, SpSbDa, SpPaChDa. Anyone who is 4 to anyone who is ego's 5, 6, 17, or 18. I may not refer to my SbChDa as *my niece.*

31. *My grandfather:* PaFa. Anyone who is *my father* to ego's 1 or 2. Terms 31–34 are each one word in my dialect. I may not refer to my PaPaFa as *my grandfather.*

32. *My grandmother:* PaMo. Anyone who is *my mother* to ego's 1 or 2. I may not refer to my PaPaMo as *my grandmother.*

33. *My grandson:* ChSo. Anyone who is *my son* to ego's 3 or 4. I may not refer to my ChChSo as *my grandson.*

34. *My granddaughter:* ChDa. Anyone who is *my daughter* to ego's 3 or 4. I may not refer to my ChChDa as *my granddaughter.*

35. *My cousin:* PaSbCh, PaPaChCh. Any 41 (*descendant*) of the 5 or 6 of any 1, 2, 31, 32, 39 (*ancestor*), or 40 (*ancestress*), without regard to whether ego and alter are in the same or different generations.

36. There is a theoretically infinite set of expressions involving terms 27–34 (*uncle, aunt, nephew, niece, grandfather, grandmother, grandson, granddaughter*) modified by the adjective *great* or repeated applications thereof:

e.g. *great grandfather, great great grandson, great great great uncle.* In my dialect the adjective *grand* is substituted for *great* as the modifier immediately preceding *nephew* and *niece* (*grand nephew, great grand nephew,* etc.) but nowhere else.[9] What these expressions denote are kin types exactly like the ones denoted by the unmodified base terms, except that the generation distance between ego and alter is increased by one for each *great* (*grand*) in the expression: e.g. *my great grandfather* (PaPaFa), *my great great grandmother* (PaPaPaMo), *my great grandson* (ChChSo), *my great great granddaughter* (ChChChDa), *my great uncle* (PaPaBr, PaPaPaSo), *my great grand niece* (SbChChDa, PaChChChDa). There is considerable dialect difference in the handling of these kinship terms. It is important to emphasize, therefore, that in my dialect such expressions as *my great uncle* and *my grand nephew* are not one word, as revealed by juncture and stress accent, and are not to be equated with *my grandfather* and *my grandson.*[10] Because the modifier *great* (*grand*) always has the same semantic effect of increasing the generation distance between ego and alter without otherwise changing the nature of the relationship, we may treat it as a distinct lexeme with a specific semantic function. Its function needs to be analyzed, but the many expressions in which it enters need not be treated as distinct lexemes in the basic corpus of kinship terms.

37. There is another set of kinship expressions that may be formed with term 35 (*cousin*) and the numerical adjectives *first, second, third,* etc., as in *my second cousin.* These are separate words in my dialect. The number selected corresponds to the lesser number of generations separating ego and alter from the sibling pair through whom they are consanguineally linked. Thus *my first cousin* may denote PaSbCh (including PaPaChCh), PaPaSbCh, PaPaPaSbCh, PaSbChCh, PaSbChChCh, etc., and *my second cousin* may denote PaPaSbChCh (including PaPaPaChChCh), PaPaPaSbChCh, PaPaPaPaSbChCh, PaPaSbChChCh, PaPaSbChChChCh, etc. None of these expressions may denote relationships that may not also be denoted simply as *my cousin.* They designate subclasses of the class of kin types designated by *my cousin.* None of the kinship expressions formed with these numerical adjectives are lexemes. They need not, therefore, be included in the basic corpus of kinship terms.

38. The expressions *once removed, twice removed, three times removed,* etc., may be added to expressions constructed with *first, second,* etc., in combination with term 35 (*cousin*). The number of times *removed* designates the number of generations separating ego and alter. Thus *my second cousin once removed* denotes PaPaPaSbChCh or PaPaSbChChCh. These expressions designate subclasses of the designata of expressions formed with *first, second,* etc.[11]

There are some additional terms that belong with the set of expressions obtainable in answer to the question "What relationship is he (she) to you?"

But they are secondary in that they are employed only in situations where ego is not readily able to specify the relationship by means of expressions formed with *my grandfather, my grandmother, my grandson,* or *my granddaughter,* together with *great* (repeated the appropriate number of times).

39. *My ancestor:* PaPaFa, PaPaPaFa, PaPaPaPaFa. Any male more than two generations removed at the senior end of the procreative chain of which ego is at the junior end.

40. *My ancestress:* PaPaMo, PaPaPaMo, PaPaPaPaMo. Any female more than two generations removed at the senior end of the procreative chain of which ego is at the junior end.

41. *(My descendant):* ChChCh, ChChChCh, ChChChChCh. Anyone more than two generations removed at the junior end of a procreative chain of which ego is at the senior end. Normally the occasion would not arise for any living ego to say "my descendant" in answer to the question "What relationship is he to you?" But it is appropriate to say "His descendant" in answer to the question "What relationship is he to him?"

Excluded from analysis because they are not fully appropriate as answers to the question "What relationship is he (she) to you?" are such kinship terms as *parent, grandparent, child, grandchild, sibling, spouse, forefather.* The linguistic and nonlinguistic (contextual) frames in which these expressions occur overlap in varying degrees with the frames in which the terms here enumerated may occur, but they do not coincide with them.[12]

Also excluded from consideration are all expressions that are relative products of the enumerated terms—*my mother's brother, my wife's uncle,* etc.,—since they are not unit lexemes. Their denotata are predictable from a knowledge of the significata of their constituent lexemes.

VIII

Analysis starts with the observation that the terms listed fall into several obvious groups. Some of these groups appear to be derivatives of others.

GROUP 1 consists of the terms 1–6 (*my father, my mother, my son, my daughter, my brother, my sister*). All and only these terms may be compounded properly with *step-, -in-law,* and *foster* to form derivative groups of terms (1a, 1b, and 1c). None of these terms may enter into constructions with the adjectives *great* or *grand,* a fact not contradicted by *grandfather, grandmother, grandson,* and *granddaughter,* which, as noted, are single words and not two words in an adjective + noun construction. None of the terms in this group may enter into constructions with the numeral adjectives *first, second, third,* etc. These observations sharply segregate this group from groups 2 and 3 below.

GROUP 2 consists of terms 27–34 (*my uncle, my aunt, my nephew, my niece, my grandfather, my grandmother, my grandson, my granddaughter*). All and only the terms in this group may enter into constructions with the adjective *great* (*grand*) to form the open-ended set of derivative terms of which *my great grandfather*, *my great uncle*, *my great great grand niece* are examples. None of the terms in this group may combine properly with *step-*, *-in-law*, *foster* or enter into constructions with the numerical adjectives *first*, *second*, etc. Expressions like *my step grandmother* and *my uncle-in-law* are meaningful to me as analogical formations, but I do not use them myself and do not accept them as standard in my culture.

GROUP 3 contains only term 35 (*my cousin*). This term alone may enter into constructions with the numerical adjectives *first*, *second*, *third*, etc., and with the expressions *once removed*, *twice removed*, etc. It may not enter into constructions with *step-*, *-in-law*, *foster*, or *great* (*grand*).

GROUP 4 consists of terms 25 and 26 (*my husband*, *my wife*). Unlike the terms in groups 1, 2, and 3, its terms may denote only affinal kin-types. They may not enter into constructions with *step-*, *-in-law*, *foster*, or *great*. Such expressions as *my first wife*, *my second husband* may occur, but here the adjectives *first*, *second*, etc., refer to temporal order of monogamous marriages and not to degree of collateral removal. Furthermore, one would never say in answer to the control question "What relationship is she to you?" that "She is my first (second) wife." "She was my first (second) wife," or "She is my former wife," or "She is my wife" are the appropriate answers to this question. We can say, therefore, that the numeral adjectives *first*, *second*, etc., with which these terms can form constructions, are the standard ordinal adjectives relating to temporal sequence and are to be considered as different lexemes from their homonyms that refer to degrees on a scale of collateral distance.

GROUP 5 consists of the secondary set of terms 39–41 (*my ancestor*, *my ancestress*, *my descendant*).

The remaining groups of terms are derivatives of the foregoing: group 1a (terms 7–12 with *step-*), group 1b (terms 13–18 with *-in-law*), group 1c (terms 19–24 with *foster*), group 2a (terms formed with *great*).

The distribution of affinal as distinct from consanguineal kin-types in these groups raises a problem at the outset of analysis. With one exception the primary groups of terms denote either exclusively consanguineal kin types (groups 1, 3, 5) or exclusively affinal kin types (group 4). Group 2 and group 2a terms denote mainly consanguineal, but also a restricted set of affinal, kin types. This inclusion of both consanguineal and affinal kin types among the denotata of terms in groups 2 and 2a suggests that analysis should deal simultaneously with consanguineal and affinal relationships. On the other hand the derivative groups 1a and 1b refer exclusively to affinal kin types in contrast with group 1, which refers exclusively to consanguineal kin types. Looking at group 1 and its derivatives, we find it convenient to analyze the terminology for consanguineal kin types first and then to

Table 1.   Relationships between Groups of Terms

TERMS DENOTING CONSANGUINEAL BASES	TERMS DENOTING AFFINAL DERIVATIVES	TERMS DENOTING OTHER DERIVATIVES
(ego)	Group 4	—
Group 1	Group 1a	Group 1c
	Group 1b	
Group 2	Group 2 in part	—
Group 2a	Group 2a in part	—
Group 3	—	—
Group 5	—	—

treat the terminology for affinal kin types as derivatives or extensions of it.

The trouble with this is that group 4 then stands out as a derivative set of terms apparently without a consanguineal base from which to be derived. As it turns out, however, this is not a problem, because group 4 stands in the same relation to "ego" as groups 1b and 1c stand in relation to group 1. According to the strategy adopted for analysis, then, the groups of terms distribute with respect to consanguineal-affinal distinctions as shown in Table 1.

Table 2 shows how groups 1, 2a, and 3 (the ones denoting consanguineal kin-types) distribute on a genealogical chart. It is immediately evident from the distribution that group 3 stands in complementary opposition to a super-group consisting of groups 1, 2, and 2a. The difference between them is of the same kind as discussed above in connection with the difference between *first, second, third,* etc., as modifiers of *my cousin*—the lesser number of generations separating ego and alter from the nearest genitor (genetrix) or progenitor they have in common. If the lesser number of generations is zero, ego and alter are in a lineal relationship; if the lesser number of generations is one, they are first-degree collaterals; if the lesser number is two, they are second-degree collaterals, etc. The dividing line between the denotata of group 3 and those of the other groups is not between collateral and lineal relationships, however, but between relationships that are two or more degrees of collateral distance as against those that are less than two degrees distant. All of the former relationships, and only these, are referred to by the group 3 term, *my cousin*.

It appears then that one of the discriminant variables in the Yankee kinship terminology is:

1. Degree of collateral distance between ego and alter, with the values;
    1.1 less than two degrees of distance (groups 1, 2, 2a, 5),
    1.2 two or more degrees of distance (group 3).

Table 2. Distribution of Yankee Kinship Terms

GENERATIONS REMOVED	DEGREE OF COLLATERAL DISTANCE				
	0	1	2	3	4
+4	2a	2a	3	3	3
+3	2a	2a	3	3	3
+2	2	2a	3	3	3
+1	1	2	3	3	3
0	EGO	1	3	3	3
−1	1	2	3	3	3
−2	2	2a	3	3	3
−3	2a	2a	3	3	3
−4	2a	2a	3	3	3

Note: The numbers on the genealogical chart represent the groups of kinship terms listed in section VIII, not including groups 4 and 5, or the derivative groups 1a, 1b, and 1c. Each vertical or diagonal line represents a lineal link and each horizontal line a lateral link.

It remains to find a discriminant variable or variables that will differentiate groups 1, 2, 2a, and 5. It is evident that the denotata of group 5
constitute a subclass of the denotata of group 2a. Therefore we may set
group 5 aside and concentrate on the difference(s) between groups 1, 2, and
2a. Inspection of Table 2 suggests that they differ according to what we
may call genealogical distance from ego. If we define a unit of genealogical
distance (marked by the solid lines in Table 2) vertically as the space between a genitor or genetrix and his or her progeny and horizontally as the
distance between two individuals with a genitor in common, then all kin
types denoted by terms in group 1 are one unit of distance from ego; all
kin types denoted by terms in group 2 are two units of distance from ego;
and all kin types denoted by terms in group 2a are three or more units of
distance from ego. Moreover, within group 2a the denotata of expressions
with only one *great/grand* are three units of distance from ego; expressions
with a *great great/great grand* denote kin types that are four units of distance
from ego; and so on with an additional unit of distance being added for each
additional *great*. We assume, furthermore, that the marriage tie does not
count as a unit of geneaological distance, but only a vertical or horizontal
consanguineal link as just defined. Thus FaBr and FaBrWi are both two
units of distance away from ego, and Br, BrWi, and WiBr are one unit of
distance away.

Genealogical distance provides a conceptual variable that includes ego
as one of its complementary values, for ego is necessarily at zero distance
from himself on a genealogical tree. Hu and Wi are also at zero distance
from ego. Thus ego is one of the consanguineal categories from which affinal
terminology can be derived, as was suggested in Table 1.

These considerations lead us to postulate as a discriminant variable in
the Yankee kinship system:

2. Degree of genealogical distance between ego and alter, with the values;
    2.1 zero distance (ego),
    2.2 one unit of distance (group 1),
    2.3 two units of distance (group 2),
    2.4 three or more units of distance (groups 2a, 5).

The results of analysis so far are shown in Table 3.

From here on, analysis deals with variables that differentiate terms
within the several groups. It is at this point that alternative ways of con-
ceptualizing the semantic structure become readily feasible.

We may, for example, sort the terms in group 1 according to:

3. Generation seniority, with the values;
    3.1 alter in a senior generation (*my father, my mother*),
    3.2 alter in ego's generation (*my brother*₁, *my sister*₁),
    3.3 alter in a junior generation (*my son, my daughter*).

On the other hand we may sort them according to:

4. Lineality of relationship, with the values;
   4.1 alter and ego in lineal relationship (*my father, my mother, my son, my daughter*),
   4.2 alter and ego not in lineal relationship (*my brother₁, my sister₁*).

Table 3

	DISCRIMINANT VARIABLES		
TERMS	1	2	DERIVATIVES
(ego)	1.1	2.1	Group 4
Group 1	1.1	2.2	Groups 1a, 1b, 1c
Group 2	1.1	2.3	
Groups 2a, 5	1.1	2.4	
Group 3	1.2	—	

Variable 4 requires that we then use some variable to distinguish *my father* and *my mother* from *my son* and *my daughter*. This can be variable 3, now with only two values:

5. Generation seniority, with the values;
   5.1 alter in senior generation (*my father, my mother*),
   5.2 alter in junior generation (*my son, my daughter*).

Which, if either, solution is preferable depends on the best means of handling the distinctions within group 2.

In any event it is obvious that the remaining distinctions to be made all can be handled by reference to the sex of alter. This discrimination applies equally to the terms in groups 2, 2a, 4, 1a, 1b, and 1c:

6. Sex of alter, with the values;
   6.1 alter male (*my father, my brother₁, my son, my grandfather, my uncle, my grandson, my nephew, my husband*, etc.),
   6.2 alter female (*my mother, my sister₁, my daughter, my grandmother, my aunt, my granddaughter, my niece, my wife*, etc.).

For the terms in group 2 there is clearly a distinction that must be made in terms of variable 5 (generation seniority), with 5.1 (senior generation) including *my grandfather, my grandmother, my uncle, my aunt,* and 5.2 (junior generation) including *my grandson, my granddaughter, my nephew, my niece.* This establishes variable 5 as one we will want to use for terms in group 1 as well.

Following the precedent established in group 1 we may then distinguish the terms in group 2 according to variable 4 (lineality) with 4.1 (lineal) including *my grandfather, my grandmother, my grandson, my granddaughter,* and 4.2 (not lineal) including *my uncle, my aunt, my nephew,* and *my niece.*

Table 4

| DISCRIMINANT VARIABLES | | | | | |
1	2	4	5	6	KINSHIP TERMS
1.1	2.1	—	—	—	ego
1.1	2.2	4.1	5.1	6.1	my father
1.1	2.2	4.1	5.1	6.2	my mother
1.1	2.2	4.1	5.2	6.1	my son
1.1	2.2	4.1	5.2	6.2	my daughter
1.1	2.2	4.2	—	6.1	my brother$_1$
1.1	2.2	4.2	—	6.2	my sister$_1$
1.1	2.3	4.1	5.1	6.1	my grandfather
1.1	2.3	4.1	5.1	6.2	my grandmother
1.1	2.3	4.1	5.2	6.1	my grandson
1.1	2.3	4.1	5.2	6.2	my granddaughter
1.1	2.3	4.2	5.1	6.1	my uncle
1.1	2.3	4.2	5.1	6.2	my aunt
1.1	2.3	4.2	5.2	6.1	my nephew
1.1	2.3	4.2	5.2	6.2	my niece
1.2	—	—	—	—	my cousin

This approach will give us the paradigm for groups 1, 2, and 3 as shown in Table 4.

There is another approach available to us. Instead of differentiating the sets of kin types designated by the terms in groups 1 and 2 with reference to discriminant variable 4 (lineality), we can do so with reference to:

7. Relative nearness of alter's generation to ego's, with the values;
    7.1 alter in the nearer generation (*my brother$_1$, my sister$_1$, my uncle, my aunt, my nephew, my niece*),
    7.2 alter in the farther generation (*my father, my mother, my son, my daughter, my grandfather, my grandmother, my grandson, my granddaughter*).

This approach gives the paradigm for groups 1 and 2 shown in Table 5.

The use of variable 4 in Table 4 has the effect of distributing the terms in rows within each group so that those designating collaterally more-distant kin types come after those designating collaterally nearer kin types. The effect of variable 7 in Table 5 is to rearrange the rows so that within each group the terms designating generationally more-distant kin types come after those designating generationally closer ones. So far there is no basis for choosing one of these models over the other. Each preserves the integrity

Table 5

DISCRIMINANT VARIABLES					
1	2	7	5	6	KINSHIP TERMS
1.1	2.1	—	—	—	ego
1.1	2.2	7.1	—	6.1	my brother₁
1.1	2.2	7.1	—	6.2	my sister₁
1.1	2.2	7.2	5.1	6.1	my father
1.1	2.2	7.2	5.1	6.2	my mother
1.1	2.2	7.2	5.2	6.1	my son
1.1	2.2	7.2	5.2	6.2	my daughter
1.1	2.3	7.1	5.1	6.1	my uncle
1.1	2.3	7.1	5.1	6.2	my aunt
1.1	2.3	7.1	5.2	6.1	my nephew
1.1	2.3	7.1	5.2	6.2	my niece
1.1	2.3	7.2	5.1	6.1	my grandfather
1.1	2.3	7.2	5.1	6.2	my grandmother
1.1	2.3	7.2	5.2	6.1	my grandson
1.1	2.3	7.2	5.2	6.2	my granddaughter
1.2	—	—	—	—	my cousin

of groups 1 and 2 and is acceptable from this point of view. The difference is that one emphasizes collateral and the other generational distance. If analysis of the rest of the terminology indicates that one of these emphases fits the data better than the other, the choice between them is clear. Otherwise these emphases remain two perfectly adequate ways of thinking about the data. Since we are talking about my culture, and I am obviously able to think in terms of either model, it cannot be argued that one is truly in my culture and the other not. Both are in my culture, and both are illustrative of how I conceptualize kin relationships, even though one model may order the totality of kin relationships more neatly than the other.

Either construction readily enables us to handle the derivative set of terms in group 2a. For either one the same derivational rule may be given:

RULE 1. Each possible kinship expression in group 2a designates a set of kin types identical in all respects with the kin types designated by the corresponding expression in group 2 except that it is as many more units of genealogical distance removed from ego as the number of times the adjective *great* (or *grand*) is used in the expression.

For either of the two constructions shown in Tables 4 and 5 we may use an alternative derivational rule in which we substitute *generations removed* for the words *units of genealogical distance removed*. The former phrasing is in keeping with variable 2 and has the esthetic advantage that the number of repetitions of *great* is the same for both lineal and nonlineal alters (regardless of their generational distance), which makes the phrasing especially attractive for the construction given in Table 4, where linearity is used as a variable. On the other hand, the second phrasing of the derivational rule is in keeping with the recognition of generation as a factor in the alternative construction shown in Table 5. In this phrasing the number of repetitions of *great* does not indicate the same number of generations that alter is distant from ego in both lineal and nonlineal relationships, but this is no problem in the construction in Table 5, because lineality is not a relevant factor there.

It seems, then, that either phrasing of the derivational rule is adequate, but the first phrasing is more consistent with the use of variable 4 (lineality) in Table 4 and the second is more consistent with the use of variable 7 (relative nearness of generation) in Table 5.

IX

The affinal relationships covered by single kinship lexemes are severely limited in extent. They do not include any relationships in which there is more than one marital tie between ego and alter, nor do they include any relationships in which ego and alter are two or more degrees distant collaterally or separated by more than two units of genealogical distance.

Affinal relationships can be readily described by means of derivational rules. We consider first the expressions with *step-* in group 1a.

The cultural ideal for family organization produces an expectation that ordinarily certain affinal kin types will be filled by the same persons as fill certain consanguineal kin types. Such convergent kin types, though conceptually different, may be called "structurally equivalent" (Goodenough 1964: 231–232). In Yankee kinship terminology we are interested in the affinal kin types that are structurally equivalent to consanguineal kin types one unit of genealogical distance from ego, where in normal expectation FaWi = Mo, MoHu = Fa, SpSo = So, SpDa = Da, PaSpSo = Br, and PaSpDa = Si. With this in mind we may state the derivational rule for group 1a as:

RULE 2. Any affinal kin type that is structurally equivalent to a consanguineal kin type denoted by a term in group 1 is denoted by an expression consisting of the corresponding term in group 1 with the prefix *step-*.

Similar considerations enable us to state the derivational rule for the set of expressions in group 1c:

RULE 3. Any relationship that is by virtue of common residence in the same household behaviorally equivalent to a relationship denoted by a term in group 1, but not also structurally equivalent to it, is denoted by the corresponding term in group 1 with the adjective *foster*.

The derivational rules for the remaining affinal relationships follow.

RULE 4. Affinal kin types that are at zero genealogical distance from ego are designated by the terms *my husband* (if alter is male) and *my wife* (if alter is female).

RULE 5. Affinal kin types that are at one unit of genealogical distance from ego and that are not structurally equivalent to consanguineal kin types are differentiated by the same discriminant variables as differentiate consanguineal kin types in group 1, and the resulting sets of kin types are designated by the corresponding terms in group 1 with the suffix *-in-law*.

RULE 6. Affinal kin types that are two or more units of genealogical distance from ego are differentiated by the same discriminant variables as differentiate consanguineal kin types in groups 2 and 2a, and the resulting sets of kin types are designated by the corresponding terms in groups 2 and 2a provided that (a) the affinal tie directly involves the senior party to the relationship and (b) the senior party is the first person in the particular relationship, or its structural equivalent, with whom the junior party has established a relationship as such; otherwise, these kin types are not denoted by kinship lexemes but by two or more lexemes in descriptive constructions (e.g. *my wife's uncle, my son-in-law's brother, my grandmother's husband, my uncle's wife*).

RULE 7. Affinal kin types that are more than one degree of collateral distance from ego are not denoted by any kinship lexemes but by two or more lexemes in descriptive constructions (e.g. *my cousin's wife, my husband's cousin*).

X

We may take the considerations expressed in the foregoing derivational rules and treat them as discriminant variables in a componential matrix:

8. Presence of a marital tie between ego and alter (relations with more than one tie are not covered by kinship lexemes), with the values;
    8.1 marital tie absent (ego, groups 1, 2 in part, 2a in part, 3),
    8.2 marital tie present (groups 4, 1a, 1b, 2 in part, 2a in part).
9. Structural equivalence of alter's kin type to a primary consanguineal kin type, with the values;
    9.1 alter's kin type structurally equivalent to a primary consanguineal kin type (group 1a),
    9.2 alter's kin type not structurally equivalent to a primary consanguineal kin type (group 1b).
10. Involvement of senior party to relationship in marital tie, with the values;
    10.1 senior party involved (groups 2 in part, 2a in part),
    10.2 senior party not involved (no lexemes).
11. Primacy of senior party to relationship as person whom junior party has actually known in the relationship, with the values;
    11.1 senior party first person in the particular relationship known to junior party (groups 2 in part, 2a in part),
    11.2 senior party not first person in the particular relationship known to junior party (no lexemes).

With these additional variables we can put all the affinal terminology into the same componential paradigm with the consanguineal terminology provided we rephrase discriminant variable 2 as "degree of genealogical distance between ego and alter or alter's structural equivalent." This is necessary in order to keep *my stepbrother* and *my stepsister* within the group of kin types that are one unit of genealogical distance away from ego. The resulting paradigm appears in Table 6.

XI

Other terms not covered in Table 6 can be handled as substitutes for terms in Table 6. Thus such expressions as *my halfbrother, my halfsister, my brother₂*, or *my full brother, my sister₂* or *my full sister*, can be substituted in Table 6 for the terms *my brother₁* and *my sister₁* and differentiated with the addition of discriminant variable 14 (for 12 and 13, see below):

14. Number of parents in common, with the values;
    14.1 both parents in common,
    14.2 only one parent in common.

Table 7 shows the set of rows now substitutable for *my brother₁* and *my sister₁* in Table 6.

We must answer the question why we chose to include the pair of terms *my brother₁* and *my sister₁* in the main paradigm shown in Table 6 rather than their substitutes as shown in Table 7. What puts the former in the "main sequence" (if I may call it that) rather than the latter? An obvious reason is that the expressions in Table 7 are not subject to the operations *step-, -in-law,* and *foster,* and do not, therefore, belong with *my father, my mother, my son,* and *my daughter* in the same way that *my brother₁* and *my sister₁* do.

The set of terms in group 5 (*my ancestor, my ancestress, my descendant*) can be substituted for the expressions denoting lineal consanguineal kintypes in group 2a (e.g. *my great grandfather, my great great granddaughter*) as shown in Table 8.

XII

If we were to use the alternative componential model, involving discriminant variable 7 instead of variable 4, it would be impossible to treat the terms in group 5 as substitutes for expressions in group 2a as we just did. No discriminations would be made then on the basis of lineality, but this is precisely what discriminates group 2a kin types covered by group 5 terms from those not so covered. This leads us to prefer the componential model utilizing variable 4 to that utilizing variable 7.

Table 6

				DISCRIMINANT VARIABLES					
1	2	8	9	10	11	4	5	6	KINSHIP TERMS
1.1	2.1	8.1	—	—	—	—	—	—	ego
1.1	2.1	8.2	—	—	—	—	—	6.1	my husband
1.1	2.1	8.2	—	—	—	—	—	6.2	my wife
1.1	2.2	8.1	—	—	—	4.1	5.1	6.1	my father
1.1	2.2	8.1	—	—	—	4.1	5.1	6.2	my mother
1.1	2.2	8.1	—	—	—	4.1	5.2	6.1	my son
1.1	2.2	8.1	—	—	—	4.1	5.2	6.2	my daughter
1.1	2.2	8.1	—	—	—	4.2	—	6.1	my brother$_1$
1.1	2.2	8.1	—	—	—	4.2	—	6.2	my sister$_1$
1.1	2.2	8.2	9.1	—	—	4.1	5.1	6.1	my stepfather
1.1	2.2	8.2	9.1	—	—	4.1	5.1	6.2	my stepmother
1.1	2.2	8.2	9.1	—	—	4.1	5.2	6.1	my stepson
1.1	2.2	8.2	9.1	—	—	4.1	5.2	6.2	my stepdaughter
1.1	2.2	8.2	9.1	—	—	4.2	—	6.1	my stepbrother
1.1	2.2	8.2	9.1	—	—	4.2	—	6.2	my stepsister
1.1	2.2	8.2	9.2	—	—	4.1	5.1	6.1	my father-in-law
1.1	2.2	8.2	9.2	—	—	4.1	5.1	6.2	my mother-in-law
1.1	2.2	8.2	9.2	—	—	4.1	5.2	6.1	my son-in-law
1.1	2.2	8.2	9.2	—	—	4.1	5.2	6.2	my daughter-in-law
1.1	2.2	8.2	9.2	—	—	4.2	—	6.1	my brother-in-law
1.1	2.2	8.2	9.2	—	—	4.2	—	6.2	my sister-in-law
1.1	2.3	8.1	—	—	—	4.1	5.1	6.1	my grandfather
1 1	2.3	8.1	—	—	—	4.1	5.1	6.2	my grandmother
1.1	2.3	8.1	—	—	—	4.1	5.2	6.1	my grandson
1.1	2.3	8.1	—	—	—	4.1	5.2	6.2	my granddaughter
1.1	2.3	8.1	—	—	—	4.2	5.1	6.1	my uncle
1.1	2.3	8.1	—	—	—	4.2	5.1	6.2	my aunt
1.1	2.3	8.1	—	—	—	4.2	5.2	6.1	my nephew
1.1	2.3	8.1	—	—	—	4.2	5.2	6.2	my niece
1.1	2.3	8.2	—	10.1	11.1	4.1	5.1	6.1	my grandfather
1.1	2.3	8.2	—	10.1	11.1	4.1	5.1	6.2	my grandmother
1.1	2.3	8.2	—	10.1	11.1	4.1	5.2	6.1	my grandson
1.1	2.3	8.2	—	10.1	11.1	4.1	5.2	6.2	my granddaughter
1.1	2.3	8.2	—	10.1	11.1	4.2	5.1	6.1	my uncle
1.1	2.3	8.2	—	10.1	11.1	4.2	5.1	6.2	my aunt
1.1	2.3	8.2	—	10.1	11.1	4.2	5.2	6.1	my nephew
1.1	2.3	8.2	—	10.1	11.1	4.2	5.2	6.2	my niece
1.1	2.3	8.2	—	10.1	11.2	—	—	—	descriptive only
1.1	2.3	8.2	—	10.2	—	—	—	—	descriptive only
1.1	2.4	8.1	—	—	—	—	—	—	group 2a terms
1.1	2.4	8.2	—	10.1	11.1	—	—	—	group 2a terms
1.1	2.4	8.2	—	10.1	11.2	—	—	—	descriptive only
1.1	2.4	8.2	—	10.2	—	—	—	—	descriptive only
1.2	—	8.1	—	—	—	—	—	—	my cousin
1.2	—	8.2	—	—	—	—	—	—	descriptive only

Table 7

DISCRIMINANT VARIABLES										
1	2	8	9	10	11	4	5	14	6	KINSHIP TERMS
1.1	2.2	8.1	—	—	—	4.2	—	14.1	6.1	my brother₂
1.1	2.2	8.1	—	—	—	4.2	—	14.1	6.2	my sister₂
1.1	2.2	8.1	—	—	—	4.2	—	14.2	6.1	my halfbrother
1.1	2.2	8.1	—	—	—	4.2	—	14.2	6.2	my halfsister

Table 8

DISCRIMINANT VARIABLES									
1	2	8	9	10	11	4	5	6	KINSHIP TERMS
1.1	2.4	8.1	—	—	—	4.1	5.1	6.1	my ancestor
1.1	2.4	8.1	—	—	—	4.1	5.1	6.2	my ancestress
1.1	2.4	8.1	—	—	—	4.1	5.2	—	my descendent

We should note, however, that if we were to use variable 7 the blocks of terms in Table 6 would remain unchanged. The effect would be to rearrange the terms within each block so that 4.2 (7.1) terms would now come ahead of the 4.1 (7.2) terms as closer to ego. The collaterally more distant to ego would now be seen as the generationally closer. Thus the possibilities for alternative componential models of my own version of Yankee kinship terminology are limited to a minor sector of the semantic structure of the system as a whole. Alternative models that would have a more radical effect on the semantic structure can be constructed only by violating the canons of analysis—in this case at the expense of the integrity of the sets of terms comprising the blocks in Table 6, an integrity we felt it necessary to preserve in order to reveal the structural relationships that the *step-*, *-in-law*, and *great* sets of expressions have with the basic sets of which they are derivatives.

XIII

The semantic structure of Yankee kinship revealed in Table 6 fits perfectly the distinction to which I referred earlier between relationships outside the immediate (nuclear) family in which lifelong obligations obtain and those in which they do not. All relationships within two degrees of collaterality (1.1 relationships) have ascribed lifelong obligations, whereas all relationships two or more degrees distant collaterally (1.2 relationships), the ones covered by the term *my cousin*, have no ascribed lifelong obligations other than a show of cordiality. Even among first cousins within the same generation there are no demands beyond this that they can make upon one another by virtue of cousinship alone. The extent to which they chose to cultivate their relationship beyond this is entirely optional. Cousins tend to have dealings with one another, therefore, by virtue of the 1.1 relatives they have in common. Given the facts of human longevity and reproduction, common 1.1 relatives bring first cousins in the same generation together much more frequently than they do any other cousins. In practice, therefore, people tend to have dealings mainly with their contemporary first cousins. When the common 1.1 relatives who bring them together have all died, there cease to be occasions for their having dealings with one another except as residential proximity, mutual friendship, or sentiment about the importance of kinship may promote them. They are no longer comembers of anyone's more immediate personal kindred based on 1.1 relationships.

That there are basic lexemes only for consanguineal kinsmen in the 1.1 set who are less than three units of genealogical removal from ego also accords with the pattern of kinship obligation. Responsibility for pre-adult children—for their survival needs, emotional development, socialization, enculturation, and education—rests first upon their fathers and mothers, their primary senior relatives. Those on whom these responsibilities next fall are the secondary senior relatives. It rarely happens that a tertiary senior relative has any occasion to assume such responsibility, though a great uncle and great aunt are sometimes called upon to do so. Thus the basic lexemes cover those relationships in which dependency rights and duties are primarily and secondarily active. Similarly, responsibility for care of the aged falls primarily on their own sons and daughters and secondarily on their grandsons, granddaughters, nephews, and nieces. An old person is rarely without junior relatives nearer than grand nephews or grand nieces on whom he can depend, and the latter are not likely to be old enough and well enough established to be able to help care for him. Thus the basic lexemes cover those relationships in which dependency rights and duties have first and second priority and are active in practice, and the relationships in group 2a (those involving *great*) are the ones in which dependency rights and duties have tertiary or remoter priority and have little chance of activation.

XIV

An examination of other subcultural variations in terminology also can prove helpful in arriving at a componential model of a particular one. I have not tried systematically to explore variations of Yankee terminology. We will know more about them as the results of D. M. Schneider's current study of

American kinship are published. One variant with which I am familiar, however, will help clarify the semantic structure of the one under analysis here.

It differs in that the terms *my aunt, my uncle, my nephew,* and *my niece* may be extended up and down the generations to any nonlineal 1.1 relatives other than those in ego's generation (*my brother* and *my sister*). The terms *my grandfather, my grandmother, my grandson,* and *my granddaughter,* however, cannot be extended in like manner to more remote lineal relatives. For these the use of *great* for the appropriate number of times is obligatory. The result of this variation requires us to introduce a new discriminant variable and modify the values for an old one (variable 2) as follows:

12. Degree of genealogical distance between ego and alter (replacing old variable 2), with the values;
    12.1 zero distance between ego and alter,
    12.2 one unit of genealogical distance between ego and alter,
    12.3 more than one unit of distance between ego and alter.
13. Number of units of genealogical distance between ego and alter beyond one, with the values;
    13.1 one,
    13.2 two,
    13.3 three,
    etc.

Omitting consideration of affinal terminology, our analysis of this variant gives the paradigm for consanguineal kin shown in Table 9.

It would be tempting here to put all the lineals (4.1) in one group and the nonlineals (4.2) together in another, as in the analysis published by Wallace (1962); but this is avoided to preserve the integrity of the set of terms for primary consanguines still needed as a base for handling the affinal terminology. Such a procedure would also obscure the way the discriminant variables intersect to produce blocks of terms which correspond with the boundary between the nuclear family and the personal kindred beyond it that includes relatives to whom lifetime obligations are owed. Variable 12 (like variable 2 in Table 6) is needed to preserve the integrity of these sets. We see here how considerations of kin-group membership, and even the way in which duties distribute over the field of kin types, can serve to delineate blocks of terms whose integrity we must seek to preserve in analysis. Pospisil (1964:400–401) has called attention to the utility of considering duty distributions as a means for selecting among alternative discriminant variables and for deciding the order in which the variables should appear as columns in the matrix table or paradigm showing the internal structure of the semantic system.

A major difference between Table 9 and Table 6 is that Table 9 brings the group 2a terms together in the same block with the group 2 terms. The necessity for this is dictated by the different distribution of *my uncle, my*

Table 9

1	12	4	5	6	13	KINSHIP TERMS
			DISCRIMINANT VARIABLES			
1.1	12.1	—	—	—	—	ego
1.1	12.2	4.1	5.1	6.1	—	my father
1.1	12.2	4.1	5.1	6.2	—	my mother
1.1	12.2	4.1	5.2	6.1	—	my son
1.1	12.2	4.1	5.2	6.2	—	my daughter
1.1	12.2	4.2	—	6.1	—	my brother₁
1.1	12.2	4.2	—	6.2	—	my sister₁
1.1	12.3	4.1	5.1	6.1	13.1	my grandfather
1.1	12.3	4.1	5.1	6.1	13.2	my great grandfather
1.1	12.3	4.1	5.1	6.1	13.3	my great great grandfather
1.1	12.3	4.1	5.1	6.2	13.1	my grandmother
1.1	12.3	4.1	5.1	6.2	13.2	my great grandmother
1.1	12.3	4.1	5.1	6.2	13.3	my great great grandmother
1.1	12.3	4.1	5.2	6.1	13.1	my grandson
1.1	12.3	4.1	5.2	6.1	13.2	my great grandson
1.1	12.3	4.1	5.2	6.1	13.3	my great great grandson
1.1	12.3	4.1	5.2	6.2	13.1	my granddaughter
1.1	12.3	4.1	5.2	6.2	13.2	my great granddaughter
1.1	12.3	4.1	5.2	6.2	13.3	my great great granddaughter
1.1	12.3	4.2	5.1	6.1	—	my uncle
1.1	12.3	4.2	5.1	6.2	—	my aunt
1.1	12.3	4.2	5.2	6.1	—	my nephew
1.1	12.3	4.2	5.2	6.2	—	my niece
1.2	—	—	—	—	—	my cousin

aunt, my nephew, and *my niece* over the field of kin types. It led me to set up variable 13 (corresponding to derivational rule 1 above) as something separate from variable 12 and to reduce the number of values for the old variable 2 (new variable 12). The results more closely accord with the fact that both group 2a and group 2 relatives are in the same kindred circle of relationships in which lifelong obligations obtain. This suggests that we might wish to reconsider my own version of Yankee kinship in the light of variables 12 and 13.

Table 10

	DISCRIMINANT VARIABLES									
1	12	8	9	10	11	4	5	6	13	KINSHIP TERMS
1.1	12.1	8.1	—	—	—	—	—	—	—	ego
1.1	12.1	8.2	—	—	—	—	—	6.1	—	my husband
1.1	12.1	8.2	—	—	—	—	—	6.2	—	my wife
1.1	12.2	8.1	—	—	—	4.1	5.1	6.1	—	my father
1.1	12.2	8.1	—	—	—	4.1	5.1	6.2	—	my mother
1.1	12.2	8.1	—	—	—	4.1	5.2	6.1	—	my son
1.1	12.2	8.1	—	—	—	4.1	5.2	6.2	—	my daughter
1.1	12.2	8.1	—	—	—	4.2	—	6.1	—	my brother₁
1.1	12.2	8.1	—	—	—	4.2	—	6.2	—	my sister₁
1.1	12.2	8.2	9.1	—	—	4.1	5.1	6.1	—	my stepfather
1.1	12.2	8.2	9.1	—	—	4.1	5.1	6.2	—	my stepmother
1.1	12.2	8.2	9.1	—	—	4.1	5.2	6.1	—	my stepson
1.1	12.2	8.2	9.1	—	—	4.1	5.2	6.2	—	my stepdaughter
1.1	12.2	8.2	9.1	—	—	4.2	—	6.1	—	my stepbrother
1.1	12.2	8.2	9.1	—	—	4.2	—	6.2	—	my stepsister
1.1	12.2	8.2	9.2	—	—	4.1	5.1	6.1	—	my father-in-law
1.1	12.2	8.2	9.2	—	—	4.1	5.1	6.2	—	my mother-in-law
1.1	12.2	8.2	9.2	—	—	4.1	5.2	6.1	—	my son-in-law
1.1	12.2	8.2	9.2	—	—	4.1	5.2	6.2	—	my daughter-in-law
1.1	12.2	8.2	9.2	—	—	4.2	—	6.1	—	my brother-in-law
1.1	12.2	8.2	9.2	—	—	4.2	—	6.2	—	my sister-in-law
1.1	12.3	8.1	—	—	—	4.1	5.1	6.1	13.1	my grandfather
1.1	12.3	8.1	—	—	—	4.1	5.1	6.1	13.2	my great grandfather
1.1	12.3	8.1	—	—	—	4.1	5.1	6.1	13.3	my great great grandfather
1.1	12.3	8.1	—	—	—	4.1	5.1	6.2	13.1	my grandmother
1.1	12.3	8.1	—	—	—	4.1	5.1	6.2	13.2	my great grandmother
1.1	12.3	8.1	—	—	—	4.1	5.1	6.2	13.3	my great great grandmother
1.1	12.3	8.1	—	—	—	4.1	5.2	6.1	13.1	my grandson
1.1	12.3	8.1	—	—	—	4.1	5.2	6.1	13.2	my great grandson
1.1	12.3	8.1	—	—	—	4.1	5.2	6.1	13.3	my great great grandson
1.1	12.3	8.1	—	—	—	4.1	5.2	6.2	13.1	my granddaughter
1.1	12.3	8.1	—	—	—	4.1	5.2	6.2	13.2	my great granddaughter
1.1	12.3	8.1	—	—	—	4.1	5.2	6.2	13.3	my great great granddaughter
1.1	12.3	8.1	—	—	—	4.2	5.1	6.1	13.1	my uncle
1.1	12.3	8.1	—	—	—	4.2	5.1	6.1	13.2	my great uncle
1.1	12.3	8.1	—	—	—	4.2	5.1	6.1	13.3	my great great uncle
1.1	12.3	8.1	—	—	—	4.2	5.1	6.2	13.1	my aunt
1.1	12.3	8.1	—	—	—	4.2	5.1	6.2	13.2	my great aunt
1.1	12.3	8.1	—	—	—	4.2	5.1	6.2	13.3	my great great aunt
1.1	12.3	8.1	—	—	—	4.2	5.2	6.1	13.1	my nephew
1.1	12.3	8.1	—	—	—	4.2	5.2	6.1	13.2	my grand nephew
1.1	12.3	8.1	—	—	—	4.2	5.2	6.1	13.3	my great grand nephew
1.1	12.3	8.1	—	—	—	4.2	5.2	6.2	13.1	my niece
1.1	12.3	8.1	—	—	—	4.2	5.2	6.2	13.2	my grand niece
1.1	12.3	8.1	—	—	—	4.2	5.2	6.2	13.3	my great grand niece
1.1	12.3	8.2	—	10.1	11.1	—	—	—	—	same as above
1.1	12.3	8.2	—	10.1	11.2	—	—	—	—	descriptive only
1.1	12.3	8.2	—	10.2	—	—	—	—	—	descriptive only
1.2	—	8.1	—	—	—	—	—	—	—	my cousin
1.2	—	8.2	—	—	—	—	—	—	—	descriptive only

The results appear in Table 10. In effect they incorporate the meaning of *great* (derivational rule 1) into the paradigm through the addition of variable 13. Its placement in the extreme right-hand column of the table consolidates groups 2 and 2a rather than keeping them as separate blocks, one a derivative of the other. The variables in the first two left-hand columns segregate the terms, as marked by the horizontal lines, into four major groups, exactly like those in Table 9, corresponding to the major concentric circles of kinsmen in ego's personal kindred. That the terms for affinal kintypes fit so perfectly within the same fourfold division underscores the primacy in Yankee kinship of the relationship between husband and wife together as alter egos at the center of their respective and overlapping personal kindreds.

Because Table 10 has the same structural organization as Table 9, comparison of the two shows exactly wherein the subcultural variants of Yankee kinship usage differ from one another: on the extent to which the application of variable 13 is obligatory. By considering variant systems and attempting to find ways of structuring them so that their differences and similarities are expressed most clearly and precisely in the resulting paradigms, we have found yet another aid to arriving at componential models that do optimal justice to the phenomena of study.

It is also evident from a comparison of Tables 9 and 10 that the basic structure of Yankee kinship is the same in each. When sufficient data on the various subcultural variants are available, comparison of their componential structures will show us to what extent they all have the same basic organization. We can then see with much greater precision than has been possible heretofore the relationship between variations in basic semantic structure of the terminological systems and variations in the social and behavioral organization of kin relationships—in the ways, that is, in which duties and group memberships distribute over the field of kin types.

There is a problem arising in the model presented in Table 10 that does not arise as clearly in Table 6. The terms in group 5 refer only to lineal kin types that are more than two units of genealogical distance away from ego, that is to the lineal kin types in group 2a. In Table 6 we can see group 5 as a substitute for the lineals in 2a, which is clearly segregated in the paradigm from group 2. But in Table 10 groups 2 and 2a are merged into a single block of terms whose boundaries do not correspond with those of group 5. We cannot fit group 5 as a substitute for any contiguous set of terms in Table 10.

This implies that there are some aspects of the kinship terminology for which the paradigm in Table 6 appears to be a "truer" model, and there are others for which the paradigm in Table 10 appears to be "truer." One model brings out one aspect of the semantic structure and another brings out another, but both aspects cannot be readily brought out in the same model.

XV

The exercise presented here illustrates my concept of the contribution of componential analysis to anthropological and behavioral science.

It enables us to summarize in a succinct way what we think we know about the categorical organization of phenomenal domains as revealed by the use of linguistic labels for the categories within them. It forces us to be precise and rigorous in stating what we think we know, thereby helping us to clarify to ourselves our knowledge and its limitations. The results of analysis, as illustrated in Table 10, portray in an objective manner complicated relationships for which otherwise we have only a subjective feel. These relationships and the structures they form thus are made much more amenable to systematic comparison for scientific purposes. Componential analysis provides a means for evaluating the adequacy of ethnographic statements regarding the cultural organizations of phenomena we presume other people to have. It imposes a set of standards or quality controls on the collection and processing of ethnographic data, thereby making it easier for independent investigators to replicate one another's data and analytical conclusions. It should be easy for any reader to test the extent to which the model of Yankee kinship here presented fits his own subculture, for example. If he analyzes his own kinship terminology using the same control question and following the same procedures and canons of analysis, we shall be in a position to undertake comparisons that are far more controlled than any made by anthropologists to date.

NOTES

[1] The analysis presented in this paper was undertaken as part of a research project entitled "Componential analysis of kin relationships," supported by the National Institute of Mental Health, Department of Health, Education, and Welfare (Grant numbers M-6126 and MH-06126-02).

[2] For the use of an equivalence rule in conjunction with componential analysis, see my handling of generation skewing in Truk (Goodenough 1956). For the systematic use of equivalence rules as a partial alternative to componential analysis, see the important paper by Lounsbury (1964a).

[3] The denotatum of any given utterance of a word is what the word points to (denotes). As I see it, this is never a "thing" but a perception or conception of something, i.e. something that is discriminated ideationally or sensually as such from what it is not. Denotata are minimal classes or categories of real or imagined objects, events, and relationships. Following Morris' (1946) usage, the set of possible denotata for a word is its designatum, a more general class of which any particular denotatum is a member. The criteria for being in the class are what the word signifies, its significatum. The semantic components are the various criteria that in combina-

tion comprise a word's significatum. These criteria are the contrasting values of perceptual or conceptual variables. Any discrimination necessarily sorts phenomena into at least two complementary classes, e.g. male and female. The criss-crossing of several such discriminations partitions a larger perceptual or conceptual universe into subuniverses. If each subuniverse is labeled with a word, then the set of labels for all the subuniverses is a terminological system, in which the significatum of any one label is made up of the particular values of the particular variables that discriminate the subuniverse it designates from all the other subuniverses in the universe. Componential analysis systematically contrasts the sets of denotata of the labels in a terminological system in order to arrive at hypotheses regarding the variables and their values that will most elegantly predict all of their respective denotata. The result is an inductively developed and validated "model" of the conceptual organization of an ideational domain, regardless of how accurately it represents the actual conceptual organization in other than the analyst's "head."

[4] For extensive discussions of this question see Wallace (1961:29–41) and Goodenough (1963:257–264).

[5] By a kin type is meant any category of relationship which can be conceived as differing in any way from another. For notational purposes it is convenient to follow Murdock (1949:133–134) and use as a base the eight genealogically closest relationships designated in standard English (father—Fa, mother—Mo, son—So, daughter—Da, brother—Br, sister—Si, husband—Hu, wife—Wi), specifying kin types as relative products of these (e.g. FaBrWi) with such additional distinctions according to relative age, sex of ego, etc., as may be necessary to handle a particular body of data.

[6] Terms of address are likely to form different terminological systems from terms of reference, as has been illustrated by Conant (1961).

[7] The genitor is the husband of the genetrix at the time of conception. If some other man is in fact the genitor, the husband of the genetrix can do one of only two things—disown the child and divorce his wife in doing so, or keep this wife and the child. He cannot disown the child and keep his wife.

[8] Thus I would refer to my stepfather as "my father" in his presence, but as "my stepfather" otherwise, unless he were the only person with whom I had established a relationship as my father, in which case I could refer to him as "my father" even when he was not present.

[9] Two of my acquaintances who grew up in Long Island use *grand* as the adjective immediately preceding *uncle* and *aunt* as well. The forms *grand uncle* and *grand aunt*, stressed as two words though written as one, also appear in Merriam-Webster (1961).

[10] In my dialect the pattern of stress and juncture in *my grand nephew* is the same as in *my great uncle* and *my great grandfather* and is not the same as in *my grandfather*. Contrast this with Conklin's (1964:39–55) treatment of what he gives as *granduncle, grandaunt, grandnephew,* and *grandniece* in his dialect. (Merriam-Webster 1961 gives these four forms spelled in this way, but with stress marks showing that *grand* is in each case a separate word.) He sees them as terms of the same order as *grandfather, grandmother, grandson,* and *granddaughter*. In such a dialect the results of componential analysis differ from those to be presented here.

[11] There is a widespread subculture in the northeastern United States in which the expressions *once removed, twice removed,* etc., have no meaning. In this subculture

the expressions *first cousin, second cousin,* etc., relate to generation distance as well as to collateral distance between ego and alter. One adds to the degree of collateral distance the number of generations removed in order to arrive at the appropriate numerical adjective. Thus a PaPaPaSbCh would be my *third cousin* by this system of reckoning, instead of being *my first cousin twice removed,* as in my subculture. I should add that this is a difference of which many people are unaware. For many people any relatives beyond first cousins in their own generation are for all practical purposes beyond the range of kinship discourse so that they are uncertain as to how to classify them except as *distant cousins.*

   [12] I do not imply that these are not kinship terms or that I would not consider them in a broader treatment of Yankee kinship. Comparison of the different contextual frames in which kinship terms are used and examination of how the denotata of the same terms shift from context to context and of what terms are limited to what contexts would be required in a fuller discussion. Since all but *forefather* are patently cover-terms resulting from the omission of sex distinctions, their inclusion would not affect the analysis presented here or the conclusions drawn from it.

REFERENCES CITED

Burling, Robbins, 1962, A structural restatement of Njamal kinship terminology. Man 62, No. 201.

———, 1963, Garo kinship terms and the analysis of meaning. Ethnology 2:70–85.

———, 1964a, Cognition and componential analysis: God's truth or hocus-pocus? American Anthropologist 66:20–28.

———, 1964b, Rejoinder (to Hymes and Frake). American Anthropologist 66: 120-122.

Conant, Francis P., 1961, Jarawa kin systems of reference and address: a componential comparison. Anthropological Linguistics 3:19–33.

Conklin, Harold C., 1962a, Comment (on the ethnographic study of cognitive systems, by C. O. Frake). *In* W. C. Sturtevent and T. Gladwin, eds., Anthropology and human behavior. Washington, Anthropological Society of Washington.

———, 1962b, Lexicographical treatment of folk taxonomies. *In* F. W. Householder and S. Saporta, eds., Problems in lexicography. Bloomington, Indiana University Research Center in Anthropology, Folklore, and Linguistics Publication No. 21.

———, 1964, Ethnogenealogical method. *In* W. H. Goodenough, ed., Explorations in cultural anthropology. New York, McGraw-Hill.

Frake, Charles O., 1960, The Eastern Subanun of Mindanao. *In* G. P. Murdock, ed., Social structure in Southeast Asia. Viking Fund Publications in Anthropology No. 29. New York, Wenner-Gren Foundation for Anthropological research.

———, 1962, The ethnographic study of cognitive systems. *In* T. Gladwin and W. C. Sturtevant, eds., Anthropology and human behavior. Washington, Anthropological Society of Washington.

———, 1964, Further discussion of Burling. American Anthropologist 66:119.

Goodenough, Ward H., 1951, Property, kin and community on Truk. Yale University Publications in Anthropology No. 46.

Goodenough, Ward H., 1956, Componential analysis and the study of meaning. Language 32:195–216.

———, 1957, Cultural anthropology and linguistics. *In* Paul Garvin, ed., Report of the Seventh Annual Round Table meeting on Linguistics and Language Study. Washington, Georgetown University Monograph Series on Languages and Linguistics No. 9.

———, 1963, Cooperation in change: an anthropological approach to community development. New York, Russell Sage Foundation.

———, 1964, Componential analysis of Könkämä Lapp kinship terminology. *In* W. H. Goodenough, ed., Explorations in cultural anthropology. New York, McGraw-Hill.

Hymes, Dell H., 1964, Discussion of Burling's paper. American Anthropologist 66:116–119.

Lounsbury, Floyd G., 1964, A formal account of the Crow- and Omaha-type kinship terminologies. *In* W. H. Goodenough, ed., Explorations in cultural anthropology. New York, McGraw-Hill.

Malinowski, Bronislaw, 1932, The sexual life of savages in northwest Melanesia. 3d ed. London, Routledge and Kegan Paul.

Morris, Charles, 1946, Signs, language and behavior. New York, Prentice-Hall.

Pospisil, Leopold, 1960, The Kapauku Papuans and their kinship organization. Oceania 30:188–205.

———, 1964, Law and societal structure among the Nunamiut Eskimo. *In* W. H. Goodenough, ed., Explorations in cultural anthropology. New York, McGraw-Hill.

Schneider, David M., G. C. Homans, 1955, Kinship terminology and the American kinship system. American Anthropologist 57:1194–1208.

Wallace, A. F. C., 1961, Culture and personality. New York, Random House.

———, 1962, Culture and cognition. Science 135:351–357.

Wallace, A. F. C., J. Atkins, 1960, The meaning of kinship terms. American Anthropologist. 62:58–60.

American Kin Terms and Terms for Kinsmen: A Critique of Goodenough's Componential Analysis of Yankee Kinship Terminology

David M. Schneider

I

The combination of a good anthropologist and an intelligent informant is very hard to beat as this paper by Goodenough clearly shows. If we really want to see just what componential analysis can do, this is the very best place to see it. It is the best place to see what componential analysis can do

Reproduced by permission of the American Anthropological Association from the *American Anthropologist*, Vol. 67, no. 5, part 2 (Special Publication), pp. 288–308 (October 1965).

for a number of different reasons. One is that this paper provides a fine instance of the great difference between a systematically undertaken adequate analysis that aims at completion and programmatic efforts that merely aim at illustration. But the most important reason this paper is the best place to see just what componential analysis can do and how it does it is that the reader can evaluate every step of the procedure.

The American reader, like the Yankee author and his informant, is a fluent speaker of the language. The American reader, like the Yankee author, is his own informant. The American reader can easily call on other informants to check the material. But the American reader can do one more thing which is perhaps most important of all, and that is to consider the product of the analysis and evaluate it in terms of his own knowledge of American culture and kinship. In other words, he can take the analytic outcome of this componential analysis and ask if it fits with a new body of ethnographic data which was not used in the analysis. This is a test we can seldom use, but it is one of the best tests of the validity of any analysis.

This point is fundamental. When Goodenough provides us with a componential analysis of Trukese kinship terms, he has collected the material himself, analyzed it himself and he is about the only person who really has any command over the basic data. Since practically none of his readers knows Truk as Goodenough does, one of the major bases for the evaluation of any analysis is therefore not generally available to his readers. He knows how his analysis fits the data and, if it did not fit, he would tell us so and tell us where it didn't fit. If there had been inconsistent data he would have resolved the inconsistencies or acknowledged them. But the evaluation by the reader would have to be based on marginal considerations—the connection between data and conclusion, redundancy, internal consistency, and of course, the great "So What!"[1]

The relationship between the basic data and the Procrustean bed in which it is displayed is an especially important one where componential analysis is concerned, for componential analysis is useful precisely insofar as it explicates the fundamental cultural categories, their conceptual organization and discriminations. The question is precisely that of native categories as cultural categories. The question is precisely how the native categories relate to each other and form a systematic whole, if they do. The question in the crudest possible terms, yet perhaps also the clearest, is of being able to define the cultural categories in terms of which the natives think.

Goodenough's paper is, therefore, the best place to see just what componential analysis can do and how it does it because it deals with data about which we all know a good deal, from a source where more data are easily available if we need them, and where the data are in a language with which we all have a fair degree of fluency.

I, however, will approach this paper from a somewhat different vantage point. I am a native speaker of some fluency, born and reared in a culture to which Yankee is very closely akin. I did my first systematic work on American kinship terminology from 1951 to 1954. From 1961 until now, I have been engaged in a comparative study of American and British kinship with Professor Raymond Firth,[2] and the American end of the work (which I did) included work on kinship terminology per se. I therefore approach Goodenough's paper as a self-styled expert on that aspect of the culture about which Goodenough is talking. I do not feel that this special vantage point guarantees that where differences arise I must be right and Goodenough wrong; on the contrary all that my special position really guarantees is the authoritative *tone* in which my views may be delivered. But by the same token I can assert that I do have data, that they have been collected and analyzed systematically, and that this is something more than merely my own impressionistic view.

I will therefore start by considering Goodenough's paper in terms of what my own study, conducted from a very different point of view, has shown. The point here is to compare two different ways of approaching what is fundamentally the same aspect of American culture to see what one can say about the way in which the other formulates it. Following this, I will try to make some more general points about what this particular instance can tell us about componential analysis in general.

II

One of the first things that anyone who works with American genealogies notices is that the system is quite clear as long as you take Ego as the point of reference and do not venture far from there. But as one goes out from Ego—in any direction—things get more and more fuzzy. This fuzziness, or fade-out, is seen in many different ways. Most fundamental, of course, is the fact that there is no formal, clear, categorical limit to the domain of kinsmen. Or, to put it in another way, the decision as to whether a particular person is or is not a kinsman is not given in any simple categorical sense. One cannot say that all second cousins are kinsmen, but all third cousins are not.

Another way in which this fade-out is seen is through the increasing uncertainty over names, ages, occupations, and locations (places of residence) the farther out the relatives are from Ego.

There is one especially interesting way in which this fuzziness of boundary is expressed, and this is through the Famous Relative. We not infrequently encountered the statement that So-and-So, a famous personage was a relative. Sometimes the relationship was traceable, sometimes not. When it was traceable, it could clearly be seen that this was the only relative of such distance on the genealogy, whereas closer relatives were unknown and unheard of.

There are really two different elements that account for the fuzzy boundary. One is the absence of any effective boundary rule, for the rule itself is infinite in its coverage. The rule is that a relative is someone related by blood or marriage. Hence, as some informants were quick to point out, everyone descended from Adam and Eve is related.

The second element is the fade-out principle, and it is really this which limits the network of kin. Ethnographically, informants express this in terms of a "close-distant" dimension, saying that certain relatives are "close" while others are "distant" and yet others so distant as not to be counted as relatives.

It is, of course, the interaction between these two elements which gives the system its flexibility and its fuzziness of boundary, for people can be counted as kin in terms of some blood relationship, traceable or presumed, and they can be lost and forgotten or, even when actually known by name, simply regarded as "too distant to count." What the Famous Relative syndrome shows is that fame works against the fade-out principle even where the traceable connection is lost, and a kinsman can be "counted" so long as a blood connection is presumed.

The organization of the terminology into different sets of basic terms, and the transformation of each of these sets by special modifiers, is one aspect of this structure. It is infinitely extendable in one respect but also restricted by considerations of "distance" or the fade-out principle in another respect.

If we consider the sets of basic terms alone they fall—as Goodenough shows so clearly—into four basic sets. The first (and here I follow Goodenough almost verbatim) consists in *father, mother, son, daughter, brother* and *sister;* the second, *uncle, aunt, nephew, niece, grandfather, grandmother, grandson, granddaughter.* The third set consists in the term *cousin*, and the fourth in the two terms *husband* and *wife.*

The first set is distinguished by the fact that it is modified only by the terms *step-, -in-law* and *foster*, and each modifier yields a derivative set of terms, i.e. *stepfather, stepmother*, etc. The second set is modified by *great* and/or *grand* and, as Goodenough notes, forms an open-ended set of derivative terms in the sense that they can proceed infinitely. The third set, *cousin* is modified in two ways, by the numerical adjectives *first, second, third*, etc., and by the expression *once removed, twice removed*, etc. These modifiers also yield an open-ended set of derivative terms which could go on indefinitely. The fourth set of terms, *husband* and *wife*, are not modified and therefore no derivative sets can be constructed from them.[3]

Let us have a closer look at the modifiers for a moment. The numerical adjectives and the removal modifiers for *cousin*, and the *great/grand* modifier for the *uncle* . . . *granddaughter* set are, in Goodenough's words "open-ended," or, as I have put it, "infinite" and without limitation. These, then, are the categorical aspects of the principle of infinite kinship extension, and it is these categories which fade out with distance in any practical application for any particular, real Ego.

The other sets of modifiers are the *step-*, *-in-law*, and *foster* terms. All three are very sharply limited in their range, and limited to categories of the first set. The fourth set, *husband* and *wife*, has no modifiers and there is no way of extending the basic terms to create derivative sets.

Briefly, then, two modifiers permit the *infinite* extension of kinship along consanguineal lines, two permit the creation of derivative sets of *sharply limited range* along affinal lines, whereas the basic affinal terms themselves (*husband* and *wife*) are *not modified* or capable of creating derivative sets.

There is one final point in connection with the fuzzy boundary and fade-out principles. Goodenough opens his section XIV by noting what he calls "subcultural variations in terminology," and by observing that he has not been able to explore this problem in great detail. He then presents one variant and, in the light of two new variables, reworks the first analysis of Table 6, making it into Table 10. The first variant system is described by Table 9. The basic difference between Goodenough's Yankee system and the variant system is in the fact ". . . that [in the variant system] *my aunt*, *my uncle*, *my nephew*, and *my niece* may be extended up and down the generations to any nonlineal 1.1 relatives other than those in ego's generation . . . ." "The terms *my grandfather*, *my grandmother*, *my grandson* and *my granddaughter*, however, cannot be extended in like manner to remoter lineal relatives. For these the use of *great* the appropriate number of times is obligatory." In footnote 11 yet another variant is noted, this time ". . . the expressions *once removed*, *twice removed*, etc., have no meaning . . . *first cousin*, *second cousin*, etc., relate to generation distance as well as to collateral distance between ego and alter . . . . For many people any relatives beyond first cousins in their own generation are for all practical purposes beyond the range of kinship discourse so that they are uncertain as to how to classify them except as *distant cousins*."

But the tentative conclusion from an inspection of the few subcultural variants which Goodenough suggests is quite clear and one with which I would most heartily concur. "It is also evident from a comparison of Tables 9 and 10 [which show the analysis of the Yankee system and the one variant analyzed] that the basic structure of Yankee kinship is the same in each. When sufficient data on the various subcultural variants is available, comparison of their componential structures will show us to what extent they all have the same basic organization."

The point is simple. The location of variant rules in the system is at the outside boundary, not in the inner core. Variant patterns govern the application of modifiers which transform the basic terms into derivative sets which seem capable of infinite extension. The variant noted in footnote 11, and especially the last variant noted in that footnote (". . . beyond the range of kinship discourse . . .") most clearly states the fade-out principle and the extreme fuzziness of the boundary.

Closely related to the fuzzy boundary and fade-out is another important principle of American kinship which also appears in the terminology. This is the principle of unbalanced, dribbling dyads. This is an important link between the problem of the fade-out principle I have just dealt with and the problem of affinity which I will raise next.

Each of the sets of kinship terms consists in a set of terms which is basic, and in some generally evaluative sense has high priority and a set of derivatives manufactured from the basic terms by a modifier which has low priority. Thus *father* takes precedence over *father-in-law*, and the set *father, mother, brother, sister, son* and *daughter* has priority over the set *father-in-law, mother-in-law . . . daughter-in-law*. So, too, cousin is a *first cousin* unless otherwise modified, and modified *cousins* are, in this very general sense, lower or lesser than the unmodified (first) cousins. Indeed the whole notion of two sets is another illustration of this principle of unbalanced dyads, for one set is basic, the other set derivative. Finally, it is important to note that the sets of basic terms are all unquestionably *kinship terms*, while the derivative terms are compounds of a kinship term plus a nonkinship term. The modifiers themselves are in no case kinship terms, though they can be treated as terms for kinsmen, and the compound of basic term and modifier, Goodenough's informant seems to suggest, can be treated as a kinship term. I will return to this point below.

The pairing of basic terms might be seen as another manifestation of this tendency toward unbalanced dyads. There is *mother* and *father, brother* and *sister, grandfather* and *grandmother, uncle* and *aunt, son* and *daughter, husband* and *wife, father* and *son, mother* and *daughter, grandfather* and *grandson, grandmother* and *granddaughter, nephew* and *niece. Cousin* does not seem to be paired, though it may be that *cousin* is paired with *Ego*. In any case, however, the pairing is related to what might be called "cover terms" which unify certain of the pairs and which unify them in different ways. First there is the *grandparent, parent, sibling, spouse, child* and *grandchild*. Here the pairs which are divided by sex are unified without regard to sex but respecting all other criteria. Goodenough notes these but excludes them from the analysis on the ground that for his informant they are not fully appropriate answers to this control question. "What relationship is he (she) to you?" The second set, which Goodenough includes as being possible answers to his control question consists in *ancestor, ancestress*, and *descendant*. It is interesting to note that in this set generation is unified but the sex distinction is maintained in ascendants, whereas both generation and sex are unified in descendants. This pattern for stipulating sex is identical in form to the way in which genealogies are recounted; uncertainty about the sex of a person on a genealogy is almost entirely confined to persons regarded as in the category of "child," as "their child." This may be in Ego's own generation as cousins, but is mainly in the generations below Ego.

What Americans call "distance" consists in a chain of unbalanced dyads, and because they are unbalanced they dribble, and dribbling means that they fade out. If all members of a set are of equal importance then the set stands as a unit. But precisely because the elements in a dyad are, with one fundamental exception, never of equal importance chains of dyads consist in chains of dyads of diminishing value and hence they fade away. The anomaly of the Famous Relative is simply a relative who by virtue of some attribute external to kinship, takes on a wholly inconsistent importance and so sticks out along the fading chain of relatives who become less important as they go farther away.

Another way to put this is that the whole system is one of chains; the elements in the chains are dyads; there are no whole, corporate units in the system at all. The terminology, as Goodenough deals with it, exemplifies this basic point, which is true whether we treat it in terms of relationships, roles, or ordered affective expressions. What is called "the family" cannot be treated as a whole unit, having corporate membership qualities, but must be treated as a system of unbalanced dyads.

Still another expression of the principle of unbalanced dyads is in the opposition between blood and marriage. Blood relationship has higher priority than that by marriage, and the particular form that this higher priority takes, among others, is in its being regarded as unbreakable. A blood relationship cannot be terminated, one by marriage can. This, I suggest, is related to the fact which I noted above. Consanguineal modifiers can go on indefinitely. They are, in Goodenough's words, "open-ended." Working from Ego out, the system is one of dribbling dyads, theoretically infinitely extendable but actually, in any particular instance, not going very far at all. But however far they do go, the links are consanguineal and not affinal; the links are by blood, not by marriage.

If we turn, therefore, to Goodenough's section XIII, it is immediately apparent that our accounts are very close to each other, with very few differences, and these may have some slight significance. Let me list those differences here. First, Goodenough contrasts life-long obligations as obtaining for all who are within two degrees of collaterality or closer, ". . . while those of two degrees of collaterality or more distance have no ascribed life-long obligations other than a show of cordiality."

I do not think that there is such a sharp break at the level of cousins, nor do I think that the difference between these two groups can be phrased in terms of the presence or absence of life-long obligations. That the re-lationship between cousins is an almost direct consequence of the relation-ship between the siblings who are the cousins' parents is true, of course, as Goodenough recognizes. But this is a good example of what I have called the principle of the dribbling dyad. It is the sibling relationship between the parents which is strong enough to create the cousin relationship between their children, and the claims of a parent on his child have a lot to do with the claims of a cousin on another cousin. It is not only that my contact with my cousin depends, and to begin with depended, on my parents' con-tact with their siblings, but it is an obligation to my parent that I treat his siblings' child as having a claim on me. Precisely what claims, and what sort of claim, is a different problem. But the break between a life-long claim and one which is not life-long may perhaps be what actually often happens in practice, but it is not—and this is most important to me—an accurate account of the conceptual and normative cultural considerations involved.

The second paragraph of section XIII is, in my view, essentially correct except that again Goodenough resorts to a functional rather than a cultural and conceptual formulation. This is, I think, an error. We both agree and remark on the fact that there is a difference between basic lexemes (basic kinship terms I called them) for consanguineal kinsmen ". . . in the 1.1 set who are less than three units of genealogical removal from Ego also accords with the pattern of kinship obligation," while derivative terms are used for the more distant kinsmen. The difference is phrased by Goodenough in terms of the responsibility for pre-adult children and for care of the aged. I suspect that he would agree—if he consulted his informant once more—that the relationship is much more diffuse than merely the specific responsi-bility for pre-adult children and care for the aged, though these are cer-tainly two specific expressions of that relationship.

Finally, Goodenough touches on another point to which I have alluded but not developed, nor is there space to do so here, though it should be mentioned. The phrase Goodenough uses is, interestingly, very much the same as the one I had come up with. I have spoken of "the pattern of solidary emphasis" and stated it in terms of priority of claims on solidarity (1959 Palo Alto Seminar Paper); while Goodenough speaks too of ". . . re-lationships in which dependency rights and duties have first and second priority and are active in practice, and the relationships in group 2a [those involving *great*] are the ones in which dependency rights and duties have tertiary or remoter priority and have little chance of activation."

I think that the differences between Goodenough and myself are very slight, and they tend to center on the fact that he shifts to functional formu-lations rather than maintaining a consistently cultural-symbolic level of analysis which I think is required. By maintaining a homogeneous level of analysis, and defining it as cultural-symbolic, the symbols which are kinship terms can be treated as part of the same ethnographic domain as the symbols which are modes and kinds of expression of relationship. I would suggest that our problem is *not* to see what correlation the cultural symbols called kinship terms have to the functional roles. Rather it is to see how the whole cultural-symbolic system is differentiated and how one set of symbols—kinship terms—relates with other sets of symbols—the norms for relations among kinsmen. But I will return to points like this below.

In sum, I think it is clear that from my own perspective, Goodenoughs' work, done wholly independently, is so very close to my own findings that I can only assume that we are both working in the same universe and that whatever differences there are up to this point are very minor indeed. In my view, of course, this confirms the value of componential analysis. In Goodenough's view, this may only confirm the fact that thus far at least I am not too bad an ethnographer.

III

The whole question of affinity is a difficult one in American kinship, and Goodenough's paper reflects this.

If we take Goodenough's Table 6 as our guide, four of the nine discriminant variables are necessary to cope with affinal terms alone. Of these four variables, three yield "descriptive only" or zero lexeme categories. Sometimes the zero lexeme is of great ethnographic significance, but the high proportion may indicate that some aspect of the analysis is problematic.

I begin, then, with some general points about affinity in American kinship.

In the first place, there are some obvious facts about which there can be almost no dispute. Informants speak of the sharp contrast between relatives by blood and by marriage, and the phrase "in-laws" is perfectly proper usage as contrasted with "relatives." Relatives "by marriage" or "in-laws" have an important place in any Ego's network. For instance, there is now reason to suspect that of the two theoretically possible ways of increasing the number of kinsmen actively engaged in a particular network, it is those who are related through marriage who constitute the major source of additional numbers, rather than the wider spread which would be obtained by tracing back farther and then out to more widely placed collateral lines. That is, the consanguineals of spouses are drawn into a network more often than distant collateral lines of consanguineal kinsmen.

But opposed to this fact is another. I have called this the Christmas-tree effect in genealogies, and it has two parts. The first is that American genealogies are often not more than three or four generations deep, and they

take the form of a squat Christmas tree or pyramid. At the top, there is often
The Ancestor, sometimes in the form of a couple, like the star on a Christmas
tree. As generations get closer to Ego, each sib-set somehow gets larger, so
that the whole thing seems to stand on a very firm, broad base. If you look
closely below the base you see the trunk of the Christmas tree; Ego's line,
his children and grandchildren, who continue to move away from Ego, in a
thin line, generation by generation. The Ancestor may or may not have had
siblings, but if he did, they are either not mentioned or they are forgotten.
Sib-sets of the Ancestor's children are larger, while the sib-sets and the collateral lines of cousins give the zero generation a considerable spread both
of cousins and of siblings.

The squat Christmas tree consists in a network of consanguineals. This
consanguineal network is adorned with spouses. But spouses only occasionally have siblings or parents, and the spouses' parents only rarely have
siblings.

The general shape is the same, whether one takes the genealogy in a
wholly nondirective way, asking simply for a list of relatives and how they
are related, and then asking "are there any more?," or if one works quite
systematically using probes of the utmost specificity, such as "and has he
any brothers? sisters? mother? father? sons? daughters? wife (or husband)?"
In the first case the tree is not very bushy. In the second case the tree is
quite bushy, and at least a third more persons are recorded on the genealogy,
but the basic shape is very much the same. It is very much the same because
informants don't remember if great-great-grandfather had any brothers or
sisters, and as far as grandfather's brother's wife is concerned, they imagine
that she must have had a mother and father but they just do not know if
she had any siblings.

The genealogy, I presume, represents an expression of something. Whatever that something is, it turns into a fundamentally consanguineal network
with spouses. In-laws are not common; in fact, they are notable by their
absence.

These two facts seem contradictory. One indicates that in actual interaction in-laws may be drawn into an active kinship network to augment it,
to make bigger family gatherings, to amplify the resources of "the family."
The other indicates that the network is conceptually consanguineal and the
only affines are spouses.

But there are some additional facts which are troublesome. One is that
the -in-law term is a modifier and, when used, it transforms a series of terms
which are basic into a set which is clearly derivative. A second troublesome
fact is that group 2 terms are the ones in which the sharp distinction between
consanguineal and affinal is not preserved but where both kintypes are included. FaBrWi and FaSi are both *aunt*. FaSiHu and FaBr are both *uncle*.
Another troublesome bit Goodenough mentions but does not resolve even

though his informant was so easily accessible, and he could have asked him directly. I quote from *uncle*. "A PaSi's or PaPaDa's second Hu is less assuredly *my uncle* than the first Hu if ego has already established a relationship with the first Hu as *my uncle*." The same is true for *my aunt*.[4] The problem, however, is simply this: What is the status of FaSi's first husband and second husband now that she is married for the third time? Are all three *"my uncle"* or only the first one with whom a relationship was established though he is no longer "around"? What seems clear is that some *uncles* and *aunts* are terminable; some spouses of consanguineal *uncles* and *aunts* may not be, properly, *my uncle* or *my aunt*. Hence it is not simply a question of the fact that these categories include both consanguineal and affinal kintypes, but that the rules governing the inclusion of the affinal kintypes are peculiarly unclear.

Still another fact of some significance is the series of "ifs" which are included in Goodenough's definition of the *-in-law* terms, these "ifs" center on two things. First, the *-in-law* relationship is *through* one or more relationships. Second, the *-in-law* relationship is through an *extant* relationship. Goodenough says: *"My father-in-law:* SpFa, SpMoHu (if married to SpMo before the marriage of ego and if SpFa is dead or in no way functioning as SpFa)." This means, I take it, that *father-in-law* is *my father* to my spouse, whether or not he is currently married to spouse's mother. Whoever stands as *my father* to spouse (it may be spouse's mother's second husband when her first is no longer acting because of death or for other reasons) is *my father-in-law*. Hence my relationship to *my father-in-law* is, first, through my spouse and, second, dependent on whether the relationship which my spouse has with him is *extant*. On one side, then, we are faced again with this odd element that ". . . a relationship . . ." plays a crucial role. On the other side, we have the best and clearest example of how these affinal categories depend on two elements, their being *through* other relations, and their dependence on an *extant* relationship.

Other *"ifs"* follow from serial monogamy. Father-in-law is *not* mother-in-law's current husband, but is spouse's father. This is in contrast to the problem of *aunt's* current *husband* and *uncle's* current *wife*. Here the relationship is in doubt according to Goodenough's informant. If I knew *aunt's* first husband as *my uncle*, Goodenough seems unsure of whether her present husband is really *my uncle* and the first one de-uncled. I have informants who claim that an *aunt's* first and discarded husband is not a relative and is not an *uncle*, but can be (and was) a very close and good "friend."

We have almost enough information now to begin to make some sense of American affinity.

First, the categories of *spouse* and *in-law* must be sharply separated, although both are affines. From the Christmas-tree effect in genealogies and the extension of the network process, this distinction between *spouses* and

-in-laws shows up quite clearly. Spouses adorn genealogies; but *in-laws* increase the size of kindred networks.

Yet from this same fact another becomes quite obvious. The distinction between *spouse* and *in-laws* is not quite enough. There are at least four kinds of affines which can be distinguished. *Spouses* of consanguineals (CA) are one, and these include Ego's own *spouse* of course. A second consists not in any *in-laws*, but only the "close" consanguines of *my spouse* (CAC₁). The third conceivable kind is the close consanguineals of any *spouse* of any of my consanguineals (CAC₂): My *aunt's husband's mother* and *father* for instance, or my *brother's wife's sister*. The fourth conceivable category is the *spouses* of the consanguines of the *spouses* of my consanguineals (CACA): My *aunt's husband's mother's brother's wife* or my *brother's wife's sister's husband*, for instance.⁵

It is these last two categories which go to fill out skinny kindred rather than more distant collaterals. But the status of these last two categories as kinsmen is very much in doubt. This doubt is a good example of the fuzzy boundary and fade-out principles at work, for their status is not a matter of strong affirmations *for*, or strong affirmations *against*, but is simply a matter of doubt. The same informant will say that on some shaky grounds these can be included as kin, but on firmer grounds they can be forgotten, not known, not counted or, as it is more often put, "really" someone else's relatives, "not really my relatives." Hence these last two categories can be ignored as affines.

The next problem is to consider the *foster* and *step-* terms. I presume that Goodenough only discusses the *foster* terms in section IX because of their close similarity to the *step-* terms, not because he regards the *foster* terms as affinal derivatives. His definition of the *foster* terms certainly rules out any suggestion that they might be considered as affinal terms. "Any relationship that is by virtue of common residence in the same household behaviorally equivalent to a relationship denoted by a term in Group 1 (Fa, Mo, Br, Si, So, Da) but not also structurally equivalent to it, is denoted by the corresponding term in group 1 with the adjective *foster*" (Rule 3).

The similarity between the *foster* derivatives and the *step-* derivatives arises from the fact that in each case a parental relationship or role is played by someone who is not "really" a parent, or, to put it more precisely, where a parental role is played by one or both parents who are not genitor or genetrix. If both parents are not genitor or genetrix, they are *foster* parents if they have not changed their position by adoption. The spouse of genitor or genetrix is a *step-* parent if the "real" parent acts as such and is known.

I have said that there are two categories of affines, *spouse* and *in-law*. I think that informants are often taken aback when presented with the fact that since a *step-child* becomes related through and by marriage he can be considered to be a kind of affine. They deny this but are often unable to explain why. One can then present them with a modified statement to the effect that *step-children* gain their position through the remarriage of one of their parents, and therefore may be considered to be "relatives by marriage." This seems logical to informants, but still leaves a feeling of uneasiness as if there were something wrong with it.

I think that this uneasiness arises in part from the fact that the *step*-relations can be conceived of in two distinct ways, both of which seem valid to informants. One is certainly, as Goodenough has suggested, that these are affinal categories which suffer from all of the rights and privileges of affinity. A woman's relationship to her husband's child by an earlier marriage, as celebrated in western European folktales, is of the essential affinal pattern. The relationship is *through* an *extant* marriage and is not a direct relationship between Ego and alter. Thus the stepmother of folklore has an abiding loyalty to her own child (the child to whom she is genetrix), and loyalty to her husband, but his child by an earlier marriage (her *step-child*) is somebody else's relative, not hers, and what she does for it she does because of her husband. The other side of this situation is simply that a parent-child relationship has certain qualities which are held to be independent of affinity, entail love and warmth; that a child has the right to expect something of a parent, even a step-parent; and that a parent's relationship should be directly to the child and not mediated by a marital tie.

Affinals remain, then, of two kinds: *spouse* and *in-law*, and the *step*-relations seem to be kinds of *in-laws*.

But the problem now arises of why FaBrWi, MoBrWi, FaSiHu, MoSiHu are *my uncle* and *my aunt*, and why SpSibCh is *my nephew* and *my niece*.

The answer to this begins with the sound ethnographic point which Goodenough makes: "A married man and woman are a single social unit whose solidarity, joint interests, and responsibilities take precedence over whatever obligations and interests either may have in any other relationship." The element in the componential analysis which corresponds to this ethnographic fact—and the ethnography is very highly condensed here—is the statement:

We assume, furthermore, that the marriage tie does not count as a unit of genealogical distance, but only a vertical or horizontal consanguineal link as just defined. Thus FaBr and FaBrWi are both two units of genealogical distance away from ego, and Br, BrWi, and WiBr are one unit of distance away. Genealogical distance provides a conceptual variable that includes ego as one of its complementary values, for ego is necessarily at zero distance from himself on a genealogical tree. Hu and Wi are also at zero distance from ego. Thus ego is one of the consanguineal categories from which affinal terminology can be derived as was suggested in Table I.

The unity of the conjugal pair is such that the differences between them are not merged or eliminated, but rather that the one implies the other. The primacy of their solidary bond to each other means that they "go together" and should act in concert. This unity has its terminological aspect, and it also has its solidarity aspect. That is, the strongest claim of loyalty and solidarity is between husband and wife, and no claim should exceed it. The categories of *my uncle* and *my aunt* are consanguineal categories. But Ego's relationship to his *uncle's wife* is through his *uncle*, and to his *aunt's husband* is through his *aunt*, and depends for its existence on their marriage being extant. This is the *through* and *extant* pattern of affinity I have mentioned. *My aunt* and *my uncle* are senior relatives and quite apart from any warmth and affection that there should be between us, they merit respect by virtue of their age and seniority. Since one is taken together with his spouse, the respect which *my aunt* and *my uncle* merit is also accorded to their spouse, for their solidarity with each other and their unity must be accepted. It is significant that courtesy kin, that is, friends of parents, are called "uncle" and "aunt," and I suggest that *my aunt's husband* and *my uncle's wife* are courtesy kin, and respect requires that they be accorded this terminological designation.

The unity of the conjugal pair really has two sides to it. On the one hand, the identity of *my uncle* and his *wife* as a conjugal pair requires that I treat them both as seniors and with respect. On the other hand, the fact that *my uncle's wife* is the spouse of one of my consanguineals puts her in the position where she can be no link to other kinsmen, where her relationship to me depends on her maintaining her relationship to *my uncle*, her husband.

That part of the Christmas-tree effect in genealogies which shows spouses who are not themselves consanguineals adorning the network of consanguines is explicable, therefore, in terms of the fundamental unity and solidarity of the conjugal pair in middle class American kinship. In the American middle class pattern of solidary emphasis, the conjugal relationship has primacy above all others.[6]

But I have gone ahead too fast. Let me return to the assertion that *uncle* and *aunt* are fundamentally consanguineal categories. I have recently been working with children as informants, and the children who have been interviewed tend to confirm what I believe the adult view to be. Adults and children alike tend to offer some form of the answer 'parent's sibling' as the definition of the terms *uncle* and *aunt*. They may say "a father's brother or sister, or a mother's brother or sister," and when asked to name "uncles" and "aunts" they do *not* tend to name the parent's siblings' spouse as falling within that category. If, however, they are pressed to name more relatives, or if they are naming relatives seriatum, or if they are asked directly, they concede that a FaBrWi is an *aunt*, a FaSiHu is an *uncle*, or they will first name the consanguineal and then the spouse.

The same is true for *nephew* and *niece*. The tendency for both children and adults is to define these as a sibling's child. It is only on pressure or direct inquiry, for instance in answer to the question, "Isn't a spouse's sibling's child a *nephew* or *niece* too?" that the response may be "of course" or the concession that this is true. *Nephew* and *niece*, then, are fundamentally consanguineal categories in American kinship; when these terms are applied to a spouse's sibling's child this is a courteous usage, and not usage as a kinship term at all.

My uncle₁ should be defined as FaBr, MoBr; *my aunt₁* as MoSi, FaSi; *my nephew₁* as BrSo, SiSo; *my niece₁* as BrDa, SiDa. These categories are opposed to *my uncle₂* who is a male friend of a parent or parents, male courtesy kinsman, respectful form of address and reference for any of the foregoing, including the spouse of *my aunt₁*, etc. *My aunt₂* would be a female of the class *my uncle₂*. And so on for *nephew₂* and *niece₂*.

The other terms in Goodenough's group 2, insofar as they include a spouse (grandfather's second wife who is not MoMo or FaMo for instance) are of the same order. These are the courteous application of a kinship term to persons who are not kinsmen. The persons in Goodenough's group 2 who are spouses are essentially courtesy kin and they are classed as courtesy kin because they are senior and because of the fundamental unity and solidary primacy of the conjugal pair.

There should be nothing surprising in this. "Father" can be used for genitor and for priest; the first is a kinsman, the second is not. "Uncle" and "aunt" can be used for a parent's sibling and for a parent's friend; the first a kinsman, the second not. "Sister" can be used for female sibling and for a female of slightly lower status—the first a kinsman, the second not. "Brother" can be used for male sibling and for a male who is a fellow lodge or church member or in a slightly demeaned status—the first a kinsman, the others not. "Son" can be used for own male child and for any younger male—the first a kinsman, the second not.

It does not follow that because a kinship term is used for FaSiHu or MoBrWi the object is a kinsman. Neither does it follow that because informants will concede that the proper term for a FaSiHu is "uncle" or "my uncle" that he is a kinsman, no more than it follows that because informants will concede that the proper term for a priest is "father" that he is a kinsman. Finally, neither does it follow that only because the question "What kin relationship, if any, is FaSiHu to you?" draws the answer "He is my uncle" that FaSiHu is a kinsman.

If this view is correct there is only one affinal category and that is Goodenough's group 4, namely, *my husband* and *my wife*. Ego's own spouse, that is, is the only true affinal in American kinship.

But what about the *in-law* and *step-* set? Have I not already accepted their affinal status? Are these really affines? Are they even kinsmen in American? What is the American term for "kinsman"? Is it "relative"? If we consider what we know about other cultures, the distinction between kinsmen and nonkinsmen is sharp and clear. Among the Nuer, for instance, the word for kinsman is *mar* (Evans-Pritchard 1951:6 and Ch. 4). The word "kinship" and "kinsman" can be found in Webster's dictionary, but Americans with whom I have talked regard these words as technical terms which seem to have crept into the vocabulary, like the word "sibling." But perhaps they are wrong. Perhaps those words are in fact going out of the vocabulary and becoming confined to technical usage by specialists like anthropologists.

I have collected a good deal of material on this subject. The word "relative" is used by some of the natives, but by no means all of them. There is, however, a general category which is fairly consistently defined, whether it is called "relative" or "people" (as in "my people"), "folks" or "kinfolk."

This is an unmarked term. "Relative" can be used either for a blood relative alone, or it can be used for "relative by blood or marriage." I have recorded the statement: "My wife is not a relative," and the statement: "My wife is a relative by marriage." The same statements are made about husbands by wives. Relative can mean both consanguineal and affinal, or it can be opposed to affinal.

But there is one more very important point about the notion of "relative," "kinship," and "kinsman." In American culture these are conceptual but not concrete categories. It is easy to get a definition of "relative" and relationship by blood or marriage in some respects. But it is very much harder to be able to say that this or that person *is* a relative, or that this or that kintype *is* a kinsman. In fact, of course, the very sharp conceptual distinction between a relative and a nonrelative, between a consanguineal and an affinal is then modified by the notion of "closeness," and it is this which has a dampening effect so that by one aspect of the definition, relationship by birth or by blood, a particular kintype must be counted as a relative, but by the notion of "closeness," it just cannot be.

Let me briefly summarize the relevant facts. First, Goodenough's fundamental point is sound and it holds, namely, there is a set of *basic* terms, and these are kinship terms, and this set is modified by modifiers like *-in-law* and *step-* and *foster* for group 1 terms. These modifiers cannot be regarded as *kinship terms*. This holds for the relationship between *all* of the basic terms in the basic sets which Goodenough has very clearly and accurately set out, and to all of the derivative terms created by the modifiers. Modifiers (*-in-law, step-, great, grand, first-second-third-, removed*) are never kinship terms in American.[7]

So much for kinship terms. This is not the same question as terms for kinsmen. Now let us turn to the ethnographic or semantic question of whether these are terms for kinsman in American.

How, then, can we deal with the simple question which has been haunting us all along? Is there but one affinal category? Are *-in-laws* and *step-*

affines or are they not? Is uncle's wife a relative by marriage or is she nothing but a courtesy kinswoman?

I cannot develop the case fully here. Suffice it to say at this point that the -*in-law* and the *step-* set of derivative terms apply to relatives in law but not to affines. There is only one affinal category in American kinship and that is spouse (*husband*, *wife*). *Uncle's* wife, *aunt's* husband, and spouse's sibling's child are not kinsmen. But kinship terms are applied to them. This is because a kinship term has at least two meanings. Its meaning$_1$ consists in the definition of that kind of kinsman. For instance, *mother*$_1$ means genetrix. Its meaning$_2$ is a kind of kinship role or relationship. *Mother*$_2$ is the name for the mother role, and it can be applied to the person who plays that role. When the person who plays the mother role is also the genetrix, then one might say that this is the special meaning of *mother*$_3$, indicated by the subscript$_3$.

Hence when *uncle's* wife is called *aunt*, she is *aunt*$_2$, not *aunt*$_1$. *Aunt*$_1$ is FaSi and MoSi. *Aunt's* husband is also *uncle*$_2$, not *uncle*$_1$. My father's brother, with whom I have an uncle-nephew relationship, is, of course, my *uncle*$_3$. (See Schneider and Homans 1955 for my very early formulation of the multiple meanings of kinship terms.)

IV

Starting from different points of view and using mainly different kinds of data, it is significant that Goodenough and I both agree on the basic facts. For all practical purposes and certainly for the purposes of this discussion, we are in almost perfect accord on the ethnography. It is of great methodological significance to consider the time and the work which went into the many interviews with many different people, the collection of genealogies, accounts of weddings and funerals and family squabbles, visiting patterns, residence patterns and religious affiliation and so forth on which I think I am basing my ethnographic statements, and then to see how closely they agree with Goodenough, whose statements are based on work with a single intelligent informant.

Just what, then, is the nature of my differences with Goodenough? How can these differences be accounted for? What does this have to say about componential analysis?

The fact that we are in basic agreement on the ethnographic material implies that we are both dealing with the same cultural universe. This is implied because we came to the same conclusions from independent work. We did not consult during its progress, we used different informants, different field methods, and, except for one area, we focused on different subjects for inquiry. The only area we both worked on is of kinship terms. But I took genealogies, accounts of weddings and funerals and Bar Mitzvahs, spontaneous listings of kinsmen, discussions of the definition of kinsmen and kinship, who is and who is not a kinsman and why, and many other subjects. The fact that Goodenough worked with a Yankee informant and I worked primarily in the midwest but a bit in New York, Cambridge and Berkeley suggests that it would not be improper to consider Yankee as indistinguishable from generalized American. We need no longer regard Yankee as an alien pocket in an otherwise American landscape.

What, then, are the differences between us?

I think that whether we take Goodenough's Table 6 or Table 10, the amount of space and the number of components, that is, the size of the analytic apparatus that is needed to deal with the derivative sets is out of proportion to their significance in American kinship and also states their position erroneously in some respects.

Table 10, and the variables 12 and 13, deal nicely with the basic four-fold division of the sets and with the infinite extension which the *great/grand* modifiers are capable of. Although the modifiers *first, second, third, etc.* and *removal* do not merit the same space on the table, they accomplish the same ends.

But Table 10 somehow seems to imply to me that *uncle* and *great great uncle* are equally relatives, and this I doubt on ethnographic grounds. That is, the *great greats* are "not very close" and I think that they fade out and become "not very closely related" if they are known and remembered and they are not likely to be remembered, though of course they may be. Table 10, that is, handles the problem of the way in which infinite extension is possible, but it does not deal with the dimension of "distance" insofar as "distance" implies something more than degrees of genealogical distance stated by components 12 and 13. Ethnographically, there is less kinship with distance.

A similar problem seems to me to characterize the affinals. I suggest that there is only one set of affinal terms, *my husband* and *my wife,* and that the primacy of the solidary bond between *husband* and *wife* accounts for all of the other usages. The spouse of a consanguineal, *my aunt's husband* for instance, is joined to that consanguineal because of the primacy of the conjugal bond between them, but that does not make the spouse kinsman to Ego. The derivative set formed by the *-in-law* modifier falls into this uncertain limbo too, and the reader will have noticed that Goodenough's *-in-law* is easily transformed into my *in-laws.* The first is a modifier for the group 1 terms. The second is used to cover anyone connected in any way by marriage (consanguineals of my affinals, spouses of my consanguineals, consanguineals of the spouses of my consanguineals) and corresponds to that part of the American definition of a kinsman which says ". . . anyone related by marriage . . . ."

The areas which I see as problematic derive this quality from the fuzzy boundary and fade-out principles. It is just because kinship and kinsmen in American are defined by the interaction of two distinct criteria that the effect is to create a scale along which there is more or less kinship, along which some are certainly kinsmen and others are "too far away to count."

There is another way in which these two problems can be stated, which raises an important question for componential analysis. The point was made that the basic kinship terms are "all kinship term" (*father* for instance) while the derivative sets are "half a kinship term" (*father-in-law* for instance), and that this seems to symbolize the fade-out principle.

As there is no clear boundary between kinship and nonkinship, relative and nonrelative, so too there seems to be no clear boundary between kinship terms and nonkinship terms. Is the lexeme *father-in-law* a kinship term or a regular "term for a kinsman"?

Goodenough says that the analysis and description in this paper are confined to ". . . kinship expressions . . ." and only to those which are ". . . used in reference . . . ." The data analyzed, furthermore, have only to do with the situation in which someone inquires of another, not in the presence of the person being inquired about, 'What kin-relationship, if any, is he (she) to you?' This invites the answer 'He (she) is my _____' or 'He (she) is not a relative.' This, then, is the control question, and this control question defines the semantic domain which is the object of the analytic procedures. Finally analysis is concerned only with the lexemes of the terminological system.

This componential analysis of Yankee kinship terminology is really aimed at a semantic domain. The semantic domain is defined by the control question, the frame within which the domain is contained and by which it is defined. The question of whether *father-in-law* is a kinship term is perhaps related to the title of Goodenough's paper, but is not immediately relevant to its content. It is presumably for this reason that there is no analysis of the word "father" insofar as this refers to a priest. One cannot say of a priest, "What kinship relationship, if any, is he to you?" and have the proper answer given, "He is my father" for the proper and true answer is "He is not a relative; he is a priest."

The title of Goodenough's paper is, therefore, misleading if it implies that it is *kinship terminology* which is being analyzed. It is, to be precise, the semantic domain defined by the control question insofar as that semantic domain is internally differentiated by something like kinship terms. It is *not* an analysis of terms for kinsmen. It is *not* an analysis of kinship terms. It is an analysis of the way in which kin types are classed by kinship terms.

Componential analysis defines the domain with which it deals in two different ways. First, it uses a control question. This control question in turn does two things. It segregates the responses it gets into or out of the domain it is dealing with so that, for instance, it is a "relative" or "it is not a relative"; it is kin or nonkin. The control question also provides the major grouping of the objects within the domain according to the terminological categories. So the answer to the control question may be "He is *my father*" or "She is *my aunt.*"

The second way in which componential analysis defines the domain is by treating the terminological categories as defined by the relative products which they differentiate. The kinship terminology is made up first of a group of primitives, and second groupings of relative products of these primitives, so that in American FaBr is among those relative products covered by the term *my uncle.*

Thus far, componential analysis defines what I would like to call an *analytic domain*. It is a way of setting up a standardized frame into which any particular culture might be more or less initially fitted for comparative purposes. It makes assumptions about the ways in which kinship systems are structured which may not be true in a particular case, but this need not be a problem since it is known in advance of any particular application.

If we say that the *semantic domain* is the particular domain as it is actually defined in a particular culture, then the *analytic domain* may thus be different from the *semantic domain* in some way or other.

This, of course, is precisely the problem with which the Yankee terminology presents us. The analytic domain assumes that the control question can separate kin and nonkin, the semantic domain of American kinship is not so easily partitioned. Because of the way the control question is stated, there is no way to find this out beforehand. That is, there is no device built into the analytic apparatus that requires the analyst to ask about this before he decides or to take note of the discrepancy in any way.

The second problem which the Yankee terminology presents is that the analytic domain assumes that the categories in the semantic domain can be defined in terms of relative products or kin types, and that such relative product definitions contain the components which differentiate the system. This turns out to be only partly true for American kinship.

Ethnographically, as I have said, the affinal kin types in Goodenough's group 2 are not really affinal kin types. Yet to treat them as affinal kin types is reasonable in terms of the assumptions built into the analytic domain since they are describable in relative product terms. Thus FaBrWi is a logical relative product, and the natives even allow that she is related as *my aunt.*

But to see these kin types, these relative products, as affinal kin types is to project a definition of affinity onto the American system which it does not have. It imposes an alien definition onto the cultural data and then analyzes the alien definition as if it were a part of American culture. To impose an alien definition onto cultural data and then to analyze it componentially does not seem a sound procedure. To regard affinal kin types in group 2 as affinals is to create an analytic problem which is not there, and it is the creation of this problem which makes the analysis, as it appears in Tables 6 and 10, so cumbersome. The system is really very much simpler than these tables suggest.

This is a vital point. Another example will be helpful. Let us assume that a careful inspection of various data lead one to believe that the kin terms *my husband* and *my wife* can be stated with reference to *my son* and *my daughter*. The phrase "she is the mother of my children" is not unheard of in American, and "he is the father of my child" is its complement. *My husband* and *my wife*, given Goodenough's ethnography (on pp. 259–261), might be defined now in terms of relative products as SoFa, DaFa (or ChFa), and SoMo, DaMo (or ChMo), where Fa = genitor and Mo = genetrix.

This should then permit me to say that *my husband* and *my wife* are consanguineal terms, terms for consanguines, and this should not surprise us in the least since it is not uncommon. The Nuer do this. A man's wife's father becomes a consanguineal kinsman on the birth of the first child, for they can now regard him as my child's mother's father. This is logically possible in both Nuer and American. Further, the usage "grandfather" and "grandmother" sometime after the couple's first child for the spouse's father and mother is not unheard of in American, and this might lend some support to the notion that these are consanguineals.

By relative product definitions, using a genealogical model, it is possible to make spouse = child's parent and to treat spouse as a consanguineal relative, and therefore to treat the terms *my husband* and *my wife* as consanguineal kin terms. But in ethnographic or cultural fact, Americans refuse to do this even when it is logically possible. They accept the argument that the spouse is related by blood or by birth through their child but they laugh uncomfortably. Even when they say that they see the logic of this, when asked if they are related to husband or wife by blood through their child, they say that they suppose that they are but they just don't think of it that way.

An analytic domain is set up so that we shall have some standard and controllable way of approaching any particular culture to begin to find out how any particular domain is structured in that culture. If we knew in advance how each culture structures kinship there would be no point in studying it. We start, therefore, with the working assumption that kinship terminology is somehow related to relative products formed from primitives which have something to do with the regulation of the reproductive and child care functions in any society. Or we take some other working assumption as a way of beginning to find out what kinship is all about in that particular society. The next problem is to then see how closely or how differently the semantic domain of the particular culture fits our working assumption, in other words, to find out what the general boundaries of the semantic domain of that culture are.

This does not mean that one cannot take a rigid analytic frame and use it for systematic comparative purposes. One can, of course, but one should not mistakenly assume that the analytic domain is identical with the semantic domain. One can compare child care, for instance, or the domain of some equally nicely defined functional universe like food distribution in which we define food analytically and ignore the native definition of food. But this is a different problem from the one which Goodenough raises for Yankee and the problem which presently engages us.

My problem here is simply to point out that although we must have a way of approaching the semantic domain of the particular culture and the particular way in which it is structured, we should not insist that the analytic domain *is* the same as the semantic domain until we have first tested this assumption and second developed some evidence for it. Indeed, we cannot tell until the analysis is all over just what the semantic domain of a particular culture consists in and how it is structured. This is, after all, the goal of the analysis, not the point of its entry.

If componential analysis made any errors in dealing with the Yankee system, it did so as a result of assumptions imbedded in the analytic apparatus itself, and not as a result of poor ethnography or sloppy workmanship. The analytic apparatus, by assuming that a relative product definition of kin terms was adequate—an assumption based on the sharp break between kinship and nonkinship built into the control question—failed to see that an *uncle's wife* need not necessarily be an affine or a kinsman at all.

But the opposite is also true. It is precisely because Goodenough did not follow his analytic apparatus rigidly that the outcome is so very good. He did not follow it in two very important places. First, he consistently introduced data from sources other than his control question and he consistently used other kinds of data than merely relative products. Second, he in effect abandoned the criterion of accurate kin term prediction as the basis for evaluating the adequacy of his analysis. At the very beginning of this analysis is the statement that, despite the fact that Wallace's 1962 analysis accurately predicted kin term applications in his Yankee system, intuitive factors led him to feel that it was not adequate.

If one final critical point can be made it is this. Componential analysis has a way of finding out what kin terms are distributed across what universe of kin types. It needs some way to inquire *systematically* into the definition of kinship and into the question of where and when kin type or relative product definitions of kin terms cease to be relevant at the level of the semantic domain as against the analytic domain. Whether greater flexibility is needed in eliciting techniques, or a better analytic domain, I cannot say here.

NOTES

[1] Since "So What!" as a criticism is as much a statement about the critic's inability to see the implications of the analysis as the failure of the analysis to have significant implications, it is a marginal consideration at best.

[2] The support of the National Science Foundation is gratefully acknowledged here. Most, though not all, of the data on which statements made here are based, were collected during this project. Earlier work is reported in Schneider and Homans 1955. The comments and suggestions that Paul Friedrich has made in many conversations and discussions and on a draft of this paper are acknowledged with gratitude. I have assimilated many ideas from him which I am unable to acknowledge individually. The views in this paper are expanded and modified in Schneider (1968). This later version employs a different treatment of basic versus modified terms, and sets forth additional ethnographic details differing from those in Goodenough's paper.

[3] I will ignore the fifth set which Goodenough singles out, *ancestor, ancestress, descendent,* since it is possibly a set of cover terms, like parent, child, sibling and not a set of basic terms. Indeed, the argument seems sound to me that to qualify as basic a term must be a *modifiable* consanguineal term, and *ancestor* is not modifiable.

[4] Incidentally, this is one of the places in the definitions where the phrase "a relationship" (". . . established a relationship . . .") appears, and this very significant phrase could perhaps have been more fully explored with the informant.

[5] The classification of affinals as CA, CAC, CACA, etc., is taken with slight modification directly from Paul Friedrich's extremely useful paper (1964).

[6] I first used the notion of Pattern of Solidary Emphasis, and noted the solidary primacy of the conjugal pair, in a paper to the Seminar on Nonunilineal Kinship, March 20, 1959, at the Center for Advanced Study (multilithed). Goodenough and I are in complete agreement on this ethnographic point. Compare his statement, "That the terms for affinal kin types fit so perfectly within the same fourfold division underscores the primacy in Yankee kinship of the relationship between husband and wife together as alter Egos at the center of their respective and overlapping personal kindreds." What we are not in perfect agreement about is the interpretation of affinal kin types and relations.

[7] Paul Friedrich differs on this point, saying that -*in-law*, and -*step*, in particular are part of the domain of kinship nomenclature, just as *father* is primarily a kinship term although used in other contexts. He feels that my kinship-term/non-kinship-term dichotomy is not tenable in its present, sharp form. I am reluctant to agree with him, yet concede that his argument has weight.

REFERENCES CITED

Friedrich, Paul, 1964, Semantic structure and social structure: an instance from Russian. *In* W. H. Goodenough, ed., Explorations in cultural anthropology. New York, McGraw-Hill.

Schneider, David M., 1968, American kinship: a cultural account. Englewood Cliffs, N.J., Prentice-Hall.

——, G. C. Homans, 1955, Kinship terminology and the American kinship system. American Anthropologist 57:1194–1208.

Rethinking 'Status' and 'Role': Toward a General Model of the Cultural Organization of Social Relationships

Ward H. Goodenough

INTRODUCTORY COMMENT

This examination of the concepts 'status' and 'role' arises from my concern with a problem in ethnographic description.[1] It is the problem of developing methods for processing the data of field observation and informant interview so as to enhance the rigor with which we arrive at statements of a society's culture or system of norms such that they make social events within that society intelligible in the way that they are intelligible to its members. My thinking about this problem has been inspired largely by structural linguistics, a discipline that has achieved a high degree of rigor in formulating descriptive statements of the normative aspects of speech behavior. I have found it useful to look upon the cultural content of social relationships as containing (among other things) 'vocabularies' of different kinds of forms and a 'syntax' or set of rules for their composition into (and interpretation as) meaningful sequences of social events.

This orientation was explicit in my account of the social organization of Truk (Goodenough 1951). Out of it developed my later work with 'componential analysis' in what might be called descriptive or structural semantics (Goodenough 1956, 1957),[2] representing an approach to constructing valid models of the categorical aspects of social norms. Here, I shall elaborate another analytical method that was first suggested in my Truk report, one aimed at a grammatical aspect of normative behavior. Hopefully it will enable us to make systematic and exhaustive descriptions of the cultural domain embraced by the expressions 'status' and 'role.'

THE POINT OF DEPARTURE

Ralph Linton (1936:113–114) defined statuses as 'the polar positions . . . in patterns of reciprocal behavior.' A polar position, he said, consists

From M. Banton, ed., *The Relevance of Models in Social Anthropology*. London, Tavistock Publications. Used by permission of the author and Associated Book Publishers, Ltd.

of 'a collection of rights and duties'; and a role is the dynamic aspect of status, the putting into effect of its rights and duties.

Unfortunately, Linton went on to discuss statuses not as collections of rights and duties but as categories or kinds of person. All writers who do not treat status as synonymous with social rank do much the same thing,[3] including Merton (1957:368–370) in his important refinement of Linton's formulation. All alike treat a social category together with its attached rights and duties as an indivisible unit of analysis, which they label a 'status' or 'position' in a social relationship. This lumping together of independent phenomena, each with organizations of their own, accounts, I think, for our apparent inability to exploit the status-role concepts to our satisfaction in social and cultural analysis.[4] For example, my brother is my brother, whether he honors his obligations as such or not. A policeman's conduct in office may lead to social events that formally remove him from office, but it does not determine in any direct way whether he is a policeman or not. Other social transactions determine what his social category or identity actually is. Furthermore, there are legislative transactions that can serve to alter the rights and duties that attach to the category policeman in its dealings with other categories without the defining characteristics of the category being in any way altered. What makes him legally and formally a policeman need not have been affected.

These considerations have led me to break with established sociological practice. I shall consistently treat statuses as combinations of right and duty only. I shall emphasize their conceptual autonomy from social 'positions' in a categorical sense by referring to the latter as *social identities*. I would, for example, speak of ascribed and achieved identities where Linton (1936:115) speaks of 'ascribed' and 'achieved' statuses. In accordance with Linton's original definition, then, the formal properties of statuses involve (1) what legal theorists call rights, duties, privileges, powers, liabilities, and immunities (Hoebel 1954:48–49) and (2) the ordered ways in which these are distributed in what I shall call *identity relationships*.

RIGHTS AND DUTIES

Rights and their duty counterparts serve to define boundaries within which the parties to social relationships are expected to confine their behavior. Privileges relate to the areas of option within these boundaries. For example, when I am invited out to dinner, it is my hostess's right that I wear a necktie; to wear one is my duty. It is also her right that its decoration be within the bounds of decency. But she has no right as to how it shall be decorated otherwise; it is my privilege to decide this without reference to her wishes. For status analysis, the boundaries (the rights and duties) command our attention and not the domain of idiosyncratic freedom (privileges).

As for powers, they and their liability counterparts stem from privileges, while immunities result from rights and the observance of duties. None of them needs to be treated as a feature of status relationships that requires analysis independent of the analysis of rights and duties.

As used in jurisprudence, rights and duties are two sides of the same coin. In any relationship A's rights over B are the things he can demand of B; these same things are what B owes A, B's duties in the relationship. Therefore, whenever we isolate either a right or a duty, we isolate its duty or right counterpart at the same time.[5]

A great deal of social learning in any society is learning one's duties to others, both of commission and omission, and the situations in which they are owed. They are matters that informants can talk about readily; they have words and phrases for them. The methods of descriptive semantics (componential analysis), referred to above, should provide a suitable means for describing the actual content of specific rights and duties with considerable rigor. But even without this, once we have established the existence of a duty for which our informants have a word or expression in their language, we can explore its distribution in identity relationships without our necessarily having its exact content clearly defined. The informant knows what he is talking about, if we as investigators do not.

SOCIAL IDENTITIES

A social identity is an aspect of self that makes a difference in how one's rights and duties distribute to specific others. Any aspect of self whose alteration entails no change in how people's rights and duties are mutually distributed, although it affects their emotional orientations to one another and the way they choose to exercise their privileges, has to do with personal identity but not with social identity. The utility of this distinction is clear when we consider the father-son relationship in our own society. The status of the social identity 'father' in this relationship is delimited by the duties he owes his son and the things he can demand of him. Within the boundaries set by his rights and duties it is his privilege to conduct himself as he will. How he does this is a matter of personal style. We assess the father as a person on the basis of how he consistently exercises his privileges and on the degree to which he oversteps his status boundaries with brutal behavior or economic neglect. But as long as he remains within the boundaries, his personal identity as a stern or indulgent parent has no effect on what are his rights and duties in this or any other relationship to which he may be party.

Every individual has a number of different social identities. What his rights and duties are varies according to the identities he may appropriately assume in a given interaction. If John Doe is both my employer and my subordinate in the National Guard, then the duties I owe him depend on whether I assume the identity of employee or of company commander in dealing with him. We tend to think of duties as things we owe to individual alters, but in reality we owe them to their social identities. In the army, what we *owe* a salute is 'the uniform and not the man.' Furthermore, what duties are owed depends on ego's and alter's identities taken together and not on the identity of either one alone, as Merton (1957:369) has observed. In our society, for example, a physician's rights and duties differ considerably depending on whether he is dealing with another physician, a nurse, a patient, or the community and its official representatives. If a status is a collection of rights and duties, then the social identity we label 'physician' occupies a different status in each of these identity relationships. Failure to take account of the identities of alters and to speak in general terms of the status of a chief or employer has been responsible for much of the apparent lack of utility of the status-role concepts.[6]

Another source of difficulty has been a tendency for many analysts to think of the parties to status relationships as individual human beings. This mistake invites us to overlook the identity of the alter in those relationships where the alter is a group and not an individual. Obviously, communities, tribes, and nations become parties to status relationships when they make treaties with one another and when they enter into contracts with individuals and subgroups within their memberships. Criminal law, as it is usually defined, concerns the duties that individuals and corporations[7] owe the communities of which they are members. Animals, inanimate objects, and purely imaginary beings may also possess rights and/or owe duties.

IDENTITY SELECTION

As Linton (1936:115) aptly observed, some identities are 'ascribed' and some 'achieved.' He was talking about how one comes to possess a particular social identity as a matter of social fact. How is it that one comes to *be* a professor or a married man, for example? Everyone has many more identities, however, than he can assume at one time in a given interaction. He must select from among his various identities those in which to present himself.[8]

As regards some identities, of course, there is no choice. Having reached a certain age, I have a duty as a member of my society to present myself as an adult and as a man in all social interactions to which I may be party. However, I am under no obligation to present myself as a professor of anthropology in all interactions. Quite the contrary.

Several considerations govern the selection of identities.

An obvious consideration is an individual's (or group's) qualifications for selecting the identity.[9] Does he in fact possess it? He may masquerade as a policeman, for example, donning the symbols that inform others of such an identity, and yet not be one. People often pretend to social identities for which they are not personally qualified, but such pretence is usually regarded as a serious breach of one's duties to fellow-members of one's peace group, duties that attach to one's identity as a member of a human community.

Another consideration is the occasion of an interaction. For any society there is a limited number of culturally recognized types of activity. The legitimate purposes of any activity provide the culturally recognized reasons for interactions, and they in turn define occasions. The same individuals select different identities in which to deal with one another depending on the occasion. For example, I may call upon someone who is in fact both my physician and my personal friend because I wish to be treated for an illness or because I wish to invite him to dinner. The purpose that specifies the occasion for the interaction determines whether I assume the identity of 'patient' or 'personal friend' in approaching him.[10]

The setting, as distinct from the occasion, might also seem to be an obvious consideration in identity selection. For example, the same individual may or may not assume the identity of chairman of a meeting depending on what other persons are present, but here we are really dealing with the factor of qualifications for assuming an identity, already mentioned. Or again, when I invite my physician friend to dinner, how I approach him depends on whether or not one of his patients is a witness to the transaction, but this is not so much a matter of identity selection as it is a matter of choosing among alternative ways of honoring one's duties and exercising one's privileges. I suspect that settings are more likely to affect how one conducts oneself in the same identity relationship than to govern the selection of identities, but this is a matter requiring empirical investigation.

An important consideration is that, for any identity assumed by one party, there are only a limited number of matching identities available to the other party. If two people enter an interaction each assuming an identity that does not match the one assumed by the other, they fail to establish a relationship. The result is ungrammatical, and there is social confusion analogous to the semantic confusion that results from story-completion games in which no one is allowed to know anything but the last word that his predecessor in the game has written down. We take care to employ various signs by which to communicate the identities we wish to assume, so that others may assume matching ones and we can interact with mutual understanding.[11] Any pair of matching identities constitutes an *identity relationship*.

It is noteworthy that different identities vary as to the number of identity relationships that are grammatically possible for them within a culture. But in all cases the number appears to be quite limited. Thus in my culture the identity relationships 'physician-physician,' 'physician-nurse,' 'physician-patient' are grammatical, but there is no such thing as a 'physician-wife' relationship or a 'physician-employee' relationship. The physician must operate in the identity 'husband' with his wife and in the identity 'employer' with his employees.

Finally, we must consider that the parties to a social relationship do not ordinarily deal with one another in terms of only one identity-relationship at a time. The elderly male physician does not deal with a young female nurse in the same way that a young male physician does, and neither deals with her as a female physician does. In other words, identities such as old adult, young adult, man, and woman are as relevant as are the identities physician and nurse. Some identities are relevant to all social interactions. In my culture, for example, I must always present myself to others as an adult and as a male. This means that I am ineligible for any identity that is incompatible with being adult and male. Among the various identities that I do possess and that are compatible with these two, not all are compatible with one another, nor are they always mutually exclusive as to the occasions for which they are appropriate. The result is that for any occasion I must select several identities at once, and they must be ones that can be brought together to make a grammatically possible composite identity. In order to avoid confusion I shall reserve the term identity for anything about the self that makes a difference in social relationships, as defined earlier. The composite of several identities selected as appropriate to a given interaction constitutes the selector's *social persona* in the interaction.[12]

The selection of identities in composing social relationships, then, is not unlike the selection of words in composing sentences in that it must conform to syntactic principles governing (1) the arrangement of social identities with one another in identity relationships, (2) the association of identities with occasions or activities, and (3) the compatibility of identities as features of a coherent social persona.

IDENTITY RELATIONSHIPS
AND STATUS RELATIONSHIPS

For each culturally possible identity relationship there is a specific allocation of rights and duties. The duties that ego's identity owes alter's identity define ego's duty-status and alter's right-status. Conversely, ego's right-status and alter's duty-status are defined by the duties that alter's identity owes ego's identity. As we shall see, one cannot deduce alter's duties from a knowledge of only ego's, except when both identities in a relationship are the same. In two separate identity relationships, ego may have the same duty-status and different right-statuses or the same right-status and different duty-statuses. When we examine the distributions of rights and duties among a society's identity relationships, we must look at every relationship twice and observe how the rights and duties are allocated from the point of view of each participating identity independently.

Every pair of reciprocal duty-statuses (or corresponding right-statuses) constitutes a *status relationship*. As we shall see, the same status relationships may be found to obtain in quite different identity relationships. We have already observed that the same identity may be in different status relationships according to the different identity relationships into which it can enter. These observations demonstrate that the structure of a society's status relationships must be analyzed and described in different terms from those that describe the structure of its identity relationships. A culturally ordered system of *social relationships*, then, is composed (among other things) of identity relationships, status relationships, and the ways in which they are mutually distributed.

THE ANALYSIS OF STATUSES

How duties distribute in the identity relationships in which people participate is a function of at least several independent considerations. For any identity relationship in which we participate in our society, for example, we must ask ourselves how much (if any) deference we owe? How much (if any) cordiality, reverence, and display of affection? How much sexual distance must we maintain? How much emotional independence? These are only some of the considerations that are relevant for the allocation of rights and duties among us. Each one of them presumably represents a single dimension of status difference in our culture's organization of status relationships. If this is so, then the several duties that in different combinations indicate socially significant differences along one such dimension will be mutually distributed in identity relationships according to the patterns of a 'Guttman scale' (Guttman 1944, 1950; Goodenough 1944).

For purposes of illustration here, I shall confine discussion to the simplest scale pattern. Suppose that the duties expressing lowest degree of deference are most widely distributed in identity relationships; suppose that the duties expressing the next higher degree of deference are next most widely distributed and only in relationships in which duties expressing the lowest degree are also owed; and suppose that duties expressing the highest degree of deference are distributed in the fewest relationships, and in all of them duties expressing lesser degrees of deference are also owed. With such successively inclusive distributions, both the social identities for every identity-relationship in which they occur and the duties expressive of deference can be ranked simultaneously against each other in a special type of matrix table known as a 'scalogram' (Guttman 1950; Suchman 1950). Our ability so to rank them is the empirical test that the duties in question are distributed in accordance with a scale pattern and that they are indeed functions of one consideration or status dimension.

We anticipate, therefore, that analysis of scales will provide a means whereby we can empirically determine what duties are functions of the same dimension and at the same time discover the minimum number of dimensions needed to account for the distribution of all culturally defined duties in a system of social relationships. As a result of such analysis, all the duties would be sorted into several distinct sets. The duties in each set would form a scale, but those in different sets would not.

Table 1 presents a hypothetical example of a scalogram such as one might obtain for one set of duties. Each distinctive combination of duties represents a different status on the status dimension represented. Identity relationships are grouped and ranked according to the combinations of duties owed by the ego-identity to the alter-identity in each, so that every identity relationship appears twice in the scalogram according to which of the two social identities in it is the ego-identity and which the alter-identity. Duties that have identical distributions and that do not, therefore, discriminate status differences on the scale are grouped into duty clusters.

The scale in Table 1 shows the distribution of duties for one person as ego in all the identity relationships in which he participates. Indeed, the procedure for gathering data for this kind of analysis requires that the informant be held constant, since there is no guarantee that different individuals have exactly the same conceptual organizations of status relationships. Data gathering and analysis must be done over again, independently, for each informant. The degree to which the resulting organizations of status relationships coincide indicates the degree of consensus among informants as to their expectations in social relationships.

Because status scales are worked out separately for each informant, they tend to be 'perfect' scales, in which no item is distributed in a way that is inconsistent at any point with the distributions of other items in the pattern of a scale. This makes the use of Guttman-scaling techniques much less complicated in the analysis of status relationships than is the case in attitude and opinion surveys, where many informants are asked the same set of questions relating to a single object and their different responses are plotted so as to rank the informants and the specific answers to the questions against each other simultaneously. Since different informants do not share the same cognitive organization of the subject under study in all respects, perfect scales cannot be obtained. Here, however, we are looking at how identity relationships and duties are simultaneously ranked against one another in the mind of one informant as revealed by the distribution of his answers. Under such circumstances almost perfect scales may reasonably be expected.

Table 1. Hypothetical Status Scale

STATUS (SCALE) TYPE	RELATIONSHIP EGO'S IDENTITY	ALTER'S IDENTITY	SPECIFIC ALTER	DUTIES AND DUTY CLUSTERS							
				I (1)	II (2)	III (3)	(4)	IV (5)	V (6)	(7)	VI (8)
1	A	X	a	Y	Y	Y	Y	Y	Y	Y	Y
	A	X	b	Y	Y	Y	Y	Y	Y	Y	Y
2	B	Y	c	Y	Y	Y	Y	Y	Y	Y	N
	B	Y	d	Y	Y	Y	Y	Y	Y	Y	N
	C	Z	e	Y	Y	Y	Y	Y	Y	Y	N
3	D	W	b	Y	Y	Y	Y	Y	N	N	N
	D	W	f	Y	Y	Y	Y	Y	N	N	N
4	D	Z	g	Y	Y	Y	Y	N	N	N	N
	E	G	h	Y	Y	Y	Y	N	N	N	N
	E	G	i	Y	Y	Y	Y	N	N	N	N
5	F	R	j	Y	Y	N	N	N	N	N	N
	R	F	k	Y	Y	N	N	N	N	N	N
	G	E	l	Y	Y	N	N	N	N	N	N
6	H	H	f	Y	N	N	N	N	N	N	N
	H	H	m	Y	N	N	N	N	N	N	N
	X	A	n	Y	N	N	N	N	N	N	N
	Y	B	o	Y	N	N	N	N	N	N	N
	I	N	p	Y	N	N	N	N	N	N	N
7	K	J	q	N	N	N	N	N	N	N	N
	J	K	r	N	N	N	N	N	N	N	N
	Z	C	s	N	N	N	N	N	N	N	N
	Z	D	t	N	N	N	N	N	N	N	N
	W	D	u	N	N	N	N	N	N	N	N
	M	I	v	N	N	N	N	N	N	N	N
	N	I	w	N	N	N	N	N	N	N	N
	I	M	m	N	N	N	N	N	N	N	N

KEY: Under 'relationship' capital letters represent specific social identities. The small letters represent specific alters. In the duty columns, Y indicates that the duty is owed by ego's identity to alter's identity, and N indicates that it is not owed. Alters b, f, and m appear in more than one identity relationship with ego. The entire scale is from the point of view of a single informant as ego.

AN EXAMPLE FROM TRUK

A scale from an informant on Truk (Goodenough 1951:113), reproduced in Table 2, provides a concrete example of a series of duties whose
distributions are functions of a single status dimension.[13] The duties are:

(a) to use the greeting *fääjiro* when encountering alter;
(b) to avoid being physically higher than alter in alter's presence, and
    therefore to crouch or crawl if alter is seated;
(c) to avoid initiating direct interaction with alter, to interact with him
    only at his pleasure;
(d) to honor any request that alter can make of ego, if alter insists;
(e) to avoid speaking harshly to alter or taking him personally to task
    for his actions;
(f) to avoid using 'fight talk' to alter or directly assaulting him, regard-
    less of provocation.

Each scale type in Table 2 corresponds to a status. Under scale type 7
are all those relationships in which none of these duties is owed (in which ego
is in duty-status 7 to alter), and under scale type 1 are those relationships in
which all the duties are owed (in which ego is in duty-status 1 to alter).

The reason ego owes the four duties that mark statuses 1–4 is because
he is not supposed to 'be above' alter. The seven scale combinations of duty
express the degree to which ego is or is not forbidden from being above alter.
The dimension in question seems best characterized as one of deference.

This scale illustrates that knowledge of ego's duty-status and alter's
corresponding right-status does not allow one to deduce ego's right-status
and alter's duty-status in an identity relationship. In the relationships
'brother'—'sister' (man to *feefinej* and woman to *mwääni*) and husband—
wife (man to Wi and woman to Hu), both brother and husband are in duty-
status 7 on the scale and sister and wife are in right-status 7. But brother is
in right-status and sister in duty-status 2, whereas husband is in right-status
and wife in duty-status 7.

COMPOSITE STATUSES

Another dimension on which status distinctions are made in Truk is
that of sexual distance. The duty scale for this dimension is shown in Table 3
as it pertains to male-female kin relationships (it has not been worked out
exhaustively for all identity relationships). Obviously, whenever any Trukese man and woman interact, the identities in terms of which they compose
their behavior call for mutual placement simultaneously on both the deference and sexual distance scales—in two different status systems at the same
time. In any relationship, therefore, it appears that the duties owed are

Table 2.   Duty Scale of 'Setting Oneself Above Another' in Truk

SCALE TYPE	RELATIONSHIP IN WHICH DUTY OWED	MUST SAY FÄÄJIRO	MUST CRAWL	MUST AVOID	MUST OBEY	MUST NOT SCOLD	MUST NOT FIGHT
1	Non-kinsman to chief	Yes	Yes	Yes	Yes	Yes	Yes
	Non-kinsman to *jitag*	Yes	Yes	Yes	Yes	Yes	Yes
2	Man to female *neji*	No	Yes	Yes	Yes	Yes	Yes
	Man to Wi's *mwääni*	No	Yes	Yes	Yes	Yes	Yes
	Woman to So of *mwääni*	No	Yes	No(?)	Yes	Yes	Yes
	Woman to *mwääni*	No	Yes	Yes	Yes	Yes	Yes
	Woman to So of Hu's older *pwiij*	No	Yes	Yes	Yes	Yes	Yes
	Woman to Wi of *mwääni*	No	Yes	Yes	Yes	Yes	Yes
3	Man to older *pwiij*	No	No	Yes	Yes	Yes	Yes
	Woman to older *pwiij*	No	No	Yes	Yes	Yes	Yes
4	Man to male *neji*	No	No	No	Yes	Yes	Yes
	Man to Wi of older *pwiij*	No	No	No	Yes	Yes	Yes
	Woman to Da of *mwääni*	No	No	No	Yes	Yes	Yes
	Woman to Da of Hu's *pwiij*	No	No	No	Yes	Yes	Yes
	Woman to So of Hu's younger *pwiij*	No	No	No	Yes	Yes	Yes
	Woman to Da of Hu's *feefinej*	No	No	No	Yes	Yes	Yes
	Woman to So of Hu's *feefinej*	No	No	No	Yes	Yes	Yes
	Woman to Hu of older *pwiij*	No	No	No	Yes	Yes	Yes
	Woman to Da's Hu	No	No	No	Yes	Yes	Yes
	Woman to So's Wi	No	No	No	Yes	Yes	Yes
5	Man to younger *pwiij*	No	No	No	No	Yes	Yes
	Man to Wi's older *pwiij*	No	No	No	No	Yes	Yes
	Woman to younger *pwiij*	No	No	No	No	Yes	Yes
	Woman to So of *pwiij*	No	No	No	No	Yes	Yes
	Woman to Hu's older *pwiij*	No	No	No	No	Yes	Yes
6	Man to Wi of younger *pwiij*	No	No	No	No	No	Yes
	Woman to own So	No	No	No	No	No	Yes
	Woman to Hu's younger *pwiij*	No	No	No	No	No	Yes
7	Man to *semej*	No	No	No	No	No	No
	Man to *jinej*	No	No	No	No	No	No
	Man to *feefinej*	No	No	No	No	No	No
	Man to Hu of *feefinej*	No	No	No	No	No	No
	Man to Wi	No	No	No	No	No	No
	Man to Wi's younger *pwiij*	No	No	No	No	No	No
	Woman to *semej*	No	No	No	No	No	No
	Woman to *jinej*	No	No	No	No	No	No
	Woman to own Da	No	No	No	No	No	No
	Woman to Da of *pwiij*	No	No	No	No	No	No
	Woman to Hu	No	No	No	No	No	No
	Woman to Hu of younger *pwiij*	No	No	No	No	No	No
	Woman to Hu's *feefinej*	No	No	No	No	No	No

KEY: Abbreviations are: Da, daughter; Hu, husband; So, son; and Wi, wife. The Trukese terms designate categories of kin. English kin terms are used only to subdivide the Trukese kinship categories when behavioral distinctions are made within them.
SOURCE: adapted from Goodenough 1951:113

Table 3.   Status Scale of Sexual Distance in Truk

STATUS OR SCALE TYPE	EGO IN RELATION TO ALTER	AVOIDANCE DUTIES				
		Sleep in Same House	Be Seen in Company	See Breasts Exposed	Have Inter-course	Joke Sexually in Public
1	Man with *feefinej*	F	F	F	F	F
2	Man with female *neji* (except Da of Wi's *mwääni*)	A	A	F	F	F
3	Man with Da of Wi's *mwääni*	A	A	D	F	F
4	Man with consan-guineal *jinej*	A	A	A	F	F
5	Man with affinal *jinej*	A	A	A	D	D
6	Man with Wi	A	A	A	A	D
7	Man with *pwynywej* (other than Wi)	A	A	A	A	A

KEY: Abbreviations used are: A, allowed; D, disapproved; F, forbidden; Da, daughter; Wi, wife. The Trukese terms designate categories of kin.

SOURCE: Adapted from Goodenough 1951:117

functions not of one but of several status dimensions at once. Indeed, in every identity relationship in which a person participates he has a duty-status and a right-status on every status dimension in his culture's system of social relationships. The particular combination of duty-statuses occupied by an identity on all these dimensions at once in a given identity relation-ship is its composite duty-status (its Duty-Status with a capital D and S) in that relationship.

Table 4.   Hypothetical Table of all Status Dimensions

DIMENSIONS	A	B	C	D	·	·	N
	1	1	1	1	·	·	1
Numbered statuses for	2	2	2	2	·	·	2
each dimension	3	3	3	3	·	·	3
	4		4	4	·	·	4
	5		5	5	·	·	5
			6	6	·	·	6
			7	7			

A complete analysis of a system of social relationships should permit us to construct a table in which every column (A, B, C, D . . . N) represents a status dimension and each number in a given column represents a status (scale combination of duties) on that dimension, as shown in Table 4. From such a table we could write the formula for every possible composite duty-status (e.g. A3-B1-C6-D7 . . . N2). We could compile an inventory of all possible identity relationships and after each one give the formulae for the composite duty-statuses (or right-statuses) of each identity in the relationship. This would provide a corpus of materials on which further analysis of cultural structure could then be undertaken.

For one thing, we could see how identity relationships group into classes according to similarities of their reciprocal composite duty-statuses. We could do the same thing for each dimension separately and see the extent to which the same identity relationships bunch in the same classes from dimension to dimension. Cross-cultural differences in the organization of such syntactic classes could then be systematically explored.

For another thing, with Table 4 in mind, we are in a position to anticipate what I am certain research will show to be an interesting feature of the cultural organization of behavior, one that is responsible for a great deal of its apparent complexity. This has to do with the compatibility of the duties on different status dimensions for ready synthesis in a composite duty-status. Suppose, for example, that in terms of the possibilities in Table 4, the composite duty-status of identity X in relation to identity Y is A4-B2-C1-D1 . . . N4, and that the nature of one of the duties defining status B2 is such that honoring it precludes the possibility of honoring one of the duties in status C1. Some accommodation will have to be made in one of three possible ways: (1) one of the duties will have to be dropped in favor of the other; (2) one or both duties will have to be capable of being honored in more than one way, with allowance for the selection of compatible alternative modes of behavior; (3) both duties may be replaced by a distinctive third one that is simultaneously an alternative for both.

For example, it is my duty on certain occasions to rise when a lady enters the room. It often happens that I am for one reason or another unable to do so, in which case I have the alternative duty to ask pardon for not rising. Here are two distinctive ways of honoring the same duty with a clear order of preference (it is wrong for me to ask pardon for not rising if I am clearly able to rise).

It is obvious that problems of this kind must arise frequently in composing actual behavior, especially when we consider that interactions often involve not a single identity relationship but several at once, for on many occasions the social personae of the participant actors are likely to consist of more than one relevant identity. Interactions involving more than two actors create even further possibilities of conflict among duties. In any social system, therefore, we can anticipate that there will be orderly procedures for handling conflicts of this kind, procedures that can be stated in the form of rules not unlike the rules of *sandhi* and vowel harmony in some languages.[14]

ROLES

From the combinations in Table 4, we can readily describe all the composite duty-statuses and right-statuses for a given identity in all the identity relationships that are grammatically possible for it. The aggregate of its composite statuses may be said to constitute the identity's *role* in a sense a little less comprehensive than but otherwise close to Nadel's (1957) use of the term. It would be equivalent to a comprehensive 'role-set' in Merton's (1957:369) terms.

When we compare identities according to their respective roles, as thus defined, some identities will obviously be found to net more privileges (fewer duties) and/or more rights in all their identity relationships taken together than others. That is, the roles of some identities will have greater possibilities for gratification than the roles of others; some roles will allow more freedom of choice in action generally than others; and some will be more and some less cramping to particular personal styles of operation. Thus, different identities may be said to have different functions in the social system as a whole and to enjoy different value accordingly. Just how they differ, and how these differences relate to informants' evaluations of them, can be precisely described in relation to the sets of formulae that characterize the several composite statuses possible for each.

FEASIBILITY OF THE METHOD

To map out a social system in this way may be possible in theory, but is it not too time-consuming and tedious for investigator and informant alike? Certainly, collecting data of this kind is tedious. Nevertheless, Mahar (1959) was able to get a purity-pollution or ritual distance scale from eighteen different informants in Khalapur, India, with very satisfactory results, neatly solving the difficult problem of empirically determining local caste rankings and the degree of cross-caste agreement in these rankings.[15] Her experience, added to my own from Truk, is encouraging.

But, we may ask, in any society we study, are there not so many duties, so many status dimensions, and so many identity relationships as to render the possibility of ever doing a complete analysis impracticable, however successful we may be in ferreting out a few scales? I do not think so. We are dealing with things that people manage to learn in the normal course of their lives without the benefit of systematic data collection and analysis. They are not likely, therefore, to be so complicated as to defy analysis.

On this point, findings in the psychology of cognition are highly suggestive. George Miller (1956) has called attention to impressive evidence that the human capacity to make judgements about where to class stimuli on unidimensional scales is severely limited. The greatest number of discriminations that can be made consistently on one dimension seems to be about seven (plus or minus two). In every interaction, on the basis of what he can observe of alter's behavior, ego has to make a judgement about where alter is putting him on every status scale, a judgement, that is, about the composite right-status that alter is ascribing to him in the relationship as alter perceives it. Ego may make these judgements for each dimension separately, but for any one dimension, the number of statuses about which he can make accurate judgements presumably will not exceed about seven. We expect, therefore, that no matter how many duties may fit into the same scale, the number of distinctive distribution combinations (scale types) they will show will be within this limit for any one status dimension. This means that when there are more than six duties in a set forming a scale, some will have identical distributions, producing duty clusters on the scale, as shown in Table 1. Seven is in fact the number of statuses I obtained for each of the two status scales from Truk (Tables 2 and 3). Mahar (1959), moreover, found that of the thirteen actions whose distributions were clearly a function of ritual distance, some had to be treated as equivalent, so that she could derive only seven scale types from them for the purpose of scoring status differences.

Proceeding from dimension to dimension, ego may make several successive judgements in assessing what composite status alter is ascribing to him. But even this procedure must become cognitively difficult and cumbersome if many status dimensions are involved.[16]

Finally, as complicatedly variable as human behavior seems to be, we must remember that the analysis outlined here is concerned only with duties (or rights). Many specific acts, I have suggested, are no more than different expressions of the same duty, like allomorphs of a morpheme in language. In this event their selection reflects syntactic rules of composition that are themselves ordered according to a limited number of principles. Much other variation in behavior reflects differences in behavioral styles, differences in the ways actors choose to elect their free options and exercise their privileges. Such variations need not concern us in deriving the formal properties of status systems.

These reasons lead me confidently to predict that the number of status dimensions in any system of social relationships will prove to be severely limited and that the number of statuses that are culturally discriminated on each dimension will prove to be in the neighbourhood of seven or less.

DUTY SCALES AS INSTRUMENTS
OF SOCIAL ANALYSIS

So far I have presented a method for constructing models of how specific cultures have organized social relationships. I have also considered the feasibility of the method. But crucial questions remain: What can we do with the models once we have constructed them? Are they just an intellectual game? Or do they enable us to understand things about behavior that eluded us before? Answer to these questions is provided by the duty scales from Truk.

Scaling duties allows us to see the circumstances under which a breach of duty will be regarded as more or less serious. We would assume from Table 2 that failure to honor a request would be least serious in Truk if alter were in right-status 4, the status in which this is the severest duty owed. It would be most serious if alter were in right-status 1, and there would be in-between degrees of seriousness if alter were in right-status 2 or 3. It is also possible that in those relationships in which a duty is the severest one owed, there is variation in the force of the obligation, its breach being forbidden in some instances and only disapproved in others. This is what we find in the second scale obtained from Truk (Table 3), one having to do with degrees of sexual distance (Goodenough 1951:117). If all four instances of 'disapproved' (D) in the scale were changed to 'forbidden' (F), eliminating this refinement, statuses 2 and 3 would merge, as would 4 and 5, and the total number of statuses discriminated on the dimension of sexual distance would be reduced from seven to five.

In every interaction, moreover, a Trukese ego has to decide to what extent he is forbidden from 'being above' alter and what is the appropriate cut-off point of his obligation on the duty scale shown in Table 2. If he wishes to flatter alter, he may act as if he were rendering one more duty than he feels is in fact required; and if he wishes to insult alter, he may render him one duty less. He must also decide what duties alter owes him and assess alter's behavior as proper, flattering, or insulting. The number of scale positions by which alter's behavior appears inappropriate measures the apparent degree of flattery or insult.

With this in mind, let us consider the occasion I encountered when an irate father struck his married daughter (right-status 2), to whom he owed all duties but the greeting *fääjiro*. Informants explained that he was angry, or he would not have done such a thing. Indeed, the fact that he was six points down the seven-point scale was a measure of how very angry he was. His daughter, it happened, was a self-centered and disagreeable young woman, whose petulant behavior had been getting on her kinsmen's nerves for some time. A good, hard jolt was just what she deserved. Being struck by her brother or husband, who were under no obligation not to strike her,

would have had little dramatic impact. That her father struck her, however, the last man in the world who should, this was something she could
not dismiss lightly. What provoked the incident was her indulgence in an
early morning tirade against her husband whom she suspected of having
just come from an amorous visit to her lineage sister next door. It is a
Trukese man's privilege to sleep with his wife's lineage sisters (he is in
duty-status 7 to them in Table 3), and men and women are not supposed
to show any feelings of jealousy when this privilege is exercised. Her shriek-
ing outburst against her husband, therefore, was another example of the
'spoiled child' behavior that made her unpleasant to live with. Witnesses
seemed to relish her undoing as full of what we would call 'poetic justice.'
I could not possibly have understood why they did so, if I had not already
worked out the status scale of 'being above' another. Nor would I have been
able to anticipate the feelings of shocked horror that people would have
exhibited had the same act been performed in other circumstances. Indeed,
relations between one informant and his older brother had been severely
strained for about a year, because the former had violated his duties and
told off his older brother (right-status 4) when the latter had exercised his
privilege and struck their much older sister (right-status 7) in displeasure
over some small thing she had done.

Methods that allow us objectively to measure such things as anger,
insult, flattery, and the gravity of offenses, and that help us to appreciate
the poetic justice of events in alien cultural contexts, such methods, I sub-
mit, are not exercises in sterile formalism. They promise to be powerful
analytical tools. They encourage me to great optimism about the possibility
of developing considerable precision in the science of social behavior.

NOTES

[1] This is a revised and expanded version of a paper entitled "Formal Properties
of Status Relationships" read at the Annual Meeting of the American Anthropological Association, 16 November 1961.

[2] For other contributions to this type of semantic analysis, see Conklin (1955,
1962a, 1962b), Frake (1961, 1962), Lounsbury (1956), Wallace and Atkins (1960).

[3] This has been thoroughly documented by Atkins (1954).

[4] The concepts have been useful for collecting and organizing data in studies of
specific social positions or limited social settings (e.g. Gross, Mason, and McEachern
1958), but they have not proved helpful in the analysis of social systems as wholes,
as Nadel (1957) has observed. See also the critique by Goffman (1961:91–95).

[5] Rights and duties correspond in part to what Nadel (1957:56) called the
"passive" and "active" attributes of roles respectively. It should be noted that some
writers have misunderstood the idea that each right has a duty counterpart by inter-

preting it as meaning that privilege also carries responsibility in the sense of *noblesse oblige*. This notion is peculiar to the former system of social 'estates' in Western Europe and is demonstrably without utility for social and juridical analysis.

⁶ This calls attention to an unfortunate tendency in the literature to treat statuses as properties of social identities and to talk about the status of a chief or employer without specifying the identity of the alter. Recognizing this problem, Nadel (1957) separated the concepts of status and role. By his definition, 'the role concept is basically a type or class concept' that 'labels and brings together numbers of individuals—human beings in our case—in virtue of certain properties they have in common' (1957:22). As he goes on to discuss it, it is clear that for him a role encompasses what I am calling a social identity and all the things associated with it, as well. He uses the term 'status' more narrowly as referring to the 'particular sets of rights and obligations falling to persons' (1957:29), but without specific regard to identity relationships, making his 'status' equivalent to Merton's (1957:369) 'role set.' Although 'status' still lacks precision as he conceived it, by abandoning status and role as complementary concepts (one the dynamic aspect of the other) and by restoring to 'role' a meaning more like that of ordinary or dramatistic usage, Nadel brought into sharper focus a useful analytical entity. How it relates to status, as I treat it here, will be clarified below.

⁷ Whenever a group is conceived as a unit having a status apart from the statuses of the individuals comprising its membership—that is, as having rights and duties pertaining to it as a party to a relationship—the group is a *corporation* for the duration of the relationship in which it enjoys status.

⁸ The sum of all the identities that a person has in social fact and in which he may legitimately choose to operate correspond to what Merton has termed a person's 'status-set' (in my terminology his identity-set).

⁹ The qualifications for a social identity are the conditions for being referred to by the linguistic expression that names the identity (Goodenough 1956).

¹⁰ Actually this example involves a further complication. Under the rules of my culture I can never approach a friend without acknowledging my recognition of our friendship. When consulting a physician for medical reasons, my dealings with him vary considerably depending on whether he is also a friend or not. This fusing of statuses attendant upon several different identity relationships that are in effect at the same time is an important matter to be considered below.

¹¹ The display of such signs, along with those that serve as credentials implying or verifying our qualifications for assuming certain identities, corresponds to what Goffman (1959:22) has termed the maintenance of 'front.' We try to assume ego-identities for which the culturally possible identity relationships accord us right-statuses and duty-statuses appropriate to the ends we wish to serve in the interaction (see the discussion of roles below).

¹² I am here using the term 'persona' in much the same sense as Goffman (1959:252) uses the term 'character' as distinct from 'performer.' Because of the many other connotations of Goffman's term in ordinary usage, it is unsuitable as a technical term.

¹³ The Trukese words in Tables 2 and 3 refer mostly to categories of kinsmen (kinship identities), which need not be explicated for present purposes. The interested reader will find them discussed at length elsewhere (Goodenough 1951, 1956).

¹⁴ For example, the phonology of Truk's language allows only for a limited number of consonant combinations in sequence without an intermediate pause. In composing phrases a speaker frequently puts together words such that one ends and the next begins with consonants that cannot occur in sequence. Either there must be a pause between them (as may happen in slow or deliberate speech), one of the consonants must undergo modification (e.g. *jesapw fejinnō* becomes *jesaf fejinnō*, *mejiwor nowumw* becomes *mejiwor rowumw*), or a vowel must be introduced according to rules of vowel harmony (e.g. *gaag cëk* becomes *gaagy cëk* whereas *jeen cëk* becomes *jeec cëk*). Thus for each word in Trukese there are several variant forms from among which selection is made according to the other words with which it is to be composed in an utterance.

¹⁵ I am grateful to Robert J. Smith for calling my attention to Mahar's paper.

¹⁶ Wallace (1961:463) suggests 'the numerical value of 2^6 for maximum size of folk taxonomies,' but whether or not this limit applies to systems of status relationships and, if so, how are matters that cannot be determined until we have a sample of these systems analyzed and described in the manner suggested here.

REFERENCES CITED

Atkins, John Richard, 1954, Some observations on the concept of 'role' in social science. Unpublished M.A. thesis, University of Pennsylvania.

Conklin, Harold C., 1955, Hanunóo color categories. Southwestern Journal of Anthropology 11:339–344.

———, 1962a, Lexicographical treatment of folk taxonomies. *In* Fred W. Householder & Sol Saporta, eds., Problems in lexicography. Supplement to International Journal of American Linguistics 28, No. 2. Indiana University Research Center in Anthropology, Folklore, and Linguistics, Publication 21.

———, 1962b, Comment (on The ethnographic study of cognitive systems). *In* Thomas Gladwin & William C. Sturtevant, eds., Anthropology and Human Behavior. Washington, D.C., Anthropological Society of Washington.

Frake, Charles O., 1961, The diagnosis of disease among the Subanunun of Mindanao. American Anthropologist 63:111–132.

———, 1962, The ethnographic study of cognitive systems. *In* Thomas Gladwin & William C. Sturtevant, eds., Anthropology and Human Behavior. Washington, D.C., Anthropological Society of Washington.

Goffman, Erving, 1959, The presentation of self in everyday life. New York, Doubleday.

———, 1961, Encounters: two studies in the sociology of interaction. Indianapolis, Bobbs-Merrill Company.

Goodenough, Ward H., 1944, A technique for scale analysis. Educational and Psychological Measurement 4:179–190.

———, 1951, Property, kin, and community on Truk. New Haven, Yale University Publications in Anthropology No. 46.

———, 1956, Componential analysis and the study of meaning. Language 32:195–212.

Goodenough, Ward H., 1957, Cultural anthropology and linguistics. Georgetown University series on language and linguistics No. 9, pp. 167–173.

Gross, Neal, Mason, Ward S. and McEachern, Alexander W., 1958, Explorations in role analysis: studies of the school superintendency role. New York, Wiley.

Guttman, Louis, 1944, A basis for scaling qualitative data. American Sociological Review 9:139–150.

———, 1950, The basis for scalogram analysis. Studies in social psychology in World War II, vol. 4, measurement and prediction, pp. 60–90. Princeton, Princeton University Press.

Hoebel, E. Adamson, 1954, The law of primitive man. Cambridge, Harvard University Press.

Linton, Ralph, 1936, The study of man. New York, Appleton-Century.

Lounsbury, Floyd G., 1956, A semantic analysis of the Pawnee kinship usage. Language 32:158–194.

Mahar, P. M., 1959, A multiple scaling technique for caste ranking. Man in India 39:127–147.

Merton, Robert K., 1957, Social theory and social structure (rev. and enlarged ed.). Glencoe, Illinois, The Free Press.

Miller, George A., 1956, The magical number seven, plus or minus two: some limits on our capacity for processing information. Psychological Review 63:81–97.

Nadel, S. F., 1957, The theory of social structure. Glencoe, Illinois, The Free Press.

Suchman, Edward A., 1950, The scalogram board technique for scale analysis. Studies in Social Psychology in World War II, vol. 4, Measurement and Prediction, pp. 91–121. Princeton, Princeton University Press.

Wallace, Anthony F. C., 1961, On being just complicated enough. Proceedings of the National Academy of Sciences 47:458–464.

Wallace, Anthony F. C. and Atkins, John, 1960, The meaning of kinship terms. American Anthropologist 62:58–80.

The Semantics of Icelandic Orientation

Einar Haugen

1. For some years now semantics has been in disrepute among responsible linguists, especially in America, thanks largely to the severe strictures passed upon it by Leonard Bloomfield. The standard set up by him for 'a scientifically accurate definition of meaning' included nothing less than 'a scientifically accurate knowledge of everything in the speaker's world' (1933:139). This admittedly impossible demand has naturally discouraged linguists from attempting many serious studies of the problems of meaning. In recent years some attempts have been made which one can only describe

From *Word*, 13:447–460 (1957). Used by permission of the author, the Linguistic Circle of New York, Inc., and the Johnson Reprint Corporation.

as half-hearted and highly speculative. Among these may be mentioned discussions by Eugene Nida (1951), C. C. Fries (1954), Rulon Wells (1954), and Shirô Hattori (1956). Nida provided a complete system of 'semes', dividing first into linguistic and non-linguistic meanings (linguisemes: ethnosemes), then each of these into semes (the meanings of morphemes), episemes (grammatical meanings), and macrosemes (the meanings of constructions). For each seme (in a particular context) he provided a sememe which was the sum of the related semes. Fries also divided into linguistic and non-linguistic (social-cultural) meanings, but included under the former both lexical and structural meanings. Wells does not offer any system for the classification of meanings, but makes a statement which may point toward a revision of the dominant Bloomfieldian view of meanings: 'I conclude that whatever Bloomfield's valid point may have been, we cannot accept his formulation of it.' Hattori's system uses sememe for the meaning of a word (or alternatively, a morpheme), but makes no provision for semes, episemes, or macrosemes, except that the overall meaning of a sentence is called a semasieme. None of these discussions goes very far in grappling with the basic question of how we know what the meaning of a form is, or how we can determine the number of semes or sememes which a form may have. Nida's system is the most elaborate, but there seems little value in having different names for the meanings of morphemes, taxemes, and constructions: it is not the meanings that are different, but the structures of the forms themselves, so that these names are generally redundant.

2. Bloomfield held out the prospect that the extension of scientific knowledge would enable us to make progress in semantics also. The model of definition, in his opinion, was the formula of the natural scientist: «We can define the names of minerals, for example, in terms of chemistry and mineralogy, as when we say that the ordinary meaning of the English word salt is 'sodium chloride (NaCl)' . . . » (1933:139). The catch here is in the word 'ordinary', which excludes all the meanings of salt that are ignored and remain largely unexplained by the scientific definition. It is of course possible to hand over to the anthropologists (a mythical body of men who will someday have analyzed everything men do) the task of defining the transferred uses of salt and similar words ('Ye are the salt of the earth'). But linguists will for a long time to come be asked to supervise the making of dictionaries, even though they have to cooperate with technicians in every field of knowledge to make them. Dictionaries are arranged by linguistic forms, not by the structure of the topics defined, and the definitions that go into them are the responsibility of linguists. Hence it should be profitable to explore the problems of semantics on a body of selected materials. As Bloomfield indicated, it may be helpful here to start with terms which are susceptible of scientific definition, or in other words, have measur-

able coordinates. This occurred to me while reading two valuable articles by Stefán Einarsson on terms of direction in Icelandic (1942, 1944). Here is a carefully collected body of information from a clearly-defined speech area concerning the meanings of the terms for the four cardinal directions (N E S W) and some others associated with them. These directions are easily determined in clear weather by any observant person and knowledge about them has been a part of western tradition as far back as we have any records. Yet Einarsson's study begins with the observation: 'There is perhaps no category of words that shows more dialectal difference of usage in Modern Icelandic than the words of orientation' (SE 37).[1]

3. Einarsson's studies bring out the fact that in addition to the meanings which jibe with the compass directions these words have meanings that vary from community to community.[2] In Einarsson's native valley of Breiðdalur in Southeast Iceland people speak of going *east* when they are actually going *northeast*, and contrast it, not with *west* but with *south*, when they are actually going *southwest* (SE 37). In the easternmost fjords of Iceland, however, the terms north and south were used approximately as on the compass. But no sooner does one pass into the northeast section than the terms are reversed, and east is used about southeast, while north is used about northwest. The reader is referred to Einarsson's articles for the details, which are sometimes quite startling, as when a man travelling directly south (from Strandir) may speak of himself as going north (to Húnavatnssýsla), or conversely, a man directed to go south (from Grindavík, on the Reykjanes peninsula) may find himself travelling due north (to Njarðvík (SE 43, 44). In his analysis of the materials Einarsson distinguishes between two kinds of meaning, the 'approximately correct' ones, which follow the compass, and the 'dialectal', also called 'pregnant', and sometimes 'incorrect' meanings, which do not. He finds a mixture of these meanings, not only in the present-day speech, but also in the sagas and other medieval texts, and he sets up tables to show the respective percentages in various sources. He discusses also the possibility of localizing sagas on the basis of their 'dialectal' terms, which might presumably betray the origin of their anonymous authors. The picture that emerges is of a usage in which all speakers retained as one meaning of the terms the 'correct' compass direction, and then added to it a confusing variety of other meanings, varying from community to community, and scarcely the same to any two speakers. It is as if one said that in Iceland N meant not only north, but also every other possible direction of the compass. If a man in Eyjafjörður says he is going N to Langanes, and the map shows that he will be travelling almost due E, then presumably one will have to say that E is one of the meanings of N, since it is, in Bloomfield's words, a part of the situation that calls forth this linguistic form. The linguist, however,

would like to raise some of the following questions and try to make the data answer them: are these meanings really as varied as they seem? Is the division into 'correct' and 'incorrect' entirely satisfactory? Are the 'pregnant' meanings truly dialectal, or can they be fitted into an overall, national system of orientation? Is it possible to reduce this multiplicity to a finite number of semes and sememes, with specified relationships in terms of their distributions? It will be the purpose of this paper to attempt an affirmative answer to this last question.

4. If we examine Einarsson's summary of the 'approximately correct usages,' they leave no doubt that the Icelanders know now the true cardinal directions and have known them since their emigration from Norway in the Ninth Century (SE 46, 282). Not only did they bring with them the terms *norðr, austr, suðr, vestr* and their derivatives, but they even had intermediate terms for finer discrimination, some of which were based on the contour of the Norwegian west coast: *landnorðr* 'NE', *útnorðr* 'NW', *landsuðr* 'SE', and *útsuðr* 'SW'. Newer terms have been created in some usages, such as *norðaustur* 'NE', etc.[3] Now in the absence of compasses it is obvious that these directions could be determined only by celestial observation. According to Einarsson this system is still used at sea, where celestial observation is the only one available. It is also used on maps, which by definition are oriented according to the cardinal directions. It is used about the weather, also a celestial phenomenon. But on the land usage is divided. It appears from Einarsson's data that celestial observation must also be the basis of orientation within an immediate neighborhood. One says e.g. north of the church (*fyrir norðan kirkjuna*) and this means the cardinal direction. There are also cases mentioned by Einarsson of tributary valleys distinguished as Norðurdalur and Suðurdalur in the midst of areas where E otherwise is substituted for N. The explanation here is presumably that the original naming took place under circumstances where valleys could be seen at once, say from their confluence or from the separating ridge, and a celestial observation made on the spot.

For the data show clearly that whenever such direct observation was impossible, the 'incorrect' orientation dominates. We may therefore hazard the guess that the 'incorrect' orientation is associated with coastwise travel (by land or sea) and can be correlated with the conformation of the land in Iceland.

5. This hypothesis is amply borne out by a careful study of the examples given. If we choose as a sample Einarsson's own native valley, we find that it is a fjord valley running NW to SE on the southeast coast of Iceland. Speakers in this valley needed to distinguish four directions, none

of which was cardinal: up and down the valley (which they called 'in' and 'out') and across the valley towards the next valley to the NE or towards the next valley to the SW. The former they called E and the latter S, thus contrasting two terms which normally are not opposites. Why these two, and not, say, N and W? The reason is clearly that the ultimate goal of the path that led them into the neighboring valleys was, respectively, E and S. It should be explained at this point that the cardinal terms are used regularly about all forms of travel into the respective quarters of Iceland. Travel from any point in one quarter to travel into another quarter is described in terms of the goal: E means going to Eastern Iceland, as administratively defined since 965 A.D. (Gjerset 1925:36).

In order to distinguish this kind of orientation from that which is used in the immediate neighborhood, we may say that there are two kinds of orientation: *proximate* and *ultimate*. Proximate orientation is based on celestial observations; but ultimate orientation is based on social practices developed in land travel in Iceland. Proximate orientation involves the immediate judgment of the eye. But ultimate orientation requires a different process. In the days when these usages were established, most travel in Iceland was on horseback over trails that crossed the valleys. Most of these valleys sent their rivers out to the roundish coast at approximately right angles, especially in the East and North. These trails were about as far from being straight lines, amenable to celestial orientation, as anything could be. Before reaching his goal, the traveller might have to proceed in all four directions of the compass as he turned and twisted to take advantage of gullies, plains, fords, slopes, and river courses, while avoiding the most rugged features of the landscape. But since Icelandic settlement consists of a thin line of localities around an uninhabitable central mass, the course taken by the traveller followed in general a line parallel to the coast. This line led all around the island into each of the four quarters, and anyone travelling along the line could say he was going in the direction of the next quarter until he actually arrived in that quarter.

6. While the direction to the next quarter might be in terms of that quarter, what about travelling within a quarter? We have seen that in Breiðdalur, Einarsson's valley, which is in the East quarter, the contrast was S (i.e. towards the South Quarter) and E, which here cannot mean 'towards the East quarter', since we are already in it. Einarsson informs us, however, that this usage goes on as far as Fáskrúðsfjörður, but here the 'approximately correct' designations of N and S appear, i.e. N takes the place of E. A glance at the map shows that this fits well with the geography: here the coast turns, as it were, a corner. The N-S usage continues northwards until one gets to Borgarfjörður, and here we find again the use of E, but now opposed to N instead of S. In other words, usage in the NE part

of the East Quarter is symmetrical with that of the SE part: in both areas
E is used of travel in the direction of the Easternmost valleys of Iceland.
But the opposite direction is N (i.e. toward the North Quarter) in the
NE, and S in the SE. The Easternmost valleys, from Fáskruðsfjörður to
Borgarfjörður, may accordingly be called the *orientation area* of the East
Quarter. Travel towards it is E, but travel within it is N-S, pointing respectively toward the North and the South Quarter, and this extends
throughout the rest of the East Quarter in both directions. The symmetry
is interrupted only by the interior area of Fljótsdalshérað (and Jökuldalur):
here is a district which borders on all three areas of the Eastern Quarter:
the NE, the E, and the SE. Travel to the first is N, to the second E, to the
third S, and in addition it uses 'out' about certain seacoast districts to the E.
The important aspect of this discussion is that the 'approximately correct'
orientation of the easternmost fjords falls into the pattern, not as a case of
celestial orientation, but as part of a system of ultimate orientation in terms
of the four quarters. Hence it is not 'correct' in Einarsson's sense, except by
coincidence; within an orientation area this is what we may expect.

7. This concept of an orientation area within a quarter as a center of
intensity for the ultimate orientation of travellers in the quarter can be
applied to the remaining quarters also. If we examine usage in the N quarter,
however, we are surprised to find that the orientation area is not the center
of the N quarter, its administrative seat, but the peninsula jutting out to
the north called Melrakkaslétta. Coming in both directions towards this
region (the district of Norðurþingeyjarsýsla) the term is N. A glance at the
map again shows why: this is the northernmost area of the North quarter.
Unfortunately we are not told what people in this district say: but one
might expect an 'approximately correct' East and West, parallel to the N-S
of the Eastern orientation area. In the part of the North Quarter that lies
to the west of the orientation area we might expect eastward travel to be
called N (which it is) and westward travel to be called W. This is true
when one gets west of Eyjafjörður, the deepest and most important of the
northern fjords.[4] But in the region east of Eyjafjörður the term 'in' (*inn*)
has taken the place of W. Two explanations are offered by Einarsson, of
which he prefers the second: (1) that the term refers to the depth of the
fjord (travel into a fjord was always 'in'); (2) that it refers to the social
dependence of the NE region on Eyjafjörður from the earliest times (in-
tensified by the growth of the city Akureyri in modern times). My own
preference would be for the first explanation, since Eyjafjörður is the deepest of all the northern fjords, and a natural ultimate orientation would include the notion of going into the fjord or the valley. But this is not susceptible of verification and is of little importance; both factors may have
contributed.

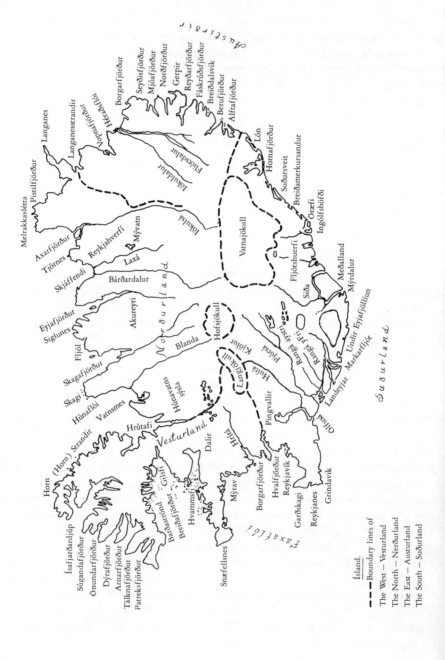

Ísland.
—— Boundary lines of
The West — Vesturland
The North — Nerðurland
The East — Austurland
The South — Suðurland

Austrátt

Borgarfjörður
Seyðisfjörður
Mjóafjörður
Norðfjörður
Gerpir
Reyðarfjörður
Fáskrúðsfjörður
Breiðdalsvik
Berufjörður
Álftafjörður

Vopnafjör

Héraðsflói

Langanes
Langanessrandir

Pistilfjörður

Jökuldalur
Fljótsdalur

Lón
Hornafjörður
Suðursveit
Breiðamerkursandur
Öræfi
Ingólfshöfði

Melrakkaslétta

Axarfjörður
Tjörnes
Skjálffendi

Reykjahverfi
Myvatn

Laxá

Bárðardalur

Jökulsá

Norðurland

Vatnajökull

Fljótshuerfi
Síða
Meðalland
Mýrdalur

Eyjafjörður
Siglunes

Akureyri

Hofsjökull
Blanda
Kjölur
Langjökull
Hekla

Rangá ytri
Rangá eystri

Þjórsá

Landeyjar
Markarfljót
Undir Eyjafjöllun

Suðurland

Fljöl
Skagafjörður
Skagi
Húnaflói
Vatnsnes
Hrútafi

Húnavatns
sysla

Vesturland
Dalir
Hvítá
Þingvallir

Ölfusá

Horn (Horn) Strandir
Gilsfi
Baðsströnd
Breiðafjörður
Hvammsfi
Myrav
Borgarfjörður
Hvalfjörður
Reykjavík
Garðskagi
Reykjanes
Grindavík

Ísafjarðardjúp
Súgandafjörður
Önundarfjörður
Dýrafjörður
Arnarfjörður
Tálknafjörður
Patreksfjörður

Snæfellsnes

Faxaflói

336

8. If we continue on to the West Quarter, it becomes apparent at once that the Orientation Area here is the extreme tips of the Vestfirðir, pointing to the NW and constituting the westernmost parts of Iceland. Information concerning usage within this orientation area is lacking. The actual directions in the West Quarter are often more N than W, but this is, as we have seen, not relevant. On the peninsula of Snæfellsnes *út* is substituted for W, which is also found in the Southern Quarter as we shall see, but this may here be due to the usual practice of calling movement towards the tip of a peninsula 'out.' The opposite to W (and *út*) is here S, if it leads towards the S quarter, N if it leads towards the N quarter. The Southern Quarter uses E for everything east of Reykjavík, but *út* for the opposite direction, instead of the expected W. This reflects two special situations in this quarter: (1) that the capital city Reykjavík is in the orientation area of the South Quarter, even though it lies in its extreme SW part and is not the southernmost part of the South Quarter; (2) that *út* is here used in a sense which the Icelanders carried with them from Western Norway, viz. W (but Njálssaga here has W and may represent the original usage). The skewing of the South Quarter is due in part to its completely different geography from the rest. Instead of a series of valleys opening up separately to the sea, we have here a wide, relatively level strip of land between an inhospitable coast and the inner wasteland. In this region the word *út* had little application in the sense of 'out to sea'; the usual route toward the sea led westward toward Reykjavík. Hence *út* took the place of west, but not in the sense of movement into the West Quarter, for which W was still used. The position of Reykjavík as a trading center for this whole area and the mecca of all Icelanders is reflected in its designation as S from all parts of the island. But actually, it is not even as an orientation the southernmost, for travel along the northern shore of the Reykjanes peninsula is considered S from Reykjavík; the opposite is 'in' (so that 'out' is sometimes used for S also).

9. It belongs in the picture to state that complementary to the four orientation areas there are four which we might call dis-orientation areas, or rather *transitional* areas between the four quarters. Between S and E, in the narrow strip of land between Vatnajökull and the sea, we learn that both *út* and *suður* are used for westward travel, thus combining usages of the S and E quarters (SE 40). But in the old Literature the usage of the S quarter is not found here, so that it may have spread eastward (SE 280). Between E and N there is the valley of Vopnafjörður, where it is reported that S is used for travel to the easternmost fjords, but E for the nearest area (SE 42). Between N and W the transition area is Strandir, the eastern coast of the Vestfirðir and administratively a part of the West Quarter. But the extreme northern extension of this coast has evidently led to an association of it with the North, and so there appears to be a divided usage,

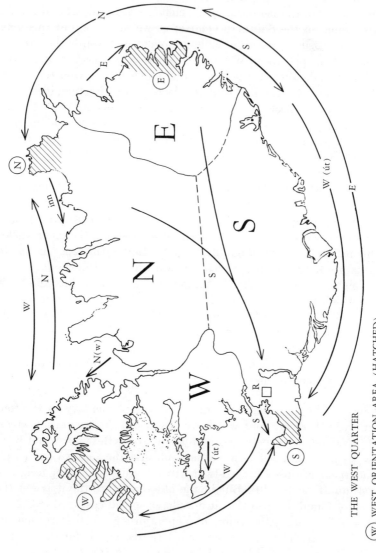

THE WEST QUARTER

Ⓦ WEST ORIENTATION AREA (HATCHED)

W̲ WESTWARD ORIENTATION

R REYKJAVIK

mostly N but also W (as in Héraðssaga Borgarfjarðar SE 43); cf. also *norðr vid Horn* from Sturlu Saga (269) and *norðarr á Strandir* from Reykdøla (SE 272). Travel from Strandir into the North Quarter is N even when it is almost due South. Between the W and the S Quarter Borgarfjörður appears to be transitional. In Breiðdalur and elsewhere in the E they call it S, but in the S Quarter they call it W; in Reykjavík usage W doesn't start before further West, and one says 'up' in Borgarfjörður, thus treating it as if it were part of the S Quarter (SE 45).

10. We conclude from this survey of the usage of cardinal terms that a common feature of all 'incorrect' and some 'correct' meanings is that they are used for *ultimate* rather than *proximate* orientation. In this situation the terms are used about destinations and directions ranged along a line of travel parallel to the Icelandic coast, such that each term applies to that part of the line which goes from one of the orientation areas in each quarter to the orientation area of the next. These areas are the geographically easternmost, northernmost, and westernmost regions of the island, plus Reykjavík and the peninsula of Reykjanes as the southernmost, though it is not geographically so. As here defined, each term has two and only two semes: one used in proximate orientation (corresponding reasonably well with the cardinal directions) and one used in ultimate orientation (for travelling, based on the four quarters of Iceland and their extreme extension in the cardinal directions). Since these two are in complementary (social) distribution and show a semantic relationship (one-to-one correspondence of orientation), they constitute only one sememe. What does this mean for the analysis of meaning? Primarily that the degree of discrimination of such terms depends on the choices available. On the sea each one depends on the identification of celestial bodies; but in land or coastwise travel the existence in most places of only two possible directions of travel reduced the possibilities of landwise orientation to two, and these were chosen not in terms of the celestially observable direction of travel, but in terms of the ultimate destination of the road, as moving towards one of the four orientation areas.

11. In so far as the usages described above are general, they can not be described either as dialectal or incorrect. Within their social situation they are correct, and they are not local, but form a proper meaning of the terms which could be regarded as universally Icelandic. There are, however, two limitations on this generality: one is the substitution of *inn* for W in the region east of Eyjafjörður, another the substitution of *út* for W in the South Quarter. These are genuinely local and dialectal, though they can be associated with other usages of the same words. To do so would require us, however, to enter deeply into the problem of the transverse terms of orientation,

those which apply to the movement up and down the valleys, or in and out. It is striking that in those regions where *inn* and *út* are substituted for W, *fram* has taken their place: in the N to mean up the valley, in the S to mean towards the sea. But the northern usage is here old, and extends into the E and W quarters as well; it is found also in western Norway, and represents a usage back probably to the first settlements of the west Norwegian valleys. In spite of its absence from most of the sagas I am therefore inclined to think it is a conservative usage (like other usages of this area). This is more probable than Einarsson's reluctant hypothesis of spread from the Fljótsdalshérað area. In the N quarter the use of *fram* in this sense permitted *inn* to be adopted for W (east of Eyjafjörður); in the S quarter the non-use of *út* in the sense of toward the sea permitted *fram* to be adopted in this sense (so also SE 281).

12. In view of the consistency in usage which has been demonstrated above, it may be questioned whether the use of so-called 'incorrect' terms in itself is sufficient to localize a saga. Both 'correct' and 'incorrect' terms may agree with local usage and at the same time be known to people from other communities, since the underlying principle is the same for the whole country. Only if an author can be shown to violate local usages of the kind mentioned in the preceding paragraph can we be sure he was unfamiliar with the region. An author telling a story from a particular region would naturally take that region as his point of orientation in telling about the movements of his characters. If a man travelled from Eyjafjörður to Húnavatnssýsla he would not say that he went N, just because he himself happened to come from Borgarfjörður where this would be the proper thing to say if one were going to Húnavatnssýsla from that region. It would be a poor author indeed who could not imaginatively place himself in the scene of his narrative and state movements in terms of this orientation. Although Ari fróði came from Snæfellsnes in the W, he quite naturally used the terms W and N about directions west and east from Eyjafjörður, as did the natives of that region (SE 266). Of course, it does not follow that these usages have remained unchanged since Old Icelandic times: Einarsson believes he has found a change in the E quarter, a S-N orientation in the SE and an E-W orientation in the NE earlier than the present-day S-E and E-N (SE 275). But the evidence is far from conclusive, since the sagas may have been under literary influence. That both the proximate and the ultimate semes came from Norway is made probable by the existence of similar usages in modern as well as ancient Norwegian. And the familiar case of the Eastern and Western Settlements of the Norsemen in Greenland falls easily into the seme of ultimate orientation: the coastwise travel from W to E was almost due S, but it led ultimately past the tip of Greenland and then across the sea to the E.

13. It is my belief that the meanings of the terms here studied have been completely accounted for (as far as the data go). These meanings are not to be equated with the totality of situations in which the words can be used, but with the diacritic features of those situations which the words trigger. The common feature of all 'incorrect' and some 'correct' meanings was found to be a social situation here described as *ultimate orientation*. Within this situation of travel in a coastwise direction around an island, most communities permitted only two choices. This meant that only two terms were necessary, those of the nearest orientation areas in either direction. These were selected, not on the basis of an exact astronomical orientation, but from the experience of travellers whose familiarity with the extremities of Iceland's four quarters provided areas of reference which corresponded to the four terms for the cardinal directions. *Meaning* may thus be defined as *the capacity of a symbol (a linguistic form) of discriminating between those messages that could be conveyed in a given social situation*. This definition is reminiscent of the formulations of recent information theory, but was arrived at independently and without benefit of the mathematical implications of that theory. The writer does not, therefore, share the regrets of Quine, as cited by Wells (249), that «we have so frequently to content ourselves with a lame partial synonym plus stage directions. Thus in glossing 'addled' we say 'spoiled' and add 'said of an egg.'» These are the prime elements of meaning: a situation (an egg) and a discrimination (spoiled): the chemical definition of addling is irrelevant (unless, of course, this is the message we happen to want).

NOTES

[1] SE denotes two papers by Einarsson (1942, 1944). The number following SE is a page reference, e.g. SE 265 refers to the first page of the second article.

[2] With the author's permission, his map of Iceland prepared for these articles is herewith reproduced [redrawn for this volume] for the orientation of the reader.

[3] Locally there are usages combining other directional terms, e.g. *út og upp* 'out and up' for NE, *inn og niður* 'in and down' for SE, etc.

[4] Einarsson notes (SE 43) that in Skagafjörður it is usual to say *austur í Húsavík*. Halldór Sigurðsson, a native of Hrútafjörður, informs me that this is common in his community also, as well as in other parts of northern and western Iceland. He also says *austur í Melrakkasléttu* and *Langanes*. Since all three of these lie east of Eyjafjörður, but within the area generally regarded as north, it is clear that Eyjafjörður serves as a kind of orientation area of its own, at least for local communities. The same speakers refer to the whole area of þingeyjarsýsla as N, but to communities within the area as E. As Einarsson points out, this situation merits further investigation.

REFERENCES CITED

Bloomfield, Leonard, 1933, Language. New York, Holt, Rinehart and Winston.

Einarsson, Stefan, 1942, Terms of direction in Modern Icelandic. Scandinavian Studies Presented to George T. Flom 37–48. Urbana, Ill., University of Illinois Press.

——, 1944, Terms of direction in Old Icelandic Journal of English and Germanic Philology, 43:265–85.

Fries, C. C., 1954, Meaning and linguistic analysis. Language 30:57–68.

Gjerset, Knut, 1925, History of Iceland. New York, Macmillan.

Hattori, Shirô, 1956, The analysis of meaning. For Roman Jakobson. The Hague, Mouton 201–212.

Nida, Eugene, 1951, A system for the description of semantic elements. Word 7:1–14.

Wells, Rulon, 1954, Meaning and use. Word 10:235–250.

4 Relevance: Psychological Reality

The final step in semantic analysis deals with the relation between arrangements and other facts. For the most part this has involved three different kinds of questions: (1) how do arrangements constructed by the anthropologist correspond to arrangements used by the people being studied; (2) how do arrangements in one semantic domain relate to arrangements in other semantic domains; (3) how are these arrangements affected by such extralinguistic factors as social context? Of these, only questions one and three have been studied in any detail. The next chapter discusses the relation between anthropologists' and native speakers' arrangements. The relation between extralinguistic facts and semantic arrangements is discussed in Chapter 5.

Once the anthropologist has completed a formal analysis and judged it complete, consistent and parsimonious, what evidence does he have that his result corresponds to the way a native speaker would isolate and arrange the features of this same semantic domain? Is this even a relevant question? Anthropologists are sharply divided on these points. Some assert a direct correspondence between the anthropologists' and native speakers' models. Others argue that there may be a correspondence between the two, but that it must be demonstrated by operations external to the methods of formal analysis. Still others maintain that the question is simply irrelevant.

Related to these problems is the fact that sometimes more than one complete, consistent and parsimonious analysis is possible for the same set of data (cf. Burling, this volume, Chapter 4). If two analyses are different, but equal on formal grounds, how can one be demonstrated to be superior? One approach involves a proof that one and only one analysis corresponds to the native speaker's model. This is achieved by psychological testing or by detailed specification of procedures indicating that one analysis is unacceptable to the native speaker. Romney and D'Andrade utilize a variety of psychological tests designed to show the relation between native speakers' and anthropologists' models of cognitive organization. Wallace and Conklin (this volume, Chapters 2 and 4) employ interviewing and eliciting techniques which enable informants to select among alternative solutions. The procedures suggested in the papers by Hymes and Frake are similar to those used by Wallace and Conklin. A different approach simply assumes that native speakers, like anthropologists, have more than one model of the system in their heads. The two models are nonidentical, but equivalent. They may even be in complementary distribution over the field of social situations and social identities. The latter position does not assume that there is necessarily one and only one analysis valid for all the members of a single culture. The identification and arrangement of semantic features may vary from individual to individual, or situation to situation, so long as one acceptable identification and arrangement is capable of being transformed into some other acceptable identification and arrangement (cf. Tyler, this volume, Chapter 5).

In essence, discussions of the relation between arrangements and other facts are concerned with the problem of relevance—the great "so what?" (Schneider, this volume, Chapter 3). But, there are many kinds of relevance and the selection of some other set of data to which a semantic arrangement could or should be relevant is basically arbitrary. Should a semantic arrangement: (1) be identical with an informant's model; (2) explain or constrain behavior; (3) correlate with behavior; (4) correlate with other semantic arrangements in the same culture or in other cultures; (5) illustrate universal laws of human thought; (6) replicate ontogenetic processes; (7) generate scientific laws? Each of these represents a valid question of relevance, but no one is a necessary question. What has not been sufficiently recognized is the fact that the anthropologist's criterion of relevance is essentially a statement of his implicit assumptions about the object of investigation— not a categorical imperative of investigation or the methods of scientific explanation.

The Meaning of Kinship Terms[1]

Anthony F. C. Wallace
John Atkins

INTRODUCTION

The meaning of kinship terms in foreign languages (or in English, for that matter) has traditionally been rendered by English-speaking ethnologists by a simple and direct procedure: each term is matched with a primitive English term (e.g., "mother"), with a relative product of two or more primitive English terms (e.g., "mother's brother"), or with a group of such primitive and/or relative product terms. Each primitive English term and each English relative product denotes an English "kin-type." Thus the meaning of the term is given by a list of nonredundant English kin-types, each of which includes one or more individuals in the group of persons to which the foreign term refers, and none of which includes any individual outside the group of persons to which the term refers. The validity of the matching derives, in general, from the prior use of a genealogical method of inquiry and from a general knowledge of the language and culture of the society. Murdock's *Social Structure* (1949) illustrates a convenient notation for such an analysis of meanings, and there is also a variety of other devices available, ranging from plotting terms on genealogical charts (each of whose points is defined by an English primitive or a relative product) to listing descriptive statements in tabular form. In Murdock's notation, the first two letters of eight primitive terms (father, mother, brother, sister, son, daughter, husband, wife) are used as the primitive symbols (Fa, Mo, Br, Si, So, Da, Hu, Wi); other kinship categories are conceived as relative products of these categories (e.g., FaBr for father's brother, SoWi for son's wife). Additional primitives (e.g., younger and older) are added as required. Similar notations are commonly used by other ethnologists and we shall call this traditional kind of notation the "kin-type notation." This process of definition is not to be confused with that of finding a convenient English rubric for a foreign term. For purposes of readable English rendering, the ethnologist may translate a foreign term into a common English one, for example, Pawnee *atías* into "my father" (Lounsbury 1956), but he is careful to indicate that insofar as it represents a native term, the English label applies not only to at least one of its own English kin-types, but also, as the case may be, to other kin-types as well.

Defining a foreign term by listing all the English kin-types to the sum of which it corresponds is, however, sometimes tedious and may yield a

Reproduced by permission of the American Anthropological Association from the American Anthropologist, Vol. 62, pp. 58–80 (February 1960).

345

veritable thicket of symbols, for one term may extend over a set of individuals which is parcelled out among dozens of English kin-types. In fact, many such lists are admittedly incomplete and conclude with an "etc." because the boundaries are not clearly or concisely definable in terms of English kin-types. Furthermore, this procedure somewhat begs the question of the principle of grouping which is inherent in the foreign concept by tacitly implying that it is the English kin-types which are grouped. And it is in the principle of grouping that, intuitively, one suspects that the meaning of the term *to its users* resides. Types of grouping of the English kin-types may be usefully classified, of course, to yield the various typologies of kinship terminology, such as Crow, Eskimo, or Sudanese. But a term may not mean to its users that collection of kin-types which the English-speaking ethnologist finds it convenient to regard as its meaning.

Recently students of social organization have developed a method called "componential analysis" for the elucidation of the meaning of kinship terms.[2] This method claims to reach a higher level of ethnographic validity than the traditional listing of kin-types. Furthermore, because this method moves much farther toward definition of the meaning of terms according to the conceptual criteria employed by their users than does mere kin-type listing, it awakens, in particular, the interest of psychologically oriented anthropologists. Therefore it is necessary to examine closely the assumptions and operations of componential analysis in order to evaluate both its utility for ethnographic studies of kinship and its adequacy as a model of semantic (and thus cognitive) process. Such an examination may suggest modifications or amplifications which will increase the effectiveness and scope of componential analysis as a tool, not only in kinship studies but in other areas of anthropological investigation as well. Such an examination may suggest also limitations on the applicability of the method. Componential analysis has so far been successfully applied primarily to definitive meaning (e.g., to the criteria by which a kinsman is recognized as belonging to a certain class). It may or may not ultimately prove to be convenient to analyze other kinds of meaning by the componential method; but we do not hope to settle such ultimate questions here. It is the more restricted purpose of this paper to use some of the resources of logical formalism to build, on a foundation of conceptualization and method provided by traditional techniques of kin-type analysis and by more recent procedures of componential analysis, toward more valid ethnographic description and more effective anthropological theories of cognitive processes in cultural behavior.

THE METHOD OF COMPONENTIAL ANALYSIS AS APPLIED TO KINSHIP

We shall consider as our source material six papers, two of them published in *Language* (Goodenough 1956, and Lounsbury 1956), one published in the AMERICAN ANTHROPOLOGIST (Romney and Epling 1958), and three delivered at the 1957 annual meetings of the American Anthropological Association and distributed there in mimeographed form (Goodenough 1957, Metzger 1957, and Jay Romney 1957). Goodenough's and Lounsbury's original papers explicate the method most fully; the other four papers illustrate and introduce modifications and extensions. We are here interested neither in exploring the historical background and contemporary analogues of the methodology, whether they be in kinship studies per se, in linguistics, Morris's semiotic, biological taxonomics, symbolic logic, or mathematics, nor in the uses and applications of the methodology in other fields of inquiry, such as the theory of typology. Nor are we primarily concerned with inter-author differences in notation and terminology except as they reflect differences in assumption and procedure.

The componential analysis of a kinship lexicon commonly consists of five steps: (1) the recording of a complete set (or a defined sub-set) of the terms of reference or address, using various boundary-setting criteria, such as a constant syntactic context, a type of pragmatic situation, or common inclusion within the extension of a cover term for "kinsmen"; (2) the definition of these terms in the traditional kin-type notation (i.e., as Fa, FaBr, DaHuBr); (3) the identification, in the principles of grouping of kin-types, of two or more conceptual dimensions each of whose values ("components") is signified (not connoted) by one or more of the terms; (4) the definition of each term, by means of a symbolic notation, as a specific combination, or set of combinations, of the components; (5) a statement of the semantic relationship among the terms and of the structural principles of this terminological system. (It should be noted here that the semantic structure of the terminological system is only one aspect of "the kinship system" of a society. The semantic structure to which we refer is a structure of the logical relationships of definitional meanings among terms and does not pretend to describe such phenomena as marital exchange or authority relations. A pair of terms may designate overlapping, mutually exclusive, identical, or inclusive sets of kin-types and the logical relations among the terms will correspondingly be those of logical independence, contrariety, equivalence, and implication. Thus the English term "uncle" designates a set of kin-types which is mutually exclusive with those denoted by "aunt," and the logical relation between the terms is that of contrariety. The structure of the terminological system is the product of these set—or logical—relationships.)

To give a simple example of the method, we shall now take a familiar group of American-English consanguineal terms in their formal and referential sense, and perform a componential analysis of their meaning. (This analysis is not offered as a definitive ethnographic statement; its purpose is to provide a readily apprehended illustration of the procedure.) Stage 1: we select: *grandfather, grandmother, father, mother, brother, sister, son, daughter, grandson, granddaughter, uncle, aunt, cousin, nephew, niece,* a group of common terms in American English, as they are used to refer to consanguineal relatives. Stage 2: we define these terms, employing the primitive kin-types Fa, Mo, Br, Si, So, Da, and the operators (:) ("refers to") and possessive relation (expressed by precedent juxtaposition, as in MoFa, which reads "mother's father"), as follows:

grandfather	: FaFa, MoFa	aunt	: FaSi, MoSi, FaFaSi,
grandmother	: FaMo, MoMo		MoFaSi, etc.
father	: Fa	cousin	: FaBrSo, FaBrDa,
mother	: Mo		MoBrSo, MoBrDa,
brother	: Br		FaSiSo, FaSiDa,
sister	: Si		MoSiSo, MoSiDa,
son	: So		FaFaBrSo, FaMoBrSo,
daughter	: Da		MoFaSiDa, etc.
grandson	: SoSo, DaSo	nephew	: BrSo, SiSo, BrSoSo,
granddaughter	: SoDa, DaDa		SiSoSo, etc.
uncle	: FaBr, MoBr,	niece	: BrDa, SiDa, BrDaDa,
	FaFaBr, MoFaBr,		etc.
	etc.		

The reader will note that for simplicity of exposition we have elected to bound the generational range of the kin-type universe at two generations above and two generations below ego. A more complete analysis would involve a larger generational range of kin-types. Furthermore, we have taken the last five terms in an extended sense, thus including the kin-types to which cousin in the sense of second-cousin-once-removed, aunt in the sense of great-aunt, and nephew in the sense of grand-nephew, and so on, refer. These five terms are actually homonyms, usable both as cover terms for an indefinitely large group of kin-types, and also as specific terms for more limited sets of kin-types. Stage 3: we observe that all but one of these terms (*cousin*) specifies sex of relative; some specify generation; all specify whether the relative is lineally or nonlineally related to ego; and nonlineal terms specify whether or not all the ancestors of the relative are ancestors of ego, or all the ancestors of ego are ancestors of the relative, or neither. From these observations we hypothesize that three dimensions will be sufficient to define all the terms: sex of relative (A): male (a_1), female (a_2); generation (B): two generations above ego (b_1), one generation above ego (b_2), ego's own generation (b_3), one generation below ego (b_4), two generations below ego (b_5); lineality (C): lineal (c_1), co-lineal (c_2), ablineal (c_3). We use Goodenough's definition of the values on this dimension of lineality: lineals are persons who are ancestors or descendants of ego; co-lineals are non-lineals all of whose ancestors include, or are included in, all the ancestors of ego; ablineals are consanguineal relatives who are neither lineals nor co-lineals

(Goodenough, private communication). Stage 4: we define the terms now by components, adopting the convention that where a term does not discriminate on a dimension,

grandfather	: $a_1b_1c_1$	grandson	: $a_1b_5c_1$
grandmother	: $a_2b_1c_1$	granddaughter	: $a_2b_5c_1$
father	: $a_1b_2c_1$	uncle	: $a_1b_1c_2$ and $a_1b_2c_2$
mother	: $a_2b_2c_1$	aunt	: $a_2b_1c_2$ and $a_2b_2c_2$
brother	: $a_1b_3c_2$	cousin	: $a\ b\ c_3$
sister	: $a_2b_3c_2$	nephew	: $a_1b_4c_2$ and $a_1b_5c_2$
son	: $a_1b_4c_1$	niece	: $a_2b_4c_2$ and $a_2b_5c_2$
daughter	: $a_2b_4c_1$		

the letter for that dimension is given without subscript. The definitions are represented paradigmatically in Fig. 1:

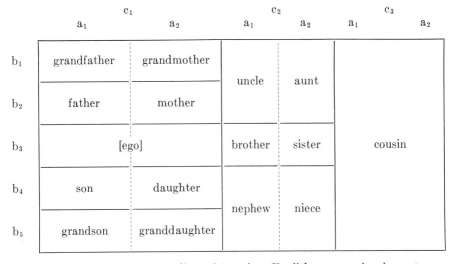

Figure 1.   A componential paradigm of American English consanguineal core terms.

Evidently each term has been so defined, with respect to the components selected, that no term overlaps or includes another; every component is discriminated by a least one term; and all terms can be displayed on the same paradigm. We do not wish to argue that this is the best representation; only that it is adequate to define the set of terms chosen.

These stages of analysis are exhibited in the several papers mentioned above with some variability of notation. Goodenough (1956), who, like us, employs an algebraic notation, drops the letter symbol for a dimension when the term does not specify a particular component on that dimension but ranges over the entire dimension; and he uses juxtaposed capital letters with numerical subscripts (with a standard prefix 'A' for each formula, indicating membership in the set of kinship terms) to indicate a commutative product (or "class product"). Lounsbury (1956) employs the commutative Boolean operators (·) and (+), a noncommutative relational operator (non-Boolean) signified by ordered juxtaposition, and the Boolean distributive law, to state the relationship of the components in those combinations where a single class product will not suffice to give the meaning of a term; Goodenough simply lists the various combinations. (See Birkhoff and MacLane 1953, for discussions of Boolean algebra, set theory, and logic, and their interrelations. "Boolean algebra" is an algebraic calculus for stating logical relationships among classes. Set theory is a calculus of the relations between groups of "elements." Both can be conceived as mathematizations of the logic of classes; and Boolean algebra is sometimes defined as the "algebra of sets".) Romney (1957) and Metzger (1957) draw matrix diagrams to represent semantic relationships; Goodenough (1956) and Lounsbury (1956) do not, preferring a tabular form of presentation. Although these and similar notational differences, as well as differences in details of procedure, would appear superficially to be merely variations in notation, they depend to some degree on differences in implicit assumptions about the logical structure of componential analysis. And assumptions about logical structure are intimately involved with the unresolved problems of analysis which we shall now consider.

ANALYTICAL PROBLEMS IN COMPONENTIAL ANALYSIS

In this section we outline five methodological problem areas which require solutions before any method of semantic analysis can become maximally useful as a tool in anthropological conceptualization and investigation. These areas will be discussed in detail in succeeding sections.

(1) THE PROBLEM OF HOMONYMS AND METAPHORS   Homonyms and metaphors are words or phrases, phonemically or graphically identical, which have different meanings (e.g., "night" and "knight" are phonemic homonyms; "light" and "light," as illumination and as not-heavy, are graphic homonyms; "to let the cat out of the bag" is both a description of one way of behaving toward felines and a metaphor implying the unintended betrayal of a secret). Goodenough (1956) and Lounsbury (1956) confront the problem of homonyms and metaphors in their analyses of Trukese and Pawnee terms. The issue is important because it concerns both the principles of finding the boundary of the system being described and also the logical nature of semantic systems.

(2) THE PROBLEM OF DEFINITION VS. CONNOTATION   All of our authors explicitly assert an interest in definitive meaning only. When the possibility

of synonyms is considered, however, the necessity of making an absolute distinction between definition and connotation may become an encumbrance.

(3) THE PROBLEM OF COMPLEMENTARITY, PARADIGMS, AND SPACES Goodenough and Lounsbury adhere to the principle that all terms should be complementary on at least one of a group of dimensions, and thus should form a paradigm. The paradigm concept can be more powerfully defined and supplemented by the notion of "logical space."

(4) THE PROBLEM OF NONCOMMUTATIVE RELATIONAL CONCEPTS Noncommutative relations are relations which cannot be reversed in order without change of meaning (e.g., "father's brother" does not have the same meaning as "brother's father"). Although the traditional English anthropological usage employs noncommutative relational operators in the kin-type notation (e.g., precedent juxtaposition in FaBr for "father's brother"), and although noncommutative relations (such as possession) may be psychologically real and linguistically recognized, none of the authors except Lounsbury (and he sparingly) uses a logic of noncommutative relations in componential analysis.

(5) THE PROBLEM OF PSYCHOLOGICAL REALITY, SOCIAL-STRUCTURAL REALITY, AND THE INDETERMINACY OF SEMANTIC ANALYSIS Goodenough (1956) points out that the componential analysis of meaning is, in fact, the analysis of cognitive structure. Romney's analysis (1957), on the other hand, seems to emphasize the structural properties of terminological systems without reference to cognitive models. These issues involve an apparent indeterminacy in analysis which in turn raises a number of basic theoretical problems concerning the purposes of componential analysis, the nature of model-building in anthropology, and the constraints on purpose imposed by the technical demands of a convenient model. Of particular importance is the distinction between "psychological" and "structural" reality.

HOMONYMS AND METAPHORS

Homonyms and metaphors enter the discussion of the meaning of kinship terms for two reasons: first, because some of the terms which signify kin relationships may, on occasion, also signify nonkin relationships (e.g., "father" may signify priest or male parent); and second, because the same term may have, or may seen to have, two or more kinship uses (e.g., "uncle" may refer both to brothers of parents and to spouses of sisters of parents). The semantic analyst therefore wishes, on the one hand, to exclude from his statement of the meaning of a kinship term those meanings which apply to nonkinship relationships, and also to avoid giving a kinship term two or more definitions when one will suffice.

Both Goodenough (1956) and Lounsbury (1956) exclude extra-kin meanings for terms by defining a universe of possible "denotata" which includes only the traditional English kin-type primitives and their relative products. A denotatum of a term, in this usage, is not a person to whom the term points, but an expression of the form FaBr, Mo, or MoSi, which stands for a class—usually a conceptually familiar class—of persons. Since the classes of denotata of the terms selected are restricted to the kin-types, metaphoric meanings and nonkinship homonyms are excluded automatically. (In a more general model, the extensions of components and terms can be persons rather than kin-types.) The Trukese analysis consequently is not concerned with the fact that some of the Trukese words are used to refer both to kin-types and to classes of individuals distinguished by their membership status in landholding corporations (a status different from, if related to, kinship) (Goodenough 1951); and Lounsbury (1956) can treat as "metaphorical extension" the Pawnee reference to corn as "Our Mother."

The situation is different where possible kin-homonyms are involved. These are homonyms within the universe of kin-type denotata. Here Goodenough and Lounsbury diverge slightly in method. They agree, initially, in refusing to regard a term which has more than one kin-type denotatum as *ipso facto* a homonym. Trukese *neji*, "child," for instance, has twelve listed denotata (others are implied by "etc."); Pawnee *atías*, "father," has fifteen listed denotata. Neither of these terms is treated as a homonym. In Goodenough's notation (which we modify here, and throughout this paper, by eliminating the constant prefix "A" signifying "kinsman"), *neji* is defined as equivalent simply to b_3 (junior generation with respect to ego). In Lounsbury's notation, *atías* is defined as equivalent to $\male \cdot \mathbf{A}^1$ (male of agnatic rank one).

But both Goodenough and Lounsbury feel that whenever a term cannot be given a "unitary definition" on the dimensions which yield significata (Lounsbury 1956:175), it is a homonym (Goodenough 1956) or a case of "polysemy" (Lounsbury 1956:175). The crucial question thus becomes: what is a "unitary definition"? For Goodenough, a unitary definition is a definition which, in the logical sense, is either a single value on one dimension, or a simple class product (a combination of *one* value from each of two or more dimensions, sometimes connected by "$\cdot$," "$\wedge$," or "$\times$," but here written by commutative juxtaposition of letters, each with one subscript, as in $a_1b_1c_1$ for male, one generation above ego, lineal—i.e., "father"). For Lounsbury, if the expression can be written as a simple class or relative product (e.g., $\male \cdot \mathbf{A}^{-1}$ or $A\,U$) without the Boolean "$+$" ("and/or," also expressed by $\vee$), it is a unitary definition. Both feel that a unitary definition is preferable, as the product of analysis, to a composite definition, because a composite definition seems to imply homonymity. Composite definitions are, in the logical sense, class sums (the referent may belong to any one of two or more alternative classes as in $a_1b_1c_1 \vee a_2b_1c_2$, for male, one generation above ego, lineal; or, female, one generation above ego, lineal—i.e., "parent").

But as a matter of fact, the terms in both Trukese and Pawnee cannot all be given unitary definitions on every definitionally adequate group of dimensions. Lounsbury, indeed, is forced to write extended composite definitions of the following kind (1956:180):

The "grandchild" class, *raktiki*, is the reciprocal of the "grandfather" and "grandmother" classes: $A^{-2}+G^{-2}+A^{-1}U^{-1}$; i.e. persons who are of agnatic rank *minus two*, or persons who are of second descending generation, or persons who are first-descending-generation uterine kinsmen to those of agnatic rank *minus one*.

And Goodenough notes that some groups of dimensions, otherwise perfectly adequate for defining the terms, yield homonymic definitions which he relates to one another by the English word "or." Goodenough and Lounsbury where possible follow an analytical convention which minimizes the apparent number of composite definitions, however: where a term does not discriminate among the values on a dimension which other terms in the set discriminate, that dimension is not regarded as semantically significant. But this invokes the danger of confusing ambiguity with irrelevance. Furthermore, considerations of economy apart, any convention of considering a dimension to be semantically nonsignificant on which no discrimination is made by some, but not all, of the terms in a lexicon invokes other difficulties, both practical and theoretical. As a practical device for reducing the number of composite definitions, the convention is of value only in special cases. It will work only if the term is ambiguous for all values on a dimension; if the ambiguity is with respect to some, but not all, values, then the ambiguity cannot be removed without redefining dimensions or selecting new dimensions. Thus, if a dimension has three values, and a term ranges over two of these values and excludes the third, then (under the convention aforementioned) the term must be treated as a homonym; only if it ranges over either three or one is it not a homonym. This problem occurs in Trukese Paradigm 4 with respect to *pwiij* (Goodenough 1956:212).

Theoretically, one may question whether terms which *can* be given either unitary definitions or composite definitions are necessarily given the unitary definition by the native user of the term, and whether the circumstance of composite definition on an English semantic matrix necessarily implies homonymity in the native cognitive world. Some terms, like *pwiij* in Paradigm 4, signify the extremes of a continuum of ordered values on a dimension and may be regarded as semantically homogeneous with respect to their extremity; their appearance as homonyms is a function of the exigencies of the paradigm. Some terms may well, in the context of a particular lexicon, signify a set of discrete unordered class products and may be used to refer to events which belong to any one of these products. But these terms likewise may not be true homonyms: they may be merely different "senses" of the term. The Trukese kinship lexicon does not happen to contain any terms which demand defining expressions involving the operator "and/or," if one follows the convention of omitting reference to semantically ambiguous dimensions. But the Pawnee terms cannot be defined without the use of the "and/or" operator. This operator must be used in order to construct a composite definition whenever two values on different dimensions cannot simultaneously complete a definition but each can separately, and whenever more than one but less than all of the values on a dimension are signified by a term. Such cases, by virtue of this fact alone, hardly qualify as true homonyms, however, any more than do terms which denote two or more kin-types, unless one wishes to insist on an equivalence between homonymity and the use of class sum ("and/or"). In general, we may observe that some terms will probably have to be componentially analyzed as class sums if a sufficiently large number of terms are taken for analysis on the same large set of dimensions. Thus "unitary definition" is an absolutely inadequate criterion for homonymity.

In order to avoid these dilemmas, we suggest the following alternative definition of homonyms: *two or more words, phonemically or graphically identical, which cannot be economically defined on the same set of dimensions without overlap or inclusion of one by the other.* (The restriction permits recognition of such homonyms as "duck" as species, and "duck" as female of that species.) Furthermore, we suggest that a policy of avoiding "homonyms" in English semantic translations is something of a red herring in analysis, interfering with the development of a consistent and logical notation, influencing the choice of either dimensions and values or the size of lexicon, and interposing an arbitrary preference for one kind of logical operator (the class product) in a situation where, in general, both class sums and class products must be used anyway. And, of course, in the interest of keeping analytical tasks within finite limits, it is always necessary initially to bound the semantic space (the range of possible meanings) by stating some major parameters (such as "kinsman"), as Goodenough and Lounsbury do, in order to exclude metaphors and to preclude reference to biological kinsmen (or kin-types) more remote than the actual native extension of the term. This may, of course, establish a semantic fence where none is intended by the native speaker, but it is justifiable to do so provided the possibility of continuity of meaning across such boundaries is recognized.

DEFINITION AND CONNOTATION

Both Goodenough and Lounsbury describe their initial purpose in the semantic analysis of kinship terms as the statement of "definitions in terms of distinctive semantic features." The individual kin-types to which a term refers are its *denotata;* the class of these kin-types is its *designatum;* and the "distinctive features of this class" constitute its *significatum* (Lounsbury 1956:168). The significatum of a term is a set of "contextual elements . . . without which it cannot properly occur. Significata are prerequisites while connotata are probabilities and possibilities. Only the former have definitive value" (Goodenough 1956:195).

The key words in the definition of significatum thus are "distinctive," "properly," and "prerequisite." A significatum is a statement of various necessary and sufficient conditions for a kin-type to belong to the class of kin-types denoted by a term. Just which conditions are considered to be necessary and sufficient will depend, in part, on the prior definition of the universe of denotata and in part on the particular set of terms being considered. In general (and synonyms excepted), each term should have a different significatum; but, as we have seen, whether a significatum need be considered as a simple class or relative product is a moot point involved in the problem of homonyms. Nor is it necessary that a significatum, unitary or composite, be unique; as Goodenough has shown, several different significata, based on different groups of dimensions, may be adequate.

A further problem must now be introduced: *synonymy*. Consider the set of English words *father, dad, daddy, pop,* and *old man.* They are all referential kinship terms which denote kin-types; all, except possibly *dad,* have nonkin homonyms or metaphoric extensions (or are metaphoric extensions of nonkin terms). (In this illustrative discussion we shall not deal with the problem of their usage in kinship address, which is recognized for all but *old man.*) All can be defined straightforwardly on the paradigm shown on page 349 as $a_1b_2c_1$ ("male, one generation above ego, lineal"). In the context of this particular paradigm, obviously, they are synonyms. But equally obviously they do not "mean" quite the same thing in colloquial usage. How then shall we consider them: as same-language synonyms with different connotations, as equivalent terms in different age, sex, and social-class languages, or as nonsynonyms?

If we elect the synonymous-with-different-connotation alternative, we must first observe that the connotata have the force of significata and are not culturally irrelevant idiosyncratic associations. A particular pattern of uses and nonuses of these terms is enjoined by the age, social group, and momentary situation of the speaker, and his usage to the discriminating listener, conveys important information about his attitudes. We do not intend to formalize the analysis of these terms here, but only to point out that if the distinguishing features of the terms are regarded as connotations, then connotations as a class must be conceived as having two sub-classes: culturally or linguistically enjoined connotations, and idiosyncratic or optional connotations.

To regard the terms as belonging to different English languages eliminates the question of synonyms but replaces it by the problem of translation and leaves the problem of signification untouched. Should a (hypothetical) lower class "pop" be translated into a (again hypothetical) middle class "dad"? Presumably the answer is "yes," since the designata of the terms are identical. But identical designata are no guarantee of identical significata. Thus we now have five componential analyses to do instead of one. And, on the other hand, it is something of a fiction to regard these terms as belonging to different languages; as a matter of fact, most speakers of American English use or recognize these terms.

Finally, we can elect to say that the terms are nonsynonymous in the same language: i.e., their significata are different. This, however, requires that we redefine the universe of denotata from simple kin-types to kin-types with qualifiers, and change the matrix of dimensions from A-B-C to A-B-C-D- . . . -N, adding sufficient dimensions to allow each term a distinctive significatum corresponding to the culturally enjoined "connotations." But, if we do this, we give a new definition of *father:* $a_1b_2c_1 \ldots n_r$ (for, in the context of *dad, daddy, pop,* and *old man, father* does not mean merely "male, one generation above ego, lineal").

We can offer no final solution to this dilemma: evidently, the definition of the universe of denotata and the choice of dimensions must be determined in part by the task of discrimination imposed by the list of terms originally selected. Thus the meaning of a term will be in part dependent on the size and composition of the particular list of terms being defined. This indicates that the meaning of a kinship term as given by a componential analysis is apt to be a minimal meaning, probably not complete in specification of culturally or linguistically relevant dimensions, and certainly devoid of most of the connotations which it will have for individuals and even subgroups in the society. This fact does not diminish the value of componential analysis as a method but suggests that the signification of a kinship term be defined as those semantic features which are in fact used to distinguish the kin-type designatum of the term from the kin-type designata of the other terms *in a given set of terms.* The significatum of a term can, in fact, be conceived to include connotations as well as definitive dimensions; there is no formal limit to the number of dimensions which may be analyzed componentially.

COMPLEMENTARITY, PARADIGMS, AND SPACES

Central to the conceptions and procedures of componential analysis is the notion of complementarity. A term may be said to complement one or more other terms if it signifies some value which the other terms definitely deny in favor of another value. For instance, English *mother* complements *father* with respect to the two values male and female: *mother* signifies female, *father* signifies male, which is equivalent to not-female, on the dimension of sex. Values which stand in a relation of complementarity thus constitute a single dimension whose two or more values are mutual contraries.

Goodenough's operating procedure, after listing a set of terms and defining the universe of kin-type denotata, is to divide the denotata into two or more groups, and the terms into two or more corresponding groups, on the basis of the complementarity of values on one dimension (for example, sex) which distinguishes the groups of denotata; then to divide each of these groups of terms into subgroups according to the principle of complementarity of their kin-type denotata on another dimension; and so on until each term stands alone as the complement of some other term on single dimension. Where a term which signifies a particular value on a dimension has no complementary term signifying another logically necessary value on that dimension, the existing term is said to be complemented by "no lexeme." The signification of each term is given by the values which specify its complementarity with respect to other terms.

Now it is evident that the stages of reduction of the set, beyond the first stage, allow a choice to the analyst: he can, on each level of analysis, utilize the same dimensions for the reduction of all the terms on that level, or he can use different dimensions for different groups. Trukese Paradigm 3 illustrates a case where the *same* dimension (L) was used to reduce the groups e_1 and e_2; Trukese Paradigm 1 (see Fig. 3) illustrates a case where different dimensions were used, after the B-level reduction: no further reduction of b_2 (since it contains only one term, reduction would require pairs of mutually complementary "no-lexemes"); b_2 reduced by D and E; $b_2d_1e_2$ reduced by F; $b_2d_1e_2f_1$ reduced by C; and b_1 reduced by C and J. Lounsbury, although he does not use the word complementarity and does not exhibit the formulas in paradigmatic arrangement, also follows the same general procedure. We are not concerned at the moment to discuss the source of the dimensions utilized: they are developed partly from standard ethnographic concepts (e.g., Kroeber 1909 and Murdock 1949), partly from concepts peculiar to the local culture and social structure; and as we have seen the choice of dimensions is in general not determinate from formal considerations: a number of sets of dimensions will, with more or less elegance, accomplish the partition of the universe of terms.

We draw attention, however, to the implications of a regular or an irregular reduction of terms. In regular reduction, not only must all remaining terms be reduced on each level of analysis, but all terms on each level must be reduced on the same dimension. If the reduction is regular on *at least one* level of analysis, then all the terms can be displayed in the same paradigm. If the reduction is *not* regular on *any* level of analysis, then the terms cannot be displayed in the same paradigm, for their significata are not logically complementary on any dimension. We refer here to Goodenough's concise definition of paradigm: "any set of linguistic forms . . . which signify complementary sememes [significata] may be said to belong to the same paradigm" (Goodenough 1956:197). Goodenough's Paradigm 1 is a paradigm according to his own and our definition, therefore, even though his dimensions F and J are logically nonindependent. Expressions whose significata do not include reference to one or more of the dimensions may by Goodenough's definition also exist on the same paradigm: *neji* (b₃), for instance is the complement of every other term with respect to generation.

A paradigm, however, is merely a mapping of a particular set of terms on a semantic space. A definite number of different sets of terms can be mapped on any given finite semantic space; and any given set of terms can be mapped on an infinite number of spaces. Thus a paradigm is essentially a logical function, comparable to a mathematical function, each term (value of the function) being equivalent to a specific cell or group of cells in a defined space.

The general properties of semantic spaces are not discussed by any of the authors considered above. We are developing a theory of semantic spaces and a suitable calculus of semantic functions, but detailed presentation here would be tedious. Nevertheless, it is necessary at this point to make some brief exposition in order to clarify the further development of this paper.

A semantic space may be initially characterized as a group of values (logical predicates) related by certain definite logical rules. Each of these values refers to a subset α_i of a set of empirical phenomena A (for example, A might be the set of all members of a community). Any values d_i, d_j, . . . d_n which refer to mutually exclusive subsets α_i, α_j, . . . α_n of A, and are therefore mutual contraries of one another, will be said to belong to a single dimension D. In fact, the group of values will subdivide into several dimensions A, B, C, . . . N. At least one of these dimensions will be logically independent of at least one other (i.e., no value or group of values on that dimension implies, or denies, a value or group of values on the other); some of the other dimensions, if any, may be logically dependent. A semantic space may now be redefined as the class product, or the relational product, or both, of the dimensions A, B, C, . . . N.

Now class-product spaces may be of at least three kinds (and all three have been used in componential analysis). Orthogonal spaces are constructed from independent dimensions. An orthogonal space may be defined as the set of class-products formed by all unique combinations of values from the N dimensions, each product including one value from each dimension, and each product not being self-contradictory. These class-products are significata, in Goodenough's and Lounsbury's sense, whose values (components) have the special property of being mutually contrary on every dimension. A set of terms whose reduction has not been regular on every level of analysis evidently cannot be represented on one orthogonal space.

A nonorthogonal class-product space is constructed from a group of dimensions at least one pair of which is nonindependent: that is to say, whenever there is a negative logical entailment of at least one value on any dimension by any value on any other dimension, the space is nonorthogonal. There are two types of nonorthogonal spaces: in the first type, all the dimensions span the same set of referents A, but at least two values from different dimensions are mutually contrary ($[a_i \rightarrow \sim b_j] \wedge [b_j \rightarrow \sim a_i]$); in the second type, each dimension overlaps at least one other dimension, and all dimensions can be arranged in an interlocking chain, but at least two dimensions span different sets of referents (A_1 and A_2), and hence at least one value on one dimension is mutually contrary with each of the n values on another dimension

$$[a_i \rightarrow \sim \{b_j \vee b_k \vee \cdots \vee b_n\}] \wedge [\{b_j \vee b_k \vee \cdots \vee b_n\} \rightarrow \sim a_i].$$

The three types of class-product spaces may be represented, for purposes of discussion here, by three simple diagrams constructed in each case from two binary dimensions containing, respectively, the values a_1 and a_2 and b_1 and b_2, as in Fig. 2:

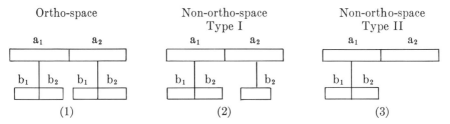

Figure 2.   Types of class-product spaces formed of two binary dimensions.

In diagram (1), the dimensions are independent and both extend over the same set of denotata. In diagram (2), the dimensions are nonindependent but both still extend over the same set of denotata. In diagram (3), the dimensions are nonindependent and the dimension B extends over only a part of the set of denotata spanned by A. (The denotata may be considered to be either persons or kin-types; the identity of the elements of the set of denotata need not be considered here.)

Now, when the space is nonorthogonal, it may be convenient to map a paradigm on it either as if it were a congeries of spaces, related hierarchically, or as a rectangular matrix with "holes" (impossible cells). When the space is orthogonal, the paradigm may most concisely be mapped on a "solid" rectangular matrix (a grid or property-space; see Barton 1955). By the hierarchical method, one representation of Trukese Paradigm 1 (corresponding to the process of reduction as given by Goodenough 1956:206) is given in Fig. 3 on page 360.

The dimensions are: B (seniority of generation): b_1 senior, b_2 same, b_3 junior; C (sex of relative): c_1 male, c_2 female; D (symmetry or parallelism of relationship to the connecting matrilineal group): d_1 symmetrical, d_2 asym-

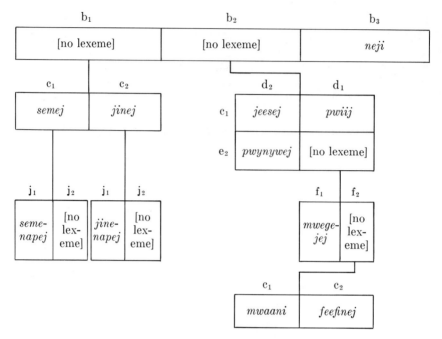

Figure 3.   Trukese paradigm 1.

metrical; E (sex relative to ego's sex): e_1 same sex, e_2 opposite sex; F (mode of relationship); f_1 consanguineal, f_2 affinal; J (collateral removal): j_1 lineal, j_2 nonlineal. This represents precisely, in logical-space form, the analysis given in Goodenough's list-form Paradigm 1 (1956:206), except that it reveals three additional "no-lexemes" (b_1, b_2, and $b_2d_1e_2$) which strict application of a complementarity rule requires.

By contrast, the analysis of Paradigm 4 appears as a single space as follows:

| | b_2 | |
	e_1	e_2
l_1		*mwegejej*
	pwiij	
l_3		[no lexeme]
l_2	*jeesej*	*pwynywej*

Figure 4.   Trukese paradigm 4.

The question now arises: can paradigms on nonorthogonal spaces, like some of those presented by Goodenough and Lounsbury and like our representation of American English (Fig. 1), be transformed by an appropriate selection of dimensions into paradigms on orthogonal spaces on which all the terms, or lexemes, in a lexicon can be represented? After considerable experimentation, we are prepared to state that it will rarely be possible to represent all the terms of any full kinship lexicon on a single orthogonal space, but that it is possible in some cases to present all of the kinship lexemes (expressions whose signification cannot be deduced from the signification and arrangement of their parts) and certain groups of "core terms" on one orthogonal space. The Trukese lexemes shown in Fig. 4, together with three others (*semej, jinej,* and *neji*), can all be represented on an orthogonal space; all of the Pawnee terms except those for "grandparents" and "grandchildren" can be shown likewise. We have tried assiduously, however, to place the forty-nine Lapp terms on one space without success, nor can all American English terms be convincingly shown on one orthogonal space.

We must also now observe that the practice of omitting reference to dimensions, as performed by Goodenough and Lounsbury, produces still another serious uncertainty. Once a space of N dimensions has been defined, the omission of a letter for a dimension should mean only that the space is nonorthogonal, Type II, and that the dimension omitted in defining a term was omitted because that dimension is irrelevant to the signification of the term. If the term is merely ambiguous as to a dimension on an orthogonal space, it should be entered without subscript; if the space is nonorthogonal, Type I, the implied value with its proper subscript must be specified. Without such a rule, the omission of a dimensional symbol may mean any one of three things: the term refers to a class sum ("and/or") of values on a dimension; the term refers to a definite single value which it shares with other complementary terms; the dimension is irrelevant to the meaning of the term.

The further analysis of the formal properties of logical and semantic spaces would take us too far afield, however, from the limited purposes of this paper, and we defer the development of the theory of semantic spaces to another occasion.

NONCOMMUTATIVE RELATIONAL CONCEPTS

The Trukese kinship lexicon contains relational linguistic forms in which two or more root morphs are connected by suffixed possessive pronouns (for example, *seme-nape-j*). These expressions are formally comparable to descriptive English expressions like "father's brother"; but some of them act not as descriptive statements but as kinship terms. Thus English "father's brother" is not a kinship term but *semenapej* is. We may also observe that Lounsbury, in analyzing Pawnee, used a noncommutative possessive relation between kintypes, which he symbolized by juxtaposing two or more symbols without writing an intervening relative product operator, with the preceding symbol "possessing" the latter. His usage is identical with traditional usage in the definition of the English kin-type denotata on which both he and Goodenough rely: FaBr, MoSi, WiBrWi, are possessive relational concepts implying an unwritten relative product operator. Goodenough does not utilize relational concepts of this kind in statements of significata (although he recognizes that the Trukese use relative products of his "lexemes" to construct other expressions in the larger lexicon). Lounsbury does depend on relative products, both to define his dimension of agnatic rank, and to state the significata for "grandparental" and "grandchild" classes. In our analysis of the English terms, furthermore, we used explicit relational concepts to define the values on the dimension of lineality, and other dimensions could have been expressed relationally.

Let us ask the general question: May not the users of many kinship lexicons cognitively define at least some of their terms relationally, even though it may be possible for the ethnographer to analyze them as class products? The answer must be "yes," both for English and Pawnee, and probably also for the Trukese full lexicon. Requests to English-speaking informants to define common English kinship terms yield responses of both class product and relational types: *father* may be defined, for instance, as "male parent," which can be analyzed as the class product "male $\wedge$ lineal $\wedge$ one generation above ego"; but *nephew* may be defined as "son of sister or brother," and *aunt* and *uncle* respectively as "sister of parent" and "brother of parent." The latter definitions are the relative products "son/sister," "son/brother," "sister/parent," "brother/parent." The adequacy of these definitions (which were provided by English-speaking informants) is beside the point: cognitively, the relation *aunt* may be reckoned by an informant not as a class product but as a relative product.

These observations lead us to ask whether many a kinship lexicon may not profitably be analyzed by a combination of class and relational calculi. There will often be a set of primitive terms, "lexemes" in Goodenough's sense, which may be exemplified by the two English sets: (a) parent, child, sibling, ancestor, and descendant, and (b) mother, father, brother, sister, son, daughter, husband, wife; and which can be defined discursively, or componentially analyzed on a single paradigm or even on a single class product space. And there will be a set of terms, some of which may be "lexemes" (but not primitives), which can be defined either as class products or as relative products of *the primitive terms of that lexicon*. The logical structure of noncommutative relations, involving the operator "/," is somewhat different from that of commutative relations involving operators "$\wedge$" (and) and "$\vee$" (and/or). In consequence, paradigms composed of relative products will have a different structure from those composed of conjunctive and disjunctive products. The details of the appropriate logical calculi, and the relative merits of relational and class-product significata and paradigms, however, are not the point of discussion here. Furthermore, the choice of one mode of analysis or another will depend on the purpose of the investigation. And it is to the matter of purpose that we now turn our attention.

PSYCHOLOGICAL REALITY, SOCIAL-STRUCTURAL REALITY, AND INDETERMINACY

Goodenough repeatedly states in his paper on Trukese terminology (1956) that the purpose of the componential analysis of kinship terms is to provide psychologically real definitions. He speaks of people having "certain criteria in mind by which they make the judgment that A is or is not B's cousin" (p. 195); he alludes to the method as a means of learning about "human cognitive processes" (p. 198); he discusses "concepts" which exist in "the Trukese cognitive world" (p. 213). In his earlier monograph on Truk he justifies the choice of components by characterizing them as "criteria" or "rules," valid in "Trukese thinking," by which the Trukese "appraise[s] his relationship with another individual." This does not contradict his prefatory caution that "he does not intend to present [the Trukese culture] as the Trukese see it." What Goodenough is avoiding is not description of Trukese practical thinking about kinsmen but Trukese rationalization about their own kinship terminology (cf. Goodenough 1951:11, 100–101). The intention of componential analysis in Goodenough's sense is to state the meaning of the terms to the native users of the terms.

Now this is a major theoretical commitment. It happens to be one which we share: a part of anthropology's mission which is of particular concern to us is the development of formal theories and methods which will describe the relationship between cultural forms and processes, and their social-structural correlates, whose locus is a society, and psychological (cognitive) forms and processes, whose locus is the individual. This commitment need not, however, be shared by all users of the method of componential analysis, or of any other method of semantic analysis; and these semantic methods do not inevitably yield psychologically real descriptions of meaning. Semantic analysis may, in fact, be profitably used for nonpsychologically oriented social-structural analysis. It is therefore particularly important to clarify the distinction between these equally valid purposes, psychological and structural, because two methodological difficulties inherent in the method itself affect these two purposes differently.

By "psychological reality" we mean what the senior author has discussed under the concept of mazeway (Wallace 1956a). The psychological reality of an individual is the world as he perceives and knows it, in his own terms; it is his world of meanings. A "psychologically real" description of a culture thus is a description which approximately reproduces in an observer the world of meanings of the native users of that culture. "Structural reality," on the other hand, is a world of meanings, as applied to a given society or individual, which is real to the ethnographer, but it is not *necessarily* the world which constitutes the mazeway of any other individual or individuals. The difference is well illustrated in the difference which sometimes obtains between descriptions of a given society by social anthropologists who are interested in predictive models of relations among groups and in related economic and demographic processes, and by ethnographers who are interested in describing the world as the individual sees it. In the province of the semantics of kinship terminology, psychological and structural reality should be related extensionally via the identity of the sets of persons (or kin-types) denoted by pairs of expressions. The statement, *the English term cousin means any nonlineal consanguineal relative who is a descendant of a sibling of an ancestor of ego* is structurally real to an anthropological observer because he can predict the usage of the term accurately from his definition, but is hardly a psychologically real definition for all speakers of the English language; yet it is extensionally equivalent to, or at least implies, many psychologically real definitions of *cousin*.

The first of the methodological difficulties alluded to above is an almost unavoidable ethnocentrism. If the analyst is writing a paper in ethnographers' English (or any language other than the idiom of his informants), he is to a degree constrained by the terminological resources of his own language in his efforts to state the meaning of a foreign expression. Even the simple kin-type denotata of which we have made such heavy use are not, to my knowledge, absolutely universal human concepts. One need not introduce here an idealistic, Whorfian linguistic relativism; the principle more closely approaches that of complementarity, in the mathematical physicist's sense. Just as the physicist cannot measure both the position and momentum of a particle under the same conditions, so the semantic analyst cannot state simultaneously the meaning of an event in his own language and in that of another person, because the two languages impose different conditions of analysis. Statements can be made in one language which will be highly predictive and therefore approximately equivalent in truth value to statements in another language; but they will not be tautologically equivalent statements in the strictest sense. Statements can be made which (in the strictest sense) are tautologically equivalent to one another in *one* language or calculus but not in two.

While preoccupation with this problem of "linguistic complementarity" leads to solipsism, ignoring it inhibits one's ability to develop increasingly proximate solutions to the second problem, that of indeterminacy. This, in semantics, is precisely equivalent to the physicist's relativity. Goodenough, for instance, exhibits three separate paradigms containing the terms *pwiij*, *mwegejej*, *jeesej*, and *pwynywej*. Each paradigm contains a different set of dimensions; one of them is an orthogonal space; one of them contains only unitary definitions, one only composite definitions, and one both unitary and composite definitions. We have produced for our own edification still other paradigms which also define the same terms. All of these analyses are extensionally valid. What then is the source of the multiplicity of solutions?

The discussion up to this point has revealed several major sources of indeterminacy: the fact that the set of all kin-type denotata has no finite boundaries; variation in the universe of denotata chosen; variation in the number and identity of terms selected from a lexicon for analysis on the same semantic space; variation in the identity of the dimensions chosen; variation as to the use of logical operators (class or relative products); variation in type of class-product space; variation as to inclusion or exclusion of "connotative" dimensions. These variations in themselves will not affect the extensional validity of the analysis: the only criteria of extensional validity available are the identity of the sets of kin-types, or of the persons, denoted by the significatum of the term and by the term itself. If a significatum denotes, in any set of denotata, the same subset as the term itself, it is an extensionally valid meaning of the term. There is, in fact, an indeterminate number of equivalent significata, both conjunctive and disjunctive, which will with equal extensional validity define any given term.

Goodenough (1956:213) seems to adopt the working principle that no evaluative discrimination is possible, that all extensionally valid definitions are equally real psychologically: "Since we can reproduce Trukese kinship usage equally well from any one of these three paradigms, we cannot eliminate from the Trukese cognitive world any one of the alternative conceptual variables E, K, D, F, and L." Romney, on the other hand, expresses disturbance over this generic indeterminacy of semantic analysis (which he believes, we think mistakenly, to be the peculiar product of Goodenough's reduction procedure) and offers a technique of analysis by "range-sets" which is said to yield a "determinate solution." Romney's technique is to define certain dimensions (in his terminology, "range-sets") by specifying a set of binary operations (such as changing sex of kin-type, taking reciprocal, etc.) which will transform the designatum of one term into the designatum of another. Since the denotata are the traditional kin-types, together with sex of speaker and age relative to ego, and a criterion of symmetry is imposed, only a limited number of such operations is possible. Dimensions with more than two variables are excluded from range-set analysis. All denotata which can be related by a single operation form a range-set; relations between the dimensions which constitute range-sets are defined by componential analysis on a logical space. This logical space does not state the meanings of terms, however; it only defines range-sets in terms of their position in the space. The result thus is simply a statement about the logical relationships among the dimensions. For instance, in his analysis of Goodenough's Trukese dimensions, Romney finds that three of them are expressible as binary operations on the kin-types; the other two are not so expressible; and not all of the dimensions are logically independent. The determinacy of this analysis by range-sets depends therefore on a special method of defining dimensions; it yields, not a semantic analysis of terms, but a logical analysis of the dimensions chosen; and it reduces only that fraction of the indeterminacy which remains after other sources of indeterminacy are held constant by stating, for a given set of terms, which dimensions can be defined as the result of binary operations on a known grouping of kin-types.

The crux of the difference between a psychologically valid description and one which is only structurally valid lies, of course, in the choice of the dimensions and logical operators (class or relative products) used in defining the space, and in the choice of the logical operators (class products, class sums, and relative products) employed in defining the terms and mapping the paradigm on the space. The ingenuity of the analyst is most severely tested in the identification of the dimensions of kinship in psychologically real spaces. Here the standard and "universal" dimensions, such as those suggested by Kroeber (1909) and Murdock (1949), must often be re-defined and supplemented by dimensions peculiar to the particular informant and his society. Such dimensions may be given by structural features of the kinship system—marriage classes, clans, land-holding lineages, and so forth—which function as principles of classification in the particular society. It cannot be emphasized too strongly that the point of the difference between psychological and structural reality lies in qualitative differences in semantic spaces and not in differences between individual and group characteristics. Psychologically real and structurally real descriptions alike can each apply to both individuals and groups.

The foregoing considerations lead to two major conclusions: first, that by working only on ethnographic data, two or more extensionally valid and perhaps even tautologically equivalent (in one language, either the ethnographer's or the native's) definitions can usually be obtained for any given term; and second, that while more than one definition may be psychologically real, in the sense of representing how users think with and about that term, one or more definitions may be real only in a structural sense, even though such definitions must be extensionally equivalent to psychologically real definitions.

A problem for research, then must be to develop techniques for stating and identifying those definitions which are most proximate to psychological reality. This is a formidable task. The formal methods of componential analysis, even with refinement and extension of their logico-semantic assumptions, will not yield discriminations between psychologically real and non-psychologically but social-structurally real meanings. It may be noted that the psychologist Osgood, who is also concerned with the meanings of some kinship terms and has developed a formal testing procedure called the "semantic differential" (Osgood 1957) avoids definitive meaning entirely and deals only with the connotative significata of fixed sets of terms (including nonkinship as well as kinship terms) on a fixed set of three dimensions (active-passive, potent-impotent, and evaluative) which define a "universal" connotative space. Ethnographers like Goodenough and Lounsbury obtain clues to psychological reality from observations on the cultural milieu of the terminology such as residence and marriage rules or historical changes. But the only way of achieving definite knowledge of psychological reality will be to study the semantics of individuals both before and after a formal, abstract, cultural-semantic analysis of the terms has been performed. Simple demands for verbal definition, the use of Rivers' genealogical method, and analysis of the system of kinship behaviors may not be sufficient here: additional procedures, by individual representative informants, of matching and sorting, answering hypothetical questions, and description of relationships in order to reveal methods of reckoning will probably all be required. This sort of information is not always obtained, or published if obtained, by ethnographers, although a good deal of it is scattered in field notes or distilled in memory. It is possible to say fairly that not only in kinship, but also in other ethnographic subjects, the degree of psychological reality achieved in ethnographic reporting is not only uneven but on the average probably rather low. Social-structural reality can be achieved; psychological reality can only be approximated. But such approximations are sorely needed. The problem of extending the psychological reality of ethnographic description is not just a "culture-and-personality" problem, it is a general anthropological issue with implications for anyone concerned with the relationship between cultural and cognitive processes. Indeed, it is a general issue for the behavioral sciences, because structurally real descriptions do not predict certain phenomena so well as psychologically real descriptions.

CONCLUSION

Semantic analysis in anthropology concerns, primarily, neither personality and culture, nor linguistics, nor culture and social structure per se, but cognitive processes in culturally organized behavior. This paper has defined two methods of semantic analysis which have been applied to kinship terms: the traditional kin-type designations and componential analysis. The methods of componential analysis are examined and illustrated in some detail with respect to their various assumptions and procedures. Its difficulties in handling five problem areas are analyzed: homonyms and metaphors; definition, connotation, and synonymy; paradigms and semantic spaces; relational logic; and indeterminacy, psychological reality, and social-structural reality. Some solutions and recommended lines of attack are suggested, based on formal semantic calculi. The distinction between psychologically and structurally real analysis is analyzed at some length. We feel that the application, in ethnographic and psychological research, of formal logico-semantic methods is not an exercise in technical virtuosity but an essential procedure for solving problems in analysis already confronting this generation of social anthropologists. In this paper, however, we are not concerned with presenting a theory of semantic spaces, or a semantic calculus, but in analyzing, evaluating, and making more effective the method of componential analysis for the practical study of cognitive processes in one aspect of cultural behavior: kinship terminology.

NOTES

[1] We wish to acknowledge our gratitude to Harold Conklin, J. L. Fischer, Walter Goldschmidt, Ward Goodenough, and David Schneider for helpful advice both in matters of analysis and of style.

[2] We realize that componential analysis has a precursor or ally in any method which aims at defining some or all of the concepts which are explicit or implicit in any terminological system (see, e.g., Edmonson 1957 and Fischer 1958). We also realize that the study of the semantics of kinship terminology is only one aspect of the study of kinship behavior. In this paper we are not attempting to trace the history of kinship studies nor to deal with aspects of kinship behavior other than the definitional meaning of kinship terms.

REFERENCES CITED

Barnett, H. G., 1953, Innovation. New York, McGraw-Hill.

Barton, A. H., 1955, The concept of property-space in social research. In P. F. Lazarsfeld and Morris Rosenberg, eds., The language of social research, Glencoe, The Free Press.

Birkhoff, Garrett, Saunders MacLane, 1941, A survey of modern algebra. New York, Macmillan.

Edmonson, M. S., 1957, Kinship terms and kinship concepts. American Anthropologist 59:393–433.

Fischer, J. L., 1958, Genealogical space. Unpublished manuscript read at annual meeting of American Anthropological Association, Washington.

Greenberg, J. H., 1949, The logical analysis of kinship. Philosophy of Science 16:58–64.

Goodenough, W. H., 1951, Property, kin, and community on Truk. New Haven, Yale University Press.

———, 1956, Componential analysis and the study of meaning. Language 32:195–216.

Goodenough, W. H., 1957, Componential analysis of Lapp kinship terminology. Unpublished manuscript read at annual meeting of American Anthropological Association, Chicago.

Kroeber, A. L., 1909, Classificatory systems of relationship. Journal of the Royal Anthropological Institute 39:77–84.

Lounsbury, F. G., 1956, A semantic analysis of the Pawnee kinship usage. Language 32:158–194.

Metzger, Duane, 1957, The formal analysis of kinship: II. special problems as exemplified in Zuni. Unpublished manuscript read at annual meeting of American Anthropological Association, Chicago.

Morris, C. W., 1955, Foundations of the theory of signs. In Otto Neurath and others, eds., International Encyclopedia of Unified Science. Vol. 1. Chicago, University of Chicago Press.

Murdock, G. P., 1949, Social structure. New York, Macmillan.

Osgood, C. E., 1957, The measurement of meaning. Urbana, University of Illinois Press.

Romney, A. K., P. J. Epling, 1958, A simplified model of Kariera kinship. American Anthropologist 60:59–74.

Romney, Jay, 1957, The formal analysis of kinship: I. general analytic frame. Unpublished manuscript read at annual meeting of American Anthropological Association, Chicago.

Wallace, A. F. C., 1956a, Mazeway resynthesis: a bio-cultural theory of religious inspiration. Transactions of the New York Academy of Sciences 18:626–638.

———, 1956b, Revitalization movements. American Anthropologist 58:264–281.

Cognitive Aspects of English Kin Terms

A. Kimball Romney
Roy Goodwin D'Andrade

The study of kinship terminology has long been of central interest in anthropology. Formal methods of description developed by linguists, such as componential analysis, have been applied with success to kinship terminologies. It has been claimed that such descriptions, in addition to representing the data in an abstract, structural, and elegant manner, uncover and represent psychological reality for the native users of these systems. For example,

> Goodenough repeatedly states in his paper on Trukese terminology that the purpose of the componential analysis of kinship terms is to provide psychologically real definitions. . . .
>
> Now this is a major theoretical commitment. It happens to be one we share: a part of anthropology's mission which is of particular concern to us is the development of formal theories and methods which will describe the relationship between cultural forms and processes, and

Reproduced by permission of the American Anthropological Association from the *American Anthropologist*, Vol. 66, no. 3, part 2 (Special Publication), pp. 146–170 (June 1964).

their social-structure correlates, whose locus is a society, and psycho-logical (cognitive) forms and processes, whose locus is the individual (Wallace and Atkins 1960:75).

This claim is, we believe, an important hypothesis: This paper reports the results of an attempt to test this hypothesis with American-English kinship terminology. However, we are equally interested in the other side of the coin, that is, in those aspects of the individual's psychological or cogni-tive structure which are not represented in formal analyses.

We begin with the presentation of two alternative componential analy-ses of American-English kin terms. Then the results of a series of psycho-logical tests, designed to measure different aspects of the individual's cogni-tive structure concerning kin terms, are related to these componential models. An attempt is made to assess the validity of each of these models and the psychological implications of componential analyses in general.

COMPONENTIAL ANALYSES OF AMERICAN-ENGLISH KINSHIP TERMINOLOGY

Wallace and Atkins, in a review of the methods of componential analysis, present a componential paradigm for American-English kin terms. The steps involved in this analysis are given as:

> The componential analysis of a kinship lexicon commonly consists of five steps: (1) the recording of a complete set (or a defined sub-set) of the terms of reference or address, using various boundary-setting criteria, such as a constant syntactic context, a type of pragmatic situation, or common inclusion within the extension of a cover term for "kinsmen"; (2) the definition of these terms in the traditional kin-type notation (i.e., as Fa, FaBr, DaHuBr); (3) the identification, in the principles of grouping of kin-types, of two or more conceptual dimen-sions each of whose values ("components") is signified (not connoted) by one or more of the terms; (4) the definition of each term, by means of a symbolic notation, as a specific combination, or set of combinations, of the components; (5) a statement of the semantic relationship among the terms and of the structural principles of this terminological system (Wallace and Atkins 1960:60).

The recorded subset which Wallace and Atkins select is made up of con-sanguineal kin terms whose denotata in kin types are given as—

Grandfather:	FaFa, MoFa	Grandson:	SoSo, DaSo
Grandmother:	FaMo, MoMo	Granddaughter:	SoDa, DaDa
Father:	Fa	Uncle:	FaBr, MoBr,
Mother:	Mo		FaFaBr, MoFaBr,
Brother:	Br		etc.
Sister:	Si	Aunt:	FaSi, MoSi,
Son:	So		FaFaSi, MoFaSi,
Daughter:	Da		etc.

Cousin: FaBrSo, FaBrDa, MoBrSo,   Nephew: BrSo, SiSo, BrSoSo,
          MoBrDa, FaSiSo, FaSiDa,   SiSoSo, etc.
          MoSiSo, MoSiDa,   Niece: BrDa, SiDa, BrDaDa,
          FaFaBrSo, FaMoBrSo,   SiDaDa, etc.
          MoFaSiDa, etc.

Wallace and Atkins point out that the range of kin types is bound (for the sake of simplicity) at two generations above and below ego and that the last five terms have been used in their "extended sense," thus including cousin in the sense of second cousin once removed, aunt in the sense of great aunt, and nephew in the sense of grand nephew, and so on. Stages 3, 4, and 5 are presented by them as follows:

> Stage 3: we observe that all but one of these terms (cousin) specifies sex of relative; some specify generation; all specify whether the relative is lineally or nonlineally related to ego; and nonlineal terms specify whether or not all the ancestors of the relative are ancestors of ego, or all the ancestors of ego are ancestors of the relative, or neither. From these observations we hypothesize that three dimensions will be sufficient to define all the terms: sex of relative (A): male (a_1), female (a_2); generation (B): two generations above ego (b_1), one generation above ego (b_2), ego's own generation (b_3), one generation below ego (b_4), two generations below ego (b_5); lineality (C): lineal (c_1), co-lineal (c_2), ablineal (c_3). We use Goodenough's definition of the values on this dimension of lineality; lineals are persons who are ancestors or descendants of ego; co-lineals are non-lineals all of whose ancestors include, or are included in, all the ancestors of ego: ablineals are consanguineal relatives who are neither lineals nor co-lineals (Goodenough, private communication). Stage 4: we define the terms now by components, adopting the convention that where a term does not discriminate on a dimension, the letter for that dimension is given without subscript. The definitions are represented paradigmatically [below]:

| | c_1 | | c_2 | | c_3 | |
	a_1	a_2	a_1	a_2	a_1	a_2
b_1	grandfather	grandmother	uncle	aunt		
b_2	father	mother	uncle	aunt		
b_3	[ego]		brother	sister	cousin	
b_4	son	daughter	nephew	niece		
b_5	grandson	granddaughter	nephew	niece		

> A componential paradigm of American English consanguineal core terms.

Evidently each term has been so defined, with respect to the components selected, that no term overlaps or includes another; every component is discriminated by at least one term; and all terms can be displayed on the same paradigm. We do not wish to argue that this is the best representation; only that it is adequate to define the set of terms chosen (Wallace and Atkins 1960:61–62).

A second method developed by Romney uses a different set of operations and yields slightly different results. This method begins with a basic set of symbols as follows:

m   represents male
f   represents female
a   represents person of either sex
=   represents marriage bond
0   represents sibling link (used only where individuals share both parents, i.e., "full" siblings)
+   represents parent link
−   represents child link
( )   represents an expansion
superscripts represent number of expansions
subscripts represent sex correspondences

These basic symbols are combined to represent kin types in the same way as standard abbreviations except that ego or sex of speaker is always explicitly indicated.

The notation and a subsequent analysis will be applied to the hypothetical English system reported by Wallace and Atkins (1960:61). The terms defined by kin types written in the present notation are:

Grandfather:	a+m+m	Uncle:	a+m 0 m
	a+f+m		a + f 0 m
			a+m+m 0 m
Grandmother:	a+m+f		a+f+m 0 m
	a+f+f		etc.,
			(also the following not included by Wallace)
Father:	a+m		a+m 0 f = m
			a+f 0 f = m
Mother:	a+f		etc.
Brother:	a 0 m		
Sister:	a 0 f	Aunt:	a+m 0 f
			a+f 0 f
Son:	a−m		a+m+m 0 f
			a+f+m 0 f
Daughter:	a−f		etc.,
			(also the following not included by Wallace)
Grandson:	a−m−m		a+m 0 m = f
	a−f−m		a+f 0 m = f
Granddaughter:	a−m−f		etc.
	a−f−f		

Nephew: a 0 m − m   Niece: a 0 m − f
            a 0 f − m   a 0 f − f
            a 0 m − m − m   a 0 m − m − f
            a 0 f − m − m   a 0 f − m − f
            etc.,   etc.,
            (also the following not   (also the following not
              included by Wallace)   included by Wallace)
            f = m 0 m − m   f = m 0 m − m
            m = f 0 m − m   m = f 0 m − m
            etc.   etc.

Cousin: a+m 0 m − m   a+f 0 f − m
            a+m 0 m − f   a+f 0 f − f
            a+f 0 m − m   a+m+m 0 m − m
            a+f 0 m − f   a+m+f 0 m − m
            a+m 0 f − m   a+f+m 0 f − f
            a+m 0 f − f   etc.

The list of kin types following each kin term will be called the *range* of
that term. An analysis of the terminological system begins with a listing of
the *range* of each term as above. The next step is to reduce the *range* of
each term to a single notational expression. (In the above example, Father,
Mother, Brother, Sister, Son, and Daughter are already single expressions.)

The rules of the reduction of *ranges* to single expressions are outlined
below.

Rule 1. *Rule of Minimum Difference within Range.* Where two kin types
within a range are identical except for a difference in sex markers in the same
position, the two kin types may be written as one with an a in the contrasting position. Apply Rule 1 before all others.

The rule may be exemplified by the range of Grandfather where the
range is indicated as:

$$a+m+m \text{ and}$$
$$a+f+m$$

The two kin types differ only in the sex markers of the medial position.
Thus, the two kin types may be rewritten as: a+a+m. The rule of minimum difference will reduce all ranges in the above system to a single expression except for Uncle, Aunt, Nephew, Niece, and Cousin. For these,
another rule is necessary.

Rule 2. *Rule of Sequence Difference within Range.* Where two expressions
are identical except for one additional "link" (i.e., a pair consisting of one
sex and one relation marker), the "link" may be written in parentheses. The
parentheses will indicate an optional expansion. This rule may be applied in
sequence but must be labeled with a superscript indicating number of reductions made.

For example, assume the following range:

$$m+f\ 0\ m$$
$$m+f\ 0\ m-m$$
$$m+f\ 0\ m-m-m$$

where it is desired to reduce these kin types to a single expression. Rule 2 provides the following convention:

$$m+f\ 0\ (m-\ )^{0,1,2}m$$

where the parentheses indicate optional inclusion of the enclosed link, and the superscripts indicate number of applications of option.

The same rule holds for "affinal" links, Thus:

$$a+m\ 0\ m$$
$$a+m\ 0\ f=m$$
$$a+f\ 0\ m$$
$$a+f\ 0\ f=m$$

reduce to $\qquad\qquad a+a\ 0\ (f=)m$

The application of these two rules completely reduces the ranges of the English system to single expressions as follows:

Grandfather	$a+a+m$
Grandmother	$a+a+f$
Father	$a+m$
Mother	$a+f$
Brother	$a\ 0\ m$
Sister	$a\ 0\ f$
Son	$a-m$
Daughter	$a-f$
Grandson	$a-a-m$
Granddaughter	$a-a-f$
Uncle	$a+a(+a)^{0,1}\ 0\ (f=)m$
Aunt	$a+a(+a)^{0,1}\ 0\ (m=)f$
Nephew	$a(=a)\ 0\ (a-)^{0,1}a-m$
Niece	$a(=a)\ 0\ (a-)^{0,1}a-f$
Cousin	$a+a(+a)^{0,1,2}\ 0\ (a-)^{0,1,2}a-a$

Before proceeding to the analysis of the structure of the above terms and expressions, two additional rules for the reduction of kin types within ranges to a single expression will be mentioned. These rules, though not necessary for the analysis of the English system, are useful for other systems.

Rule 3. *The Rule of Paired Sequence Difference within Ranges.* This rule is used widely for the analysis of systems recognizing the parallel vs. cross distinction. It may be thought of as an extension of Rule 2. Where two expressions are identical except for "paired links," the "paired links" may be written in parentheses. The parentheses will indicate an expansion, and superscripts will indicate number of expansions. In addition, the subscripts i and j will be used on the sex markers to indicate appropriate handling of sex when the expression is expanded.

Take for example the following hypothetical range:

$$a+m\ 0\ m-a$$
$$a+f\ 0\ f-a$$
$$a\ 0\ a$$

Rule 3 provides the following single expression:

$$a(+a_i)^x\ 0\ (a_j-)^y a$$
$$\text{where } x=y=0,\ 1$$
$$\text{and } i=j$$

The subscripts i and j may also be used for relative sex of speaker.

Rule 4. *The Rule of Reciprocals Within Ranges.* Where two expressions differ only by the fact that they are complete reciprocals of one another, either expression may be written between slashes and be taken to represent both. In the present notation, a reciprocal of any kin type is found by writing the expression in reverse order and changing all $+$'s to $-$'s and *vice versa*, without changing 0 and $=$ links.

For example, if a range included the kin types $m+f\ 0\ m$ and $m\ 0\ f-m$, they could be reduced to the single expression, $/m+f\ 0\ m/$. In practice, we have found it most convenient to put the ascending generations between slashes.

Perhaps at this point the rationale behind the development of this new notational system can be stated clearly. This notational system contains exactly the same information as the traditional systems. The difference is that in this notation, all information is represented explicitly. For example, if one wished to program a computer with the traditional notation to identify those kin terms which refer solely to male kin types, it would be necessary to give the machine special instructions that the symbols "Fa," "Br," "So," and "Hu" stand for males (as well as other things). Such additional instructions are not necessary for the notation given here.

Structural Analysis of Terms. We return to the task of completing a structural analysis of the expressions given above. A structural analysis may proceed on the basis of a set of rules in much the same way that within-range reductions were made. The essential difference is that the operations at this stage of analysis reveal structural principles rather than produce reduced expressions of ranges. The following rules are to be applied in ordered sequence as listed. They apply to the reduced expressions produced by procedures outlined above.

Sex of Relative. If two expressions are identical except for the final sex marker, then *sex of relative* is a distinctive variable. Whenever a distinctive variable is discovered by any of the procedures in this section, it is noted for the appropriate terms. Then the expressions involved are combined and carried along in the analysis.

For example, the expressions for Grandfather and Grandmother above are $a+a+m$ and $a+a+f$, and they differ only by the final sex marker. Hence, *sex of relative* is a distinctive variable. It may be marked as R and takes the values R_1 male and R_2 female. We then mark Grandfather as R_1 and Grandmother as R_2. We now combine the expressions into $a+a+a$ (or more simply, $++$), which is carried along for further analysis.

Sex of Speaker. If two expressions are identical except for the initial sex marker, then *sex of speaker* is a distinctive variable. It may be marked as S and takes the values S_1, male speaking, and S_2, female speaking. Where a variable is nowhere recognized in a system, it would not be marked anywhere. Thus S does not appear in the description of English.

Relative Sex. If two expressions are identical except for the fact that in one, sex of speaker is the same as the relative and in the other, it is different, then *relative sex of speaker* is the distinctive variable. It may be marked as D and takes the values D_1, different, and D_2, the same.

Relative Age. If two expressions are identical except for relative age, then *relative age* is a distinctive variable. It may be marked as A and takes the values A_1, relative older than ego, and A_2, relative younger than ego. (Sometimes relative age of intervening relatives is criterial.)

Reciprocity. If two expressions are identical except for being reciprocals, then *polarity* is a distinctive variable. It may be marked by P and takes the values P_1, senior or ascending generation, and P_2, junior or descending generation.

Sex of Intervening Relative. Where two expressions are identical except for intervening relative, then *cross vs. parallel* is a distinctive variable. It may be marked by C and takes the value C_1, cross, and C_2, parallel.

Further Differences in Expressions. Let us summarize the appearance of the analysis of English to this point. The application of the procedures in this section produce the following:

TERM	EXTRACTED COMPONENTS	REMAINING EXPRESSION
Grandfather	R_1P_1	
Grandmother	R_2P_1	$/++/$
Grandson	R_1P_2	
Granddaughter	R_2P_2	

Father	R_1P_1	
Mother	R_2P_1	
Son	R_1P_2	/+/
Daughter	R_2P_2	

Uncle	R_1P_1	
Aunt	R_2P_1	
Nephew	R_1P_2	/+(+) 0 /
Niece	R_2P_2	

Cousin	R P	+(+) 0 (−)−

Brother	R_1P	
Sister	R_2P	0

In order to complete the analysis, it is necessary to have a small list of common distinctive variables that characterize systems. Examples of such variables include direct vs. collateral, generation, etc. Up to this point the steps in the analysis are explicit. The procedures have reduced 15 kin terms to five range-sets. We know of no way to specify a single best solution for the classification or arrangement of these five range-sets. Taste, previous knowledge of the system, emphasis on core kin types, and other factors affect the outcome. Three possible solutions are shown in Fig. 1:

Primary	Secondary	Tertiary
/+/	/++/	+(+) 0 (−)−
0	/+(+) 0 /	

Figure 1.   First analysis of American kinship system.

This solution stresses the distinction between relatives in the nuclear family and those outside the nuclear family. This is a simplification of Parson's picture of the American kinship system where "primary" relatives correspond to his "inner" circle (Parsons 1943:179).

The second solution (Fig. 2) corresponds to the distinction referred to by Wallace and Atkins above (1960:62).

	Lineal	Co-lineal	Ablineal
±2	/++/	/+(+) 0 /	+(+) 0 (−)−
±1	/+/		
0	ego	0	

Figure 2.   Second analysis of American kinship system.

The third solution (Fig. 3) is the one we prefer and the one that will be used in the remainder of the paper. It emphasizes the core or kernel kin type and hence treats "cousin" as a zero generation relative.

	Direct		Collateral		
	male	female	male	female	
+2	GrFa	GrMo	Un	Au	+
−2	GrSo	GrDa			
+1	Fa	Mo	Ne	Ni	−
−1	So	Da			
0	Br	Si	Co		0

Figure 3.   Third analysis of American kinship system.

Note that the dotted lines in Fig. 3 represent the relations between terms obtained with simple operations on the notation scheme. Since the notation scheme represents the genealogical elements, it may be assumed that terms joined by dotted lines are somehow "closer" than terms separated by solid lines. (Although Wallace and Atkins use dotted lines between sex pairs, e.g., mother and father, they are not derived from steps in the analysis.) The dotted lines arise from the analytic procedures. Terms within solid lines (separated only by dotted lines) are defined as constituting a *range-set*.

COGNITIVE IMPLICATIONS AND INDIVIDUAL BEHAVIORAL MEASURES

There appear to be two separate issues with respect to the cognitive implications of the analyses presented above. The first issue deals with the problem of alternative componential structures, while the second issue involves the selection of behavioral measures that would be affected if a componential analysis were isomorphic with cognitive structure.

There are two possible solutions to the first issue; that is, either one analysis is more efficient than the other in providing a cognitively accurate representation, or individuals have more than one cognitive structure with which they may operate. If the individuals in a culture have alternative cognitive structures, it is possible that either different individuals have arrived at different cognitive structures or that the same individual operates with alternative structures.

It is our feeling that there will usually be several alternative analyses possible for any set of kin terms. If we are to talk about psychological or cognitive implications of an analysis, we must specify what these implications might be. Probably some analyses will be more useful for some purposes and less useful for others. Thus there may be no single best solution for a given system.

It should be pointed out that differences in Romney's and Wallace and Atkins' analyses are due to more than one factor. One difference is due to the definition of components, especially in the definition of collaterality. Another source of difference is that Romney uses an entirely different component (reciprocity) as a basic means of aligning range sets. These alternative results highlight the fact that componential analysis is not an automatic method of uncovering individual cognitive structures. Slight differences in the operations or the definition and number of components imply different pictures of psychological reality. We feel that the solution to this problem lies in further behavioral measures of individual cognitive operations.

As Wallace and Atkins (1960:78) say,

> But the only way of achieving definite knowledge of psychological reality will be to study the semantics of individuals both before and after a formal, abstract, cultural-semantic analysis of the terms has been performed. Simple demands for verbal definition, the use of Rivers' genealogical method, and analysis of the system of kinship behaviors may not be sufficient here: additional procedures, by individual representative informants, of matching and sorting, answering hypothetical questions, and description of relationships in order to reveal methods of reckoning will probably all be required.

Following this suggestion, we have collected a variety of data on English kinship from large samples of high school students, utilizing a number of different techniques. The techniques that we have used include the following:

1. A listing of kin terms in free recall.
2. The semantic differential.
3. Direct judgments of similarity and difference with the triad method.

The general prediction we have made from componential analyses to cognitive measures is that the more components any two terms have in common, the greater will be the similarity of response to these terms. This prediction is derived from the assumption that the components of a term constitute the meaning of that term for an individual; hence, the more components which are shared, the more similar the meaning. We use component at two levels of contrast: first, as a dimension, e.g., generation or sex; second, as a value on a dimension, e.g., zero generation or male sex. Context should make clear which level is being referred to.

At this point we have not differentiated between denotative or referential meaning and affective or connotative meaning (although we believe
componential analysis would correspond most closely to denotative meaning). Nor have we attempted to prejudge which measures of similarity
actually measure similarity in meaning. These issues will be discussed later
in the paper as data are presented.

Table 1.   List of Basic Relatives in Order
of Mean Position in the Lists with Percentage of Subjects Listing Term (n = 105)

TERM	PERCENT
1. Mother	93
2. Father	93
3. Aunt	92
4. Brother	90
5. Sister	87
6. Uncle	98
7. Grandmother	97
8. Grandfather	94
9. Cousin	98
10. Niece	61
11. Daughter	31
12. Nephew	65
13. Son	29
14. Granddaughter	17
15. Grandson	17

Listing Task. One task we set for a group of 105 high school students was
to "list all the names for kinds of relatives and family members you can think
of in English." We were interested in the types of inferences we could draw
concerning the cognitive structure of the kin terms from the order, frequency
of recall, and productiveness of modifiers (such as "step-," "-in-law," etc.).

The "saliency" of kin terms is not considered explicitly in most formal
analyses but is of interest from a psychological point of view. There are two
indices of saliency available in the listing data. The first is the position of a
term in the list. We assume that the nearer the beginning of a list that a kin
term occurs the more salient it is. The second index of saliency is the per cent
of subjects who remember the term. We assume that the more salient terms
will be recalled more frequently. Table 1 lists the basic kin terms in the rank
order of their mean position in the freely recalled list. ("Mother," for
example, occurs nearest the beginning of the list, on the average.) In addition, the per cent of subjects listing the term at all is indicated.

It can be seen that there is fair correspondence between the two measures of saliency. The main discrepancies center upon the terms uncle, grandmother, grandfather, and cousin, all of which are remembered by more subjects than would be expected from their position in the list. It is of interest to note that *son* and *daughter* are low in saliency for high school students and that less than a third of them remember to include these terms.

One overwhelming regularity in the order of items in the individual lists was the adjacent occurrence of pairs of relatives differing only in the component of sex, e.g., pairs like father-mother, son-daughter, uncle-aunt, etc. These pairs occured 98 percent of the time on individual lists containing both

Table 2. Percentage of Subjects Modifying Kin Terms with Common Modifiers (Frequencies below 10 Excluded)

	STEP	IN-LAW	GREAT	HALF	SECOND
Father	55	54	—	—	—
Mother	55	57	—	—	—
Son	20	28	—	—	—
Daughter	20	30	—	—	—
Brother	55	73	—	28	—
Sister	50	63	—	25	—
Grandfather	—	—	78	—	—
Grandmother	—	—	77	—	—
Grandson	—	—	33	—	—
Granddaughter	—	—	33	—	—
Uncle	—	—	63	—	—
Aunt	—	—	52	—	—
Nephew	—	—	10	—	—
Niece	—	—	10	—	—
Cousin	—	—	—	—	60

terms. This suggests that an immediate constituent analysis is appropriate to list data and that these pairs may be taken as an immediate constituent vis-a-vis other terms in the list.

The listing task also allowed inferences about the cognitive structure of the terms from an analysis of the modifiers occurring with the various kin terms. Modifiers that occurred with a frequency of as much as 25 percent with any term are given in Table 2 with percentage of occurrence of each term (frequencies below 10 percent are excluded as being idiosyncratic or a variant usage).

Note that kin terms within the same range-set (terms bounded by the solid line in Romney's analysis) always occur with identical modifiers. Also note that every range-set takes different combinations of modifiers except for most distant generation sets separated by direct-collateral distinction (i.e., *Grandfather*, etc., set not distinguished from *Uncle*, etc., set by modifiers).

The number of modifiers is maximum for "close" sets and minimum for "distant" sets. *Brother* and *sister*, for example, take three modifiers while the more distant *cousin* takes only one. This conforms to the anthropological assumption that maximum terminological differentiation will occur with "close" relatives and progressively less differentiation with "remoter" relatives (or, more generally, that greater lexical differentiation will occur in areas of most interest and importance).

The classification of kin terms produced by partitioning of terms on the basis of sharing identical sets of modifiers is shown in Fig. 4.

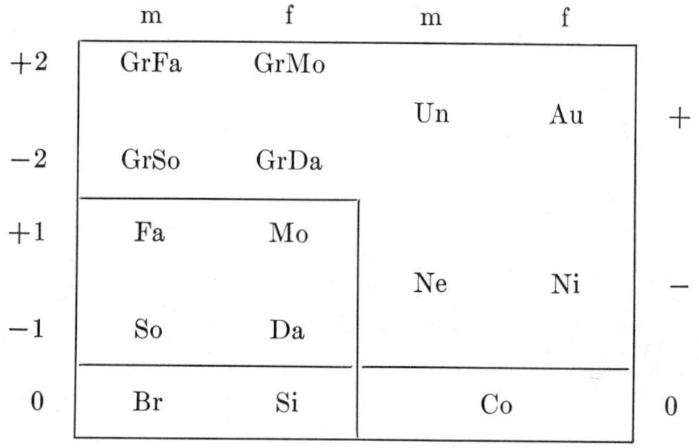

	m	f	m	f	
+2	GrFa	GrMo			
			Un	Au	+
−2	GrSo	GrDa			
+1	Fa	Mo			
			Ne	Ni	−
−1	So	Da			
0	Br	Si	Co		0

Figure 4

One of the implications of these data is that all kin terms occurring with the same modifier may be thought of as occurring in a similar response environment. Thus, for example, the fact that "half-brother" and "half-sister" occur (while no other kin term occurs with "half") may be seen as a kind of "response similarity" between "brother" and "sister." The fact that no range-sets are partitioned by any modifying word together with the fact that sets of terms occurring with the same modifier are bounded by components (or combinations of components) may be interpreted as supporting the idea that terms are classified by components.

Semantic Differential. Next, Osgood's semantic differential procedure (Osgood, Suci, and Tannenbaum 1957) was used to investigate the effect the componential composition of a term has on other verbal responses made to that term. The issue here deals with the nature of the verbal stimulus to which a subject responds when he makes a rating on the semantic differential. That is, do subjects make a semantic differential rating for the term *father* on the basis of the components which constitute the referential meaning of the term, or do they respond uniquely to *father* as an indivisible lexical item?

In order to put this issue to test, the following methods were used. First, bipolar adjective ratings for *good-bad, nice-awful, kind-mean, heavy-light, hard-soft,* and *fast-slow* were obtained for the concepts *father, mother, brother, sister, man, woman, boy, girl,* and *myself.* The sample consists of 86 six to thirteen-year-old children. The ratings were obtained in an interview in which each child was asked, "Is a *father (mother,* etc.) *good* or *bad (hard* or *soft,* etc.)?" If the child answered, "*Bad,*" he was then asked, "Is a *father* very *bad* or just a little bit *bad?*" From these responses, a five-point-scale rating was constructed with the mid-point consisting of instances in which the child rejected the first question or said "both" or "neither."

An intercorrelation matrix and factor analysis was computed on the Fortran Bi Med Program for adjective scales and was rotated to simple structure using the Verimax program. Two clear factors were found, each composed of three sets of adjectives, which correspond to the evaluation and potency dimensions (see Table 3).

For the second step of the analysis, factor scores were computed for each individual for each concept. Scores were computed by adding the raw scores for the three bipolar adjective scales for each factor.

Table 3.   Rotated Factor Analysis for Semantic
Differential Bipolar Adjectives

	FACTOR LOADING		
	I	II	III
Good-bad	.64	.00	− .04
Nice-awful	.61	.01	− .01
Kind-mean	.65	.00	.02
Hard-soft	− .20	.56	.19
Heavy-light	.00	.58	− .25
Fast-slow	.10	.64	− .04

Figure 5 presents the mean Evaluation and Potency scores for each concept plotted on a two dimensional space. The scores for *myself* were found to be significantly different for boys and girls and so were plotted separately.

From the spatial arrangement of the concepts on the two factor dimensions, it can be seen that there is a tendency for sets of concepts to cluster together. However, such clustering offers little evidence that these children were responding to the components of the terms.

However, if subjects were responding uniquely to each item, then it would be impossible to predict the factor score for one item from the factor score of any other. To the extent that subjects are responding to the components, then, a factor score for an item which represents the response to a particular component will predict the factor score for another item which shares the same component. For example, if subjects are responding to the female component in the terms *woman* and *sister* on the potency dimension, the potency score for *woman* should be correlated strongly with the potency score for *sister*. (The potency scores need not be identical for *woman* and *sister*, they should merely covary.)

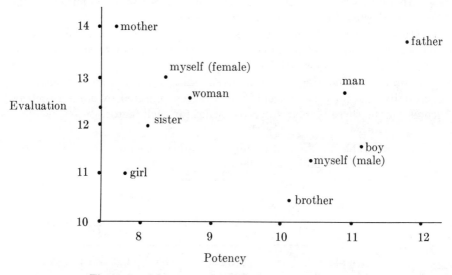

Figure 5.   Mean semantic differential factor scores.

To test the hypothesis that the componential structure of this set of terms would be reflected in the correlations between factor scores for different items, a correlation matrix and a factor analysis of this matrix was computed. (While a factor analysis of a set of factor scores may seem overly complex, the purposes of the two analyses are simple and different. The first factor analysis was computed to find out which sets of adjectives go together. The second factor analysis was performed to find which kin and person term scores go together.)

The results are presented in Table 4. Again, the Fortran Bi Med and Verimax programs were used.

In Table 4, beneath each set of factor loadings, the component which the majority of items have in common is presented. Only two terms are inconsistent with the majority of factor items; the potency score for *self* (for girls) which appears with a low factor loading in a set of terms which are otherwise all males, and the evaluation score for *sister*, which occurs with a low factor loading in a set of terms which are otherwise all young males.

While the consistent groupings of scores by components indicate that to some degree subjects rate terms as if they were rating the components of these terms, still the data contain some anomalies. The set of "young" terms (brother, sister, boy, girl, self, for boys and girls) does not emerge as a factor,

Table 4. Factor Loading for Semantic Differential Concept Scores on Evaluation and Potency (All Loadings above ∓ .30 Reported)

Factor 1.	.80	Evaluation score for *man*
	.78	Evaluation score for *mother*
	.77	Evaluation score for *woman*
	.60	Evaluation score for *father*
		("adult" component)
Factor 2.	.81	Potency score for *man*
	.80	Potency score for *self* (for boys)
	.71	Potency score for *father*
	.70	Potency score for *brother*
	.54	Potency score for *boy*
	.43	Potency score for *self* (for girls)
		("male" component)
Factor 3.	.84	Potency score for *sister*
	.75	Potency score for *girl*
	.66	Potency score for *woman*
	.42	Potency score for *self* (for girls)
	.30	Potency score for *mother*
		("female" component)
Factor 4.	.97	Evaluation score for *self* (for boys)
	.73	Evaluation score for *boy*
	.55	Evaluation score for *brother*
	.35	Evaluation score for *father*
	.35	Evaluation score for *sister*
		("young and male" components)
Factor 5.	.84	Evaluation score for *self* (for girls)
	.82	Evaluation score for *girl*
	.45	Evaluation score for *sister*
	.30	Evaluation score for *woman*
		("young and female" components)

but is split by sex into two factors, as if the components of youngness and sex interacted to form a unique connotative meaning. A second unpredicted result of the factor analysis is that kinship terms did not separate from personal status terms, although semantically these are separate domains. However, perhaps the technique of the semantic differential makes the separation of domains unlikely, since adjectives are selected for their applicability across a wide range of domains.

Triads Test. In order to investigate further the internal cognitive structuring of American-English kin terms, a sorting test was devised, adapted from procedures used in psychophysical measurement (Torgerson 1958) and in clinical psychology (Kelley 1955).

This test is called the triads test and consists of presenting sets of three terms to the subject who is instructed to designate which of the three terms is the most different in meaning. For example, a subject would be presented with the triad, *father, son, nephew,* and asked to pick out the term which is most different in meaning. (In our sample, 67 percent of the subjects selected *nephew* as most different, 22 percent selected *father* and 2 percent selected *son.*)

This task of choosing the most different of three items is a slightly more complex variety of the frequently used procedure of asking persons to state whether two items are the *same* or *different.* Here, the person is asked which two of three objects are *more* similar, or which one is *more* different. The ambiguity in this type of task concerns the question of "same or different with reference to what?" The instructions requested the subject to pick out the term which is most different *in meaning.* We wished to have the subject sort terms on the basis of similarity in referential meaning. In this respect, this procedure differs from the listing task which is thought to measure the strength of association. Similarity in referential meaning may, of course, affect the strength of association, but other conditions such as frequent contiguity in normal speech are also likely to increase association frequencies.

It is not possible to prove that all our subjects always sorted on the basis of referential meaning. However, we have interviewed a handful of subjects about their reasons for their classifications, and the subjects' verbalizations seem consistently referential. For example, one subject (untouched by anthropological knowledge) gives the following criteria for her sorting:

> father-uncle-cousin: "a father is the most different; uncles and cousins are both offshoots"
>
> father-son-brother: "a brother is most different because a father has a son and a son has a father, but a brother has a brother or sister"
>
> brother-son-grandson: "a grandson is most different, because he is more remote"
>
> grandson-brother-father: "a grandson is most different because he is moved down further"
>
> nephew-son-grandson: "a nephew is most different because he is offside.(I: What is offside?) Not in the same line."

Given that subjects do sort predominantly on the basis of referential meaning, what predictions can be made from a componential analysis about the triads test? First, let us restate our assumptions, as follows:

(1) The referential meaning of a term for an individual consists of the components of that term.

(2) The more components held in common by any two terms, the more similar the terms in referential meaning.

Given these assumptions, what predictions can be made from a componential analysis? Consider the simple subset of kin terms presented in Fig. 6.

Only two components are involved, sex and generation. *Father* and *mother* share an identical component for generation, but differ on sex. *Father* and *son* share the identical component of sex but differ on generation. However, *father* and *daughter* do not share either component. (Although they do,

	Male	Female
Ascending Generation	Father	Mother
Descending Generation	Son	Daughter

Figure 6.   Subset of American kin terms.

of course, share other components not in contrast for this subset of terms, such as reciprocity, direct lineality, etc.) Therefore, the prediction is that the term *father* will be classed as more similar to *mother* than to *daughter* and classed as more similar to *son* than to *daughter*. This will hold true no matter what strength is given to the component of sex compared to the component of generation. That is, even if a person regards sex differences as trivial and generation differences as extreme, so long as some strength is given to sex differences, *father* will be classed as more similar to *son* than to *daughter*.

If we then present all possible triads for this set of four terms and ask subjects to select the most different in meaning in each triad, we should find fewer cases in which *mother* and *son* or *father* and *daughter* were classed together than the other possible pairs. The empirical results, for a sample of 10 high school students, is presented in Table 5.

Table 5.   All Possible Triads for the Set Father, Mother, Son, Daughter

1.	father	(0)*	mother	(4)	son	(6)
2.	father	(3)	mother	(0)	daughter	(7)
3.	father	(5)	son	(0)	daughter	(5)
4.	mother	(3)	son	(7)	daughter	(0)

* Figures in parentheses indicate the number of times a term was selected as most different in meaning from the other two terms in the triad by 10 subjects.

From this table we can compute an average (mean) for the number of times each pair of kin terms are classed together by summing the number of times any two terms are classed together (i.e., are *not* circled) and dividing by the number of subjects. For example, in the table above, *father* and *mother* are classed together six times in the first triad and seven times in the second triad for a total of 13 pairings for 10 subjects, or a mean of 1.3 pairings. Figure 7 presents these mean figures. The empirical data conforms well to the predicted results. In no case did any subject cross two components. (The same results were found for the subset of terms *uncle, aunt, niece,* and *nephew.*)

Since the componential analyses by Romney and by Wallace and Atkins differ slightly, they imply slightly different predictions. In order to test these predictions, it would have been most effective to use all the kin terms

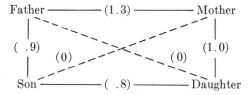

Figure 7.   Pairing of selected kin terms. Frequencies in parentheses represent mean number of times a pair of terms were classed together.

contained in the analyses. However, the major drawback of the triads method is that the number of triads increases drastically with the number of items. The formula for computing the number of triads in n items is

$$\frac{n!}{3!(n-3)!}$$

Thus, while there are only 56 possible triads for eight kin terms, there are 455 possible triads for 15 kin terms. Therefore, two questionnaire forms were used, each containing eight kin terms. Part of the data for the first questionnaire, which contained the terms *father, mother, son, daughter, uncle, aunt, niece,* and *nephew* has already been presented. The main purpose for using this set of terms was to ascertain that pairs of relatives, such as *father-mother* or *niece-nephew*, which have identical components except for sex, would be classed together with high frequency. The results indicated clearly that these sex pairs are classed together with very high frequency. This finding makes it possible to reduce the subset of kin terms to only one sex since the addition of the opposite sex kin terms into the sorting task is not likely to change the results.

The second questionnaire contained the eight male terms, including *cousin,* used in Romney's and in Wallace and Atkins' componential analyses (*grandfather, father, brother, son, grandson, uncle, cousin, nephew*). The triads test was given in questionnaire form to 150 public high school students. 116 forms were accepted for analysis. Forms which were incomplete or which showed clear position preference or which were from students whose cultural backgrounds might have unusual designations for English kin terms were rejected. The results are summarized in Table 6 for total number of times each pair of terms was classed together across all triads.

Table 6.   Mean Number of Times Each Pair of Kin Terms Were Classed Together

	FATHER	BROTHER	SON	GRANDSON	UNCLE	COUSIN	NEPHEW
Grandfather	3.9	1.0	1.4	4.3	1.5	.6	.9
Father		2.4	3.9	1.6	2.0	.6	.6
Brother			3.8	1.6	1.6	1.7	1.5
Son				3.1	.6	1.4	1.2
Grandson					.7	1.1	1.7
Uncle						3.5	3.7
Cousin							4.2

Chance expectancy = 2.0.
N = 116.

The distribution of mean responses for this table has a possible range from zero to 6.0, with 2.0 responses expected in each cell by chance. The observed table has a skewed (or almost bimodal) distribution of responses, with only eight pairs occurring with a frequency above expectancy, and nineteen pairs occurring below expectancy. A schematic representation of which pairs are classed together more frequently than expected by chance is presented in Fig. 8.

The schematic diagram presented in Fig. 8 is not the best spatial representation possible for picturing degree of similarity, since an effective representation would have all high-frequency pairings occurring in adjacent spaces. When the high-frequency pairings are plotted on the two componential analysis diagrams, it can be seen that in Romney's analysis all high-frequency pairings are between terms which differ in only one component. In Wallace and Atkins' analysis several high-frequency pairings cross more than one component (see Fig. 9).

While these results support our assumptions concerning componential analyses, there remain questions which cannot be answered solely by plotting high frequency pairings. First, we might ask if the low and middle frequency pairings also conform to our componential model. In addition, we would like to know if the triad data could be treated in some way so that it would yield directly a cognitive model of American-English kin terms.

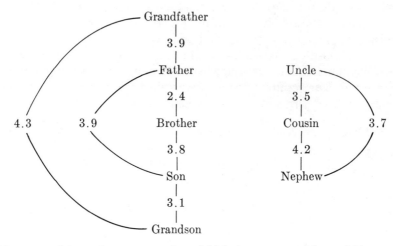

Figure 8. Schematic representation of high frequency pairings of kin terms.

Both of these questions can be answered by the use of a multi-dimensional scaling technique described by Torgerson (1958:Ch. 11), developed expressly for the treatment of triadic data. This technique produces a distance model consisting of a set of absolute distances (of undetermined units) between all pairs of stimuli in the universe treated. These distances give the relative location of the stimuli in an n-dimensional space—where n is the minimal number of dimensions needed to define uniquely the geometrical model. It *does not* yield a spatial model, e.g., it does not give the absolute projections of each point on axes referred to a known origin. The distance model is sufficient for our purposes, however, since we need only know the distances between points, and not their absolute locations in the n-dimen-

Table 7. Interpoint Distances between Male Relatives for 116 American-English Subjects (Absolute Distances Estimated with c = 3.6)

	GrFa	GrSo	Fa	So	Br	Un	Ne	Co
GrFa	0	2.696	2.786	3.913	4.288	3.755	4.275	4.448
GrSo		0	3.793	2.881	3.782	4.215	3.572	3.861
Fa			0	2.544	3.248	3.422	4.334	4.344
So				0	2.943	4.205	4.807	3.620
Br					0	3.779	3.733	3.680
Un						0	2.980	3.099
Ne							0	2.801
Co								0

Componential analysis of consanguineal male American kin terms.
Adapted from Wallace.

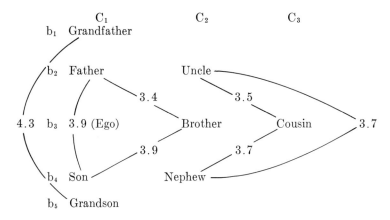

Componential analysis of consanguineal male American kin terms.
Adapted from Romney.

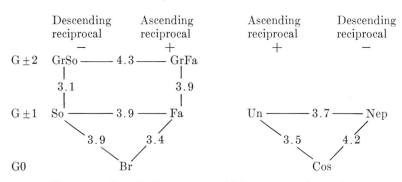

Connecting lines indicate terms which were paired together
in the triad list with high frequency. Numbers represent
mean frequency of pairing.

Figure 9.   Alternate analyses of American kin terms.

sional space. (We are indebted to William H. Geoghegan for all calculations
for the triad data. He also aided the interpretation and helped to write this
section.)

The distance model is expressed, in Table 7, as a full set of interpoint
distances in matrix form. These distances are generally in inverse relation to
the frequency of pairing data presented above. That is, the more frequently
any two items are paired together, the less the distance between them. The
problem of conceptualization may be simplified considerably with a "picture" of the model that allows visualization. The eight points may be repre-

sented in a three dimensional space. If these points were distributed *randomly* there would be an infinitely high probability that *seven* dimensions would be required to define uniquely their position, By adding the proper constant to the interpoint distances the dimensionality could be reduced to *six*—no less. So we may regard it as significant when we find that only *three* dimensions are required to define uniquely the interpoint distances of our eight kinship terms.

These dimensions correspond to the three components of generational difference, reciprocity, and collaterality. Perhaps it would be more exact to say that the direction of change of reciprocity in the model (ascending to descending) is roughly orthogonal to the direction of change of generation (from zero to one to two); and that the two of these are in turn roughly orthogonal to the direction of change of collaterality (direct to collateral). The modifier "roughly" is used because the position of some of the terms is slightly ambiguous. /Br/, for example, lies halfway between ascending and descending reciprocal, and halfway between direct and collateral. Even so, Fig. 10 below, showing the relative positioning of the terms in a three dimen-

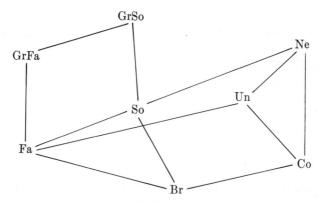

Figure 10.   Spatial representation of male American kin terms from triad data.

sional space, tentatively confirms the validity of assigning these three dimensions to the model. In Fig. 11 are illustrated the spatial distance models (geometrical constructions) that might ideally be expected from two componential analyses. The first shows the Romney analysis and the second, the Wallace and Atkins version. (The positions shown are *relative*.) It can be seen that the greater correspondence with the mathematical model occurs for the Romney version.

The Romney analysis involves three dimensions, while the Wallace and Atkins version involves only two (since the latter do not consider reciproc-

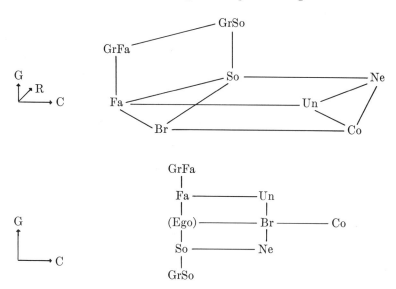

Figure 11.   Spatial representation of male American kin terms from formal analysis.

ity), The mathematical model clearly necessitates the dimension of reciprocity to define the positioning of points.

In general, the use of sorting procedures as a means of investigating similarity in referential meaning seems to be a potentially effective method. For American-English kin terms, the prediction that the more components any two terms hold in common, the more likely the two terms will be classed together as similar in meaning, was supported. Also, the triad data indicate that subjects use a set of distinctions that are in the main isomorphic with the components uncovered in semantic analyses. Finally, there is some evidence that components have differential strengths in classing together and separating terms.

Further work is necessary to validate the method fully, however. Geoghegan (1963) has shown that the data may be contaminated in various ways; for example, different subjects may have different cognitive models, or connotative as well as denotative meaning may be used by subjects in making their judgments, etc.

SUMMARY AND SPECULATIONS

Beginning with the initial problem of two alternative componential analyses for American-English kinship terms, we have attempted to explore the cognitive or psychological implications of componential analyses. A series of simple tests have been administered to individual subjects, with the general hypothesis that terms which share components will receive similar responses. This prediction was based on the assumptions that the components isolated by a formal analysis define the meaning of a term and that an individual's response to a term is affected by that term's meaning. In general, it appears that much of our data supports these assumptions, and that one of the componential analyses fits the data better than the other. However, we also found several areas of psychological interest about which a formal analysis would provide no information whatsoever, such as the saliency of a term as measured by its position in a freely recalled list or by percentage of recall.

A major conclusion of this paper is that people respond to kinship terms as if each term contained a bundle of distinct meanings. Historically, componential analysis was developed to handle exactly this type of situation. We would not need a componential analysis of American-English kinship terms if the terms were morphologically segmented into separate referential meanings. If we had such a system, we might say, "Listen, true-lineal-male-of-first-ascending-generation-ego-speaking-formally, I need the car tonight." In a system of this type, a componential analysis would be superfluous, and an adequate analysis would be to try to state the referent for "true," "lineal," etc.

We call the components of a lexeme its *sememes*. That is, we consider kinship lexemes to be composed of sets of sememes and componential analysis, a means of isolating this set of sememes.

The question of interest here is to ask *how* these sememes become part of the individual's cognitive system. In the psychological lexicon, it would seem that the sememes of kin terms function as *discriminative stimuli* for individuals. Our equation of component or sememe with discriminative stimuli is based on the fact that the test data presented above indicate that individuals make differential responses to the components of kin terms, not just to the unique term. Of course, for kin terms, many of the components are relational in character rather than absolute, which means that the discriminative stimulus consists in these cases of a relational concept, e.g., reciprocity.

The original question can now be rephrased as "how do the sememes of American-English kin terms become discriminative stimuli?" The answer would seem to be that *the sememes are learned as discriminative stimuli through precisely the same set of operations which allows the analyst to uncover components.* That is, a discriminative stimulus is most efficiently learned when a subject is repeatedly presented with events which differ or contrast in one particular feature and in which the subject's responses to the contrastive stimuli are differentially reinforced. What both the individuals who use the native system and the analyst do is learn the set of contrasts which signal a difference (although the reinforcement for the analyst may be only a neat system, while the reinforcement for the individual in the system are approval and understanding). Thus both the analyst and the native speaker learn that only females are *aunts* and only males are *uncles*. Furthermore, both might also be trained to notice that for every "kind of person" who can be an *aunt*, there is an identical (except for sex) "kind of person" who can be an *uncle*.

E.g. "aunt"   MoSi, FaSi, MoBrWi, etc.
      "uncle"   MoBr, FaBr, MoSiHu, etc.

However, not all American-English kin terms have ranges of kin types which match except for one feature. Only those distinctions which in Romney's method of analysis are termed *range-sets* can be matched up in this way. The range of the term *uncle* can be matched to the range of the term *aunt*, but the range of *uncle* cannot be matched to *father*. This difference in the conditions of contrast is perhaps related to the fact that individuals tend to class together in the triad procedure and in the use of the affix "in-law," "step," etc., those terms or sets of terms whose ranges have an exact match except for one feature. Such sets of terms are not only easy to learn to distinguish, but they are also easy to learn to re-classify together as one unit versus other units. (E.g., *parents* vs. *child*, *sibling* vs. *cousin*, *father* and *son* vs. *uncle* and *nephew*, etc.) Thus, the ease of contrastiveness and regrouping may account for the differential strength of various components in sorting kin terms.

However, from other evidence, the mere fact of repeated presentations of material which differs only in one feature, but which is *not* differentially reinforced, is not enough to train in a discriminative stimulus. For example, although we are repeatedly presented with human faces which differ slightly from left side to right side, we typically fail to notice the asymmetry, since such an easy observation is not contingent on any reinforcement. Both contrastiveness and differential reinforcement seem to be necessary conditions for learning a discriminative stimulus. As a related speculation, we suggest that the differential saliency of various sets of kin terms noted in the listing task is a result of the differential frequency, strength, and type of reinforcement received for using these terms.

A further implication of the notion that componential analysis may isolate discriminative stimuli is that other types of components found in the analysis of non-semantic material, such as the distinctive features of phonemes, or the shape dimensions of orthographies, may also be considered as potential discriminative stimuli. However, simply because the analyst can put together a series of items and find in them a verbalizable set of contrasts does not imply that these contrasts function as discriminative stimuli for any other individual. If the users of these items rarely have the opportunity to place them in contrast, or if there are no reinforcing consequences in doing so, then the analyst has trained himself on a discriminative stimulus which is uniquely his.

Finally, it should be mentioned that persons may learn more discriminative stimuli to class and segregate kin than the contrasts found only in the lexical system. The use of such distinctions as "close" or "nuclear family" is a case in point. Nor are kinship contrasts always so clear that they force all individuals to learn the same simple discriminative stimuli. However, the fact that individuals may develop more discriminative stimuli than the componential analyst finds necessary and the fact that both may face equivocal contrasts, would seem to be a topic for further research.

REFERENCES CITED

Geoghegan, William H., 1963, A distance model for the American-English kinship system. Unpublished ms.

Goodenough, Ward H., 1956, Componential analysis and the study of meaning. Language 32:195–216.

Kelly, George A., 1955, The psychology of personal constructs. New York, Norton.

Osgood, C. E., G. J. Suci and P. H. Tannenbaum, 1957, The measurement of meaning. Urbana, University of Illinois Press.

Parsons, Talcott, 1943, The kinship system of the contemporary United States. *In* Parsons, Essays in sociological theory. New York, Free Press.

Torgerson, Warren S., 1958, Theory and methods of scaling. New York, Wiley.

Wallace, A. F. C., J. Atkins, 1960, The meaning of kinship terms. American Anthropologist 62:58–79.

The Problem of the Psychological Validity of Componential Analyses[1]

Anthony F. C. Wallace

INTRODUCTION

What is the purpose of a componential analysis of a terminology? In initial formulations (see Goodenough 1956, and Lounsbury 1956) this purpose was stated clearly: it was a semantic analysis, an analysis of meaning; and, furthermore, not any and all kinds of meaning, but meaning of a par-

Reproduced by permission of the American Anthropological Association from the *American Anthropologist*, Vol. 67, no. 5, part 2 (Special Publication), pp. 229–248 (October 1965).

ticular kind. The kind of meaning which componential analysis aimed to expose was, first of all, *intensional* or *definitional meaning:* that is to say, the minimal information about the object to which a term referred, either sufficient to justify the utterance of the term in reference, or necessary to infer from its use. It did not aim to reveal *extensional meaning* (merely a listing of individual referent objects, such as particular people, episodes of illness, potatoes, etc.) nor *connotational meaning* (which, in an arbitrarily restricted domain, the semantic differential technique of Osgood and his associates aimed to reveal). Furthermore—and this restriction is central to the argument of this paper—the aim of componential analysis was to discover the intensional meaning of terms *for their native users.* In other words, it was supposed to make statements about concepts in the native's "cognitive world." The methodological promise of componential analysis, and a large part of the reason for its popularity, lay precisely in its claim to be a systematic, reliable technique for revealing what words mean to the people who use them, not merely in the domain of kinship, but in any other lexical domain with a taxonomic structure.[2]

In some recent papers (e.g. Burling 1964a, and Lounsbury 1964a) and in discussion among practitioners of the art, however, a drawing-in-of-horns has begun. The claim that a componential analysis represents a native speaker's cognitive world is now often avoided (see Burling 1964a, 1964b; Frake 1964; Hammel 1964; Hymes 1964; Lounsbury 1964a). One reason for this shyness has been, I think, the traditional lack of interest of anthropologists in testing the validity of hypotheses by experimental research methods. One major intent of this paper is to demonstrate that the validity of a hypothesis about native cognitive worlds can be tested empirically. (For another attempt along these lines of empirical testing, see Romney and D'Andrade 1964.) Another reason for avoiding the psychological issue seems to be a reluctance to recognize the implications either of accepting or of rejecting an interest in native "cognition."

Let us consider the implications of rejecting an interest in native cognition as an aim of semantic analysis via componential, or any other, method. Such a refusal renders trivial the claim that the analysis is semantic at all. If all that can be said of the product of these operations is that they predict a certain kind of verbal behavior, there is certainly no need to call the results semantic. If the analyst claims, in effect, that the meaning of the terms is merely their meaning to him and that he has no way of demonstrating what they mean to anyone else, and in particular to their native users, the sense of semantic employed is minuscule. And if he matches terms with categories in a "universal" frame, all that he can show is that the objects referred to by certain terms have certain social, biological, or other objective characteristics: i.e., that they are male, older or younger than the speaker, related to him by blood or by marriage, and so on. While all this is by no means useless information to a student of the society, it is gratuitous to call it semantic, in any anthropological sense, since the only cognitive process considered is that of the analyst himself.

To take an example outside the domain of kinship let us suppose that a primitive people—such as the Seneca Indians—have a word which refers to petroleum, a substance which they collect from the surface of pools and use as a liniment. To the contemporary Chinese chemist petroleum is a substance with certain physical and chemical properties. Both the Chinese and the Seneca words for petroleum refer to this same substance, but it would be silly to cite the Chinese chemist's definition of petroleum as the "meaning" of the Seneca word, even though the matter referred to displays the characteristics given in the chemist's definition. Yet a componential analysis employing as the "frame of reference" the periodic table of the elements and the laws of chemical combination can be used just as reasonably to define the "meaning" of all the words for all material objects in all the languages of the world, as a mechanically applied universal frame of kin-types and transformation rules can be used to define the "meaning" of all the words for kinfolk in all the languages in the world. The result in both cases may be useful information, in the one instance about technology and in the other about sociology, but they should not be confused with anthropological semantics.

And lest the example appear far-fetched, it is well to keep in mind that the root of componential analysis was the use of a standard frame for the definition of phonemes. Individual phonemes are defined as cells in a taxonomic structure whose dimensions are independent variations in the muscular positioning of various parts of the mouth and upper respiratory apparatus while air is being inhaled or exhaled. Yet the linguist does not say that a phoneme's "meaning" to the native speaker is defined by the statement of the physical disposition of the vocal apparatus during its enunciation.

If, however, the componential analyst does claim that he is saying something about what words mean to other people, he must recognize that he undertakes a very difficult task. First of all, he needs to be clear about what it is that he is assaying. He is trying to make statements about the speaker's behavior and not about the objective characteristics of objects to which the speaker refers. He is not merely trying to pair noises made by informants with classes of objectively identified objects; he is trying to describe an information process in which symbols received by the speaker are related predictably to symbols produced by the speaker. He wishes to fill in the schema of a terminological system of the following kind:

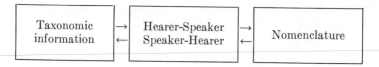

When such a schema can be filled in for a particular lexical domain, by various methods including the use of componential analysis, one can say that a *semantic* analysis has been done. Needless to say, this is not likely to be an analysis of the whole behavior system which involves those objects denoted by the terminological system, and whether one wishes to call the results a contribution to the study of cognition, or psychology, or culture, or language, is not very important. The principal reason for my own inclination to call such a schema "cognitive" is that the process by which the speaker relates taxonomic information to nomenclature is latent or perhaps unconscious: i.e. he cannot give a clear and correct verbal statement of his own rules of semantic procedure (although he can give valuable clues on proper inquiry), and the rules must therefore be inferred and their validity—their "psychological" validity—tested by techniques of a sort more commonly employed by psychologists than anthropologists. But it is not essential in this discussion to argue about the value of considering culture as cognition, even though I regard this as a worthwhile assumption.

From this point of view the dispute over whether properly conducted componential analysis yields only one true analysis ("god's truth") or a multitude of equally true analyses ("hocus pocus") is also beside the point. One or many, their psychological validity—in distinction to their sociological, mineralogical, biological, or whatever objective validities may be relevant—must be established by means independent of the mechanics internal to componential analysis itself. Nevertheless awareness of the problematic nature of psychological validity sprang historically from the apparent indeterminacy of the results of componential analysis. The publications on componential analysis to date, and no doubt the unpublished experience of others like myself, suggest that the application of its procedures to lexical and denotative data does not automatically yield a unique description of a native cognitive (or semantic) system (Wallace and Atkins 1960, Burling 1964). This is not to say that such descriptions are inaccurate in predicting the usage of a native speaker. As we have argued, the question is whether the anthropologist is able not only to predict which objects will be referred to by which terms but also to predict what criteria the native speaker will employ in determining the appropriate term to use. The problem was first recognized as a serious practical issue because componential analytic procedures, as classically described by Goodenough (1956) and Lounsbury (1956), generally yield two or more distinct descriptions of any given lexical domain. Which, if any, of these alternative descriptions are valid as descriptions not just of the distributions of terms over denotata but of the criteria by which the native speaker classifies these denotata? The classic methods do not give any way of answering the question.

There have been two kinds of responses to this situation. On the one hand, because of the difficulty of investigation some have disclaimed interest in psychological matters and confined their attention rigorously to what Wallace and Atkins (1960) have called "structural reality." In the case of kinship terms structural reality implies merely such sociological character- istics of kinsmen of Ego as can be inferred from arrays of kin-type deno- tations. From this point of view, the parsimony, elegance, and accuracy with which a terminological usage can be predicted are the criteria by which the relative merit of alternative descriptions is to be judged (Burling 1964 and Lounsbury 1964). Using kinship terms as the example, the anthropolo- gist says in effect: "If you point out to me any pair of persons in this com- munity, and give me certain items of information about each of them, I can predict whether or not they will consider themselves to be kinfolk, and by what terms they will refer to one another." On the other hand, one may say that both structural and psychological reality are of interest, and that be- cause the procedures of componential analysis as classically described, while adequate for producing structural descriptions, are insufficient to produce demonstrably-valid psychologically real descriptions, it is necessary to de- velop new techniques. The anthropologist, in this posture, wants to say: "If you point out to me any pair of persons in this community, and give me certain items of information about each of them, I can predict whether or not they will consider themselves to be kinfolk and by what terms they will refer to one another. Furthermore, the items of information which I am using are the same items as they themselves employ in determining whether they are kinfolk and by what terms they should refer to one another."

In this paper I am not urging that the only worthwhile goal of compo- nential analysis is the production of psychologically valid semantic descrip- tions. Sociological information is certainly of interest to the ethnographer (and to the cross-cultural sociologist). But I am asserting that *if* the anthro- pologist wishes to claim that he has produced a valid description of a cogni- tive (semantic) system, he needs to use additional techniques beyond those of the classic method of componential analysis. First, there must be tech- niques for identifying dimensions of classification and logical operations which *are* demonstrably real to the native speaker. Second, there must be techniques for demonstrating that a given logical operation or dimension of classification, however derived by the anthropologist, is *not* employed in the native speaker's semantic calculus.

Kinship terminology will be used as the material for illustrative analysis according to the principles described in Wallace and Atkins (1960). But I do not want to confuse the methodological issues relevant to componential analysis as such with the methodological issues relevant to the study of kinship as such. They overlap rather than coincide. Although kinship ter- minology is, in a sense, the backbone of any human kind of culture, never- theless, as Schneider emphatically insists, kinship terms are obviously not by any means the whole of any kinship system, and their analysis by componential or other means does not exhaust the description of kinship. The kinship terminology, and the taxonomy of which it is the nomenclature, are related to kinship groups, to the mutual rights and duties of kinsmen, and to the relationship of kin relationships to other sorts of relationships—political, economic, or whatever—in society; but describing the terminology does not complete the description of the kinship system. One reason for the popularity of kinship terms in componential analysis is their amenability to being run through useful methodological exercises. Methodologically, indeed, kinship terms have been to the cultural anthropologist what rats have been to the experimental psychologist: small warm objects readily manipulated in elegant research designs yet (hopefully at least) sufficiently similar to larger entities to justify their use as models of processes in a bigger world.

IDENTIFICATION OF PSYCHOLOGICALLY REAL DIMENSIONS

In the classic method of componential analysis as applied to kinship, the procedure is simply to sort kin-types into complementary sets matched with complementary groups of terms. Since the kin-types are treated as if they were objects ("denotata"), psychological considerations do not seem to arise. But most semantic analysts, whether or not they wish to claim psychological reality for their analyses, probably make use of some plausible assumptions about the meaningfulness of these kin-types to some sort of "human nature": for instance, that maternity, sex, and marriage at least are universally recognized and relevant kinship relationships or properties. Thus when the analyst finds that some kin-type and kin-term sets sort out neatly into "male" and "female" distributions, he does not hesitate not only to use this discovery as a convenient aid to the construction of his own predictive model of usage, but also to attribute his distinction to the native speakers (explicitly or implicitly). To avoid doing so, indeed, would demand a more rigorous hocus-pocus-manship than even the most positivistic anthropologists probably possess, and hardly requires subscription to a Berkeleyan idealism. But this raises the more general problem of justifying the use of *any* universal set of conceptual denotata as a meta-language into which all kinship terminologies can be translated. Universal frames of reference—whether they be kin types, or the periodic table, or the Linneaean system of classification—are valuable for the service they perform to nonpsychological science, but they cannot automatically claim a psychological universality; they are not inevitable as cognitive categories of a "human mind."

Beyond relying upon their implicit assumptions about human nature, most analysts probably (and some certainly, by their own declaration—see Hymes 1964) make use of their knowledge of other areas of the particular culture under consideration to identify dimensions of kinship classification.

Thus knowledge of the determinants of inheritance of property may provide a guide to native conceptions of descent; marriage rules may help to define the dimensions involved in distinctions among children of parents' siblings; the existence and nature of kin groups (such as sibs) may provide evidence of distinctions that "cut across" dimensions of lineality and generation, or may corroborate the plausibility of other dimensions already hypothesized. More generally the distinctions mentioned as taxonomically relevant in many contexts will yield useful suggestions to the student of one taxonomic area.

But beyond such clues as are derived from notions about human nature and miscellaneous knowledge of the culture, there seems to be no generally followed procedure for eliciting directly from the native speaker a statement of what are, for him, the dimensions of the taxonomy whose nomenclature is under investigation. (The eliciting technique of Metzger and Williams, currently under development, is however intended to solve this problem—see Metzger and Williams, 1963. Also the technique of Romney and D'Andrade for measuring semantic saliency should be mentioned—see Romney and D'Andrade, 1964.) One such procedure, of course, is to ask the informant how he knows that such and such a real person, to whom he refers by the term "K" (kinsman-of-certain-class), is really his "K." Another such procedure is to ask the informant what the term "K" means (i.e. how he defines the term). Obviously such procedures will yield neither consistent nor complete information on a lexical domain, both because of interpersonal communication difficulties and because of the well known difficulty of explicating own behavior. But the straightforward revelation by an informant that he thinks in terms of lineality, generation, sex, or whatever, is positive evidence for the psychological reality of at least these dimensions for him.

In most kinship analyses, and in any other componential analytic enterprise which uses a standard set of reference objects (such as "kin types"), the above procedures do not replace, but rather guide, the sorting of denotata in the direction of a psychologically valid description. Where the use of a standard set of reference objects is inconvenient or technically impracticable (as may be the case with many lexical domains), the procedures indicated above may be the only way in which a componential paradigm can be formulated.

IDENTIFICATION OF PSYCHOLOGICALLY REAL LOGICAL OPERATORS

As was pointed out in an earlier publication (Wallace and Atkins 1960), anthropologists doing componential analysis seem to choose class-product or relative-product operators without much concern for the native's logical mode. Class-product logic is the logical mode in which most scientific analysis in the Western tradition is conducted and, whether or not the Western layman customarily uses this rational framework in his folk taxonomies, the

Western scientist turns to the algebraic formula and the class-product space as the most familiar manner of technical conceptualization. But the classic procedures of componential analysis provide no means for determining the logical modality of the native speaker's taxonomy. Thus supplementary inquiry is again necessary in order to determine how the native speaker "reckons" the criteria for determining the taxonomic classification, and hence the appropriate terminology, for a reference object.

The methods for determining the native speaker's mode of reckoning are similar to those needed for discovering the dimensions of his taxonomy: observing the use of one kind of logical operator or another in other linguistic and cultural contexts; in the instance of kinship terminology, asking him how he knows that a given real person is his kinsman, and that he should be referred to by the term "K"; and asking him to define the term "K." Once again, in an inquiry concerned with psychological reality, it is not enough to know that the ethnographer—and therefore, possibly, the native speaker— *can* predict usage by a particular model. It is necessary to know how the native speaker *does* go about choosing the term to be used.[3]

TESTING THE PSYCHOLOGICAL VALIDITY OF THE ANALYSIS

It is not possible to show that a given analytic model is the only one which the native speaker can, or does, employ. But it is possible to show that a native speaker can use one model and cannot use another. Showing that a native speaker cannot use a certain model does not in any way imply that the model is not adequate to predict his usage; its structural validity is to be tested by other criteria embodied in the classic method of componential analysis.

Inasmuch as terminological usage can be predicted adequately by several models, only some or none of which may be psychologically valid, the test of prediction of such usage is useless in discriminating between psychologically valid and psychologically nonvalid paradigms. In question is *how* the native speaker, confronted by a reference object, reckons to choose the appropriate reference term. Therefore the test must require the native speaker to display—verbally, in writing, or in visible manipulation—the reckoning procedures which he employs. This reckoning procedure, or calculus, involves three stages: first, the selection of sufficient relevant information about the reference object; second, the organizing of the data so as to define the object's class or relationship; and third, the choice of the term appropriate to that class. We are here chiefly interested in the first two stages of the process, which involve respectively the dimensions and logical operations required for the solution of the problem.

It should be possible to state the general principles on which such tests should be based, even though scientific ingenuity probably can devise dozens of particular procedures appropriate to various problems and research situations. There seem to be two kinds of tests corresponding to the two real-life situations of choosing a term from a knowledge of the reference object's characteristics and of inferring from the use of a term the characteristics of the class of reference objects to which it refers. With respect to the first type of test, the first principle is to supply in series different sets of restricted information about the reference object in order to discover what dimensions the native speaker considers to be relevant and sufficient to reckon the choice of term. The second principle is to require the native speaker to make manifest the procedures he uses to reckon with the information supplied in order to discover the logical operations he performs. With reference to the second type of test, the first principle is to supply different sets of terms, in series or simultaneously, in order to discover what dimensions of information the native speaker can infer from the terms. Once again the second principle is to require the native speaker to make manifest his reckoning procedures.

The use of such tests as these can demonstrate that a given speaker cannot—therefore does not—make use of certain dimensions of information and/or certain logical operations in the taxonomic domain under investigation, and that he can use others. These tests cannot demonstrate, however, that he does use this particular psychologically valid calculus in other situations outside of the test context. Nor should the impression develop that such tests are substitutes for other kinds of ethnographic field work; indeed, as the foregoing discussion should have made clear, despite their psychological flavor these tests can be developed only after standard ethnographic information is collected.

In the following sections I shall illustrate the use of such testing procedures on data collected from a Japanese informant. The purpose of the illustration is not to provide a complete analysis of Japanese kinship terminology but to display how alternative componential paradigms may be tested for psychological validity in the case of a particular native speaker.

THE CASE OF A JAPANESE INFORMANT
by
Anthony F. C. Wallace and John Atkins

In the course of the studies which led to an earlier paper (Wallace and Atkins 1960), John Atkins and I attempted to work out techniques, according to some of the criteria outlined above, for distinguishing between psychologically valid and nonvalid paradigms. We were not interested in demonstrating the classic method of componential analysis but only in developing

devices to handle the problem of testing the psychological validity of paradigms once derived by whatever method. For this purpose we worked with
a Japanese informant, Miss Hiroko Kameyama, who was temporarily in
this country as a Fulbright Fellow at the University of Pennsylvania.[4] An
English major in the School of Education, and an excellent speaker of the
English language, she kindly devoted nearly 30 hours of her time to the task.
The interviews were conducted jointly by both authors in the summer of
1958 in an office at the Eastern Pennsylvania Psychiatric Institute, and for
the most part were recorded on tape. The following protocol of interviews
was followed:

Interview A

Initial conversation was aimed at establishment of rapport and explanation
of the scope and purposes of the investigation, definition of mutual roles, and agreement on a tentative schedule.

A first approximation was elicited of the desired lexicon of individual and group
referential kinship terms customarily used by the informant in Japan. Each term
was written by the informant in English letters and also in Japanese ideographs on
a separate file card.

The informant was questioned systematically as to the extensional relationships
of all obtained words and phrases (i.e. all pairs of terms were classified as being
either equivalent, contrary, one inclusive of the other, or overlapping with respect
to the individuals who could be referred to by them).

Interview B

Additional group and individual terms were offered by the informant.

Extensional classification was amplified and corrected.

A family tree, displaying genealogical relationships of the informant to all her
significant relatives, was constructed.

Interview C

The informant brought a slightly revised and more elegantly drawn genealogical
chart to the interview. She assigned to each relative a kinship term. This yielded a
set of more or less incomplete kin-type definitions of most of the terms.

The informant was asked to give her definition in Japanese of each term. This
request led to considerable discussion of the nature of the task and the most effective
method of recording the data. The informant finally elected to take home with her
the set of cards representing the individual terms of reference and to write out in
Japanese her concise definition of each, with a strictly literal and a "good" (idiomatic
English) literal translation following each Japanese definition.

Interview D

The informant returned with definitions written out for 98 terms (including
synonyms and a number of specialized terms for such kinship categories as "divorced
daughter who has returned home"). She also brought with her a Japanese friend,
the newly-arrived wife of a Japanese student, to "check the accuracy" of her Japanese definitions. The friend's "corrections" were added in red ink to the informant's
definitions. The friend had apparently been invited because the informant felt she
might give a more accurate representation of "correct" Japanese usage. (The in-

formant never completely accepted our view that her task was to give personal usage; she felt that she was a representative of Japan and should be "correct.")

The definitions were discussed with, and between, both informants.

Miss Kameyama was asked to "sort" the file cards containing the referential terms. Through faulty instruction by the ethnologists, she proceeded to arrange all the cards on what turned out to be one large paradigm, rather than to classify them successively on a series of dimensions. Further card sorting procedures were abandoned in order to complete more immediately relevant tasks.

Interviews E and F

"Loose ends" were identified and tied up: missing definitions, additional terms, uncertainties of spelling, etc.

The informant was asked to discuss explicitly the Japanese usage of the relational connective *no* and the way in which various logical operations were expressed in Japanese syntax.

The informant gave her English definitions of the English kinship terms which she had used to define the Japanese terms.

The product of these rather elaborate procedures was a set of referential kinship terms (female speaking): thirty consanguineal terms, three step terms, and six affinal terms; a larger set of cover terms used for referring to classes of kinsmen; and a number of terms for organized groups of kinfolk.[5] The kin terms proper can be used to denote individuals in expressions of the sense: "[He or she] is my _____." Table 1 presents a group of 18 of these terms, with their Japanese and literal English definitions, selected by the investigators because their kin-type extensions approximately corresponded to the English terms discussed in Wallace and Atkins' earlier paper (1960). The criteria of extensional comparability was important because the tests of psychological validity involved an English paradigm.

The kin-type extensions (derived from her genealogical assignments and from her corrected definitions) are as follows:

sofu	FaFa, MoFa	*oji*	FaBr, MoBr, FaFaBrSo, MoFaBrSo, etc.
sobo	FaMo, MoMo	*oba*	FaSi, MoSi, FaFaBrDa, MoFaFrDa, etc.
chichi	Fa	*itoko*	FaBrSo, MoSiDa, FaFaBrSo, etc.
haha	Mo	*oi*	BrSo, SiSo
ani	El Br	*mei*	BrDa, SiDa
ane	El Si	*o-oji*	FAFaBr, FaMoBr, MoMoBr, FaFaFaBrSo, etc.
otōto	Yo Br	*o-oba*	FaFaSi, FaMoSi, MoMoSi, MoFaFaBrDa, etc.
imōto	Yo Si	*mago*	SoSo, SoDa, DaSo, DaDa
musuko	So	*musume*	Da

Table 1. Japanese Consanguineal Kinship Terms with Definitions and Translations

NO.	JAPANESE TERM	JAPANESE DEFINITION (AS WRITTEN BY INFORMANT)	ENGLISH TRANSLATION	APPROXIMATE ENGLISH EQUIVALENT
1	chichi	otoko-oya	Male parent	Father
2	haha	onna-oya	Female parent	Mother
3	musuko	otoko no ko (domo)	Male child	Son
4	musume	onna no ko (domo)	Female child	Daughter
5	sofu	chichi-kata haha-kata ni yorazu, oya no chichi	Independent of [whether] on father's side or mother's side, father of parent	Grandfather
6	sobo	chichi-kata haha-kata ni yorazu, oya no haha	Independent of [whether] on father's side or mother's side, mother of parent	Grandmother
7	ani	oya no musuko no toshiue no mono	Son, older than one's self, of parent	Elder brother
8	ane	oya no musume de toshiue no mono	Daughter, older than one's self, of parent	Elder sister
9	otōto	[oya no mosuko no toshishita no mono]	[Son, younger than one's self, of parent]	Younger brother
10	imōto	oya no musume de toshishita no mono	Daughter, younger than one's self, of parent	Younger sister
11	oji	chichi-oya no kyōdai, mata tokinawa chichi-oya no itoko mo sasu	[male] Sibling of father or cousin of father	Uncle
12	oba	chichi no onna kyōdai; haha-oya no onna kyōdai	Female sibling of father; female sibling of mother	Aunt
13	itoko	chichi-kata haha-kata ni yorazu, oya no kyōdai no musuko de toshiue no mono; . . . no musuko de toshishita no mono; . . . no musume de toshiue no mono; . . . no musume de toshishita	Independent of [whether] on father's side or mother's side, parent's sibling's son [whether] older or younger than one's self, or daughter, [whether] older or younger than one's self	Cousin
14	oi	kyōdai-shimai no musuko	Son of sibling	Nephew
15	mei	kyōdai-shimai no musume	Daughter of sibling	Niece
16	o-oji	chichi no oji	Uncle of father	Great-uncle (paternal)
17	o-oba	chichi-kata no sofubo no onna kyōdai matawa chichi no oba; haha-kata no sofubo no onna-kyōdai matawa haha no oba	On father's side, female sibling of grandparent or aunt of father; on mother's side, female sibling of grandparent or aunt of mother	Great-aunt
18	mago	[ko no ko]	[Child of child]	Grandchild

Let us attend now to the task of formulating a model of the informant's definitions which most closely corresponds to her cognitive structure, under the conditions of this experiment. The closest approximation to psychological reality, in componential form, should be a componential analysis in the informant's language, in this case Japanese. The following dimensions are explicitly mentioned in the informant's definitions: "side" of family— *chichi-kata* ("father's side") and *haha-kata* ("mother's side"); sex of relative —*otoko (no)* ("male") and *onna (no)* ("female"); relative age of relative with respect to Ego—*toshiue no* ("elder") and *toshishita no* ("younger"); variety of nuclear relationship—*oya (no)* ("parent"), *ko* ("child"), *kyōdai* ("sibling"). But these dimensions, and conjunctive and disjunctive operators, do not in themselves yield a componential analysis of all the terms. Another device on which the informant relies heavily is the relative product, which she constructs by the use of the operator *no* to connect various primitive terms like *ona, ko, otoko,* and *onna* (which she does not define formally at all) and other terms defined on the "original" matrix. Four of the terms are defined on two dimensions (it is interesting to note that the "side" dimension, although it is referred to repeatedly, is not required in any definition). The remaining 14 terms are defined as relative products of the primitive dimensional values, the four core terms, and one another. The outcome thus is a systematic chain-like paradigm involving three sets of elements: a group of primitive, undefined kinship and nonkinship terms which define a space; a group of four terms for members of the nuclear family defined on this componential space; and a group of terms for other consanguineal relatives, defined by single or disjunctively-summed relative products. The results (including the informant's "errors") are seen in Table 2.

Although this model of the informant's verbal definitions can be translated literally into an English model, of more interest are the possible analytical transformations. One of these (involving, however, a "correct" redefinition of *oji* and *o-oji* to include mother's brother, and maternal great uncles, respectively, and further specification by the informant of kin-type extensions not listed on the genealogical chart) yields a paradigm which, with the exception of the age-classified sibling terms, is mapped on the same dimensions as the English paradigm given earlier (see Wallace and Atkins 1960). The graphic representation, on the "English" dimensions, is given in Fig. 1.

To judge from the verbal definitions, however, such an Anglicized model probably fails correctly to represent the informant's psychological reality, even though it yields within certain extensional limits "correct" predictions of Japanese usage. For one thing, it neglects the significant, though apparently redundant, references in the original model to "side" of family (father's or mother's). The basic structure of the terminology is bilateral of Eskimo type (but with "Hawaiian" generational classification of nonlineals of older

Table 2. Componential Analysis Following Informant's Definitions

I. Primitives
   Components (arranged as values on dimensions):
   A: *chichi-kata*(α_1); *haha-kata* (α_2)
   B: *otoko* (*no*) (β_1); *onna* (*no*) (β_2)
   Γ: *toshiue no mono* (γ_1); *toshishita no momo* (γ_2)
   Δ: *oya* (*no*) (δ_1); *ko* (δ_2); *kyodai* (*no*) (δ_3)
   Operators
   Relative product ("/"): *no*
   Logical sum (disjunctive) ("$\vee$"): *ni yorazu; mata;* serial enumeration of homonyms
   Logical product (conjunctive) ("$\wedge$"): *de;* sometime *no;* also represented in informant's syntax by juxtaposition of components, with or without connecting hyphen

II. Nuclear Terms

	oya	*ko*
otoko (*no*)	*chichi* (ν_1)	*musuko* (ν_3)
onna (*no*)	*haha* (ν_2)	*musume* (ν_4)

III. Relative products derivative from I and II
   sofu: $(\alpha_1 \vee \alpha_2) \wedge (\delta_1/\nu_1)$
   sobo: $(\alpha_1 \vee \alpha_2) \wedge (\delta_1/\nu_2)$
   ani: $(\delta_1/\nu_3) \wedge \gamma_1)$
   ane: $(\delta_1/\nu_4) \wedge \gamma_1)$
   otōto: $(\delta_1/\nu_3) \wedge \gamma_2)$
   imōto: $(\delta_1/\nu_4) \wedge \gamma_2)$
   oji: $(\nu_1/\delta_3) \vee (\nu_1/itoko)$
   oba: $(\nu_1/[\beta_2 \wedge \delta_3])$
   itoko: $(\alpha_1 \vee \alpha_2)\ (\gamma_1 \vee \gamma_2)\ \vee (\nu_2/[\beta_2 \wedge \delta_3])[(\delta_3/\nu_3) \vee (\delta_1/\delta_3/\gamma_3/\nu_3)$
      $\vee (\delta_1/\delta_3/\nu_4) \vee (\delta_1/\delta_3/\nu_4)]$
   oi: (δ_3/ν_3)
   mei: (δ_3/ν_4)
   o-oji: (ν_1/oji)
   o-oba: $(\alpha_1 \wedge [\text{sofubo}/(\beta_2 \wedge \delta_3)] \vee (\nu_1/\text{oba}) \vee (\alpha_2 \wedge [\text{sofubo}/(\beta_2 \wedge \delta_3)]\ (\nu_2/\text{oba}))$
   mago: (δ_2/δ_2)

Informant also gave a complex definition of kyōdai (δ_3) employing the additional disjunctive operators *to* and *matawa onaji*, and using the terms defined in III, as follows: *ani to otōto, matawa onaji oya no ko; ane to imōto, matawa onaji oya no ko.*

It is also noteworthy that in the informant's usage, relative products involving *no* are sometimes used in much the same sense as in poetic or archaic English expressions of the following kind: "eyes of blue." These constructions are formally relative products but (both in English and in Japanese) are regarded as nearly equivalent to idiomatic or nonidiomatic expressions (like "blue eyes") employing the conjunctive (product) as the operator.

	Lineal		Colineal		Ablineal	
	Male	Female	Male	Female	Male	Female
Second Ascending Generation	*sofu*	*sobo*	*o-oji*	*o-oba*	*o-oji*	*o-oba*
First Ascending Generation	*chichi*	*haha*	*oji*	*oba*	*oji*	*oba*
Ego's Generation	[ego]		Elder *ani* Younger *otōto*	Elder *ane* Younger *imōto*	*itoko*	
First Descending Generation	*musuko*	*musume*	oi	mei	[no term but descriptive expression *itoko no ko*]	
Second Descending Generation	*mago*		[no term but descriptive expressions: *oi no ko; mei no ko*]		[no term but descriptive expression: *mata-itoko*, or *toen* ("distant relative")]	

Figure 1.   "Anglicized" componential paradigm of certain Japanese cosanguineal terms.

generation than Ego), and it does not require distinction as to "side." This "side" dimension is significant to the informant, however, because like many Japanese she belongs to a patri-clan or *kazoku* (translated as "family" by the informant, in somewhat the sense of "family" intended in such English expressions as "he came of good family"). At birth the individual becomes a member of the *kazoku* of his father, and the male normally retains membership in it throughout his life. On marriage, however, women are "adopted" into the *kazoku* of their husbands; occasionally males are adopted into their wives' or other *kazoku*. One suspects that the urge to classify relatives according to "side" (i.e. unilineally) is also active in an interesting incompleteness or asymmetry in her definitions of *oji* ("uncle) and *oba* ("aunt"). *Oji* is ascribed by the informant to father's side only; *oba* is ascribed to both sides. Thus she gives no term for the kin type mother's brother. *O-oji* ("great-uncle") and *o-oba* ("great-aunt") are similarly asymmetrically defined, for there is no term assigned to great uncle on mother's side. The other informant, and the primary informant herself, later spontaneously corrected this asymmetry. In this asymmetry we may be seeing, in the psychologically real structure of the informant's usage in verbal definition, the reflection of a possible functional strain on Japanese kinship terminology which a more complete and more "accurate" structural analysis of the terminology, such as is given by the Anglicized model, would have ignored. Even though the coexistence of patri-clans with a bilateral kinship terminology is a perfectly practical arrangement, it seems for this informant to present a disharmony which she attempts to smooth by redefinition of terms. Furthermore, we may note that the psychologically real analysis possesses a different logical structure from the Anglicized structural model, and depends in part on different primitive dimensions and operators. The informant simply does not *intend* "ablineal same generation as Ego" when she defines the term *itoko:* this is a meaning which the term has to the ethnographer, an equivalent meaning perhaps, but not the psychologically real meaning.

The ethnographer usually is less concerned with verbal definitions of terms than with the conditions under which the terms are used in the practical business of everyday living. The individual in a society must be able to do more than merely apply kinship terms as namelike labels to his own familiar relatives (although doubtless in his early life he has used them as names), or to define them more or less correctly for didactic purposes. He must be able to classify personally unfamiliar individuals with respect to their kin relationship to himself, on the basis of certain kinds of information about them. He must be able to classify the relationship between two other persons (a different relationship, in most cases, from either of their relationships to him) on the basis of the same kinds of information. He must be able to infer the relevant characteristics of relationships between himself and others, and between others, which are implied when he hears a term employed. As Goodenough succinctly summarizes the problem of everyday usage, "What do I have to know about A and B in order to say that A is B's cousin?"

With respect to the problem of psychological and structural reality, however, it is important to recognize the difference between the sets of criteria which the individual-in-society *does use* to make such judgments, and other sets which he *could use,* and which the ethnographer may formulate, but which the individual-in-society has not in fact learned to use. As we have indicated, the formal procedures of componential analysis do not in themselves differentiate between psychologically and merely structurally valid criteria, and the componential analyses in the literature do not attempt seriously to provide evidence to prove that the definitions presented are real to anyone except the ethnographer. Psychologically real dimensions may be hypothesized from knowledge of the social structure of the society, features of its language, themes and principles of discrimination which are operative in many contexts. These sources of information are skillfully employed by Goodenough, Lounsbury, and others in the choice of dimensions. But the acid test is to impose a task in which given criteria must be matched with terms. If the informant cannot use these criteria to sort the terms, or sort the criteria by use of the terms, it is necessary to conclude that they do not form part of his psychologically real cognitive world with respect to these terms.

Ideally, the best test of the psychological reality of a proposed semantic paradigm is to observe whether the subject can apply the kinship terms correctly when he is supplied only with information implying the dimensions and values of the space on which the proposed paradigm is mapped. If he can use this information to sort the terms correctly, the semantic space from which the information is drawn must be considered as psychologically real. Thus if a male Trukese informant is asked the correct term to use in referring to a relative of opposite sex, of the same generation, symmetrically related (in the sense of Goodenough's definition of symmetry), and consanguineal, he should reply "feefinej." But an obvious methodological difficulty interferes: failure to respond correctly may imply that the concept is psychologically unreal, or that the translation into Trukese has been clumsy, or that the informant does not understand and accept the task; while a successful response may imply either that the concept has for some time been psychologically real, or that the informant has just learned it from the ethnographer's question. Thus a safer procedure requires that the ethnographer avoid describing the concepts which he wishes to evoke and instead ask the informant to apply his own concepts to the sorting of the terms themselves. Such a procedure, although not directly testing the informant's ability to label certain concepts, tests whether or not the concepts in question are present and semantically related to the terms, by setting the informant a series of term-sorting tasks which cannot be performed correctly without the use of those concepts.

In order to test the hypothesis that the ethnographer can formulate structurally real definitions of kinship terms which are not psychologically real to the informant, let us return to the analysis of the terminology used by our Japanese informant. In the course of further interviewing it became apparent that a second paradigm, employing different dimensions of lineality and consequently being mapped on a different semantic space, would accommodate the terms. This paradigm is given in Fig. 2. The dimensions A and B cover, respectively (as in Wallace and Atkins 1960) sex (a_1 = male, a_2 = female) and generation (b_1 = second ascending generation, b_2 = first ascending generation, b_3 = Ego's generation, b_4 = first ascending generation, and b_5 = second descending generation). The dimension D divides the terms into "flesh-relatives" (*nikushin*) (d_1) and non-"flesh-relatives" (*kinshin*) (d_2); and the value d_1 is further divided by the dimension E into direct lineals (e_1) and siblings (e_2). Direct lineals are reduced as before by sex and generation; siblings are of Ego's generation and are reduced by dimension F into relative age (f_1 for "elder" and f_2 for "younger"). The non-flesh-relatives are also reduced by sex and generation, with no terms for

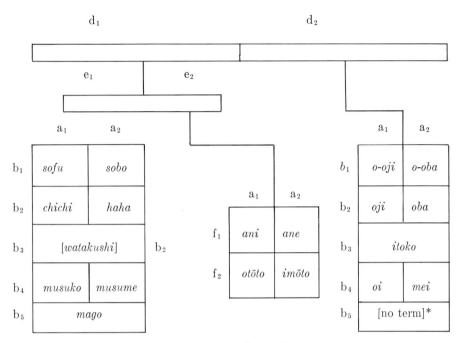

Figure 2.   Alternative componential paradigm of Japanese consanguineal core terms.

* Descriptive expression was used by this informant: *itoko no ko* or *oi no ko* or *mei no ko*.

two (or more) generations below Ego. The main structure of this paradigm was spontaneously drawn by the informant (minus the sex dimension) to aid her in reckoning during the tasks described in the following paragraphs.

The task now given to the informant was to state the principle on which various groups of terms had been divided into two parts. The groupings were preselected, with the two alternative paradigms in mind, so as to present the informant with pairs of subgroups which differed only on one dimension. Thus, for instance, the pair of groups

A	B
sofu	*sobo*
chichi	*haha*
musuko	*musume*
ani	*ane*
otōto	*imōto*

differ with respect to the sex of the relatives to whom the terms in Group A and Group B refer. The instructions given to the informant were to imagine that the terms referred to relatives of her own, whether or not she actually had such relatives living, and then to describe what the relatives referred to by terms in Group A had in common which was different from what the relatives referred to by terms in Group B had in common. If there was more than one criterion, she was asked to give them all. She was to exclude personal attitudes or special relationships which might be true in her own or some other particular family but would not necessarily be true in all Japanese families. Eighteen pairs of term-groups, some of them formulated on the basis of information provided during the performance, were presented in order to provide sortings produced by value differences on all of the dimensions from both the "Anglicized" model (Fig. 1) and the putatively "Japanese" model (Fig. 2) dimensions of sex, generation, relative age, *nikushin* vs. *kinshin*, and lineals vs. siblings. She was frankly unable to explicate the "senseless" sortings. Finally, even after the principles of the Anglicized model had been suggested to her, she was unable to explicate the one sorting which could be rationalized *only* by the Anglicized dimension of lineality (lineals, colineals, and ablineals). This sorting was:

ani
imōto
mei   *itoko*
otōto
ane
oi

Her response to this, after some preparatory expressions of doubt as to the homogeneity of the left-hand column, was: *"Mei* and *oi* would be better on the right hand column. That's all, I guess."* Where the sortings could be explicated by concepts drawn from either model, she used the "Japanese" model and did not give as alternatives the "Anglicized" dimensional concepts. In addition to the explication of the principles of sorting, the informant, as indicated earlier, gave valuable additional information in commentary on the task and in explaining her method of reckoning kin, which was useful in further specifying details of the "Japanese" model and in providing additional test sortings.

The technique adopted evidently was best suited for a highly literate, bilingual, and cross-culturally sophisticated informant. It may not be usable in detail as a wholesale research device, but we suggest that comparable sorting and explication tasks can be devised to suit local circumstances where it is desired to assess the degree of psychological reality of a putative paradigm. It should be noted also that such sorting procedures depend on having made some prior componential analyses of the terms in question which will serve as a baseline for the sorting procedures themselves.

Our conclusion with respect to the relative psychological realities of the two alternative analyses of the Japanese terms considered here is that the second model (the so-called "Japanese" model in Fig. 2) was psychologically real to our informant, but that the first (the "Anglicized" model in Fig. 1) was not psychologically real to her, despite its extensional equivalence, because she did not have available to her the "lineality" dimension (lineal, colineal, and ablineal, as defined in Wallace and Atkins 1960).

DISCUSSION: THE USES OF PSYCHOLOGICALLY AND STRUCTURALLY REAL ANALYSIS

A set of scientific propositions about human behavior may be more or less "true" in the sense that they yield accurate predictions of certain future events under specified conditions. The calculus by which these proportions are combined to yield these predictions may be said to simulate human behavior. The classic method of componential analysis enables the ethnographer to simulate the taxonomic behavior of his subjects. A successful simulation procedure has what I call "structural validity": it permits accurate prediction of a terminological event because it correctly identifies sufficient sociological, or other objectively defined, characteristics of the reference objects. But successful simulation of a process leading to any specifiable event can often be accomplished in a number of ways. If one wishes to replicate the actual process by which the subject himself produces the event, one must in effect identify, among the several successful simulacra of the process, that one (or those ones) which in specific ways replicate the procedures of the subject. A simulacrum which replicates psychological process, in addition to predicting the event, has what I call psychological validity.

In areas of ethnographic inquiry other than kinship studies, the distinction between psychological and structural validity is commonly, if informally, made; indeed, his attention to psychological reality is the hallmark of the anthropologist in contrast to the sociologist. No competent ethnographer is confused by the fact, for instance, that a mourning ceremony may have as its "purpose," in the native cognitive world, the appeasement of the vengeful soul of the departed relative, even though its "function" is not the appeasement of a soul but the termination of a socially disruptive mourning process. To confuse the native's cognitive and affective processes with the ethnographer's knowledge of their functional consequences for the social structure would pave the way for the most ancient of explanatory fallacies: the assumption that the "real" explanaton of an action which actually has a certain effect is a motive on the part of the actor to produce just this effect. In primitive societies this assumption is expressed in animistic theories of causation. In contemporary social science it is expressed, above all, in the looser varieties of psychoanalytic and structural-functional "explanations" of human behavior.

Thus it is necessary to take the position that psychologically real propositions may be held by an individual without some of their tautological or extensional equivalents, or implications, being psychologically real in any sense to him, although these equivalents and implications may be structurally real and apparent to the ethnographer. And it must be emphasized that this distinction is not to be confused with contrasts of "ideal" norms vs. "real" behavior, or with "individual" vs. "group" data: the distinction applies equally well to all four of these data categories. In other words, merely structurally valid statements are true statements about a society; psychologically valid statements are true statements about a society and also are true statements about individuals' cognitive processes.

These observations lead to a question which, as Goodenough has indicated, is pertinent to problems of culture change. What is the cultural and psychological status of the unrealized tautological or extensional equivalents, or implications, of sets of culturally accepted propositions about "reality"? In the Trukese case, he points out that there are several equivalent models available for the analysis of Trukese terminology, and he infers from this that the various dimensions are not only the *Anlagen* of culture change, but are conceptually active in the Turkese cognitive world, even though they may not be mentioned explicitly or observably used by his informants. From our position as expounded above, however, it is safer to say that some of these dimensions *at present* may not be psychologically real elements of any given Trukese mazeway, although they are implied logically by existing Trukese concepts, and thus perhaps may be elicited readily under suitable conditions. The relationship between what is now psychologically real, and what is logically implied by the existing psychological reality but is not now a part of psychological reality, is perfectly exemplified in our own culture in such a field as mathematical research. At a given point in time, certain axioms and proven theorems are psychologically real to mathematicians. Mathematicians consciously strive to discover new, as yet unrealized, implications of these axioms and theorems, for the avowed purpose of expanding various cultural frontiers in pure and applied mathematics. The same principle applies to the sort of recombinations which Barnett (1953) analyzes in the field of material culture, to those which I have discussed in connection with religious innovation (Wallace 1956), and to the notion of cultural fulfillment and depletion which Kroeber and others concerned with the philosophy of history have utilized in the definition of concepts like "climax," "golden age," "fatigue," and "cycle." From this standpoint much culture change is the product of the working through of the logical implications of an existing semantic system, with occasional recasting of the problem when new "axiomatic" propositions are introduced (such as, in material culture, the realization of the principle of the wheel or, in religion, the postulation of a new deity or new attributes of an old one). Furthermore, our informant's "error" (concerning the asymmetry of *o-oji* and *o-oba*) suggests that we should be interested in "incorrect" inferences from culturally accepted axioms: such logically inconsistent derivations also may yield cultural innovations which require justifying assumptions in the form of new axioms.

Structural analyses and psychologically real analyses of semantic systems thus should bear very different significances to the ethnographer. Structural models which reveal certain logical or functional implications for his behavior and for the sociocultural system, of which the informant may be unaware, may provide the ethnographer with convenient heuristic devices for teaching himself or his readers to make useful predictions about peoples' behavior, and may yield clues as to likely and unlikely directions of past or future cultural change, including the production or elimination of inconsistencies. Psychologically valid analysis, on the other hand, approximates the cognitive world of the persons under study, and reveals properties of individual and system behavior, including inconsistencies and asymmetries, and some of the actual cognitive operations of the users of the culture which abstracted structural analysis simply ignores. Furthermore, a psychologically real model makes possible more extensive and reliable predictions of behavior in certain situations than does a merely structurally real model.

NOTES

[1] This is a revised version of a paper presented to the conference on componential analysis in Palo Alto in June 1964. It benefits from the writer's listening to tapes of the discussion and from correspondence with Harold Conklin, Robbins Burling, and David M. Schneider, who was the principal discussant. In the revision—particularly of introductory sections—various points made by discussants are taken up; grateful acknowledgment is owed to E. A. Hammel and the discussants for the opportunity to revise with their very useful comments before me.

[2] Throughout this paper, the words "taxonomy" and "taxonomic" refer in a generic sense to the principles by which phenomena are systematically classified and sorted, and the word "paradigm" refers to the graphic representation of a taxonomy. Conklin's useful distinction between what I call orthogonal and non-orthogonal taxonomies or spaces employs "taxonomy" to refer to a perfectly non-orthogonal space and "paradigm" to a perfectly orthogonal one (see Conklin 1962).

[3] It must be pointed out here that asking a native speaker for his definition of terms is not equivalent to letting him do the componential analysis; that it does not presume that the definitions are "correct"; that it is not "ethno-semantics" or any other kind of "ethno-" science. Informant's definitions are useful only as clues to dimensions of taxonomy which *may* prove to be valid in the paradigm as eventually formulated on the basis of this and other evidence. The disqualification of infor-

mant's definitions as a source of information would be no more reasonable than the ruling out of his answers to genealogical inquiries or census questions, which also are notoriously liable to error.

[4] The Japanese materials were collected and analyzed with the collaboration of John Atkins. To Miss Hiroko Kameyama we are deeply indebted for her skillful cooperation in an exacting inquiry.

[5] To the best of my knowledge, no systematic published componential description of the meanings of Japanese kinship terms exists in English, although several community studies list some of the terms and the circumstances of their use. Befu and Norbeck, for instance, provide no semantic analysis, simply translating *itoko* as "cousin," *oji* and *oba* as "parents' siblings," etc., and omitting some of the terms included here (Befu and Norbeck 1958). Nor does Smith (1962) provide more than English translations of the Japanese terms. I am indebted to a letter and discussion with Harold Conklin for clarification of some of the problems of the Japanese analysis.

REFERENCES CITED

Befu, Harumi, Edward Norbeck, 1958, Japanese usages of terms of relationship. Southwestern Journal of Anthropology 14:66–68.

Burling, Robbins, 1964, Cognition and componential analysis: God's truth or hocus-pocus? American Anthropologist 66:20–28.

Barnett, Homer G., 1953, Innovation. New York, McGraw-Hill.

Conklin, Harold C., 1962, Comment (on the ethnographic study of cognitive systems, by C. O. Frake). *In* W. C. Sturtevant and T. Gladwin, eds., Anthropology and human behavior. Washington, Anthropological Society of Washington.

Frake, Charles O., 1964, Further discussion of Burling. American Anthropologist 66:119.

Goodenough, Ward H., 1956, Componential analysis and the study of meaning. Language 32:195–216.

Hammel, E. A., 1964, Further comments on componential analysis. American Anthropologist 66:1167–1171.

Hymes, Dell H., 1964, Discussion of Burling's paper. American Anthropologist 66:116–119.

Lounsbury, Floyd, 1956, A semantic analysis of the Pawnee kinship usage. Language 32:158–194.

Metzger, Duane, G. E. Williams, 1963, A formal ethnographic analysis of Tenejapa Ladino weddings. American Anthropologist 65(5):1076–1101.

Romney, A. Kimball, R. G. D'Andrade, 1964, Cognitive aspects of English kin terms. American Anthropologist 66, No. 3, Pt. 2:146–170.

Smith, Robert J., 1962, Stability in Japanese kinship terminology. *In* R. J. Smith and R. K. Beardsley, eds., Japanese culture: its development and characteristics. Viking Fund Publications in Anthropology No. 34. New York, Wenner-Gren Foundation for Anthropological Research.

Wallace, A. F. C., J. Atkins, 1960, The meaning of kinship terms. American Anthropologist 62:58–80.

Cognition and Componential Analysis: God's Truth or Hocus-Pocus?[1]

Robbins Burling

I

Many anthropologists have been attracted by procedures of formal semantics, such as componential analysis, and some have noted the possibility of alternative solutions (Goodenough 1956:211ff.; Wallace and Atkins 1960:75ff.). To my knowledge, however, none have given consideration to the total number of alternative solutions that are logically possible, and to the implications of that number for the problem of indeterminacy, and to the implications of indeterminacy for semantic analysis. Componential analysis is applied to a set of terms which form a culturally relevant domain and proceeds by recognizing semantic distinctions (components) which apportion the terms of the set into contrasting sub-sets, such that every item is distinguished from every other item by at least one component. Subsets can be arrived at in many alternative ways, however, and in the following discussion I will first consider the wide number of possible choices (II). Then I will consider the relation of the number of possibilities to the "cognitive" status of solutions, and conclude by stating what limited but real value I consider componential analyses to have (III).

II

My first objective will be to clarify the ways in which the items in a set may be distinguished from each other and divided among individual cells. The theoretical possibilities are most easily understood by considering very small sets of items. If we have a set of only one item, there is no problem of partitioning at all. Two items can presumably be distinguished in only one way, allowing only one possible division of a set of two terms. If there are three items in the set (call the items *a*, *b*, *c*) the possibilities become slightly more complex. For a first partition, one has three obvious choices: use a component which separates *a* from *b* and *c*; one which separates *b* from *a* and *c*; or one which separates *c* from *a* and *b*. As a matter of fact, any two of these components acting together will partition the set of three items completely, so that, to start with, there are three possible componential analyses of a set of three items (Fig. 1). However, one further possibility must also be allowed for. After a first partition (which, let us say, separates

Reproduced by permission of the American Anthropological Association from the *American Anthropologist*, Vol. 66, pp. 20–28 (February 1964).

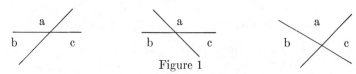

Figure 1

a from *b* and *c*) it is possible to make a second partition which distinguishes *b* from *c*, but which is irrelevant for *a*. Such components have been regularly used in analyses which have actually been carried out. For instance, in giving a semantic analysis of the third person singular pronouns in English, one might first suggest an animate/inanimate distinction to separate *it* on the one hand from *he* and *she* on the other. A second component, separating male from female can distinguish *he* from *she*, but sex is simply irrelevant for *it*. If we recognize this type of secondary partitioning, which makes use of a component that is significant for some but not all of the items in the set, three additional methods of discretely partitioning a set of three items become possible—for instance, a component distinguishing *a* from *b* and *c*, together with a second component separating *b* from *c* but irrelevant for *a*. This makes six possible analyses in all (Fig. 2).

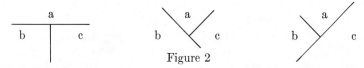

Figure 2

When we consider a set of four items, the possibilities increase considerably. In the hope of keeping the discussion as clear as possible, I will arbitrarily label the items *a*, *b*, *c*, and *d*, and I will call any partition which is significant over the entire set a "primary component." A component which is significant for less than the total number of items of the set I will call a "secondary component." A secondary component can only act after the particular sub-set to which it applies has been set off and distinguished either by one of the primary components or by a more inclusive secondary component. The initial partition of any set must always be made by a primary component. To label particular components I will use abbreviations of the following type: *ab/cd* means a component that divides the set of four items into two sub-sets, *ab* on the one hand and *cd* on the other. Secondary components can be labeled by such formulae as *bc/d*, which would indicate a component which acts after *a* has been separated from the others and which is not itself applicable to *a* but which distinguishes *b* and *c* from *d*.

In a set of four items, seven different primary components can be recognized. These fall into two distinctive types, which I will call *Type I* and *Type II*, respectively.

Type I	a/bcd	b/acd	c/adb	d/abc
Type II	ab/cd	ac/bd	ad/bc	

These primary components can be combined in various ways to produce "discrete" but "non-redundant" solutions to the set. By a "discrete" solution I mean an analysis which apportions each item into a separate cell and which distinguishes between every pair of items by at least one component. By a "non-redundant" solution I mean an analysis in which no component can be eliminated without breaking down the distinction between at least one pair of items. Both discreteness and non-redundancy have implicitly been considered desirable in componential analysis. The discrete but non-redundant solutions, using the primary components only, are as follows:

A. Any three Type I components: 4 possible solutions.
B. Any two Type II components: 3 possible solutions.
C. Any one of the Type II components may be combined with any of four pairs of Type I components. The Type I components must be chosen to partition the sets already set up by the Type II components. For instance, ab/cd can be combined with any one of the following pairs of Type I components, but with no others:

a/bcd and c/abd
a/bcd and d/abc
b/acd and c/abd
b/acd and d/abc

Combining each of the three Type II components with the four appropriate Type I components gives: 12 possible solutions: $3 \times 2 \times 2$.

Taking A, B, and C together, we have, so far, 19 ways of apportioning the four items into discrete cells by using primary components only. If secondary components (which do not cut across the entire set) are used as well, the possibilities increase. We can recognize two types of secondary components, those which make a distinction among three items and those which distinguish only two. These can be added to the earlier types and called Types III and IV. There are, respectively, 12 and 6 Type III and Type IV components, as follows:

Type III		a/bc	b/ac	c/ab
		a/bd	b/ad	d/ab
		a/cd	c/ad	d/ac
		b/cd	c/bd	d/bc
Type IV	a/b	a/c a/d	b/c b/d	c/d

Several new possibilities now arise by which components of the several Types can be combined to obtain discrete but non-redundant solutions.

D. Any two Type I components acting together may be combined with any one of four Type III components: a/bcd and b/acd, for instance, may be combined with any of the four Type III components which distinguish c from d.

E.g. a/bcd, b/acd, c/ad
24 solutions: $(3 + 2 + 1) \times 4$

E. Any two Type I components acting together may be combined with one particular Type IV component:

E.g. a/bcd, b/acd/ c/d
6 solutions: $(3 + 2 + 1) \times 1$

F. Any Type I component when acting with any Type II component may be combined with any one of four Type III components: a/bcd with ab/cd fails to distinguish only c and d. Any of the four Type III components which do distinguish cd from d will complete the job.

E.g. a/bcd, ab/cd, c/bd
48 solutions: $4 \times 3 \times 4$

G. Any Type I component acting together with any Type II component can then be combined with one particular Type IV component. I.e. once a choice of the Type I and Type II components has been made, one and only one of the Type IV components will complete the partitioning:

E.g. a/bcd, ab/cd, c/d
12 solutions: $4 \times 3 \times 1$

H. Any Type II component may be combined with the two Type IV components which redivide the sub-sets specified by the Type II component.

E.g. ab/cd with a/b with c/d
3 solutions: $3 \times 1 \times 1$

I. Any Type I component together with any one of three Type III components (one of the three which do not include the item designated by the letter to the left of the slash in the Type I component which was chosen) can then be combined with one particular Type IV component to complete the partitioning.

E.g. a/bcd with b/cd with c/d
12 solutions: $4 \times 3 \times 1$

In D through I, by combining primary and secondary components, we have added 105 possible analyses to the 19 which use primary components only for a total of 124 ways in which a set of four terms can be discretely but non-redundantly apportioned into cells by the application of components. Clearly with five or more items the possibilities would rapidly become astronomical.

One hundred and twenty-four possible analyses for four items may seem surprising, but they do not exhaust the complications. Others deserve at least brief mention: 1) *Homonomy*. Analysts of kinship terminology have occasionally found it expedient to provide two different formulae for a single term and suggest that it has (by such an analysis) two different meanings. 2) *Empty semantic spaces*. Authors of some semantic analyses have pointed out that when a number of components cross-cut each other in several ways, it may be found that there is no lexeme at all for some particular combination of components. 3) *Non-binary components.* There is no necessary reason why an analysis must be confined to binary distinctions, although some workers seem to have felt them to be esthetically more pleasing and my discussion has been limited to them. 4) *Parallel components.* There seems no reason to suppose that in real systems only a single distinction can separate the same sub-sets, though in the abstract formulation given here only one distinction is possible. 5) *Redundancy.* Finally, there seems no real reason to limit the available analyses to the non-redundant ones, except that by admitting redundant analyses, we open the way to vastly increased possibilities: ab/cd/ ac/bd, and a/bcd form a discrete analysis of four items. It is redundant since the third component can be eliminated without destroying the discreteness of the solution. Redundant components have not traditionally been allowed in semantic analyses, though it is difficult to justify this limitation as a matter of principle. Homonomy, empty spaces, non-binary distinctions, parallel components, and redundant solutions all add considerable complexity to the possibilities for analysis of a set of terms. In principle, the number of possible analyses becomes infinite.

III

Readers may doubt whether this abstract and formalistic argument has any great relevance to the practical analysis of real systems. Later, I will try to suggest that it does, but since its relevance is entirely dependent upon one's objectives in conducting a semantic analysis, we must be clear about our objectives before considering its relevance.

Anthropologists who have advocated the use of componential analysis and similar formal methods as a way of studying the meaning of sets of terms seem to have had two contrasting objectives. Their first and more modest goal has been to specify the conditions under which each term would be used. The problem has been posed in the following way: What do we have to know in order to say that some object is to be called by a given term?[2] That is, analysts have searched for a set of rules which would unambiguously state the criteria by which it could be decided whether or not a particular term could be applied to some object, and the test for the validity of the analysis has been the accuracy with which it predicts such naming. If it can be used to predict what term will be used for a particular object, then this is taken to justify the analysis.[3]

The more ambitious objective of the method is to use it to lead us to an understanding of the criteria by which speakers of the language themselves decide what term to use for a particular item. This view was suggested in Goodenough's original paper (1956:196) when he said, "[the semantic analyst] aims to find the conceptual units out of which the meanings of linguistic utterances are built . . ." and more forcefully by Wallace (1962:352): "The problem is to define the taxonomic system itself—that is, to explicate the rules by which users of the terms group various social and genealogical characteristics into concepts." Frake (1962:74) described one of his papers as containing ". . . some suggestions toward the formulation of an operationally-explicit methodology for discovering how people construe their world of experience from the way they talk about it."

These two objectives differ in an important way. Specifically, any of hundreds or thousands of logically alternative solutions might predict which term can be used, but the success of that prediction does not demonstrate that the speaker of the language uses the same scheme, or indicate whether or not all speakers use the same one.

It is a long and difficult leap from an analysis which is adequate in the sense of discriminating which term should be used to denote an object to that particular analysis which represents the way in which people construe their world. I will try to suggest briefly that the difficulty is not a purely hypothetical one by considering the attempts that have been made to analyze such sets as botanical and disease terminology. Conklin (1962) and Frake (1961, 1962) have suggested that such terms can be arranged into a hierarchical taxonomy. In colloquial English, for instance (not necessarily in the special English of taxonomic botany), we have a class of objects which we call plants, and within the class of plants we have a class of trees. Within the class of trees is a class of "needled trees" (which, in my part of the country where little account is taken of broad-leafed evergreens, seems nearly synonymous with "evergreen"). "Needled trees" include "pines" and "pines" in turn include "jackpines." At each taxonomic level are other coordinate terms: "Flowers" and "bushes" may be coordinate with "trees"; "palms" and "leafy trees" with "needled trees"; "spruce" and "hemlocks" with "pines"; and "white" and "Norway pines" with "jackpines" (Fig. 3). Taxonomies existed for plants in all languages long before Linnaeus codified the idea and laid the basis for systematic biology.

Plants							
Etc.	Bushes	Flowers	Trees				
Etc.			Leafy Trees	Palm Trees	Needled Trees		
Etc.			Etc.	Etc.	Spruce	Hemlock	Pine

Figure 3

A taxonomy of the sort suggested by this example constitutes a special form of componential analysis. After a primary component has been used to divide the entire set of terms, the next distinction is a secondary component which divides one of the sub-sets but which typically does not cross the first component into the other sub-set. Each component operates only within a single undifferentiated set which has been set off by earlier components but which is not yet divided itself. Intersecting components may be used for botanical terminology as well as for kinship, but they have less commonly been recognized.

It is my feeling that the analyses of terms into hierarchical taxonomies that have lately been discussed have rather glossed over the problems of indeterminacy. In fact, in my example I also glossed over some difficult problems of this sort. I am not at all certain, for instance, that "flower" and "bush" are really coordinate to "tree." Perhaps on the basis of size English speakers distinguish "trees" from "bushes," and "bushes" from "plants" (homonymous, but not synonymous with "plants" used as a general cover term for the entire set), and then on the basis of use, divide "plants" into "flowers," "vegetables," and "weeds." What about "cedars"? Are they "needled trees"? Not really, of course, but they are not "leafy trees" either. Should "balsam," "hemlock," and "spruce" be classed together as "short needled trees" (Christmas trees) as opposed to "pines"? Or should they all have equivalent taxonomic status? What is the essential "cognitive" difference between hemlock and spruce? Is it gross size, type of needle, form of bark, or what? I do not know how to answer these questions, but they are the types of questions which must be answered before any single semantic analysis can claim to represent the cognitive organization of the people, or even claim to be much more than an exercise of the analyst's imagination. The questions which I raise about English botanical terms represent precisely the sort of indeterminacy that arose in the abstract example which began this paper.

Analyses of terms in exotic languages may obscure the range of possible alternatives. For instance, Frake (1961) discusses some disease terms in Subanun, a language of Mindanao, and he makes appealing suggestions for their analysis; yet I cannot help wondering if he does not convey an unjustified certainty in the particular analysis he offers. Frake gives a diagram (1961:18) of the same form as my diagram of English plant terms (Fig. 3), in which certain skin diseases are assigned to various taxonomic categories and sub-categories. Not knowing the language, the reader can hardly question the data, and yet he may still wonder if this diagram is any less subject to question than my diagram of plant terms. This is particularly the case since Frake does not give a complete analysis of all disease terms, but limits himself to examples which illustrate the problems he is considering, and he implies that once having solved the problems one may easily provide the full analysis. In fact, in my judgment, the field of structural semantics has had a surfeit of programmatic articles, glowing with promise of a new ethnography (Conklin 1962; Frake 1961, 1962; Wallace and Atkins 1960; Wallace 1962), and a dearth of substantive descriptions of whole systems or definable subsystems.

Students who claim that componential analysis or comparable methods of semantic analysis can provide a means for "discovering how people construe their world" must explain how to eliminate the great majority of logical possibilities and narrow the choice to the one or few that are "psychologically real." I will not be convinced that there are not dozens or hundreds of possible analyses of Subanun disease terms until Frake presents us with the entire system fully analyzed and faces squarely the problem of how he chooses his particular analysis. In the meantime, I will doubt whether any single analysis tells us much about people's cognitive structure, even if it enables us to use terms as a native does.

The hope that we could somehow use our knowledge of language to gain understanding of the workings of the human mind has had a long history. Whorf's ideas have fallen into disrepute largely because the relationships which he claimed to see between patterns of language and patterns of thought could be checked only from the side of language. The language patterns were there to be sure, but how, except through intuition, could one tell whether the patterns corresponded to anything else? Structural semantics has the advantage over Whorf's more naive ideas in that it attempts to relate two observable types of data with one another—language use and events in the non-linguistic world. I cannot see that it has any advantage over Whorf's procedures in gaining an understanding of cognition.

This conclusion may sound harsh, but it does not imply that "structural semantics" is useless. There is a real problem of formulating rules which will predict the use of terms, or to put it another way, of specifying the relationship between terms, on the one hand, and events and situations in our extra-linguistic experience, on the other. In still other words, it is legitimate to try to specify precisely what terms "mean." The exercise of carrying out a formal analysis, moreover, is certainly useful in checking the completeness and adequacy of one's data, in exactly the same way that writing up a grammatical statement may make one aware of previously unimagined possibilities, whether or not these are attributed to the speaker. If nothing else, a precise statement of the objects to which terms are applied is certainly a help to someone wishing to learn the language or use behavior which will be effective. I am convinced that componential analysis and other formal semantic methods can help us in this task. As we learn more about all aspects of language use and its relation to non-linguistic events and as we bring studies of various semantic domains into harmony with each other and take wider and wider account of all aspects of behavior, we may be able to narrow down the alternatives. I expect, however, that a large degree of indeterminacy will always remain. I can be proven wrong by analyses which admit to no alternatives, but until such analyses are given, I will regard it as gratuitous to attribute our analyses to the speakers.

Linguists, in referring to attitudes toward grammatical analyses, have sometimes made a distinction between the "God's truth" view and the "hocus-pocus" view (Householder 1952). When a linguist makes his investigation and writes his grammar, is he discovering something about the language which is "out there" waiting to be described and recorded or is he simply formulating a set of rules which somehow work? Similarly, when an anthropologist undertakes a semantic analysis, is he discovering some "psychological reality" which speakers are presumed to have or is he simply working out a set of rules which somehow take account of the observed phenomena? The attitude taken in this paper is far over on the "hocus-pocus" side. It is always tempting to attribute something more important to one's work than a tinkering with a rough set of operational devices. It certainly sounds more exciting to say we are "discovering the cognitive system of the people" than to admit that we are just fiddling with a set of rules which allow us to use terms the way others do. Nevertheless, I think the latter is a realistic goal, while the former is not. I believe we should be content with the less exciting objective of showing how terms in language are applied to objects in the world, and stop pursuing the illusory goal of cognitive structures.

NOTES

[1] Freedom to pursue the ideas presented in this paper was provided by a grant under Section 602 of the National Defense Education Act. The paper has benefited from many lengthy discussions with Paul Friedrich and Ward Goodenough, and both of them, as well as William Sturtevant, and Ruben Reina, read earlier drafts of the paper and offered numerous suggestions.

[2] Goodenough states: "The problem of determining what a linguistic form signifies is very well illustrated by kinship terms. In essence it is this: What do I have to know about A and B in order to say that A is B's cousin?" (1956:195).

[3] ". . . Paradigms 1, 3, and 4 [which each analyze Trukese kinship terms in a somewhat different fashion] are all valid, in that they all enable us to predict what can and what cannot be a denotation for each of the lexemes therein." (Goodenough 1956:212–213).

REFERENCES CITED

Conklin, Harold C., 1962, Lexicographical treatment of folk taxonomies. *In* Fred W. Householder and Sol Saporta, eds., Problems in lexicography. Supplement to

International Journal of American Linguistics, Vol. 28, no. 2. Bloomington, Indiana University Research Center in Anthropology, Folklore and Linguistics, Publication 21.

Frake, Charles O., 1961, The diagnosis of disease among the Subanun of Mindanao. American Anthropologist 63:113–132.

———, 1962, The ethnographic study of cognitive systems. *In* Thomas Gladwin and William C. Sturtevant, eds., Anthropology and human behavior. Anthropological Society of Washington. Washington, D.C.

Goodenough, Ward H., 1956, Componential analysis and the study of meaning. Language 32:195–216.

Householder, Fred W., 1952, Review of "Methods in structural linguistics" by Zellig S. Harris. International Journal of American Linguistics 18:260–268.

Wallace, Anthony F. C., 1962, Culture and cognition. Science 135:351–357.

Wallace, Anthony F. C., John Atkins, 1960, The meaning of kinship terms. American Anthropologist 62:58–80.

Discussion of Burling's Paper

Dell H. Hymes

This paper makes an original and important contribution to the development of componential analysis, when it shows that there exist a large and expanding number of logical possibilities for the internal structure of members of a set, and when it draws some implications from that fact for cognitive validity. The paper, it seems to me, however, is an accurate criticism only of some, not all, existing practice. I do not share the author's pervading skepticism, and should like to stress ways in which the difficulty he raises can be and is being met.

The main thing is to observe that the total number of logical possibilities is fully pertinent only if all solutions have an equal chance of being arrived at. Not all solutions do have an equal chance of being arrived at, however, if the practice of the work by Conklin and Frake, cited in the paper, is followed. One must consider here the point made in Conklin (1955), as to finding out what questions members of the culture themselves ask in categorizing experience, a point which he has elaborated, contrasting semantic structure with arbitrary arrangement, in comments to Frake (1962), regarding analysis of American coins. In general, componential analysis, as practiced and advocated by Goodenough, Conklin, Frake, is question-dependent, dependent upon the questions asked by participants in the culture (cf.

Collingwood 1939, Ch. V, regarding analysis of ideas generally as answers to questions which must themselves be discovered).

One major consequence of such practice is that investigation allows members of the culture to reveal the existence of various types of relations among members of a set, e.g., hierarchical relations of class inclusion (cf. again Conklin 1962 and Frake 1961). The point is that the revealing of a type of relation eliminates some logically possible alternative solutions. Taking hierarchy as an example, if a and b are found to be kinds of c, then $c/a + b$ holds; both $a/b + c$ and $b/a + c$ are eliminated.

Another major consequence is the attention given to techniques for eliciting and ascertaining cognitively pertinent features, by use of native drawings, culturally relevant objects, etc. Again, the point is that the discovery of semantic content for componential dimensions may serve to eliminate some logically possible alternative solutions. If a contrasts with b as to one feature, and both with c as to another, then again $c/a + b$ is indicated (although the kind of relation, hierarchical or other, remains open thus far), not $a/b + c$ or $b/a + c$. (Cf. again the implications of the two analyses succinctly treated by Conklin [1962]).

Another way of coming at the status of the difficulty raised by Burling is to distinguish between (a) making the right *sorting*, which can be formal and cognitively empty, since it involves only putting the discriminated items into relation with each other, and (b) making the right *assignment* of semantic features to the dimensions of the sorting. Logical possibilities, as discussed here, apply only to the former. There are, indeed, great problems of indeterminacy and dubious validity, since, even if the one and only right sorting is achieved, its semantic basis may be unknown or unknowable. To use an example for which I am indebted to a conversation some years ago with Fred W. Householder, Jr., I may be able to predict that you will sort berry A and berry B, but not know whether by size, color, shape, imagined taste, or what; and to predict that you will group berry A and berry B together as against berry C, and group all as subtypes of berry type D, yet still be no wiser as to why. In fact, however, sorting and assignment are interdependent in the empirical field investigations of Frake and Conklin, and contextual and other evidence can be obtained which permit facts of sorting and the semantic content of the relationship, to give evidence for each other, in the course of developing a theory for the set as a whole. Given a set—and it is vital to note that the existence and conditions of relevance of a set must also be empirically determined—the possible sortings, and the possibly pertinent semantic features, are both finite in number; and one sorting usually will eliminate some features as possible, while particular features usually will eliminate some sortings.

The distinction between sorting and assignment is in effect a distinction between a model, taken as accounting for the way in which the set is organized, and an explanation, which is involved in prediction of naming, thus making the organization intelligible or motivated. Within the range of logically possible alternatives, all are equivalent as models in the sense that each satisfies the criterion of sorting out the terms of the set. Even if one sorting and one model can be decided upon, no explanation or interpretation of how the sorting is done is given. Burling notes this, but does not seem to realize that explanation is involved in the prediction of naming, which he discusses and advocates as a goal, and which he seems to think can be accomplished by any logically possible model.

If an analyst claims only to have found a set of components which make a distinction everywhere native speakers do, the spectre of many logically possible cognitive alternatives is real; but prediction of naming has not been accomplished. To predict naming is to treat the analysis as generative, as accounting for the acceptability and non-acceptability of acts of naming, including, by implication, acts of naming novel objects. To predict the naming of novel objects introduces the possibility, indeed necessity, of discriminating among alternative solutions in terms of the semantic features validly pertinent to designating an item as X, Y or not in the set. In favorable cases, one can vary the possibilities and get responses which eliminate a good deal of indeterminacy, pin-pointing pertinent features, e.g., by triad tests as Romney has done with American kinship. (Note that the problem is in principle the same as that being investigated in acoustic phonetics with regard to alternative orderings of a phonemic system, and the criteria actually employed by native hearers to distinguish the members.)

There are, of course, additional considerations which give credence to the validity of an analysis, such as informant explicitness and consistency. Frake's problem in Subanun was the opposite of the predicament described by Burling. There was no difficulty in getting agreement as to the criteria discriminating different terms; rather, the difficulty was in getting agreement on the term to be used in a given instance of predicting naming. All knew the criteria for being an instance of X, but might disagree as to whether or not a given instance met the criteria. Also, it is impressive when an analysis brings order out of confusion, supported by contextual evidence, as in the case of Haugen's analysis (1957) of Icelandic terms of orientation on the basis of Einarsson's data, and Frake's resolution of the seeming confusion of usage of a term, once the fact of implicit answers at different levels of the native hierarchic taxonomy was found (1961).

It remains that not all indeterminacy may be removed, and, as Goodenough has noted, the fact may itself be significant. Some areas of experience are more elaborately and more consistently terminologized than others, and this in itself tells us something interesting about the cognitive system of a group. Sometimes overt variation in accounts given by informants can be explicated, providing the basis for experimental test. Thus, Miss Joan Davlin has found a remarkable variety of reasons and reasoning for the distinction between "books" and "magazines," but the major criteria can all be referred to an underlying distinction in the temporal dimension as to periodicity of publication. The latter contrast seems to be the source of the major features recognized and used by informants, though itself not offered by any.

In sum, Burling's skepticism and analysis is a valuable corrective to simplistic and band-wagon approaches to componential analysis, which, when valid, is hard work indeed. One must balance skepticism with the positive things that can be done, however, unless one intends the skepticism to apply not only to a new technique (new techniques seem often to spur such skepticism), but to most of anthropology, whenever it refers to values, orientations, attitudes, beliefs, or any other notion which imputes the presence of something inside people.

So far as the best current work is concerned, the strategy is to discover questions which reveal native sortings and the features which discriminate semantically for native speakers, and to integrate the two. The analyst who follows such a strategy is never in the situation of having to consider all logically possible sortings. His field procedure secures elimination of many of them by members of the culture, and he does all he can to devise questions, techniques, predictions which will discriminate among the alternatives that may remain.

The full force of Burling's critique applies only to that part of current practice which consists, so to speak, of sitting at a desk with a set of terms uncertainly constituting a native set, and playing with analysis into dimensions uncertainly corresponding to native features. (Burling has made this point very well recently in *Man* [1962].) There are people whose conception of componential analysis answers to the description, but they are not the ones cited in the present paper.

REFERENCES CITED

Burling, Robbins, 1962, A structural restatement of Njamal kinship terminology. Man 62:122–124.
Collingwood, R. G., 1939, An autobiography. London, Oxford University Press.
Conklin, Harold C., 1955, Hanunóo color categories. Southwestern Journal of Anthropology 11:339–344.
————, 1962, Comment [to Frake (1962)], 86–91.
Frake, Charles O., 1961, The diagnosis of disease among the Subanun of Mindanao. American Anthropologist 63:113–132.
————, 1962, The ethnographic study of cognitive systems. *In* Thomas Gladwin and William C. Sturtevant, eds., Anthropology and human behavior, 72–93. Washington, Anthropological Society of Washington.
Haugen, Einar, 1957, The semantics of Icelandic orientation. Word 13:447–459.

Further Discussion of Burling

Charles O. Frake

Given two competing ethnographic statements (the operational derivation of each from an ethnographic record being equally clear), the best statement is the one which most adequately accounts for the widest range of behavior. If two statements differ in their implications for behavior, then a choice between them can only be made in one way: by testing them against the behavior of the people being described. I can see no other criterion of "reality" or "truth"—be it psychological, structural, or God's—available to the investigator or, for that matter, to persons in a society learning to be "native actors." A person learning to speak and behave in a culturally appropriate manner is "just fiddling with a set of rules which allow him to use terms [and otherwise behave] the way others do." If this is hocus-pocus, then there is no God's truth—either for the investigator or his subjects. The important thing is to write ethnographic statements whose implications for behavior are explicit and which can therefore be tested against competing statements.

I agree with Burling that the field has had more than its share of programmatic statements. Substantive descriptions are badly needed, and the intent of the programmatic statements was presumably to stimulate the production of such descriptions, not to generate more programmatic statements.

Reproduced by permission of the American Anthropological Association from the *American Anthropologist*, Vol. 66; pp. 119 (February 1964).

5 Relevance: Context

Human communication involves the transaction of semantic components within a specified environment. This environment includes relevant features from the linguistic and extralinguistic context. Features of context thus far identified include: (1) the social identities of the speaker and hearer; (2) the social situation; (3) the channel (for example, writing and speech); (4) message form (for example, poetic and instructional); (5) the code (grammatical structure); and (6) the topic (Hymes, 1964:216). In semantic analysis these features are initially relevant because their variation may directly influence both the gathering of data and its subsequent analysis. For example, failure to control for social situation may lead to the neglect of factors which alter the distribution or arrangement of semantic features. Even more important is the fact that there may be more than one possible arrangement depending on features of context. Analysis of context involves two separate aspects; identification of contexts relevant to the people being studied, and the relation of context to other aspects of semantic structure. The first requires specification of the kinds of social identities, social settings, social scenes, topics and means of communication recognized by native speakers. The second concerns the relationship between variations in semantic features of context and other semantic features. The important point here is that context itself is a part of the semantic system. Such analysis aims at discovering selective variation of semantic features in response to features of context. Since most of the work in cognitive anthropology has focused on features of social identity, social situation and topic, the papers in this chapter do not include detailed discussion of the remaining features.

The paper by Frake is an important contribution to ethnographic techniques for the description and analysis of social settings. Characteristics of such settings are related to the distribution of social identities and roles. Application of Goodenough's (this volume, Chapter 3) idea of complementarity and contrast in the distribution of social identities and roles is partially dependent upon prior descriptions of social settings along the lines suggested by Frake. Moerman's paper is an extraordinarily sensitive analysis of a single concept in Thai-Lue culture. Moerman seeks an understanding of "loss of face" through analysis of credibility, purposes and consequences, style, subject, and hearing situation. Both Gumperz and Tyler discuss structures underlying multiple codes in the communication system of a single speech community and delineate sets of rules for transforming codes. In both papers transform rules are used as a measure of semantic distance.

REFERENCES CITED

Hymes, Dell, 1964, Language in culture and society. New York, Harper & Row.

Communication in Multilingual Societies

John J. Gumperz

No one would claim that there is a one-to-one relationship between languages and social systems, yet we continue to think of speech communities as discrete, culturally homogeneous groups whose members speak closely related varieties of a single language. To be sure, no human group of any permanence can exist without regular and frequent communication. But such communication does not necessarily imply monolingualism. Recent ethnographic literature deals increasingly with stable multilingual societies, where populations of widely different cultural and linguistic backgrounds live in close geographic proximity. They are subject to the same political authority, attend the same schools, exchange services and cooperate in many other respects. But they carry out their joint activities by means of not one, but a variety of languages. (Leach 1954, Salisbury 1962, Ferguson 1964, Rice 1962). A major contemporary linguistic problem is the description of the verbal skills involved in speakers' concurrent use of the languages used in such communities.

Whenever all members of such a community do not have equal facility in all the languages in use there, language choice is, of course, determined by requirements of intelligibility. But we also have evidence to show that a majority, or at least a significant minority of residents, can frequently communicate effectively in more than one language, and that they alternate among languages for much the same reasons that monolinguals select among styles of a single language (Rubin 1961; Fishman 1965). That is to say, the same social pressures which would lead a monolingual to change from colloquial to formal or technical styles may induce a bilingual to shift from one language to another. Where this is the case, the difference between monolingual and bilingual behavior thus lies in the linguistic coding of socially equivalent processes. In one instance speakers select among lexical or phonetic variants of what they regard as the *same* language; in the other case, speakers choose between what they view as *two* linguistic entities. We shall now inquire into the special verbal skills required by interlanguage shift and what differentiates them from the skills needed to shift among styles of the same language.

Since the classification of speech varieties as belonging to the same or different languages is in fact determined largely on socio-political grounds (Ferguson and Gumperz 1960), it can easily be shown that the purely qualitative distinction between monolingualism and bilingualism is by no means adequate to answer our question. Language pairs like Serbian and Croatian in Yugoslavia, Hindi and Urdu in India, Bokmal and Nynorsk in Norway, all of which have figured prominently in recent accounts of language conflict, are, for example, grammatically less distinct than some forms of upper- and lower-class English in New York. An individual who shifts from one member of such a pair to the other is bilingual in a social sense only. On the other hand, colloquial and literary varieties of Arabic would be regarded as separate languages were it not for the fact that modern Arabs insist on minimizing the differences between them. Thus speakers' views of language distinctions may depart considerably from linguistic reality.

Even when two speech varieties are obviously grammatically distinct, convergence resulting from language contact over time materially affects their distinctness. Scholars working in the Balkans where multilingualism has long been widespread, have frequently noted considerable overlaps in lexicon, phonology, morphology, and syntax among local varieties of Slavic and adjoining dialects of Greek, Rumanian, and Albanian. They also point out that these relationships are independent of historical relatedness (Sandfeld 1931).

The effect of convergence on the structure of languages is often questioned. Structural linguists have tended to criticize writings on convergence on methodological grounds. Edward Sapir's view that the grammatical core of a language is relatively immune to diffusion is still widely accepted. Nevertheless, more recent, structurally-oriented studies by Weinreich (1952) and Emeneau (1962) reveal a number of clear instances of grammatical borrowings. Such borrowings are particularly frequent in those cases where we have evidence of widespread multilingualism.

Ethnographically oriented work on bilingual behavior further shows that not all varieties of a language are equally affected. Casual styles of either language tend to be less distant than more formal varieties. Diebold, for example, finds that phonological interference is greatest in code switching situations (1963). The colloquial Canadian French expression, *Pourquoi tu l'a fait pour?* cited by Mackey (1965) is a close translation equivalent of the English, *What have you done that for?* John Macnamara cites a similar example from rural dialects of Irish English, where sentences such as *I have it lost* for *I lost it* can be explained as direct translation equivalents of Gaelic. Both formal Canadian French and educated Irish English avoid such translation equivalents. Charles Ferguson (1964) in his discussion of diglossia— the use of grammatically separate varieties among educated residents of several societies—states that the varieties concerned in each case constitute a single phonological structure, in spite of their grammatical differences.

There is ample reason to suppose, therefore that whenever two or more languages are regularly employed within the same social system, they differ significantly from the same languages as spoken in separate social systems, They are grammatically more similar and at the same time show greater intralanguage differentiation. Language distance is not a constant but varies with the intensity and quality of internal communication. Any answer to our question about the skills required in language switching therefore requires empirical investigation by methods, which do not depend on any prior assumption about linguistic or social reality on the part of the analyst.

MEASURES OF LANGUAGE DISTANCE

Much of the linguistic research on bilingualism to date relies on measures of interference, "the use of elements from one language while speaking or writing another" (Mackey 1965). The usual procedure is to search the bilingual performance for features of pronunciation, grammar and lexicon not present in the monolingual standard, which can be attributed to second language influence. Interference analysis has provided important insights into the more general processes of borrowing (Weinreich 1953) and its effect on linguistic change. It also serves as an important tool in language pedagogy, where the object is to study what is involved in the monolinguals' learning of a new language and acculturating to a different monolingual community. Interference measurements of all kinds however assume that the the structure of the standard is known and that speakers have direct access to the standard and seriously attempt to imitate it. These assumptions are justified for the ordinary second language learner or for isolated speakers of minority languages, whose significant contacts are largely with the surrounding monolingual community and who can thus be expected to conform to its norms. They do not however, apply in our case. Members of stable bilingual communities interact largely with other bilinguals and it can be shown that such interaction generates its own norms of correctness (Ervin-Tripp 1964). Although learning through prestige imitation takes place in all societies, the particular linguistic object of this imitation in bilingual societies must be established through empirical research; it cannot be assumed.

A second technique of interlanguage comparison is that of contrastive analysis, which finds extensive application in the preparation of pedagogical language texts (Kufner 1962, Moulton 1962, Stockwell and others 1965). This method consists of a direct point by point comparison of the two systems at each component of structure. Differences are evaluated according to their place within the respective system (whether they are phonetic, phonemic, syntactic, and so forth). They are then counted under the assumption that "what the student has to learn equals the sum of the differences established by this comparison" (Banathy, Trager and Waddle 1966). Prediction of the hierarchy of difficulties is thus based on the linguist's analysis of their structural importance. For example, the fact that in Spanish the segments [d] and [đ] are in complementary distribution, with the former occurring initially in words like *dar* and the latter medially in words like *lado,* whereas they contrast in English words like dare and there, may lead to the diagnosis that the Spanish-speaking student has the problem of assigning phonemic status to two phonetic entities which are allophones and not phonemes in his own language (Banathy, Trager and Waddle 1966). But the assignment of phonemic status to a linguistic feature is generally based on the performance of "ideal speakers living in a homogeneous community" (Chomsky 1965). Since bilingual speakers are excluded from consideration here, ordinary structural categories can hardly be used to predict bilingual performance.

The fact that bilingual communities show more than the usual amount of intralanguage diversity also raises some doubt about the carry-over of traditional elicitation techniques into fieldwork in bilingual situations. If the linguist, as is commonly done, simply seeks out individuals who speak both languages well and asks them to repeat utterances in the two languages, he is likely to elicit largely formal (maximally distinct) styles. Colloquial expression like the French and Irish expressions cited above are quite likely to be suppressed as unsuitable as long as speakers themselves perceive of the interview situation as a formal encounter. Since the rules of language choice are largely beyond conscious control, even repeated requests to speak and behave informally are not likely to produce the desired results.

If instead of starting with the a priori assumption that two languages are distinct, we take the opposite view and treat them as part of a single whole, many of the difficulties cited above can be avoided. This means that in his fieldwork the linguist would disregard the speaker's view of the languages as distinct entities, and treat them as part of the same *linguistic repertoire* (Gumperz 1964). The distinction between grammars and languages current in recent linguistic theory provides some justification for this approach. A grammar is a theoretical construct, a set of rules which underlie verbal performance. A language consists of the set of utterances generated by the grammar. Implicit in the notion of grammar is the assumption that some rules are universal, that is, characteristic of human behavior as a whole, and others are language specific. If we say that grammars may show varying degrees of relatedness we are only carrying this notion a little bit further. We then assume that bilingual behavior reflects both an underlying set of general rules which apply to the entire linguistic repertoire and lower order non-shared language specific rules. It is the task of linguistic analysis to discover the dividing line between these two sets of rules.

Recent work on machine translation provides a technique for accomplishing this, which enables the investigator to focus directly on the relationship between two sets of texts without requiring any a priori linguistic or social assumptions. In some earlier work in machine translation, it had in fact been assumed that grammatical information could be disregarded. But this assumption was soon proved wrong when it was shown that grammatical analysis is the most efficient way of organizing the information required for translation so as to fit into a computer's storage capacity (Lamb 1965). If we then ask what is the minimum coding necessary to translate the speaker's performance in Language A to the same speaker's performance in Language B we must in fact do a linguistic analysis. But note that a grammar in these terms is merely an information storage device; it is not an independently patterned organic entity. Its categories are justified only to the extent that they facilitate the translation process. The best solution is simply that which provides the simplest translation rules. Since the greater the grammatical overlap, the easier the translation process, it is simplest to assume that there is a single underlying system from which the differences of the two languages can be derived. Language distance can then be measured as a function of the number of nonshared rules.

If translatability measures are based only on a single set of texts, the number of grammatical rules needed will be an arbitrarily restricted selection. But the greater the number of speakers measured, and the greater the variety of contexts in which the texts are collected, the more complete will be the body of rules. Translatability measures thus are akin to sociological forms of measurement in that they depend for their validity on sample size and on interaction processes and are therefore ideally suited for socio-linguistic analysis where interspeaker variation is the central problem.

CASE STUDIES

During the last few years, we have experimented with translatability measures in several societies. Although our results are still preliminary, they are of sufficient general interest to warrant reporting here. The following data collection procedure was employed. Conversational texts in two languages were collected from bilingual speakers interacting in natural settings. Texts in Language A were then translated into Language B, and texts in Language B were rendered into Language A, by a second group of bilinguals. We were interested in determining the minimum number of differences necessary for utterances to be perceived as distinct languages by their speakers. Translations were therefore edited to maximize the number of translation equivalents and minimize the language distance without destroying grammaticality in either language. A third group of bilinguals was therefore asked to check each translated text individually to judge its acceptability.

A preliminary study of Hindi-Punjabi bilingual college students in Delhi shows that both languages are analyzable in terms of a common set of grammatical categories, (Pronouns, Adverbs, Inflectional Patterns, and so forth) and in terms of identical rules for their combination in sentence structures. They furthermore have the same articulatory base. Texts in the two languages differ only in the morphophonemic rules which determine the phonetic shape of relevant words and affixes. Here is an extreme example (morpheme boundaries are indicated by a dash, word boundaries by a space. The following abbreviations are used in these and other examples: Lit. E: literal English; H: Hindi; P: Punjabi; M: Marathi; K: Kannada; T: tense; ADJ: adjective; ADV: adverb; AGR: agreement; AUX: auxiliary; DAT: dative; GEN: genitive; OBL: oblique; N: noun; NP: noun phrase; PN: pronoun; PP: post position; S: sentence; VS: verb stem; VP: verb phrase; PART: particle; PPL: participial suffix).

1. "He doesn't eat."

P	oo	naii	khaa–	nd–aa	
	PN	ADV	VS	T	AGR
H	woo	naĩĩ	khaa	t	aaa
Lit. E.	he	not	eat- ing		

2. "He is in the house."

P	oo	kar–	wic	hæ	g–aa	
	PN	N	PP	AUX	PART	AGR
H	woo	ghar	mẽẽ	hæ		
Lit. E.	he	house	in	is		

Note that in the above sentences even content words such as 'eat' and 'house' are identical. Differences lie primarily in the function words (i.e., words referring to grammatical relations such as 'in') and inflectional endings. The position of these items within the sentence is the same in each case. Only the Punjabi particle *g–aa* in sentence 2 does not have a direct Hindi equivalent in that context. However *g–aa* does occur elsewhere in Hindi (Gumperz 1964a).

An even more striking example of linguistic overlap is found among bilingual speakers of Kannada and Marathi, two genetically unrelated languages belonging to the Dravidian and Indo-Aryan stocks, respectively. Our data on these languages was collected in the course of some three months' fieldwork in a village in Sangli district of Maharashtra State, India. The village is located about seven miles from the border of Mysore State in an area where, according to historical records, Kannada and Marathi have been in contact for more than a thousand years. Both languages possess a standard literature and both have, at one time or another, served as the administrative language of the area and the religious language for various groups there. Since 1955, when the present boundaries between Mysore and Maharashtra were established, Marathi has become the main literary language of the region and the sole medium of primary and secondary education.

Approximately 70 percent of the population of our village are native speakers of Kannada. The majority of these are members of the dominant Jain caste, a group of cultivators and entrepreneurs. A significant minority of Muslim village residents, furthermore, speak a form of Deccani Hindi. There is also a small community of lower caste speakers of Telugu. A sizable group of untouchables speaks only Marathi. The linguistic repertoire thus includes local dialects of Kannada, Marathi, Telugu and Deccani Hindi. Telugu and Hindi, however, are spoken only by their native speakers. Marathi, and to a slightly lesser degree Kannada, serve as media of intergroup communication. Literacy is relatively widespread in the village, and the Jains and other higher castes, whatever their native language, have a good command of standard Marathi. With the exception of a few Jain priests, however, no one can read or write Kannada.

Since we were fortunate enough to obtain lodging in a village home and to participate in many activities, we were able to record natural speech in a wide variety of styles varying from formal recitations to unguarded chatter. All texts were transcribed and analyzed in terms of grammatical categories suitable for serving as input data for the machine translation program devised by Douglas Johnson (1965) and based on the work of Sydney Lamb (1965). Here are some sample sentences along with constituent structure diagrams:

3. "We told about our poverty."

Lit. E.	this	us	of	poverty		told		we
K	id	nəm	də	gəribstiti	heḷ	Ø	dew	nawr
M	he	am	cə	gəribstiti	sahgit	l	ə	ami

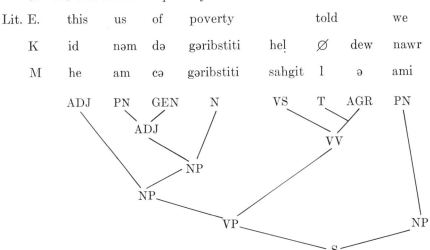

4. "I have a beedi (cigaret)."

Lit. E.   me   of   near   beedi   is
K   nən   də   hatyag   biḍi   eti
M   majh   ə   jəwəḷ   biḍi   hay

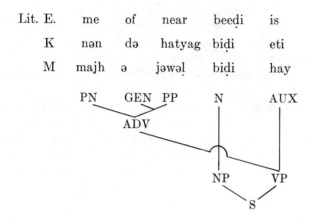

5. "I cut some greens and brought them."

Lit. E.   greens   a little   having cut   having taken   [I] came
K   təpla   jəra   khod   i   təgond   i   bə   Ø yn
M   pala   jəra   kap   un   ghe   un   a   l   o

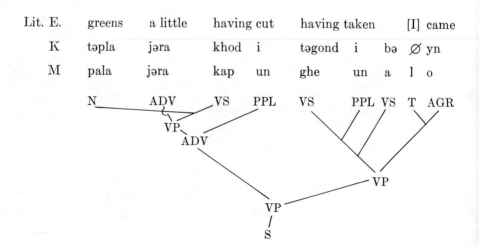

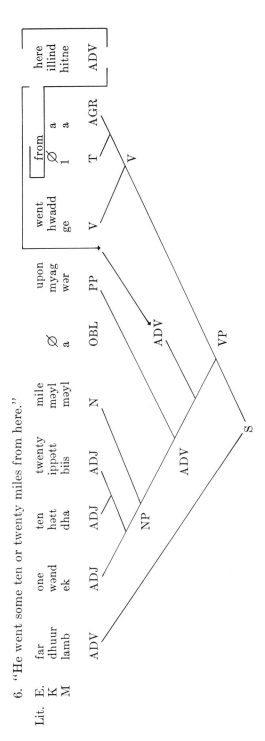

6. "He went some ten or twenty miles from here."

In contrast to the previous examples, the above sentences are lexically distinct in almost every respect. Yet they show identical grammatical categories and identical constituent structures. It is possible to translate from one to the other by a simple process of word for word or morph for morph substitution. The similarity is even more striking by comparison with the English which differs radically from the Indian languages, for example in the way in which possession in sentence five and the verbal action in sentence six are coded grammatically.

We were able to analyze our whole extensive corpus of bilingual texts without having to postulate grammatical categories or rules for one language which were not present in the other language. Independent phonetic perception tests further showed that native speakers were unable to keep the two languages apart on phonological grounds alone. The identity is furthermore not merely confined to grammatical form, it also extends to semantic domains relating to grammatical categories. Nouns in both languages appear in two numbers, singular and plural, and three case forms are oblique, one which carries little or no semantic load, a genetive and a dative which do. The local Kannada dialect has lost the objective case, which is characteristic of standard Kannada and of other Dravidian languages. There are two major gender-like categories: human and nonhuman. The latter is in turn subdivided into masculine and feminine. Here the local Marathi dialect seems to have lost the three gender distinction of standard Marathi by transferring all masculine and feminine nouns with nonhuman referents to the neuter category and thus merging with the Dravidian system.

The following lists of pronouns and common postpositions gives further evidence of the semantic identity of the two languages.

Pronouns:

M	K	E
mi	na	I
tu	ni	you (sing.)
apən	tan	reflexive
ami	nawr	we exclusive
apən	tawr	we inclusive
tumi	niwr	you (pl.)
hew	iiw	he, this one
tew	aw	he, that one
hi	iki	she, this one
he	id	it, this one
hyani	iwr	they (human)
kon	yar	who
kay	yan	what

Postpositions:

M	K	E
−la	−gi	to
−at	−ag	in
−mage	hindgi	behind
−wər	myag	on
−khali	tyag	under
−jəwər	hətyag	near

Note that both languages share distinct reflexive and nonreflexive, inclusive and exclusive and proximate and nonproximate categories. Both pronouns and postpositions are furthermore exact translation equivalents, so that a Marathi item is always replaceable by its Kannada equivalent wherever it occurs.

It is interesting to note that, when examined separately by historical linguists specializing in South Asian languages, our texts are characterized as somewhat deviant but nevertheless easily identifiable specimens of Dravidian and Indo-Aryan, respectively. Genetic relationships among languages are established largely through a process of matching at the morphophonemic level. Since this is the area of structure where the two varieties differ most, it is not surprising that historical linguists in the past have failed to make systematic analyses of the underlying similarities.

To be bilingual in either Hindi-Punjabi or Kannada-Marathi—as these languages are spoken in our experimental community—a speaker simply needs to internalize two sets of terms for the same objects and grammatical relationships. He can switch from one language to the other by merely substituting one item in a pair for the other without having to learn any new grammatical rules other than the ones he already controls. If we contrast this form of bilingual communication with the rather complex selection among phonological, syntactic and lexical variables, which Labov's recent work in New York has revealed (1966), it seems clear that there are at least some circumstances where bilingualism may require less skills than the normal process of communication in some monolingual societies.

In evaluating the significance of the above data, it must be kept in mind, however, that our sample was somewhat biased when compared to what is normally understood as bilingual behavior. In attempting to see whether it is possible for one speaker to speak two languages using the same set of grammatical categories, we confined ourselves only to those speech varieties which are regularly used in bilingual interaction. If we take into account literary varieties or varieties used in religious ritual and other activities that are language specific, a number of new differences arise. In more formal Punjabi, for example, we would have to account for word tone at the phonetic level and for additional differences in lexicon and in the system of function words (Gumperz 1964b). In educated Marathi and Kannada, even when it is used among Marathi-Kannada bilinguals, differences in gender and in rules governing adjective-noun agreement not found in casual village speech will arise. Since the linguist's grammars rely heavily on educated speech, contrastive analysis based on these grammars will show considerably more language distance than our data reveal. The formal varieties concerned, however, are learned primarily through formal education; not all members learn them equally well. Translatability measures can account for this by successively sampling different groups of speakers in different settings. However, as we said before, language distance when measured in this way is not a constant. It varies both with social context and social class.

Because of the special circumstances of long and continuous contact between speakers of the languages concerned, our Indian examples are not likely to have too many parallels elsewhere. More recent work among Spanish-English bilinguals in New York shows somewhat different results. The two languages in this case are quite distinct phonetically. There are further more obvious differences in syntax. Where, for example, Spanish distinguishes between two verbs of "being," *ser* and *estar*, English has only one.

In the realm of verb tenses, Spanish has a number of special subjunctive forms and an inflected future which do not occur in English. It is interesting to note though that in the conversational speech of the uneducated the inflected future is dropped in sentences like "I will write" in favor of the periphrastic construction which, like the English, is formed with the verb *ir* "go" as the auxiliary. Similarly the only subjunctive form which occurs with any frequency is the conditional which serves as the direct translation equivalent of English constructions with "would." Social interaction seems to lead to increased translatability also with English and Spanish.

On the whole, however, the speech of the Spanish-English bilingual in New York approaches our usual image of bilingual behavior. In spite of some overlap, the systems concerned are distinct in every component. Nevertheless, even in this case, the translatability approach raises some new questions about the nature of bilingual skills. To give a phonological example, much of the difference between the two languages results from the presence in one language of articulations not occurring in the other. Thus Spanish lacks the [š] of English *shoe* and English lacks the [ñ] of Spanish *baño*. Further distinctions however emerge when we compare the articulation of phonetically equivalent words. Thus the word photo will be [fowtow] in English and [foto] in Spanish in the same speaker's pronunciation. Whereas in Marathi-Kannada such pairs would be undistinguishable. Spanish-English bilinguals maintain two parallel sets of phonetically similar articulation ranges corresponding to functionally equivalent phones.

It would seem that the necessity of keeping the above ranges separate is an important problem in Spanish-English code switching. Comparison of the formal speech of educated bilinguals with that of uneducated bilinguals or with the same speakers in informal speech shows in fact that these distinctions are frequently collapsed.

SOME GENERAL FEATURES OF BILINGUALISM

Different as the above bilingual situations are, they nevertheless share certain common characteristics. All repertoires maintain an unusually large number of variants at the morphophonemic level. In actual sentences, moreover, the variants never appear in all combinations. Regardless of how large or small the number of nonshared rules, however, differences in the phonological realizations of morphemes play an important part. Even in Hindi-Punjabi where the list frequency of differences is relatively low, differences are very noticeable because they affect affixes and common function words with high text frequency. Variants furthermore never occur in isolation, but in co-occurrent patterns, so that if a Hindi-Punjabi bilingual begins a sentence with *oo* "he," he must also use the participle affix *–nd–*. The alternate affix *–t–* does not co-occur with *oo*. The rigidity of such co-occurrence rules reinforces the perceptual distinctness of codes. In spite of the underlying grammatical similarities, therefore, the shift between codes has a quality of abruptness which to some extent accounts for the speaker's view of them as distinct languages. Such codes seem ideally suited for communication in socities which stress cultural distinctions, while at the same time requiring regular and frequent interaction. In stylistic switching, co-occurrence rules also exist, but they seem less strictly defined, and transitions between styles are more subtle. Stylistic variation, furthermore, is signaled less by morphophonemic distinctions than by differences at the lexical level.

CONCLUSION

Our listing of the variant linguistic correlates of bilingualism was intended to be suggestive rather than exhaustive. Nevertheless the view that language distance is a function of social interaction and social context raises some interesting general problems. The common view that multilingualism wherever it occurs also reflects deep social cleavages is clearly in need of revision. If we wish to understand the social significance of language behavior, we must go beyond popular language names and simple language usage statistics. Furthermore, if in spite of surface appearances, as our Indian examples indicate, language is not necessarily a serious barrier to communication, why do such differences maintain themselves over long periods of time? What is it within the system of roles and statuses or in the norms of social interaction that favors the retention of such overt symbols of distinctness? Under what conditions do such symbols disappear?

Of more direct practical value is the question of the relative importance of social and language barriers to communication. Intralanguage variation clearly plays an important part in bilingual behavior and measures of bilingual competence must account for it if they are to be socially realistic. Furthermore, the common assumption that uneducated speakers of minority languages learn better when instructed through the medium of their own vernacular is not necessarily always justified. Instructional materials in these vernaculars may rely on monolingual norms which are culturally quite alien to the student and linguistically different from his home speech. Considerably more research is needed on these and similar questions. We hope that our discussion highlights the importance of ethnographically oriented linguistic measurement in this task.

NOTES

The research reported herein was supported by grants from the National Science Foundation, Division of Social Science, and from the U.S. Office of Education Language. Thanks are due to Joshua Fishman and Roxana Ma for assistance and criticism. This paper is an expansion and revision of a previous paper: "On the Linguistic Markers of Bilingual Communication," *The Journal of Social Issues*, 1967, 23:48–57.

REFERENCES CITED

Banathy, Bela, Trager, Edith, and Waddle, Carl D., 1966, The use of contrastive data in foreign language course development, pp. 35–56. *In* A. Valdman, ed., *Trends in language teaching*. New York, McGraw-Hill.

Chomsky, Noam, 1965, Aspects of the theory of syntax. Cambridge, MIT Press.

Ervin-Tripp, Susan, 1964, An analysis of the interaction of language topic and listener. *In* John J. Gumperz and Dell Hymes, eds., The ethnography of communication, American Anthropologist: 66, (6), Part 2: 103.

Ferguson, Charles A., Gumperz, John J., 1960, Introduction. *In* Linguistic diversity in South Asia. Indiana University Publications in Anthropology, Folklore and Linguistics, 1960, Publication 13.

Ferguson, Charles A., 1964, Diglossia. *In* Dell Hymes, ed., Language in culture and society, pp. 429–439, New York, Harper.

Fishman, Joshua, 1965, Who speaks what language to whom and when. *La Linguistique*, 2:67–88.

Gumperz, John J., 1964a, Linguistic and social interaction in two communities. *In* John J. Gumperz and Dell Hymes, eds., The ethnography of communication. *American Anthropologist*, 66, (6), Part 2: 137–153.

Gumperz, John J., 1964b, Hindi-Punjabi code switching in Delhi. pp. 1115–1124. *In* Horace Lunt, ed., *Proceedings of the ninth international congress of linguists.* The Hague, Mouton.

Johnson, Douglas, 1965, Memorandum on morphologies. Machine translation project. Berkeley, University of California. In mimeograph form.

Kufner, Herbert L., 1962, The grammatical structures of English and German. Chicago, University of Chicago Press.

Lamb, Sydney, 1965, The nature of the machine translation problem. Journal of Verbal Learning and Verbal Behavior, 4:196–210.

Leach, Edmond, 1954, Political systems of highland Burma. London, Harvard University Press.

Mackey, William F., 1965, Bilingual interference: its analysis and measurement. Journal of Communication, 15:239–249.

Moulton, William, 1962, The sounds of English and German. Chicago, University of Chicago Press.

Rice, Frank A., 1962, Study of the role of second languages. Washington, D.C., Center for Applied Linguistics.

Rubin, John, 1961, Bilingualism in Paraguay. Anthropological Linguistics, 4:52–58.

Salisbury, Richard, 1962, Notes on bilingualism and linguistic change. Anthropological Linguistics, 4:1–13.

Sandfeld, K., 1930, Linguistique Balkanique. *In* Collection Linguistique de La Societé de Linguistique de Paris, 31.

Stewart, William, 1962, Functional distribution of Creole and French in Haiti. *In* E. P. Woodworth and R. J. diPietro, eds., Linguistics and Language Study Monograph No. 15. Washington, D.C., Georgetown University.

Stockwell, Robert P., Bowen, J. Donald, and Martin, John W., 1965, The grammatical structures of English and Spanish. Chicago, University of Chicago Press.

Stockwell, Robert P., Bowen, J. Donald, 1965, The sounds of English and Spanish. Chicago, University of Chicago Press.

Weinreich, Uriel, 1953, Languages in contact. New York, Linguistic Circle.

A Little Knowledge

Michael Moerman

The moral of this paper[1] is that while a little knowledge may be dangerous, a great deal of knowledge can be devastating. The most dangerous knowledge comes from what is conventionally regarded as adequate ethnography.

From *Contributions to Ethnomethodology*, edited by Harold Garfinkel and Harvey Sacks. To be published in 1971 by Indiana University Press. Used by permission of the author and Indiana University Press, Bloomington, Indiana.

In *We, The Tikopia,* Firth (1963:2) eloquently describes the ignorant anthropologist who arrives at a feast of information from which he can select an occasional appetizer. The image suggests a hope, which most of us share, that progressive familiarity with the culture one studies produces knowledge. It is perhaps charmingly naive for the discipline which prides itself on having realized that it would not be a fish who discovered water to assume that cultural immersion (the longer, the better; one just soaks it up) produces scientific knowledge.

To become familiar with a culture is to find no surprises in it and to regard native explanations as analyses instead of as data. Consider, for example, the initially unexceptionable statement by Oscar Lewis that in the village he knows so well:

> In the past few years the [Catholic nuns] who have come to the village have been making a house-to-house campaign to try to unite separated couples and to marry couples who have been "living in sin." They have met with little success, for *Tepoztecans resent their activities as undue interference in personal matters* (Lewis 1963:78).

It seems clear that the phrase I have emphasized is meant to explain what precedes it. But even if we assume that it is not merely a projection of American opinions into Tepoztecans and that the resentment was expressed by them as their explanation of their own behavior, the statement still tells us little about Tepoztlan because the statement is probably true tautologically in all societies. People resent "undue interference in personal matters" in that it is this reaction which usually permits natives and their observers to refer to "personal matters," i.e., to the matters which a person considers it illegitimate for specific others to concern themselves with in specific ways. The ethnographer's task is to delineate these specifics in the society he describes. The question which Lewis should have asked of his data is, what is it about nuns and about marriage in Tepoztlan which makes some people resent this concern? It may be that nuns are regarded as outsiders and marriage as a village matter. It may be that Tepoztecans consider education or contemplation to be the proper sphere of a nun's behavior, while form of marriage is understood to involve a secular balance between present and desired status on the one hand, and available cash on the other. Readers can suggest other answers more ingenious and perhaps more correct. The point is that we cannot answer the question because Lewis never asked it of his data. On the basis of my own mistakes as an ethnographer, I would suggest that Lewis never asked the question because he knew Tepoztlan so well that it did not surprise him that Tepoztecans resented the nuns' concern with their marriages. Let me give you an instance of the price of familiarity from my own fieldwork in Ban Ping, a Thai-Lue village where my wife and I lived for 14 months in 1960–1961 and to which I returned for a month in 1965.

After having been in Ban Ping for ten months, we took a trip to Bangkok. Immediately upon our return to the village, Pearl, our "adopted daughter," volunteered the information that Sue, a divorcee with two children, was pregnant. Villagers had noticed her large stomach and begun to gossip; the elders had talked about the matter. We were also told that Sue had named Sam, the unmarried son of our best friend, Sol, as the father. The issue was ethnographically important in that a native considered the event to be immediately and interestingly reportable, and in that her account made voluntary reference to the event's importance to other villagers (gossip, participation of elders). Its interest to the anthropological profession lies in its indication of what kinds of evidence (large stomach) villagers thought appropriate and in its involving the First Principles of sex and legitimacy.[2] Personally, it was expected that I, as Sol's friend, should participate in hearings, offer advice and, if necessary, support. Were it not for the reported gossip and participation of elders, as well as subsequent activities, Pearl's excited narrative might have been stimulated largely by her expectation of my personal and professional[3] interest, and thus not be a sign of the event's ethnographic importance.

Since the event, for whichever reason, was clearly important, it should be no surprise that my notes on the case occupy over 40 typed cards (each 7" × 4") and two seating plans. Let us consider a portion of my record of the first formal hearing, which occurred at Sue's house.[4]

Transcript #1:

> At 0800, Karl, Sue's father, not looking at [the] group and talking as if to himself, says: "I have called the old men to talk about this subject."

> James [elder man in Sue's faction]: "It would be good if they married." Grandfather Norm [in Sue's faction] and Grandfather John [in Sam's faction] agree.

> Silver [in Sam's faction]: "If they'll marry, let them marry." [i.e., It would be a good idea, and that would be the end of it.]

> Grandfather Norm: "If they don't marry, I won't accept a settlement. se na se ta[5] [Literally: lose face, lose eyes.] [I] will take [him i.e., Sam,] to jail.

> Grandfather John: "Ask the boy whether he'll marry her."

> Sam: "I can't marry. I won't marry."

Grandfather Norm's reference to loss of face surprised no one, least of all me who accepted it, as the villagers seemed to, and wrote it down with no further comment and no query. So well did I understand this part of Ban Ping's culture that I could have and did employ the phrase se na se ta in a manner and in situations quite acceptable to the natives (cf. Goodenough

1957:168). But in addition to the by no means clear distinction between folk and analytic categories, one must distinguish between natives and anthropologist. Although, or, more correctly, *because* I knew Ban Ping well enough to feel (appropriately) that Norm's statement was appropriate, I cannot satisfy myself that I know what makes his statement appropriate and expectable. Somewhat more specifically, what did Grandfather Norm intend, what was he understood to mean, and how did he come to say, "I will lose face?" To set about learning this, I found it necessary to consider three issues: the credibility of his statement to himself and to his listeners, the situated purposes and consequences of his statement, and the locally defined situation (Goffman 1964) in which his statement was made. These issues are all so closely related and my present understanding of them so *ad hoc*, that it is most honest to discuss them in the order in which they occurred to me.

CREDIBILITY

How could Norm credibly claim that he would lose face unless the pair married? One component of this question, which lies outside this paper, is: how is it that what Sue does or what happens to her can affect Norm's face? More generally, how can one person's behavior affect another's reputation? My hunch is that one person is concerned to control another when the latter's behavior implicates the former's reputation. In Ban Ping, spoken titles (of reference and address) record and manipulate this implication. In the present case, Norm can be labeled Sue's "paternal grandfather," Sue labeled as Norm's "granddaughter."

If you will grant, as the villagers seemed to, that what happens to Sue can lose face for Norm, the remaining component of credibility is: why should non-marriage cause loss of face? If, as I reported, everyone in the village including the influential elders already knows that: a) Sue has become pregnant out of wedlock,[6] that, b) Sam has been accused of and has not denied paternity, and that, c) Sam has made a hearing necessary through not legitimizing the union, what is involved in loss of face? Consider further, that, a) everyone knows that Sue now has no husband but does have two children by different men and, b) many villagers believe that she has been having intercourse with a number of bachelors and young married men. What face is left to be lost by Sam not marrying Sue?

Stimulated by what we know of other cultures, let us consider some of the ways in which being an unwed mother might create disabilities. I am sure that my anthropologist colleagues would ridicule a bald attempt to explain the actions by the American feeling that it is naughty to have an illegitimate child. I am equally sure that they, like me, often assume that when members of another society act as we do, they do so for reasons like our own. The form which this assumption usually takes is that anthropologists rarely try to explain (and may even fail to notice) behavior which appears to be just like American behavior.

Are there any Ban Ping offices, groups, activities from which Sue would be excluded because she has no husband? I know of none. Would its illegitimacy significantly affect the status of her child? In response to an abstract question about illegitimacy, an informant replied:

> There is no stigma to illegitimacy. The child is reared just as is one born in wedlock. Such a child is called "a child of the road" because he was not conceived in the proper place—a mosquito net at home.

More concretely, I should mention that a former village headman is both a "child of the road" and the product of an incestuous union. His pedigree did not prevent his election to and long tenure in office, nor was it ever referred to, in public or privately, even by his most heated critics who did accuse him of stealing, excessive borrowing, undependability, irresponsibility, and addiction to gambling and drunkenness.

Support and inheritance do not seem to be importantly involved. The techniques and resources for land acquisition available in Ban Ping make inheritance of relatively less consequence than it is in many other peasant rice-growing communities (Moerman 1968). Moreover, both support and inheritance are determined by rearing and not begetting. An adopted child inherits from and is supported by those who raise him; he has no patrimony from his biological parents, although they or their beneficiaries may elect to give the child a token share of the estate. The rights of children of divorced parents are similar. Marriage is rather brittle in Ban Ping and children usually stay with their mother and her family should their father leave. The father may send them an occasional gift and the mother and her kin may complain about failure of support. But there is no sanction, aside from ineffective gossip, by which to enforce the mother's claim which men are rarely, if ever, criticized for ignoring.[7]

There are, then, no specific sanctions directed against the illegitimate and their mothers. Further, I would argue that the concepts of illegitimacy, adultery, and fornication among the Lue and among the Central Thai (Hamburger 1965:56–58) are different from and less precise than our own. Both peoples permit polygyny and call wives other than the first, "lesser wives." Both lack a word which we would translate as concubine or mistress. Both use "lesser wife" for any woman other than coresident spouse with whom a man has fairly regular sexual relations, regardless of whether the man pays for her favors or whether her identity or her existence is regarded as known to his coresident spouse, (his "wife"). Persons whom we would term concubines or mistresses, the Thai term "lesser wife." Most events which we would term adultery, the Thai term as polygyny. The offspring of such unions do not by sole virtue of their illegitimacy suffer disabilities of support and inheritance. It is up to the father which, if any, of his children he will protect and support. The relative insignificance of illegitimacy and of adultery permits a woman who has a child to be called a "mother," *mE* in Lue. If the child's father does not live with her, then she is either a widowed mother, (*mE maj*), or a divorced, abandoned one, (*mE hang*). Either term implies that she once had a husband who was father to the child. If, however, it is impossible to suppose that a husband was father to the child, the woman, since she cannot be categorized as a "maiden" (*saw*), is either a "wanton," (*jing lin hi*), or a "whore," (*jing khaj hi*).

If Sam succeeds in asserting his refusal to be taken as Sue's husband, then Sue cannot subsequently be supposed to have been Sam's wife. The categorial choice between "wanton" and "whore" is thus not irrelevant to the credibility of Sue's, and thereby Norm's, loss of face, but is not sufficient to explain it. First, Sue is already a divorcee (*mE hang*) by virtue of her previous marriages.[8] Secondly, although "whore" and "wanton" are labels for the category of which mothers who have never been married are members, they need never be used as terms for addressing or referring to particular persons: teknonymous terms for women are always permissible in Ban Ping. Nevertheless, Sam's refusal to marry her does help to make Sue a subject of gossip and to maintain and develop her previous reputation as a "wanton" and a "bad woman," (*mE jing haj, mE jing bO di*), which, had Sam married and stayed with her, she would gradually have lost. It is in this sense that marriage to Sam might have made an honest woman of Sue.

I say "might have" for the following reasons. As a general ideal, as fact for 25 other cases in which my genealogical data indicate short liasons or pregnancies out of wedlock, and—on the part of some informants—as an ideal statement even for Sue, marriage ends all gossip. "People don't say anything anymore. If there is a real marriage, then the subject is closed." Sue's case, however, is special in two respects. First, if a woman's marriages are too brief or her divorces too numerous, "people say that she is no good." Although there is a Lue proverb: "Thrice ordained, thrice left the order, it's bad to take him as a friend; thrice married, thrice divorced, it's bad to take her as a wife," it would be a mistake to regard the disreputable frequency as a quantifiable one. So, for example, one 40-year-old woman about whom I could neither hear nor elicit any relevant criticism, has been three years married to her fourth husband, having left or been left by the previous three, to none of whom was she married for more than two years and to one of whom for less than three months. Another, a 30-year-old divorcee, has had three husbands, two of them for less than three months.

The second reason why marriage to Sam might not have salvaged Sue's reputation is that her reputation was already too bad. Some of Sam's contemporaries claim that even had he married her for only a few days (a possibility discussed below), Sam would have "lost face because many men have known her body, have had intercourse with her." In 1965, after Sue had married a non-Lue from another area, village gossips said:

> If anyone wants to sleep with a woman, they are told to go to Sue because she's a bad woman. Sam didn't want to marry her because people would talk about him and say that his wife was a bad woman . . . . Sue's husband can never know when he leaves the house whom his wife might be sleeping with.

The propositions that three divorces damage a reputation and that marriage ends gossip are both "true as a rule" in two senses characteristic of social rules. First, counter instances do not disprove them (Helmer and Rescher 1960:8). Second, a member can use the rules to argue, but not to clinch, the correctness of his judgments about actions, events, and persons.

Sue's bad reputation and the fact that a husband's intelligence is implicated by his wife's morality were presumably among the major reasons for which Sam was unwilling to marry Sue. Sam's adamance is especially striking in that Norm and the other elders argued for no more than a *cu* ("pretend," "artificial," "bogus") marriage. They first suggested that the couple live together just long enough to let Sam till Karl's fields, a matter of about seven months. They argued next that the couple live together for only two or three months until the harvest season was over. At a subsequent hearing, the chief headman (*kamnan*), a sophisticated market-dweller, suggested that Sam stay with Sue for only a few nights and pointed out to the litigants (including Sue) that the costs of a wedding feast, when averaged over those nights, would come to less than the price of a prostitute.

As can be seen from the suggestion, for a marriage to be *cu* does not involve its rites of initiation (as does the distinction between *aw kan* and *tEngngan* marriage). To characterize a marriage as *cu* is, I think, to say that the husband initially intended it to, and was able to make it, last only a very short time. This double condition probably provides further motive for Sam's refusal, for as a villager subsequently pointed out: "When one marries *cu*, he can't be sure that the woman will let him leave her. She can follow him wherever he goes and not leave him."

The double condition also suggests that some marriages become *cu* only, and "defeasably," in retrospect. The ascription of an instance to its category (for example: This is a marriage. This is a *cu* marriage. This is a fellow American.) is "'*defeasable*'" in the sense that it "is subject to termination or '*defeat*' in a number of different contingencies (which cannot be exhaustively specified in advance) but remains intact if no such contingencies mature" (Hart 1952:148). To phrase it somewhat differently, in addition to their "*et cetera* clause," (Garfinkel 1964:248) social rules, and members' procedures for subsuming cases to them, have an "unless clause" which members can cite in order to reclassify a case or to explain their having, "as it turned out" retrospectively, misclassified it.

There is no reason not to believe that Norm's listeners thought his, "I'll lose face" appropriate within its setting. The major component of its acceptability is, I think, its credibility. (Compare, "Waitress, unless the eggs are really soft-boiled I'll kill myself.") This credibility results mainly from Sam's refusal to accept a demand or request for marriage. When divorce is so easy and so final, when, in reversal of all precedent, Sue's kinsmen offered Sam the use of her father's fields as a sort of "husband-price," when the marriage behavior demanded was for Sam to go to her house with a suitcase and a new shirt and sleep with her for a few nights, then the very ease and temporary nature of the marriage makes its refusal all the more insulting.

When I returned to Ban Ping in the summer of 1965, Norm was dead and the whole affair rather cold. Nevertheless, I solicited some opinions about whether Norm had lost face and, if so, why. Of these opinions, Sol's is representative. "Yes," he replied, "Norm did lose face. He lost face because we wouldn't marry them." Sol denied that Norm would not have lost face had he not made the statement and, when I asked him why Norm did make the statement, he replied: "He said *se na se ta* because he would *se ta* before us in that they wanted to marry us and we didn't want to marry them." Before returning to Ban Ping, I had hoped that villagers' judgments on this matter would be somehow definitive. I would now argue that this hope is illusory. At the very least, it is quite possible that another informant, or Sol at some other time, might have answered my question differently. Further, I see little reason to assume that any answer, even Norm's had he been asked at the moment when he made the statement, would give us Norm's single major motive. I see no reason to assume that he had one.

Let us momentarily examine one implication of the preliminary "conclusion" that Norm lost face because Sam refused his offer of marriage. For Norm's remark to have been acceptable to natives, it either required no explanation other than the situation in which it was made (that is, it is conventional in a hearing for a party to say, "*se na se ta*"), or it has to have been heard as credibly and specifically motivated. The main credible motive that the villagers and I can find is Sam's refusal, which, like Norm's statement, is within, and inseparable from, the hearing situation. Had Sam not refused, there would have been no hearing; had there been no hearing, Sam could not have publicly refused.

I can go no further toward establishing the basis of credibility, to himself and to his listeners, of Norm's statement, "If [they] don't marry, [I] won't accept a settlement. [I would] lose face," We have yet to consider a), why he would make the statement, b), why he would follow it by saying, "I will take him to jail," and, c) how it could come about that shortly after his statement, once Sam had adamantly refused to marry, the discussion at this and subsequent hearing should devolve about the size of the settlement payment. A related question is whether Norm's statement is a performative (Austin 1962), in the sense that his very assertion that he will lose face if they do not marry may create a situation in which he does lose face when they do not marry.

PURPOSES AND CONSEQUENCES

An initial answer to the questions asked above is that Norm made his statement, and was understood to have made it, for purposes of negotiation.[9] Elsewhere, (Moerman 1966:154), I have suggested that:

> One of the features of Ban Ping, and an aspect of its "looseness," is that individuals are often expected to give primacy to their divergent private interests and are never publicly accused of inconsistency or hypocrisy for the rhetoric which conceals their selfishness.

An amplification and a refinement of that remark is appropriate here. I think that one striking way in which the Lue use speech is the extent to which statements can *legitimately* be intended to manipulate those to whom they are made and to mask the motives of their maker. To the Lue, I would guess*[9] that the question: "Why did he say that?" (*pin sa, pirn wa* . . .) would most often elicit not a diagnosis of the unconscious origin of a statement or of its maker's barely conscious general attitude, but would elicit an imputation of its maker's conscious motive of self-interest.

Among the Lue, there are many situations in which statements are legitimately expected to have and are understood as having the purpose of masking their maker's desires* (cf. Evans-Pritchard 1956). Further, if a statement has moral value, then that value resides not in the accuracy with which it reports the maker's desires* nor in the accuracy with which it reports some other condition of the world,* but in the nature of the desire it serves* and/or in its efficacy in fulfilling those desires.* Transparency, not hypocrisy; ineffectiveness, not inconsistency; illicit desires, not illogicality are criticisms relevant to Lue rhetoric* (cf. Albert 1964). Furthermore, persons are held less accountable for their remarks than for the purposes* and consequences* of their remarks. I do not assert that the Lue conceal their desires in order to manipulate their listeners more than do we. I do assert, a), that they regard such concealment for purposes of manipulation as legitimate,* b), that they call it eloquence,* c), that it has no simple relation to what they call lying,* and d), that while it may be impolite for a listener to call attention to a speaker's motives,* to do so does not discount his statement,* as it does for the American when, for example, he says about a salesman's praise for a used car, "He's just trying to unload it on me."

I further maintain that however much these uses of speech obtain to common conversations, they obtain even more to legal hearings.* Consider, for example, the following case. In February 1961, there was a hearing at

which Al and his wife Kate were divorced. Jim, a former headman, dominated the proceedings. He spoke pleasantly to Al, suggested alternatives to
him, referred to precedents, piously mentioned the importance of kinship
bonds, and when Al left, called after him:

Transcript #2:

> Don't say goodby completely. Come back to visit. Come to this house
> or to my house to eat rice and drink water. Whenever you pass by, come
> and visit your kinsmen here.

Throughout the hearing, he assumed a posture of impartiality. As soon as
Al left, however, Jim:

> raised great laughter by saying: I spoke all the time so that he couldn't
> answer. I didn't know how little he could speak, otherwise I would have
> given him more chance. I was afraid that he'd mention the traditional
> customs. [During the hearing Jim had made numerous references to
> modern Thai law] by which he wouldn't have to give [his wife] anything.

An old man then explained to me:

> In the old days, the old folks would talk together and the family would
> divide their property equally. But in this case, one side collapsed [in
> that] there is only one side, since Al comes from Laos and has no kins-
> men [here].

Then, as was also done for me at another hearing, he gesticulated what I take
as the Lue model of adjudication. Pressing together the fingertips of his two
hands, he likened them to the roof of a house, and showed how the structure
collapsed and one side overlay the other when the weaker gave way.

The purpose of a hearing, the business of adjudication, the meaning of
justice is mutually acceptable compromise. My notes of hearings contain
numerous instances of ethnocentrically blatant hyperbole, inconsistency,
and backing-down. Because no Lue ever criticized such statements, I suggest
that they were accepted, even more than statements are in other Lue situations,* as instrumental devices for purposes of bargaining, negotiation, and
manipulation. This, I think, is how Norm's statement about loss of face and
his subsequent threat were taken.[10] This is why it was followed by an
adamant demand and why making the statement did not cause him to lose
face when his demand was not met.[11]

My analysis of Norm's statement is summarized in Table 1 which indicates the suppositions I have made. One component of "loose social structure" (a) in Ban Ping is that persons often cannot be made to do what they
are unwilling to do. Sam's stated unwillingness to marry Sue (b) makes it
(c) unlikely that he will marry her. Norm's reputation is implicated by what
happens to Sue (d). Because of the relationships among refusal of marriage,

Table 1. How Grandfather Norm Could Say, "I will lose face"

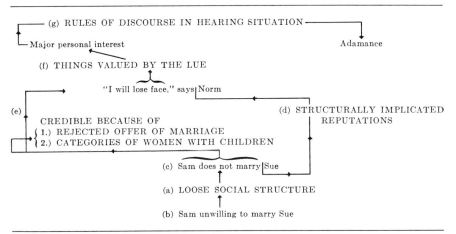

Upper case statements are my suppositions for tying together the village events reported in lower case.

unwed motherhood, and reputation, Norm and his listeners find it credible that absence of marriage would cause loss of face (e). Face is a major interest (f) to the Lue. At a hearing, one is expected to advance one's interests and to be especially unyielding about major ones (g), hence the credibility of Norm's position despite, or perhaps because of, his excessive threat (jail) and demand (marriage).

THE HEARING SITUATION

The analysis, so far, raises questions more interesting than any it answers. To assert that the rules of discourse change during a hearing is to assert that a hearing is a recognizable unit.[12] Ban Ping, like many peasant villages, lacks specifically legal officers, costumes, rooms, emblems, or lexicon. It is therefore not surprising that the boundary-markers of a hearing and the ways in which hearing-time differs from the time that precedes and follows it are both predominantly rules of interaction.

Consider the scene before Karl opened the hearing, a scene like the ones which preceded the approximately 20 hearings I witnessed. The platform on which Lue houses are built extends well beyond the front of the house (see Fig. 2). One reaches the platform by climbing a staircase which gives onto the part of the platform furthest from the house. This part of the platform is a roofless but railed verandah (*can*) whose floor is made of narrow separated parallel boards. Close to the house is the *xatop*, the edge of a raised and roofed porch with a solid floor which is built onto the open porch to cover about one third of it. The eastern half of this raised porch is enclosed by a half-wall or railing (*fa phanak*) and is called the *xOm* or *hoxOm;* the rest of the raised porch is called the *sik*. The *xOm* is divided from the *sik* by an invisible line which runs from the edge of the *fa phanak*, through the central house-post (*saw dang*), and continues within the interior of the house as the *ping*, a raised and visible floor beam which runs the length of the interior of the house and separates the sleeping room (*somnOn*) on the east from the rest of the interior (the *na pOng*), which contains the hearth.

For the sake of brevity and as a consequence of incomplete analysis, we may speak of increasingly private areas as one moves; house compound, *can; sik, xOm; na pOng*, deep (beyond hearth) *na pOng; somnOn*. Semi-colons indicate discontinuities, the crossing of which may require specific invitation. Villagers say that hearings take place in *xOm*. Observationally, the old men who discuss the case are seated there, male litigants sit on the *sik*, female litigants and witnesses sit on the *xatop* or stand on the *can*. When persons first arrive at the compound where the hearing is to be held, they immediately climb the stairs to the house platform. Although the most senior of them sometimes go directly to the *xOm*, it is more common for participants to stay on the *can, xhatop* and *sik* until shortly before the hearing begins. The hearing usually begins at least a half hour after most participants have arrived, and usually at least a quarter of an hour after all have arrived and seated themselves in the *xOm*, the representatives of opposite sides facing each other in order of decreasing age.[13] Since all of the participants are always present before the hearing begins and since they are usually in place for at least a little while before it begins, it should be possible to observe the ways in which the formal opening of a hearing changes the behavior of its participants. Some changes, I have suggested, relate to the rules of discourse, specifically to the legitimate instrumentality of statements* and to the negotiability of publicly taken positions.* There are others, which also need further field verification.

All hearings I attended began and ended quite abruptly. The abrupt start can be seen in *Transcript 1*, which also suggests the two most striking changes that characterize hearing-time. One of these changes is in the style of conversation, the other is its subject. When Karl opened the hearing of Sue and Sam, he began to talk about the business of the hearing (subject) and he did not look at the other participants (style).

SUBJECT Before the hearing opens no one present ever mentions its subject or, except for an occasional *soto voce* and/or very brief two-person exchange, even alludes to it. This restriction is not binding upon nonpar-ticipants (usually women, children, and young men) who sometimes observe the participants and the proceedings from positions in or near the compound in which the hearing occurs. Those who will participate in the hearing sit about the *can, sik,* or even the *xOm* talking about crops, prices,

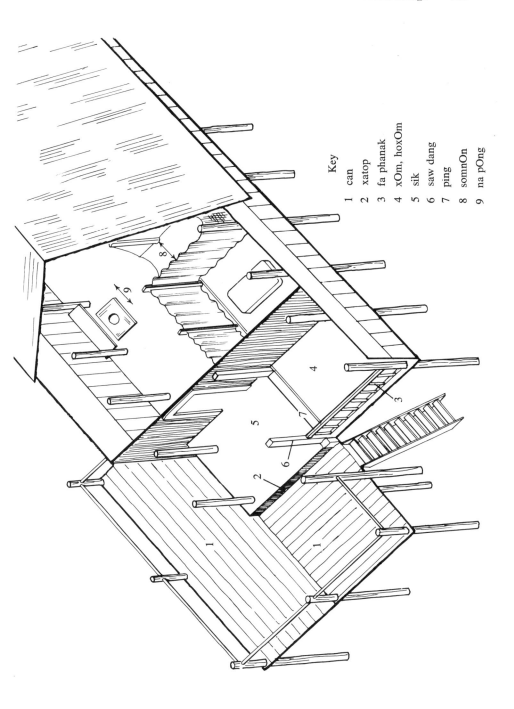

Key

1 can
2 xatop
3 fa phanak
4 xOm, hoxOm
5 sik
6 saw dang
7 ping
8 sommOn
9 na pOng

weather, lottery results or other common topics of conversation irrelevant to the subject of the hearing. Near them—at the far end of the *can*, below the house, outside the compound fence—there are often nonparticipants talking or whispering about the hearing's subject and participants. On their way to the hearing compound, participants sometimes discuss the case and its precedents among themselves. When a nonparticipant, who knows full well where they are going and what they will do there, greets them with the conventional, "Where are you going?" they answer, "Visiting." They sometimes add the direction in which they are walking, but name the house to which they are going much less often than villagers do when they are "really" just going visiting.* Their reticence is respected by the questioner: I have never heard anyone followup his question, as is sometimes done at other times, by asking "To visit whom?" or "To visit about what?"

On the basis of these "observations," I would say that public discussion of its subject matter is a significant feature, even a defining feature, of the hearing itself. Similarly, it seems to be illegitimate to talk about the business of a village meeting until the meeting has been opened. Whenever a village meeting (of which there were about 25 during our first stay in Ban Ping) was called I would regularly try to ask those attending it what it was to be about. Even when everyone in the village could be presumed to know the subject and/or the occasion of the meeting (for example, the headman's monthly report on District affairs, a cause célèbre), the answer I almost always received was: "I don't know, it hasn't been announced yet." While one might reason from these observations to Thai notions of predictability, (cf. Phillips 1965:81) I think it better to confine ourselves to discussing what kinds of predictions the Thai consider it legitimate to make in public, and to what kinds of statements seem to differentiate one local class of occasions (a class which I cannot define, but which includes hearings and meetings) from other such classes. Whatever our interpretation, it is quite striking that while they are at the hearing compound, participants do not discuss the subject of the hearing either before the hearing starts or after it ends.

In some unusual circumstances (exemplified by *Transcript 2* but not yet analyzed) it seems to be legitimate to make post-hearing statements about the hearing itself, but even then the issues raised or resolved in the hearing are not discussed. That participants may talk about the subject only during hearing-time need not mean either that they must talk about the subject or that they may not talk about other subjects. It does mean, however, that unlike non-hearing time, talk about matters other than subject-related issues communicates one's attitude toward those issues. A participant who talks of non-hearing subjects during the hearing-time signals* displeasure, refusal, or delay, or so it seems from the way in which such "irrelevant" remarks seem to frequently follow a demand and to sometimes be followed by a watering-down of that demand or by a repetition of the demand by someone other than the person who first made it. This observation raises a matter of the style of hearings, and specifically of their involvement contour.

STYLE   It is my impression that Lue hearings tolerate more nonsubject remarks than we do* at our meetings and trials. This should not surprise us, since I have indicated that "irrelevant" remarks are quite relevant to the business of the hearing (cf. Phillips 1965:73). It is more important to point out that this impression is of no interest whatever, since an ethnographer's purpose in writing about the Lue is not to differentiate them from the Americans, but to formulate rules which permit a stranger to recognize and use Lue categories as the Lue seem to. Lue seem to differentiate between hearings and other Lue occasions. Two observed features of behavior which I, an outsider, find associated with this distinction is that the involvement contour of hearings is quite even and the intensity of involvement rather high.

By evenness of involvement, I record my observation that most statements are about the subject of the hearing. During a long hearing,* conversation about other matters is not infrequent but this, I think, is a manifestation of the tactical relevance of irrelevant statements to which I have already referred. Since the goal of a hearing is to obtain a compromise, to say that a hearing takes a long time is to say that the compromise is not reached quickly. The way to reject a proposal or to gain time for considering it is to talk about irrelevant subjects. In any event, it is my impression that compared to casual conversations* and to village meetings,* participants in hearings keep more to the subject and maintain a more constant emotional tone and decorum.

I also maintain that the intensity of involvement is high relative to other Lue social occasions, but here ethnocentrism makes valid observation almost impossible. The Thai value and aspire to passivity and non-involvement, whether expressed as the Buddhist virtue of *ubekha* or the folk-phrases "cool-heart" and *chirj-chirj*. They eat slowly and with long pauses, talk softly, maintain pleasant neutral facial expressions, and avoid tears and loud laughter. Moreover, and perhaps as one of the cues which elicits from Western anthropologists the diagnosis of "loose social structure" or "permissiveness," they permit a greater variety of more intensive "side activities" in more situations than we do. During hearing-time participants smoke, chew betel or pickled tea leaves, and hold occasional momentary soto voce two-person conversations. But such side activities are also common at all occasions including Buddhist temple services (except when actually chanting or holding the hands in the attitude of prayer and reverence). It is my impression that during hearings two-person conversations are short and uncommon, resistance to diversion by external events great, simultaneous public statements rare, walking about non-existent, and wearing a shirt (or its equivalent, a folded cloth over the left shoulder) standard, *relative to other Lue occasions*. That is, locally appropriate (and, in some cases, locally recognized) indices show that hearing-time is contrastively formal and highly involved.

Let me emphasize what I mean here. The common casual observation that the Thai are noisy in temple is really a false comparison masking as a description, for were the Thai not noisier than some other people—real or imagined—the observation would not have been made. That the Thai sometimes blink, sleep, or talk is nowhere recorded in the literature. I suppose that the observations means: "The Thai I saw in temple were noiser than Methodists are supposed to be in church." Many of our social science observations become reportable phenomena, and most of our social science comparisons (practical as opposed to spiritual, pragmatic as opposed to magical, guilt as opposed to shame) are made, on the basis of covertly comparing what we like to believe is true of white middle-class Americans with what we see in the behavior of natives. It is perhaps true, and clearly testable, that the decibel level of a Thai Buddhist congregation is higher than that of a Los Angeles Methodist congregation, and lower than that of a Jamaican Pocamania congregation. As a description and comparison of human activity, such a statement is without significance. If I am correct in asserting that the Thai are quieter in temple than they are in other locally delimited situations, then however loud they sound to Methodists and however quiet to Pocamanians, the Thai whether ethnographically or for purposes of comparative ethnology (since [cf. Goodenough 1956:37] such comparisons should be based on intracultural contrastive analysis), are quiet in temple.

My last point about style, like the one about subject, struck me with sufficient force to be entered in hearing transcripts. First, participants talk relatively softly. Second, they often do not look at one another while they talk. My transcripts indicate that a), only young men look directly at the person they are talking or listening to; b), that most participants seem to be looking at no one in particular, or even to be staring into vacant space; and that c), the individual who, despite his absence of such formal attainments as temple service or literacy, seems to be most respected and influential in hearings, meetings, and private decisions often keeps his eyes closed while he talks or listens to remarks addressed to him. I will call this eye-separation, rather than eye-avoidance because "eye-avoidance" implies that we know its meaning (duplicity, humility, and so on) or, minimally but still more dangerously, that it has some determinable meaning with respect to speaker and/or statement. At the present stage of analysis, I would maintain that its meaning, like that of sitting in place or talking about the subject, is in respect to the kind of situation (a hearing) in which it occurs. Observation of its differential incidence does, however, suggest that eye-separation is a sign of and perhaps a cause of being a respected hearing participant. To the extent that the rule of eye-separation is general for hearings or for participants of high status, one would expect its violation to have meaning with respect to statements and status, but I do not know whether it does,* or if it does, what those meanings are. Eye-separation is binding mutually and generally. That is, speakers do not look at listeners; listeners do not look at speakers. If it is a limitation on expressive messages (Goffman 1963), it is a two-way limit. I phrase this conditionally because it is possible that the Lue do not regard the eyes as windows to the soul. There is no compelling reason to reject the hypothesis that voice tone and word choice are such important expressive signs to the Lue that they avert their eyes in order to be able to better concentrate on them. Alternatively, one might hypothesize that expressive signs are unimportant because most of what they signify for Westerners (credibility, wealth, education, class, political persuasion, unbudgeable bias) is already known by every participant about every other participant by virtue of the very communality which makes hearings an effective means of adjudication. Or, again, since the Thai strike most sympathetic observers as being exquisitely sensitive to the nuances of interpersonal confrontations and also as being extremely devoted to keeping such confrontations amicable, one might hypothesize that eye-separation permits them to give uncensored information by not muting opinion differences which eye-contact would make unpleasant if the speaker and listener received each other's expressive messages. Again, it might be the case that adequate expressive message is carried by the voice, but that eye-separation permits the receiver to pretend that he did not get the message.

As was the case with alternative explanations of resentment of the nuns in Tepoztlan, the alternative hypotheses seem about equally plausible. But I have not come quite full circle, for there is no anthropologist other than myself who can be criticized for not having the data of which to ask the right questions. I am not at all sure what the right questions would be, but I think that I know what such data should look like.

If we assume, as our faith in a science of ethnography requires, that Lue life is not random, then we can hope to discover some order in adequately complete records of that life in vivo. The stipulation "in vivo" is intended to exclude the bulk of conventional fieldnotes which consist of dubiously situated answers to questions which no native ever asks another. It is also intended, perhaps pathetically, to effect a compromise between the analyst's procedural need for stable data that can be continually reexamined and the apparent fact that the native meanings and relevances of social life—the analyst's goal—are situated. My own experience in writing this paper suggests that even unusually detailed fieldnotes, an ability "to operate in a manner acceptable to . . . members" (Goodenough 1957), prompt follow-up questions, and the luxury of a return to the field site produce arbitrary tokens of the motile and ephemeral situations in which actions occur and from which they derive their native significance. The ethnographer's task in the field is to freeze for analysis the bubble of situated action.

It is clear that the primary questions should be those which the ethnographer asks *himself* in order to coherently describe the organization he finds in the data of natural social life. The answers should perhaps be formulated as rules that predict (or "generate")[14] further acceptable behavior. The ethnographer can then use informants to verify each rule by asking whether the observed behavior from which the rule was explicated constitutes a coherent class and whether the behavior predicted by the rule is acceptable and a member of that class.

NOTES

[1] This paper is a revision of one read at a conference on "Interpersonal relations in South and Southeast Asia" sponsored by the Institute for International Studies of the University of California in 1965. For their comments on that earlier version, I am indebted to the conference participants. Subsequent versions have benefited from criticisms by Jasper C. Ingersoll, Ranier Lang, Edward Leddel, Lyle Steadman, and Paul Steinberg.

I am pleased to be able to thank the Foreign Area Training Fellowship Program of the Ford Foundation for sponsoring my first field trip, and the UCLA Academic Senate's Committee on Research, together with the University of California's Center for Southeast Asia Studies, for helping to support my second. Work on this paper was supported in part by ARPA (order #836) monitored by the Air Force Office of Scientific Research (AFOSR–66–1167; 68–1428).

[2] There is no need to remind my fellow initiates that the anthropological faith affirms the fundamental importance of these institutions to all created societies.

[3] Deliberate missionaries of self-aware faiths sometimes proselytize by means of "living a life of Christian witness." The anthropological field worker, as an accidental missionary of unconscious faith, proselytizes in similar fashion. By asking for (and enthusiastically responding to) information about kinship terms, social classes, ranks of prestige, etc., the skillful fieldworker quietly teaches previously benighted natives that these data are significant. Thus, "living a life of professional witness" is sometimes effective, but it is, of course, more efficient to develop respondents into research assistants by training them to draw proper genealogies, to intelligently sort prestige-ranking cards, to keep correct household budgets, etc.

[4] Throughout this paper, uncited quotations are fieldnotes edited only by translation, explanatory insertions (in brackets), deletions (indicated, . . .), and altered proper names.

[5] For the present paper, an elaborate orthography is inconvenient and an exact phonology unnecessary. In transcribing Thai and Lue words, I have ignored tone

(which is phonemic in Lue) and vowel length, but have maintained the following conventions of Thai transcription.

LETTER IN TEXT	APPROXIMATE AMERICAN SOUND
a	*father*
e	sp*a*de
E	p*a*d
i	mach*i*ne
o	*ro*te
0	*caugh*t, d*o*g
u	*too*
aj	fl*y*
aw	c*ow*
ir	b*ir*d (but without the "r" sound)
ue	Extremely high front vowel, no English equivalent.
b	*b*oy
c	*J*ohn (but unvoiced), mat*ch*es (but unaspirated)
d	*d*og
f	*f*oe
h	*h*ill. Also indicates aspiration of preceding stop.
j	*y*et
k	s*c*old
l	*l*ip
m	*m*oo
n	*n*il
ng	si*ng*
p	s*p*ade
s	*s*ill
t	s*t*op
x	a*ch* (as in German)

[6] Harvey Sacks first suggested that this village knowledge makes Norm's loss of face problematic, and thereby stimulated the line of thought which developed into this paper.

[7] Sue's child, a girl, died in infancy. In response to my question, Sol replied that, "Had she lived and come to visit us we would have given her food *just as we do any child who comes to visit*" (emphasis added). To a further question he replied, "Yes, she would have called me *pOpu* [a kin term restricted to father's father]." Another 1965 informant furnished as an abstract rule, the statement that a "road child" does not inherit. My present summary of the relevant data is: if A is B's acknowledged child, A has a claim against B and against B's close kinsmen, but A's illegitimacy or B's leaving A's mother can be used by B and his kinsmen to diminish A's claim.

[8] Ranier Lang made this suggestion, which my 1960 fieldnotes and 1965 informants confirmed.

[9] This statement, and subsequent ones marked with an asterisk, are assumptions required to explain the data. As analytic propositions, they cannot be tested simply by asking an informant whether they are true. Rather it is necessary to

collect a corpus of data, delimit coherent domains within it, and demonstrate that such propositions explain the data of those domains better than alternative propositions do. I have now collected such a corpus (of tape recorded natural village conversations) but it does not enter into this paper.

[10] I do not feel that this statement can be proved or disproved simply by asking an informant to react to it. Nevertheless, I feel that there must be some ways, which I cannot yet specify, in which native judgments must influence the formulation and help provide the verification of such statements. Specifically, I feel (but cannot demonstrate) that the following excerpt from 1965 field notes supports my statement about how Norm's utterances, and similar hearing utterances, are understood by villagers.

Sol [in response to my question, "Why did Grandfather Norm say, 'I will take him to jail'?"]: Norm said, 'I'll take him to jail' in order to make us fear him, in order to *lOk* ["bother," "disturb," "create a nuisance," commonly used of haunting spirits] us, to make us fearful and afraid so that we would either marry or offer him a great deal of money. In the same way, he said [subsequently] that he would take the issue to the headman, the chief headman, the provincial capital. But we knew that it wasn't a major crime and that people don't go to jail for it, [we all knew that] it was only an unmarried woman, not someone's wife, that unless she had agreed to the intercourse it would never have happened.

R? Lots of people talk in order to *lOk* like that during a hearing [*rirng*].
R? [He said, 'I will lose face'] so that we would pity (*du*) him.

[11] Harvey Sacks suggests that the hearing may be "ahistorical" in that only its outcome, and not the events within it, are accountable. It occurs to me that it might be characteristic of occasions which "set things right" to stand outside of history. Once things are set right—through marriage, reconciliation, the payment of compensation—it is not legitimate to refer back to the maneuvers which produced the settlement or, sometimes, even to the cause (for instance, pregnancy, quarrel, or injury) of the occasion.

[12] A Ban Ping hearing is a "focussed interaction" in that the parties to it concentrate on the subject which it is their business to discuss and to try to resolve. Throughout this section, I borrow, twist, and squander the ideas of Erving Goffman (1961, 1963).

[13] When male elders visit a home, they usually sit in the *xOm*, the oldest against the east wall or in the northeast corner and the others "below" him in order of decreasing age. So only the division into factions is hearing-specific.

[14] Chomsky's informal examples (1964:65–66) tempt me to claim that my rules would have "descriptive adequacy," but such a claim cannot be sustained, since the formal conditions for such adequacy (Chomsky 1965) (i)–(iv) of pp. 30–31) are not transparently applicable and since the necessary (*ibid.*, p. 41) motive of explanatory adequacy seems unattainable. That the powerful and fashionable approach of transformational generative grammar seems unavailable to the ethnographer perhaps follows from its ontological assumption that "most facts of interest and importance . . . [are] neither presented for direct observation nor extractable from data by inductive procedures of any known sort" (*ibid.*, p. 18). If the intended data of a transformational generative grammar consist of unordered native intuitions, then

the closest analogy I can see between it and the procedures I suggest is that my rules should produce such data, and thereby meet a stronger test of observational adequacy (Chomsky 1964:79–80, 62, n. 8) than the mere listing and corpus index which elsewhere (in the same article) is called observationally adequate.

REFERENCES CITED

Albert, Ethel M., 1964, Rhetoric, logic, and poetics in Burundi: culture patterning of speech behavior. American Anthropologist, 66.6, Pt. 2:35–54.
Austin, J. L., 1962, How to do things with words. Oxford, Clarendon Press.
Chomsky, Noam, 1964, Current issues in linguistic theory. In J. A. Fodor and J. J. Katz, eds., The structure of language. New York, Prentice-Hall.
———, 1965, Aspects of the theory of syntax. New York, M.I.T. Press.
Evans-Pritchard, E. E., 1956, Sanza: a characteristic feature of Zande language and thought, Social Anthropology and Other Essays. New York, Free Press, 1962.
Firth, Raymond, 1963, We, the Tikopia. New York, Beacon Press.
Garfinkel, Harold, 1964, Studies of the routine grounds of everyday activities. Social Problems 11:225–250.
Goodenough, Ward H., 1956, Residence rules. Southwestern Journal of Anthropology, 12.1:22–37.
———, 1957, Cultural Anthropology and Linguistics, Georgetown University Monograph Series on Language and Linguistics, No. 9.
Goffman, Erving, 1961, Encounters: two studies in the sociology of interaction. New York, Bobbs-Merrill.
———, 1963, Behavior in public places. New York, Free Press.
———, 1964, The neglected situation. American Anthropologist, 66.6, Pt. 2: 133–136.
Hamburger, Ludwig, 1965, Fragmentierte Gesellschaft: die Strucktur der Thaifamilie. Kolner Zeitschrift fur Soziologie und Sozial-Psychologie, 17:49–72.
Hart, H. L. A., 1952, The ascription of responsibility and rights, In Anthony Flew, ed., Logic and language. Oxford, Basil Blackwell.
Helmer, H., Rescher, N., 1960, On the epistemology of the inexact sciences. The Rand Corporation. R–353.
Lewis, Oscar, 1963, Life in a Mexican village. Urbana, Illini Books.
Moerman, Michael, 1966, Ban Ping's temple: the center of a "loosely structured" society. Anthropological Studies in Theravada Buddhism, Yale Southeast Asia Cultural Report Series, No. 13.
———, 1968, Agricultural change and peasant choice in a Thai village. Berkeley and Los Angeles, University of California Press.
Phillips, Herbert P., 1965, Thai peasant personality. Berkeley and Los Angeles, University of California Press.

A Structural Description
of Subanun
"Religious Behavior"

Charles O. Frake

The purpose of this paper is not to present anything approaching a complete description of Subanun "religion" but rather to raise the question of what kind of statement would constitute an adequate ethnographic description of an aspect of a culture.[1] This is not, I think, a trivial question to ask. A theory of how to describe cultural behavior implies a theory of culture. Ethnography, the science of cultural description, can potentially fill a role as critical to our general theoretical understanding of the nature of culture as has modern descriptive linguistics toward our understanding of the nature of language.

A description of a culture, an *ethnography*, is produced from an *ethnographic record* of the events of a society within a given period of time, the "events of a society" including, of course, informants' responses to the ethnographer, his queries, tests, and apparatus. *Ethnographic technique*, ignored in this paper, is the task of devising means for producing an adequately ample record of events. *Ethnographic methodology* is the task of devising operations for producing an ethnography from an ethnographic record. *Ethnographic theory* is the task of devising criteria for evaluating ethnographies. These three aspects of the ethnographic task are independent. The adequacy of the record and the validity of the methodology cannot be determined unless the data are subjected to analysis and the results tested against the criteria of the theory during the course of field investigation. The production of an ethnography should imply a task more challenging than "writing up one's notes."

When an ethnographer first enters a strange society, each encountered event is new, unanticipated, improbable, and, hence, highly informative in the communication-theory sense. As he learns the culture of the society, more and more of what happens becomes familiar and anticipatable. The ethnographer can plan his own activities on the basis of these anticipations. The more he learns of a culture, the more his anticipations match those of his informants. Similarly for a person born in a society, as he learns his culture, the events of his life become more probable, becoming parts of familiar *scenes* which he and his fellows plan for, stage, and play their roles in. To describe a culture, then, is not to recount the events of a society but to specify what one must know to make those events maximally probable. The problem is not to state what someone did but to specify the conditions under which it is culturally appropriate to anticipate that he, or persons occupying his role, will render an equivalent performance. This conception of a cultural description implies that an ethnography should be a theory of cultural behavior in a particular society, the adequacy of which is to be evaluated by the ability of a stranger to the culture (who may be the ethnographer) to use the ethnography's statements as instructions for appropriately anticipating the scenes of the society. I say "appropriately anticipate" rather than "predict" because a failure of an ethnographic statement to predict correctly does not necessarily imply descriptive inadequacy as long as the members of the described society are as surprised by the failure as is the ethnographer. The test of descriptive adequacy must always refer to informants' interpretations of events, not simply to the occurrence of events.

With this criterion of descriptive adequacy in mind the formulation of an ethnographic statement would seem to include at least the following tasks:

1. Discovering the major categories of events or *scenes* of the culture.

2. Defining scenes so that observed interactions, acts, objects, and places can be assigned to their proper scenes as roles, routines, paraphernalia, and settings.

3. Stating the distribution of scenes with respect to one another, that is, providing instructions for anticipating or planning for scenes.

These three methodological problems will be discussed with reference to a portion of the Subanun record, a record which is inadequate at several points because much of this analysis was completed only after I had left the field.

The Subanun are a pagan people practicing swidden agriculture in the mountainous interior of Zamboanga Peninsula on the island of Mindanao in the Philippines. The data of this paper pertain only to the Eastern Subanun of the Gulu Disakan and Lipay regions northeast of Sindangan Bay in the interior of Zamboanga del Norte Province, studied in the field in 1953–1954 and 1957–1958. In terms of segmentation and stratification, Subanun society displays remarkable simplicity. Each nuclear family is the focus of a partially unique and variable network of social ties with kin and neighbors which constitutes, for that family, the "total society." This maximal, nondiscrete sphere of social relationships has no corporate organization and is not segmented into lineages, age-sets, secret societies, territorial districts, political factions, or the like. Despite this simplicity of their social structure, the Subanun carry on constant and elaborate interfamily social activities—litigation, offerings, feasts—all well-lubricated with ample quantities of rice wine. Warfare is lacking (Frake 1957, 1960; Christie 1909).

THE IDENTIFICATION OF "RELIGIOUS BEHAVIOR"

One of the most frequent and regularly recurrent events in the Subanun record is eating. Most, *but not all*, Subanun events which we should consider instances of "eating" as a category of activity fall into an easily distinguishable Subanun scene, a 'meal'.[2] To qualify as a 'meal' a scene must include at least one actor, the 'eater,' and a 'cooked starchy-staple food.' A meal characteristically marks a clear interruption of other activity, requiring the performers to squat before a setting of food on the floor or ground; it is scheduled at least once daily; it requires prior planning and preparation; and, although one actor is sufficient, it is generally staged as a social performance.

In the typical recorded meal, those participating in the role 'joint eaters' belong to a single nuclear family, the side dish is a nonmeat food, the staple may be a root crop or a cereal, and no 'rice wine' (*gasi*)[3] is served. These are *ordinary meals*. If one of the features of an ordinary meal changes, the others change as well. Meals with multifamily joint eaters, meat side dish, cereal staple, and 'rice wine' are *festive meals* or, simply, *feasts*.

Festive meals occur at irregular intervals and must be occasioned; i.e., there must be a legitimizing event which serves as a reason for the feast. It is always appropriate to ask in Subanun, "What is the reason for this feast?" To ask, "What is the reason for this meal?" would sound somewhat odd in uncontrived contexts. Festive meals substitute for ordinary ones. A meal is scheduled at least once daily. If there is a legitimizing occasion and the necessary components are procurable, a festive meal is staged; otherwise an ordinary meal is staged. A central part of Subanun planning involves anticipating festive occasions so that the necessary components for staging a feast be procurable whenever a legitimizing event occurs. The occurrence of one of the components, as an event, can itself be a reason for a feast, requiring the mustering of the other essential components. If a wild pig (meat-side-dish component) is caught in a trap, its consumption requires a feast. If guests congregate (multifamily-performance component), they must be feasted. The festive meal itself occurs in a context of a wide range of other activities: competitive drinking, displays of verbal art, singing, dancing. All activities occurring from the arrival to the departure of participants in a feast together constitute a *festivity*.

During some festivities occur episodes which themselves seem to be feasts, but of a rather special sort. The festive provisions are set up on distinctive paraphernalia and the 'eaters,' though sometimes audible, are not visible to the ethnographer nor, by report, to the ordinary Subanun. Feasts of this sort whereby 'mortals' feed the various categories of 'nonvisible' or 'supernatural' inhabitants of the Subanun universe, the Subanun call *kanu*, here glossed as 'offerings.' During the course of a festivity, one to several offerings may be performed. A festivity during which offerings occur is a *ceremony*. A ceremony may be *simple* or *complex* depending on whether one or more than one offering is held. This contrast between simple and complex ceremonies is not matched by a lexical distinction in Subanun, but is necessary in order to describe the denota of names for types of offerings and ceremonies. Ceremonies are named for one constituent offering. Thus *beklug* denotes a particular kind of offering or a ceremony in which the *beklug* offering is one of many constituents. If a Subanun offering name is given as "instructions to perform," one must know from context whether the referent is an offering or a ceremony and, if a ceremony, whether it is simple or complex. The term *kanu* may likewise, depending on context, refer to an offering or to a ceremony.

A ceremony, then, is one kind of festivity. Other kinds are 'litigation,' 'labor-recruiting feasts,' 'game-sharing feasts,' 'meat-division feasts,' and 'hospitality feasts.' Several kinds of festivities may be jointly held. If for some reason it is necessary to provide a feast, it is often economic to discharge as many festive functions as possible during its course. Thus a legal case and an offering may occur during a festivity originally staged as a hospitality feast.

To the naïve observer an offering may seem like a minor episode in a festive event. But when one considers how offerings and ceremonies vary in paraphernalia, social participation, routines, planning, and programming, and when one considers the range of events which are relevant to staging ceremonies, it becomes clear that the behavioral complex centering on offerings penetrates deeply into many crucial areas of Subanun life. The programming and staging of ceremonies forms a major segment of Subanun cultural activity comparable in scope and content to the traditional ethnographic category of "religion." This comparability suggests (but does not require) the term *religious behavior* as a label for this activity, and it suggests *Subanun religion* as a label for what is described by an ethnographic statement which accounts for this behavior. But the only criterion of whether a particular act is an instance of *religious behavior* is its relevance to the programming and performing of 'offerings.' The ethnographic (in contrast to the ethnological) issue is not whether instances of *religious behavior* so defined conform to any particular cross-cultural notion of "what religion is," but whether they do in fact comprise a meaningful descriptive category of Subanun cultural activity and, if so, how is this category to be described.

THE PERFORMANCE OF AN 'OFFERING'

The first step in describing Subanun *religious behavior* is to describe the performance of offerings themselves in terms of discovered categories of constituent locales, objects, performers, and acts. Only a brief outline of the constituent structure of offerings as performances can be presented here.

SETTINGS   There are no special buildings, rooms, or outdoor areas reserved for staging offerings. Offerings may be held inside nuclear family residences, in house yards, in fields, in forests, or on stream banks, the specific locale depending on the type of offering as well as on sociological, ecological, and meteorological conditions.

PROVISIONS   A festive meal must be provided for both mortal and supernatural participants. A feast for supernaturals requires special components: the staple must be of rice, eggs are added to the required meat side dish, the proffered wine (or fermented mash) must be of rice and be ritually prepared, the proffered betel quids must be prepared with domesticated betel-pepper leaf and areca palm nuts (mortals often use substitute ingredients). Some categories of supernaturals take their food raw, others in a cooked state. These provisions are first offered to the invited supernaturals on an altar, then removed and consumed, generally as part of a larger feast, by humans. (The supernaturals conveniently consume only the 'intangible essence,' *seŋaw*, of food and drink.) The kind and quantity of provisions within these constituent categories varies with type of offering, with the kind of event occasioning the offering, with the whims of individual supernaturals, and with particular bargains struck beforehand between mortal host and supernatural guest. From an economic standpoint the side dish, requiring sacrifice of valuable livestock, is the most significant feature of an offering. The market value of pigs and chickens slaughtered for the offering and accompanying feast provides a direct index of the occasion's importance.

PARAPHERNALIA   Humans settle for a banana leaf on the floor, but the supernaturals demand elaborate devices from which to partake of their meals. The Subanun construct at least thirty types of altars, varying in number of platforms, method of construction, materials employed, means of support or suspension, decoration, and size. Sometimes the type of altar is determined by the deity being propitiated. Thus the 'raw-food-eating gods' (*kemuŋluq*) always eat from a platformless *seleŋsaŋan*, but a personal 'guardian god' (*tipun*) generally prefers a *bibalay* altar, the defining attributes of which are rectangular shape, no sides, stick floor, and parallel legs. More often the type of altar or altars is specific to a particular kind of offering or ritual occasion, and a variety of supernaturals will in turn eat from it during the ceremony. Some more elaborate offerings require special equipment other than altars: various kinds of barriers to inhibit the movements of malevolent supernaturals, folded cloths to capture lost souls, miniature wooden replicas of weapons, model rafts and canoes, decorative and rustling leaves. With few exceptions all of this equipment is constructed anew (usually in a rather slipshod fashion) for each offering and then discarded. Since human drinking and feasting cannot proceed until the offering is completed, the few Subanun who are prone to spend time lavishing care on the construction of ritual paraphernalia become the butt of criticism from their more secular-minded fellows. Every offering also requires a resonant porcelain bowl (struck rhythmically to announce the occasion to the supernatural guests) and incense (the fumes of which augment the aroma of the offering as a lure).

PARTICIPANTS   The participants in an offering all belong to the category of 'persons' (getaw), those 'living things' (tubuqan) with whom one can establish communicatory relations. A dichotomous dimension of reported conscious visibility divides 'persons' into two subcategories with fundamentally distinct roles in offerings. 'Persons' reported to be consciously visible to the ordinary Subanun are 'mortals' (kilawan). 'Persons' whom the ordinary Subanun are reportedly unable to see consciously are 'supernaturals' (kanaq kilawan). Only the exceptional perceptual powers of certain prominent 'mediums' can reportedly record a conscious visual image of the 'supernaturals.' Others may 'see' a supernatural without being aware of it—a possible cause of illness if the unconscious image is particularly terrifying. The nonempirical nature of Subanun 'supernaturals' refers only to the visual sense; these beings are (reportedly) able to make an impression on one's auditory and tactile senses.

The English word 'supernatural' thus serves as a *label* for the *Subanun* category of 'persons' reportedly not consciously visible to the ordinary Subanun. There are, of course, in the verbally revealed Subanun universe many creatures ('persons' and 'nonpersons') which the ethnographer feels confident he will never see and which many informants admit they have never seen (but only because they have never encountered them, except perhaps in the dark). Some of these "natural" (i.e., visible) but rarely encountered phenomena play an important role in Subanun life, but they do not appear at offerings and hence are not relevant to the present discussion. Only by attending to Subanun criteria can we assign the bow-and-arrow-wound-inflicting *menubuq* pygmies to the category 'supernatural' and the body-dismembering *meŋayaw* marauders to the category 'mortal.' Neither class appears to the ethnographer to have any empirically substantiatable members in the Subanun habitat at the present time, though they both may once have had. Yet to discuss both categories together as aspects of Subanun *religion* because they are both "supernatural" according to the ethnographer's notions would seriously distort the structure of Subanun culture.

At the most general level of terminological contrast the Subanun classify 'supernaturals' as 'souls' (gimuud), 'spirits' (mitubuq), 'demons' (getau-telunan), and 'gods' (diwata) (cf. Table 1). Two semantic dimensions suffice to define these four categories in terms of necessary and sufficient contrasts in verbal descriptions:

1. Inherent connection with mortals

   1.1. Inherently connected with a living mortal
   1.2. Once inherently connected with a mortal now dead but still remembered by at least one living mortal
   1.3. Not inherently connected to a living or remembered mortal

2. Habitat connection with mortals

   2.1. Regularly residing with mortals in 'this world' (*glumbaŋ*)
   2.2. Not regularly residing in 'this world'

Using the numbering of the outline above, the four categories are definable as follows:

'Souls'	:	1.1	
'Spirits'	:	1.2	
'Demons'	:	1.3	2.1
'Gods'	:	1.3	2.2.

'Souls' play a role in offerings through attempts to use offerings to recapture, for the sake of their owner's health, lost souls lured away by fragrant blossoms, attractive supernaturals, and the offerings of sorcerers. ('Souls,' a kind of 'supernatural,' must be distinguished from *gina* 'life stuff,' associated with consciousness, cognition, and emotion but not a 'person' who attends offerings.)

After death the soul survives to become a 'spirit,' a bodiless soul who wanders about 'this world' until sent on a tour of sacred places and other worlds by a series of offerings performed on his behalf by survivors. Becoming eventually forgotten in the sky world, he then acquires the necessary attributes of a 'god' (cf. definitions above). It is the spirits of the recent dead—close kin whom he remembers personally and toward whom he still has ritual obligations—that concern a Subanun. When he dies, others will remember him, and those he remembered will be forgotten. Ties between spirits and mortals are reformulated in successive generations rather than continuing through time as an ancestor cult—just as the corporate social groups of Subanun society, the nuclear families, do not survive through successive generations as descent groups but are constantly dissolving and reforming (Frake 1960).

Remembered spirits are important to the Subanun because they are the closest friends a mortal has among the supernaturals. They willingly attend seances for sentimental reunions with their loved ones (though even they demand an offering of food and drink). At seances they typically act as intermediaries between mortals and less friendly supernaturals, often filling a role not unlike that of a legal authority in arbitrating a dispute between

Table 1. Categories of Participants in Subanun
'Offerings'

'persons' *getaw*
  *1. 'supernaturals' *kanaq kilawan*
    1.1. 'souls' *gimuud*
    1.2. 'spirits' *mitubuq*
    1.3. 'demons' *getau-telunan*
    1.3.1. 'ogres' *menemad*
    1.3.2. 'goblins' *memenwa*
    1.3.3. 'pygmies' *menubuq*
    1.4. 'gods' *diwata*
    1.4.1. 'sky gods' *getau-laŋit*
    1.4.2. 'raw-food-eating gods' *kemuŋluq, meŋilaw*
    1.4.2.1. 'sunset gods' *getau-sindepan*
    1.4.2.2. 'sea gods' *getau-dagat*
    1.4.2.3. 'ocean gods' *getau-laud*
    1.4.3. 'sunrise gods' *getau-sebaŋan, tumiag*
    1.4.4. 'underworld gods' *getau-bayaq*
    2. 'mortals' *kilawan*
  *2.1. 'functionaries' *sug mikanu dun*
    2.1.1. nonprofessional functionaries
    2.1.2. 'professional functionaries' *belian*
    2.1.2.1. 'invocators' *bataq belian*
    2.1.2.2. 'mediums' *gulaŋ belian*
    2.1.2.2.1. 'shamans' *guleligan*
    2.1.2.2.2. 'interviewers' *meninduay*
    2.2. 'assistants' *gimpaŋ*
  *2.3. 'beneficiaries' *sug pikanuan dun*
    2.4. 'audience' *sug suminaup dun*

---

* Marks categories which must be represented at any offering.

plaintiff (the offended supernatural) and defendant (the mortal offender and victim of the plaintiff's wrath). Spirits respond to emotional appeal "for oldtimes' sake" and consequently tend to be less greedy in their demands than other supernaturals. They can be troublesome, however, if their mortal kin shirk their ritual obligations. Also they may become so afflicted with the prevalent Subanun sentiment of 'loneliness' (*bugaq*) that they desire to transform a mortal loved one to spirit status, a transformation few mortals are willing to undergo, no matter how fond they were of the departed. Several informants have voiced a suspicion, founded on their remembrance of the deceased, that the spirit in such cases is not always as sentimental as he pretends; he has merely discovered a neat wedge for extorting food and drink from his survivors.

'Demons,' while not usually so viciously malevolent as the 'raw-food-eating gods,' are dangerous because they live so close at hand. Any chance encounter with them is likely to result in illness, and the disturbance of many of their habitats caused by swidden activities requires regular propitiation.

Of greatest importance among the 'gods' are the various types of 'raw-food eaters' (see Table 1) who periodically ascend the streams of Subanun country to inflict severe illness and epidemics and through their 'pets,' the rats and locusts, cause agricultural disasters. Their annual 'new year's' propitiation at strategic river confluences provides a common ritual interest for all settlements whose drainages converge upon a single convenient blocking place.

Other 'gods,' especially the 'sky gods,' are generally much less malevolent if not actually friendly. Perversely, they do not participate nearly so regularly in human affairs, although some exert important control over rice growth. During the course of an illness-studded life, most adult male Subanun acquire a personal 'guardian supernatural' (*tipun*), frequently a 'sky god,' who must receive annual propitiation at harvest time for the sake of the health of the man's family and rice.

'Gods' and 'demons' come in large numbers of varieties distinguished by habitat specifications, appearance, malevolence, diet, altar preferences, natural phenomena under their provenience, and so on. The verbal expositions of this pantheon vary greatly from informant to informant and from region to region. To present any one of these systems in all of its detail as "the Subanun pantheon" would do violence to cultural reality. The striking feature of Subanun theology is that, at any but the most general levels (see Table 1), it is not a consistent body of cherished lore at the tip of everyone's tongue. Beyond the generalizations given here, Subanun 'supernaturals' are, with some exceptions, diffuse in their functions. Almost any supernatural can cause almost any ailment or interfere in almost any activity. Consequently an elaborate and precise taxonomy of supernaturals correlated with their functional roles need not be shared by all participants in the performance of an offering. Individuals and groups can differ considerably in their theological speculations with little consequence for the practical conduct of *religious behavior.*

Direct observation and Subanun descriptions of role performances both make it clear that a 'mortal' participant in an offering occupies at least one of the following roles: 'functionary,' 'assistant,' 'beneficiary,' or 'audience' (see Table 1).

The 'functionary' has the task of extending the invitation to the supernatural guests once the offering has been prepared. He invokes the supernaturals by incantation, bowl striking, and incense burning. The functionary, furthermore, assumes the responsibility of supervising all proceedings connected with the offering to ensure their proper performance. Every adult male household head has frequent occasion to serve as functionary for simple household ceremonies. Women rarely assume this role in fact, except during one type of agricultural offering, but are not proscribed from it by custom. A person must always act as his own functionary in offerings to his personal 'guardian god' (*tipun*).

The complexity of Subanun religious techniques, however, demands specialized knowledge of functionaries for all but the simplest offerings. A 'professional functionary' (*belian*) is an acknowledged specialist in religious techniques who regularly acts as a functionary for offerings involving beneficiaries outside his own household. If a 'professional functionary' has one or more supernatural 'familiars' (*bilaq*) and can thereby conduct seances, he is a 'medium' (*gulaŋ belian*, or simply *belian* if context makes the level of contrast clear); otherwise he is an 'invocator' (*bataq belian*, literally, "a little bit of a professional functionary"). There are two kinds of 'mediums': 'shamans' (*guleligan*), who are 'possessed' (*tenaqan*) by their familiars, and 'interviewers' (*meninduay*) who carry on conversations with the supernatural guests as the latter partake of the offering.

Of the special statuses which a Subanun can achieve, that of 'medium' is the most formalized in method of recruitment and in social acknowledgment. It can never, however, replace a Subanun's full-time occupational role of farming. There are two routes, open to any adult man or woman, for becoming a medium: by 'training' (*pigubasan*) and by 'revelation' (*gemaw*). All mediums of my acquaintance selected the former route, involuntarily, when the supernaturals imposed the role upon them as the price of recovery from an illness. In this manner the gods recruit new members to the profession which is so essential to their well-being. A person so selected assists a qualified medium and acts as an 'invocator' until the gods inform him that he is ready to assume a medium's role himself. A medium of the other type (*gemaw*) allegedly receives his training direct from the gods and needs no apprenticeship.

The Subanun expects a good medium to exhibit certain peculiarities of 'habitual behavior' (*kebetaŋ*). His personality should emphasize to a fault the Subanun virtues of a quiet, passive, rather phlegmatic approach to interpersonal relationships with the consequence that he becomes, by Subanun evaluation, somewhat impractical in daily affairs. These traits of the personality type called *melemen* are the polar opposites of the forceful aggressiveness (*gembeluq*) required of a legal authority (Frake 1957). Hence the same person cannot easily occupy both the role of mediator with the supernaturals and the role of mediating among human disputants. Furthermore, by Subanun standards, the personality expected of a medium is more commendable, if less entertaining, than that of the extroverted legal authority.

Almost every settlement has someone who can assume the role of 'invocator' for certain ceremonies, but, in the area of my fieldwork, over half of the settlements lacked resident mediums. Mediums must therefore extend their services beyond their own settlements on a community-wide or even a region-wide basis, depending on their reputation. The travel required takes sufficient time from the medium's agricultural and technological tasks at home to counterbalance what material rewards his profession brings—a problem paralleling that of prominent legal authorities. Probably the most important material reward for mediums is the opportunity they have to attend a large number of feasts and drinking parties without any obligation to reciprocate. In addition, when called upon to perform special ceremonies for the cure of illness, they collect a small fee. They receive no fee for communal ceremonies in which they themselves are beneficiaries.

The other roles assumed by participants at an offering are functions of the particular social context; they are not permanent attributes of a person's status in the society at large. 'Assistants' are any persons who, under the functionary's supervision, prepare and set up the food and material equipment for the offering. They are recruited for the occasion from apprentice mediums, personnel of the beneficiary's household, the beneficiary himself, or simply from people "who like to do that sort of thing." The 'beneficiary' is the person or persons for whose benefit the offering is being given. The beneficiary may be one person, a household, a settlement, or even an entire region, depending on the purpose of the offering. The responsibility of providing a locale for the ceremony, of securing the necessary provisions, and of recruiting assistants falls to the beneficiaries. Any person or family intending to assume the role of beneficiary must make a contribution to the offering.

The 'audience' comprises all persons who are present because of the offering but who have no special role in its actual performance. It may include uninvited people who "happened to drop by" (in unexpressed anticipation of a feast), but it is largely composed of people with a special interest in the beneficiary. Major ceremonies of illness and death provide the only formalized occasions which bring large numbers of a person's dispersed kindred together as participants in a single event. Scheduled agricultural and prophylactic ceremonies, on the other hand, recruit audience and group beneficiaries along lines of local group affiliation. Except during seances, the majority of the audience and even beneficiaries, when these are in large number, generally show very little interest in the proceedings of the offering proper; that is the task of the functionary and his assistants. A Subanun offering is a technique for accomplishing a practical purpose. It is not an obvious source of inspiration or a forceful expression of ultimate values to an awe-stricken congregation. There are, of course, sources of inspiration and forceful expressions of values in Subanun life, but they are more likely to be communicated during secular gatherings around rice-wine jars after the offering is completed. Seances, however, rival legal disputes as foci of lively interest: they provide all persons present with an opportunity to interrogate, beg, cajole, bargain, and debate with the supernaturals themselves.

ROUTINES   To complete a description of the constituent structure of offerings there should be an analysis of the actions or routines followed in the performance. Such a description, however, would require a much more detailed discussion of offerings in all their varieties than is possible here. Consequently I merely list below the categories under which such a description of routines would be organized:

1. Preliminary staging talk
2. Assembly of participants
3. Preparing of provisions and paraphernalia
4. Setting up of offering
5. Invocation
6. Seance, if any
7. Removing provisions

(Routines 4–7 repeated for each offering of the ceremony)

8. Festivities (routines of festive eating, drinking, singing, etc.)
9. Dispersal of participants
10. Postperformance critique

THE DISTRIBUTION OF 'CEREMONIES'

If we assume that the foregoing description adequately accounts for the identification and performance of offerings within ceremonial contexts, the problem remains of formulating a statement which accounts for the scheduling of ceremonies in relation to other scenes of the culture. A distributional analysis seeks to answer the question: what does the occurrence of a given event imply to the knower of the culture about the occurrences of other possible events in the system? A statement of the distribution of ceremonies will specify what features of a Subanun's experience are relevant to the staging of a religious performance of a given kind at a given time.

Formulating a statement of the distribution of religious scenes requires examination of the ethnographic record for observed and reported events which, by the criteria already formulated, are instances (or "tokens") of this scene. Next we list the other scenes regularly occurring before and after religious scenes. To judge the extent to which the occurrence of one scene implies another, the record of observed sequences must be checked against the record of informant's statements about anticipated sequences

and of their interpretations of actual sequences in terms of these anticipations. This list of scenes provides a distributional *frame* for the set of
events labeled 'religious scenes' or 'ceremonies.' The diagram A| |B, where
A is the set of scenes regularly anticipated before ceremonies and B the set
regularly anticipated after ceremonies, represents the frame. Such a distributional frame specifies the necessary conditions for anticipating the occurrence of a ceremony. Note that these conditions depend not only on the
actual occurrence of an anticipated event, but also on plans made for producing or coping with future events. The model of distributional structure
is a two-sided, before-and-after frame, such as that required in linguistic
description, and not a Markov chain in which the probability of an event
is a sole function of the outcome of the preceding event. In acting as well as
in speaking persons have an image of the pattern to be completed and make
plans accordingly (cf. Miller and others 1960).

Description of a frame requires a statement of: (1) the probability of
the events that comprise the frame, (2) the alternative scenes, other than
ceremonies, that can be anticipated to occur in the same frame, (3) the
alternative kinds of ceremonies that can be anticipated to occur given the
occurrence of *a* ceremony.

The significance of ceremonies in Subanun life relates strikingly to the
probability of events which, in terms of legitimate cultural expectations,
imply ceremonies. Among the most probable events of Subanun life are those
that make up the scenes of the annual agricultural cycle: swidden slashing,
felling, burning, planting, protecting, and harvesting. The annual staging of
each of these scenes in this order by each family is an essential feature of
the Subanun ecological adaptation. These scenes and their constituents provide a frame for scheduling about nine annual complex ceremonies, the exact
number varying locally. Each of these ceremonies is of a specific named kind
with prescribed settings, kinds of provisions, paraphernalia, routines, and
social participation. These ceremonies are *scheduled ceremonies*. Their distribution has the following characteristics:

1. The scenes of the distributive frames are highly probable.
2. Each frame calls for a specified kind of ceremony.
3. There are no anticipatable alternatives to any of these ceremonies.

Thus the annual occurrence of a given kind of scheduled ceremony is
highly probable, and learning that a given scheduled ceremony has indeed
occurred is not very informative (it is not "news") to the person who knows
the culture. The occurrence of a scheduled ceremony is, in effect, a structural
marker of the anticipatable sequence of scenes in Subanun culture. It signals that events are unfolding as scheduled. (Compare the linguistic frames
marked in the following English utterance: "I want | | go | | Hawaii."
The person who knows English can legitimately anticipate only one form,
to, in the first slot; whereas in the second slot a number of alternatives can

be anticipated: *to, through, by, near, away from,* etc. The actual occurrence of a given form in the second slot is less probable and much more informative about the nonlinguistic world than the occurrence of a form in the first slot which can inform us only whether or not the utterance is correctly constructed [cf. Ziff 1960:41–42].)

To the Subanun, the occurrence of a scheduled ceremony not only signals the expected unfolding of events, but it is also necessary if future anticipations of probable events are to be fulfilled. The failure of one of the scenes of the agricultural cycle to occur as anticipated is a sign of a major *crisis*—an unanticipatable occurrence with far-reaching consequences for future anticipations. If harvesting does not follow swidden planting and protecting, then a crisis—drought, locusts, crop disease, human sickness—has occurred. The anticipated structural sequence of scenes has been broken. Correspondingly, to the Subanun, the failure properly to stage the correct ceremony on schedule can only lead to crisis. Unanticipated crises are caused by the supernaturals when *their* anticipations of regular feasts are not met. The explicit rationale for performing scheduled offerings is to prevent the occurrence of crises, to ensure the proper unfolding of events.

The performance of scheduled ceremonies is necessary to prevent crises, but, as is obvious to any Subanun, it is by no means sufficient to do so. Serious crises do occur. The distributive frames of many ceremonies are composed of unscheduled events that disrupt the ordinary routine of activities. Since their scheduling in relation to other scenes cannot, with great probability, be planned in advance, ceremonies occupying such frames are *unscheduled ceremonies.* Their distribution has the following characteristics:

1. The events which comprise the distributive frame are relatively improbable in the sense that other events could more legitimately have been expected at that time instead.

2. In a given frame there are often alternative courses of action to staging a religious scene.

3. Given the staging of a religious scene, a variety of types of ceremonies can occur in many of these frames.

Thus, knowing Subanun culture, one cannot predict when the conditions for an unscheduled ceremony will occur, and given the occurrence of such conditions, one cannot directly predict if a ceremony or an alternative scene will be staged, and given the staging of a ceremony, one cannot directly predict what kind of ceremony will be held. In a typical unscheduled situation there are a number of alternative courses of action—a range of doubt over what to anticipate. When a particular course of action is selected from these alternatives, the decision is highly informative—it is news—even to one who knows the culture.

The occurrence of illness exemplifies an unscheduled frame. Oversimplifying somewhat (by ignoring disease stages and states of 'relapse' and 'recuperation') the anticipated outcomes of an illness are continued sickness, cure, or death, giving the frame:

sickness | diagnosis | continued sickness
cure
death

All English terms comprising the frame are labels for categories of events as identified by the Subanun. The alternatives anticipatable are:

1. No formal therapy
2. 'Medication' (one or more of about eight hundred alternatives)
3. 'Religious' therapy
    3.1. Consulting the supernaturals
    3.2. 'Ritual contract'
    3.3. Performance of a 'contracted offering'
    3.3.1–61+. (List of alternative types of offerings)

The initial choice is made in relation to the anticipatable outcome, or prognosis, predicated by diagnosis, and subsequent choices are made in relation to the results of previous choices (Frake 1961). 'Medication' (*kebuluŋan*), relying on the special power inherent in certain, generally botanical, substances, comprises a set of techniques conceptually distinct both from reliance on 'skills' (*kependayan*) and from appeals to the supernaturals through offerings. These three contrasting techniques are applicable to a wide range of endeavors apart from illness: agriculture, technology, social control, love-making, etc.

Because of the greater expense and more elaborate planning required, religious therapy for illness is resorted to only if medication fails or its failure is immediately obvious from prognosis. If religious therapy does occur, it is informative of the seriousness of the case. The particular kind of ceremony required, if any, cannot be determined from diagnosis, but only by consulting the supernaturals through divination or seance.

Once a patient has learned he must perform a specific kind of ceremony and has ritually acknowledged his intention to do so, he has acquired a *binalag*, a term appropriately glossed as 'ritual debt,' for a Subanun's procrastination and legalistic evasion with *binalag* obligations closely parallels his handling of ordinary 'debts' (*gutaŋ*) with his fellow mortals. The 'ritual acknowledgment' (*penebiin*) of a *binalag*, which generally follows considerable haggling with the supernaturals, can be labeled 'ritual contract.' It is sound policy to contract to pay one's ritual debt *after* one is cured. In this way one is assured that the supernaturals will abide by their side of the agreement. The Subanun knows that even the most generous offering does not always cure his afflictions, and that, if he pays his ritual debts while he is sick, the supernaturals may keep him sick in the hope of extorting more and more from him.

But in this contest between mortal and supernatural, the former shows no more conscientiousness in fulfilling his obligations than the latter. Once he is cured, the Subanun patient becomes very reluctant to expend his resources on the supernaturals. Yet most Subanun have had enough experience with relapses of sickness to be somewhat wary of neglecting their ritual obligations without making an effort to do it legitimately by obtaining an extension of the contract through assiduous divination or through pleading with the supernaturals during a seance. Obtaining an extension often means an increase in the offering at interest, but despite past experience, the Subanun frequently hopes that with enough extensions his supernatural creditors will eventually forget about the debt and not inflict illness on him again in an effort to recover it. These hopes are generally in vain. The supernaturals hound their debtors with the same diligence as mortal creditors. Sooner or later, the Subanun who has neglected a ritual debt becomes ill. Then he remembers his outstanding obligations, which are likely to be numerous, and, if indications from seances and divination are affirmative, he may actually perform the contracted offering. But he may also acquire a new obligation pertinent to his new illness and penalizing him for the long delay in paying the debt for the old. With the new obligation, depending on the course of the illness, he may go through the same delaying tactics until he is once again afflicted. Because of these tactics of debt evasion, in many a crisis ceremony of disease the beneficiary is indeed sick but not with the illness that originally incurred the obligation to perform *that* ceremony. (There are, of course, many complexities and deviations from this simplified description that cannot be dealt with here.)

SUMMARY

In contrasting religious scenes with alternative and complementary kinds of cultural activity, it becomes clear that the entire behavior complex of which 'offerings' are the ultimate constituents serves the Subanun essentially as a technique, a way of getting things done. To build a house, to grow crops, to cure disease, or to make love, a Subanun may rely on his own 'skills' (*kepandayan*), resort to the 'medicinal' properties of certain substances (*kebuluŋan*), or call upon the supernaturals for assistance (*kanu*). Religion, generally the most expensive and complex of these techniques, belongs especially to the context of crises or potential crises—unanticipatable events with severe consequences and uncertain outcomes. The regular performance of scheduled ceremonies is designed to prevent crises. Unscheduled ceremonies are staged to cope with crises and put events back on their proper course.

The rationale for *religion* (i.e., 'offering'-focused behavior) as a technique lies in the belief that one can accomplish an end by inducing others to act in his behalf. This principle, valid enough in social relationships, the

Subanun extend by peopling the universe with unseen beings who have the power to inflict and thereby cure illness. These beings, the 'supernaturals,' are terminologically a species of 'persons' (*getaw*), and they can be influenced by methods resembling those proved effective in social relationships among mortals: offering food and drink, verbal appeals, attention to paraphernalia. A unique network of relationships, canalized by ritual obligations incurred through illness and the threat of illness, links each Subanun with the supernatural inhabitants of the universe, just as his network of social ties is patterned by secular obligations. The supernaturals sanction their demands with their power over health, whereas one's mortal fellows generally employ subtler sanctions of public opinion. In both cases the sanctions prove effective: social relationships are maintained, the supernaturals are fed, and the Subanun patient, if not cured, is perhaps consoled.

These characterizations of Subanun *religion* are summaries of the distributional properties of a structural segment of Subanun cultural activity with respect to contrasting and complementary activities. They are not, in intention at any rate, simply intuitive impressions of "the meaning of religion in Subanun life" unrelatable to operations performed on ethnographic data. As an adequate ethnographic statement the present paper is deficient in detail and rigor. It merely suggests some of the methodological features of such a statement.

NOTES

[1] A shorter version of this paper was read at the Tenth Pacific Science Congress, Honolulu, 1961. The notions of ethnographic method presented here owe much to Bruner (1957), Conklin (1962), Garfinkle (n.d.), Goodenough (1957), Miller and others (1960), Pike (1954), Barker and Wright (1955), and Goffman (1958).

[2] English terms appropriated as labels for descriptive categories are marked by single quotes or italics, the former indicating glosses, i.e., English terms which substitute for, but do not define, Subanun expressions. Frequently used glosses and labels appear unmarked after initial mentioning, but they always carry only whatever meaning has been assigned to them in this paper. The fact that a descriptive category is not given a gloss here does not mean that the Subanun cannot or do not talk about that category and its members. Evidence from Subanun discussions of scenes as well as from verbal and nonverbal performances within scenes was used in isolating all descriptive categories. But frequently the problem of how the Subanun talk about something is more complex than simply a question of "whether they have a word for it." For example, a variety of Subanun expressions may be used to point to an event as being a *feast* in contrast to an *ordinary meal*. Any reference to the provision of 'rice wine' (*gasi*) will suffice, as will a specification of a kind of *festivity*, such as 'labor-recruiting feast' (*pesilut*), during which the 'meal' is consumed.

[3] *Gasi* is a rice-yeast-fermented beverage made of a rice, manioc, maize, and/or Job's-tears mash. It contrasts in linguistic labeling, drinking technique, and social function with palm toddy (*tubaq*) and sugarcane wine (*sebug*).

REFERENCES CITED

Barker, R. G., H. F. Wright, 1955, Midwest and Its Children: The psychological ecology of an American town. New York, Harper & Row.
Bruner, J. S., 1957, Going Beyond the Information Given. *In* Contemporary approaches to cognition: a symposium held at the University of Colorado. Cambridge, Harvard, pp. 41–70.
Christie, E. B., 1909, The Subanuns of Sindangan Bay. Manila: Bureau of Science, Division of Ethnology, Publication 6.
Conklin, H. C., 1962, Lexicographical treatment of folk taxonomies. *In* Fred W. Householder and Sol Saporta, eds., Problems in lexicography. Bloomington, Ind.: Indiana Research Center in Anthropology, Folklore, and Linguistics, Publication 21.
Frake, C. O., 1957, Litigation in Lipay: A study in Subanun law. Proceedings of the Ninth Pacific Science Congress, Bangkok. (In press.)
————, 1960, The Eastern Subanun of Mindanao. *In* G. P. Murdock, ed., Social Structure in Southeast Asia. Viking Fund Publications in Anthropology, no. 29, Wenner-Gren Foundation for Anthropological Research, Inc., pp. 61–64.
————, 1961, The diagnosis of disease among the Subanun of Mindanao. American Anthropologist, 63:113–132.
Garfinkle, Harold, n.d., Reflections on the clinical method in psychiatry from the viewpoint of ethnomethodology. Paper presented at a conference on ethnoscience, Stanford University, 1961.
Goffman, Erving, 1958, The presentation of self in everyday life, University of Edinburgh Social Science Research Centre, Monograph no. 2.
Goodenough, W. H., 1957, Cultural anthropology and linguistics. *In* Paul L. Garvin, ed., Report of the seventh annual round table meeting on linguistics and language study. Georgetown University, Monograph Series on Languages and Linguistics, no. 9, pp. 167–173.
Miller, G. A., Eugene Galanter, and K. H. Pribram, 1960, Plans and the Structure of Behavior. New York: Holt, Rinehart and Winston, Inc.
Pike, W. L., 1954, Language in relation to a unified theory of the structure of human behavior, part I, preliminary ed. Glendale: Summer Institute of Linguistics.
Ziff, Paul, 1960, Semantic analysis. Ithaca, N.Y.: Cornell.

Context and Variation in Koya Kinship Terminology [1]

Stephen A. Tyler

The analysis of kinship terminologies has traditionally operated only with the genealogical denotata of the nominal stems of kin terms, with little reference to the social and linguistic contexts in which kin terms are used. Such analysis has usually resulted in the delineation of a single, unitary structure. Problems of variation are seldom systematically accounted for; one reason for this failure is that an explanation of variation requires information on social and linguistic environments. Focusing on variation

> *indicates that there is no single, unitary structure of kin terms defined*
> *solely on the basis of genealogical components. This implies that typological*
> *analysis or formal analysis based on genealogical criteria alone is apt to*
> *obscure important data. It also indicates that the traditional "genealogical*
> *method" is an inadequate field method—if the ethnographic aim is to predict*
> *"who will be called what."*

Kinship terminologies, like most other linguistic phenomena, are usually analyzed as a single unitary structure. Variant forms may not be altogether excluded, but they are seldom explained, either formally or functionally. The following is a typical example:

> . . . the language is particularly prolific in terms of endearment . . .
> for the formal "father," Sinhalese has *appa, appocci,* and *tatta* as alterna-
> tives for *piya*. . . . When *complications* of this sort are *ignored*, the struc-
> tural pattern of Sinhalese kinship terminology is identical to that of the
> Tamil. . . . Practical usage does not correspond strictly to this formal
> design . . . the terms *ayiyā* (elder brother) and *malli* (younger brother)
> may be used *indiscriminately*, even of individuals who should, accord-
> ing to formal principles, be classed as *massinā* (cross-cousin) [Leach
> 1960:125–126, English italics ours].

There is no mention of the environment in which these alternate forms occur, nor is there any indication that the kin types denoted by these alter- nate forms are structurally equivalent. Aside from notable exceptions (Schneider 1953, 1955; Frake 1960; Swartz 1960; Fischer 1964), anthropol- ogists seem to have remained content with the simple environmental differ- entiation of terms of reference and terms of address. Other than this rather rudimentary classification, interest in variant forms has been expressed in terms of historical reconstruction (Spoehr 1947) or culture change (Bruner 1955). This is not to denigrate these approaches; for as long as one is con- cerned only with typology, historical reconstruction, or culture change, the methods may be adequate. But in the realms of functional and formal analy- sis many significant data are neglected by these methods. For example, it is the boast of formal analysts that formal analysis will provide the minimum information for deciding "who will be called what" in any given kinship sys- tem (Lounsbury 1964:352). Yet I know of no formal analysis that has dealt adequately with the problem of variation. To be sure, problems of synonymy and homonymy have been discussed (cf. Wallace and Atkins 1960:64–65, 67–68), but no system has been fully analyzed to account for these factors. To some extent this failure may be attributed to the fact that most formal analysis has been concerned with lexical items or, more appropriately perhaps, with the nominative stems of kin terms. It is my contention that, so construed, formal analysis does not provide the minimum information for deciding who will be called what in any kinship system (cf. also Swartz 1960:397; Hymes 1964a:26; 1964b:97–98).

Elsewhere I have argued that a part of the variation occurring in kinship terminologies can be explained by the contradictions entailed in the role systems of the class of kinsmen denoted by a given term (1964a; cf. also Schneider 1956:17). In this paper I want to explore further implications of role specificity for variations in terminology. Specifically, I will attempt to relate terminological variation to the contexts in which terms of reference are used. In essence the problem of variation here is the same as that, for example, in phonology. What are the restrictions on the occurrence of a given form, and/or in what environments does a given form occur? My general aim is to provide a statement of the contexts in which variant forms occur, and thus to fulfill one part of the minimum requirement of the ethnography of kinship—the prediction of who will be called what.

THE ECOLOGY OF THE SPEECH COMMUNITY

Following Gumperz (1962, 1964), the delimitation of the "natural unit" to be used is based on patterns of communication. Within any given geographical area it is possible to arrive at any number of such units, depending on the level of abstraction desired; but for the purposes of this paper the communication matrix is limited to direct face-to-face contacts among people who are socially defined as kinsmen. Justification for this procedure lies in the fact that such a limitation partially obviates the necessity for a rigorous definition of communication networks on the basis of frequency counts.

Starting from any ego in a Koya village it is possible to trace a widely ramifying group of people who are classed as kinsmen (*cuTTaaku*).[2] In this particular region the class of kinsmen may include people who are non-Koya. It may include members of various Telugu-speaking castes and Koya- and Telugu-speaking members of the Christian caste.

In villages along the banks of the Godavari River and in close proximity to the road from Bhadrachallam to Nugur, members of all these groups are resident. Within the villages, it is common for each group to be physically separated into distinct hamlets, which are named for the subgroup occupying them. All the constituent groups of the population are further segmented by occupational specializations and kin-group alignments. Occupational specialists include blacksmiths, stoneworkers, and religious performers and practitioners; kin-group alignments include clans, lineages, phratries, and castes.

TYPES OF VARIATION

At the level of abstraction that refers to the whole Koya tribe, it is possible to demonstrate that variations in the use of terms of reference for kinsmen occur at the phonological, morphological, and lexical levels. For example, the term *aaNe* (SiSo) among the Gommu Koyas is realized in another dialect area as *aaNDe*. In still other areas there is an isogloss D/R, especially in pronominal endings. Thus, GuTTa Koya has *eelaaRi* (Ysi) and Gommu Koya has *eelaaDi*. Other variants occur in morphology, particularly with reference to the distribution of plurals. More important, however, for present purposes, are the variations occurring within a communication network where dialect differences are minimal.

Within a group of socially defined kinsmen and, further, within the subset that interacts with some frequency, there exist lexical and morphological variations inexplicable by simple reference to dialect differences. Table 1 records a set of alternate lexemes used by a single informant for the group of people classed by him as kin.

Lexical Variation—I

Taken in traditional terms, the items in list one are Telugu and the items in list two are Koya. Isolating the terms in this fashion, however, is misleading, for all forms occur in the linguistic repertory of a single speaker. Considered as such, certain complications arise. For almost the entire set of kinsmen there would appear to be alternate lexemes. The problem would be simple if a bilingual Koya used items from list one when speaking Telugu and items from list two when speaking Koya. We would then have a simple case of code switching in which a Koya speaker employs the Koya terms when speaking to another Koya and the Telugu terms when speaking to a Telugu. Since most Telugus know little if any Koya, the relationship would be asymmetrical. In a given linguistic interchange involving the use of kin terms, the speaker's choice of the appropriate term would be determined by: (1) the kin relation obtaining between the speaker and hearer (or between the speaker or hearer and the person referred to), and (2) the linguistic repertories of both speaker and hearer. Thus, given a Koya speaker and a Telugu hearer, the term chosen would be Telugu. Such switching would be facilitated if the semantic structures of the two codes were identical. The situation to be described, however, is somewhat more involved.

The semantic distance between the two kinship codes is relatively slight. A componential analysis reveals the structure of the two codes (see Table 2). The components are: (1) sex; (2) generation; (3) cross *vs.* parallel; (4) relative age. For convenience, the component of relative sex of speaker is omitted and the relative age of linking relative is subsumed under relative age. The relative effectiveness of each component is indicated in the preceding table. It will be noted that the parallel-cross distinction does not obtain in the Telugu system at the $+2$ and -2 generations. In all other respects, the two systems are coordinate. Hence, in terms of semantic structure, the transform

Table 1

	TELUGU	KOYA
Fa, FaBro, MoSiHu	ayya	eyya
	taNDri	tappe
	nayana	
	naana	
Mo, MoSi, FaBroWi	amma	evva
	talli	talluru
FaFa	taata	daadaal
MoFa	taata	taataal
MoMo	avva	kaako
FaMo	avva	emma
FaSi, MoBroWi, WiMo, HuMo	atta	pooye
MoBro,FaSiHu, WiFa, HuFa	maama	maamaal
Ebro, Emale parallel cousin	anna	enna
Ybro, Ymale parallel cousin	tammuDu	tammuNDu
Esi, Efemale parallel cousin	akka	ekka
Ysi, Yfemale parallel cousin	cellelu	eelaaDi
	celli	
Efemale cross cousin, EbroWi	vodina	enge
Yfemale cross cousin, YbroWi	maradalu	eendaaDi
Emale cross cousin, EsiHu	baava	baaTaal
Ymale cross cousin, YsiHu	baamaaradi	eruNDu
So (x)BroSo, (o)SiSo	koDuku	marri
	kummaruDu	peeka
	abbayi	
Da (x)BroDa, (o)SiDa	ammayi	mayyaaDi
	kuturu	piikiDi
	biDDa	
(x)SiSo, DaHu, (o)BroSo	alluDu	aaNe
(x)SiDa, SoWi, (o)BroDa	kooDalu	koDiyaaDi
SoSo	manamaDu	tammuNDu
DaSo	manamaDu	eruNDu
SoDa	manamaraal	eelaaDi
DaDa	manamaraal	eendaaDi

These are minimal ranges for the terms. For a fuller treatment, as well as formal analysis and discussion of morphology, see Tyler (1964a; 1964b; 1965). (x) indicates male speaker; (o) indicates female speaker; E and Y denote elder and younger respectively.

Table 2

TELUGU

	Male	Female	Male	Female
+2	taata		avva	
+1	ayya	amma	maama	atta
0	anna	akka	baava	vodina
	tammuDu	cellelu	baamaaradi	maradalu
−1	koDuku	kuturu	alluDu	kooDalu
−2	manamaDu		manamaral	
	Parallel		Cross	

KOYA

	Male	Female	Male	Female
+2	daadaal	emma	taataal	kaako
+1	eyya	evva	maamaal	pooye
0	enna	ekka	baaTaal	enge
	tammuNDu	eelaaDi	eruNDu	eendaaDi
−1	marri	mayyaaDi	aaNe	koDiyaaDi
−2	tammuNDu	eelaaDi	eruNDu	eendaaDi
	Parallel		Cross	

Certain aspects of morphology have been omitted here. For details, see Tyler (1964b). In Koya O, tammuNDu is analyzed as a homonym of −2 tammuNDu. Similarly for the other −2 categories (cf. Tyler 1964a).

(for a Koya speaker) from one system to the other is fairly simple. It entails only the following rules:[3]

$$1. \quad \begin{cases} a+m+m \\ \qquad\qquad \to a+a+m \\ a+f+m \end{cases}$$

$$2. \quad \begin{cases} a+m+f \\ \qquad\qquad \to a+a+f \\ a+f+f \end{cases}$$

$$3. \quad \begin{cases} a-m-m \\ \qquad\qquad \to a-a-m \\ a-f-m \end{cases}$$

$$4. \quad \begin{cases} a-m-f \\ \qquad\qquad \to a-a-f \\ a-f-f \end{cases}$$

Using a reciprocal operation, these can be simplified to:

$$5. \quad \begin{cases} a*m*m \\ \qquad\qquad \to a*a*m \\ a*f*m \end{cases}$$

$$6. \quad \begin{cases} a*m*f \\ \qquad\qquad \to a*a*f \\ a*f*f \end{cases}$$

To complete the statement, it is necessary to provide data on the environment in which this transform is permissible. Since we have said that such a transform occurs when a Koya speaker refers to a kinsman in a linguistic interchange with a Telugu-speaking kinsman, this can be formulated as follows:[4]

$$\begin{cases} a*m*m//K-T/a*a*m \\ a*f*m// \end{cases}$$

This is to be read: the kin types $a*m*m$ and $a*f*m$ in the environment of a Koya speaker and Telugu hearer are realized as $a*a*m$.

K-T is only one of the possible environments in which such a linguistic interchange may occur. The remaining environments are:

$$//K-K/ \qquad\qquad //k-T/$$
$$//K-k/ \qquad\qquad //k-t/$$
$$//k-K/ \qquad\qquad //K-t/$$
$$//k-k/$$

The speaker is indicated by the first alphabetical symbol, the hearer by the second. K indicates Koya, k Koya Christian, T Telugu, t Telugu

Christian. Since our interest here is only in those situations where Koyas are speakers, the remaining environments are not discussed.

For all significant environments the distributional statement is:

$$7. \begin{cases} a^*m^*m//K-T/ \\ a^*f^*m//k-T/a^*a^*m \\ \qquad //K-t/ \\ \qquad //k-t/a^*a^*m \text{ or } \begin{cases} a^*m^*m \\ a^*f^*m \end{cases} \\ \qquad //else/ \begin{cases} a^*m^*m \\ a^*f^*m \end{cases} \end{cases}$$

The added variation in k-t requires a further restriction on the social environment. To my knowledge, this variation occurs only where a Koya Christian male is married to a Telugu Christian female. In these cases, the linguistic repertories of husband and wife in kinship terminology tend toward isomorphy, and code switching probably occurs only when the presence and composition of an outside audience evoke it. In the presence of his wife's relatives, for example, the husband would use the appropriate Telugu term in speaking to her.

In general, at the level of semantic structure these two transform rules plus the accompanying distributional statement enable one to predict the appropriate denotata of a term. Once these operations have been performed, the lexical realization of the remaining categories involves only a simple process of substitution, or word-for-word translation. For example, *aaNe*//k-T/*alluDu*. Realization of the appropriate lexeme can be predicted on the basis of the foregoing rules, with the exception of k-k and k-t. For k-k, the following additional statements are necessary:

$$a-f-m//k-k/manamaDu$$
$$a-f-f//k-k/manamaraal$$

Lexemic realization in k-t for the categories a-f-m and a-f-f is dependent on the transform occurring in statement number seven, above:

$$\text{For} \begin{cases} a^*m^*m//k-t/a^*a^*m \\ a^*f^*m \end{cases} \rightarrow a-f-m//k-t/manamaDu$$

$$\begin{cases} a^*m^*f//k-t/a^*a^*f \\ a^*f^*f \end{cases} \rightarrow a-f-f//k-t/manamaraal$$

$$\text{For} \begin{cases} a^*m^*m//k-t/ \begin{cases} a^*m^*m \rightarrow a-f-m//k-t/eruNDu \\ a^*f^*m \end{cases} \\ a^*f^*m \end{cases}$$

$$\begin{cases} a^*m^*f//k-t/ \begin{cases} a^*m^*f \rightarrow a-f-f//k-t/koDiyaaDi \\ a^*f^*f \end{cases} \\ a^*f^*f \end{cases}$$

Since Koya and Telugu are both Dravidian languages, many of the kin terms are cognate. Some are related by quite simple sound changes, for example, Telugu *a-*, Koya *e-* (*avva, evva*); Telugu *-D*, Koya *-ND-* (*tammuDu, tammuNDu*). Note, however, that the semantic range of these cognate forms varies. *amma* in Telugu denotes Mo, while Koya *emma* denotes FaMo; Telugu *taata* denotes FaFa and MoFa, while Koya *taataal* denotes only MoFa. Given the phonological similarity of these terms, one might expect a certain amount of interference. This does not seem to be the case here—although it could be argued that in other areas, where differences occur in the extent to which Koyas dominate the ecology of the speech community, interference stemming from these sources could be a cause of changes in the terminological system. This, however, is outside the domain of this paper.

Lexical Variation—II

The second type of lexical variation relates more to situational variants within a kinship code than it does to varieties of codes. In the preceding schedule of terms, it will be noted that within each of the codes certain categories have alternate lexemes. These occur with terms for father, mother, younger sister, son, and daughter in the Telugu code, and for father, mother, son, and daughter in the Koya code. There are two problems involved here: (1) Are the denotata of all variant forms equivalent; (2) if so, are there environments that limit the distribution of some variants?

In the case of *taNDRi/nayana/ayya/naana*, the first two denote father and father's brothers, with appropriate morphemes denoting relative age, that is, $a + m(om)^{0,1}$ (see note 5). *naana*, however, denotes only an actual father $(a + m)$, and *ayya* denotes father's brothers $(a + mom)$, but not father. In summary:

$$taNDRi/nayana \text{ denotes } a+m(om)^{0,1}$$
$$naana \qquad\qquad \text{denotes } a+m$$
$$ayya \qquad\qquad \text{denotes } a+mom$$

Since *ayya* and *naana* are not structurally equivalent to the other terms, they need no longer concern us here. *taNDRi* is generally regarded as the more formal and respectful term; *nayana* is less respectful and more informal. The major variable for these two then is the extent to which one wishes to confer respect on the referent. In summary statement:

$$a+m(om)^{0,1}//F/taNDRi$$
$$//If/nayana$$

(*F* indicates formal and *If* informal. The set of situations in which informality is permissible for this range is unrecorded.)

For *eyya/tappe:* *eyya* denotes $a+m(om)^{0,1}$
tappe denotes $a+m$
For *evva/talluru:* *evva* denotes $a+f(of)^{0,1}$
talluru denotes $a+f$

For *amma/talli* I have been unable to isolate significant differences in either denotata or environment, other than a general impression that *talli* more frequently denotes a+f and may be more formal than *amma*. For lack of better data, these two will be considered synonymous in the domain of kinship reference.

It should be noted that all these structural differences have the effect of transforming the system at the +1 consanguineal level from bifurcate merging to bifurcate collateral.

cellelu/celli differentiate at both structural and environmental levels. *cellelu* denotes Ysi and younger female parallel relatives, that is, $a(+a_i)^{0,1}o$ $(a-_j)^{0,1}f^y$ (i=j), while *celli* denotes only aof^y unless one's female parallel relatives reside in the same patrilaterally extended household. In this case the structural differentiation is negated.[6] *celli* in reference to a Ysi is further differentiated from *cellelu* as "sweet" (*tiyyani*) usage. I have little data on the specific environments in which "sweet" usage is permissible, but believe its use is restricted to the home among consanguineal kin. In terms of the speaker's intention, *celli* denotes an intimate relation between speaker and Ysi. These distributions are formulated as:

$$a(+a_i)^{0,1}o(a-_j)^{0,1}f^y//In/celli$$
$$(i=j)   //PEH/celli$$
$$//H/celli$$
$$//else/cellelu$$

(*PEH* indicates patrilateral extended household, *In* intimacy, *H* in the home. The ordering of rules is as given.)

The remaining variants denoting son and daughter do not yield to this kind of analysis on the basis of the data available to me, but it is probable that similar kinds of differentia account for the variability here as well.

Note that the highest frequency of variation occurs among categories of kin who are apt to be members of the same household. This is in line with the general expectation that maximum differentiation occurs in areas of high interest and interaction. Further, for the population being discussed, it is precisely between the reciprocals Fa/Ch and Mo/Ch that the greatest role inconsistencies occur.[7]

Morphological Variation

Both in Koya and Telugu, the referential use of kin terms involves not only the selection of the appropriate noun stem, but also the selection of appropriate possessive pronouns and derivative suffixes. (Thus, in Koya and Telugu a kin term may consist of possessive pronoun + noun stem ± derivative suffixes.) It can be argued that this is in the domain of syntactic function, but it is easier in the present context to treat the whole problem under morphology. Whether syntactic or morphological, the main point is that the mere knowledge of the appropriate noun stem and its denotata is not sufficient to generate acceptable statements of kinship reference.

The distribution and use of possessive pronouns and derivative suffixes in first person reference have previously been discussed for Koya (Tyler 1964a). The first and second person possessive pronouns in Koya and Telugu do not differ. They are: *maa-* "our, my" formal; *naa-* "my" informal. Second person possessive pronouns are *nii-* "your" informal, *mii-* "your" formal. The derivative suffixes occurring with kin terms for Telugu are: *-ayya*, "sir"; *-gaaru*, "sir, madam"; for Koya: *-aal*, "mature male."[8] Table 3 indicates the distribution of first person possessives and derivative suffixes for Telugu.

Possessive Pronouns

For Koya, the distribution of possessives is similar to the above, with the exception that *maa-* and *naa-* may alternate for elder female relatives.

The alternation of *naa-/maa-* for *baava* and *vodina* is paralleled in Koya, and the reasons for the alternation seem to be identical. On the one hand, these are elder relatives whom one should respect, but on the other hand, they are people with whom a joking relation is permissible. Since a female is given somewhat more latitude in a joking relation, sex of speaker is a determinant. The next determinant is audience composition. This involves two factors: (1) the presence or absence of the referent, and (2) the presence or absence of the speaker's elder consanguineal relatives and/or the presence or absence of nonkin. If the referent is absent, *maa-* is used; if present, *naa-*. The latter is abandoned when the speaker's elder consanguineal relatives or elder nonkin are present. The major situational determinants are weddings and a festival, the *Bhima paNDum*. One phase in a wedding ceremony involves a form of group singing in which the bride's party and the groom's party sing competing rounds. As the songs frequently refer to the sexual attributes of a *baava* or *vodina*, these terms occur in the songs with the informal possessive *naa-*. Since Christians no longer use the Koya ceremony, the significant environments for this variation are K-T and, with the appropriate semantic transform, K-K. During the Bhima festival a mock marriage is performed. At this time the distribution of *maa-/naa-* is the same as for a real wedding.

These distributions may be formulated as:

$$a + a_i o a_j - a^e, \ (i \neq j), \ PP^1 // f - /naa-$$
$$//R/naa-$$
$$//WS/naa-$$
$$//else/maa-$$

(*f* denotes female speaker, *R* referent present, *WS* wedding songs, and *PP*[1] first person possessive pronoun.)

Table 3

(TELEGU) STEM	FIRST PERSON POSSESSIVE		DERIVATIVE SUFFIX	
	maa-	*naa-*	*-ayya*	*-gaaru*
taata*	+	+	+	+
avva	+	+		+
naana	+		+	+
nayana	+			+
taNDRi	+			+
ayya	+			+
amma	+			+
talli	+			+
maama	+		+	+
atta	+			+
anna	+		+	+
tammuDu		+		
baava	+	+	+	+
vodina	+	+		+
akka	+		+	+
cellelu		+		
baamaaradi		+		
maradalu		+		
koDuku		+		
abbayi	+	+		
kummaruDu		+		
ammayi	+	+		
kuturu		+		
biDDa		+		
alluDu		+		
kooDalu		+		
manamaDu		+		
manamaraal		+		

* Where *maa-* and *naa-* alternate, derivative suffixes do not occur when *naa-* is used. This differs substantially from the system in T-T and t-t, and wherever T- or t- is speaker. In these cases *maa-* does not alternate with *naa-*.

Alternation of *maa-/naa-* with terms in the +2 generation is largely a function of the age of the speaker. Between grandparents and grandchildren there is usually a close, intimate relationship. The care of children is frequently entrusted to elder grandparents who are no longer able to work actively in the fields. Consequently, young children use *naa-* when referring to these relatives. The social setting and audience composition may also be important here. It is my general impression that mature speakers use *naa-* in reference to these kinsmen in the home among other household members.

My principal informant asserted that this was the case, but since my access to Koya homes was limited, I have little to substantiate this. These rules may be summarized as:

$$PP^1//I-/naa-$$
$$//H/naa-$$
$$//else/maa-$$

(*I* denotes an immature speaker, *H* inside the home.)

The alternation of *maa-/naa-* for *ammayi* and *abbayi* is unexplained.

The use of possessive pronouns in second person kinship reference, unlike that in first person reference, confers status or respect on the hearer, not on the referent of the term. The pronouns in question are: *mii-* "your" formal; *nii-* "your" informal. The pronouns are the same for both Telugu and Koya. The following example should indicate the process involved here.

K−T: *mii tammuDu ee pani ceestunnaaDu,* "what work is your Ybro doing (now)?" Since a Ybro is low status, one might expect agreement between the possessive pronoun and the noun stem, that is, *nii tammuDu* rather than *mii tammuDu*. Because *nii tammuDu* occurs in other situations, *nii-* and *mii-* are not inalienable in the sense that *naa-* and *maa-* are. The important variable here concerns the relative statuses of speaker and hearer. Briefly, the sources of status are education, wealth, occupation, categorical membership in kin groups, and personal characteristics. Since all sources of status are not isomorphically distributed in specific population segments or kin categories, the use of possessive pronouns in second person reference cannot be predicted simply on the basis of categorical membership in K, k, T, t groups or from knowledge of the kin relation obtaining between speaker and hearer. The precise details of this system cannot be delineated in this brief paper. Suffice it to say that when the speaker's status is lower than the hearer's, *mii-* occurs; when higher, *nii-* occurs. If the status of speaker and hearer are approximately equivalent, *mii-* and *nii-* are in free variation. Between old or ritual friends, *nii-* is used irrespective of status differences. This may be formulated as:

$$PP^2//L-H/mii-$$
$$//H-L/nii-$$
$$//F-F/nii-$$
$$//E-E/nii-, \ mii-$$

(*L* indicates low status, *H* high status, *E* equivalent status, *F* friends, and *PP*² second person possessive pronouns.)

Derivative Suffixes

Derivative suffixes in Koya and Telugu differ in the lack of a Koya equivalent for *-gaaru*. Where *-gaaru* occurs for females in Telugu, Koya has

ϕ. With the exception of its occurrence with Esi, Telugu -*ayya* is identical in distribution to Koya -*aal*.

Unfortunately, data are not at all certain here, but the most important variable seems to be the definition of the situation. In part, this is determined on the basis of audience composition. First, if the referent of a given term is present, derivative suffixes are used; when the referent is absent, they are used less frequently. Secondly, if the audience consists of people whom the speaker wants to impress by his knowledge of respectful behavior, the derivative suffixes will be used. The strength of this situation is such that one of the most disparaging comments one can make about another is that he is not respectful. Since one of the most critical audiences consists of one's elder affines, the presence or absence of elder affines is usually sufficient to predict the appropriate use of derivative suffixes. Further, among affines, those who are related to ego by only a single affinal link (in contradistinction to those with whom a series of such affinal links may be traced) are apt to be more critical.[9] These distributions may be formulated as follows:

$$DS//R/DS$$
$$//A^1/DS$$
$$//A^2/\phi, DS$$
$$//\text{else}/\phi$$

(*DS* denotes derivative suffixes, *R* referent present, A^1 single link affines, A^2 multiple link affines, and ϕ no DS.)

In more general terms, certain social gatherings are considered to be more formal than others. Marriages, for example, are formal occasions. Formal behavior, however, is required only in specific phases of the wedding ceremony, or only from the central actors. The rules of formal behavior are not enjoined for peripheral actors—in fact, the reverse is usually the case. Analysis of these situations is too complex for brief summary, but enough has been said to indicate that a general rule may be formulated:

$$DS//F/DS$$
$$//\text{else}/\phi$$

(*F* denotes a formal situation.)

CONCLUSION

This paper does not conclude that the rules presented are sufficient to predict who will be called what. There are too many gaps, both in data and in analysis. Yet, sketchy and incomplete as this analysis is, it should at least indicate that the appropriate use of Koya kin terms cannot be predicted solely on the basis of a formal analysis predicated on the assumption of genealogical reckoning. There are many contextual factors to be taken into consideration. Among these are: social setting, audience composition, sex and age of speaker/hearer, linguistic repertories of speaker/hearer, and—most difficult of all—something that might be called the speaker's intention. Many of these and others have previously been discussed (Ervin-Tripp 1964:86–94; Gumperz 1964:143–147; Hymes 1964b:15–25) and need not receive further comment here.

Even though the Koya case may seem rather extreme, it should demonstrate that less complex types of variation can probably be easily handled by analysis of the sort used in this paper. In addition, it should emphasize that problems of variation (or of general ethnography) call for somewhat different field techniques than those that have traditionally been used. There must, for example, be a greater emphasis on the recording of kin terms as they are used in concrete and/or simulated ethnographic situations (cf. Conklin 1964; Hymes 1964b:11). The anthropologist armed only with a genealogy and an informant or informants and using traditional methods of questioning cannot hope to cope with the problem of variation. This is not intended as a blanket condemnation of such methods. They are useful in collecting some kinds of data and can provide a base of information on which it is possible to build, but it should be abundantly clear from other publications (e.g., Frake 1962; Metzger and Williams 1963) that if our aim is ethnographic description, then field methods must be adequate to the task.

Finally, these data show that much of what has usually been simply regarded as unimportant variations on the basic structural pattern of a terminological system consists of highly important differentiations, not only in denotata but in role expectations as well. This should be sufficient indication that an overemphasis on typology or on genealogically based formal analysis can obscure relevant functional aspects of kinship terminology.

NOTES

[1] The research on which this paper is based was carried out in India in 1962–1963, supported by a Foreign Area Training Fellowship from the Ford Foundation. An earlier version of this paper was presented at the Timber Cove Conference on "Approaches to Interpersonal Relations in South and Southeast Asia," April 9–12, 1965, sponsored by the Institute of International Studies, University of California, Berkeley. It has benefited not only from the comments of other conference participants, but from specific suggestions made by David M. Schneider, Gene Hammel, John Gumperz, and Alan Beals. Davis colleagues Yehudi Cohen and David Olmsted read earlier drafts and provided useful comments.

[2] The transcription is broadly phonetic. Long vowels are marked by double vowels, retroflex consonants by upper case letters. Further linguistic details are contained in Tyler (1968).

[3] The notation system used is that developed by Romney (1964). m indicates male, f female, a any sex, $+$ an ascendant link, $-$ a descendant link, o a sibling link.

Since grandson is the reciprocal of grandfather, the reciprocal operation (*) says to read * as $\pm$. The first member of an expression is ego; e.g., English *father* would be $a+m$.

[4] The notation$// /$ denotes "in the environment of." Thus,

$$a+f+m//K-t/a+a+m$$
$$a+m+m//$$

indicates that $a+m+m$ and $a+f+m$ in the environment of a Koya speaker and a Telugu hearer are both realized as $a+a+m$.

[5] Parentheses indicate an optional expansion; superscript numbers denote the number of times the expansion may be employed. Thus $a+m(om)^{0,1}$ will generate $a+m$ and $a+mom$.

[6] Superscript y denotes younger, e elder. Subscripts i and j indicate appropriate handling of sex. That is, since i = j, then the expression reads $a(+m)^{0,1}o(m-)^{0,1}f^y$ or $a(+f)^{0,1}o(f-)^{0,1}f^y$ but neither $a(+m)^{0,1}o(f-)^{0,1}f^y$ nor $a(+f)^{0,1}o(m-)^{0,1}f^y$.

[7] For further discussion of this point, see Tyler (1964b).

[8] There are others, for example, $-Du$, $-Di$, $-a(a)l(u)$, etc.; but for the most part these are not optional in the same sense as *-aal*, *-gaaru*, *-ayya*. The English glosses are only handy approximations.

[9] The distinction here is between "affines" who are consanguineally related to ego and "affines" who are related to ego only by a marriage link. For example, WiFa may be an actual MoBro, as opposed to cases in which an actual MoBro is not also WiFa. The former are terminologically distinguished from the latter by the prefix *meena-*.

REFERENCES CITED

Bruner, Edward M., 1955, Two processes of change in Mandan-Hidatsa kinship terminology. American Anthropologist 57:840–850.

Conklin, H. C., 1964, Ethnogenealogical method. *In* Explorations in cultural anthropology. W. H. Goodenough, ed. New York, McGraw-Hill.

Ervin-Tripp, Susan, 1964, An analysis of the interaction of language, topic, and listener. *In* The ethnography of communication. John J. Gumperz and Dell Hymes, eds. American Anthropologist 66, no. 6, pt. 2.

Fischer, J. L., 1964, Words for self and others in some Japanese families. *In* The ethnography of communication. John J. Gumperz and Dell Hymes, eds. American Anthropologist 66, no. 6, pt. 2.

Frake, C. O., 1960, The Eastern Subanun of Mindanao. *In* Social structure in Southeast Asia. G. P. Murdock, ed. Chicago, Quadrangle Books.

———, 1962, The ethnographic study of cognitive systems. *In* Anthropology and human behavior. T. Gladwin and W. C. Sturtevant, eds. Washington, Anthropological Society of Washington.

Gumperz, John, 1962, Types of linguistic communities. MS.

———, 1964, Linguistic and social interaction in two communities. *In* The ethnography of communication. John J. Gumperz and Dell Hymes, eds. American Anthropologist 66, no. 6, pt. 2.

———, n.d., Hindi-Punjabi code-switching in Delhi. MS.

Hymes, Dell, 1964a, A perspective for linguistic anthropology. *In* Horizons of anthropology. Sol Tax, ed. Chicago, Aldine.

————, 1964b, Toward ethnographies of communication. *In* The ethnography of communication. John J. Gumperz and Dell Hymes, eds. American Anthropologist 66, no. 6, pt. 2.

Leach, E. R., 1960, The Sinhalese of the dry zone of Northern Ceylon. *In* Social structure in Southeast Asia. G. P. Murdock, ed. Chicago, Quadrangle Books.

Lounsbury, F. G., 1964, The formal analysis of Crow- and Omaha-type kinship terminologies. *In* Explorations in cultural anthropology. G. P. Murdock, ed. New York, McGraw-Hill.

Metzger, Duane, and Gerald Williams, 1963, Tenejapa medicine: the curer. Southwestern Journal of Anthropology 19:216–234.

Romney, A. K., Roy G. D'Andrade, 1964, Cognitive aspects of English kin terms. *In* Transcultural studies in cognition. A. K. Romney and R. G. D'Andrade, eds. American Anthropologist 66, no. 3, pt. 2.

Schneider, D. M., 1953, Yap kinship terminology and kin groups. American Anthropologist 55:215–236.

————, 1955, Kinship terminology and the American kinship system. American Anthropologist 57:1194–1208.

Schneider, D. M., and J. M. Roberts, 1956, Zuni kin terms. Monograph 1, Notebook No. 3, Laboratory of Anthropology. University of Nebraska.

Spoehr, A., 1947, Changing kinship systems. Anthropological Series, Chicago Natural History Museum, vol. 33, no. 4.

Swartz, Marc J., 1960, Situational determinants of kinship terminology. Southwestern Journal of Anthropology 16:393–397.

Tyler, S. A., 1964a, Formal analysis of Koya kinship terminology. M. B. Emeneau saṣṭipūrti volume, B. H. Krishnamurty, ed. Centres of Advanced Studies in Linguistics, Poona.

————, 1964b, Koya kinship: the relation between rules and behavior. Unpublished Ph.D. dissertation, Stanford University.

————, 1965, Koya language morphology and patterns of kinship behavior. American Anthropologist 67:1428–1440.

————, 1968, Koya: an outline grammar. University of California Publications in Linguistics, vol. 54.

Wallace, A. F. C., John Atkins, 1960, The meaning of kinship terms. American Anthropologist 62:58–80.

Name Index

505

Subject Index